The Library Juice Press
Handbook of
Intellectual Freedom

The Library Juice Press

Handbook of

Intellectual Freedom

Concepts, Cases, and Theories

Mark Alfino and Laura Koltutsky, Editors

Library Juice Press
Sacramento, California

Published in 2014 by Library Juice Press.

Library Juice Press
PO Box 188784
Sacramento, CA 95818

http://libraryjuicepress.com/

This book is printed on acid-free, sustainably-sourced paper.

Layout by Martin Wallace.

The image used on the cover is "Stigma Poem No 5," by Nadia Plesner. Nadia Plesner fought a legal battle with Louis Vuitton for the right to use their brand images as an element of her work. Her case went to the Hague, where the European Court of Justice decided in her favor in 2011.

Library of Congress Cataloging-in-Publication Data

The Library Juice Press handbook of intellectual freedom : concepts, cases and theories / edited by Mark Alfino and Laura Koltutsky.
     pages cm
  Includes bibliographical references and index.
  Summary: "Provides a grounding in the philosophical, historical, and legal development of the concept of intellectual freedom by providing current thinking on a range of intellectual freedom concepts, cases, and controversies"-- Provided by publisher.
  ISBN 978-1-936117-57-4 (alk. paper)
1. Intellectual freedom. 2. Intellectual property. 3. Privacy, Right of. 4. Academic freedom. 5. Freedom of information. 6. Censorship. 7. Libraries--Censorship. I. Alfino, Mark, 1959- , author, editor of compilation. II. Koltutsky, Laura, author, editor of compilation. III. Title: Handbook of intellectual freedom.
  JC598.L534 2014
  323.44--dc23
                                                              2014000835

Contents

Acknowledgements

Both Laura and I would like to thank our authors first. Special thanks to Rory Litwin, Toni Samek, Robert Hauptman, as well as other Advisory Board members, Mary Minow, Alvin Schrader, Jim Kuhn, Laura Quilter, Elizabeth Buchanan, Siva Vaidhyanathan, and Tara Robertson.

Laura Koltutsky would like to thank her employers, her colleagues, her family, and all of the teachers in her life. Special thanks to Toni Samek and Hope Olson who helped me to find my professional voice.

Mark Alfino would like to acknowledge the support of Gonzaga University for this work, as well as the ongoing support of his family, friends, and colleagues.

Advisory Board

Contributors

Mark Alfino is a Professor of Philosophy at Gonzaga University. He has written on a wide range of topics, including information ethics. His writing has appeared in *Library Trends*, the *Journal of Information Ethics*, *Social Theory and Practice* and other journals. He co-authored *Information Ethics for Librarians* (McFarland 1997) with Linda Pierce and co-edited *McDonaldization Revisited: Critical Essays in Consumer Culture* (Praeger 1998, with Caputo and Wynyard).

Elizabeth Buchanan holds an endowed Chair in Ethics and is Director of the Center for Applied Ethics at the University of Wisconsin-Stout. She has been a Visiting Research Fellow at the University of Oxford's E-Social Science Center, and has been a Lecturer at the Upper Austrian University of Applied Science in Hagenberg, Austria since 2010.

John Buschman is Dean of University Libraries at Seton Hall University. He holds a Doctor of Liberal Studies from Georgetown University where he was Associate University Librarian for Scholarly Resources & Services prior to moving to Seton Hall. He is author of, among other books, *Dismantling the Public Sphere: Situating and Sustaining Librarianship in the Age of the New Public Philosophy* (Libraries Unlimited/Greenwood 2003) and most recently *Libraries, Classrooms, and the Interests of Democracy: Marking the Limits of Neoliberalism* (Scarecrow/Rowman & Littlefield, 2012).

James V. Carmichael, Jr. is Professor of Library and Information Studies at The University of North Carolina at Greensboro. He received his undergraduate and master's degree from Emory University and his doctorate from The University of North Carolina at Chapel Hill. He has written extensively on southern library history, gender issues, and gay library history.

Olivier Charbonneau is an Associate Librarian at Concordia University, primarily interested in copyright issues as well as questions of open access and social media. In addition to his role as liaison librarian for the John Molson School of Business, he is a doctoral student at the Faculté de droit, Université de Montréal. He keeps a French blog about his research at www.culturelibre.ca and an English blog at www.outfind.ca about his liaison role.

Joanna Cornwell is a litigation associate at Winston & Strawn, LLP, who joined the firm's Chicago office in 2012. She counsels clients on compliance with privacy and data security laws and regulations as well as complex commercial and patent litigation matters. Prior to law school, she worked for four years in several government policy and information technology consulting positions and was certified as an Information Privacy Professional (CIPP).

Joe Cutbirth is Assistant Professor of Communication at Manhattan College, where he directs the journalism program and is a fellow at the Manhattan College Ethics Center. His research examines the efficacy of nontraditional media and nontraditional media narratives in political discourse. He worked nearly 20 years as a journalist and communications professional before earning his Ph.D. at Columbia University.

Susan Forde is and Associate Professor and Head of the School of Humanities at Griffith University, Australia. She is the author of *Challenging the News: The Journalism of Alternative & Community Media* (Palgrave Macmillan, 2011) and the co-author of *Developing Dialogues: Indigenous and Ethnic Community Broadcasting* (Intellect 2009, with Meadows & Foxwell). She currently leads the media and journalism research program in the Griffith Centre for Cultural Research.

Loretta M. Gaffney is a Lecturer and Visiting Researcher at UCLA's Dept. of Information Studies, where she teaches courses on intellectual freedom, reading research, and youth services librarianship. A former middle school librarian, she defended her dissertation, "Intellectual Freedom and the Politics of Reading" in 2012. Loretta's current research projects include teen reading, school librarians' knowledge, and Tea Party-related book challenges in libraries and schools.

Leonard Hammer is a Senior Lecturer at the Rothberg International School, Hebrew University and the David and Andrea Stein Visiting Professor for Modern Israel Studies at the Judaic Studies Department, University of Arizona. He has written about freedom of conscience and religion as an international human right and also on topics such as sacred space and migrant workers.

Kathrine Henderson is the research librarian for the State of Arizona, Office of the Auditor General. She conducts research across many disciplines with the purpose of determining best practices for state agencies, boards, commissions and authorities. She also provides legal research in areas such as legislative intent and documentation of changes to statute and rule. Prior to joining the office in

2008, she was the Instructional Programs Librarian for Thunderbird School of Global Management.

Dale A. Herbeck is the Chairperson of the Communication Department Studies Department at Northeastern University, where he teaches courses on argumentation, communication law, cyberlaw, and freedom of expression. He is co-author, with Thomas L. Tedford, of *Freedom of Speech in the United States*, a past editor of Free Speech Yearbook, and a former chair of the National Communication Association's Commission on Freedom of Expression.

Robert P. Holley, Professor, School of Library & Information Science, Wayne State University, has been actively involved in intellectual freedom for many years including diverse publications on this topic. He has also held multiple positions within the ALA Intellectual Freedom Round Table including chair and headed the ACRL Intellectual Freedom Committee for four years.

Emily J. M. Knox is an assistant professor in the Graduate School of Library and Information Science at the University of Illinois at Urbana-Champaign. Her research interests include intellectual freedom and censorship, the intersection of print culture and reading practices, and information ethics and policy.

Laura Koltutsky is an associate librarian at the University of Calgary. She has been active within the Intellectual Freedom and Social Responsibility communities of the American Library Association since graduating with her Master of Information Studies degree from the University of Alberta. Laura's research interests include intellectual freedom, academic libraries, and the integration of technology and information literacy.

Tomas A. Lipinski holds multiple degrees in law and in library and information science, having worked as a lawyer and a librarian. In 2013 he is Director of the School of Library and Information Science at Kent State University. His most recent monograph is *The Librarian's Legal Companion for Licensing Information Resources and Services* (2012). In 2014 he will be a Visiting Professor, at the College Doctoral, Université Lille Nord de France, Lille, France.

Susan Maret is currently a Lecturer at the School of Library and Information Science, San Jose State University, where she teaches a variety of subjects, including a course on freedom of information and government secrecy. She is the editor of *Government Secrecy, Research in Social Problems and Public Policy* (Emerald 2011) and with Jan Goldman, *Government Secrecy: Classic and Contemporary Readings* (Libraries Unlimited 2009).

Svetlana Mintcheva is Director of Programs at the National Coalition Against Censorship, a 40-year old alliance of U.S. national non-profit organizations. She is the founding director of NCAC's Arts Advocacy Program. She is the co-editor of *Censoring Culture: Contemporary Threats to Free Expression* (New Press 2006). She teaches part-time at New York University. Her current research focuses on ethics, censorship and the notion of "offense."

Lauren Pressley is the Associate Director for Learning and Outreach at Virginia Tech University Libraries. She frequently writes and presents on the future of libraries and their role in education, and is author of *So You Want to be a Librarian.*

Douglas Raber is currently the Director of the Marion Public Library in Marion, Iowa. He was a member of the faculty of the School of Information Science & Learning Technologies at the University of Missouri and the School of Information Sciences at the University of Tennessee. From 2003–2005 he served as Interim Director of SIS at Tennessee and in 2005 received the Tennessee Library Association/SIRS Freedom of Information Award for the active promotion of intellectual freedom in Tennessee. He is the author of *Librarianship and Legitimacy; The Ideology of the Public Library Inquiry* (Greenwood 1997) and *The Problem of Information* (Scarecrow 2003).

Neil Richards is a Professor of Law at Washington University in St. Louis, where he writes and teaches about privacy law, free speech, and technology. He is the author of numerous scholarly and popular articles and the book *Intellectual Privacy* (Oxford University Press 2014). He holds graduate degrees in law and history from the University of Virginia, and is a former law clerk to Chief Justice William H. Rehnquist.

Robert Tiessen is a Librarian at the University of Calgary. He first became interested in copyright when he was Head of Access Services at the University of Calgary. He has spoken at conferences on the issue of libraries and copyright, and is an active member of the Canadian Library Association's Copyright Committee.

Introduction

The guiding intuition behind the collection of articles in this book is that thought and action about intellectual freedom needs to be informed by a broader and more complex range of topics and theoretical reflection than it typically has been. If we were looking for confirmation of the relevance of this intuition from almost five years ago when this project began, we would find it in the news from this month and this year.

At the time of this writing, Germany and Brazil are introducing resolutions to the United Nations calling for international standards for digital privacy following revelations that the heads of their governments were subject to surveillance by the National Security Agency (NSA) of the United States of America. The NSA is facing public scrutiny within the United States for a wide range of programs, many of which the public has learned more about because of leaks by whistleblower Edward Snowden, who received temporary political asylum in Russia this past August. A year before the first Snowden leaks, Julian Assange was taking up residence in the Ecuadorian Embassy in London, where he enjoys protection from extradition to Sweden to face charges, which would expose him to extradition to the United States. Assange is the publisher and founder in 2006 of WikiLeaks, which in 2010, leaked copies of illegally obtained diplomatic cables between the United States and other countries amongst other documents.

Privacy and secrecy are specific topics in this collection and recur as themes in several articles because these developments are part of a larger pattern of changes in politics, technology, publishing, and communication in the past twenty to thirty years that have challenged traditional cultural assumptions about intellectual freedom. Our traditional political and social practices related to intellectual freedom, are unquestionably undergoing rapid change. These changes apply as well to legal practices which govern intellectual property, privacy, defamation, and, of course, fair use. It is not as though we never knew that governments spy on each other, but that we might now begin to wonder what practices a commitment to intellectual freedom should lead us to tolerate. It is hard to be committed to intellectual freedom without also being committed to the availability of reliable information for decision-making. We are experiencing change and disruption across a broad range of social and legal practices which affect the availability of reliable information. Moments of disruption in the status quo can affect intellectual freedom positively or negative, and are also opportunities to ask whether we should adopt new principles or conserve our current ones in the face of change. Conceptions of individual freedoms have evolved through time beginning with the Enlightenment. It is therefore understood that in the future intellectual freedom will not look like its origins, so there is work to do to redefine, readdress and remedy a lack of awareness of intellectual freedom principles.

To think about intellectual freedom in new ways and to respond to these new challenges we sought authors who were already experts on intellectual freedom as well as authors who could connect their specific area of expertise to intellectual freedom. In some cases this was quite challenging for our authors and for ourselves, as editors. The idea and even the terminology of intellectual freedom are shaped significantly by the professional cultures of librarianship, but we were primarily interested in other domains of knowledge and practice that might help us internationalize and complicate the North American paradigms and practices of intellectual freedom.

The result is a collection of twenty one articles which all present concepts, theories, and cases relevant to the reassessment and re-theorizing of intellectual freedom that our times seem to demand. We recommend this work to you as much for the distinct and independent treatments of each topic as well as for a highly inter-related set of readings which might support further intellectual work on intellectual freedom in the coming years.

The articles themselves were grouped (retrospectively) into four categories based on their treatments: 1) "Humanities and Politics;" in which we offer a philosophical overview of intellectual freedom, articles on Gramsci, Habermas, Feminism, and an assessment of the politics of neo-liberalism in relation to intellectual freedom. 2) "Media, Access, and Property" offers articles on alternative media, intellectual property, the internet and intellectual freedom, and the open access movement. 3) "Law, Rights, and International Approaches" includes work on the theory and cases of international courts related to the freedom of conscience, as well as the topics of hate speech and secrecy. Concluding chapters explain the nature of privacy and its importance to intellectual freedom—Richard's and Cornwell's, "Privacy and Intellectual Freedom"—and give an account of defamation law and some of the ways it can impede free expression—Dale Herbeck's, "Defamation Law and Intellectual Freedom." 4) "Arts, Social Culture, and Professional Life" covers a diverse range of topics, including religion, art censorship, sexual information and intellectual freedom, sexual orientation, libraries, journalism, and academic freedom.

In what follows we offer a very brief summary of the specific chapters and some of the connections that have emerged among them. In section one, Mark Alfino's chapter on "Philosophies of Intellectual Freedom" seeks a philosophical understanding of intellectual freedom by drawing on resources across the Western tradition but also specifically in the tradition of Mill and some of his critics. Critical insight about the philosophical traditions of intellectual freedom can be found in Gramsci's thought, which Doug Raber presents in his chapter entitled, "Gramsci and Intellectual Freedom," which also makes a critical comparison of Gramsci's and Mill's views. In other articles we also find implicit or explicit critique of the mainstream Millian tradition (see Koltutsky, Forde, Charbonneau, Lipinski and Henderson, for example). Lauren Pressley's "Feminism and Intellectual Freedom" is one of two articles that consider the emergence of social and political movements in relation to intellectual freedom. (See Carmichael for the other.) The section concludes with Laura Koltutsky's article on the politics of neoliberalism and intellectual freedom, which shows how neoliberal politics have altered perspectives on the goals of intellectual freedom from its liberal democratic origins.

All of the authors in Section 2 are concerned with various ways in which access, ownership, and the dissemination of information alter practices and ideas important to intellectual freedom. "Alternative Media and Intellectual Freedom," by Susan Forde, looks at the emergence and commitments of so-called alternative or "radical" media. Here, as with Gramsci, we encounter journalism with a critical attitude toward a classic liberal approach to intellectual freedom. (Another treatment of journalism, from the standpoint of the nature of the profession, can be found in Joe Cutbirth's chapter, "Journalism and Intellectual Freedom.") Robert Tiessen's chapter, "Intellectual Property and Intellectual Freedom," identifies and discusses ways in which the application of contemporary intellectual property law, both in the US and internationally, is having unintended and negative impacts on intellectual freedom. Elizabeth Buchanan's contribution, "The Internet and Intellectual Freedom," uses a local intellectual freedom incident at her home campus (and its dissemination and magnification through the internet) as a way of exploring some of the differences the internet makes to intellectual freedom cases. A final chapter by Olivier Charbonneau on "The Open Access Movement and Intellectual Freedom" develops the themes of access and property by showing how advocates of open access theorize open access content from a legal and economic perspective.

Section 3 includes contributions on law, rights, and international forms of intellectual freedom. A number of articles in the collection address international aspects of intellectual freedom (in addition to work about German and

Italian thinkers by Buschman and Raber, Tiessen, Lipinski and Henderson, Herbeck, and Alfino (on Academic Freedom) all consider international aspects of intellectual freedom in relation to their specific topics. But Leonard Hammer's article, "Intellectual Freedom from an International Perspective," considers legal theory supporting international case law on the freedom of conscience based on both United Nations and European covenants and conventions on human rights. Lipinski and Henderson review both philosophical and legal aspects of hate speech and its jurisprudence, including school speech codes, in "Hate Speech and Intellectual Freedom." They treat hate speech in part as a "market failure" in relation to the goals of intellectual freedom.

Susan Maret's "Intellectual Freedom and US Government Secrecy," provides a critical look at both historical and theoretical approaches to secrecy as these emerged from the practices of secrecy developed especially since the mid-20th century in the US government. Privacy can initially be thought of as a set of rights which allow individuals to keep information about themselves secret. But understanding privacy, especially in relation to US constitutional law and digital privacy, provides a more complex picture. In "Privacy and Intellectual Freedom," Richards and Cornwell use both jurisprudential history and theoretical argument to suggest that privacy needs to also be thought of as a set of controls for the flow of information to us. This discussion provides critical resources for looking at contemporary practices such as "frictionless sharing" and issues such as reader privacy and the impacts on privacy of the US Patriot Act. The section concludes with Dale Herbeck's article on "Defamation and Intellectual Freedom." After giving the reader sufficient understanding of defamation law, Herbeck shows how variations in defamation standards, for example, can impact intellectual freedom. This chapter also discusses intentional strategies for using defamation and libel law to intimidate or penalize expression. This includes so-called SLAPPs (Strategic Lawsuits against Public Participation).

The final section of this collection covers a diverse range of topics, from the arts and social culture to professional life. But reading through these chapters reminds us how much of a culture's intellectual freedom is realized in practices that only intersect with law and politics, but also have their own unique characteristics and implications. For example, Emily Knox's article, "Religion and Intellectual Freedom," shows how the practices of reading in a religion can support intellectual freedom and can be a rationale for broadening our stereotype of both religion and its relationship to intellectual freedom. This suggests new ways that librarians might respond to religionists and non-religionists. In "Art Censorship and Intellectual Freedom," Svetlana Mintcheva brings readers up to date on the kinds and cases of censorship found in a wide range of visual and performing arts. In each case some of the theoretical issues peculiar to each type of censorship are given, often drawn from the controversies of the underlying cases themselves.

Sex is never just another topic. Bob Holley's "Sex and Intellectual Freedom" helps us see why, by showing and exploring some of the ways that we treat sexual topics differently in spite of intellectual freedom commitments. This "cultural consent" not to discuss many sexual topics has implications for the ability of many people to understand their sexuality and promote sexual health. Sex, identity, and gender expression also have implications for intellectual freedom if you are part of a group that experiences "non-mainstream" sexual orientation and gender expression, such as Lesbian, Gay, Bisexual, and Transgender/transsexual (LGBT) individuals. By tracing the practices of naming and labelling of these groups, Jim Charmichael's "Sexual Orientation, Gender Expression and Intellectual Freedom" helps us understand the challenge of claiming intellectual and social space as a group in order to have freedom to express and theorize one's orientation and gender identity.

The last three articles in the collection all explore intellectual freedom in relation to professional life, specifically, librarianship, journalism, and academics. Loretta Gaffney's "Libraries and Intellectual Freedom" discusses the politics and media strategies of conservative groups that emerged during the mandatory filtering era of the Children's Internet Protection Act in the US. Disturbingly, many of these media campaigns target librarianship itself, often intentionally ignoring the intellectual freedom commitments of the profession or implicitly calling into question the moral commitments of professional librarians who oppose filtering.

Joe Cutbirth looks at the development of the profession of journalism and helps readers locate the role that journalists play in promoting intellectual freedom. Journalists sometimes do die for telling the truth and this often supports a popular intuition that journalists are trained truth seekers, but Cutbirth suggests that it is more helpful to think of journalists as "agents of the public sphere" (a concept from Habermas also discussed by Buschman). Finally, Alfino looks at the future of academic freedom in the professoriate, examining traditional defenses of it in light of the decline of tenure and other trends in higher education. Specific topics, such as religious "exemptions," internationalization, donor effects, and recent legal history are addressed in Alfino's article.

Whether these articles are read collectively or individually, each author tries to define how intellectual freedom has a role in their practice, their professions and their lives. The Handbook of Intellectual Freedom: Concepts, Cases and Theories was developed to take a broader view of modern society and to analyze intellectual freedom from a critical perspective. As we have worked with this book it has become profoundly obvious that challenges to intellectual freedom are by no means diminishing in number and that disparate fields have recognized this reality. It is heartening to realize that regardless of corporate and government attempts to limit access to information and to reduce personal privacies there is both awareness of and resistance to these efforts.

Part One

Theories from the Humanities and Politics

Philosophies of Intellectual Freedom

Mark Alfino

Intellectual Freedom is widely and correctly held to be one of the central achievements of the Enlightenment tradition in Western European thought. While the Enlightenment crystallized the modern conception of freedom of thought and conscience, the elements of this unique historical compound can be found in traditions of church scholarship and debate in the major religions of the West, in the culture of the university (Maguire 1998), in the history of public controversies involving the expression of ideas, toleration of religion, and the limits of the power of the state. Intellectual freedom places fundamental value on the autonomy of the individual to hold and express beliefs without fear of political or social punishment. This requires valuing mind and inquiry. One result of inquiry is knowledge, and the possession of knowledge, especially foreknowledge, has often been valued as divine or a sign of contact with the divine. Western sources for thinking about the value of mind and inquiry go as far back as the values of Periclean Athens and Platonic thought. Political and social cultures which have grown from the Enlightenment and its precursors have generally enshrined intellectual freedom in a set of more recognizable freedoms—especially freedom of speech, freedom of religion, and freedom of association. These relatively new political freedoms come to us from a broader political philosophical discourse of the self and involve an extensive scheme of legal protections of the individual against the power of the state.

But they also come together in the social culture of intellectual freedom. We can start our investigation informally by asking, "What is it like, fundamentally, to grow up in a culture of intellectual freedom?" The average individual in a political community shaped by basic liberties such as intellectual freedom rarely experiences this freedom through formal interaction with political and legal institutions. Rather, to grow up in a social culture with intellectual freedom, especially when it is not resisted by family or religious culture, is to acquire a distinctive sense of the acceptability of maintaining one's independence of thought and privacy of thought. It involves hearing affirmations of one's right to think differently and to develop one's own thinking. It involves experience of a culture of discussion and debate. A child in such a culture expects to be encouraged to develop a personal point of view as a part of his or her growth, and an adult in such a culture expects equal respect for his or her beliefs and tolerance for legitimate differences of opinion.

In the social culture of intellectual freedom, intellectual autonomy is taken seriously and social norms and legal rules support the detailed social construction of the autonomous self. In this sense, intellectual freedom entails a commitment to education and a concept of personal intellectual development. Inquiry is valued fundamentally in the social culture of intellectual freedom, at least in words and aspirations. In addition to formal learning, social etiquette and conversational values presume that nothing is in principle excluded from inquiry. One may learn that it is not respectful to challenge your dear old uncle's views over the holiday meal, but you would not learn that there are views which cannot be challenged, which cannot be investigated or written about and discussed among adult participants. By contrast, we know that individuals who grow up in cultures without intellectual freedom or in which such freedom was interrupted, for example, in Soviet era Eastern European countries, China, or some modern Arab political states, may feel the importance of this freedom as deeply, but learn a very different set of rules—rules about what topics it is never acceptable to speak publicly about, as well as what views are unacceptable to hold. This briefest sketch, even if it presents somewhat simple contrasts, shows us that intellectual freedom permeates the social practices of a culture's concept of the self and the model of the individual's development. Philosophers tend to want to know what rationales or theories support a culture's self-image and practice. What foundations can we give our idea and practice of intellectual freedom?

On a practical level, the social culture of intellectual freedom is sustained by a political and legal structure that articulates, administrates, and protects it. As a political achievement, intellectual freedom requires protections and legal remedies for unjust treatment for one's opinions and expression and against efforts to censor expression or unjustly limit access to information and discussion. Of course, the perpetrator of these injustices is often the state, so the political culture of intellectual freedom also typically includes a legal and juridical framework for challenging actions of the state which contravene its commitment to the basic liberties associated with intellectual freedom, especially speech, religious exercise, and freedom of association.

We must also acknowledge, at the start of the inquiry, that intellectual freedom exists in a dynamic relationship with other political and social forces. Our description of the social culture of intellectual freedom above was something of an idealization. One's religious experience, family life, social and economic status will affect how prominent the concept of intellectual freedom is in one's life. One's life experiences and temperament will matter. For example, outspoken academics, who rely on the job protections of tenure, and citizens or public figures who exercise their free speech rights to say something controversial experience their intellectual freedom in different ways from each other and from most of their peers who do not engage in such expression. Good philosophical accounts take into account both the idealizations of theory and the realism and complex phenomenology of our experience.

A philosophical investigation of intellectual freedom seeks to explore and evaluate our best understandings of and justifications for intellectual freedom. To do this, we must work from an accurate characterization of the historical, social, and political traditions within which it developed. Intellectual freedom has a history. Because its advocates generally see it as one of the best ideas in human history, there is a natural temptation to enlarge the historical narrative, to suppose that its roots are as broad and deep as the Western tradition itself. The trial of Socrates might be suggested as the first great moment in the history of intellectual freedom in the West, but we will see that that is a complicated statement to make.

While Enlightenment thought is a major focus of our philosophical analysis, a richer and more diverse political history is implicated in the Enlightenment development of intellectual freedom than we will have space to consider in this article. The history of the professional author, the religious wars and revolutions of Europe in the 17th and 18th centuries, the rise of science in public discourse[1], and the growth of knowledge during this period all contribute in complex ways to the formation of the modern concept of intellectual freedom. We will mention some of these themes as we gather resources for the main philosophical analysis of intellectual freedom, but each of these topics, if studied in detail, would provide more insight into the nature of intellectual freedom.

In the present article I will survey briefly some of the major philosophical expressions of the idea of intellectual freedom. Flashes of insight from ancient and modern culture shape the intellectual landscape that takes its current form in the Enlightenment and becomes recognizable to us in the twentieth century as "intellectual freedom." A major focus of our inquiry will be John Stuart Mill's defense of "liberty of thought and discussion" in *On Liberty*, which, I argue, gives a pivotal synthesis of historical themes along with a theoretical framework that should inform contemporary discussions

---

1   The rise of the "public sphere," as discussed also by Buschman and Cutbirth in this volume.

and controversies in intellectual freedom. Contemporary competing views, especially from John Rawls and the social contract tradition of political rights will be set in juxtaposition with Mill's work. After the survey of historical philosophical sources for the concept of intellectual freedom, which occupies section one below, the philosophical work of our inquiry will remain largely still to do. Do the philosophical resources of the past and present still provide a secure foundation for intellectual freedom? What are the principle philosophical problems in articulating the value or scope of intellectual freedom today? Have the past twenty years of the internet and the growth of digitial media changed anything fundamentally about our understanding of or reasonable aspirations for intellectual freedom? Good answers to these questions, which are attempted in sections two and three, develop what I call the "dual foundations" view of intellectual freedom. In section four, we test this view by reference to some contemporary problems in intellectual freedom.

Before searching the historical record for philosophical insights and resources, it might be useful to say something about the value of philosophical investigation of intellectual freedom. First, there is the possibility of increased self-understanding about the idea itself. We sometimes assume that if a concept or idea is central to social and political life then it must be well understood, but this is not always the case. Philosophical analysis can help with definitions and self-awareness about discrepancies in meaning of even seemingly well-known and widely held concepts such as intellectual freedom. But the specific value of understanding foundations goes beyond this kind of clarity. When librarians, lawyers, academics, and others advocate the rights and liberties associated with intellectual freedom in particular controversies—a contested book, a cancelled speech, an unjust dismissal—they need to know what ideas their advocacy commits them to. When librarians advocate the right to read as part of a commitment to intellectual freedom, for example, is it because they believe that we should all share a commitment to a certain kind of activity (reading), becoming a certain kind of person (a reader), or is reading purely instrumental to other goals, such as becoming a better citizen or increasing personal well-being through development of imagination or acquisition of knowledge? Perhaps the basis of our commitment is more formal than this? Do we advocate intellectual freedoms as a *right*, apart from any theory of the utility of it? Each of these justifications will take us to different commitments, only some of which are compatible with each other. Our best account of intellectual freedom should not only be self-consistent but also aspire to the sort of objectivity that compels assent. If we lack a compelling account of the objective value of intellectual freedom, we will have nothing persuasive to say in response to the objector who feels that our advocacy is arbitrary or based more on hopes than reality.

Ultimately, there are very practical reasons for wanting to clarify the foundations of intellectual freedom. As we shall see, at times the basis of intellectual freedom has been given in theological terms, anthropological terms, political terms, and, more recently, in epistemological terms. There is nothing specifically wrong with any foundational defense of intellectual freedom that includes insightful and true premises and a solid rationale, but if the goal is to locate the best philosophical theory about intellectual freedom (or features of the best theory), as it is in this philosophical inquiry, then we need to pay particular attention to the presuppositions at work in various defenses of this idea. Presumably clarity about the basic nature and grounding of intellectual freedom will help us determine which battles to engage in the name of this freedom. It may also help us to discern a future for intellectual freedom in light of a rapidly changing information environment. The best philosophical theory of intellectual freedom for our day and place will ultimately combine a historical retrieval of insights and ideas with our best contemporary understanding of the value of freedom of conscience and expression.

Philosophical Resources for Intellectual Freedom

When we look for historical sources and philosophical resources for thinking about intellectual freedom, most of the evidence that we easily recognize as such does seem to come from a specific and well known strand of the Western tradition, beginning in Greek culture of sixth century B.C.E. and running through the development of Western European political history.[2] Social codes and practices concerning who may speak in a group or under what conditions one has a "claim" to say something (and protection after saying it) are universal among human societies. Intellectual freedom is not reducible to a set of social codes and practices, but as we have already seen, they can be partially descriptive of it. In saying that intellectual freedom is a tradition of the West, we are focusing on the unique development of these universal social and political practices as they lead to their mature expression in the Enlightenment and in contemporary rights-based societies around the world.

In this review of historical viewpoints, I will illustrate what I take to be a standard historical view: that the tradition of intellectual freedom of the Enlightenment brought together ancient and longstanding values about the

2   It will help to use a broad conception of this tradition. As Swan points out, there are elements of intellectual freedom in Egyptian and Sumerian culture (Swan 1994, 280). Also, the "Western tradition" is, famously, not a single or simple thing, and it is what it is in part because of interactions with cultures outside of itself.

importance of deliberation, tolerance, speech, and expression with the modern political tradition of universal rights. Within a relatively very short span of Western political history, and in no small part because of widespread experience of violent and persistent religious and political warfare, the political self in many European states became a bearer of rights for liberty of thought and conscience. In the philosophical parallel to this political history, European intellectuals produced major statements and treatises on the importance of knowledge, expression, and tolerance, especially from the beginning of the 17th century to the end of the 19th. In reconstructing some ideas from this tradition, we will be supplying ourselves with resources for the philosophical analysis in section two of the inquiry.

Before treating the modern philosophical history we should look at the ancient. The development of the status of the citizen in ancient Athens can be taken as a historical starting point for our discussion of intellectual freedom. In response to social unrest in the early sixth century B.C.E., the reforms of Solon moved Athens toward establishing the status of the citizen and his (and eventually, under Pericles, her) legal obligations and benefits. Solon's reforms did not completely address the social unrest that motivated them, and toward the end of the sixth century Cleisthenes literally reorganized the political map of Athens to dilute the influence of nobles over poor citizens and to undercut older tribal divisions of the polity. Crucially, the reforms placed emphasis on local and collective discussion, speech situations in which citizens were expected to advance considerations for laws and policies (Martin 1996, 87). By the time of Pericles, 50–60 years later, additional reforms were undertaken, including measures to allow the poor to take advantage of their democratic opportunity to serve in government (Martin 1996, 115). This increased the value of speech as a fundamental technology of political life, and brought with it questions about the protection one enjoyed for candid speech.

In recent decades, attention has been given by scholars to the concept of *parrhesia*, or "frank speech" and a related term, "isegoria," both of which are originally associated with Athenian democracy, but which also surface in many places throughout the Graeco-Roman period, including Platonic dialogues, Euripedes' plays, Epicurus, and, later, Roman writers such as Seneca and Philodemus, who wrote a treatise, *On Parrhesia*. The problem of frank speech in a world of political tyrants is logically and rhetorically complex. How does a tyrant get candid advice? If he asks you for criticism, how do you know that he will not kill you for your candor? Ancient authors recognized, in addition, that distinguishing frank speech from flattery might be difficult to do rhetorically, especially in a world that does not already protect candor (Konstan 2004, 20).

Konstan cites examples of ancient attitudes toward candor in speech and its role in Athenian democracy. Parrhesia was a recognized right of a citizen to speak in public and related to another concept, "isegoria," which refers to the equality of standing of citizens to address an assembly. Parrhesia has a range of meanings. In the Philodemus text it is principally about the problem of candor between teachers and disciples. Marcus Aurelius echoes this in a reflection on learning the importance of enduring the frank speech of others. Epictetus mentions parrhesia as a political good that might be taken away by bad law (2004, 28). We have good evidence that parrhesia is part of the cultural concept of self in the ancient world and that its usages cut across many categories of social, political, and philosophical discourse.

In Foucault's treatment of parrhesia, both in lectures at the Collège de France in 1981–1982 and at University of Berkeley in 1983, parrhesias is explored across these categories of discourse. In the earlier lectures, Foucault considers, for example, the ancients' awareness of the rhetorical problem of speaking truth to power. How does the Prince distinguish truth from flattery without protecting frank speech? In the lectures at Berkeley, eight months before his death, Foucault initially gave an analytic treatment of parrhesia. He notes, for example, that parrhesia comes up in contexts in which telling the truth involves a danger, such as the danger to journalists so vividly discussed in this volume by Joe Cutbirth. It is connected fundamentally to the decision to expose the self in words that could risk disapproval or punishment from a tyrant, a majority, or another, more powerful citizen or group. Foucault's wide ranging lectures show how the concept of parrhesia arose across six plays of Euripides, the Platonic dialogue *Laches*, and in the public practice of the Cynics. Foucault's insight, as usual, is to identify layers and dimensions of social practice which both constitute and interact with philosophical and other hegemonic discourses. One realizes from his treatment that intellectual freedom is fundamentally connected with danger to the self yet also defining for a self.

Shifting from this broad philosophical cultural analysis to "official" philosophical culture, one could say that the spirit of the Platonic dialogues embody a commitment to the value of intellectual freedom, at least in so far as it promotes mind and inquiry. Plato constantly has the Socrates of the dialogues inviting interlocutors to give candid answers to his questions and to let the arguments go wherever they may. The historical Socrates seems to have spent considerable time in public engaging in open discourse with others about a wide range of topics. His own defense against the charges of corruption brought against him is that he was on a religious mission to learn the meaning of the Oracle at Delphi, who declared Socrates to be the wisest human. This mission compelled him to engage in frank speech (especially questioning) with figures of authority who were regarded as wise. He tries to persuade his peers in the jury that this activity, natural philosophy, is beneficial to Athens. Famously, Socrates declares that he would rather die than stop engaging in philosophy. Socrates deserves his status as a hero of candid speech and commitment to principle. We should note, however, that neither he nor Plato were supporters of their culture's democracy, and it is unlikely that they would have responded to a call for universal protections for intellectual freedom with enthusiasm. The spirit of inquiry in the dialogues seems to imply a favorable view of intellectual freedom, especially to a modern ear, but you can believe that some people should engage in free inquiry without believing that everyone should. Plato's endorsement of the noble lie and a stratified society would suggest that he falls in this camp. In spite of this, Plato advocates discussion virtues which are important to a culture of intellectual freedom, and appears to have modeled them within the Academy, if the tone of the dialogues is an accurate guide. But for Plato, the discussion virtues of free and open inquiry are part of a method for pursuing truth. There is no broader agenda in Plato for promoting liberty of thought and expression for its own sake.

In this selective survey of ancient philosophical resources on intellectual freedom we find the roots of intellectual freedom in the political traditions of Athens which articulate the standing and protection of the citizen. More generally, intellectual freedom is part of the dynamic of truth and power, the relationship of the critic to the tyrant, the dissenter to the state. Even in the case of the tyrant seeking advice, the dynamics of "frank speech" and danger are at work. The logic of this dynamic qualifies the tyrant's power. Finally, we find it in the open pursuit of the truth modeled in the Platonic dialogues.

These representative, yet briefly presented details of political and cultural life from ancient Greece and the Hellenistic and Roman periods do not paint a complete picture of the overall historical development of intellectual freedom. For example, there are traditions of intellectual discourse, both following from the post-Socratic schools (such as the Cynics) and from major religious traditions within which open questioning and frank speech were encouraged. These traditions eventually intersect in the history of the university. To the extent that traditions of inquiry are part of the development of modern intellectual freedom, these two sources would be important to discuss, among others. Like the Platonic tradition, they model discussion virtues related to the pursuit of truth. Standing to speak is not conferred as a matter of egalitarian principle or because of a universal individual right, but because one has earned the status to speak (or to "profess") or has found oneself in a situation requiring a Socratic-like commitment to truth.

The historical transition to modern European thought through the Renaissance and the early scientific revolution looks, in retrospect, like the incubation period of the modern concept of intellectual freedom. The recovery (and re-invention) of ancient culture in the Renaissance included a retrieval and revalorization of Greek and Roman heroes of speech and principle such as Socrates, even as it would eventually find its own heroes, ranging from Galileo to renaissance heretics such as Giordano Bruno. Francis Bacon's 1605 treatise, *The Advancement of Learning*, is an early work (possibly the first published in English) imagining the growth and spread of knowledge from the new methods of science. Baconian thought about progress in knowledge, like the general culture of scientific inquiry which follows it in the 17th and 18th centuries, increasingly presumed that inquiry must be freed from prior constraints, such as those imposed by traditional culture and our lack of independent thought. In the same spirit, almost 200 years after Bacon, Kant would boldly declare, in *What is Enlightenment?*, that the age of Enlightenment promises nothing less than the liberation of humankind from its bondage through ignorance. "Nothing is required for this enlightenment, however, except freedom; and the freedom in question is the least harmful of all, namely, the freedom to use reason publicly in all matters" (Kant 1949). Kant directly connects freedom of conscience and expression with the use of reason and the spread of knowledge for the improvement of human well being.

By the time of Bacon's treatise, a revolution had already occurred within Christianity in the form of the Protestant schism. Luther's advocacy of direct study of the bible had obvious and direct implications for free intellectual culture. While the right of conscience within religious thought was not invented by Protestants, the Reformation placed new emphasis on the individual's personal relationship to the Bible. That relationship came to be thought of as a protected matter of individual conscience within a congregation of worshippers. The achievement of a universal culture of intellectual freedom in Europe would have to wait through wars of religion, the growth of social consensus about religious tolerance and separation of church and state, but the introduction of a less hierarchical, less Platonic model of the pursuit of religious truth, such as we find in Protestantism, clearly influenced the growth of intellectual freedom in Europe.

A singular text for pursuing this point is Milton's *Areopagitica*, "A Speech for the Liberty of Unliscensed Printing," 1644, which offers a religious defense of freedom of the press. Milton argues for liberty of thought and expression because it is crucial for the purpose of revealing the meaning of God's creation. He advocates state protection for non-seditious speech and a general protection of freedom of conscience. Like Locke in his *Letter on Toleration*, he allows for suppression of Catholic thought, but Milton's work represents an important treatment of intellectual freedom from a religious philosophical perspective (Jones 1949). Later Enlightenment statements of religious freedom, such as Jefferson's, will echo this argument from religious purpose.

Some of the best philosophical resources for the modern conception of intellectual freedom come from statements of the need for religious toleration in light of political experience. John Locke's famous *Letter on Toleration* (1689) and Thomas Jefferson's *Bill for Establishing Religious Freedom* (1779) and *First Inaugural Address* (1801) are among the more important sources for seeing both continuity with the past and new arguments. Locke's letter comes after the religious conflicts which led to the Glorious Revolution of 1688. Fear about the growing influence of France and Catholicism came to a head with the accession of James II and his pro-Catholic policies, including the 1687 Declaration of Indulgence, also known as the Declaration for the Liberty of Conscience, which promoted freedom of religion. As is well known, the Glorious Revolution brought the Protestant, William of Orange, to the throne and restructured both the relationship of the monarch to parliament and the relationship of religion to government.

Locke begins his argument for religious toleration much as Jefferson would almost 100 years later, by invoking religious arguments. The Gospels should be sufficient, Locke implies, to show Christians that faith must work by persuasion rather than force. Locke argues that allowing the magistrate to enforce a single religion's norms by law creates more social unrest than separating, as much as possible, the duties of civil government from the proper office of religion—the care of souls. While Locke expresses concern (as will Mill almost 200 years later) about the dual loyalties of Catholics, it is important to note that at the level of belief, Locke supported toleration. Most of the things we would want to prevent a religious group from doing (Locke considers a faith that might want to sacrifice babies) can be justified without proscribing religious belief. The idea that a stable society can allow great latitude of belief would not have seemed as intuitive to Locke's audience is it might to a contemporary citizen of a stable rights-based democracy. But Locke advocates tolerance even of a religion whose believers Locke's contemporaries might otherwise distrust. "If a Roman Catholic believe that to be really the body of Christ which another man calls bread, he does no injury thereby to his neighbor. If a Jew does not believe the New Testament to be the word of God, he does not thereby alter anything in men's civil rights." (Locke 1689) We will see Mill's even stronger version of these principles of separation and tolerance, but it is important to note that Locke conceives of matters of private belief and faith as protected by our fundamental liberties. Locke considers numerous arguments of the day for letting the government enforce a common religion and morality, but he consistently shows that limited state involvement in religion makes the most sense of social life given the long history and recent experience of man, especially in matters of religious conflict.

Jefferson drafted *The Virginia Act For Establishing Religious Freedom* three years after drafting the *Declaration of Independence* and ten years before supporting the Bill of Rights as amendments to the U.S. Constitution. A reading of this short text, in conjunction with his First Inaugural Address, shows both continuities and differences with Locke's Letter. Like Locke, he begins by invoking a religious argument, "that Almighty God hath created the mind free, and manifested his Supreme will that free it shall remain, by making it altogether insusceptible of restraint" (Jefferson 1949a). He echoes several of Locke's arguments concerning separation of civil government from religion.

Perhaps because of the occasion of Jefferson's text, which introduces an affirmation of religious freedom as a legislative act, there is a more specific concern with the implications of religious practices for a citizen's standing. The act itself is worth quoting in full to show this concern, which is similar to Locke's, but more pronounced.

> We the General Assembly of Virginia do enact, that no man shall be compelled to frequent or support any relig[i]ous Worship place or Ministry whatsoever, nor shall be enforced, restrained, molested, or burthened in his body or goods, nor shall otherwise suffer on account of his religious opinions or belief, but that all men shall be free to profess, and by argument to maintain their opinions in matters of religion, and that the same shall in no wise diminish, enlarge, or affect their civil capacities. (Jefferson 1949a)

In addition to proscribing compulsion, there is a focus on the positive expression of the individual's views and beliefs and the danger that religious belief could either enlarge or diminish someone's power as a citizen. Consistent with the idea of *parrhesia*, Jefferson's act is intended to provide protection for the potentially dangerous practice of frankly expressing or living out one's views about religion. Significantly, this protection is needed from both government and one's peers, whose social behaviors could be as tyrannical as an oppressive ruler.

One finds a similar echo of *parrhesia* in Jefferson's First Inaugural Address, in which he said, "If there be any among us who would wish to dissolve this Union or to change its republican form, let them stand undisturbed as monuments of the safety with which error of opinion may be tolerated where reason is left free to combat it" (Jefferson 1949b). Jefferson is boasting that this form of government, which would protect even those who advocate its dissolution, is ultimately "the strongest Government on earth" (Jefferson 1949b, 143). In both this quote and in his earlier bill, Jefferson affirms freedom of speech and conscience as part of a process of engaging and combating error. As we will see, this epistemological dimension of intellectual freedom becomes more prominent in Mill's thought in *On Liberty (1859)* and in very recent interpretations of it.

John Stuart Mill's short treatise, *On Liberty*, was not written in the haste of an immediate political crisis. It was an enlargement, worked on over a period of about 5 years, of a shorter essay on the same topic, the limits of the authority of the state over the individual.[3] Mill wants to know the legitimate principles defining and governing basic human liberties. He thinks of human liberty in term of three domains: the "inward domain of consciousness," the "liberty of tastes and pursuits," and freedom of association. It is important to note that Mill includes thought, expression, and conduct in his concept of liberty (Mill 1977, 18:226). The introductory chapter frames the political question of the limits of the state over the individual in terms of the following famous principle: ". . . the sole end for which mankind are warranted, individually or collectively, in interfering with the liberty of action of any of their number, is self-protection" (Mill 1977, 18:223).

The central and most famous arguments relevant to intellectual freedom occur in the next Chapter entitled, "On Liberty of Thought and Discussion." There Mill argues for promoting liberty of thought and discussion of ideas, whether they are true or false. Mill follows that with a chapter, "Of Individuality," which discusses the general value of individuality given our natures and the value to society of allowing so-called "experiments in living" (Mill 1977, 18:261). The text concludes with two more chapters. One frames the *social* question of the limits of society over the individual by distinguishing between circumstances in which an individual must bear negative social consequences for his or her views or free acts (such as shunning) and our obligation to tolerate others and avoid making their lives "uncomfortable." (Mill 1977, 18:279). The last chapter considers quite a few practical applications of the main philosophical principles of the text, including cases involving truth in advertising, medications and poisons, compulsory education, and other matters. From the structure of the discussion alone it should be clear that Mill sees himself addressing basic liberty at both the political and social levels. He is concerned, for example, about the state acting against an individual who speaks out against it or holds an unpopular opinion, but he is also wondering how we are supposed to relate to each other socially if we disagree fundamentally with each other's views or lifestyle. This is the problem of living out a commitment to human liberty in a world in which one's commitment to truths may lead one to want to shun or act against those whose differences are perceived as a threat.

---

3   The circumstances of authorship are of more than passing interest to our inquiry. The text was authored during a relatively short period of time in which Mill was finally married to his long time partner, Mrs. Harriet Taylor, and enjoyed relative seclusion with her from society. Their relationship was a scandal, but Mill credits her with tremendous influence on his thought, including the entire argument for his famous, *The Subjugation of Women*. It is hard to imagine that Mill would not be thinking of his own need for liberty of association and intellectual partnership, and its constraint by social traditions, as he worked on *On Liberty* in close quarters with Harriett, during the last five years of her life (Shields 1956, xi–xii).

The main argument in Chapter Two of "On Liberty" may be summarized as follows: The silencing of the expression of opinions is a bad thing in every case. It is bad when the opinion is false, when it is true, and when there is a mix of truth and falsehood in it. In the first case, when the opinion is false, silencing it is bad for two reasons. First, it "robs the human race" of the opportunity to determine for itself that the opinion is false. But second, it assumes that we can know with absolute certainty that an opinion is false. This requires that we believe ourselves to be infallible. Mill argues eloquently that an assumption of infallibility about one's opinions is a bad basis for finding truth, a bad basis for limiting *others'* pursuit of truth, and incompatible with what we know about how humans come to have any certainty about their knowledge at all. We only get justified certainty by following principles of "corrigibility, open-mindedness, and epistemological modesty" (Finnochiaro 2005, 90). These principles are crucial to finding and maintaining truth, therefore an attitude of infallibility, which would be needed to limit expression, is not justified in itself or as a basis for limiting inquiry or expression.

Mill considers many objections here, but one early one is particularly important for our discussion. Suppose a group replies to Mill by saying that they are not assuming infallibility by acting on their views, but only acting on beliefs they honestly hold to be true. Could they then limit expression of other views? After all, our faculty of judgment is there to use and it might even be our duty to stand up for what we believe true or to prevent the dissemination of claims we believe to be false, especially if we regard them as dangerous. It may not be assuming infallibility so much as the right to act on views one believes true (Mill 1977, 18:230). One might imagine a case in which someone does have the requisite epistemic humility, but has good reason to think that the harms of not acting on one's knowledge are greater than the benefit of leaving some questions open. In response to this kind of challenge, Mill develops part of a theory of truth, which we will be able to trace through his discussion. He distinguishes between asserting a view because it has survived a process of validation and refutation, on the one hand, and assuming it true for the purpose of preventing future refutations or challenges to its validity on the other. Mill argues that if you pay attention to how the human mind works, you will realize that we only come to truth or certainty at all by a social process of discussion, interpretation, and the collision of our ideas with others.

> *The steady habit of correcting and completing his own opinion by collating it with those of others, so far from causing doubt and hesitation in carrying it into practice, is the only stable foundation for a just reliance on it. . . . (Mill 1977, 18:232)*

The argument, then, is that the person who advocates suppression of inquiry because he claims to have the truth is not acting consistently with the process that produces truth, even if he is not assuming infallibility. That is not to deny that there will still be situations in which we must restrict or regulate speech, and Mill does advocate restrictions on commercial speech when the potential for harm is great (Mill 1977, 18:294).

Later in the chapter Mill considers the hypothetical case in which the opinions in question *are actually true* and not just believed true. Surely in that case we are entitled to close off discussion of dissenting views. But here Mill adds significantly to his theory of truth, really a "social epistemology," a theory about how social life advances or hinders the pursuit of truth. He argues that our understanding of truth depends upon a continuous process of interpretation and discussion without which the truth would be a "dead dogma, not a living truth" (Mill 1977, 18:243; Finocchiaro 2005, 91). Even if we need to enforce restrictions on, say, the sale of poisons, we need to keep reviewing and thinking about arguments and evidence for the restriction, in order to maintain a social understanding of the nature of the truth on which our restriction is based. The point, then, is not that we never restrict or condition liberty, but that we never assume that a truth we hold, whether about the harms of some prohibition, or even about the basis of liberty itself, does not need continual review, rethinking, and restatement.

What follows in the text is one of the most passionate and well reasoned accounts of the importance of continual and ongoing discussion of beliefs. Mill implies that the person who merely learns truths, without engaging in the dialectical process which produces them, has a deficient understanding. Every truth depends, for its complete understanding, on the explication of its grounds and of diverse points of view about it. Mill describes the difference between rote learning of truth and the active engagement of the mind in understanding a truth to help make his point (Mill 1977, 18:242-252).

The last case, in which the opinion is partially true and partially false, is the easiest for Mill to address. After all, in such cases, we are clearly in the process of sorting out true and false claims, arguments, and theories. In the typical case there are partial truths to be distilled from larger claims, as well as claims judged likely or certainly to be false. Again, Mill has a very temporal and social model of truth and discourse here: ". . . in revolutions of opinion, one part of the truth usually sets while another rises" (Mill 1977, 18:18, 252). In discussing this case, he uses the example of how a robust and open discussion of Christian morality, for example, might reduce religious and philosophical misunderstanding (Mill 1977, 18:256-257).

Part of the elegance of Mill's argument lies in the way he systematically considers cases in which we are tempted to extend the power of the state to suppress opinion. Throughout the main argument, he is concerned about assumptions which arguments for suppression make about the nature of truth and theories about how truths are discovered, held, justified, and applied. These two concerns underlie the four major sub-arguments Finocchiaro finds in Chapter Two of *On Liberty* (Finocchiaro 2005, 95). First, there is the assumption of "infallibility," which comes up most directly in the case of suppression of "known" falsehoods, but which also occurs as a temptation when we have universal acceptance of truths. The positive argument is: Human knowledge is generally fallible. If we appreciate the fallibility of knowledge we will value social practices which favor the discussion and review of many ideas and beliefs, including some which we are sure to be false. Second, Mill places fundamental value on the act of giving supporting reasons for a view (presenting views with justifying or explanatory rationales) as a means of knowing truth and sharpening our understanding of error. Not only is this a common Enlightenment conceit, which we found in Bacon and Kant, but Mill's exposition clearly shows that he is thinking about the production of truth as a social process which requires various kinds of tests and challenges. Third, Mill argues that we cannot maintain the practical meanings of ideas without thinking them through in ongoing critical discussion. This is a more basic point than the previous one since he is claiming something about the minimum requirements for even *maintaining understanding* of ideas, much less winnowing truth from its mixture with falsehood. Finally, Mill bases some of his arguments on a view about the typical case in which we find that truth and falsity are mixed. The general fact that our views and competing views often both have partial truth and insight should support intellectual freedom.

There is much more to Mill's argument for intellectual freedom than the central arguments of Chapter Two, "On Liberty of Thought and Discussion" suggest. In his fascinating discussion of individuality, Mill offers a set of arguments for the importance of individuality and the correlative importance of a society tolerating different lifestyles. Individuality relates to the second and third domains of intellectual freedom, the "liberty of tastes and pursuits" and "freedom of association." For what good is it to express an idea and not be at liberty to pursue it in one's life and with other like-minded individuals? But Mill goes further than arguing against restrictions on intellectual freedom that would limit individuality. He also believes that individuality is a measure of the vitality of a free society. We should want individuality in others, even if we are ourselves traditionalists or conformists (Mill 1977, 18:267). Individuality can wax or wane in a society and Mill argues that we should want genuine individuality and avoid excessive conformism. In this famous passage, Mill advocates so-called "experiments in living." His worry about the chilling effect of custom on individuality is again reminiscent of Bacon's critique of tradition.

When Mill returns to his larger argument in Chapter 4, "Of the Limits to the Authority of the Society over the Individual," his focus is on how society should treat viewpoint and lifestyle diversity. In the introduction he had argued for limiting the state's interference with fundamental liberties. Now he asks how our social relations ought to accommodate diversity. Mill's views on this are still inspiring to many. He acknowledges that society can punish people by exclusion and shunning, and that sometimes this is justified. "We have a right, also, in various ways, to act upon our unfavorable opinion of anyone, not to the oppression of his individuality, but in the exercise of ours" (Mill 1977, 18:278). On the other hand, Mill argues that we owe a kind of civility and fairness even to those whose views and behaviors we regard as flawed. If the effects of their actions are purely self-regarding, we might take into account that the person may already be bearing the punishment of their mistaken beliefs and actions. In any case, we should acknowledge that even the negative examples of others' folly are valuable to us. In a Millian society, we would adopt social attitudes toward others and their self-regarding behaviors which parallel the restraint and toleration we show over differences of opinion about truth and knowledge.

Mill's *On Liberty* deserves its reputation as a critical text in the development of the modern conception of intellectual freedom. His position brings together ancient themes in intellectual freedom, such as parrhessia, with a contemporary understanding of the need for universal liberties, the importance of limiting state and social coercion in protecting these liberties as rights, and the Enlightenment ideal of promoting human and social well-being through the growth of knowledge. These are crucial elements of our contemporary understanding of intellectual freedom, and Mill's synthesis of them is clear and relevant to contemporary discussion, as we shall see in Section III. Also, it is remarkable how much of Mill's reasoning is focused on a view about how truth and knowledge are produced through social interaction, a social epistemology. Mill's ultimate goal may be to defend liberty, but many of the reasons we ought to defend liberty turn out to have to do with the fact that limitations of liberty tend to be justified using beliefs or attitudes that are inimical to the discovery, validation, and understanding of new truths, on which the progress of society depends.

But Mill's defense of freedom of thought, expression, and conduct is hardly the last major defense of these values among recent or modern philosophers and jurists. Mill's discussion has a focus on thought and expression that is unique for its time and gives it a deserved pre-eminence in discussions of intellectual freedom. But for the general defense of rights, the main tradition of the Enlightenment is not the positivist and utilitarian one running from Comte through Mill to the present. Rather, the more extensive tradition of justifying basic liberties as rights comes to the Enlightenment from the earlier tradition of natural law. The Enlightenment developed the idea that our basic rights are justified by supposing them to be the result of a "social contract" which reflects the principles of justice that "any rational person" would agree to.

The social contract tradition was developed in diverse ways through the writings of philosophers such as Hobbes, Locke, Kant, and Rousseau. In the twentieth century, John Rawls is credited with reviving this tradition by conceiving of the original contract as a hypothetical situation in which we try to agree upon basic principles of justice. In order for the agreement to reflect our rational judgement, as opposed to our judgement biased by particular facts about ourselves and our place in society, Rawls asks us to imagine that we choose principles of justice from behind a "veil of ignorance"—in other words, without knowing our ethnicity, natural abilities, share in good fortune, or even whether we will be part of a liked or disliked group. We do, however, retain knowledge about human nature and psychology as we consider various principles. In his major works, *A Theory of Justice, Political Liberalism,* and *Justice as Fairness,* Rawls establishes this framework and tries to show that rational agents would choose two basic principles of justice. First, they would choose a scheme of basic liberties which would include "freedom of thought and liberty of conscience; political liberties (for example, the right to vote and to participate in politics) and freedom of association, as well as rights and liberties specified by the liberty and integrity (physical and psychological) of the person; and finally, the rights and liberties covered by the rule of law" (Rawls 2001, 44; cited in Amdur 2008, 106). Basic liberties are contrasted, for example, with secondary rights such as those governing the sorts of property that can be owned. Basic liberties can only be restricted in order to promote liberty. So, for example, we cannot restrict someone's liberty because it threatens economic development, but we could restrict liberty if its exercise limited others' liberties. As Robert Amdur notes, both Mill and Rawls put a high value on freedom of conscience, thought, and discussion (Amdur 2008, 107), so it is reasonable to ask what difference their distinct justifications might make to the actual practice of intellectual freedom, when competing values are at stake.

As we turn to critical issues in the philosophical discussion of the foundations of intellectual freedom, we will engage Rawls' specific criticism of Mill. For now, however, we have put on the table most of the philosophical resources we will need to work with in the second section, where we will begin the philosophical part of the inquiry, the goal of which is to determine the best philosophical justifications for intellectual freedom.

Two Philosophical Problems in Intellectual Freedom

We want clarity about the foundations and theory of intellectual freedom for all of the reasons identified at the outset—to know what situations really involve intellectual freedom, to justify public practices connected with intellectual freedom, and to know how to develop our ideas of intellectual freedom in relation to new knowledge and technology. As an historical and cultural concept, intellectual freedom and the rights which support it need continual discussion and assessment, especially as our critical understanding of the Enlightenment deepens in light of contemporary cultural experience. The present offers both new versions of old problems and new problems. Our intellectual freedom controversies are not identical to the problems of religious toleration growing out of the wars of religion in Europe, but we clearly have an analogue of that problem in contemporary challenges by various groups, including fundamentalist religionists, to the culture of free speech and expression. In a global information environment, philosophical inquiry offers a non-arbitrary approach to these challenges.

In our own era, two kinds of foundational problems have become prominent. First, there are significant differences between rights-based and utility-based defenses of intellectual freedom. The contest of arguments between rights theorists, such as Rawls, and modern day defenders of Mill needs to be joined. After presenting recent versions of the argument from the professional literature, I will argue that there is no simple choice between the two distinct theoretical approaches, and that the differences between them are often exaggerated, at least in the case of intellectual freedom. Put positively, there may be a coherent "dual foundation" to intellectual freedom which fuses both traditions to some extent.

Second, a traditional goal of justification regarding basic liberties is to find "neutral foundations"—that is, a basis for intellectual freedom that is neutral with respect to different concepts of the good life. If our advocacy of intellectual freedom is based on a particular theory of persons or the best way to live, even a theory with considerable evidence held by a majority of people, then we might wonder if it can ever claim more authority than the collective bias that represents it. Are there entirely neutral foundations for intellectual freedom? I will argue that the search for entirely neutral foundations for intellectual freedom is mistaken. We ought to search for a broad and overlapping consensus regarding the most neutral principles possible, but we ought to also use our best current knowledge of human nature and the production of knowledge to inform principles and practices. There are real limits to the neutrality of foundations. As we will see, the difficulty of articulating neutral principles for intellectual freedom parallels the problem of defending neutrality in librarianship. Our best resolution to these foundational issues will help justify a practical contemporary understanding of intellectual freedom.

Returning to the first problem, defenders of traditional theories of human rights argue persuasively that persons have rights by virtue of their intrinsic nature. Respecting rights involves respect for the intrinsic value of the individual. Contemporary theorists of rights, such as Rawls, argue that if we exclude morally irrelevant information by adopting a perspective behind a "veil of ignorance," we will all discern the same principles of justice needed to realize the conditions of respect for our nature. Notice that nothing in this account refers to the production of human happiness. Rights traditionally rest on obligations to respect the autonomy of individuals to act for or against their happiness. Maybe the KKK and its supporters are happier on the day they march through town, but the overall happiness of the community might plummet. For the traditional defender of rights, these effects are strictly irrelevant. Thus, the defense of rights is traditionally thought to be based on a deontological (or duty-based) as opposed to a eudaimonistic (or happiness-oriented) theory of value.

Since the development of utilitarian thought in the 19th century, especially since its statement in Mill's *Utilitarianism* (1863), there has been an alternative way of thinking about rights. Utilitarians are committed first and foremost to the principle of utility, which obligates us to promote human well-being for the greatest number possible. The warrant for this principle depends upon the following two basic claims: 1) that each person's happiness is as valuable to that person as every other person's happiness is to them; and 2) that the goal of human society is fundamentally the promotion of human well being. In other words, utilitarianism is traditionally committed to the equality and priority of human well being. Promoting human well being as a matter of moral duty commits the utilitarian to an *extrinsic* theory of value, in contrast to the *intrinsic value* of respect for persons at work in rights theories. Our moral choices involve acting on values by which human beings seek to promote their happiness. Utilitarians recognize rights, but they defend them as policies for promoting human well-being. They generally argue that if the traditional defender of rights is honest about the situations in which violating someone's rights would be justified, (imagine an armed citizen trying to decide whether to kill someone who is about to detonate a nuclear bomb), she would reconsider her commitment to intrinsic value, or at least to an absolute defense of rights without considerations of utility. For utilitarians in the Millian tradition, respecting rights is good policy for promoting human well-being.

The rights theorist, not surprisingly, will claim that the utilitarian is misunderstanding the basic reason why members of a society would insist on protections for basic liberties. We could value rights as a means to achieve happiness, but the *real* rationale for acknowledging rights is that by doing so we represent ourselves to each other as moral persons. A commitment to basic rights is fundamentally about recognizing a set of moral facts about individuals and making this recognition part of the basis for our social contract. In other words, the contractarian rights theorist, such as Rawls, is saying that a rational person would put the recognition and equal protection of basic rights ahead of any cooperative venture for promoting happiness. The former is something I should want guaranteed, recognized, and protected apart from any effort I make to secure the latter. The basic criticism, then, is that the utilitarian cannot provide a firm enough foundation for the basic liberties underlying intellectual freedom, ". . . the case for liberty is itself precarious, relying as it does on the result of utilitarian calculations. Even if the calculations appear to support liberty today, tomorrow a new set of calculations could demonstrate that repression produces greater overall utility" (Amdur 2008, 108). Martha Nussbaum echoes this criticism when she writes that Mill makes free thought and discussion "hostage to contingent facts concerning what best promotes truth and progress" (Nussbaum 2004, 326; cited in Amdur 2008, 108).

The theoretical tensions between rights theories and utilitarian theories are, in an important sense, fundamental and irresolvable. There really are different choices and motivations for advocates of each theory, and the basic theories of value seem incompatible. We find similar versions of this theoretical dispute in the library literature on defenses of intellectual freedom. In a 1990 Library Trends article, David Ward eloquently defends a traditional rights-based view. In addition to the general arguments already discussed, Ward argues that a rights theory can distinguish better between, for example, our negative duty to refrain from censorship (his example was the case involving censorship of the *Satanic Verses*) and our positive duty to promote expression. Ten years later, Tony Doyle's article, "A Utilitarian Case for Intellectual Freedom in Libraries," makes a thorough set of reply arguments to Ward and the traditional view in general. Doyle considers it an advantage of the utilitarian approach that it *does* give us a basis for affirming positive duties to promote truth and exchange of ideas in the interest of promoting human well-being. After all, a limitation of rights theories for the advocate of intellectual freedom is that they traditionally do not give fundamental value to the positive promotion of truth and discussion. Respecting rights traditionally involves more restraint than active promotion of specific ends. Yet, this exchange does more than duplicate the traditional arguments for or against utilitarian and deonotological thought on rights. Doyle's response highlights the possibility that the advocate of intellectual freedom may have a broader agenda than the rights theorist. Intellectual freedom, for Mill as for most advocates today, involves more than respecting the features of our nature that make us want to exchange ideas and information. It involves actually promoting and encouraging expression and conduct.

While there may be no way to resolve the fundamental conflict between utilitarians in general and rights theorists in general, recent commentators on the conflict between Rawls and Mill provide new ways of thinking about this problem as it arises for the defense of intellectual freedom. In the case of intellectual freedom, the differences between these two thinkers' theories of value may not be as great as typically supposed. Mill does seem to throw down a challenge early in *On Liberty* when he writes, "I forgo any advantage which could be derived to my argument from the idea of abstract right, as a thing independent of utility. I regard utility as the ultimate appeal on all ethical questions; but it must be utility in the largest sense, grounded on the permanent interests of man as a progressive being" (Mill 1977, 18:224). Clearly, Mill is a utilitarian, but he is also appealing to a conception of human nature that he considers anything by contingent. Robert Amdur argues that Mill has multiple defenses for intellectual freedom, not just a utilitarian one. As Amdur points out from a passage in which Mill discusses the basic value of choosing, "Mill's point is not simply saying that people who choose for themselves are likely to make "better" choices than others could make for them, but also that choosing itself is important. One becomes a fully developed human being only when one makes choices for oneself" (Amdur 2008, 109). After discussing Rawls' criticisms of Mill, and especially Rawls' later reworking of his theory of the priority of liberty, Amdur concludes, "In reworking his argument for the priority of liberty, Rawls seems to be relying on something very similar to Mill's ideal of the person." (2008, 114).

Henry West, writing on, "Mill's Case for Liberty," argues, as do other commentators such as Gerald Gaus, that Mill has both an intrinsic and extrinsic theory of value. Mill can coherently claim, says West, that human development of a certain sort is necessary to genuine human happiness and that development is therefore intrinsically valuable. The conditions which bring about that development— free and open discussion and information flow— could then be valued both for facilitating development and the pursuit of well-being (West 34). This could be part of what Mill means by appealing to the *"permanent* interests of man as a progressive being."

Of course this does not permanently settle disputes between traditional social contract theorists of rights and utilitarian theorists of rights. In the traditional framework of Enlightenment thought, it might be considered incoherent to advocate a dual foundation for basic liberties. After all, as soon as someone introduces *two* foundations for an idea, we can reasonably ask which of those foundations should be appealed to in a particular case. When the Klan wants to march, is it the total sum of happiness or the promotion of human development that we should favor?

On the reading we have been developing, this kind of question would never be posed. Mill defends intellectual freedom as essential to *both* our recognition of the intrinsic value of developing deliberative abilities *and* to our use of these abilities to secure human happiness. In a Millian society, the marching of the KKK is a positive opportunity for people to review and refresh their commitments to the truths of equality.[4] This is a psychologically challenging position because it requires us to defeat our immediate impulse to judge the falsity and worthlessness of the offensive speech and to infer that exposure to falsehood is bad for human well-being. But we need to recall that for Mill's position, false views are never really worthless because they stand as opportunities for sharpening our understanding of truth. Likewise truths are never self-sufficient, but always in need of rehearsal. For Mill the progress of society toward a greater happiness depends upon several key commitments, including our adoption of habits of mind that look at differences of viewpoint as opportunities to develop our deliberative skills and make or reinforce real human choices. The dual foundations approach developed here commits us to a basic endorsement of the development of human capacities for deliberation in distinction from their ability to produce happiness, as well as a confidence that this development is an essential means to promote human well-being. While Mill abjures appeal to "the abstract idea of a right," he relies heavily on a concrete conception of human development and progress. He uses basic liberties as a way of protecting this conception of human choice, much as a rights theorist might protect autonomy or privacy rights (Mayes and Alfino 2003). Philosophers today who advocate a "capabilities approach" to virtue theory might be seen as contemporary kindred spirits to Mill in spite of their deeper theoretical differences. (Nussbaum 2000, 2004; Sen 1991)

But this leads us to the second major theoretical problem facing philosophies of intellectual freedom today, and that is the neutrality problem. The version we confront in the immediate case is this: If we have to believe everything Mill says about either human development or social progress to endorse his case for liberty, then we will have to acknowledge that his theory is not at all neutral with respect to different conceptions of the good life. Mill's ideology of progress is inspiring to those who share his view, but, traditionalists of one sort or another might argue that developing the capacity for rational autonomous choice is not an unqualified good because it often

---

4   Hate speech is still a challenging problem for both approaches since hate speech can incite behavior that violates rights as well as diminishing human happiness. But as Jonathan Riley claims in "Racism, Blasphemy, and Free Speech," Mill can argue that the net social benefits of a liberal doctrine of free speech are greater than the short term harm to even deeply held feelings about respect for persons (Riley 2008).

leads people to question their family, ethnic, or religious culture, for example. From the perspective of the traditionalist, the Millian society might not look neutral. Mill's frequent and overtly expressed disdain for tradition might be cited as evidence of his partiality. It clearly reflects the author's Enlightenment bias in favor of the use of reason and empirical methods to examine and, in many cases, debunk traditional thought.

The traditional defense against this kind of non-neutrality charge, which is available to both the Rawlsian and the Millian, is that the traditionalist should want a system of equal liberty because it is the one in which his or her views (and lifestyle) are likely to receive the most protection. This is clearly a rational choice, but it may not be the traditionalists' first choice, which might have been to influence the society fundamentally rather than just be tolerated by it. Just as the defense of tolerance must allow us to be intolerant of intolerance, so also perhaps one must be non-neutral about neutrality itself.

Mill achieves what scholars on the question of neutrality in liberalism call "first-level neutrality"—his position is generally neutral with respect to different conceptions of the good life. But commentators acknowledge that his defense of liberty, what might be called "second-level neutrality," is anything but neutral, in spite of Mill's own intention to avoid principles based merely on "preference" (Gaus 2008, 92). As Gaus and others have pointed out, Mill takes a very modern view of what counts as a harm (harm to the body) and this leads him to discount psychic or spiritual harm, for example, of the sort that a vegetarian might feel from knowing that others are eating meat or that a religionist might feel knowing that his fellow citizens are heretics or non-believers. In applying a utilitarian perspective to what counts as a harm, critics have argued, the Millian is abandoning neutrality (Gaus 2008, 93).

A broader version of this criticism of Mill was made by Sir Karl Popper in his *The Poverty of Historicism*. Popper was insightfully attentive to the hidden assumptions in Mill's historical narrative of human social progress, which we have already noted permeate the text of *On Liberty*. Such historicist and utopian theories assume that trends and regularities in human history are like laws of nature. Popper's skepticism about this assumption is still relevant today, though his thesis might now be considered over broad. But if Mill's justification of neutrality is ultimately based on a particular, and now dated, view of progressivism, then what hope is there for second-level neutrality in our justification of intellectual freedom?

At first glance the problem of "neutral justifications for neutrality" might seem hopelessly distant from the actual disputes of librarians or other information professionals who observe various sorts of neutrality in their professional roles. Typical challenges to neutrality are challenges to first-level neutrality. A patron challenges a book; a student challenges the choice of topics in a course, for example. But groups and individuals do sometimes make deeper critiques of the culture of intellectual freedom and these critiques are often just below the surface in censorship challenges. Behind attacks on intellectuals and others during the McCarthy era, we find an ideology with an inflated sense of its own certainty about its vision of cultural imperatives, just as Mill would have predicted.

The best approach to the problem of second-level neutrality for intellectual freedom is to acknowledge, as we have already, that complete neutrality is probably an illusion. Some norms of rationality might always be challenged and any updated theory of progress will still be quite speculative and gather some of its authority from shared cultural experience. We live in a world of contested truths.

The Social Epistemology of Intellectual Freedom

There are resources for such a defense of neutrality in Mill's work, especially in light of recent scholarship on this issue. Essentially, we can pair down Mill's somewhat extravagant theories of progress to a few simple claims that might be easier to defend. David Brink argues, for example, that Mill's core defense of freedom of expression could be focused on the need to develop our capacities for deliberation and choice, to which Mill assigns a fundamental and, perhaps, intrinsic value. Like Frederick Rosen in "The Philosophy of Error and Liberty of Thought," Brink connects Mill's defense of intellectual freedom to his work on informal logic and epistemology. Rather than focus on Mill's arguments for the utilitarian effects of truth on social progress, this interpretation suggests that Mill has a kind of "social epistemology"—a view about the way truth is produced by social processes. Evidence for this reading is not hard to find. The entire organization of the argument for freedom of thought and expression is based on the truth conditions of the beliefs in question. Neutrality can be justified in terms of rights and utility, but it can also be more narrowly justified as a way of developing the capacities for judgment that simultaneously serve the individual and the social discovery of truth. As Gaus puts it, we have "shared epistemic interests" (Gaus 2008, 98) in social processes that produce truth.

We can justify a minimal non-neutrality by acknowledging this shared interest and acknowledging that there are no infallible accounts of how to achieve truth. This justification of neutrality is independent of a specific method of achieving truth, but it does presuppose a commitment to the idea that truth and inquiry matter in the broadest sense. To be sure, this is not a neutral view, it is a kind of epistemology, a commitment to at least a *kind* of theory about truth and the conditions of its production (that they involve social communication, freedom of association, and experimentation in lifestyles). If a challenger to this view accepts the premise that we have shared epistemic concerns, but disputes elements of Mill's specific view of truth, the floor remains open for discussion, re-examination, and reconsideration. In other words, by endorsing a general commitment to knowledge and inquiry and an attitude of open-ended revisability about the actual norms and methods for determining truth, a Millian can claim neutrality about the justification of neutrality, while still offering a default theory (the best current one) of how truth is produced or maintained. We do not so much need to be utilitarians or social progressivists to justify neutrality as we need to believe in the fundamental importance of the pursuit of truth (both theoretical and practical) and the absence of any absolute and infallible approach to knowledge. Even people who believe themselves to possess such knowledge should be able to acknowledge that its demonstration is not an accomplished fact. This way of approaching neutrality provides the best justification for intellectual freedom because it allows us to take advantage of the "dual foundations" approach to the rights/utility problem while minimizing the criticism that one has to believe in a highly contingent theory of progress or a specific moral theory in order to justify intellectual freedom.

Basing intellectual freedom in part on a commitment to the intrinsic value of deliberative capacities and in part on a commitment to truth and inquiry may make the theory open-ended and neutral. We do have considerable agreement, across many different conceptions of the good life, that the development of deliberative capacities is intrinsically and extrinsically valuable. Contemporary virtue theorists advocating the "capabilities approach" have developed a broad theory of the importance of human capabilities to the exercise of obligations and values. This theory also fits with contemporary research in moral psychology on human development.

In its non-neutral commitment to truth and inquiry, Mills' theory of intellectual freedom accomplishes something truly significant in the history of thought on intellectual freedom. As we said at the outset, the history of intellectual freedom can be thought of as the record of human cultures coming to value mind and inquiry. That is one of the reasons intellectual freedom has its own distinctive development within the academy in the form of academic freedom. By treating inquiry as a broadly distributed social process, by thinking of every individual as engaged in inquiry about the best way to live, Mill invites us extend universally the kind of respect and protection that we have traditionally reserved for academics.

The librarian or other information professional working from this framework for intellectual freedom should ideally be able to work with anyone committed to the pursuit of truth through a process of epistemic justification. By endorsing authoritative knowledge sources and representing established methods of inquiry and justifications of knowledge (along with challenges and controversies, of course), the librarian is not violating neutrality. As my co-author Linda Pierce and I argued in an earlier work, neutrality in librarianship cannot entail passivity and agnosticism about truth and authoritativeness, but neither can it tolerate the canonization of some set of beliefs or theories as infallible (Alfino and Pierce 1997, 131). Professional advocates for intellectual freedom, especially librarians, have fundamental obligations to respect the decisional autonomy of others while accurately representing the authoritativeness of diverse credible points of view and knowledge claims. The interpretation of intellectual freedom which emerges from the two philosophical problems we have been working on in this section models the pursuit of truth and knowledge as part of the fabric of our social life. As others in this volume have noted (see Hammer, for example), to be "free" intellectually is not only a matter of the absence of constraint. It is also the positive liberty to develop capabilities for deliberation and choice. This happens only within a social world that supports this pursuit through education and the free flow of knowledge, ideas, and culture.

Applying a philosophy of intellectual freedom to contemporary and emerging challenges to intellectual freedom

One way to critically evaluate the view of intellectual freedom we have been developing is to see how conceptually relevant or insightful it is for contemporary problems and challenges in realizing intellectual freedom. For this exercise, I have chosen two contemporary public policy problems which raise intellectual freedom concerns: 1) The 2010 US Supreme Court decision in *Citizens United v. Federal Election Commission* which overturned some legislative restrictions on campaign financing and on the use of media during an election, and, 2) The role of private corporations, such as Google, in setting or managing information policy globally. After looking at these specific issues, I consider a recent and novel challenge, from a postmodern perspective, to the theory we have been developing.

Many political commentators in the U.S. have felt that laws that regulate speech in the electoral process have been on a collision course with the First Amendment for some time. After all, laws such as the Bipartisan Campaign Reform Act of 2002 forbade corporations from television electioneering right before primary elections for Federal offices. In the case at hand, a private non-profit corporation, *Citizens United,* sought distribution of an anti-Hillary Clinton video close to a Democratic Party presidential primary. The FEC forbade the distribution (which was through pay-per-view cable) and the group appealed to the Supreme Court, which overturned the BCRA's restrictions, allowing corporations to spend unlimited funds to electioneer for or against political candidates right up to election day.

Much of the focus of criticism has fallen on the court's willingness to grant free speech rights to corporations, which is a departure from a long history of legal and juridical practice. Emphasis will naturally fall on the empirical claims that opponents of the decision (and the original advocates of campaign regulation) made, that unequal access to the media during an election process will have a distorting effect on the voters' deliberations. But we also need to consider, as the majority points out in their decision, that allowing news media, which are dominated by a few powerful corporations, unlimited access to the election process while excluding a citizens' group which forms a corporation from airing a video seems counter-intuitive for anyone worried about unequal access. Perhaps a less restrictive form of regulation (allowing corporate free speech but requiring disclosure of interests) envisioned by the court majority would actually improve the ability of voters to deliberate. One of the traditional concerns of intellectual freedom, dating back to Periclean Athens, is the "standing" of the parties engaging in protected speech in relation to power and influence. The *Citizens United* case is so important for intellectual freedom because it combines this classical issue with the question of the quality of deliberation in democratic political process under contemporary technological conditions. So our philosophical work seems to track this issue well, and even suggests some of the key issues that need to be joined to assess dilemmas raised by free speech and unequal influence.

Questions about the relative power of speakers (corporate or otherwise) have been a traditional feature of intellectual freedom discussions, back to the concept of *parrhesia*. Likewise, censorship cases are a traditional source of challenge to intellectual freedom, as addressed by several authors, especially Mintcheva, Buchanan, and Tiessen. Internationally, many governments make requests of Google to suppress search results that identify content deemed unacceptable to the government or culture. Google filters search results pointing to pro-Nazi and Holocaust-denial sites in France, Germany, and Poland, for example, because in each of those countries it is unlawful to publish such content. It has a more difficult time deciding how to comply with requests from authoritarian or repressive governments (Goldman 2010). In negotiating with countries over filtering, Google and similar services face a trade-off between compliance and access. Countries can block Google in its entirety, which affects revenue for Google and curtails intellectual freedom.

The ability to control electronic access through filtering of search results represents a new frontier of censorship. In the traditional paradigm, it was the nation-state that was the reference point for the controversy. Intellectual freedom typically involved controversies between authors or groups within the country and their government about a particular work. To be sure, there have always been "outside agitators" to blame for unwelcome new ideas. But now we have emerging global practices related to the flow of information that develop outside of the consideration of national policy.

Google is, in one sense, like a traditional publisher, but it has a standing in this process which is similar to a political entity. Google wields much greater power than a traditional publisher to promote or inhibit intellectual freedom. The future of this issue is hard to predict, but this controversy highlights a key feature of a modern philosophy of intellectual freedom—access to knowledge is affected by the information policies of powerful agents. While this has always been true, the geopolitics of information policy in a networked world give new expressions to this principle.

Both of these examples present specific and unique challenges that are well captured in the philosophical view we have been developing, but they also share a common problem that lies at the heart of the modern idea of intellectual freedom as a social epistemology. Traditionally, intellectual freedom advocates have emphasized negative rights—freedoms from restriction on expression and association—over positive rights—claims that we ought to choose, as a matter of right, social practices that improve our collective access to information and culture. Should we just refrain from restricting liberty or should we also use public policy and law to promote rights to access? While arguments for positive informational rights are clearly implied in the "social epistemology" interpretation we have been developing, the political tradition of liberalism has historically treated negative rights as more fundamental. Rawls' view is typical of the rights tradition; he articulates fundamental liberties as negative duties, duties which enjoin others from interfering with us, but do not obligate others to act on our behalf. Mill also reflects Enlightenment thinking about the independence of the individual. Recall that for Mill the state is only justified in interfering with individuals who are causing harm to others. But contemporary theorists, such as Julie Cohen, have argued that access to information and culture through digital media represents a basic commitment of a society to respect the autonomy of the individual. A positive information rights advocate argues that we have a positive duty to promote the individual's access to informational and cultural resources.

Julie Cohen's important paper, "Information Rights and Intellectual Freedom," provides an example of a positive information rights argument, challenging our concept of what intellectual freedom should commit us to in a global networked environments and markets. Cohen wants to challenge the assumption that a fully "propertied" approach to intellectual freedom, one that eliminated "fair use" for example, would be the best way to promote intellectual freedom. In her recent book, *Configuring the Networked Self: Law, Code, and the Play of Everyday Practice,* Cohen develops this argument by suggesting that if we take a realistic look at the creative process, we will see that it involves use and expression of cultural material that help constitute the "self" in a networked world. As more culture is expressed in digital media, a fully propertied digital environment would unduly and illogically constrain creative production, which is the opposite of one of the social aims of copyright protection, for example.

To appreciate Cohen's argument it is important to understand that she thinks of intellectual freedom in terms of the promotion of "autonomy and decisional independence." Autonomy for her is not merely the abstract possibility of being "self-legislating," but an embodied and variably realized set of capacities to engage in informed deliberation and decision making about one's life. She points out that traditional rights defenses, including Rawls, have emphasized the protection of autonomy through arguments against constraints against liberty, but a complete understanding of autonomy as an actual capacity requires us to consider also positive means for promoting it by assuring the quality and accessibility of "information flows". As Cohen puts it: "Intellectual freedom is a function of the autonomy that individuals enjoy with respect to information flows to, from, and about them" (Cohen 2010). If autonomy is thought of in this way, then supporting information rights, and by extension intellectual freedom, is not just a matter of avoiding negative constraints (such as censorship), but involves assessing information markets in terms of their effectiveness in improving deliberative decision making for individuals.

For Cohen, some of the culprits in limiting information rights are to be found in the Digital Millennium Copyright Act and international agreements defining copyright infringement. In some cases, the legal and political processes governing these agreements seemed to be unjustifiably eliminating areas of copyright free use of intellectual property. In her new work she explores a broad range of considerations about the implications of over-privatization of digital content (Cohen 2010). She identifies with the capacities view of human flourishing mentioned earlier (Nussbaum 2004 & Sen 1991) and uses this view to give more content to the idea of autonomy and the development of the self. Intellectual freedom includes more than discrete knowledge that individuals need to govern themselves and their practical affairs. It also includes the ability to access and "play" with culture. But this kind of intellectual freedom requires that property rights be kept "incomplete" in the tradition of fair use allowances. With greater sensitivity to the constitutive power of networks to shape the self, and with a more developed sense of human flourishing, Cohen argues, we can ask more critical questions about how intellectual property rights in digital content affect the self and the development of autonomy in the self (Cohen 2010).

Julie Cohen offers a significant critique of copyright and intellectual property by emphasizing a more complete account of how individuals actually interact with culture to produce culture. This is at once a broader concern than we have been considering since it does not involve assessing the effects of policy on knowledge production and dissemination, but rather asks more fundamental questions about the effect of "propertied culture" on the ability of the individual to build and fashion a self. While technology and thought about intellectual property has certainly change since Mill's day, Cohen's concern is reminiscent of Mill's view that a healthy society would be tolerant of a diversity of lifestyles (so-called "experiments in living"). For Cohen, the networked culture of advanced capitalism poses a new range of threat to intellectual freedom by limiting access and "play."

Conclusion

Intellectual freedom was originally about establishing the "standing" and protection of individuals to speak candidly. We might even say that its root value is the importance of being able to tolerate candid expression. In that sense, the problems of *parrhesia* remain central to the modern context. As we have seen, Enlightenment thought on intellectual freedom grows out of a similar practical problem—the need to tolerate diverse religious viewpoints and to promote the growth and spread of knowledge following the scientific and political revolutions of that period. While philosophical and political theory tracks this problem in both the traditions of rights and utility, a real innovation of Mill's approach, highlighted in recent scholarship, was the re-focusing of the problem of liberty on the conditions needed to pursue inquiry through a social network which values individuality and individual discernment of the truth. In light of the role of information networks in education and contemporary life generally, we could say that Mill's approach was prescient. In contemporary intellectual freedom controversies, we are often concerned about the quality of, access to, and equality of access to information resources which enable individuals to develop their autonomy and capabilities.

In this shift of focus to the conditions of inquiry, we may also be moving, as recent information rights advocates like Julie Cohen have argued, toward an acknowledgement of positive information rights, not only to knowledge, but also to culture. Believing in intellectual freedom without assuring that individuals have access to the best resources for inquiry and the pursuit of their personal and cultural identity may be as problematic as valuing mind and inquiry, but not valuing widespread access and cultivation of it.

References

Alfino, Mark , and Linda Pierce. 1997. *Information Ethics for Librarians*. Jefferson, North Carolina: McFarland and Company.

Amdur, Robert. 2008. Rawls' critique of 'On Liberty'. In *Mill's On Liberty: A Critical Guide: Mill's On Liberty: A Critical Guide*. ed. Ten, C. L. Cambridge: Cambridge University Press.

Bacon, Francis. 1949. *The Advancement of Learning (1605)*. ed. Jones, Howard Mumford. *Primer on Intellectual Freedom*. Cambridge: Harvard University Press.

Cohen, Julie. *Berkman Luncheon Series: Configuring the Networked Self* [cited March 20, 2010. Available from http://cyber.law.harvard.edu/events/luncheon/2010/01/cohen.

Cohen, Julie. 2001. Information Rights and Intellectual Freedom. In *Ethics and the Internet*, edited by Anton Vedder, 11–32. Antwerp: Instersentia.

Cohen, Julie. 2012. *Configuring the Networked Self*. New Haven: Yale UP.

Doyle, Tony. 2001. A Utilitarian Case for Intellectual Freedom in Libraries. *Library Quarterly*.44–71.

Finocchiaro, Maurice A. 2005. Mill's 'On Liberty' and Argumentation Theory. In *The Uses of Argument: Proceedings of a Conference at McMaster University, 18–21 May 2005*. Hamilton: Media Production.

Foucault, Michel. *Discourse and Truth: The Problematization of Parrhesia* [cited January 17, 2010. Available from http://foucault.info/documents/parrhesia/.

Gaus, Gerald F. 2008. State Neutrality and Controversial Values in 'On Liberty'. In *Mill's On Liberty: A Critical Guide: Mill's On Liberty: A Critical Guide*. Cambridge: Cambridge University Press.

Goldman, David. *Banned . . . by Google* [cited March 20, 2010]. Available from http://money.cnn.com/2010/03/18/technology/google_china_censorship/.

Jefferson, Thomas. 1949. *Bill for Establishing Religious Freedom*. In *Mill's On Liberty: A Critical Guide: Mill's On Liberty: A Critical Guide*. ed. Ten, C. L. Cambridge: Cambridge University Press.

Jefferson, Thomas. 1949. *First Inaugural Address*. In *Mill's On Liberty: A Critical Guide: Mill's On Liberty: A Critical Guide*. ed. Ten, C. L. Cambridge: Cambridge University Press.

Jones, Howard Mumford, ed. 1949. *Primer on Intellectual Freedom*. Cambridge: Harvard University Press.

Kant, Immanuel. 1949. *Critique of Practical Reason and Other Writings in Moral Philosophy*. Chicago: University of Chicago Press.

Konstan, David. 2004. Parrhesia: Ancient philosophy in opposition. In *Mythos and Logos: How to Regain the Love of Wisdom*, ed. Anderson, Albert A., Steven V. Hicks, and Lech Witkowski. 19–35. Amsterdam: Rodopi.

Locke, John. *A Letter Concerning Toleration* 1689. http://etext.lib.virginia.edu/
etcbin/toccer-new2?id=LocTole.xml&images=images/modeng&data=/
texts/english/modeng/parsed&tag=public&part=all (accessed March
20, 2010).

Martin, Thomas R. 1996. *Ancient Greece.* New Haven: Yale University Press.

Mayes, Randy, and Mark Alfino. 2003. Reconstructing the right to privacy.
Social Theory and Practice 29, no. 1: 1–18.

Mill, John Stuart. 1977. *On Liberty. Essays on Politics and Society.* Toronto: University of Toronto Press and Routlege & Kegan Paul.

Milton, John. 1949. *A speech for the liberty of unliscensed printing (1644).* In
Mill's On Liberty: A Critical Guide: Mill's On Liberty: A Critical Guide. ed.
Ten, C. L. Cambridge: Cambridge University Press.

Nussbaum, Martha. 2000. *Women and human development: the capabilities approach.* Cambridge: Cambridge University Press.

Nussbaum, Martha. 2004. *Hiding from humanity: Disgust, shame, and the law.*
Princeton: Princeton University Press.

Plato. *Apology.* trans. L. A. Post. ed. Edith Hamilton and Huntington Cairns,
The Collected Dialogues of Plato. Princeton, NJ: Princeton UP.

Popper, Karl. 1957. *The Poverty of Historicism.* London: Routledge & Kegan
Paul.

Rawls, John. 1999. *A Theory of Justice.* Rev. ed. Cambridge, Mass.: Harvard
University Press. Reprint, Revised Edition.

Rawls, John. 2001. *Justice as Fairness: A Restatement.* Cambridge: Harvard
University Press.

Riley, Jonathan. 2008. Racism, Blasphemy, and Free Speech. In *Mill's On
Liberty: A Critical Guide: Mill's On Liberty: A Critical Guide.* ed. Ten, C. L.
Cambridge: Cambridge University Press.

Sen, Amartya. 1991. *On Ethics and Economics.* London: Blackwell.

Shields, Currin V. 1956. Introduction. In *On Liberty,* ed. Currin Shields. Indianapolis: Bobbs-Merril Co.

Swan, John. 1994. Intellectual freedom. In *Encyclopedia of Library History,*
280–285. New York: Garland Publishers.

Ward, David. 1990. Philosophical issues in censorship and intellectual freedom. *Library Trends* 39, nos. 1–2: 83–91.

West, Henry R. 2008. Mill's case for Liberty. In *Mill's On Liberty: A Critical
Guide: Mill's On Liberty: A Critical Guide.* ed. Ten, C. L. Cambridge: Cambridge University Press.

Gramsci, Hegemony, and Intellectual Freedom

Douglas Raber

An examination of Antonio Gramsci's thinking regarding intellectual freedom presents some interesting challenges. Like other socialist theorists of the late 19th and early 20th centuries, including Marx himself, Gramsci does not explicitly address the concepts of free speech or intellectual freedom at any length. These topics are implicated in his work but they were not his explicit concern. Gramsci's thought turns in a more practical and materialist direction and it is set in the context of a dispute within the turn-of-the-century socialist movement that must be understood if we are to understand the implications of Gramsci's work for the concept of intellectual freedom.

That dispute turned on questions raised within the movement regarding whether the constitutional freedoms of capitalist democracies represented genuine advances toward human justice or were tools the bourgeoisie used to manage relations between its factions and justify its collective dominance over subordinate classes. On more than one occasion in the heat of struggle, Gramsci demonstrated distinct Leninist tendencies suggesting that free speech granted by the ruling class was not to be trusted, that it nevertheless might be an effective tool in the class struggle, and that its suppression might be justified to prevent the enemies of the working classes from achieving their oppressive goals. We will have to revisit this dispute and we will have to extrapolate by way of a Gramscian exploration of John Stuart Mill to get hold of Gramsci's understanding of intellectual freedom. Had Gramsci ever addressed Mill explicitly, he might have argued that Mill was on the right track but that he needed to make a more historically grounded argument.

Antonio Gramsci and his Marxism

Born in Sardinia in 1891, Gramsci came of age in Turin; one of the points of what later became known as the Red Triangle (Turin, Milan, and Genoa,

Italy). He was actively engaged in the pre-war European socialist movement, joining the Italian Socialist Party in 1913. By 1914 he was writing for socialist newspapers and earning a reputation as an effective political journalist. Even at this early stage of his writing Gramsci displayed the creativity that characterized his integration of theory and practice (Gramsci 1977). In the journal *L'Ordine Nuovo* he took a Leninist direction, and he played a major role in the founding of the Italian Communist Party in 1921 which allied itself with the Communist International (Comintern) established by Lenin and the Bolsheviks in Moscow two years earlier. In a way, Gramsci was an incidental theorist.

Antonio Gramsci wrote the main body of his theory in a prison cell where he was held by Mussolini's Fascist state for his revolutionary activity as head of the Italian Communist Party (PCI) from 1924 to 1926. Throughout *The Prison Notebooks*, Gramsci refers to Marxism as the "the philosophy of praxis" in order to confuse his guards and disguise his purpose (1992). He was afraid that otherwise he might be denied writing materials. Even in prison, Gramsci did not intend his writing to be an abstract reflection on political problems. He wrote to provide a practical guide for Western European revolutionary practice. In this regard he was not different from other leaders of the late 19th and early 20th century socialist movements, including Marx.

Gramsci's philosophy of praxis, however scattered it may be across many different texts written for many different purposes, offers a surprisingly coherent understanding of how modern capitalism works. His work provides a profound reinterpretation of the relationship between the Marxist concepts of base and superstructure and allows new insights into the relations between the material conditions of human existence and human consciousness as aspects of human history.

For Gramsci, the philosophy of praxis—Marxism—begins with the notion that human being and history are products of human labor, and that human nature is not a fixed quality. The production and reproduction of life and value constitutes the material foundation for human existence, and all are aspects of culture—the "complex of social relations" that constitute human nature as phenomenon of 'becoming' (man 'becomes', he changes continuously with the changing of social relations)" (Gramsci 1971, 355). The social relations of production that organize human labor constitute the economic *structure* or *base*. The relations of production are the material conditions under which life is produced and reproduced and they have personal consequences for individuals. Their nature plays a dominant role in determining life outcomes, or as Laswell put it so well, who gets what, when and how (1990).

One's relationship to the means of production plays a dominant role in determining one's life possibilities. In capitalist societies, life possibilities depend crucially on whether one is an owner of the means of production or sells one's labor for wages. Class, if not class consciousness, is an objective historical phenomenon related to private property and its ownership. Industrial capitalist societies are characterized by the historical dominance of relations of production by the *bourgeoisie*, the industrial property owning class, and the subordination of the *proletariat*, a class constituted by working men and women who are compelled for their survival to sell their labor, and in effect their lives, to the bourgeoisie at exploitative terms. These relations allow the bourgeoisie to extract *surplus labor* from the proletariat. The proletariat produces greater value than it consumes to sustain its life, and the bourgeoisie appropriates this surplus as its own private property, a privilege of ownership of the means of production.

Even Marx recognized that by the late nineteenth century the division of labor within capitalism had created a diversity of different classes whose members bear different kinds of relationships to the means of production. These classes include but are not limited to small business owners, professionals, landowners, and agricultural workers. Their relationship to the means of production can be ambiguous and their actual nature, relative size and influence, and role in organizing a particular society depend upon historical conditions unique to that society. The position of the bourgeoisie as the capital owning class, however, is dominant and the relations of production between the bourgeoisie and other classes are structured by the bourgeoisie to favor its interests and ends as a ruling class. This condition constitutes the essential injustice of capitalist societies. Value is created by the many and appropriated by the few for their personal benefit. The final contradiction that drives the history and politics of capitalist societies is the contradiction between the social nature of the production of value, and life, and the nature of its appropriation, control, and use as private property. This contradiction is the source of both the economic crises and social problems that plague capitalist societies.

Relations of production between classes, the economic base, provide the foundation for the social organization of particular capitalist societies and give rise to particular and unique *superstructures* in particular places and at particular points in human history (Gramsci 1971, 55–90). The superstructure consists of social, political, and cultural practices through which the ruling class exercises its control over society as whole. It includes not only the state and its associated juridical and coercive institutions, but also the social and cultural institutions and practices typically associated with the idea of civil society, including churches, schools, news and entertainment media, social organizations, and libraries. Its role is twofold; to secure the historical reproduction of capitalist relations of production and to reduce or eliminate the need for state coercion to achieve this end by securing the consent of the proletariat and other subordinate classes regarding the legitimacy of the relations of production. The superstructure is an ideological apparatus that is necessary and historically organic to a given structure. It is the glue that keeps capitalist structures from falling apart because of tensions generated by their internal contradictions (Gramsci 1971, 375–377).

The concepts of structure and superstructure arise from Marx's assertion that relations of production constitute "the economic structure of society, the real foundation, on which rises a juridical and political superstructure" (Marx 1973, 503). The ideas that dominate and govern a particular moment in history are the ideas of the class that dominates and governs the means and relations of material production (Marx 1970a, 64–5). Given these kinds of statements, it is not difficult to see how some interpreters of Marx arrive at the conclusion that Marxism implies economic determinism, but one must also recall that Marx insists that "[m]en are the producers of their conceptions, ideas, etc.—real, active men, as they are conditioned by a definite development of their productive forces and of the intercourse corresponding to these . . ." (Marx 1970, 47). His point is simply "that circumstances make men just as much as men make circumstances" (Marx 1970, 59).

Early twentieth century revolutionary theory however, manifest in the International Communist movement led by the Soviet Union, insisted on a determinist interpretation of Marx. Gramsci (1971, 158–168) argued that this approach to understanding capitalism was not really different from that offered by liberal *laissez faire* economics and he dismissed both as *economism*. While he credited Lenin, to whom he had to refer as Ilyich, with great insight regarding the contemporary practicalities of revolutionary theory, especially the role of the Party as an agent of change, there were two points of theory about which Gramsci was not convinced. The dominant view held that the base is organized by and for the interests of the ruling bourgeoisie and the superstructure is simply the political instrument for class rule. Such parliamentary forms as exist are primarily intended to provide a means for bourgeois factions to air and resolve their differences. Genuine popular participation is always constrained or even prohibited. Given the political role of the superstructure then, social change depends on revolution at the base by the proletariat and the assumption of their historical role as the class whose rule will end class rule. History awaits the dictatorship of the proletariat to be followed by the end of private property, the dissolution of classes and the withering away of the state.

It was Gramsci's genius to see two things. First, as opposed to the relatively simpler structures of mid to late nineteenth century capitalist societies, complex, modern twentieth century capitalism makes class difficult to discern and renders class identity ambiguous. The base and the values of the capitalist relations continue to provide the dominant ideological foundations

of capitalist social formations, but class as a social and psychological phenomenon, if not an economic one, becomes indeterminate as individuals become who they will in the context of historically determined class structures.
Second, and as a result, superstructures can and do influence real material
change in the nature of the capitalist economic base. What people believe
and value and how they choose to behave is not entirely or exclusively determined by the dominant relations of production, nor by their objective role in
those relations.

Gramsci understood that the superstructure, rather than merely an instrument of domination, is a relatively autonomous historical phenomenon
and potentially a site of political conflict whose outcome can alter relations
of production. Ideology, rather than being merely an effect of relations of
production designed to reproduce those relations, can also serve revolutionary ends by serving as a cause of their change. For Gramsci, the philosophy
of praxis identifies the space within which human beings make their own
history; it explains the determinants of that history, but does not imply that
history is determined. "The claim, . . ." he writes, "that every fluctuation of
politics and ideology can be presented and expounded as an immediate expression of the [economic] structure, must be contested in theory as primitive
infantilism, and combated in practice with the actual testimony of Marx"
(Gramsci 1971, 404).

The Historic Bloc and Hegemony

The concept of the *historic bloc* is central to Gramsci's marxism. It provides
the foundation for his analysis of the *hegemony* exercised by the bourgeoisie
over capitalist social formations as well the revolutionary *war of position* that
can be conducted against bourgeois hegemony. At any given moment in the
life of a social formation there is only one historic bloc. It organizes the base,
dominates the superstructure, and manages the relations between them. Its
purpose is to reproduce the means and relations of production from which
it derives its resources, political power, intellectual/cultural power, and, as
Gramsci calls it, its ethico-political hegemony. The base and structure provide an historic bloc with its material content, and the superstructure gives
it moral and intellectual form (Gramsci 1971, 377). The historic bloc is constituted by and represents political alliances, but it cannot be reduced to a
mere political alliance (Sassoon 1980, 119–25). It is a "complex, contradictory,
and discordant *ensemble* of the superstructures [that] is the reflection of the
ensemble of the social relations of production" (Gramsci 1971, 366). An historic
bloc is an ensemble of social groups, intellectual and ideological forces organized around the historic interests of the "fundamental social group" that
organizes and leads the bloc (Gramsci 1971, 115–16).

An historic bloc, then, is not merely a structural phenomenon that somehow determines social outcomes. A bloc, in addition to its control of the means of production, depends on ideological principles and political alliances that are subject to constant negotiation, challenge, and change. It is characterized by diverse interests whose particular fortunes and influence will vary as an outcome of political contests both within the bloc, and between the bloc and its historical challengers, including the proletariat. It organizes and asserts its hegemony over society largely by controlling the terms and agenda of political discourse, but its own internal divisions combined with events and behaviors beyond its control can and do create historical imperatives to which it must respond. "Hegemony" is a concept Gramsci uses to clarify the nature of an historic bloc's power. This power is dominant, but not dominating. It is far from total and it is exercised by setting political agendas rather than dictating political outcomes. Gramsci writes

> [T]he supremacy of a social group manifests itself in two ways, as 'domination' and as 'intellectual and moral leadership.' A social group dominates antagonistic groups, which it tends to 'liquidate,' or to subjugate perhaps even by armed force; it leads kindred and allied groups. A social group can, and indeed must, already exercise 'leadership' before winning governmental power (this indeed is one of the principal conditions of winning such power); it subsequently becomes dominant when it exercises power, but even if it holds it firmly in its grasp, it must continue to 'lead' as well. (1971, 57–8)

In effect, an historical bloc represents a kind of social contract among the bourgeoisie, the social groups it needs to maintain its dominant position, and the subordinate classes. It will exercise coercive power if necessary but that is a risky and costly means of social control. As a result, the situation of the historic bloc is relatively stable but subject to changing economic and political conditions that can lead to renegotiation at any moment.

But this why there are always positions within social formation from which arise challenges to the historical bloc. Challenges can arise from traditional segments of society generally seeking a return to an ideologically constructed mythical past. Others may arise from marginalized and radicalized segments seeking a transformation to a utopian future. Some will arise from within the bloc itself as different interests that constitute it assert different visions of the bloc's future. Factions with different immediate interests exist within historic blocs, and each will seek its own power within the bloc (Poulantzas 1978, 77–85). Contests between factions can result in an historical instability of the bloc's hegemony, allowing either progressive or reactionary forces to take advantage of the weakness and possibly gain a governing influence over the bloc, even if they cannot alter the relations of production at the base. Some factions within the historic bloc might actually occupy socially progressive and politically leading positions that challenge the bloc's legitimacy outright despite personal consequences. Alternatively, weaknesses manifest in a bloc's hegemony can also lead to authoritarian and totalitarian solutions to problems of political instability, as for example when the military or powerful charismatic leader steps in to rule on behalf of the bourgeoisie (Marx 1968, 95–180).

The key to Gramsci's thought in this regard lies in his rejection of economic and historical determinism. Rejecting the idea that inexorable laws determine inevitable outcomes in human affairs, Gramsci argues that in addition to its economic aspects, human existence is characterized by an ethical-political, or as he frequently refers to it, an "intellectual" reality, manifest in and through superstructures (Gramsci 1971, 8–9, 161, 258, 333–34, 366–67). As discussed earlier, the historical relations between base and superstructure are dialectically determined. Causes and effects work in both directions, despite the relative predominance of the base. Gramsci writes: "Between the premise (economic structure) and the consequence (political organization), relations are by no means simple and direct: and it is not only by economic facts that the history of a people can be documented. It is a complex and confusing task to unravel causes and in order to do so, a deep and widely diffused study of all spiritual and practical activities is needed" (Gramsci 1958, 280–81).

Recent Marxist theory manifests a controversy over whether base and superstructure should be regarded as inherent categories of historical existence or as cultural and intellectual constructions. This issue turns on another controversy regarding the role of classes as agents of history (Laclau and Mouffe 1985; Derrida 1994). Both problems are related to the failure to realize a genuine socialist hegemony (Stiglitz 1996), and to the postmodern turn of thought in late capitalism (Jameson 1991). This situation is about much more than merely the collapse of the Soviet Union and the resilience of western capitalism. By the mid-1970s many western Marxist scholars and socialist activists, largely because of the influence of Gramsci's thought, had already come to regard the Soviet Union as a practically and theoretically bankrupt historical model, and were searching for a new way to understand the West (Claudin 1975, 598–602).

According to Gramsci, however, the location of a historical subject in a social formation, an individual or a social group, is an objective but not a determinate phenomenon. There are objective, but not necessarily historically determined political interests. Of course, Gramsci asserts that the relations of production have a powerful and dominating material influence on the course of history. This notion is central to Gramsci's concept of hegemony, but he insists that historical subjects are located, and more importantly, willfully locate themselves in the nexus of historically conditioned productive and social relations that constitute hegemony. Louis Althusser's structural-ism (Althusser and Balibar 1970) has been criticized for merely substituting an idealist essentialism for economic determinism (Laclau and Mouffe 1985, 97–105), as a result leaving "little room for a revolutionary subject," (Fields 1988, 141) but it seems clear that he was working from Gramsci's ideas when he used the psychoanalytic concept of overdetermination to describe the dialectic moment in which base and superstructure, economic and intellectual reality interact to create the actual historical location of a subject in a social formation.

The political location of a subject depends on objective historical conditions *and* what the subject thinks about those conditions (Althusser 1970, 87–128). Class membership, that is, a subject's location in a social formation with regard to the relations of production, is a fundamental but not determining factor. It plays a large, but not exclusive, role in the construction of a subject's political interest. A subject's political reality, while ideologically constructed and ordinarily reflecting the ideas of the dominant hegemony, is also the source of the superstructure's power to influence the base and alter if not the relations of production, at least the outcomes of production. It can be a location that subjects actively contribute to and construct. It can provide a historical position within the superstructure from which the dominant hegemony and the relations of production which support it can be challenged.

In Althusser's language, the relations of production are in the last instance the determinant force within social formations, but it is an instance which usually never fully arrives because of willful, counter-determinant resistance to their logic. The continued dominance of capitalist relations of production is no more assured than is their radical transformation (Schumpeter 1950). The goal of the contest between labor and capital is to alter the relations of production that unnecessarily limit human freedom—to change the social formation at its base in order to realize and take full advantage of the social nature of the production of human values, and thus to transcend the commodification and private appropriation of human labor. The outcome of this contest will be determined by what Gramsci calls the "war of position." This is not a war of violent civil strife. It is necessarily a protracted struggle of ideological and political practice that ordinarily takes place on the terrain of civil society, but in some instances can occur within the state itself (Gramsci 1971, 108–11, 120, 229–39). The historic bloc of capitalist societies displays ideological and political vulnerabilities that can be identified, exploited and attacked by progressive political forces in the cause of economic and social justice.

The existence of factions shows that capitalist relations of production can be organized in a variety of ways, and more and less progressive choices are available. Combined and uneven development, both within and between

national social formations, means that different peoples will organize themselves in different ways (Trotsky 1957, 4–6, 13–14; 1962, 6–10). In other words,
not everyone lives in or through exactly the same historical moment. As a
result, superstructures vary, and some capitalist social formations will be
more progressive than others. Politics at the level of the superstructure can
be used to effect what Gramsci (1971, 366–67) calls a "catharsis", or "the passage from the purely economic (or egoistic-passional) to the ethico-political
moment," and in this moment the base can be "transformed into a means of
freedom, an instrument to create a new ethico-political form and a source of
new initiatives." Ideas have power, and the progressive material reform of
the relations of production that genuinely improve the life outcomes of the
oppressed is possible, even though such change may fall short of revolutionary transformation.

According to Gramsci (1971, 235, 243), the political means of accomplishing these ends lies in challenging capital's hegemony within the "trenches"
of the superstructure, particularly in the realm of civil society, as a means
to the seizure of social, cultural, and finally state power. This is the terrain
of a war of position. He argues that progressive social groups and individuals must "penetrate" civil society of the dominant hegemony, seize positions
within it, and "turn" its institutions toward progressive and transformative
ends. Gramsci writes:

> The massive structures of modern democracies, both as State organiza-
> tions, and as complexes of association in civil society, constitute for the
> art of politics as it were the 'trenches' and the permanent fortifications of
> the front in the war of position: they render merely 'partial' the element
> of the movement which before used to be 'the whole' of war. (1971, 243)

Gramsci's understanding of the art of politics follows from his understanding of the dialectical relations between base and superstructure. Change is
not a matter of reforming the base so that reform of the superstructure may
follow. The art of politics is a matter of reforming base and superstructure
simultaneously through political action that accompanies a change of political consciousness (Gramsci 1975, 1328). The fact that western capitalism relies
on the discourse of democracy to legitimate its hegemony also creates an
opening for a politics that demands the meaningful extension of democracy
at the level of the base.

Marxism and the Ambiguity of Intellectual Freedom

The theoretical subtlety of *The Prison Notebooks* was not always present
Gramsci's work, especially during his years as activist in the Italian Socialist and Communist Parties. His early, Leninist influenced political writings

reveal the ambivalence toward formal democracy and civil liberties that marked the socialist dispute over the meaning of these phenomena for revolutionary strategy. In retrospect it's clear that Gramsci doubted the authenticity of Western European commitment to intellectual freedom rather than the value of the idea itself.

In 1916, while editor of *Avanti*, the official newspaper of the Italian Socialist Party, Gramsci urges his readers to "boycott the bourgeois press with the same unity and discipline that the bourgeoisie boycott the newspapers of the workers . . ." (Gramsci 1916). Gramsci warns the workers that these papers served the dominant class and always portrayed the workers, as well as their actions for justice, as subversive. The intent of the bourgeois press was not to inform, but to explain and justify the policies and actions of the ruling class.

Gramsci's real targets, however, were the workers themselves and their complicity in their own oppression. He calls for them to wake up and criticizes and laments the fact that they "regularly and daily give their pennies to the bourgeois newspapers, thus assisting in creating their power." He argues that too often the workers passively accept the dominant class' version of the truth. It is not clear that if the means had been available Gramsci would have gone as far as urging the suppression of the bourgeois press for the facts they "either keep quiet about, or travesty, or falsify in order to mislead, delude or maintain in ignorance the laboring public" (Gramsci, 1916.) For Gramsci it is clear that this condition raised questions about the legitimacy of the bourgeois press and that the workers ought to avoid reading bourgeois newspapers and take up the socialist press instead, notably *Avanti*.

At first glance, Gramsci appears to be at best suspicious of the bourgeois press; at worst his attitude seems to be outright illiberal. A liberal contemporary might have responded by saying that the goodness of democratic societies is to be found in the fact that Gramsci is free to make his case and even publish it in a newspaper. A free marketplace of ideas makes possible democratic discourse and political choice. After all, the dominant newspapers will be those that dominate the market—people choose their news by choosing where to spend their money. It would appear as if Gramsci may have ceded the high moral ground, unless the marketplace is rigged and the appearance of competing ideas is used merely to cover the actual lack of competition.

Gramsci was trying to find his way in the dispute between evolutionary and revolutionary socialism and their competing strategies for social change. The former provided the theoretical and practical foundations of modern European social democracy while the latter informed the development of Bolshevism, the Russian Revolution and the rise of international communism. The contest between the two approaches represents the primary schism within the early socialist movement, a conflict so intense that each side often saved its most venomous rhetoric for the other rather than direct it at their common enemy, the European bourgeoisie.

This was a dispute about appropriate revolutionary strategy as much as one between contesting theoretical analyses of capitalism. The documenting literature is vast and engaged every significant socialist figure of the time, but is neatly represented on one side by Eduard Bernstein's *Evolutionary Socialism; A Criticism and Affirmation* (1961) and on the other by Lenin's *What Is To Be Done? Burning Questions of Our Movement* (1969). Bernstein was a member of the German Social Democratic Party (SPD) and an elected member of the Reichstag from 1902–1918 and again from 1920–1928. Lenin led the Bolshevik Revolution in Russia and served as Chairman of the Council of People's Commissars of the Soviet Union until his death in 1924. It must be noted that the historical context of each man's political activity and writing is important to explaining and understanding the arguments of these books, but an exploration of that context is beyond the scope of this essay.

Bernstein argued and acted on the assertion that "[s]ocial democracy has to-day in Germany, besides the means of propaganda by speech and writing, the franchise for the Reichstag as the most effective means of asserting its demand" (Bernstein 1961, 194). Extra-parliamentary action would be required to realize a socialist future, but in Bernstein's view, there is no genuine liberal thought that is not always already an element of socialism. Likewise, political equality alone is not sufficient for socialism; it also depends on the freedom from economic compulsion.

"In this sense," Bernstein says, "one might call socialism 'organizing liberalism,' for when one examines more closely the organizations that socialism wants and how it wants them, he will find that what distinguishes them . . . is just their liberalism, their democratic constitution, their accessibility" (Bernstein 1961, 153–154). Violent class-based revolution can move more quickly and along the way satisfy the passion for justice, but revolutionary change brought about through legislation guided by the intellect is more likely to bring about lasting achievement (1961, 217–218). Bernstein sums his position simply; "Legislation works as a systematic force, revolution as an elementary force" (1961, 218).

From Lenin's perspective, Bernstein's argument represents opportunism; a willingness to trade off socialist ideas and goals for political power based on the misguided assumption that revolution can be accomplished from within capitalist social formations rather than in opposition to them. Lenin's rhetoric is more strident. By way of dismissing what was then referred to as "freedom of criticism" within the socialist movement, Lenin asserts that

> . . . *if we judge people, not . . . by the high-sounding appellations they give themselves, but by their actions and by what they actually advocate,*

> *it will be clear that "freedom of criticism" means freedom for an oppor-*
> *tunist trend in Social-Democracy, freedom to convert Social-Democracy*
> *into a democratic party of reform, freedom to introduce bourgeois ideals*
> *and bourgeois elements into socialism.* (Lenin 1969b, 10–11)

Lenin did not reject the advantages bourgeois democracy provides to the socialist revolutionary movement; a parliamentary state with accompanying civil liberties is a "convenient arena" for class struggle precisely because of the freedoms it provides (Meyer 1957, 59–61). He also writes, "Democracy is of enormous importance to the working class in its struggle against the capitalists for its emancipation. But democracy is by no means a boundary not to be overstepped; it is only one of the stages on the road from feudalism to capitalism, and from capitalism to communism" (Lenin 1999).

Still, the goal was not to accept whatever reforms the ruling class might grant in an effort to co-opt the proletarian struggle; the goal, as Marx wrote in *The Communist Manifesto*, was "to win the battle of democracy" (Marx and Engels 1968, 52). The state, even in a democratic form, is always an instrument of class rule. Capitalist democracies are "always hemmed in by the narrow limits set by capitalist exploitation, and consequently always remains, in effect, a democracy for the minority, only for the propertied classes, only for the rich. Freedom in capitalist society always remains about the same as it was in the ancient Greek republics: freedom for the slave-owners" (Lenin 1999). According to Lenin, reforms won from the ruling class are not to be trusted. The intention behind them is the production and re-production of class rule.

Ambivalence regarding democracy and formal civil liberties is characteristic of early Marxist thought. Freedom, and by implication intellectual freedom, tends to be discussed in terms of negating the obstacles preventing development of human potential and the realization of a just social formation, one that embraces the individual and collective dialectic of human natures. Likewise, self-determination is necessarily an individual and collective characteristic of genuine freedom, and can only be realized through a socialist transcendence of the constraints of capitalist relations of productions. This view has led Marxists to deny the value of bourgeois political and legal freedoms and in some cases, notably in the former Soviet Union, has led to their suppression, "all too often in the name of freedom itself" (Lukes 1983, 146–147).

The apparent willingness of the left to find a necessary reason for the suppression of speech creates an opening for a critique from the right. Contemporary conservative views of Gramsci provide an interesting perspective. They offer the claim that the left's assertion of "political correctness" to judge the value of speech and action is at the heart of a Gramscian strategy that intents to "win the world *voluntarily* to Marxism." By condemning traditional Western, Christian culture as "repressive," "Eurocentric," and "racist" and, thus, unworthy of our continued devotion," and holding in its place an "unalloyed primitivism in the guise of 'multiculturalism,'" the left intends to establish the revolutionary cultural hegemony necessary for seizing state power (Thornton 1999).

The strategy involves suppressing intellectual freedom to subvert and delegitimate traditional culture so that it can no longer support "the integrity of the national heritage" and serve as a means of imparting that heritage and reproducing traditional culture. According to this view, the threat from socialism has never been greater. One take from this perspective argues that a subversive threat is present even in what might at first appear to be ordinary moderate left-of-center politics. The Romantic Poet's weblog, for example, claims that the Obama Administration advances a socialist agenda. Another observer claims that Gramsci and John Maynard Keynes inform a "Gramscian conspiracy" that includes the left-wing infiltration of universities, the press, the courts, and Hollywood in order to conduct a culture war:

> What is taught is that objective truth is a fiction and the only thing that matters is "narratives." Thus the goal of journalism is to promote progressive "narratives." . . . This is prima facie evidence of the Gramscian conspiracy—that the media would silence free speech in the interest of promoting the progressive agenda. . . . [T]o the socialist it is necessary to control all channels of communication to dominate the "superstructure" and prep the masses for the socialist revolution. (Reasonsjester 2009)

Arguably, these sources do not represent a mainstream political discourse but they do deploy words in what can be regarded as a cultural war of position in order to authentically speak for the meaning and value of 'national heritage' and intellectual freedom. They speak as if defending a position under an attack, and they launch a counter attack. But even as they strike out at a perceived form of censorship they assert explicit parameters for and set limits to what ought to be acceptable as public discourse.

These examples demonstrate an approach to the problematics of 'political correctness' and 'intellectual freedom' manifest by both right and left that reveals the nature of these concepts as being essentially contested (Connolly 1993, 10–44). They further reveal an essential political dynamic of late capitalist society. The superstructure is the battleground of politics if not revolution, and ideas and discourse are the weapons deployed. Intellectual freedom can be defined as an abstraction more easily than it can be realized as a social practice.

It is not likely that Thornton can grasp the possibility that his own "traditional, Christian" society might be an exercise of cultural hegemony on behalf of a dominant historic bloc and the primary means of constraining genuine intellectual freedom. But in a way not anticipated by Thornton, or others who make a similar case, the critique he represents introduces the problematic of intellectual freedom that Gramsci might have pursued. The fact, as Thornton says, that workers and peasants proved to be little interested in revolution and instead were much more attuned to "such things as faith in God and love of family and country" is potentially evidence of the effectiveness of capitalist cultural hegemony that Gramsci bemoaned when he urged the workers not to subscribe to bourgeois newspapers.

The conservative perspective of Gramsci and his legacy is important and revealing, and ultimately points to an essential ambiguity in the idea of intellectual freedom; in capitalist social formations not all speech is equal, nor is it equally free because not all speakers are equal or equally free despite formal rights. By assigning entire classes of people to material conditions that prevent them from realizing freedom from necessity, capitalist social formations betray the formal freedoms they apparently offer. For those whose lives are determined by material necessity, the struggle to sustain life in the face of immediate needs tends to take precedence over exercising opportunities to speak out against that condition. Outright censorship need not be in play to silence a voice.

Despite their obvious differences, one can see that Bernstein and Lenin embrace at least one idea in common; one whose source is found in the work of Marx. If freedom, including intellectual freedom, is to have any real meaning at all, the formal conditions of democracy including the universal franchise, equality before the law, and civil liberties—among them the right to free speech—must be accompanied by freedom from necessity. Otherwise, one is only as free as one can afford to be. Formal rights and freedoms make little difference to real persons if they lack the means of self-determination. In characteristic terms, turning the accepted view upside down, Marx wrote,

> *Just as religion does not make the man, but man makes the religion, so the constitution does not make the people, but the people makes the constitution. . . . Man is not there for the benefit of the law, but the law for the benefit of man. . . . That is the fundamental character of democracy.*
> (1970, 65)

Marx might have added that intellectual freedom does not make us who we are. Rather, we make it what it is, and it can be made in many different ways depending on what can be legitimately spoken under its regime and who has the resources necessary to allow them to speak. Progressive and even revolutionary potential exists in capitalist democracies, but formal political freedoms and declarations of rights do not make us free. Real subjects, acting freely, determining their lives according to human nature imbue the merely formal with real, historical meaning. Ideological principle without grounding in economic and historical reality is without substance.

A Gramscian Reading of Mill

In any social formation certain institutions exist for the purpose of situating and contextualizing public discourse. These institutions include schools at all levels, the church, the press, publishing, entertainment, libraries, and museums; in effect, any organization or institution engaged in moral/intellectual discourse regardless of whether the discourse is popular or scholarly. Some of these agents are private and organic to the historic bloc, but many are public, state institutions. In common, they are fora of public communication; together they constitute the "public sphere" (Habermas 1991) and they act to organize and distribute public discourse. They are the means we use to talk about ourselves and to create and sustain identities among other kinds of social relations. They are also means of social control. They are arenas in which legitimate public discourse is separated from the illegitimate. They are the social locations in which limits to thought and speech are set. In short, they are the means by which the dominant historic bloc of a social formation exercises power and guarantees its reproduction. From Gramsci's perspective they represent the battle ground of class struggle in advanced 20th century industrial societies.

In societies with cultural traditions of free speech, such as those of Western Europe and the USA, these institutions are identified with norms of intellectual freedom. They are ostensibly designed to allow the free discourse necessary for reasoning and democratic political discourse and action. The expected outcome, following from the application of reason to the problems of living, is the realization of the Enlightenment's promise of the good life. Gramsci, like Marx, was firmly rooted in the same Enlightenment mode of thought. He could not accept the irrationality of Soviet Marxism grounded in "scientific" economic determinism but neither was he blind to the ideology that informed western capitalism and the irrational outcomes that followed from that ideology.

From Gramsci's perspective, the institutions of public discourse are the sites and the weapons, and also the stakes in a "war of position" among the competing interests and factions struggling for dominance and the control and/or liberation of capital and the means of production that determine who is free from necessity and who is not. They require free discourse to work rationally and to justify the historic bloc's dominant position, but the work they do is always already an integral part of their historical location and role regarding production and reproduction of the historic bloc and its dominating culture and social position. This work is inevitably distorted by ideology masked as reason. Intellectual freedom is not an absolute, uncontested, un-distorted phenomenon, nor can it be. It is and will be historically conditioned as an idea, an action, and as an individual as well social reality until it no longer serves the politics of necessity that characterize capitalist social formations society.

The problematic of intellectual freedom is actually a specific instance of the general problematic of freedom in capitalist democracies. This problem can be usefully explored by a Gramscian interrogation of John Stuart Mill's classic text *On Liberty*. In that work Mill addresses a very broad problem; the morally appropriate relationship between society and the individual. From Mill's utilitarian perspective, the individual's interest and welfare must be privileged over the interest and welfare of society because the greatest social good can be realized only by allowing individuals to pursue their own vision of the good life. Each individual life constitutes an existential space from which society can and ought to be justly excluded. In that space, the actions of individuals affect only themselves or if others are involved it is "only with their free, voluntary, and undeceived consent and participation." This sphere is, in Mill's words, "the appropriate region of human liberty" (Mill 1975, 13).

Presumably, this is the region of intellectual freedom, and it must possess certain characteristics. It must allow for "liberty of conscience in the most comprehensive sense." Individuals must be free to think whatever they like about whatever they like. And the freedom to *express* what one *thinks* is so intimately related to liberty of conscience that thought and its expression cannot be meaningfully separated. In Mill's view, this test of liberty finds its ultimate manifestation in contests over freedom of moral and religious thought. It must allow, as he says, for the liberty of "tastes and pursuits." There is no reason to expect that each of us will define the good life in the same way. Excepting the pursuit of desire that causes harm to another, each must be allowed to pursue their self-determined desires. Finally, the region of human liberty must allow for freedom of assembly. People must be free to act together, or not, to achieve an end they desire in common. Mill also writes:

> No society in which these liberties are not, on the whole, respected, is free, whatever may be its form of government; and none is completely free in which they do not exist absolute and unqualified. The only freedom which deserves the name is that of pursuing our own good in our own way, so long as we do not attempt to deprive others of theirs, or impede their efforts to obtain it. Each is the proper guardian of his own health, whether bodily, or mental and spiritual. Mankind are greater gainers by suffering each other to live as seems good to themselves, than by compelling each to live as seems good to the rest. (1975, 14)

The main subject of *On Liberty* then is a solution to the problem of guaranteeing individual liberty, but there is another aspect to this problem that Mill implies without fully exploring. The problem is revealed in Mill's insistence that the liberties he identifies as necessary to a genuinely free society must be absolute and unqualified. From Gramsci's point of view, however, those liberties cannot be either absolute or unqualified as long as society is governed by necessity and dominated by an historic bloc, as is the case of all capitalist societies.

Mill begins his first chapter of *On Liberty* with a brief history of despotism and the human struggle to be free from despotic governance but at no point does he suggest that governance is unnecessary. Society does have legitimate claims upon individuals; at the very least to prevent harm from coming to the individuals that constitute society. There is a need for social authority; there is a need for the state acting as the people in their interest. Mill writes:

> *The struggle between Liberty and Authority is the most conspicuous feature in the portions of history with which we are earliest familiar . . .*

And later,

> *There is a limit to the legitimate interference of collective opinion with individual independence: and to find that limit, and maintain it against encroachment, is as indispensable to a good condition of human affairs, as protection against political despotism. But though this proposition is not likely to be contested in general terms, the practical question, where to place the limit—how to make the fitting adjustment between individual independence and social control—is a subject on which nearly everything remains to be done. All that makes existence valuable to anyone, depends on the enforcement of restraints upon the actions of other people. Some rules of conduct, therefore, must be imposed, by law in the first place, and by opinion on many things which are not fit subjects for the operation of law. That these rules should be, is the principal question in human affairs; but if we except a few of the most obvious cases, it is one of those which least progress has been made in resolving.* (1975, 3; 6)

Gramsci would not disagree with the substance of Mill's argument, although he would suggest that the struggle between liberty and authority is merely one form taken by the class struggle at one point in human history. He might also have stressed that rules of conduct, especially those imposed by opinion are inevitably rules that privilege the interests of the historic bloc and are based on its opinions.

Furthermore, Gramsci's thought also resonates with Mill's contention that general happiness depends on finding the right balance between authority and liberty and that we have not been especially successful at finding that balance. Mill actually confronts a number of problems in his pursuit of the rules of social conduct that will guarantee the right balance between liberty and authority, not the least of which is a consideration of how an apparently legitimate authority can in fact be as oppressive as any despotism. This too, is a problem with which Gramsci was familiar. In reading Mill we can witness the emergence of Gramsci's problematic.

Mill explicitly warns against the tyranny of the majority, and along the way introduces another issue that arises in the context of an historic bloc's cultural dominance—protection of the rights of minorities. From here follow issues of multiculturalism and identity politics, although Mill, who was writing in the 19th century, cannot be held responsible for failing to address them. The tyranny of the majority, however, is a phenomenon whose potential Mill lived with, and it he reveals it as a very subtle and powerful enemy of freedom.

Let's assume a state—a social authority—exists and exercises power by the consent of the governed. We can be even more specific and assume that this state is an elected representative government. Is this an adequate guarantee of individual liberty? Maybe not. Mill observes that in the case of government by the people, "the 'people' who exercise power are not always the same people with those over whom it is exercised" (1975, 5). It may instead be a government of "each by the rest." Mill makes a crucial distinction. This kind of government, a popular government in fact, practically expresses "the will of the most numerous, or the most active *part* of the people . . ." (1975, 5). By identifying the most active part of the people as actual governors of the people, Mill implies a Gramscian argument. From Gramsci's perspective, in a capitalist social formation the most active part of the people will be the bourgeois historic bloc.

It is entirely possible, for example, for a popular government by consent of the majority of its citizens to suppress the rights of minorities, or even to suppress themselves. The majority can vote to end democracy at any time, or to severely restrict the application of its principles. More dangerous to liberty, however, is the possibility that a government of the people, based on the will and consent of the majority is in fact dominated by a smaller coalition of people—Gramsci's historic bloc for example—who "succeed in making themselves accepted as the majority." This end can be accomplished if the coalition has the resources necessary to establish its world view as the prevailing world view even if in fact this view and the actions that follow from it are harmful to all of society except the group that seeks domination. If capital in its various forms—material, cultural, and political—is unevenly distributed in a society, as Gramsci argued it is in capitalist societies, then this outcome is to be expected. The historic bloc dominated by the minority bourgeoisie achieves the end feared by Mill because it controls the means of production through the mechanism of private property; its dominance is legitimated by the rule of law, and the social order is justified by the existence of formal freedoms, especially constitutionally guaranteed free speech.

At the very least the protection of individual and minority rights is critical and necessary for democratic society. Social obligation and personal freedom must be balanced but given the potential power of society—acting through the state—personal liberty must be privileged over social authority. But even the formal protection of individual rights may be problematic if society is dominated by an historic bloc. Mill observes that society can exercise its own mandates without using the coercive apparatus of the state and in so doing may penetrate private life far more deeply than does political oppression. This too is an observation that could equally well have been made by Gramsci fifty years later. Gramsci would add that coercion penetrates social as well as individual life, but Mill and Gramsci both agree that the power they observe is subtle, representing a cultural assault on individuality that subverts the very norms on which it claims to be based.

One may be free to think differently from one's family, friends and immediate associates, but it can be very difficult to speak up and say so. One may not agree with one's legitimately selected leaders, or at least be suspicious of what they say, yet it can be very difficult to find the time and energy to research the policy issues that demand attention or actively participate in politics. At a certain point utility appears to be better served by trusting the voice of one's representative. It can be difficult to challenge received opinion, to disagree with prevailing opinion and feeling. This is why Mill insists, in addition, to the formal and constitutional protection of individual rights, "there needs protection also against the tyranny of the prevailing opinion and feeling." But as Mill suggests, finding the means to balance individual liberty against this kind of collective power has been difficult. He also gives us a clue about where to look for explanations for the failure of systems of formal rights:

> Wherever there is an ascendant class, a large portion of the morality of the country emanates from its class interests, and its feelings of class superiority. The morality between Spartans and Helots, between planters and negroes, between princes and subjects, between nobles and roturiers, between men and women, has been for the most part the creation of these class interests and feelings. (1975, 8)

At this point, Mill and Gramsci are remarkably in sync. Mill's "ascendant class" and Gramsci "historic bloc" dominate social formations organized by themselves for themselves. Their opinions and feelings come to be the prevailing opinions and feelings. They suppress cultural challenge and minority opinion by force of social pressure rather than by means of formal censorship. The latter is an unnecessary and extreme measure. Custom, Rousseau called it convention, is the means by which this tyranny is exercised. Mill says it works like this:

> The likings and dislikings of society, or of some powerful portion of it, are thus the main thing which has practically determined the rules laid down for general observance, under the penalties of law or opinion. And in general, those who have been in advance of society in thought and feeling, have left this condition of things unassailed in principle, however they may have come into conflict with it in some of its details. They have occupied themselves rather in inquiring what things society ought to like or dislike, than in questioning whether its likings or dislikings should be a law to individuals. (1975, 8)

As it turns out, most people have little interest in challenging common notions, even if those notions demand that they sacrifice their liberty to the interests of society, or at least a part of society, in the name of a common good. Regarding decisions about the appropriate use of state power in the intervention of civic affairs, as of the mid-19th century, Mill concluded, ". . . one side is at present as often wrong as the other; the interference of government is, with about equal frequency, improperly invoked and improperly condemned" (Mill 1975, 10).

Things have not changed much, and in late capitalist democracies we still struggle with finding the right balance between authority and liberty, between social obligation and personal freedom. Mill is suggesting his system of liberty, including liberty of thought and discussion, as a reasonable means to the end of that balance. But to make his case, he also reveals how a modern tyranny of prevailing opinion and feeling might work. Note carefully the arguments Mill anticipates that can and perhaps will be mounted against his case. Especially note just how reasonable they can sound and then consider how difficult it might be to actually establish the conditions for the liberty of thought and discussion called for by Mill or the freedom from necessity called for by Gramsci.

A final point that Mill and Gramsci would agree upon: A relationship exists between speech and knowledge. Free speech is the means of knowledge as an end. For enemies of freedom, or at least freedom other than their own, speech itself is not the strategic object of their efforts. Control of speech, through sanction, approval, restraint, or any number of other actions short of outright use of state power to censor is merely a tactical means of controlling knowledge. Specifically, it is the means of controlling the criteria of determining and legitimating truth and thus asserting cultural hegemony. What we know to be true may be quite wrong but that falsehood may serve the interests of a powerful group within society and so remains true. A distinct separation between power and knowledge is difficult to make in modern societies, further contributing to the ambiguity and irony of intellectual freedom.

False Metaphors and Repressive Tolerance: An Example of Exercising Hegemony

In capitalist democracies the metaphor of a "marketplace of ideas" often represents formal intellectual freedom; a fair competition between speakers and ideas is assumed to exist, each having its turn in public discourse, and then based on rational comparison and deliberation the people choose which one is true, fair, moral, or right—whatever is at stake. Mill was not entirely convinced that this metaphor was accurate or useful. Gramsci would dismiss it as an ideological construct intended to disguise the oppressive work of the dominant culture. Capital and labor do not enter the labor market on equal terms and neither do ideas.

From Gramsci's perspective it is not surprising that in capitalist social formations, economic issues are privileged over social issues; a prevailing assumption is that social issues cannot be addressed, especially by government, unless the economy is strong enough to provide sufficient surplus wealth. In society, power and privilege gain access to resources as often as merit and need. In business, the needs of firms and shareholders tend to come before the needs of employees and consumers. In law, property rights tend to be privileged over human rights. *Citizens United v. FEC* neatly reveals how all of these privileges come together. It is a case that goes to the heart of how the historic bloc of American society practically defines political speech and reveals the way the formal mechanisms of bourgeois democracy act to privilege and constrain speakers. Gramsci would not have been surprised by the U.S. Supreme Court's decision in this case.

The case involved a private corporation, Citizens United, which with contributions from other private interests had funded the production and distribution of a film attacking Hillary Clinton during the 2008 presidential primary election campaign. The Federal Elections Commission (FEC), acting under authority granted to it by the Bipartisan Campaign Reform Act (BCRA)—also known as the McCain-Feingold Act—ruled that broadcast of the film was illegal. Citizens United took the FEC to court and the case made its way to the U.S. Supreme Court. In a summary prepared for the State of Connecticut by its Office of Legal Research, Kristin Sullivan and Terrance Adams write:

> In a 5-4 decision, the U.S. Supreme Court ruled that corporations and unions have the same political speech rights as individuals under

the First Amendment. It found no compelling government interest for prohibiting corporations and unions from using their general treasury funds to make election-related independent expenditures. Thus, it struck down a federal law banning this practice and also overruled two of its prior decisions. (2010)

The Court's decision in *Citizens United* called into question state laws that prohibited corporations from making independent expenditures from their general treasury for election campaign purposes.

The practical result of the Court's decision in *Citizens United* is that corporations and unions, or anyone else for that matter, can spend as much as they desire and can for political advertising supporting or attacking a given candidate for office in order to influence the outcome of an election. On its face this might seem like a fair outcome, but from a Gramscian perspective it is clear that in capitalist democracies one's capability for public speech is not unrelated to the amount of capital that can be spent for it. In effect, *Citizens United* merely granted formal recognition to a principle already in place—that spending on public speech was in itself a form of speech constitutionally protected by the First Amendment. A government imposed limit on how much money can be spent by whom and for what in public discourse is now to be regarded as an illegitimate constraint of speech as guaranteed by the First Amendment. After *Citizens United v. FEC*, with regard to political speech, speakers with the most money tend to have their speech privileged.

Citizens United confirms what Gramsci believed was already in place in capitalist social formations—that voices are never equal in ways that matter. Formal equality has little if anything to do with real equality. The bourgeoisie and its partners in the historic bloc have always held a privileged position in the fora of public discourse. Ownership of media, prestige of speakers, capital necessary to reach audiences and distribute messages have always been largely in the hands of the historic bloc. Large organizations, including labor unions, have always had more power to assert a louder voice than individuals. Formal equality of persons and voices has always been betrayed by the accumulation and application of capital to speech in capital social formations. From a Gramscian perspective, *Citizens United* merely matches formal practice to material practice and in effect does not alter the reality of free speech or the distortion of its meaning in capitalist social formations.

Once again, Mill and Gramsci are in sync. Mill argues that to meet the conditions of genuinely free speech, minority opinions are to be "encouraged and countenanced" (Mill 1975, 46) for at least two reasons. They are likely to represent neglected social groups that are in danger of exclusion from their fair share of social benefits and civic participation, and they are likely to be the ideas of challenge and change, and capable of bringing us a step closer to the truth, either because they are correct or because in refuting them we will know ourselves and our world more completely. There is a practical and utilitarian value to the truth associated with the protection of minority opinion. Gramsci's theory suggests the reasons why this condition is not likely to prevail in a capitalist social formation and implies that a society that uses a market metaphor to describe its practical realization of intellectual freedom is acting in bad faith.

Jill Gordon draws attention to Mill's avoidance of a marketplace metaphor to talk about the conditions of free speech and his emphasis on the "treatment afforded to ideas held by a minority of the people," (1997, 238) and raises explicit doubts about whether such a market can meet the conditions that Mill establishes as necessary for genuine liberty of thought and discussion. A market aggregates the choices of individual producers and consumers, each assumed to have perfect information regarding products and prices. The aggregation of choice by means of free exchange between producers and consumers results in the most efficient way of providing and equitably distributing the best products at the best prices. It is economic. Gordon warns us that in this concept the notion of "... 'best' is ... defined solely *ex post facto* as that product which does so triumph or prevail in the marketplace" (Gordon 1997, 236).

Consider a couple of questions. In real markets, does the "best" product always prevail? Products can sometimes not be very good or effective, but nevertheless successful. If we claim that the market produces the best and most efficient results we also have to ask for whom? How? From what perspective is the "best" to be judged? These questions raise problems for applying a market metaphor to the conditions necessary for liberty of thought and discussion.

Like Gramsci, Gordon observes that individuals never enter a market with equal buying power (1997, 241). The market's determination of good is a quantitative rather than qualitative choice. In markets, the will of the people is always the will of some people. Even mass markets depend on exclusions. In some instances, needs may go unmet because producers will not try to reach consumers if profit margins are too narrow or non-existent. Gordon observes, again as Gramsci might have, that products and opinions can be excluded from markets and denied to consumers, including consumers of ideas, without the mechanism of formal exclusion. Neither ideas nor products need be officially prohibited to prevent their distribution. The law of supply and demand will set the price (cost) of certain opinions in a way that makes them too expensive to produce, distribute, or acquire. Minorities, and their ideas, can be excluded from the market, or at least their entry made exceedingly difficult, as both buyers and sellers.

Publishers, for example, often reject manuscripts not because their arguments challenge the status quo, but simply because of an expectation of limited demand and limited, if any, return on investment. Once published, libraries often fail to select material not because it might be offensive to anyone, but again because of the expectation of limited demand. Unless an idea already has widespread acceptance, establishing its presence can be difficult. Truth may sometimes require affirmative assistance.

But what does it mean to say that the capitalist historic bloc, even in western democracies, uses the superstructure, including the "marketplace of ideas" as a metaphor for intellectual freedom, to exercise dominance over an entire social formation? Among other things it means that the purpose of a great deal of social activity, especially communication, is to maintain the base; specifically, to rationalize and legitimize capitalist relations of production, to make it unimaginable that any other set of economic relations could be possible. Public agendas, if not public discourse, are dominated by questions of interest to the historic bloc: how to grow the economy, the appropriate role of government with regard to private enterprise and social welfare, international finance, and globalization. Factions of the historic bloc use these issues to seize or negotiate competitive advantages while the bloc as whole uses them to reproduce its privileged position at the level of the base.

From a Gramscian perspective, public discourse in capitalist social formations involves exclusions by means of cultural marginalization rather than coercion. Capitalism, its possible forms finding expression in social settings as different as communist China and the United States, possesses its own rationality, logic, and values that exclude or at the least attempt to exclude challenges. Its discourse is not planned or directed or organized as an explicit instrument of oppression. It is merely what members of the bloc think and say to one another about the world and their responsibility for it, but through assertion and dismissal this discourse attempts to identify challenge to its premises as irrational, illogical, or morally wrong. Herbert Marcuse identifies the mechanism at play as "repressive tolerance" (Marcuse 1969, 95–137).

From a Gramscian perspective, repressive tolerance may allow and in some instances constitutionally guarantees dissenting and challenging expression, but that expression will be ideologically characterized and commonly understood as false, incorrect, inappropriate, or irrelevant. The extent of the historic bloc's success in this project—the extent that its discourse is persuasive and accepted by the social formation as an accurate representation of it real nature—is the extent to which the bloc's hegemony is complete and it can rest assured that its particular interests will be accepted as universal.

Challenges are then regarded as "special interests" posing as universal in order to deceive and justify the attempt to exploit public interest to serve private gain. Ironically, the bloc's own special notions of right and good are accepted as true; its way of doing things, instead of being revealed as historically developed and conditioned, are seen as the only sensible way of doing them. Under these circumstances, Marcuse closes his argument with the observation that "free competition and exchange of ideas . . . become a farce" (Marcuse 1969).

Conclusion: Late Capitalism and the Possibilities of Freedom

Antonio Gramsci did not explicitly address let alone attempt to define the concept of intellectual freedom and his work raises some doubt about what it really means. Article 19, Universal Declaration of Human Rights offers a very broad definition that likely resonates with what most people commonly think of as intellectual freedom:

> *Everyone has the right to freedom of opinion and expression; this right includes freedom to hold opinions without interference and to seek, receive and impart information and ideas through any media and regardless of frontiers.* (United Nations 1948)

The American variant of this notion is reflected in American librarianship's commitment to intellectual freedom as a core responsibility of the profession. In the most recent edition of the ALA *Intellectual Freedom Manual* Candace Morgan writes:

> *The First and Fourth Amendments to the U.S. Constitution are integral to American librarianship. They are the basis of the concept librarians call intellectual freedom. Intellectual freedom accords to all library users the right to seek and receive information on all subjects from all points of view without restriction and without having the subject of one's interest examined or scrutinized by others.* (2009)

But the Freedom to Read (2009) statement, after a fashion, sounds as if it was based on a reading of Gramsci:

> *. . . [E]fforts at suppression are related to a larger pattern of pressures being brought against education, the press, art and images, films, broadcast media, and the Internet. The problem is not only one of actual censorship. The shadow of fear cast by these pressures leads, we suspect, to an even larger voluntary curtailment of expression by those who seek to avoid controversy or unwelcome scrutiny by government officials.* (ALA 2009)

Although there are instances of formal censorship in the USA, the First Amendment provides reasonable protection of speech. Sexually explicit content is more likely to draw attention and sanction than political speech, and even then print is not likely to cause the same kind of trouble that visual images do. Voluntary curtailment of speech is more likely, either self-imposed as a matter of passive and unthinking acceptance of convention or in response to social norms and peer expectations. In democratic social formations, this phenomenon is a much greater threat to intellectual freedom than official censorship or forcible prior restraint of speech.

Gramsci probably would have agreed with Marcuse's rather bleak conclusion about the marketplace of ideas and that the Freedom to Read statement more accurately captures the reality of intellectual freedom than do formal statements that merely assert its value as an abstract principle. But he also would have asserted that possibilities for transformative political action exist. Of course the historic bloc has advantages over its competitors and challengers. Most of the state ideological apparatus as well as the largely privately owned culture and communication industries that constitute the public sphere will privilege the bloc's discourse and structuring of reality (Adorno 1991). It is important to recall, however, that a historic bloc is not a "ruling class," and neither the state ideological apparatus nor the public sphere exist merely as extensions of the bloc's interests. Modern, twentieth century capitalism is characterized by contradictions and factions within its historic bloc as well as by a structure of economic complexity and superstructure of social and political diversity.

Beliefs and values are independent historical phenomena. In capitalist democracies the superstructure is vulnerable to alternative discourses, at least partly because of the liberal values that characterize the ideologies of historic blocs in these kinds of social formations. The state, the culture and entertainment industries, even the public sphere are ideologically overdetermined institutions—locations that can be and to an extent always are sites of political conflict in the war of position conducted on the ground of the superstructure. The outcome of these conflicts can alter these institutions and the social relations they govern, including relations of production. The modern capitalist state has monopoly control over the means of coercive violence, but to maintain its position, the historic bloc relies more on ideological persuasion than on coercion. It is precisely this need to rely on intellectual and moral leadership, however, that opens the historic bloc to a challenge of its legitimacy on its own terms, and suggests potentially progressive historical roles for various groups that might challenge the hegemony of the historic bloc.

For some time now, the historic bloc of western capitalism has employed two broad legitimation strategies in the effort to solve the problems of protecting and extending its hegemony and moral authority, and reproducing capitalist relations of production, including its own position as a privileged historical subject in the social formation. The first involves grounding the institutions of the state and civil society on a "rational/legal" basis (Weber 1946, 78-9, 196-209, 293-95). The second is to grant concessions to popular demands for social and political participation and economic security, if not equality.

Outstanding historical examples of both strategies in action include the governing policies of Roosevelt's New Deal and Johnson's Great Society. Both regimes offered a constrained but real partnership in the bloc to formerly excluded historical subjects by creating more permeable class boundaries for individuals. These regimes recognized the grievances of historically excluded social groups, and represented themselves symbolically as extensions of a historical discourse of democracy. They both had lasting consequences for the nature of the American social formation and contributed to the realization of genuinely progressive economic and political outcomes. Gramsci identifies this strategy as one of "passive revolution". It allows the bourgeois dominated historic bloc to find ways to further develop the social formation's productive forces, thus reinforcing its hegemony in response to crisis and "the relative weakness of the rival progressive force" (1971, 106-7, 119-120, 222).

The political strategies of late capitalism are overdetermined, driven not just by considerations of practical politics seeking a social equilibrium and the maintenance of capital's power, but also by a widespread acceptance of the discourse of democracy's legitimacy, even among the members of the historic bloc (Laclau and Mouffe 1985). The essential relations of production—the base—may change only very slowly, but new superstructural arrangements imposed by political action can lead to the redistribution of wealth and privileges. These changes may include greater degrees of social participation, recognition of the legitimacy of interests that challenge the hegemony of the historic bloc, and the redress of social and economic inequalities.

For social formations in which freedom is a meaningful idea whose social determination has material consequences for a subject's life chances, intellectual freedom is an essentially contested concept (Connolly 1993). While the idea in itself is central to the nature of the social formation, even more important are the contests over the meaning of the idea and their implications for everyday social and political life. These contests can and do determine the extent to which difference, in language, lifestyle, ideology, personal expression, social and ethnic identity, and individuality are genuinely tolerated and accepted in a social formation. They determine the manner and extent to which the freedom to think as one chooses, free of fear of sanction or constraint, actually exists.

References

Adorno, Theodor W. 1991. *The culture industry*. London and New York: Routledge.

Althusser, Louis. 1970. Contradiction and overdetermination. In *For Marx*. New York: Vintage Books.

Althusser, Louis and Etienne Balibar. 1970. *Reading capital*. Trans. Ben Brewster. New York: Pantheon Books. (Orig. pub. 1968.)

American Library Association. 2009. The freedom to read. In *Intellectual freedom manual, 8th edition*. Chicago: American Library Association. http://ifmanual.org/ftrstatement (accessed September 15, 2012).

Bernstein, Eduard. 1961. *Evolutionary socialism; A criticism and affirmation*. Trans. Edith C. Harvey. New York: Schocken Books. (Orig. pub. 1899.)

Claudin, Fernando. 1975. *The Communist movement: From Comintern to Cominform. Part two*. New York: Monthly Review Press.

Connolly, William E. 1993. *The terms of political discourse*, 3rd ed. Princeton: Princeton University Press.

Derrida, Jacques. 1994. *Specters of Marx: The state of the debt, the work of mourning, and the new international*. New York: Routledge.

Fields, Belden A. 1988. In defense of political economy and systemic analysis: A critique of prevailing theoretical approaches to the new social movements. In *Marxism and the interpretation of culture*, Ed. Cary Nelson and Lawrence Grossberg. Urbana and Chicago: University of Illinois Press.

Gordon, Jill. 1997. John Stuart Mill and the 'Marketplace of Ideas'. *Social Theory and Practice* 23, 235–249.

Gramsci, Antonio. 1958. *Studi gramsciani*. Rome: Instituto Gramsci.

_____. 1916. Newspapers and the workers. Avanti, December, 22. Gramsci Links Archive. http://www.marxists.org/archive/gramsci/1916/12/newspapers.htm (accessed September 5, 2012).

_____. 1971. *Selections from the prison notebooks*. Ed. and Trans. Quintin Hoare and Geoffrey N. Smith. New York: International Publishers.

_____. 1975. *Quaderni del carcere*. Vols. 1–4. Ed. Valentino Gerratana. Turin: Einaudi.

_____. 1977. *Selections from political writings (1910–1920) with additional texts by Bordiga and Tasca*. Comp. and Ed. Quintin Hoare, Trans. John Mathews. New York: International Publishers.

_____. 1992. *Prison notebooks*. Vols. 1–3. Ed. Joseph A. Buttigieg. Trans. Joseph A. Buttigieg and Antonio Callari. New York: Columbia University Press.

Habermas, Jurgen. 1991. *The Structural transformation of the public sphere: An inquiry into a category of bourgeois society.* Cambridge, Mass.: MIT Press.

Jameson, Frederic. 1991. *Postmodernism, or the cultural logic of late capitalism.* London: Verso.

Laclau, Ernesto and Chantal Mouffe. 1985. *Hegemony and socialist strategy: Towards a radical democratic politics.* London: Verso.

Lasswell, Harold D. 1990. *Politics; Who gets what, when, and how.* Gloucester, Mass.: Peter Smith.

Lenin, V. I. 1969a. *Imperialism: The highest stage of capitalism.* New York: International Publishers. (Orig. pub. 1917.)

_____. 1969b. *What is to be done? Burning questions of our movement* New York: International Publishers. (Orig. pub. 1917.)

_____. *The State and revolution: The Marxist theory of the state and the tasks of the proletariat in the revolution. "The Economic Basis of the Withering Away of the State. 4. The Higher Phase of Communist Society.,* 1999. *Collected works,* vol. 25. Lenin Internet Archive. http://www.marxists.org/archive/lenin/works/1917/staterev/index.htm (accessed September 5, 2012). (Orig. pub. 1918.)

Lukes, Steven. 1983. Emancipation. In *A Dictionary of Marxist thought.* Ed. Tom Bottomore. Cambridge: Harvard University Press.

Marcuse, Herbert. 1969. Repressive tolerance. In Robert Paul Wolff, Barrington Moore, Jr., and Herbert Marcuse, *A critique of pure tolerance.* Boston: Beacon Press, 95–137. http://www.marcuse.org/herbert/pubs/60spubs/65repressivetolerance.htm (accessed Sept 5, 2012).

Marx, Karl. 1968. The Eighteenth Brumaire of Louis Bonaparte. In *Karl Marx and Frederick Engels, selected works.* New York: International Publishers.

_____. 1970. *Critique of Hegel's philosophy of right.* Ed. J. O'Malley. Cambridge: Cambridge University Press.

_____. 1970a. *The German ideology. Part one.* New York: International Publishers.

_____. 1973. Preface to a contribution to the critique of political economy. Vol. 1 of *Selected works.* Moscow: Progress Publishers.

Marx, Karl and Frederick Engels. 1968. Manifesto of the Communist Party. In *Karl Marx and Fredrick Engels: Selected works.* New York: International Publishers. (Orig. pub. 1848.)

Meyer, Alfred G. 1957. *Leninism.* New York: Frederick A Preager Publishers.

Mill, John Stuart. 1975. *On Liberty* New York: W.W. Norton & Company. (Orig. pub. 1869.)

Morgan, Candace D. 2009. Intellectual freedom: An enduring and all-embracing concept. In *Intellectual Freedom Manual, 8th edition.* Chicago: American Library Association. http://ifmanual.org/ (accessed September 15, 2012).

Poulantzas, Nicos. 1978. *Political power and social classes.* London: Verso.

Reasonsjester. 2009. Antonio Gramsci: Mentor of the new left. Point Counterpoint blog. http://pointvscounterpoint.blogspot.com/2009/03/antonio-gramsci-mentor-of-new-left.html. (accessed July 10, 2012).

Romanticpoet's Weblog. Just another wordPress.com weblog. Gradualism through Fabian socialism and Antonio Gramsci (Italian communist) to absolute government control. (accessed July 10, 2012).

Sassoon, Anne Showstack. 1980. *Gramsci's politics.* New York: St. Martin's Press.

Schumpeter, Joseph A. 1950. *Capitalism, socialism, and democracy.* 3rd ed. New York: Harper.

Stiglitz, Joseph E. 1996. *Whither socialism?* Cambridge, Mass.: MIT Press.

Sullivan, Kristin and Terrance Adams. 2010. Summary of *Citizen United v. Federal Election Commission.* March 2, 2010-R-0124. Office of Legislative Research.

Thornton, Fr. James. 1999. Gramsci's grand plan. *The New American,* July 5, http://www.freerepublic.com/focus/news/823368/posts (accessed September 5, 2012).

Trotsky, Leon. 1957. *The history of the Russian revolution.* Vol. 1. Ann Arbor: University of Michigan Press.

_____. 1962. The permanent revolution. New York: Pioneer Publishers.

Weber, Max. 1946. *From Max Weber: Essays in sociology.* Ed. and Trans. H.H. Gerth and C. Wright Mills. New York: Oxford University Press.

United Nations. 1948. Universal declaration of human rights. http://www.un.org/en/documents/udhr/ (accessed September 15, 2012).

Habermas and Intellectual Freedom
Three Paths

John Buschman

Jürgen Habermas' fundamental (and continuing) contributions in the late twentieth and early twenty first centuries to philosophy, political theory, communications theory, critical social theory, legal theory, and critical education studies among other fields are well known. Space will not be used here to introduce his biography or corpus of work, other than to refer the reader to his entry in the free online *Stanford Encyclopedia of Philosophy* or a shorter précis this author wrote a few years ago (Buschman 2010). Since his has been such a long and productive career that includes significant engagement with contemporary public issues, someone with a passing familiarity with him might well assume that Habermas had long ago weighed in on intellectual freedom (IF)—or academic freedom, its close cousin with which it is much entangled (Buschman and Rosenzweig 1999). However, he has not meditated on the role of either—nor a justification for them, and Habermas has largely passed over educative institutions[1] in his career (1992, 438) beyond broadly

---

1   There are two working assumptions around which much of this chapter is built. First, that any rounded conception of intellectual and/or academic freedom largely presumes the rights and protections within democratic societies. Second (in something of a feedback loop), contemporary democracies rely on and produce varieties of institutions, which Mara enumerates as three: 1) educative (the focus here, encompassing libraries, schools and universities), 2) enabling (encompassing voting, political participation), and 3) elicitive (juries, school boards, etc.) (2008, 132). The context of intellectual and academic freedom in classrooms and of libraries is thus situated here as a function of public educative institutions in a democratic society. As it was put, intellectual freedom is "indispensible to librarians, because they are trustees of knowledge with the responsibility of ensuring the availability of information and ideas . . . [and] so that teachers may freely teach and students may freely learn" (Association of College and Research Libraries and American Association of University Professors in Buschman and Rosenzweig 1999, 38).

noting that "market success is being replaced by professional success result-ing from formal education . . . [in the] ideology of achievement" (1976a, 381). When he has somewhat turned to the topic, Habermas wrote primarily about the German student protests of the 1960s and the new roles of the German university in a democratic capitalist society. He broadly reflected on the role of free speech in those protests, the "beneficent but archaic freedoms" of the university, and that the "link between our postwar democracy and the tra-ditional university—a link that seems . . . attractive—is coming to an end" (Habermas 1970, 4–5). He comes closest to IF in a later reflection on the evolu-tion of the university: it is a lifeworld[2] and so the relationship between the "dimension of critical self-reflection [and] the relations of research processes . . . [should] be rendered transparent," noting the historic example of the "ex-emplary significance given to scientific autonomy" in teaching and research which resulted in a free exchange of knowledge: the "stimulating and pro-ductive power of discursive disputes" (Habermas 1987a, 16–17, 21; Ostovich 1995).

His other persistent focus has been the "contradictory steering impera-tives [which] assert themselves through the purposive-rational actions not of market-participants, but of members of [school] administration" whose legit-imacy is declining since curricula are no longer self-evident (Habermas 1975, 68, 71). It is in the context of those cross-cutting economic and bureaucratic pressures that school and teacher autonomy (presumably also in the form of intellectual and academic freedom) is eroded (Habermas1987c, 371–373) ab-ermas wishes to uncover the "affinity [between] the enterprise of knowledge . . . [and] the democratic form of decision-making" (Habermas in Ostovich 1995, 473), but he admits that the enterprise "can get along perfectly well without that fond notion it once had of itself" (Habermas 1987a, 18). Beyond these indirect comments, Habermas does not address the issue extensively. That, however, is not meant to imply that Habermas has little or nothing to say about the place, nature, or importance of IF.

There are three paths within his work that provide insight into the topic, and they become increasingly sophisticated, reflective and critical as they are presented and framed here. The final result is a nuanced and supple con-textualization of IF, the forces that militate against its full realization and a

---

2   Mara describes the lifeworld concept as "the 'reservoir' of societal meanings that surround and enable communicat[ion]. . . . And it constitutes the informal but structured communicative networks that allow discursive interactions among the differentiated spheres of complex societies" (2008, 143). There is a very useful compilation of references to and quotations of Habermas' concept, the clearest of which describes the function of the lifeworld: "the propagation of cultural tradi-tions, the integration of groups by norms and values, and the socialization of succeeding generations" (Habermas in Brookfield 2005, 1143, 1140–1145).

deeper understanding of the relationship between IF and democratic capacities. We will begin with the logical support for IF within Habermas' concept of the public sphere, then move to neopragmatic appropriations of Habermas' thoughts and their meaning for IF, and finally his ideas of systematically distorted communications and the strong implication for IF as a critical counterweight. Those are three of the paths within Habermas' corpus chosen here to lead us to and reflect on IF.

It has been my habit at this stage in presenting Habermas to demur about the comprehensiveness, connectedness, complexity and breadth of his thought in relationship to what is presented here. However, Habermas is utilized in the way adopted here in so many fields—and they proceed to redact his work in the same way as those of us who in the LIS field do—that it is perhaps time to simply put him to use and let our colleagues and the process of discursive exchange hone our ideas about and appropriations of him. Finally, some of those précis are cited here in order to save time and space and proceed more directly down the three paths Habermas takes toward IF. The reader is encouraged to use the bibliography and go beyond this chapter.

Path One: The Public Sphere

Habermas' investigation into the public sphere presents a "stylized picture," historically situated, of its development as an essential element of democratization (1989, xix; Hohendahl 1974). The public sphere itself is "a child of the eighteenth century"—that is, of the Enlightenment, and conceptually it is an abstraction, only fleshed out in its practices and effects (Habermas 1989; xviii; 1974). The briefest way into the concept is to describe what was reacted against: historically, the "public face of the . . . state was splendour, its core was shrouded in secrecy. The combination . . . was raised to the level of a political philosophy by Machiavelli, but it was a commonplace of . . . statecraft. A positive role was given to the secrets of the state" (Peters 1993, 547). As for the state's pomp and splendor, they are embodied in the "ceremony and imposingness" of monarchy and were often staged: from jousting matches to the courtly conduct which reached its height in the Versailles of Louis XIV (Peters 1993, 545).[3] Thus was power and hierarchy depicted as legitimate and virtuous, justified by being "capable of public representation" (Habermas 1989, 8). The increasing interests of merchants in the policies of increasingly mercantile governments set up a tension "between the authorities and the subjects[, an] ambivalence [between] public regulation and private initiative" (Habermas 1989, 24). In response, those mercantile interests began to coalesce and then communicate about those policies, becoming in the process

---

3   A contemporary manifestation of this phenomenon can still be seen in ecclesial "ritual, liturgy, mass, and processions" (Habermas 1989, 8).

a grouping "situated between the absolutist state and bourgeois society, i.e., between the world of social labor and commodity trade . . . consist[ing] of discoursing private persons who critically negate political norms of the state and its monopoly on interpretation" and information (Hohendahl 1979, 92). That for Habermas is the indispensable seedbed of democratic functions: "a historical process whereby the shift from premodern feudal, absolutist rule to forms of modern representative democra[tic] public opinion, based on publicly available information and debate, developed both as a check on, and as a source for the legitimacy of government" (Garnham 2001, 12856).[4] Thus "a discursive or deliberative model replace[d] the [traditional liberal] contract model: the . . . community constitutes itself not be way of a social contract but on the basis of a discursively achieved agreement" in Habermas' theory of modern democratic origins (1996, 449).

The *process* of that shift brings us into the arena that IF would eventually flesh out. Habermas is careful to distinguish between "plebiscitary-acclamatory" forms of public assent to ruling that twentieth century dictatorships were so successful at manipulating; they represent a controlled and "regimented public sphere" (1989, xviii). By this Habermas means the manipulations of a "stylized . . . show . . . [and] symbols to which . . . one can not respond by arguing but only by identifying with them," and in this sense those controlled and false choices are non-literate (1989, 206, xviii).[5] Historically, the public sphere then was strongly connected to the "intellectual press" and literate, free exchange of opinion, observation, and argumentation in that venue; in other words, a key element of the public sphere (and thus the development of political democracy) was reasoned argument carried out in publication (Habermas 1974, 53). Those journals contained not merely information (prices, the travels of princes, incoming and outgoing ships), but also "pedagogical instruction and even criticism and reviews"; soon the writers began "to think their own thoughts, directed against the authorities," and then they "readied themselves to compel public authority to legitimate itself before public opinion" (Habermas 1989, 25). Habermas sees in the historical

---

4   Habermas put it this way: "By mobilizing citizens' communicative freedom for the formation of political beliefs that in turn influence the production of legitimate law, [communicative] obligations of this sort build up into a potential that holders of . . . power should not ignore" (1996, 147).

5   This distinction represents an effective answer to the red herring set up by Buckland: libraries are important to democratic regimes, "but so is oil," and they are "important assets in nondemocratic regimes" as well; there are the historical examples of Lenin's librarian wife or the enthusiasm of Mussolini's minister of education—thus any theoretical approach that frames these institutions in IF terms in service to democracy is *de facto* falsely essentializing this relationship in his argument (2009; 2008).

development of the public sphere the instituting of "rational legal principles
. . . which were binding for all"—that is, the restriction of public authority in
the interests of private, discursive autonomy (Hohendahl 1974, 46; Habermas
1974, 52–53). It is in this sense that the public sphere was literate and literary
in its development, and that essential interest continues to this day: "without the flow of information gained through extensive research, and without
the stimulation of arguments based on . . . expertise . . . public communication loses its discursive vitality" (Habermas 2007; 1985a, 97). Democracy for
Habermas is not merely choosing from among elites through voting in occasional elections and exercising private liberties within a framework of legal
protections; rather, "the legitimate exercise of political power [is] trace[d] to
the free communication of citizens" (Cohen 1999, 387).

Habermas is ever concerned with restrictions and blocks on communication, and the "administrative solution favoured by Habermas is to facilitate
access . . . for a discoursing public" in the interests of the health and functioning of democracy (Rodger 1985, 207; Habermas 1994).[6] It is this mantle that
librarianship has taken up and instantiated in its practices and in its IF ethos.
Habermas enumerates five basic categories of rights:

1. those developed autonomously and politically to ensure "equal
    subjective liberties"

2. those that result from the autonomy "of the status of a member in a[n]
    association of consociates under law"

3. those that "result . . . from the actionability of rights and . . . legal
    measures"

4. those ensuring "equal chances at participation in the processes of
    opinion- and will-formation;

5. and those "that secure the conditions of . . . social, technical and
    environmental protection, that are necessary . . . for an equal chance
    to use [those] civil rights" just noted (Baynes 1995, 211).

---

6   Habermas recognizes that formally democratic representative democratic bod-
     ies can function, but become utterly disconnected to a functioning public sphere
     (that is, a legitimate and justified political order): essentially a "state based on the
     rule of law but without democracy" (1992, 431). The problems with and objections
     to his model are summarized and reviewed by Lefrançois and Ethier (2010) and
     Garnham (2001). Essentially the issues come down to objections that empirical
     experience is not as tidy as a theoretical description allows, and the related point
     that the "public" of the public sphere was never exclusive to male bourgeois—a
     point Habermas (1992) has long ago conceded and integrated into his theory.
     I agree with Hohendahl's contention that Habermas has provided an essential
     historical category that has allowed us to understand the historical transition to
     democracy in the west (1974), and thus "even when Habermas has been contra-
     dicted, it is usually within the framework of his theory" (1979, 89).

In turn, librarianship instantiates and articulates a set of principles and practices that, if they do not constitute a precise one-to-one parallel to Habermas' enumerations of rights, they broadly articulate them in the form of IF and its purposes in the democratic roles that libraries play:

- Libraries house and further rational discourse through the organization of collections which is coupled with the principle of unfettered information access and transparency.

- The field enacts the principle of critique and rational argumentation through the commitment to balanced collections, preserving access to them over time, and furthering inclusion through active attempts to make collections and resources reflect historical and current intellectual diversity.

- By their very existence libraries potentially verify (or refute) claims to authority in making current and retrospective organized resources available to check the bases of a thesis, law, book, article, policy etc. continuing the process of debate which lies at the heart of the public sphere and democracy.

- The field has sought to reach out to those not served to make access to information and education more widely and universally available, thereby continuing to ground communicative and democratic processes. (Buschman 2003a, 47; 2005)

Coupled with Habermas' earlier comments on the necessary freedom of educative institutions in democratic societies, that these institutional locations form smaller lifeworlds themselves in need of free communicative exchange, the importance of informed (that is, research-based) public opinion formation, and the articulated role of rights, and Habermas' theory of the public sphere welds a justification for IF strongly to the needs and just functioning of democratic societies and their educative institutions.[7] This then is the most direct route to IF within Habermas' work.

Path Two: Habermas as Neopragmatist

From the very beginning Habermas' work could be characterized as practical and pragmatic in the sense that it is "directed principally toward society"

---

7   It also provides an empirical answer to Garnham's claim that Habermas and deliberative democrats generally valorize direct participation and do not deal well with intermediary arrangements and their roles (2001, 12589–12590). Habermas' look at the role of educative institutions as lifeworlds and the articulations of rights carried out within associations has, I would argue, answered some of this line of questioning.

and concerned in its analysis with "implications . . . for our life together" (Haught 1988, 25). Specifically, he has plumbed the "practical interest [in] improving mutual understanding and preserving intersubjectivity of understanding," (Habermas in Frankel 1974, 47), and in pursuing that practical interest, he has drawn specifically on Pragmatism to ask: "How shall we employ what we know to direct our practical behavior so as to test these beliefs and make possible better ones? The question is seen as it has always been empirically: What shall we do to make objects having value more secure in existence?" (Dewey in Habermas 1973, 272). In other words, at a very high level of abstraction (Wood 1985, 147-148), Habermas has long been in sympathy and congruence with the tradition of the American Pragmatists, and he further identified and articulated many of the same problems of the intertwined relationship between the functions of democracy and the development of a capitalist economy as Dewey (1927; Habermas 1996, 171, 316). A good deal of this can be encapsulated in the meaning of his word "scientism," which for Habermas signifies that thought, investigation, and rationality "must be identified with science" alone; the scientistic society has welded these techniques to production and the shaping of social practice so as to obviate utterly "democratic planning as a steering mechanism" within the enormous scale of modern economies in putatively democratic societies (1971, 650–652; 1970, 81–85). Thus reason becomes exclusively instrumental action in service to economic ends, excluding reason—understood in Haberasian practical terms as of communicative reaching of mutual understanding, problem solving, and life-making that underwrites the health of the lifeworld and democratic functioning: "to the extent that practical questions are eliminated, the public realm loses its political function" (Habermas 1970, 104).[8]

The Neopragmatic appropriations of Habermas make a decisive move back toward a less boxed-in position and toward IF, drawing from his insistence on communicative rationality's "stubbornly transcending power, because it is renewed with each act of unconstrained understanding" (Habermas 1982, 221). It is instantiated in pragmatic and practical terms in a "substantial-ethical procedural democratic theory"—that is, the search for the means to enact

---

8   Habermas clearly links these concepts to that of the lifeworld: "To the extent that action coordination, and with it the formation of networks of interaction, takes place through processes of reaching understanding, intersubjectively shared convictions form the medium of social integration" (1996, 35). White's contention that this analysis of "'scientism' may have made some sense in the heyday of logical positivism, but [is] not very telling [in terms of] contemporary philosophy of science" is far too narrow and academic (2004, 316). There is an empirical reality outside of intellectual currents in the form of the economy, its functioning, and its tight relationship with Big Science that this critique still speaks to in effective ways.

and replicate democracy and its ethos in fair, neutral, and rational discursive ways (Bernstein 1996 1145). Habermas "relies on a particular conception of human excellence; the best way of life is the autonomous life" (Mara 1985, 1053): "Only in an emancipated society, which had realized the autonomy of its members, would communication have developed into that free dialogue of all with all which we always hold up as the very paradigm of a mutually formed self-identity, as well as the ideal of true consensus. To this extent the truth of statements is based on the anticipation of a life without repression" (Habermas 1966, 297). People cannot realize their autonomy (or their interest in it—the same way in which they have a practical interest in mutual understanding) based "on their collective tutelage to social relations, institutions or values to which they cannot adopt a detached, critical attitude, and which they cannot accept [or justify] on rational grounds" (Wood 1985, 148–149). Therefore, if "autonomy and responsibility in the evaluation of individual and social choices" are to be rational and healthy and deliberative, then educative institutions have a substantive role to play in fostering those baseline capacities (Mara 1985, 1038; 2008, 132, 141; Warren 1993, 214–216; 2002, 692; Englund 2000; 2006; Gutmann 1987). That act of fostering autonomy has a political trajectory—there is a strong connection between a democratic ethos, political autonomy, inclusion, individual autonomy, and self-rule (White 2004, 321–323; Bernstein 1996).

Those educative institutions—libraries and schools and universities in this case—are the best sites to discursively sort through "real interests . . . without either entailing some form of authoritarianism, or giving up entirely on . . . [a] normative viewpoint" (White 2004, 312). "Normativity and communicative rationality intersect with one another" in this process (Habermas 1996, 5). Neopragmatist uses of Habermas make this not merely a question of problem-solving (that slides too easily toward the authoritarianism critique to which the Frankfurt School was vulnerable), but rather the "bringing forward complex questions of problem constitution" (White 2004, 319)—or as Brown put it, expanding those things that are say-able and ask-able in the first place (2006, 693–694). This approach does not abjure addressing power, specifically in the form of "the interesting question . . . [of] the conditions that prevent [the] wholly natural and predictable process [of learning and autonomous development] from happening" (Brookfield 2005, 1151, 1149; White 2004, 315). In the terms of our concerns here, educative institutions have a role to play in revealing how "the relations of power embodied in systematically distorted communication[9] can be [addressed] by the process of critique" (Habermas 1973, 9). "Without the capacity for critical reflection we are unable to separate our identity from the steering mechanisms of

---

9   A fuller meaning of this phrase will be addressed more fully in the next section.

money and power that have invaded the lifeworld," and the specific functions of IF within educative institutions furthers that neopragmatic process of problem-formulation in the interests of individual and political and communicative autonomy (Brookfield 2005, 1155). Specifically, IF in our educative institutions is interwoven tightly with the characteristics of deliberative communication and democracy:

- The representation of all voices and viewpoints in adequate, articulated way;

- The confrontation of those voices/viewpoints with one another in a non-coercive way;

- The ablility for the "force of the better argument" to emerge and be accepted (or creating the spaces for it), or at least be acknowledged as the best contemporary contingency;

- Space/the ability to question or investigate authority, tradition, or received wisdom;

- Safe space/ability to do all of the above without oversight or control from political or religious authorities, or for that matter teachers, librarians, etc. (Habermas 1996, 305–306; Brookfield 2005, 1161; Englund 2006, 512).

"Every association that institutionalizes such . . . procedure[s] for the purposes of democratically regulating the conditions of its common life thereby constitutes itself . . . as . . . an association that agrees to regulate . . . its common life impartially" (Habermas 1996, 306). In other words, coming somewhat in parallel now to the nature and role of IF drawn from the development of the public sphere, there is a communicative-, democratic-, and individual-autonomy-interest in IF in Neopragmatist-Habermasian terms that is tightly interwoven with the lifeworlds of educative institutions and their positive roles in the formation and continuation of democratic societies.

Path Three: On Systematically Distorted Communication and IF as a Counterweight

Much of the theoretical basis of what has been conveyed about Habermas and discourse or understanding is captured and systematized in his theory of communicative action (1984; 1987c). Put as simply as practicable, the theory "sets itself the task of seeking out the rationality embedded in everyday communicative practice and of reconstructing a comprehensive concept of [it] from the validity basis of speech" (Habermas 1985b, 176). Communicative action can be summarized as: 1) "meaning is tied to the truth conditions of statements"; 2) truth/validity does not consist in mere facts; that is, expressive and normative speech can be validly and rationally judged; 3) those judgments are real; that is, they actualize the truth or falsity of the statement: we either accept what is conveyed, or reject it (Young 1990, 103). In turn, truth/validity comes about through meeting some key requirements that have a familiar affinity with IF: no one affected is excluded; all included should have equal possibility to speak/make validity claims and must be willing to hear/empathize with others' claims; power differences among participants are neutralized and have little effect on reaching agreement; participants must be transparent about their intentions and goals (Flyvbjerg 1998, 213). We can see that Habermas utilizes his theory of communicative action in his definition of democratically-valid and rational arrangements sketched out previously. More specifically, a theory of communicative competence that is routinely achieved[10] sheds considerable light on systematically distorted communication: e.g. communicative incompetence, deviance, and speech or psychological pathologies (Habermas 1976b; Young 1990, 106–115). While those form the baseline of analysis in intersubjective communication problems, Habermas wishes to extend the concept to the *social* level: "the communicative practice of everyday life is one-sidedly rationalized into a utilitarian lifestyle. . . . As the private sphere is undermined and eroded by the economic system, so is the public sphere by the administrative system" (Habermas 1987c, 325). He makes a series of distinctions between communicative action oriented toward understanding/consent/cooperation and strategic or instrumental communication oriented toward success/manipulation/the reaching of goals (Habermas 1970, 92–93; 1985b, 169–172).

> [T]here is an expansion of social subsystems that coordinate action through the media of money (capitalist economy) and administrative power (modern, centralized states). . . . [T]hey increasingly invade areas of social life that have been or could be coordinated by the medium of understanding or "solidarity." Modernization in the West has thus generated a pathology: an unbalanced development of its potential . . . [or the] "colonization of the lifeworld" that brings in its wake a growing sense of meaninglessness and dwindling freedom. (White 1995, 8)

In turn, Habermas contends that these social patterns have become strong enough to influence the ability to form personal relationships and a healthy

---

10   That is, communicative competence is a non-extraordinary part of the lifeworld. The citation to Young here gives an exceptionally clear and concise idea of Habermas' technical working-through of these ideas, including the key area of developmental issues of import for the young, which has implications for IF in the schools as well.

lifeworld: "processes of monetarization and bureaucratization penetrate[d] the core domains of cultural reproduction, social integration, and socialization" (1987b, 355). Put another way, the "authority of markets" and other forms of strategic/instrumental action result in "nondiscursively created identities" (Warren 1993, 211). These ideas bring us very much closer to the statement by Brookfield above about the interesting question of what stands in the way of a natural and progressive development of communicative competence and mutual understanding. On a social level, systematically distorted communication is that which persists and "maintain[s] legitimacy despite the fact that [it] could not be validated if subjected to rational discourse" (Schroyer in Held 1980, 256). This in turn brings the question of systematically distorted communication much closer to issues of IF. Though Habermas has described the colonization of the lifeworld in systemic and theoretical terms (broadly, as a crisis of legitimation),[11] Dryzek points out that his framework need not be only theoretical, and can in fact help identify and frame empirical circumstances and cases as systematically distorted communication (1995, 100–103). A selection of examples puts us even closer to the issues and concerns of IF. Given Habermas' deep concern with the Nazi past of Germany and its twisting postwar path toward democracy, two of the most revealing examples/ analyses of systematically distorted communication and the counterweight of IF concern that era.

Gross examined the history of a 1995 exhibition curated and sponsored by the Hamburg Institute for Social Research on the role of the German Werhmacht in the Eastern Front during World War II, and specifically the varieties of public response to it. The exhibition generated protest, academic

---

11   That the state intervenes in the economy means that the original wellspring of its democratic legitimacy (the neutrality of the function of the market and those who find success in it) is utterly obviated, therefore the "political system [is obliged] to maintain stabilizing conditions for an economy that guards against risks to growth and guarantees social security and the chance for individual upward mobility [resulting in] manipulation [to limit] private law, secure the private form of capital utilization, and bind the masses' loyalty to this form" (Habermas 1970, 102; 1976a; 1989). As a heuristic, I would argue that this quasi-Marxist formulation still holds analytic power on certain levels. At the other end of his theoretical spectrum, in terms of culture "we are witnessing an increasing substitution of images for words, and also that inter-mingling of categories such as advertising, politics, entertainment, [and] information. . . . The banal coalesces with the unreal [in a] high-tech style [of] the highly personalized, consumeristi-cally polished bizarre" (Habermas 1985a, 97). Thus are politics defined in terms of the market and entertainment, and the public sphere is distorted and obviated for Habermas, leading to a paralyzed civil society and "a mood of antipolitics" (2006, 422; 1985a).

disputation, and parliamentary debate, resulting, in his analysis, in systematically distorted communication in the form of academic nitpicking about the provenance and sensationalism of the exhibition photographs from historians, parliamentary rhetoric conveying patriotic pieties about the past and excuse-making (the atrocities in the East were the work of a minority), and the reemergence of racist Neo-Nazi justification for the actions. "Given the heavy burden of the German past, efforts are understandable to re-shape that past in the interest of a more comfortable present. Among these . . . none is more prominent than the myth of a 'Wehrmacht free of moral taint,' a German army that fought . . . with honor and dignity, along side but separated by a moral gulf from those who behaved very differently" (Gross 2006, 310). The Institute could not have been more scrupulous or open in revealing its research and documentation processes and corrections, but he contends that "in the deepest of senses, these are all *German* atrocities" and there remains an empirical "uniqueness of the German crime" (Gross 2006, 319–320). Gross implicitly makes clear that IF was a vital part of the process, and the process genuinely pointed toward a discursive assembling of a public sphere around a vital issue of social memory and the public reckoning with history needed for the health of German democracy. But Gross also points to the prevalence of obviating factors: that historians and parliamentarians used power and manipulative methods to cloud and blunt the point of the exhibition, calling to mind Habermas' worries about the effects of media culture on rational exchange. In the end, the role and existence of IF is a necessary but not a sufficient condition for constitution of a public sphere and/or the accuracy of public representation and memory—i.e. it was only a partial counterweight to systematically distorted communication. Power and manipulation must still be overcome.

The second example ironically concerns the opposite end of the political spectrum: those opposing the Iraq war quoted Hermann Goering, Nazi Minister of Propaganda on the manipulations of leaders: "Voice or no voice, the people can always be brought to the bidding of the leaders. That is easy. All you have to do is tell them they are being attacked" (Goering in Buschman 2003b, 65). As superficially appealing and convenient as the quote was for the political purposes at hand, and as "verified" as a "true" "Urban Legend" by Snopes.com at the time, there were significant problems with the quote, and its use. First, Goebbels was the Propaganda Minister for the Nazis, not Goering; second, upon even minor investigation the provenance of the quote was dubious, "based on a private conversation (eventually written up) by [a] sympathetic interlocutor, not while Goering was in power, but while . . . on trial for war crimes . . . said . . . by way of rationalization of his alleged lack of direct responsibility . . . [and] not said in his strutting role as second in command to Hitler" (Rosenzweig in Buschman 2003b, 67). The convenient and telling "quote" exhibited media-like trivialization in its "verified" status which screened entirely its context. Information seekers often "turn away from any question that requires a bit of . . . effort [and] research . . . [and] without [investigation the] Goering quote would have been 'verified' as 'fact' . . . and that would have been that" (Buschman 2003b, 71). The "quote" incident was a different-but-classic case of systematically distorted communication, and IF in this case serves as a goad—a different kind of counterweight to the blithe recitation of "known" facts.

Under this broad analysis, the opportunity to identify numerous contemporary and historical instances of systematically distorted communication (that which cannot be legitimately maintained when subjected to rational discourse) is quite broad and many are of particular interest in terms of IF:

- Annette Gordon-Reed traces historical work that undermined the worth of "fully formed [black] persons with innate worth and equal humanity that links them directly to us all" (Gordon-Reed 2008, 32): "I stand at the end of this writing, literally aghast at what American historians have done" to the role of African-Americans in history (Du Bois in Gordon-Reed 1997, ix). In the process, "historians, journalists, and other . . . enthusiasts have . . . shamelessly employed every stereotype of black people and distortion of life in the Old South to support their positions . . . (and continue to do so today)" (Gordon-Reed 1997, xiii). She asks, "in what universe could the humanity, family integrity, and honor of slave owners count for more than the humanity, family integrity, and honor of slaves?" (Gordon-Reed 2008, 32)

- Similarly, "women . . . had been prominent in late eighteenth century salon society and elite public spheres, but were widely excluded from nineteenth and twentieth century public space; this was mirrored by a commensurate bias in political thought [and it took] feminist struggles [to] ma[ke] gender a basic political issue in new ways" (Calhoun 2001, 12596).

- Historically, people have often identified their social and "political location . . . through opposition [to] the Other as an adversary"; it is the lack of experience or intellectual grounding or information with difference that allows "misunderstanding, mudslinging, name-calling, and petty searches for insidious motivations . . . [and to] stereotype the Other . . . in ways that allow . . . grasp and confirm[ation of] place and identity"—recently this is particularly the case with religious differences and disagreements (Warren 1996, 252; Habermas 2003).

- American voters have persisted in wrongly believing the Bush Administration assertion of the role of Saddam Hussein in the 9/11 attacks and other such "facts" (Shenkman 2008), higher levels of education do not necessarily lead to more accurate information or opinions on issues or the voting of one's interests (What do you know? 2011), and initiatives are often couched in purposefully confusing language to deter or confuse voters (War by initiative 2011).

- Neil Postman has been the most explicit in exposing the specifics of Habermas' critique of the non-rational and non-discursive underpinning of media, and particularly advertising, which is "immune to truth[:] propositions are as scarce as unattractive people"; an advertisement is "not a series of testable, logically-ordered assertions. It is a drama . . . of handsome people selling, buying, and eating . . . and being driven near to ecstasy by their good fortune" (Postman 1988, 42).

- The work of Maret copiously illustrates the IF interest as against government secrecy "manifest[ed] by way of assorted stealth methods: lying, the withholding of information, information pollution and manipulation through propaganda as well as bureaucratic rules that formalize information classification" affecting social and democratic ability to oversee everything from toxic waste and other forms of pollution to military and diplomatic and security decisions made on our behalf (2002, 74; 2011).

Nor is this a specifically recent and American phenomenon. McCullough recounts the utter frustration of ardently democratic and republican Americans in Paris at the commencement of the imperial Franco-Prussian War in 1870 who could not accept that "singing the 'Marseillaise,' the hymn of the French Revolution, had any connection with any of the Napoleons [but now] was the emperor's song" (2011, 258). The role of IF is less central in this path, though no less consequential. In a Habermasian frame, IF is an important element in the constitution of a rational society (whether in the institution of the library, the school, university, or the broader society) "where reason is understood as communicative praxis" (Ostovich 1995, 476). This is opposed by (and therefore IF has a role as a counterweight to) "the powerful [who] can prevent conflict . . . not by direct confrontation, but by surreptitiously manipulating sources of information and by tacitly shaping . . . beliefs" (Gross 2006, 327). That manipulation can take the form, as we have seen, of "detached and manipulated [discourse]—especially through the visual media—because they are [not] sustain[ed by] processes of argumentation" (Warren 1989, 521).

IF has a role to play in the conditions under which these media operate and make their "claims," and the key terrain at stake is autonomy: "the discovery, articulation, and exploration of concerns, as well as formulation of new understandings . . . must not itself be subject to . . . control [by] specialized interests, routines, and vocabularies"—the methods and grammar of media and its financial base in marketing being prominent in considerations here (Cohen 1999, 409). So situated, IF has a role to play as a counterweight to systematically distorted communication in a variety of subtle ways, but always in the interest of "the freedom to move from a given level of discourse to increasingly reflected levels[:] a progressive radicalization" of the process of discovery, inclusive of revealing the non-linguistic/non-rational bases of positions held or the grammar of media messages (McCarthy 1976, 482).

Conclusion

In some ways, Habermas has done us a favor by not weighing in on IF and academic freedom *tout court*. As a result we are forced to grapple with the concept and the practice in much less black and white terms. IF thus becomes much less of a trump played at key points effectively ending discussion by the assertion of a right. Rather, IF so contextualized in Habermasian terms has a deeper relationship to the democratic functioning of educative institutions in democratic societies, and is played out in complex ways with more interests at stake than a simple moralism about the ability of an individual to solipsistically get information or merely have available alternative viewpoints. IF has a social function within much larger social and political functions, and Habermas helps us to think about it and enact it in our inevitably more complex social and ethical environments.

References

Baynes, Kenneth S. 1995. Democracy and the *Rechsstaat*: Habermas's *Faktizität und geltung*. In *The Cambridge companion to Habermas*, ed. Stephen K. White, 201–232. Cambridge, UK: Cambridge University Press.

Bernstein, Richard J. 1996. The retrieval of the democratic ethos. *Cardozo Law Review* 17, 1127–1146.

Brookfield, Stephen. 2005. Learning democratic reason: The adult education project of Jürgen Habermas. *Teachers College Record* 107, no. 6: 1127–1168.

Brown, Wendy. 2006. American nightmare: Neoliberalism, neoconservatism, and de-democratization. *Political Theory* 34, no. 6: 690–714.

Buckland, Michael. 2008. Letter to the editor. *Journal of the American Society for Information Science and Technology* 59, no. 9: 1534.

– – –. 2009. Review of *Self-examination: The present and future of librarianship*, by John M. Budd. *Library Quarterly* 79, no. 2: 271–272.

Buschman, John. 2003a. *Dismantling the public sphere: Situating and sustaining librarianship in the age of the new public philosophy*. Westport, CT: Libraries Unlimited.

– – –. 2003b. Historical accuracy and the web: A PLG-net exchange. *Progressive Librarian*, no. 22: 65–72.

– – –. 2005. On libraries and the public sphere. *Library Philosophy & Practice* 7, no. 2: 1–8.

– – –. 2010. The social as fundamental and a source of the critical: Jürgen Habermas. In *Critical theory for library and information science: Exploring the social from across the disciplines*, eds. Gloria J. Leckie, Lisa M. Given, and John E. Buschman, 161–172. Santa Barbara, CA: ABC-CLIO/Libraries Unlimited.

Buschman, John, and Mark Rosenzweig. 1999. Intellectual freedom within the library workplace: An exploratory study in the U.S. *Journal of Information Ethics* 8, no. 2: 36–45.

Calhoun, Craig. 2001. Public sphere: Nineteenth- and twentieth-century history. In *International encyclopedia of the social & behavioral sciences*, eds. Neil J. Smelser and Paul B. Baltes, 12595–12599. New York: Elsevier.

Cohen, Joshua. 1999. Reflections on Habermas on democracy. *Ratio Juris* 12, no. 4: 385–416.

Dewey, John. 1927. *The public and its problems*. Athens, OH: Swallow Press.

Dryzek, John S. 1995. Critical theory as a research program. In *The Cambridge companion to Habermas*, ed. Stephen K. White, 97–119. Cambridge, UK: Cambridge University Press.

Englund, Tomas. 2000. Rethinking democracy and education: Towards an education of deliberative citizens. *Journal of Curriculum Studies* 32, no. 2: 305–313.

– – –. 2006. Deliberative communication: A pragmatist proposal. *Journal of Curriculum Studies* 38, no. 5: 503–520.

Flyvbjerg, Bent. 1998. Habermas and Foucault: Thinkers for civil society? *British Journal of Sociology* 49, no. 2: 210–233.

Frankel, Boris. 1974. Habermas talking: An interview. *Theory & Society* 1, no. 1: 37–58.

Garnham, Nicholas. 2001. Public sphere and the media. In *International encyclopedia of the social & behavioral sciences*, eds. Neil J. Smelser and Paul B. Baltes, 12585–12590. New York: Elsevier.

Gordon-Reed, Annette. 1997. *Thomas Jefferson and Sally Hemings: An American controversy*. Charlottesville: University Press of Virginia.

———. 2008. *The Hemingses of Monticello: An American family.* New York: W.W. Norton & Co.

Gross, Alan. 2006. Habermas, systematically distorted communication, and the public sphere. *RSQ: Rhetoric Society Quarterly* 36, no. 3: 309–330.

Gutmann, Amy. 1987. *Democratic education.* Princeton, NJ: Princeton University Press.

Habermas, Jürgen. 1966. Knowledge and interest. *Inquiry* 9, no. 1–4: 285–300.

———. 1970. *Toward a rational society: Student protest, science, and politics.* Boston: Beacon Press.

———. 1971. Why more philosophy? *Social Research* 38, no. 4: 633–654.

———. 1973. *Theory and practice.* Boston: Beacon Press.

———. 1974. The public sphere: An encyclopedia article (1964). *New German Critique* no. 3: 49–55.

———. 1975. *Legitimation crisis.* Boston: Beacon Press

———. 1976a. Problems of legitimation in late capitalism. In *Critical sociology: Selected readings*, ed. Paul Connerton, 363–387. New York: Penguin.

———. 1976b. Systematically distorted communication. In *Critical sociology: Selected readings*, ed. Paul Connerton, 348–362. New York: Penguin.

———. 1982. A reply to my critics. In *Habermas: Critical debates*, eds. John B. Thompson and David Held, 219–283. Cambridge, MA: MIT Press.

———. 1984. *The theory of communicative action: Reason and the rationalization of society.* Boston: Beacon Press.

———. 1985a. A philosophico–political profile. *New Left Review* no. 151: 75–105.

———. 1985b. Remarks on the concept of communicative action. In *Social action*, eds. Gottfried Seebass and Raimo Tuomela, 151–178. Dordrecht, NL: D. Reidel.

———. 1987a. The idea of the university—learning processes. *New German Critique* no. 41: 3–22.

———. 1987b. *The philosophical discourse of modernity: Twelve lectures.* Cambridge, MA: MIT Press.

———. 1987c. *The theory of communicative action: Lifeworld and system: A critique of functionalist reason.* Boston: Beacon Press.

———. 1989. *The structural transformation of the public sphere: An inquiry into a category of bourgeois society.* Cambridge, MA: MIT Press.

———. 1992. Further reflections on the public sphere. In *Habermas and the public sphere*, ed. Craig J. Calhoun, 421–461. Cambridge, MA: MIT Press.

———. 1994. Hannah Arendt's communications concept of power. In *Hannah Arendt: Critical essays*, eds. Lewis P. Hinchman and Sandra Hinchman, 211–229. Albany: State University of New York Press.

–––. 1996. *Between facts and norms: Contributions to a discourse theory of law and democracy.* Cambridge, MA: MIT Press.

–––. 2003. Intolerance and discrimination. *I.CON* 1, no. 1: 2–12.

–––. 2006. Political communication in media society: Does democracy still enjoy an epistemic dimension? The impact of normative theory on empirical research. *Communication Theory* 16, no. 4: 411–426.

–––. 2007. How to save the quality press? Sightandsign.com. May 21. http://www.signandsight.com/features/1349.html (accessed April 17, 2008).

Haught, John F. 1988. Reading theology. In *A clashing of symbols: Method and meaning in liberal studies,* ed. Phyllis O'Callaghan, 23–29. Washington, DC: Georgetown University Press.

Held, David. 1980. *Introduction to critical theory: Horkheimer to Habermas.* Berkeley: University of California Press.

Hohendahl, Peter Uwe. 1974. The Public Sphere (1964). *New German Critique* no. 3: 45–48.

–––. 1979. Critical theory, public sphere and culture. Jürgen Habermas and his critics. *New German Critique* no. 16: 89–118.

Lefrançois, David, and Marc-Andre Ethier. 2010. Translating the ideal of deliberative democracy into democratic education: Pure utopia? *Educational Philosophy & Theory* 42, no. 3: 271–292.

Mara, Gerald M. 1985. After virtue, autonomy: Jürgen Habermas and Greek political theory. *The Journal of Politics* 47, no. 4: 1036–1061.

–––. 2008. *The civic conversations of Thucydides and Plato: Classical political philosophy and the limits of democracy.* Albany: State University of New York Press.

Maret, Susan. 2002. The channel of public papers : control of government information and its relation to an informed citizenry. PhD diss., The Union Institute Graduate College.

–––. 2011. *Government secrecy.* Bingley, UK: Emerald.

McCarthy, Thomas. 1976. A theory of communicative competence. In *Critical sociology: Selected readings,* ed. Paul Connerton, 470–497. New York: Penguin.

McCullough, David G. 2011. *The greater journey: Americans in Paris.* New York: Simon & Schuster.

Ostovich, Steven T. 1995. Dewey, Habermas, and the university in society. *Educational Theory* 45, no. 4: 465–477.

Peters, John Durham. 1993. Distrust of representation: Habermas on the public sphere. *Media, Culture & Society* 15, no. 4: 541–571.

Postman, Neil. 1988. The contradictions of freedom of information. In *Alternative library literature, 1986/1987,* eds. Sanford Berman and James Danky, 37–49. Jefferson, NC: McFarland.

Rodger, John J. 1985. On the degeneration of the public sphere. *Political Studies* 33, no. 2: 203–217.

Shenkman, Rick. 2008. 5 myths about those civic-minded, deeply informed voters. Outlook. *Washington Post.* September 7.

War by initiative. 2011. *The Economist,* April 23.

Warren, Mark. E.1989. Liberal constitutionalism as ideology: Marx and Habermas. *Political Theory* 17, no. 4: 511–534.

– – –. 1993. Can participatory democracy produce better selves? Psychological dimensions of Habermas's discursive model of democracy. *Political Psychology* 14, no. 2: 209–234.

– – –. 1996. What should we expect from more democracy? Radically democratic responses to politics. *Political Theory* 24, no. 2: 241–270

– – –. 2002. What can democratic participation mean today? *Political Theory* 30, no. 5: 677–701.

What do you know? 2011. *The Economist,* April 23.

White, Stephen K. 1995. Reason, modernity, and democracy. In *The Cambridge companion to Habermas,* ed. Stephen K. White, 3–16. Cambridge, UK: Cambridge University Press.

– – –. 2004. The very idea of a critical social science: A pragmatist turn. In *The Cambridge companion to critical theory,* ed. Fred Rush, 310–355. Cambridge, UK: Cambridge University Press.

Wood, Allen W. 1985. Habermas' defense of rationalism. *New German Critique* no. 35: 145–164.

Young, Robert E. 1990. *A critical theory of education: Habermas and our children's future.* New York: Teachers College Press.

Feminism and Intellectual Freedom

Lauren Pressley

Feminism and intellectual freedom have a long history of intersections in issues, leaders, and resolutions. This chapter cannot take a view of the entire history of these intersections, but will instead emphasize relatively contemporary issues, faced by those interested in both feminism and intellectual freedom in the early 2000s in the United States.

Although feminists and those interested in intellectual freedom often have shared a common cause, there are surprisingly few articles, book chapters, or books written about this specific combination of interests at this point in time. There are books about leaders in these areas and mentions of gender related issues in intellectual freedom works and notes about access to information in feminist texts, but rarely do the two come together in a single, unified work. This chapter seeks to fill this gap.

It is evident that intellectual freedom is an internationally recognized issue from several statements. The International Federation of Library Associations (IFLA) declared that "human beings have a fundamental right to access to expressions of knowledge, creative thought and intellectual activity, and to express their views publicly" (International Federation of Library Associations 2011). The United Nations Declaration of Human Rights includes this concept in a number of articles—most notably Article 19 (United Nations 1948).

The American Library Association (ALA) asserts that "intellectual freedom is the right of every individual to both seek and receive information from all points of view without restriction. It provides for free access to all expressions of ideas through which any and all sides of a question, cause or movement may be explored" (n.d.).

Feminist approaches deeply intertwine with this. Throughout history there have been challenges for those looking for access to information discussing the feminist perspective, information about sexual health, and even childbirth. If information is restricted, censored, or confidentiality and privacy is violated due to gender or related issues, there is a feminist intellectual freedom issue at hand. From women's lack of access to education in some countries, to the inability to find information about controversial topics like abortion or sexual content in some communities in the United States, restricting access to information can impact all women's access to information making intellectual freedom a feminist issue.

Today, much of this information is readily available in many contexts, but can still be challenging to locate for portions of the population or in environments more hostile to the idea of feminism. Even feminism, itself, is called into question in some communities and institutions and those people interested in feminist approaches may have a harder time accessing information. The very field of Women's Studies, which studies the world from a feminist perspective, is called into question from time to time. Academic environments that are hostile to this perspective, inevitably impact the ability of researchers and students to do feminist work and produce feminist information. If less information is produced, less is available. This reciprocal relationship emphasizes the importance of understanding of intellectual freedom from a feminist perspective.

Gender issues are well covered in librarianship's professional statements on intellectual freedom, perhaps due to the feminized nature of the field. These include an official interpretation of the *Library Bill of Rights on Access to Library Resources and Services Regardless of Sex, Gender Identity, Gender Expression, or Sexual Orientation* (American Library Association. Office for Intellectual Freedom 2010) as well as feminist representation on various professional associations such as the Committee on the Status of Women in Librarianship for the American Library Association (ALA), the Feminist Task Force of the Social Responsibilities Round Table of the ALA, the Women's Studies Section of the Association of College and Research Libraries, and Women, Information and Libraries Special Interest Group of the IFLA.

This chapter begins with an explanation of feminism, outlines a history of intellectual freedom from a feminist perspective, and concludes with a discussion on the intersection of feminist and intellectual freedom issues.

Defining Feminism

In the most general terms, feminists are interested in equality. Within the body of feminist thinkers' and activists' work, there are many nuanced approaches and definitions. However, generally speaking, those who define themselves as feminist are both intellectually committed to the principles of feminism and support a political movement that aims to ensure justice for women and the end of all sexism (Haslanger, Tuana, and O'Connor 2011, 1).

That being the case, sometimes "feminism" is meant to refer only to a specific historical/political movement or a general belief that there are injustices against women (Haslanger, Tuana, and O'Connor 2011, 3). This essay does not mean to use "feminism" in such narrow and specific ways, but instead in the broader term that women are at times disadvantaged compared to men and that this is, in fact, unjustified (James 1998, 576).

An important theme in contemporary feminism is that the feminism of the 1960s is now commonly viewed as a feminism of a white, middle-class woman. Betty Friedan's *Feminine Mystique*, a classic of that era, did not address issues facing working class women or most women of color (hooks 2000, 1–3). Feminists today look at the intersectionality of women's issues, which is why we see feminist groups concerned with race, class, sexuality, and women in other countries. This interest in intersectionality can extend to concern about how the marginalization of women impacts men and masculinity as well.

Waves

Though this essay focuses on contemporary feminism, it is important to recognize that there have been many feminist movements, interpretations, and viewpoints all contextualized by their culture and community. The history of the feminist movement can be described in "waves."

It is generally accepted at the "first wave" of feminism took place in the twentieth century, focusing on civil and political equality, which gave way to the "second wave" of feminism around the 1960s and 1970s which focused on sexual rights and equality within the family (Walters 2005, 137). The often used phrase "the personal is the political" is a slogan that was frequently used by second wave feminists, addressing the very fabric of our personal lives; how we interact with family, in relationships, in our everyday life, is a political act that has implication for all women. This era was rich in feminist activist work with the founding of the National Organization for Women, working towards the Equal Rights Amendment (ERA), and the beginning of the Gay and Lesbian Rights movements (Tuana 2011, 3). The late 1960s and 1970s saw the beginning of legislative efforts including the legalization of abortion, the publication of Kate Millett's *Sexual Politics*, and the beginning of feminist philosophy and theory in the United States (Tuana 2011, 4).

"Third wave" feminism arose in the late 1990s and rejects the essentialism of previous feminist movements and in doing so includes the perspective of women of color and poorer women than previously included in feminist work (Zack 2006, 193). This is the feminism of most activists and scholars in the contemporary United States and is the view of feminism this chapter will use in discussing intellectual freedom.

In practice

Understanding feminism as a perspective on the world leads to seeing its application in activism, theory, and at the intersections of the two. Although feminist activists and theorists utilize different tools in their approaches to disrupting patriarchal systems, in many cases the two bodies intersect and work together for the cause.

Activism

Feminist activists have been central to the feminist movement in the United States from its beginning. From the earliest First Wave discussions in the 1840s about equal access to education through the twentieth century focus on improving equity in the political, educational, and economic systems for women (McAfee 2011, 2). The very practice of speaking out on these issues and in some cases participating in political discussion, civil disobedience, and being sentenced in response to feminist actions, illustrates the emphasis on activism more than theory for these earliest American feminists. Their emphasis was working towards equality in the daily lives of women.

Second wave feminists continued this work, but emphasized the private sphere. As feminists began turning their focus to private issues rather than the public ones of access to education, voting, and other societal inequities, second wave activists worked for access to birth control and abortion and to equality in private family lives. This movement pulled from the language of the civil rights movements and on women's solidarity movements for a new approach to feminist activism (McAfee 2011, 2–3).

Today, "third wave" feminist activists focus on the intersections of marginalized groups, hesitating to describe one state that all women have achieved or should aim for. Feminists emphasize choice in women's lives and can focus on a myriad of interrelated issues. These issues might include class issues, the politics of sexuality, global issues that impact women, achieving legal equity through pay equity, domestic violence laws, or even private equality through co-parenting children or taking control of reproductive choices.

Theory

The feminist activists of the 1960s laid the groundwork for the development of feminist philosophy in the United States in the 1970s (Tuana 2011, 2). While feminist activists are working to attain equality in the world, current feminist theorists are working to help reconceptualize what we know from a feminist perspective, or at least not an overly masculine worldview. For example, in philosophy, feminists reject the field's emphasis on epistemology over ethics and instead argue that the two are connected (10). Further, feminist ethicists argue for new approaches to ethics that do not rely on masculine assumptions of the past.

In ethics, Alison Jaggar argues that ethics as a field has ignored the female perspective in showing more concern for men's issues, trivializing the private world of family and care, for indicating that men are more morally developed, that culturally masculine traits are more valuable than those that are culturally feminine, and that ethics as a field prefers "male" ways of reasoning (1992, 363–364). Jaggar's line of argumentation is feminist in that it both emphasizes the connectedness of ethics to epistemology and it argues for a new approach that both decentralizes the "male" approach of the past while incorporating a "female" understanding of ethics. This example demonstrates a feminist approach to thinking and is helpful when considering feminist perspectives on intellectual freedom.

History of Intellectual Freedom From a Feminist Perspective

Intellectual freedom has never been defined by the American Library Association, but is rather understood as a collection of principles that support intellectual freedom (Krug and Morgan 2010, 12). Even with that being the case, it is plain to see that the general principles of intellectual freedom have been part of the feminist movement from its earliest days.

In the United States, one of the earliest documents of the feminist movement is Mary Wollstonecraft's 1789 work, *A Vindication of the Rights of Women*. This document also holds intellectual freedom issues at its core. In this document, Wollstonecraft argued for the education of women, in essence, for the ability of women to have access to education and information in order to contribute to society. This work was published at a time in which education was not guaranteed to females and there was debate about what women should even learn beyond those skills necessary to domestic life.

Not quite half a century later, in the 1830s, Dr. Charles Knowland wrote a pamphlet, *Fruits of Philosophy: An Essay on Population*. This pamphlet discussed the physiology of sex and birth control. At that point in time this information was not freely available to everyone, despite its centrality to women's existence, and Knowland was subsequently fined and imprisoned (Semonche 2007, 16). Information about how to control reproduction, and thus women's bodies, continued to be dangerous to share and was restricted in society, even nearly a century later. In 1916 Margaret Sanger opened the first birth control clinic in the United States, only to be raided, closed, and arrested for making such information and service available (Price 2006).

In the 1920s, legislation was introduced in New York proposing an environment in which prosecutors could base an indictment on any one passage of a book that could be described as "filthy" or "disgusting" (Semonche 2007,

9). This legislation was unpopular with publishers and other interested parties argued against it. It was in this environment and era that the American Library Association (ALA) began developing a code of ethics in 1928, and was formally suggested in 1930 (Krug and Morgan 2010, 21).

In 1937 the documentary, "*The Birth of a Baby*," followed a woman from when she learned of her pregnancy until the birth of the child. Like the Knowland publication and Sanger's work, the film provided access to information about reproduction. The movie was supported by prominent medical experts, yet was banned by New York censors and the State Commission of Education due to being "Indecent, immoral, and . . . tend[ing] to corrupt morals" (Semonche 2007, 114). Amid this environment, in 1939, the ALA adopted the *Library Bill of Rights*, at the time called the *Library's Bill of Rights* (Krug and Morgan 2010, 15).

In 1940 the ALA established the Intellectual Freedom Committee, then called the Committee on Intellectual Freedom to Safeguard the Rights of Library Users to Freedom of Inquiry with the official charge "to recommend such steps as may be necessary to safeguard the rights of library users in accordance with the Bill of Rights and the *Library's Bill of Rights*, as adopted by Council" (15). This organization continues to monitor intellectual freedom issues and examine how individuals' access to information is impacted by ALA policy and make recommendations to improve access.

Meanwhile, in 1952 Simone de Beauvoir's *The Second Sex* introduced feminist philosophy in Europe. Just over ten years later Betty Friedan's *The Feminine Mystique* introduced a similar movement in the United States. These texts gave feminist arguments to mobilize around and helped to define issues of inequality.

Many areas of society were impacted by the activity in the intellectual freedom and feminist movements. In the library world, 1961 saw an amendment to the *Library Bill of Rights* that "an individual . . . should not be denied or abridged [use of a library] because of his race, religion, national origin, or political views" (54). In a cascading effect, 1967 saw both the establishment of the Office of Intellectual Freedom within ALA and an amendment to the *Library Bill of Rights* that broadened it to include social views and age (17–22). In 1969 the Freedom to Read Foundation was incorporated to further protect against censorship (27).

Developments around intellectual freedom and feminism continued steadily in the 1970s. In 1970 ALA Council passed a "Policy on Confidentiality of Library Records" and the Intellectual Freedom Committee charge was changed "to recommend such steps as may be necessary to safeguard the rights of library users, libraries, and librarians, in accordance with the First Amendment to the United States Constitution and the *Library Bill of Rights* as adopted by the ALA Council. To work closely with the Office for

Intellectual Freedom and with other units and officers of the Association in matters touching intellectual freedom and censorship" (15–18). These moves had strong, positive impacts for those interested in feminist issues of access to information, both in the ability to seek information confidentially, even if it was controversial or had a history of censorship around it, but also in the emphasis of the Intellectual Freedom Committee on specifically taking steps to safeguard users' access to information.

In 1971 ALA asserted "the confidentiality of the professional relationships of librarians to the people they serve, that these relationships be respected in the same manner as medical doctors to their patients, lawyers to their clients, priests to the people they serve," and that "no librarian would lend himself to a role as informant, whether of voluntarily revealing circulation records or identifying patrons and their reading habits" (18). Professional librarians would agree that this is a logical stance, but it is also very clear in these statements that even if seeking information about topics that are taboo or generally thought to be in bad taste, patrons would not need to worry about their privacy. Patrons could then seek information about physical development, sex, birth control, or other sensitive issues with an expectation of confidentiality. Further in 1971, the Social Responsibility Round Table Task Force on Gay Liberation recommended that libraries and ALA members serve any minority individual, whether it is an ethnic, sexual, religious, or "any other arbitrary classification" holding obvious positive implications for feminists as well (17).

The 1970s continued to see further movement around intellectual freedom issues and the intersection of feminist principles as well. In 1973 the Intellectual Freedom Round Table, a grassroots, membership group within the ALA, was established (24). In 1974 the ALA endorsed the Equal Rights Amendment (ERA) with the argument that "women constitute 82% of the library profession" (32). The same logic applied when in 1978 the ALA endorsed the "ERA Extension Resolution" and when in 1979 it established the ERA taskforce charged with assisting and consulting with "ALA Chapters in carrying out the commitment to passage of the Equal Rights Amendment in ways best suited to the individual states." Finally, at the end of the 70s, in 1979, the ALA passed a draft statement on professional ethics (21).

Things slowed down a bit in the 1980s, but nonetheless continued to improve. In 1980 the *Library Bill of Rights* was updated to encompass all discrimination based on "origin, age, background, or views" (17). This change more clearly included gender within the *Library Bill of Rights*. In 1988 ALA Council adopted a resolution supporting ALA's commitment to Article 19 of the Universal Declaration of Human Rights which also holds a view that all people have a right to information, personal opinions, and expression (33).

In 1991 ALA Council adopted "The Universal Right to Free Expression" (34) and in 1993 adopted *Access to Library Resources and Services Regardless of Sex, Gender Identity, Gender Expression or Sexual Orientation, an interpretation of the Library Bill of Rights.* This interpretation was amended 2000, 2004, and 2008 (American Library Association Office for Intellectual Freedom 2010, 85). The interpretation of the *Library Bill of Rights* finally made explicitly clear that regardless of sex, gender identity, gender expression, library patrons should be protected and have full intellectual freedom in their use of the library. This stance was so strongly held by ALA that in 1995 the Midwinter conference was withdrawn from Cincinnati where voters repealed a gay rights ordinance. The Association felt it was wrong to sponsor their meeting in a city that withdrew legal protection from gay colleagues (Krug and Morgan 2010, 25).

In the past decade, things have been slower for feminist work in intellectual freedom, perhaps because so many of the major issues have been resolved. In 2001 the Intellectual Freedom Committee formed a privacy subcommittee (22). Most recently, in 2005, ALA Council passed a *Resolution on Threats to Library Materials Related to Sex, Gender, Gender Identity, or Sexual Orientation* finding:

> *RESOLVED, that the American Library Association affirms the inclusion in library collections of materials that reflect the diversity of our society, including those related to sex, gender identity, or sexual orientation; and be it further*

> *RESOLVED, that the American Library Association encourages all American Library Association chapters to take active stands against all legislative or other government attempts to proscribe materials related to sex, gender identity, or sexual orientation; and be it further*

> *RESOLVED, that the American Library Association encourages all libraries to acquire and make available materials representative of all the people in our society.* (American Library Association 2005)

Intersection of Feminist Ideas and Intellectual Freedom

Obviously, from the earliest professional discussions of intellectual freedom among librarians, there have been feminists working towards equality in both private and public spheres including in access to information and education. In the 1960s and 1970s both groups were particularly active and saw large changes that positively impacted each other.

Today, when thinking of intersections between feminism and intellectual freedom, one of the chief documents to consider is the *Access to Library Resources and Services Regardless of Sex, Gender Identity, Gender Expression, or Sexual Orientation: An Interpretation of the Library Bill of Rights*[1]. Principally, this document lays out the primary concerns for gender in intellectual freedom issues to be around censorship, free access to information, and privacy and confidentiality.

Censorship

In this chapter, we have already discussed the challenge of providing access to information about reproductive issues over time, and we have seen that the library community has responded to censorship issues and made statements against it. Specifically, in *An Interpretation*, the ALA states that

> *Library services, materials, and programs representing diverse points of view on sex, gender identity, gender expression, or sexual orientation should be considered for purchase and inclusion in library collections and programs. (ALA policies 53.1.1, 53.1.9, and 53.1.11). The Association affirms that attempts to proscribe or remove materials dealing with gay, lesbian, bisexual, and/or transgendered life without regard to the written, approved selection policy violate this tenet and constitute censorship.* (American Library Association Office for Intellectual Freedom 2010, 84)

This statement clearly shows how libraries can avoid censorship, whether accidental or intentional.

However, today some censorship issues are not as clearly cut as a censor showing up at the library demanding a book be removed. The very existence of academic Women's Studies programs are threatened at times. When this issue arises, it tends to be built around arguments about indoctrination and anti-American thoughts (Weber 2008). This is important to recognize as Women's Studies programs not only expose people to information, but also open up a stream of faculty to be producing new information on the topic—information that would not exist if it was not accepted as part of academic processes. Without these programs, libraries would not have collection development policies designed to develop strong feminist collections and even if the information did exist, it might not be available from the library because without Women's Studies programs librarians would not have collection development policies designed to collect these materials. This insidious approach to limiting others' access to information is not censorship in the traditional sense, but does hold the same potential to limit access to information.

---

1   Referred to as "An Interpretation" throughout this section of the essay.

And sometimes feminists, themselves, are the cause of censorship. Some feminists, notably Catharine MacKinnon and Andrea Dworkin, have taken legal actions against pornography, later being labeled as censorious in their activism. Being feminist does not automatically equate with having an interest in absolute intellectual freedom, though in many cases—as we have seen—there is a significant intersection of interests.

Free Access to Library Materials

It is very clear that libraries must offer access to diverse information to all patrons. *An Interpretation* clearly states

> *Librarians are obligated by the Library Bill of Rights to endeavor to select materials without regard to the sex, gender identity, or sexual orientation of their creators by using the criteria identified in their written, approved selection policies.* (ALA policy 53.1.5, American Library Association Office for Intellectual Freedom 2010, 83)

It goes on to say

> *A person's right to use a library should not be denied or abridged because of origin, age, background or views . . . it is intended that: "origin" encompasses all the characteristics of individuals that are inherent in the circumstances of their birth . . . and "views" encompasses all the opinions and beliefs held and expressed by individuals. Therefore, Article V of the Library Bill of Rights mandates that library services, materials, and programs be available to all members of the community the library serves, without regard to sex, gender identity, gender expression, or sexual orientation. This includes providing youth with comprehensive sex education literature.*

And finally,

> *Libraries which make exhibit spaces and meeting rooms available to the public they serve should make such facilities available on an equitable basis, regardless of the beliefs or affiliations of individuals or groups requesting their use. This protection extends to all groups and members of the community the library serves, without regard to sex, gender identity, gender expression, or sexual orientation.* (ALA Policy 52.5.2, 84)

Access to library materials also has a parallel in feminist philosophy: the concept of "access equality," that,

> *women should have equal access either to*
>
> i)   the full range of existing social institutions or to

      ii) a full range of social institutions which have been reformed or transformed so that women can access these institutions on equal terms (Stone 2007, 198)

This framework has specific applications for information access, that women should have equal access to libraries and information centers, to college and universities, and to the services therein. Further, women should be able to use all of these services on equal terms, even if it means that the institutions themselves need to adapt to more easily serve women and men on equal footing. It might appear that libraries are well situated as most library staff are women. However it is well known and discussed in feminist literature that women will often take on masculine traits or worldviews in order to be successful (Lorde 1984, 112) and it will be worth examining any organization to see if it is welcoming, even if the majority of employees are women themselves.

This concept introduces an insidious access issue that mirrors the one addressed in the censorship section above. Feminist philosophers raise the issue of gender-based knowledge and whether it is possible to have access to gender-based knowledge other than your own (Anderson 2011, 11). You can imagine this to mean access to what it is like to be part of a men's locker room for women or to know the experience of childbirth for men. Less foreign is the idea that there is gender-based information available in social settings that you may or may not have access to based on your gender (10). In this case you can imagine social norms or mores that make it easier or harder for members of a minority group to participate in information sharing. Feminist epistemologists consider these types of knowledge based in the fact that women have a gendered access of information that is different from men due to their position as women both biologically and due to their role in different societal processes (4–5). Feminist thinkers examining these lines of thought might question the ability to know what information can even be found based on different sets of knowledge going into the search process, and could argue for more of a need to provide access to information that would be impossible to get outside of a text.

Privacy and Confidentiality

Privacy and confidentiality also have important connotations for feminists. As many feminist causes have been controversial over time such as access to education, voting, reproductive information, or information about birth control. It has been important to be able to seek that information without fear of being found out.

Today it is more likely that a young girl who is curious about what is happening to her body or a teenager too embarrassed to ask about sex might want access to information that is readily available but embarrassing to ask others about. Like previously politically dangerous information, today's users need to know that their confidentiality will be maintained even if the consequences today might be more about embarrassment rather than legal challenges.

Today, with internet filters on many public computers, we also have to recognize the challenge that they can pose to finding gender specific information. Filters on public computers likely filter out websites that mention breasts or vaginas, yet a student researching breast cancer or trying to find information about *The Vagina Monologues* will not be able to access information either, due to that same filter. And even worse, even though these students have socially acceptable reasons to seek this information, they might not feel comfortable asking for help in bypassing the filter if that is an option, or seeking paper-based resources if that is available to them. Confidentiality is not mentioned nearly as often as access and censorship in library documents on intellectual freedom, but it is still a critical aspect of intellectual freedom for our users.

Conclusion

As feminism continues to evolve in light of today's interests and recognition of inequalities, many feminist theorists have discussed the narrowness of a feminism that only addresses the needs of a fraction of all women. We begin to see the inclusion of race, class, ethnicity, sexuality, and a variety of different "others" that intersect with women's issues, and that only in recognizing these intersections is it possible to fully represent the female perspective and understand the feminist approach.

As such, to fully understand the intersectionality of feminism and intellectual freedom, it is necessary to understand how these other perspectives intersect with it as well. Within this book, there are other chapters[2] that one should familiarize themselves with to have the broadest understanding of a feminist approach to intellectual freedom. With a full understanding of the complexity of today's feminism, it is clear that there are many points of intersection among social issues that impact women and intellectual freedom.

---

2   Specifically: Lipinski and Henderson's "Hate Speech," Hammer's "Intellectual Freedom within the International Human Right to Freedom of Thought, Conscience, and Religion Intellectual Freedom within the International Human Right to Freedom of Thought, Conscience, and Religion," Knox's "Religion and Intellectual Freedom," Holley's "Sex and Intellectual Freedom," and Carmichael's "Sexual Orientation and Gender Expression."

References

American Library Association. 2005. Resolution on threats to library materials related to sex, gender, gender identity, or sexual orientation (ALA Policy 53.12). http://ifmanual.org/resolutionthreatsgi (accessed February 22, 2013).

———. Intellectual freedom and censorship q & a. http://www.ala.org/Template.cfm?Section=basics&Template=/ContentManagement/ContentDisplay.cfm&ContentID=60610 (accessed January 12, 2013).

American Library Association Office for Intellectual Freedom. 2010. Library bill of rights: Interpretations. *Intellectual freedom manual.* Chicago, IL: American Library Association, 62–198.

Anderson, Elizabeth. 2011. Feminist epistemology and philosophy of science. In *Stanford Encyclopedia of Philosophy.* Stanford, CA: The Metaphysics Research Lab. http://plato.stanford.edu/archives/spr2011/entries/feminism-epistemology (accessed January 12, 2013).

Haslanger, Sally, Nancy Tuana, and Peg O'Connor. 2011. Topics in feminism. In *Stanford Encyclopedia of Philosophy.* Stanford, CA: The Metaphysics Research Lab. http://plato.stanford.edu/archives/win2011/entries/feminism-topics/ (accessed February 12, 2013).

hooks, bell. 2000. *Feminist theory from margin to center.* 2nd ed. Cambridge, MA: South End Press.

International Association of Library Associations. 2013. IFLA statement on libraries and intellectual freedom. http://www.ifla.org/en/publications/ifla-statement-on-libraries-and-intellectual-freedom (accessed January 22, 2013).

Jaggar, Alison. 1992. Feminist ethics. In *Encyclopedia of ethics.* Garland Reference Library of the Humanities. Ed. Lawrence C. Becker and Charlotte B. Becker. New York: Garland Publishing.

Krug, Judith F. and Candace D. Morgan. 2010. ALA and intellectual freedom: A historical overview. In *Intellectual Freedom Manual* 8th ed. 12–36. Chicago, IL: American Library Association.

Lorde, Audre. 1984. Sister outsider: Essays and speeches. 1st ed. Trumansburg, NY: Crossing Press.

McAfee, Noëlle. 2011. Feminist political philosophy. In *Stanford Encyclopedia of Philosophy.* Stanford, CA: The Metaphysics Research Lab. http://plato.stanford.edu/archives/win2011/entries/feminism-political/ (accessed February 12, 2013).

Price, Diana A. 2006. Celebrating 90 years, and the struggle continues. *National Organization of Women* http://www.now.org/issues/reproductive/101606sanger.html (accessed January 22, 2013).

Semonche, John E. 2007. *Censoring sex: a historical journey through american media.* Lanham, MD: Rowman & Littlefield.

Stone, Alison. 2007. *An introduction to feminist philosophy.* Malden, MA: Polity.

Tuana, Nancy. 2011. Approaches to feminism. In *Stanford Encyclopedia of Philosophy.* Stanford, CA: The Metaphysics Research Lab. http://plato.stanford.edu/archives/spr2011/entries/feminism-approaches/ (accessed February 13, 2013).

United Nations. 1948. The Universal Declaration of Human Rights. New York: United Nations.

Walters, Margaret. 2005. *Feminism: A Very Short Introduction.* Oxford, UK: Oxford University Press.

Weber, Cynthia. 2008. Academic freedom and the assault on interdisciplinary programs: Re-articulating the language of diversity. *Women and Language* 31, no.2: 51–6.

Zack, Naomi. 2006. Can third wave feminism be inclusive? Intersectionality, its problems and new directions. In *The Blackwell Guide to Feminist Philosophy.* Ed. Eva Feder Kittay, Chichester, UK: John Wiley & Sons.

Neoliberalism and Intellectual Freedom

Laura Koltutsky

Intellectual freedom is an intangible concept that attempts to define a critical need for all. How the concept is interpreted and codified is different in many nations. After World War II there was an acknowledgement by the United Nations that there was a need for a stated standard of behavior for nations. This resulted in the creation of the Universal Declaration of Human Rights and in 1948 the states of the United Nations chose to include intellectual freedom in the *Universal Declaration of Human Rights* within Article 19: "Everyone has the right to freedom of opinion and expression; this right includes freedom to hold opinions without interference and to seek, receive and impart information and ideas through any media and regardless of frontiers" (General Assembly 1948).

This was a crucial recognition of the fundamental nature of intellectual freedom in modern life. These precepts were built into modern liberal beliefs but were based upon earlier ideas of 18th century Enlightenment thinkers such as Rousseau and Voltaire. Mark Alfino's chapter on "Philosophies of Intellectual Freedom" in this work goes into greater detail of how Enlightenment thinkers helped to create our modern ideas of intellectual freedom.

> *The fundamental premise of liberal democracy is the sovereignty of the people. Governance by the people is exercised through communicative freedoms of speech, assembly, and press; it relies on norms of publicity that emphasize transparency and accountability, it consists of the deliberative practices of the public sphere.* (Dean 2009, 21)

The modern context for intellectual freedom is itself a local construct within individual states and may have very different definitions by populace and governments, therefore defining what intellectual freedom is may be impossible. John Rawls points out that freedom or liberty is a concept of which there are many conceptions (Rawls 1971, 5). Liberal conceptions of freedoms likewise vary with political freedoms taking precedence over economic freedoms. Jeremy Waldron outlines this idea, "Certainly a strong commitment to liberty in the economic sphere is more likely to be associated with political conservatism than with liberalism, particularly as those terms are understood in North America (1987, 129). The focus of this chapter is to explore how neoliberal politics have changed perspectives on the goals of intellectual freedom from its liberal democracy origins. I am focusing on the post World War II time period to present day. As a means of interpreting how neoliberalism has altered societal perspectives on intellectual freedom, I have also chosen to look at its impacts on universal or mass education.

Universal education is enshrined in the *Universal Declaration of Human Rights* in Article 26. "Everyone has the right to education. Education shall be free, at least in the elementary and fundamental stages. Elementary education should be compulsory" (General Assembly 1948). It would seem obvious that liberal democracies would make education a priority for its citizens. In modern times, universal education has become fractured and distorted by school options that can become obstacles to the goal of an informed citizenry.

John Rawls felt that there was an educative imperative to maintain such an informed citizenry. "Rawl stresses that society should . . . pay enough attention to the education of children: children are future citizens. . . . As future citizens it is essential that they acquire the capacity to understand the public political culture of society and the capacity to participate in its institutions" (Lehning 2009, 146). When schools are focused on standardized test results, rankings, and an ever-shifting curriculum the goal of creating an informed citizenry is not the priority. Michael Apple's writings have focused on the economics and power dynamics of education. He outlines this tension between education and power brokers. "Education is a site of struggle and compromise. It serves also as a proxy for larger battles over what our institutions should do, who they should serve, and who should make those decisions" (Apple 2000, 58).

Neoliberals would argue that their policies of privatization, accountability and school choice will better serve modern society. Jane Fowler Morse addresses the tension between economic needs and the promotion of intellectual freedom:

> On the one hand, I agree with Mill that intellectual freedom is primary. On the other hand, economic freedom is meaningless without ideas, even though freedom of thought without sufficient economic support is ineffectual, as Marx believes. Unfortunately, intellectual freedom is not always protected, suppressed by repressive governments, a narrow patriotism, bigotry, and lack of access to education. Significantly, intellectual freedom is also limited by an unequal distribution of resources and economic or political control of information. (Morse 2001, 201)

Liberalisms

Modern liberalism can be differentiated from classical liberalism, as they emphasize different aspects of enlightenment ideals. James L Richardson outlines liberalism generally in *Contending Liberalisms in World Politics*.

> *Viewed historically, liberalism is first and foremost normative: a body of ideas about social and political values, the principles that should govern political life, the grounds for political legitimacy. The cluster of values now identified with liberalism came into being over a long period; particular values were articulated in specific historic contexts.* (2001, 18)

In attempting to define the goals of modern liberalism, I believe it would be a mistake to try to define it too closely as these goals are dependent on their time and place. Jeremy Waldron describes the difficulty to trying to define liberalism, "To say that a commitment to *freedom* is the foundation of liberalism is to say something too vague and abstract to be helpful, while to say that liberals are committed fundamentally to a particular *conception* of liberty is to sound too assured, too dogmatic about a matter on which, with the best will in the world, even ideological bedfellows are likely to disagree" (1987, 131). Milan Zafirovski tried to create a classification scheme suggesting that "the defining attributes and constitutive components of liberal society and modernity, comprise the following: integral liberty; egalitarianism; social justice; democracy, social pluralism; social universalism; individualism; rationalism, progressivism, modernism and optimism; humanism and secularism; pacifism and the like" (2007, 46). These components are necessarily broad and some of them may shift in importance depending on events and cultures. Jeremy Waldron suggests, "Freedom or liberty is a concept of which there are many conceptions. Since some of these conceptions are not associated with the liberal tradition, it is unsatisfactory to say simply that liberals are committed to (equal) liberty and leave the matter there" (1987, 130). It would seem that within liberalism there is room for disagreement about the definition and/or emphasis on liberty but that it is nonetheless an integral belief to many who call themselves liberals.

Classical liberalism, "focuses on the idea of limited government, the maintenance of the rule of law, the avoidance of arbitrary and discretionary power, the sanctity of private property and freely made contracts, and the responsibility of individuals for their own fates (Ryan 1993, 293). Thorsen suggests that classical liberalism is primarily interested in minimizing the state's role in economic matters except for those that cannot be minimized such as "armed forces, law enforcement and other non-excludable goods. . . . This kind of state is sometimes described as a 'night-watchman state', as the sole purpose of the minimal state is to uphold the most fundamental aspects of public order" (Thorsen 2010, 192). Walter Lippman described classical liberalism as being focused on continuing with laissez-faire principles. "Laissez-faire was the necessary destructive doctrine of a revolutionary movement. That is all it was. It was, therefore, incapable of guiding the public policy of states once the old order was overthrown" (Lippmann 1944, 185). Laissez-faire economics are most frequently associated with the work of Adam Smith, a Scottish philosopher and the author of *The Wealth of Nations* (1776). Anthony Quinton suggests that classic liberals, "favour theory, above all classical economics, with its apparent implication that an unfettered market will lead to the greatest possible satisfaction of human needs and desires and the most productive use of resources" (2007, 285). These beliefs have formed the core of neoliberal principles.

Walter Lippman also addressed the conservative presumption that legal regulation was unnecessary.

> I suppose that a solitary man cast ashore on an undiscovered island could be said to have freedom without law. But in a community there is no such thing: all freedom, all rights, all property, are sustained by some kind of law. So the question can never arise whether there should be law here and no law there, but only what law shall prevail everywhere. (Lippmann 1944, 186)

Friedrich A. Hayek, an Austrian economist, recognized that conservatism or classical liberalism was flawed, and that he, himself, was not a conservative. In *The Constitution of Liberty*, Hayek states, "Personally, I find that the most objectionable feature of the conservative attitude is its propensity to reject well-substantiated new knowledge because it dislikes some of the consequences which seem to follow from it—or, to put it bluntly, its obscurantism (Hayek 1960, 404). This wish to not only suppress new ideas but to create a bleak worldview has assisted in the acceptance of globalization as the new normal. Hayek also recognized that in contrast with conservatives, "The liberal regards democracy as a protective device for guaranteeing the rule of law. It offers a procedure for the peaceful change of government and a check on arbitrary rule by ensuring that the coercive power of the state is only employed for 'ensuring obedience to the rules of just conduct approved by most or at least by a majority" (Bellamy 1994, 422). Classical liberals view the role of government to be minimal and ideally to allow markets to define policy direction. "It is argued that . . . since the 'market' knows best . . . private decisions, including those of speculators, would bring about financial discipline and force governments to adopt 'healthy' policies such as balancing budgets, especially by cutting social expenditures (Raffer 2011, 45).

There was a shift in the post World War II period to international cooperation in economic policy. The Bretton Woods Conference in 1944 led to the creation of an economic cooperation framework. Two of the institutions that came out of this meeting are the International Monetary Fund IMF and the International Bank for Reconstruction and Development IBRD. The IMF, an international organization established in 1947 to promote, alongside the General Agreement on Tariffs and Trade (now the World Trade Organization or WTO), the expansion of international trade in a way consistent with the maintenance of balance of payments equilibrium by individual member countries. This has involved the Fund in negotiating the removal of restrictions (such as foreign exchange controls) on the convertibility of currencies, the establishment of 'orderly' exchange rates between members' currencies and the provision of borrowing facilities and international reserves to members in balance of payments difficulties These institutions, which became known as the Bretton Woods Institutions, have become tied to both neoliberalism and globalization. A fixed exchange rate based on the gold standard was integral to the Bretton Woods Agreement which thirty two countries signed in 1946. This agreement lasted until 1971 when the gold standard was abandoned by the United States. This agreement helped to form the basis of remarkable economic security of its member states.

The Bretton Woods Institutions were based in part on the work of John Maynard Keynes. A British economist, Keynes wrote *The General Theory of Employment, Interest and Money* in 1936 after watching Britain struggle to recover from the Great Depression of the 1930s. Keynes thought that governments should only interfere with market forces when absolutely required. He also believed that this would be a temporary need with the market resuming its role when it was able. Keynes believed that, "The outstanding faults of the economic society in which we live are its failure to provide for full employment and its arbitrary and inequitable distribution of wealth and incomes" (Keynes 1951, 372). His writings were central to the development of the future social welfare state.

Keynesian economics became the dominant model in Western nation states after World War II until economic and political disruptions in the 1970s caused some states to reduce expenditures on the welfare state. "The 1950–1970 was a period of relatively high economic growth and low levels of unemployment, with generally moderate inflation. . . . The welfare state had taken root in Europe and major reforms in social security and health systems were also instituted in the United States under the drive for the Great Society" (ul Haque 2004, 6). In the United States the federal government declared War on Poverty and passed the Elementary and Secondary Education Act, the Civil Rights Act, the Voting Rights Act, the Fair Housing Act, the Clean Air Act, the Clean Water Act and created Medicare, Medicaid, Head Start, Job Corps, the Environmental Protection Agency, Occupational Health and Safety in the 1960s and 1970s era. Suzanne MacGregor identifies these changes as having developed from shifting political priorities.

> *In political debate, the progressive voice argued for a move from the night watch-man state to a social-service state and thence to a welfare state, which some saw as a step towards socialism. It was thought that to bring about a full welfare state, governments would need to emphasise education as a key social service, accept responsibility for ensuring full employment and pursue policies of economic growth and redistribution of income from rich to poor.* (2005, 142)

Many European countries, in particular the Scandinavian states, went much farther down this path of modern liberalism.

The Development of Neoliberalism

Neoliberal beliefs have sometimes been referred to as a "thought collective" rather than a branch of conservatism. While difficult to pin down its origins, meetings held in both France (1938) Colloque Walter Lippman and Switzerland (1947) Mont Pelerin helped the participants to define the goals of neoliberal policies. The Colloque Walter Lippman was organized by French philosopher, Louis Rougier, and was held in Paris in August 1938. The Colloque was to be centered around discussion of Lippman's newest book, *The Good Society*. Walter Lippmann's ideas around how societies could adapt to ever changing conditions had been well received in 1938 and had recently been translated into the French language. The Colloque Walter Lippman did not result in agreement on new political goals and those in attendance split into two factions with Hayek and Lippman disagreeing with their French hosts. The division was described here, "On one side were 'those for which neoliberalism was fundamentally different, in its spirit and its program of traditional liberalism' (these included Louis Rougier, Auguste Detouf, Louis Marlio, William Rpke, and Alexander Rstow), and on the other side were defenders of the "old liberalism" headed by Louis Baudin, Jacques Rueff, and the Austrian School (Friedrich Hayek, Ludwig von Mises)" (Denord 2009, 49).

The Mont Pelerin Society (MPS) was created in 1947 at a meeting in Switzerland organized by Friedrich A. Hayek Members of the Mont Pelerin Society are often tagged as neoliberals although they refer to themselves as liberals of the classical school. According to the MPS website the group's goals were modest. "Its sole objective was to facilitate an exchange of ideas between like-minded scholars in the hope of strengthening the principles and practices of a free society and to study the workings, virtues, and defects of market-oriented economic systems (Mont Pelerin Society, "About MPS").

These two meetings allowed for academics, economists and business people to meet and discuss how post World War II economies should develop and the role of government in economic decision making. After the Colloque Walter Lippman in 1938 there was much discussion of how to define the new doctrine. "To be neoliberal" was supposed to imply the recognition that 'laissez-faire' economics was not enough and that, in the name of liberalism, a modern economic policy was needed" (Denord 2009, 48). Miran Zafirovski suggests, "In a sense, 'neo-liberalism' is a sort of 'liberal name' or rather misnomer for neo-conservative 'free-market' ideas and economic policies, in America and Great Britain, as epitomized by Reaganism and Thatcherism" (2007, 324). In tying their new doctrine to earlier forms of classical liberalism (if only with language), neoliberals were to begin a battle with modern liberalism.

The domination of the conservative base that supports neoliberal policies has evolved largely in the past thirty years and this has impacted western cultures in significant ways. "Conservatives arguably played key roles in dismantling the New Deal-era welfare state; in scaling back the unionization of American workers; in strengthening in other ways the hand of industry, raising American economic competitiveness, and at the same time likely exacerbating social inequality" (Gross 2011, 326). Jodi Dean describes this time as "the 'structural crisis' in the world economy . . . and the failure of Keynesianism 'to develop public understandings of the economy which could compete with the neoliberal rhetoric of free markets'" (Dean 2009, 53).

James L. Richardson outlines the effect that neoliberalism has had internationally.

> Its effect on political practice has been varied, but even though it has not always been successful in reducing the level of state expenditure, the neoliberal offensive has succeeded in eroding the legitimacy of the welfare state and, more broadly, the public sector and in impoverishing publically funded institutions, especially universities and libraries for which there is no mass electoral lobby. (Richardson 2001, 42)

This shift in thinking is also outlined by Pierre Bourdieu in *Acts of Resistance: Against the Tyranny of the Market*. He describes neoliberalism as "a very smart and very modern repackaging of the oldest ideas of the oldest capitalists. . . . This new kind of conservative revolution appeals to progress, reason, and science (economics in this case) to justify the restoration and so tries to write off progressive thought and action as archaic" (1998 34–5). Paulo Freire in *Pedagogy of Freedom* railed against complacency. "Now in our time, it is essential and urgent that people unite against the threat that looms over us. The threat, namely, to our own identity as human persons caught up in the ethics of the marketplace" (1998, 115).

In this environment, neoliberalists took advantage of the confluence of world events such as the Vietnam War and economic turmoil to advocate for their belief system. This definition of neoliberalism in David Harvey's, *A Brief History of Neoliberalism* assists in understanding both the political and economic goals of this belief system.

> *Neoliberalism is in the first instance a theory of political economic practices that proposes that human well-being can best be advanced by liberating individual entrepreneurial freedoms and skills within an institutional framework characterized by strong private property rights, free markets and free trade. The role of the state is to create and preserve an institutional framework appropriate to such practices.* (Harvey 2007, 2)

This placement of the market as the predominant defining force of political decision making was tied to events of the early 1970s such as the dissolution of the Bretton Woods Agreement, rising inflation, and unemployment. Rather than blaming the markets, neoliberals blamed Keynesian economic policies that nation states had used to move towards increasing employment, strong social programs, and a more collaborative relationship between labor and industry. Ronaldo Munck describes how democracy was restructured so that informed citizenship was no longer a goal but rather a hindrance. Politics became a commodity, one to be managed but not the end goal. Civil society was deemphasized and subverted into refuting the need for government involvement. Language became important whereby community organisations became social capital and citizens became consumers (Munck 2005, 66).

Intellectual Freedom Implications

Teaching students to think critically is time intensive and does not give an immediate payoff to administrators and politicians as does standardized testing. Teachers who are asked to "teach to the test" are already balancing teaching the curriculum with the pressures of meeting standards set by those from outside the classroom.

> *My concern stems from what my colleagues and I have found. Almost every school mission statement these days boasts broad goals related to critical thinking, global citizenship, environmental stewardship, and moral character. Yet beneath the rhetoric, increasingly narrow curriculum goals, accountability measures, and standardized testing have reduced too many classroom lessons to the cold, stark pursuit of information and skills without context and without social meaning.* (Westheimer 2010, 6)

Students are not being well served by policies that create learning environments where they focus on passing tests that rarely evaluate any critical thinking skills. Critical thinking can not be learned through constant testing. Problem based learning, portfolios, and inquiry are all teaching strategies that require time and thought to be successfully implemented in the classroom. At the moment time in the classroom is a rare commodity. "In the United States, whole subject areas—in particular those that tend to embrace multiple perspectives and complex narratives—have been virtually been eliminated from the class schedules of many students" (Ibid).

Effective citizenship is a goal of universal education but what skills does a citizen need in the modern world? It would seem that more often than not there is a focus on creating future workers and ensuring that students can compete in the global marketplace. The ability to critically evaluate information is being devalued. "In addition, a democratic society needs an education system that helps to sustain its democracy by developing thoughtful citizens who can make wise civic choices. By its very nature, as Dewey (1916) pointed out, a democratic society is continually changing—sometimes for the better, sometimes for the worse—and it requires citizens who are willing and able to distinguish between the better and the worse" (Noddings 2005, 11). When math and reading are the priorities for standardized testing it follows that class time will be spent focusing on those areas. Social studies is by its nature able to help students explore ambiguity and to develop an understanding of political processes and responsibilities within a democratic system. Would it not be helpful to know if our students are learning these skills? Yet the Common Curriculum still only tests Math, English, and Language Arts and it seems unlikely that other subjects will be added by the 2014 deadline. Critical thinking can be taught in any subject and effective educators can help students make connections to concepts that reoccur in other areas. One of the biggest losses of these neoliberal approaches is the child focused classroom where many people of my generation thrived. Children are individuals, not simply future workers or human capital and that seems to have been lost in the reforming process.

> Clearly some aspects of the market wish to promote learning—the learning of skills considered appropriate to different strata in the labor market. The point here is that capital seeks to repress those aspects of critical thought, such as those embodied in critical pedagogy, in socialist/Marxist analysis, which are inimical to its own continuation. (Hill 2007, 125)

Vivian Collinson studied exemplary American secondary teachers trying to create learning environments that supported intellectual freedom within their classrooms. "The exemplary teachers used collective inquiry as the primary process for fostering intellectual freedom in their classrooms and for reinforcing the 'generic' learning they seemed to consider necessary: the values of humility and responsibility, along with attitudes of curiosity and open-mindedness" (Collinson 2012, 113). The challenge for educators is always to balance the needs of the students to be engaged with preparing these students to succeed on the mandated standardized tests and to meet accountability standards like No Child Left Behind.

Neoliberalism and Education

Neoliberal beliefs have been able to shift perceptions of the purpose of education within a society. "'Consumer choice' is the guarantor of democracy. In effect education is seen as simply one more product like bread, cars, and television. . . . Thus democracy is turned into consumption practices" (Apple 2000, 60). Citizens have been supplanted by consumers and critical thinking skills are deemphasized in schools that are pressured to prepare students for the global marketplace. Milton Friedman, a mercantalist economist from the Chicago School, had proposed school vouchers in the 1970s but the U.S. did not implement them at that time. "More than thirty years ago, Friedman used schools to illustrate his general belief that unregulated market forces of supply and demand can do a better job than government programs in helping meet society's needs" (Henig 2001, 59). Friedman felt so strongly about school choice that he created the Friedman Foundation for Educational Choice in 1996 to promote and support school choice programs. "Friedman . . . argued that public schools had become lazy public monopolies. Public schools are monopolies because most parents are impeded from exercising their option to switch to the alternative, private providers . . . when added to a continued legal obligation to support public education through their taxes" (Ibid). That said, education has a role to play in increasing human capital. "The key force in human capital development obviously has to be education. It is the main public investment that can foster both economic efficiency and civic cohesion. Education isn't a static input into the knowledge economy, but is itself becoming transformed by it" (Giddens 2000, 73).

Margaret Thatcher, Prime Minister of Britain was a believer of neoliberal principles. Susan George in a 1999 speech stated that "The central value of Thatcher's doctrine and of neo-liberalism itself is the notion of competition—competition between nations, regions, firms and of course between individuals. Competition . . . is supposed to allocate all resource, whether physical, natural, human or financial with the greatest possible efficiency" (George, 1999). Conservatives, neoliberals amongst them, suggest that Thatcher needed to take down the unions and the welfare state for the well being of the country, which was in economic crisis. Her deflection of government responsibility was evident in her political decisions which included trying to privatize government services like education. The New Right governments of the 1980s and 1990s in England created an educational service market, which was neither entirely public nor entirely private. "Levacic (1995) suggested that the distinguishing characteristics of a quasi-market for a public service are the 'separation of purchaser from provider and an element of user choice between providers'" (Gordon and Whitty 1997, 454). The end goal was to privatize educational services but to maintain some controls at the same time. "The 'swollen' bureaucratic state of Keynesianism is being replaced by what Neave (1988) termed the 'evaluative state,' which seeks to steer the system at a distance. Under this model, the quasi-market finds ways to intervene at the same time as appearing to eschew interventionism" (Ibid, 455). In this way the government of Margaret Thatcher attempted to privatize education and to remove it as a public good provided to its citizens.

Ronald Reagan, President of the United States, followed the lead of Margaret Thatcher and Milton Friedman and became an advocate of "trickle down" economics. This theory suggested that if the rich were given economic benefits in the form of lower taxes, this money would then be reinvested in businesses creating jobs and allowing wealth to be transferred to the less affluent. Unfortunately, the economy was not served well by trickle down economics as the wealthy chose to bank their savings rather than act as the economic engine. Neoliberal policies that reduced the welfare state created bigger problems for the middle class and the poor. "As the neoliberal state withdraws from the provision of public services, individuals are increasingly made responsible for managing personal financial risk related to areas such as health care, retirement, and education" (Ambrosio 2013, 321). The end result of Reagan's neoliberal belief system was that the rich have become richer creating an even larger economic divide. "In 1977, the top 1 percent of American families had average incomes 65 times as great as those of the bottom 10 percent. A decade later, the top 1 percent was 115 times as well off as the bottom decile" (George 1999).

Both Great Britain and the United States elected moderate governments in the 1990s. President Bill Clinton, a Democrat and Prime Minister Tony Blair of the Labour Party did attempt to ameliorate some of the perceived damage done by previous governments. This new political belief was named "The Third Way" or new progressivism. Clinton attempted to pass legislation that would have brought about single provider health care but the legislation failed to gain enough support to pass. He also tried to create voluntary national education standards but was similarly unsuccessful. National education standards are still a contentious topic in the United States, No Child Left Behind does not include national standards but funding was attached to meeting outcomes set by the federal government.

The creation of charter schools was a priority for President George W. Bush, he couched this in terms of increasing local control and accountability. He outlined his strategy in a prominent education journal *Phi Delta Kappan* in October 2000, "Schools that do not teach and will not change must have some final point of accountability—a moment of truth when their federal funds, intended to help the poorest children, are divided up and given to parents for tutoring or a charter school, or some other hopeful option" (Bush 2000, 122). Immediately after Bush won the election, he put into motion his educational objectives with the No Child Left Behind Act of 2002. As you will see in the section on school choice Bush's ideas were carried forward through his terms in office and into President Obama's presidency. Barack Obama not only continued on with No Child Left Behind but supported the creation of the Common Core Standards which are even tougher on schools that are struggling to meet the No Child Left Behind performance measures.

School Choice

There is an element of condescension in the marketing of school choice to a largely poor and socially disadvantaged audience. School choice has always existed for the wealthy through a parallel private school system. School choice as a new idea for other social groups holds a tinge of charity. Kathryn McDermott and Kysa Nygreen looked at selected urban schools through the lens of new paternalism. The term "new paternalism" came from the book, *The New Paternalism: Supervisory Approaches to Poverty* by Lawrence Mead who "identified the 'new paternalism' with 'close supervision of the dependent' (p. 1) and an assumption that people receiving welfare benefits need 'direction,' not just financial assistance (p. 2)" (McDermott and Nygreen 2013, 85). New paternalist urban schools have three common elements: increased instructional time, deliberate cultivation of a college-going culture, and an emphasis on the non-academic social development of students "or what many of these institutions call 'character' education" (Ibid 86-7). Education reform in this context does not require society to invest much in the way of resources and new paternalism is perceived to solve another traditional problem with education. "New paternalism also resonates with a growing belief that improving public education requires a break with the priorities of traditional educational institutions, such as schools of education and especially teachers' unions" (Ibid, 88). McDermott and Nygreen also outline how character education is applied in urban schools whereby "middle class" values are being promoted, "Not only will it help students to achieve upward mobility, but it is also the common sense thing to do . . . but U.S. history suggests that something discriminatory could be going on if the "need" for different treatment of low-income students of color is "obvious" to people whose children will not experience this treatment" (Ibid, 90).

Neoliberals believe that school choice will benefit the working poor and minorities, and it is the best way to resolve the public school crisis. That somehow school choice will create a solution for problems created by much broader socio-economic challenges such as poverty and underfunded schools. "Choice is being used skillfully as the enticement into the most important education-policy debate of this decade. The word is being recreated as conveying such innocent, inherent integrity that it cannot be opposed" (Barlow and Robertson 1994, 187).

> *Much as advocates of globalization use the phrase there is no alternative or TINA, school choice advocates suggest that the public education system has failed and charter schools have had to fill the gap. In truth, recent research has indicated that charter school students are matching or even scoring worse on standardized tests than public school students.*
> (Bifulco and Ladd 2004)

Charter schools have an economic advantage over the public school systems in that they don't have to meet the same state standards as traditional public schools. This is done to promote innovation and to reduce administration load on the new charter schools. Teachers with subject and state certifications are not mandatory in all charter schools. These teacher standards are based on each state's teacher certification requirements. According to a 2004 study done by the Education Policy Center at Michigan State University, teacher experience in charter schools is another area of concern. In that national study they determined that teachers within charter schools have roughly half the years of teaching experience as their public school colleagues (Burian-Fitzgerald and Harris 2004).

Public school systems such as the Houston Independent School District have developed their own charter schools and specialized programs to "compete" for students, who have now become a commodity. Parents can now choose from several programs but the term "choose" may not accurately reflect the admissions process. Public charter schools can set their own admissions criteria and in effect restrict entry to only the most qualified students. Open admissions, done by lottery as shown in the documentary, *Waiting for Superman*, are to fill a limited number of seats after filling the majority with other assessment criteria. A 2012 Reuters report by Stephanie Simon looked at national charter school admissions in the United States. Some of the admission strategies identified in the article included the following:

•   Applications that are only available just a few hours a year

- Lengthy application forms, often printed only in English, that require student and parent essays, report cards, test scores, disciplinary records, teacher recommendations and medical records
- Demands that students present Social Security cards and birth certificates for their applications to be considered, even though such documents cannot be required under federal law
- Mandatory family interviews
- Assessment exams
- Academic prerequisites
- Requirements that applicants document and disabilities or special needs.

Criteria like these can and have led to large numbers of students being rejected by charter schools and specialized programs or resulted in students and their families choosing not to apply. Other researchers have noted that open admissions based upon a lottery can still result in less diversity. "However, how a school advertises and what requirements it imposes (e.g. parental involvement contracts) may narrow the range of students who seek admission. In addition, many charter schools may "recruit" students by word-of-mouth, raising further questions about homogeneity and access" (Bulkley and Fisler 2003, 332).

As a librarian and a teacher I have been privileged to work with preservice teachers and Education faculty in Houston, Texas. It is impossible to escape discussion about school performance in Texas. Public schools live and die by their standardized test scores that are judged by the populace to be a measure of effective learning. Teachers could and did argue that all the standardized tests in the world can not evaluate learning in its complete and complex reality. Unsurprisingly, these test scores tended to trend higher in wealthier neighborhoods with "better" public schools. As schools are funded through local property taxes, affluent neighborhoods have an advantage in school funding.

Public school systems may choose to develop their own magnet programs which allow schools to focus on certain approaches in an attempt to help students who are not successful within traditional public schools. As a result of school funding being based on student populations these programs are critical to maintaining or increasing funding. Mary Nash-Wood reported on local magnet schools in a *Shreveport Times* article. In Shreveport, Lousiana, the Caddo Parish School Board had created eight magnet schools as a response to diminishing enrollment. Only six percent of the district's African American students attend these magnet schools and while sixty five percent of the district's student base live in poverty only twenty six percent of magnet school students live in poverty. Standardized test admission was the primary reason given for African American students' failure to be accepted at the magnet schools. Walter Lee, former Caddo Superintendent stated, "The magnet system today is nowhere what we envisioned when we created the program. . . . The program has many purposes, but the main idea was to create an integrated environment, and that's not what we see today"(Nash-Wood 2012).

The Houston Independent School District created their own system of school choice offerings; traditional neighborhood schools, magnet schools, vanguard programs, charter schools, Montessori, International Baccalaureate programs, Houston Innovative Learning Zone programs, Career Academies, STEM, language programs, and Fine Arts Programs. On the *HISD News Blog* on August 14, 2013, the latest offering was proudly featured, the HISD Energy Institute High School. "The school is the first of its kind in the nation and represents a collaborative effort between a public school district and industry leaders. The high school will provide students with a rigorous STEM (science, technology, engineering, and math) curriculum, hands-on learning, and externships in the fields of geoscience, alternative energy, and offshore technology" (HISD 2013). Is the HISD Energy Institute High School an exemplary program or the complete subordination of curriculum to industry?

Neoliberals have turned the idea of school choice into a reality whereby their ideas for education reform, increased testing, school vouchers, and more accountability sound reasonable. School choice seems like a positive change to many parents as they equate increased choice to increased quality. Reformers appealed to minority parents claiming that public schools were responsible for holding their children down, unable to achieve their maximum potential. There is a deliberate use of language to suggest that teachers' unions, government bureaucracies, and academics are misleading them. Why should these people know any more about what your child needs than you do? Efforts at marketing school choice as the only responsible decision that parents can make contributes to a fear-based decision making environment. What parent does not want to ensure that their children will be successful in the modern workplace?

A powerful argument used by proponents of school vouchers is that minorities, the poor, and the primarily urban students will obtain better educations through school vouchers. The most effective strategy of all would be to raise all children out of poverty, as that has been proven to be the largest determinant of educational success. Bruce J. Biddle and David C. Berliner outlined numerous studies that supported the premise that stronger socio-economic supports for public schools and their students would improve student success rates.

> To illustrate, a study of 11th grade achievement scores among school districts in Oklahoma found that student poverty and per-student revenues within schools were associated with achievement. Effects for the former were roughly twice the size of those for the latter (Ellinger et al., 1995). Similar results were found for the determinants of 8th grade achievement scores among school districts from across the United States that participated in the Second International Study of Mathematics Achievement (Payne & Biddle, 1999). And Harold Wenglinsky (1997a), using data drawn from the National Assessment of Educational Progress, found that average student socioeconomic status and per-student expenditures within school districts were both associated with level of mathematics achievement in the 8th grade, but that the effects for socio-economic status were again larger than those for per-student expenditures (Biddle and Berliner 2002, 53).

Charter schools can not move students out of the socio-economic context in which they live. Poverty will always negatively affect learning regardless of where a child is being taught. "Resistance to equitable funding for schools has also been supported by several belief systems about the causes of poverty. One of these, the ideology of *individualism*, holds that success and failure result mainly from individual effort rather than social circumstance" (Ibid, 51). This mythology places the blame on the impoverished student and their family rather than acknowledge a failure on the part of government. This creates an uneven playing field that seems weighted towards failure before education can try to ameliorate poverty's effects.

Educational Reform and Accountability

"For most people, education may be the most important element of their social status, and their educational background will have a greater direct impact on their overall life chances than any other element but nationality" (Boli 1985, 145). Publically funded education has been increasingly targeted by neoliberals since the 1970s. As a public good provided by governments to its citizens, universal education was a priority for all nations. So what has changed in the political world for the modern reality of universal education to have developed? Margaret Thatcher followed the lead of neoliberals when she changed this understanding of the relationship between society and social services like education when she stated, "there is no such thing as society. . . . There are individual men and women, and there are families. And no government can do anything except through people, and people must look to themselves first" (Thatcher 1993, cited in Gillborn and Youdell 2000, 39). . . . By reducing success to individual merit, schooling becomes one more consumer choice where one benefits from choosing wisely" (Hursh 2007b, 26). There was a profound shift in the purpose of universal education. Education was no longer a public good that benefited all of society but a commodity to be privatized, where productivity measured by standardized tests became the goal. "Within this milieu, schooling for the masses became education for human capital preparation while democratic education was essentially reserved for the economic elite" (Hyslop-Marigison and Sears 2006, 3).

As part of their efforts neoliberals have denounced government funding, teachers, and state based curriculum standards for being ineffectual. "The contemporary reform movement in America is driven mainly by political conservatives who are concerned about morals and economics. . . . Significantly, they have also adopted a free-market model for schools, claiming that schools themselves must be subjected to a competitive format" (Rust and Jacob 2005, 240–41). If the reformers can't privatize education they will do the next best thing—drain government and teacher influence through the creation of charter schools within the public systems. "Privatization should not be seen as simply a reduction in the breadth of state activity, but rather as an active policy of extending market discipline. . . . The decommodified spaces of education are being eroded as part of the elimination of any spaces outside of market relations" (Sears 2003, 18–21).

Accountability is a relative concept and in this neoliberal context charter schools have a different level of accountability. The presumption is that if charter schools are not being accountable, than they won't succeed within the educational "marketplace". Charter schools are presented as giving the public educational choice but there are also associated risks to choosing from the marketplace. Government authorizers who approve the creation of charter schools do not follow the same set of criteria nationwide. "Overall, market-based accountability seems to be operating roughly as advocates anticipated, and the role of government in ensuring school quality through applications, monitoring, and renewal is less clear and more varied across authorizers and states (Bulkley and Fisler 2003, 330).

Public schools face a vastly different accountability environment whereby if they do not measure up to standards they have failed. The implementation of No Child Left Behind (NCLB) in 2002 was supported by both the Republican and Democratic parties in the United States. David Hursh describes how and why there was a perceived need for such legislation. "I show how NCLB, like other recent education policies promoting standardized testing, accountability, competition, school choice, and privatization, reflect the rise and dominance of neoliberal and neoconservative policy discourses over social democratic policy discourses (Hursh 2007a, 494). NCLB created a set of criteria that many states perceived to be an unfunded mandate. The individual states had to pay for yearly testing in every school and if the Annual Yearly Progress AYP was unacceptable, the federal government would pay for tutoring and for highly qualified teachers to work with those schools. If these schools didn't meet the criteria set by NCLB for five years in a row, the possible NCLB sanctions included the following, of which the school must choose one.

- Reopen the school as a public charter school
- Replace all or most of school staff, including the principal
- Enter into a contract with an entity, such as a private management company, with a demonstrated record of effectiveness to operate the school
- Have the state take over
- Impose another major restructuring of the school's governance arrangement

The United States Common Core standards published in 2012 were designed in many ways to replace the NCLB. An increasing number of states had asked for and received a waiver from having to meet NCLB so they had grown increasingly pointless. The Common Core standards are tougher than those demanded by NCLB and were created without teacher consultation or academic review. The Council of Chief State School Officers, and the National Governors' Association were the initiating bodies. "The work groups were staffed almost exclusively by employees of Achieve, testing companies (ACT and the College Board), and pro-accountability groups (e.g., America's Choice, Student Achievement Partners, the Hoover Institute)" (Mathis 2010, 5). At this point, the group has only developed standards for math and English language arts with other subjects to be incorporated by the 2014 deadline.

Race to the Top is a federal 2009 grant program with a competitive bidding process that pits state against state in the first round and school districts against each other in future rounds. The "successful" applicants were given millions of dollars to innovate their programs with very specific government goals including increasing the number of charter schools. Applications by states that had incorporated the Common Core Standards would gain benefit from having done so. Teachers will be paid bonuses based on their student's standardized test scores (Onosko 2011, 5). These new tests are being created by some of the testing groups involved in developing the Common Core standards. They stand to make money off the initial tests but in addition to the testing, vast databases of student and teacher data will need to be created

(Mathis 2011, 3). It is unclear exactly what information will be collected but the companies involved have gone to great efforts to reassure stakeholders that it will be kept safe and not sold to outside groups.

Race to the Top is the last in a long list of American education reform measures since the 1970s. None of these have accomplished what they purport to do—to create an even playing field. By some measures they are actually achieving at the same level or even worse within the new charter school structures. Joe Onosko suggests that Race to the Top has negative implications for citizenship.

> *The plan threatens our democracy due to students' reduced capacity for informed decision making. . . . For example, skilled analysis and decision making about a U.S. foreign-policy issue requires citizens to draw upon a variety of conceptual frameworks, including political, geographic, economic, and historical understanding related to the issue. How will our nation's future citizens acquire these understandings given the erosion that has occurred in social studies and science curricula during NCLB, erosion that will continue due to Obama's desire to increase penalties for teachers and administrators who fail to improve test scores in language arts and mathematics?* (Onosko 2011, 9)

Conclusion

Michael Apple states, "In summary, I argued strongly that education was not a neutral enterprise, that by the very nature of the institution, the educator was involved, whether he or she was conscious of it or not, in a political act" (Apple 2012, 19). Teachers are the frontline workers and their knowledge should play a role in defining learning objectives in collaboration with their communities. Neoliberal reforms tried to remove educators' judgement from the equation. Hiring less experienced, less qualified teachers to work shorter careers in public charter schools may be perceived to be innovative but persistent turnover is another feature of chartered schools which research has proven to have detrimental effect upon students (Exstrom 2012). Experienced teachers saw the detrimental effects of these reforms and many have chosen to work around them. To do the best they can for their students with what influence they have over curriculum and assessment. They wait for a time when child centered learning again becomes the priority. Noam Chomsky points out, "Once its institutional structure is in place, capitalist democracy will function only if all subordinate their interests to the needs of those who control the investment decisions. . . . And with popular organizations weakened or eliminated, isolated individuals are unable to participate in the political system in a meaningful way" (Chomsky 1992, 348). A major failing of neoliberalism is the assumption that the individual self-interest will trump any other motivation. Universal education is and has been provided to the masses for over a century and it is up to citizens to determine what their goals are for their educational system.

The voices of citizens have been diminished but not destroyed. Liberal democracies have gone through similar cycles of restrictions and openness. Nick Couldry, points this out in *Why Voice Matters: Culture and Politics after Neoliberalism*, "The challenge for a post-neoliberal politics, then is not to neglect government, or reduce the scope of its decision-making, but to offer ways of rethinking how government can use more effectively its populations' resources for cooperation, including the enhanced resources that now exist online for social production" (Couldry 2010, 148). It is this idea of government and its citizens working together to demand shared goals that meet the needs of the many that gives me hope. It is within this public sphere that liberal democracies need to reflect on these collective potentialities if there is to be hope for a free society of the future.

Intellectual freedom may be difficult to define but we need to remain vigilant to the threats against its principles of unfettered access to information and freedom of expression. Democracy needs to have citizens who are capable of making informed decisions in their lives. Amy Gutmann describes the concept of deliberative democracy.

> *Accompanying the ideal of autonomous persons is an ideal of politics where people routinely relate to one another not merely by asserting their wills or fighting for their predetermined interests, but by influencing each other through the publically valued use of reasoned argument, evidence, evaluation and persuasion that enlists reason in its cause."* (2007, 527)

Universal education has become a contested battleground because the stakes are so very high. "We are at a critical point in educational history. We face, to a heightened degree, the enduring contradiction of a dynamic economic system which needs its workers to acquire knowledge and skills, but is terrified lest they become truly educated" (Wrigley 2009, 79). Public schools can serve as an equalizing force but only if that is the cultural will of the populace. School vouchers, educational reform, and oppressive levels of standardized testing are not going to help societies develop an informed citizenry. "The citizen is not the same as the consumer, and freedom is not to be equated with the freedom to buy or sell in the marketplace. Markets do not create or sustain ethical values, which have to be legitimized through democratic dialogue and sustained through public action" (Giddens 2000, 164). States that have developed from enlightenment ideals and who had successfully integrated modern liberalism before turning to neoliberalism, still have a decision before them. Is it more important to create informed citizens who are capable of participating in their societies or creating workers for the market economy?

References

Ambrosio, John. 2013. Changing the subject: Neoliberalism and accountability in public education, *Educational Studies: A Journal of the American Educational Studies Association* 49: 316–333.

Apple, Michael W. 2000. Between neoliberalism and neoconservatism: Education and conservatism in a global context, In *Globalization and education: Critical perspectives*. Ed. Nicolas Burbules. 57–77. New York: Routledge.

– – –. 2012. On analyzing hegemony, In *Knowledge, power, and education: The selected works of Michael W. Apple*, Edited by Michael W. Apple. 19–40. New York, NY: Routledge.

Barlow, Maude and Heather-Jane Robertson. 1994. *Class warfare: The assault on Canada's schools* Toronto,ON: Key Porter Books.

Bellamy, Richard. 1994. 'Dethroning politics': Liberalism, constitutionalism and democracy in the thought of F. A. Hayek. *British Journal of Political Science* 24, no. 4 (October): 419–41.

Biddle, Bruce J. and David C. Berliner. 2002. Unequal school funding in the United States. *Educational Leadership* 59, no. 8 (May): 48–59.

Bifulco, Robert and Helen F. Ladd. 2006. The impacts of charter schools on student achievement: Evidence from North Carolina. *Education Finance and Policy* 1, no. 1: 50–90.

Boli, John, Francisco O. Ramirez, and John W. Meyer. 1985. Explaining the origins and expansion of mass education, *Comparative Education Review* 29, no. 2 (May): 145–70.

Bulkley, Katrina and Jennifer Fisler. 2003 A decade of charter Schools: From theory to practice, *Educational Policy* 17: 317–42.

Bush, George W. 2000. Gov. George W. Bush's plans for education in America, *Phi Delta Kappan* 82, no. 2 (October): 122–25.

Burrian-Fitzgerald, Marisa and Debbi Harris. 2004. Teacher recruitment and teacher quality: Are charter schools different? Education Policy Center at MSU. East Lansing, MI. http://education.msu.edu/epc/forms/Policy-and-research-Reports/report20.pdf (accessed June 10, 2013).

Bourdieu, Pierre. 1998. *Acts of resistance: Against the tyranny of the market.* Trans. Richard Nice. New York, NY: New Press.

Chomsky, Noam. 1992. *Deterring democracy.* New York, NY: Hill and Wang.

Collinson, Vivienne. 2012. Exemplary teachers: teaching for intellectual freedom. *Pedagogies: An International Journal* 7, no. 2: 101–14.

Couldry, Nick. 2010. *Why voice matters: Culture and politics after neoliberalism.* London, UK:Sage Publications.

Dean, Jodi. 2009. *Democracy and other neoliberal fantasies: Communicative capitalism and left politics.* Durham, NC: Duke University Press.

Denord, Francois. 2009. French neoliberalism and its divisions: From the Colloque Walter Lippmann to the Fifth Republic. In *Road from Mont Pelerin: The making of the neoliberal thought collective.* Ed. Phillip Mirowski and Dieter Plehwe Cambridge, MA: Harvard University Press.

Exstrom, Michelle. 2012. Teaching in charter schools. *National Conference of State Legislatures.* (July). http://www.ncsl.org/documents/educ/teachingincharterschools.pdf (accessed August 27, 2013).

Freire, Paulo. 1998. *Pedagogy of freedom: Ethics, democracy, and civic courage.* Lanham,MD: Rowman & Littlefield Publishers.

General Assembly. 1948. Universal Declaration of Human Rights. New York: United Nations.

George, Susan. 1999. *A short history of neo-liberalism: Twenty years of elite economics and emerging opportunities for structural change.* Bangkok: Conference on Economic Sovereignty in a Globalising World. http://www.tni.org/article/short-history-neoliberalism (accessed June 20, 2013).

Giddens, Anthony.2000. *The Third Way and its critics.* Cambridge, UK: Polity Press.

Gordon, Liz and Geoff Whitty. 1997. Giving the 'Hidden Hand' a helping hand? The rhetoric and reality of neoliberal education reform in England and New Zealand, *Comparative Education* 33, no. 3: 453–67.

Gross, Neil, Thomas Medvetz, and Rupert Russell. 2011. The contemporary American conservative movement. *Annual Review of Sociology.* 325–54.

Gutman, Amy. 2007. Democracy. In *A companion to contemporary political philosophy* Ed. Robert E. Goodin, Philip Pettit, and Thomas Pogge. 521–31. Malden, MA: Blackwell Publishing.

ul-Haque, Irfan. 2004. *Globalization, neoliberalism and labour.* Geneva: United Nations Conference on Trade and Development.

Harvey, David. 2007. *Brief history of neoliberalism.* Oxford, UK: Oxford University Press.

Hayek, Friedrich A. 1960. *The constitution of liberty.* Chicago, IL: University of Chicago Press.

Henig, Jeffrey R. 2001. *Rethinking school choice: Limits of the market metaphor.* Princeton, NJ: Princeton University Press.

Hill, Dave. 2007. Educational perversion and global neoliberalism. In *Neoliberalism and education reform*. Ed. E. Wayne Ross and Rich Gibson, 107–44. Cresskill, NJ: Hampton Press.

HISD. 2013. Energy Institute High School officially opens today. *HISD News Blog* August 14. http://blogs.houstonisd.org/news/2013/08/14/energy-institute-high-school-officially-opens-today/ (accessed August 28, 2013)

Hursh, David. 2007a. Assessing No Child Left Behind and the rise of neoliberal education policies, *American Educational Research Journal* 44, no. 3 (September): 493–518.

———. 2007b. Marketing education: The rise of standardized testing, accountability, competition, and markets in public education, In *Neoliberalism and education reform*. Ed. E. Wayne Ross and Rich Gibson, 15–34. Cresskill, NJ: Hampton Press.

Hyslop-Margison, Emery J. and Alan M. Sears. 2006. *Neo-Liberalism, globalization and human capital learning: Reclaiming education for democratic citizenship*. Dortrecht, NL: Springer.

Keynes, John M. 1951. *The General theory of employment, interest and money*. London, UK: Macmillan and Co.

Lehning, Percy B. 2009. *John Rawls: An introduction*. Cambridge, UK: Cambridge University Press.

Lippman, Walter. 1944. *The Good Society*. New York: Grosset & Dunlap. (Orig pub. 1938).

Mathis, William J. 2010. *The 'Common Core' standards initiative: An effective reform tool?* Education and the Public Interest Center & Education Policy Unit.. Boulder, CO: http://nepc.colorado.edu/files/PB-NatStans-Mathis.pdf (accessed July 24, 2013).

MacGregor, Susanne. 2005. The welfare state and neoliberalism. In *Neoliberalism: A critical reader,* Eds. Alfredo Saad-Filho and Deborah Johnston, 142–48. London, UK: Pluto Press.

McDermott, Kathryn A. and Kysa Nygreen. 2013. Educational new paternalism: Human capital, cultural capital, and the politics of equal opportunity. *Peabody Journal of Education* 88: 84–97.

Mill, John S. 1991. *On liberty and other essays*. Oxford, UK: Oxford University Press.

Mont Pelerin Society. About MPS. https://www.montpelerin.org/montpelerin/mpsAbout.html (accessed July 21, 2013).

Morel, Nathalie, Bruno Palier, and Joakim Palme. 2011. Beyond the welfare state as we knew it? In *Towards a social investment welfare state?: Ideas, policies and challenges*. Eds. Nathalie Morel, Bruno Palier, and Joakim Palme, 16–45. Bristol, UK: Policy Press.

Morse, Jane Fowler. 2001. Intellectual freedom and economic sufficiency as educational entitlements. *Studies in Philosophy and Education* 20: 201–11.

Munck, Ronaldo. 2005. Neoliberalism and politics, and the politics of neoliberalism. In *Neoliberalism: A critical reader,* Eds. Alfredo Saad-Filho and Deborah Johnston, 60–69. London, UK: Pluto Press.

Nash-Wood, Mary. 2012. Racial disparity evident in magnet schools. *Shreveport Times.* December 16.

Noddings, Nel. 2005. What does it mean to educate the whole child? *Educational Leadership* (September): 8–13.

Onosko, Joe. 2011. Race to the Top leaves children and future citizens behind: The devastating effects of centralization, standardization, and high stakes accountability, *Democracy & Education* 19, no. 2: 1–11.

Quinton, Anthony and Jane Norton. 2007. Conservatism. In *A companion to contemporary political philosophy.* 2nd ed. Ed. Robert Goodin, Philip Pettit, and Thomas Pogge. 285–311. Malden, MA: Blackwell Publishing.

Raffer, Kunibert. 2011. Neoliberal capitalism: A time warp backwards to capitalism's origins? *Forum for Social Economics* 40, no. 1: 41–62.

Rawls, John. 1971. *A theory of justice.* Cambridge, MA: Harvard University Press.

Richardson, James L. 2001. *Contending liberalisms in world politics: Ideology & power.* Boulder, CO: Lynne Rienner Publisher.

Rust, Val D. and W. James Jacob. 2005. Globalisation and educational policy shifts. In *International handbook on globalization, education and policy research: Global pedagogies and policies.* Ed. Joseph Zajda et al. 235–52. Dordrecht, NL: Springer.

Ryan, Alan. 1993. Liberalism, In *A companion to contemporary political philosophy.* Eds. Robert E. Goodin and Phillip Pettit. Oxford, UK: Blackwell Publishers.

Sears, Allan M. 2003. *Retooling the mind factory: Education in a lean state.* Toronto, ON: Broadview Press.

Simon, Stephanie. 2013. Class struggle—how charter schools get students they want. *Reuters Special Report* February 15. http://www.reuters.com/article/2013/02/15/us-usa-charters -admissions-idUSBRE91E0HF20130215 (accessed July 12, 2013).

Thorsen, Dag Einar. 2011. The neoliberal challenge. *Contemporary readings in law and social justice* 2, no. 2: 188–214.

Waldron, Jeremy. 1987. Theoretical foundations of liberalism. *Philosophical Quarterly* 37, no. 147: 127–50.

Westheimer, Joel. 2010. No child left thinking: Democracy at risk in Canada's schools. *Education Canada* 50, no. 2 (Spring): 5–8.

Woods, Phillip A., Carl Bagley and Ron Glatter. 1998. *School choice and competition: Markets in the public interest.* London, UK: Falmer Press.

Wrigley, Terry. 2009. Rethinking education in the era of globalization. In *Contesting neoliberal education: Public resistance and collective advance*, Ed. Dave Hill, 61–82. New York, NY: Routledge.

Zafirovski, Milan. 2007. *Liberal modernity and its adversaries: Freedom, liberalism and anti-liberalism in the 21st century.* Leiden, NL: Koninklijke Brill NV.

Part Two

Media, Access, and Property

Journalism for Social Justice
Discussing the Alternative Media and Intellectual Freedom

Susan Forde

The notion of intellectual freedom is one which is central to the work of alternative media practitioners—indeed, they might see it as their core purpose due to their demonstrated commitment to providing the public with a broad range of information and context to news and current affairs that (they believe) the public cannot receive elsewhere (Atton & Hamilton, 2008; Forde, 2011). Much of the literature surrounding the notion of 'intellectual freedom' is centred around librarianship, primarily focusing on the importance of removing censorship, providing public access to a broad range of views, and not restricting thought or expression. Dresang summarises:

> *Intellectual freedom as a concept in librarianship means freedom to think or believe what one will, freedom to express one's thoughts and beliefs in unrestricted manners and means, and freedom to access information and ideas regardless of the content or viewpoints of the author(s) or the age, background, or beliefs of the receiver. Intellectual freedom is closely allied with the U.S. brand of democracy, which depends upon the rule of an informed citizenry that is able to deal with conflicting ideas and ultimately to make wise choices.* (2006, 169–170)

Certainly, the principles expressed here by Dresang draw essential connections, which media scholars also draw, between democracy and intellectual freedom. The US Office for Intellectual Freedom notes that 'citizens must also be able to take part in the formation of public opinion by engaging in vigorous and wide-ranging debate on controversial matters' (2010, xvii). What is key in this discussion for alternative, independent and community media workers—and what occupies the bulk of this chapter—is the concern about the connections between intellectual freedom, an 'informed citizenry', the ability of the citizenry to actually *engage (participate)* in the deliberations and debates, and the connection between these issues and a highly function-ing democracy. This is at the heart of the work that alternative media schol-ars do—we investigate the underpinnings, the practices, and motivations of alternative media work in order to develop arguments around its importance to democracy and an informed public. To that end, this chapter will exam-ine the increasingly important role that alternative and community media forms are playing in developing an open public sphere; in creating spaces for marginalised voices; and in providing a forum for views and opinions that do not receive attention from more mainstream outlets. In this, they have an incredible amount in common with those who stretch for broad-ranging intellectual freedom within our society.

Before examining this intersection, it is important to establish parame-ters for this discussion. Most alternative and community media scholars are regularly asked—what do you mean by 'alternative media'? Alternative to what? Indeed, one of the key scholars in our field John H. Downing rejects the term 'alternative' as an oxymoron because, at some point, everything is alternative to something else (2001, ix). He prefers the term "radical media" to describe the media of social movements and social change which will also be included in this discussion here. Nevertheless, I intend to stick with the term 'alternative' because I believe convention establishes a broad understanding for what that term means. It encompasses radical, community, grassroots, in-dependent, citizens' media forms—all of them variously committed to their own, and their audiences', intellectual freedom. Indeed, if we consider the aims of publications such as Australia's independently owned news maga-zine *The Monthly* (Warhaft, 2006), and the Australian-based but global online alternative publication *Eureka Street* (Cranitch, 2006), they describe a journal-ism which focuses on providing news and information relevant to the needs of the community members; 'to engage these members in public discussion, and to contribute to their social and political empowerment' (Jankowski 2003, 4). In that, they have everything in common with notions of creating an informed citizenry and of giving that cohort the opportunity to engage in wide-ranging debate in the public sphere about civic issues.

Alternative and community media

I will intersperse the terms 'alternative' and 'community' throughout this work, as both describe sub-sections of the media and journalism that form the backbone of this essay. Numerous scholars have made useful attempts at defining the sector (for example, Atton 2002; Atton & Hamilton 2008; Rodriguez

2001; Downing 1984 and 2001; Couldry & Curran 2003; Howley 2010; Kidd and Rodriguez 2010), and all generally agree that while there are differences between the structure, format and *raison d'etre* of many of these outlets, they have traits in common (Forde 2011). Independent and alternative media are often characterised by their reliance on strong notions of social responsibility (Atton 2003, 267) and their journalists generally demonstrate stronger commitment to the idealistic norms of journalism than their mainstream counterparts (Forde 1997a). Their work is consistent with Jankowski's definition of 'community' media, focusing on providing news and information relevant to the needs of the community members; 'to engage these members in public discussion, and to contribute to their social and political empowerment' (Jankowski 2003, 4). Rodriguez refers to citizens' media which sees localised media outlets integrated into communities, with audience members participating in production of content for their (often troubled) community members; Atton refers to the not-for-profit, often amateur 'alternative' media; Downing deals specifically with politicised radical media which usually exists within social movements, and indeed, forms their 'lifeblood' (see also D'Adamo, 2006 for a practitioner's perspective on this). As Howley reinforces, community media serve as "an exceptional vehicle to explore the way local populations create media texts, practices and institutions to serve their distinctive needs and interests" (2010, 3). Clemencia Rodriguez argues that alternative media forms, what she calls 'citizen's media', need to be defined by what they *are*, not by what they *are not* (Rodriguez 2001); and says the terms 'community media, alternative media, autonomous media and radical media all fit within the broad definition of 'citizens' media' (Rodriguez 2010, 132). Rodriguez overwhelmingly focuses on the *processes* of participation, organisation, and connection between people as the key defining characteristic of citizens' media, and does not really address 'what it is responding to'—more it is, a consideration of the *mediations* that occur, rather than the media itself (2003,190). Research conducted with colleagues at Griffith University found similarly—the processes of creating content, the creation of community that occurred in doing this, was just as important (if not more) than the actual content being produced (Meadows, Forde, Ewart, Foxwell 2007). In line with the descriptions and definitions above, we can perhaps conclude with the recognition that alternative and community media are examples of a consistent and long-serving 'disruption' to media power and by extension, to existing social and economic power.

Alternative journalism and freedom of expression

The specific journalistic practices of such alternative media outlets can also be considered as part of this discussion. It is here, within the practices of the journalists, that the intersections with intellectual freedom are expressed daily. Research conducted in the 1990s found independent press journalists self-reported that they undertook their duties for the higher ideals of autonomy, the chance to help people, and editorial freedom rather than the superficial concerns expressed by mainstream journalists such as the pay, fringe benefits, the chance to 'get ahead' and job security (Henningham 1996, 211) and (Forde 1997b). Furthermore, alternative media journalists are more committed to the active public and 'citizens' form of their craft in that Australian independent news journalists nominate 'providing context to the news', 'motivating the public' and 'giving a voice to the voiceless' as their primary journalistic aims (Forde 1997a, 118). Again here, connections with the importance of intellectual freedom in both the librarianship context and the broader social context is evident—Dresang refers to the tension between what we might term 'absolute' intellectual freedom and 'conditional' intellectual freedom which takes account of the impact of the published word on marginalised and oppressed groups. In essence, absolute intellectual freedom defends the right of anyone to express their view, regardless of the impact of that view on others. A more conditional intellectual freedom—which we certainly see in evidence in the anti-racist, anti-sexist, equal opportunity alternative media suggests 'that there might be limitations to that principle when it does not encompass respect for marginalized social groups. A tension, over the years, for the in-library practice of intellectual freedom has arisen from conflicting social values' (Dresang 2006, 170-171). In contrast, the Office for Intellectual Freedom finds that intellectual freedom 'implies a circle, and that circle is broken if either freedom of expression or access to ideas is stifled (2010, xvii).

Dresang's summary, however, is reflected in alternative media's realisation of 'intellectual freedom'. John Downing's classic study for example, *Radical Media*, which provides the foundation for much contemporary analysis of alternative and community media forms, finds that many forms of radical media do not encourage increased freedom for media. Far left political media, such as the socialist publications, demand allegiance to the Party and its key doctrines. So for many radical media editors and journalists, their intellectual freedom is quite limited to working within the boundaries set by a socialist ideological framework (Downing 1984). We may argue they are no more constrained than the journalist writing for a commercial, 'professional' news organisation—but certainly, there is evidence that their political expression and their angle on stories and comments is significantly dependent upon the view of the Party. To that end, Downing suggests for radical media to be more representative—for our purposes, to be more 'intellectually free'—they should ensure the following conditions apply to their work (1984, 17). Chris Atton repeats these conditions in his important and foundational 2002 work, *Alternative Media* (2002, 20):

1. the importance of encouraging contributions from as many interested parties as possible, in order to emphasise the 'multiple realities' of social life (oppression, political cultures, economic situations);
2. that radical media, while they may be partisan, should never become a tool of a party or intelligentsia;
3. that radical media at their most creative and socially significant privilege movements over institutions
4. that within the organisation of radical media there appears an emphasis on prefigurative politics

Downing's analysis, in essence, focuses on radical media's connections to social movements which are 'the lifeblood of these media, and they are the movements' oxygen' (2001, 390). This allows Downing's work to ignore forms of alternative media not connected to a particular social movement— he excludes music fanzines, for example; political opinion blogs; individual websites espousing personal opinions, etc. The late-American intellectual and author Gore Vidal offers a useful perspective on the term 'radical' used widely by Downing, drawing connections between 'radicalism', 'liberalism' and politics and concluding that the information imparted to the public was necessarily limited, and 'stifled':

> *The word 'radical' derives from the Latin word for root. Therefore, if you want to get to the root of anything you must be radical. It is no accident that the word has now been totally demonized by our masters, and no one in politics dares even use the word favourably, much less track any problem to its root. But then a ruling class that was able to demonize the word 'liberal' in the past ten years is a master at controlling—indeed stifling—any criticism of itself. 'Liberal' comes from the Latin liberalis, which means pertaining to a free man. In politics, to be liberal is to want to extend democracy through change and reform. One can see why that word had to be erased from our political lexicon. (Vidal, 1992)*

News media researcher Thomas Patterson (1992) examines this notion of freedom within the media in more detail, although his focus is on the mainstream rather than the alternative media. His work is important to this study, however, as he draws essential conclusions about what 'freedom of the press', or 'freedom of expression' really means in the news media context. Patterson's work looks for signs of diversity in news coverage in countries which apparently had a high level of press freedom—freedom of expression, of access, of voice. Patterson found that more than two-thirds of journalists defined freedom of expression in terms of their own, and their news organisations' rights rather than the public's right to diverse information which reflected a narrow professionalism which did not take account of journalists' place in the larger democratic scheme (1992, 15).

Patterson also finds evidence that increased professionalism has caused greater homogeneity in news content. He blames professionalism for the failure of the news media to create a diverse marketplace of ideas—in his survey, United States journalists ranked highest on the professionalism index (determined by their attitudes to objectivity, impartiality, neutrality) and also ranked lowest on the diversity index (1992, 9). His international study of professional values across a range of countries found that, in the nations such as the United States, 'the same news stories are highlighted each day by the great majority of newspaper and broadcast organizations from coast to coast' (1992, 4). Patterson believes this narrowness can be attributed directly to the requirement for 'professional and objective' journalism, which forces news reporting to be driven increasingly by events rather than issues. Relatively minor editorial decisions such as which facts and events are more important do not constitute diversity of information, and are 'a far cry from a competitive marketplace of ideas' (1992, 4). Zelizer notes that the 'sixth sense' or 'nose for news' that most journalists use as a way of defining their work is a leading reference point for the industry (2005, 68) but Patterson interprets this as common definition of news, developed out of professional training and experience which again, sees the same top stories appearing each day across a huge range of media outlets (1992, 4). Gurevitch and Blumler further argue that adherence to professional definitions of news values act as a powerful force for conformity and ensure journalists all arrive at the same decision when considering—'What is the most significant news today?' (1990, 282) (Zhong and Newhagen, 2009).

I.F. Stone, a United States journalist who established the successful alternative publication *I.F. Stone's Weekly* in 1953, wrote of the mainstream media:

> The fault I find with most American newspapers is not the absence of dissent. It is the absence of news. With a dozen or so honourable exceptions, most American newspapers carry very little news. Their main concern is advertising. The main interest of our society is merchandising. All the so-called communications industries are primarily concerned not with communications, but with selling. . . . Most owners of newspapers are businessmen, not newspapermen. The news is something which fills the spaces left over by the advertisers. The average publisher is not only hostile to dissenting opinion, he is suspicious of any opinion likely to antagonize any reader or consumer. (Johnson 1971, 6)

This is particularly relevant to isolated and marginalized communities—". . . if we have been effectively shut out from official public communication, if we are women, First Nations, refugees, children, undocumented workers, who is there

who has any sense of obligation to listen to us, to the specifics of our experience, to our framing of the world?" (Downing 2007). The American Library
Association Office for Intellectual Freedom notes that providing "intellectual
freedom" to immigrants is the only way to provide them with information
that they require to become productive members of society (2010, xvii). Community media has fulfilled this role in the life of immigrants, refugees ad
asylum seekers for some time—not just in providing new arrivals with news
of their home country, but more specifically providing community-building
and networking opportunities for immigrants to create their own important
social connections in their new country, usually with others who have mi-
grated before them. There is also a strong recognition that the ability of community media—particularly community radio—to provide essential service
information to immigrants in their native language is key to the successful
settlement of immigrants and refugees (Forde, Foxwell, Meadows 2009). It is
also key to their ongoing sense of social well-being and general 'satisfaction'
with life (Meadows and Foxwell 2011).

A consideration of the alternative media and freedom of expression, then,
suggests intellectual freedom within the alternative media sector is not absolute (particularly in the radical political sections of the alternative media).
There is also evidence here which, predictably, proves that in countries where
freedom of expression is assumed to be at a near-ideal level—for example, in
advanced democracies such as the United States and the United Kingdom, in
fact there is very little diversity in the breadth of views presented or in the
actual definition of 'what is news' in those countries leading to significant
homogeneity of news and information. Finally, this part of the discussion
suggests that isolated and marginalised groups are most likely to suffer from
this 'shutting out' from official public communication due to the narrow definitions of news—and it is here that community media in particular is picking
up the ball and properly representing or giving voice to these communities.
It is important to consider this final point in more detail, as it is in their social
justice role that the alternative media best demonstrate their commitment
to more completely informing the citizenry, and to creating a broader, more
inclusive public sphere.

Alternative journalism and its public role

Librarian scholar Emily Knox, fittingly notes that information professionals around the world 'approach intellectual freedom as a social justice issue' (2011, 49). And so it is with alternative media and their journalists—their
overwhelming commitment to covering the news they see fit, to providing
context to news already in the mainstream, and providing a voice for the marginalized, the downtrodden (Downing 2003) is related to their foundational

commitment to social justice. If intellectual freedom is inexorably tied to freedom of access to information, then it is a core calling of the alternative journalist. One alternative media worker, Jessica Lee from the successful New York alternative newspaper *The Indypendent*, explained:

> *I consider myself a journalist and I guess from certain perspectives you could consider what we do as social justice journalism or activist journalism. Just because we give regular people, people in the grassroots movements more of a voice in our articles than you might see in a different publication.* (personal interview, 2009)

The Council of Europe clarified in a 2009 declaration that the key motivation and rationale for the further development of community media in the European Union was due to the proven role the sector could play in improving social cohesion and intercultural dialogue (Council of Europe 2009) and see also (Lewis 2008). This section of the chapter turns to the evidence from alternative journalists which bears out their commitment to social justice and their perception of their role as a conduit to provide the public with information they would otherwise not have access to through more mainstream media outlets. The evidence presented here is based on 19 qualitative interviews with alternative media journalists from Australia, the United States and the United Kingdom.[1] The interviews usually lasted about an hour, and recordings were transcribed and evaluated through the qualitative software program NVivo. Through this analysis, I have presented data elsewhere (Forde 2011) which investigates the role of the alternative journalist in the contemporary media landscape in more detail. For the purposes of this work, I wish to focus specifically on that evidence from the journalists which emphasizes a commitment to 'freedom of information', to social justice, to 'filling the gaps' of the mainstream all which point to an overriding connection with the essence of intellectual freedom. There is a juncture where I believe alternative media and the absolute form of intellectual freedom depart, and I will discuss this in the closing section of this chapter.

In the mid to late 1990s, mainstream and alternative journalists' attitudes to their role in society were compared. The two groups shared several broad perceptions of their role, notably that their job was to 'uncover and investigate problems' and to 'impart information to others'. However, a range of more proactive roles which were presented to both sets of journalists began

---

1   Personal interviews were carried out with journalists in Australia, the United States and the United Kingdom throughout 2009 and 2010 as part of a project called 'Rethinking Journalism'. Data from some of these interviews is quoted in sections of this chapter and is presented in more detail in the author's monograph, 'Challenging the News: The Journalism of Alternative & Community Media' (Palgrave Macmillan, 2011).

to highlight the differences between the two cohorts. The aspects of 'influencing the public', 'influencing public policy decisions' and 'championing particular values and ideas' were rated as much more important by alternative journalists. More than three-quarters of the independent press sample felt it was either very or quite important to influence the public, where only 49 percent of the mainstream sample considered this important. Overall, 10 years ago alternative press journalists nominated that 'providing an alternative view', 'contextualising the news', 'motivating audiences and providing access for audiences' and 'balancing the mainstream' were key themes of their work. In 2010, those themes still resonate although the general description to 'provide an alternative view' is now, through the qualitative data, a little more complete in its form as 'covering stories others won't cover'. Importantly, a new theme has emerged which was previously not nominated by either mainstream or alternative journalists—which is to provide local news to a local audience. This was also identified by both community broadcasting volunteers and journalists; and community broadcasting audiences as a key function of, particularly, community radio news (Meadows et al 2007). This theme also re-occurred in discussions about news values.

It was expected that those publications primarily run to provide investigative journalism, and publications such as the UK's *The Spark* ethical quarterly would identify their overarching role to provide longer-form journalism. However, alternative journalists nominated this as their role even when they were providing daily journalism, such as at Australia's *crikey.com*. Proprietor and journalist Eric Beecher refers to the publication's role as looking 'under the bonnet' (i.e., under the hood) of Australian politics to get the story behind the story. Similarly, Jeff Clarke at Northern California Public Broadcasting in the USA, which runs daily news and current affairs programming, identifies a key difference between what his organisation does, and what the mainstream journalists do that he worked with more than 30 years ago as a broadcaster for commercial radio and television, and prior to that with the American Forces Radio & Television service:

> *I think the real essence and the real difference between independent journalists, public broadcasting journalists and the mainstream media is there are different levels of depth and quality in the arena that independent journalists are handling, versus the what I would call the 'mile-wide and inch-deep' coverage that we get in the normal mainstream media. Both have a purpose but I think where we have excelled in the public broadcasting landscape has been to really provide a level of intelligent information that really covers the ground of a specific story or issue, or conflict in a way that allows people to make up their own minds . . . people want to get behind the headline and really see the depth of story.*
> (personal interview, 2010)

Carol Pierson, from the US National Federation for Community Broadcasters notes that individual stations' abilities to carry out good, in-depth alternative journalism depends entirely on their resources, but it was an overarching goal of most of the stations to provide contextualised news and deeper analysis as much as they could:

> . . . *we were definitely looking at more [substantial] stories than what a lot of the commercial stations were covering, which tends to be a lot of accidents and crime and those kinds of stories. So we were looking at stories that were about issues that made a big difference in people's lives . . . we also wanted to do longer pieces and more in-depth reporting so we gave people more time to work on stories.* (personal interview, 2009)

The 'more time' factor is an issue, and is one that is perhaps an advantage of alternative journalism that needs to be recognised. Many mainstream journalists, given similar circumstances, might also be able to write long-form, investigative journalism. The reality is however, that the chances of mainstream media organisations investing time in journalists producing one strong story a week; or perhaps taking several weeks or even months to work on a significant investigative piece is dwindling. Newsrooms are being downsized all over the world and there is irrefutable evidence that mainstream organisations—particularly commercial ones—no longer see the economic benefit in investigative journalists delving 'behind the story'. In fact, the opposite is the case with demand increasing, every day, for more news, more quickly, due to the insatiable appetite and unlimited news hole of news websites (Paterson 2006; Barker 2009; Johnston and Forde 2009; Gawenda and Muller, 2009; Australian Press Council 2008). So while it may not be the 'fault' of mainstream journalists that they are not doing more in-depth journalism, which alternative journalists strongly identify as one of their key roles in society, it is certainly the case that this content that alternative journalists are producing is becoming more important as mainstream newsrooms scale down even further and journalists become 'disseminators' rather than 'gatherers' of original news (Barker, 2009).

In particular, when speaking about their 'motivations' for what they do the large majority of alternative journalists put their work in the context of what I have termed 'enhancing journalism and democracy'. Indeed, many of the journalists identified that they were not, and could never be, in the business for the money or the dependable wage—but more that most people working in the alternative journalism industry were doing so out of a sense of the potential for social change. Carlton Carl from the *Texas Observer,* and Carol Pierson from US community broadcasting's representative body the National Federation of Community Broadcasters illustrate:

> *. . . everyone draws a salary, they're not huge salaries. One certainly wouldn't go to work for the* Texas Observer *to get rich and it's unlikely that anybody would ever go to work for the* Texas Observer *if they didn't share our mission for enhancing equality and justice and so forth [Carl].* (personal interview, 2009)

> *Well I would say that it's not so much the good pay that it's much more a real dedication to getting information that's important to people so they can act responsibly in a democracy and have an insight into what's going on [Pierson].* (personal interview, 2010)

Peter Barr from community station RTR in Perth, Australia just wants to 'pay my rent and buy some fruit' and if he can do that, he will continue to work in his position at RTR because he would rather be just getting by, financially, than doing well and feel 'stifled and bored' (personal interview, 2009).

When Professor John Henningham conducted the first national survey of Australian journalists in the early 1990s, he applied a long-tested quantitative survey to his sample of more than 1000 journalists which replicated work by David Weaver and Cleve Wilhoit in the United States (1986; 1991; 1994; 1996; and Weaver et al 2003). One of the questions he asked was designed to test journalists' commitment to the public service ideals of journalism, with a series of questions which probed respondents about why they chose journalism as a career. Most nominated their ability at writing as the primary reason for becoming journalists, while issues related to the glamour and excitement of journalism were second most important. Less than four percent of journalists nominated the desire to serve the public (tested by categories such as 'finding the truth', 'putting things right' etc) as an important reason for entering journalism (1996, 210). Henningham concluded: 'Hence, a strongly service-oriented notion of journalism was not found among Australian journalists . . . ' (1996, 210). The responses of alternative journalists lay in direct contrast, as alternative press journalists were found to be significantly more committed to the public role of journalism—to serving the public interest, influencing public policy through information and providing background and context to information in the public arena. In 2009 and 2010, those values held true and perhaps appeared stronger through these qualitative interviews across three continents than they did through the original Australian-based quantitative survey. Anderson found similarly in her study of information-based programming on 4ZzZ community radio in Brisbane, Australia that the values of agitating for action, educating audiences, and organising communities of like-minded people were key roles of some parts of the community radio sector (2005).

This study reinforces that alternative journalists see their primary role as providing context and depth to information already (perhaps cursorily) available in the public sphere; and to both educate *audiences* about issues and campaigns, and potential *contributors* on the practices of alternative journalism. Most importantly, these functions are underpinned by a driving desire to motivate audiences to participate—whether in demonstrations, community life, or other forms of political action. It represents an "imagining" of journalism as a key player in facilitating the public's involvement in democracy, in a variety of ways.

Concluding thoughts: Alternative media, democracy and intellectual freedom

The evidence from alternative journalists working in a range of alternative and independent media outlets suggests a number of areas where we might say alternative media is intersecting with the core meaning of intellectual freedom. Firstly, alternative journalists are undoubtedly highly committed to providing the public with access to information they might not otherwise find or hear about. To be specific, they see it as one of their key roles to uncover information not currently covered by mainstream commercial or publicly funded outlets—to give air to stories that have so far remained hidden. I refer to this as the alternative journalists' motivation to uncover "the scoop", a huge investigative story that is broken by an independent outlet. On another level, they are committed to following the news agenda of larger, mainstream outlets with a purpose of delivering information and context that they consider has not yet received the air-time it deserves. That is, they believe strongly in "filling the gaps" left by the mainstream media, in providing the behind-the-scenes story about government policy, perhaps covering a story about more illegal boat arrivals from the perspective of the refugee, rather than the government which is usually mouthing concerns they perceive to exist in the community at large.

Again, I see this as a demonstration from the alternative media that their concern is to provide access to information for the public—to enhance democracy by widening the public sphere of debate. Importantly, research into community media audiences makes a third point—not only are alternative media committed to providing access to information, but one of their key functions is to provide access (itself) so that people feel free to participate in media production thereby dissolving the audience-producer boundary. Through their informal structures and the nature of the organisation as rooted in the community, ordinary audience members feel welcome and able to participate in media production, to ring the station and talk to the announcer, to offer input to programming—to assist in the creation of community through their involvement in the community media outlet (Meadows, Forde, Foxwell, Ewart 2007). I believe their contribution to dissolving the audience-producer boundary is further evidence of the role alternative and community media are playing in delivering key aspects of intellectual freedom—they are, without doubt, giving voice to voices otherwise unheard (and importantly, people are listening).

The American Library Association reports that intellectual freedom is (and I will cite at length here, as this is a key concluding thought):

> . . . the right to seek and receive information from all points of view, without restriction, even those ideas which might be highly controversial or offensive to others. As a personal liberty, intellectual freedom forms the foundation of our democracy. It is an essential part of government by the people. The right to vote is not enough—we also must be able to take part in forming public opinion by engaging in open and vigorous debate on controversial matters. (1999, 1)

This description echoes that provided by Dresang in the opening comments of this chapter, tying the notion of intellectual freedom to the US First Amendment, core to the protection of individual liberty and right to freedom of expression. In many countries, however—and in the alternative media—there is a caveat on freedom of expression, on intellectual freedom. It is that every citizen should have the right to express themselves freely and to be heard but that this should occur within a context which is not designed to incite hatred against particular groups in society; or which is designed to deliberately misinform. In essence, the intellectual freedom that I assess is being practiced by alternative journalists is not so much rooted in an absolute right to say whatever they think, regardless of the consequences—but more, to deliver news, opinion and analysis which is based in truth and which is gathered out of a genuine desire to *improve* the quality and breadth of discourse in the public sphere. While the industry is diverse, the research evidence suggests this truth-seeking mission and the overarching motivation to *improve* public sphere debate is central to our analysis of how alternative media conceptualises and carries out 'intellectual freedom'.

References

American Libraries Association. 1999. Why Intellectual Freedom. *American Libraries* 30, no. 6: 1–12.

Anderson, Heather. 2005. Agitate Educate Organise. The roles of information-based programming on 4ZzZ. *3CMedia* 1: 58–72.

Atton, Chris. 2003. What is Alternative Journalism? *Journalism* 4, no. 3: 267–272.

———. 2002. *Alternative Media*, London, UK: Sage.

Atton, Chris and James F. Hamilton. 2008. *Alternative Journalism*, London, UK: Sage.

Australian Press Council. 2008. *State of the News Print Media in Australia Report*, http://www.presscouncil.org.au/uploads/52321/state-of-the -news-print-media-2007.pdf (accessed February 2, 2009).

Barker, Geoffrey. 2009. The crumbling estate. *Griffith Review* 25: 117–123.

Couldry, Nick and James Curran. 2003. The paradox of media power. In *Contesting Media Power: Alternative Media in a Networked World*, Lanham, MD: Rowan & Littlefield.

Council of Europe. 2009. *Declaration of the Committee of Ministers on the Role of Community Media in Promoting Social Cohesion and Intercultural Dialogue,* Accessed February 11, 2009. https://wcd.coe.int/ ViewDoc.jsp?id=1409919

Cranitch, Tom. 2006. *Personal interview with the author,* recorded June 6.

D'Adamo, Chuck. 2006. Intellectual Freedom and Media Independence: Some Alternative Press History. *Library Juice Concentrate,* ed. Rory Litwin, 107–118. Duluth, MN: Library Juice Press.

Dresang, Eliza. T. 2006. Intellectual freedom and libraries: Complexity and change in the twenty-first-century digital environment. *Library Quarterly,* 76 no. 2: 169–192.

Downing, John. 2007. Grassroots Media: Establishing priorities for the years ahead. *Global Media Journal* (Australian edition), 1 no. 1. http://www.commarts.uws.edu.au/gmjau/iss1_2007/pdf/ HC_FINAL_John%20Downing.pdf [Accessed April 30, 2010].

———. 2003. Audiences and readers of alternative media: The absent lure of the virtually unknown, *Media, Culture & Society* 25, no.5: 625–645.

———. 2001. *Radical Media: Rebellious Communication and Social Movements,* Sage: Thousand Oaks, CA.

———. 1984. *Radical Media: The Political Experience of Alternative Communication,* Boston: South End Press.

Forde, Susan. 2011. *Challenging the News: The Journalism of Alternative and Independent Media,* London: Palgrave Macmillan,.

———. 1997a. A descriptive look at the public role of the Australian independent alternative press. *AsiaPacific Media Educator* 3): 118–130.

———. 1997b. Characteristics and ethical values of Australia's independent press Journalists. *Australian Studies in Journalism* 6: 104–126.

Forde, Susan, Foxwell, Kerry, and Michael Meadows. 2009. *Developing Dialogues: Indigenous and ethnic community broadcasting in Australia,* Bristol, UK: Intellect.

Gawenda, Michael and Denis Muller. 2009. The Black Saturday bushfires: How the media covered Australia's worst peace-time disaster. *Centre for Advanced Journalism, University of Melbourne.* http://caj.unimelb.edu.au/ sites/caj.unimelb.edu.au/files/executive-summary-how-the-media.pdf (accessed March 12, 2010).

Gurevitch, Michael and Jay G. Blumler. 1990. Political communication systems and democratic values. In *Democracy and the Mass Media,* ed. Judith Lichtenberg, Cambridge, UK: Cambridge University Press.

Henningham, John P. 1996. Australian journalists' professional and ethical values. *Journalism and Mass Communication Quarterly* 73, no. 1: 206–218.

Howley, Kevin. 2010. Introduction. In *Understanding Community Media,* edited by Kevin Howley, Los Angeles, CA: Sage.

Jankowski, Nicholas W. 2003. Community Media Research: A quest for theoretically-grounded models. *Javnost* 10, no. 1: 1–9.

Johnson, Michael L. 1971.*The New Journalism: The Underground Press, the Artists of Nonfiction, and Changes in the Established Media,* Lawrence, KS: University Press of Kansas.

Johnston, Jane and Susan Forde. 2009. "Not wrong for long": The role and penetration of news wire agencies in the 24/7 news media landscape," *Global Media Journal* Australian Edition 3 no. 2: http://www.commarts.uws.edu.au/gmjau/2009_3_2_toc.html (accessed April 30 2010.

Kidd, Dorothy and Clemencia Rodriguez. 2010. Volume1: Introduction. In *Making Our Media: Global Initiatives Toward a Democratic Public Sphere, Volume 1,* ed. Clemencia Rodriguez, Dorothy Kidd and Laura Stein, 1–22. Cresskill, NJ: Hampton Press.

Knox, Emily. 2009. Intellectual Freedom. *Public Services Quarterly* 7, no. 1–2: 49–55.

Lewis, Peter M. 2008. *Promoting Social Cohesion: The Role of Community Media.* Council of Europe, Media and Information Society Division, Directorate General of Human Rights and Legal Affairs Council of Europe.

Meadows, Michael. and Kerrie Foxwell. 2011. Community broadcasting and mental health: The role of local radio and television in enhancing emotional and social wellbeing. *The Radio Journal* 9, no. 2: 89–106.

Meadows, Michael, Susan Forde, Jaqui Ewart and Kerry Foxwell. 2007. *Community Media Matters: An audience study of the Australian community broadcasting sector,* Griffith University: Brisbane. http://www.cbonline.org.au/in-print/community-media-matters -report/

Office for Intellectual Freedom. 2010. *Intellectual Freedom Manual,* 8th Ed. Chicago, IL: American Library Association.

Paterson, Chris. 2006. News Agency Dominance in International News on the Internet. *Papers in International and Global Communication,* Centre for International Communications Research, no. 01/06. http://folders.nottingham.edu.cn/staff/zlizaw/Readings/Week%209/ Paterson%202006.pdf (accessed January 2, 2009.

Patterson, Thomas E. 1992. Irony of the free press: Professional journalism and news Diversity. Paper presented at the American Political Science Association meeting, Chicago, IL, September.

Rodriguez, Clemencia. 2010. "Knowledges in Dialogue: A Participatory Evaluation Study of Citizens' Radio Stations in Magdalena Medio, Colombia." In *Making Our Media: Global Initiatives Toward a Democratic Public Sphere* Rodriguez, eds. Dorothy Kidd, Clemencia Rodriguez and Laura Stein, 131–154. Cresskill, NJ: Hampton Press.

———, 2003. "The Bishop and his Star: Citizens' Communication in Southern Chile." In *Contesting Media Power: Alternative Media in a Networked World,* eds Nick Couldry and James Curran, 177–194. Lanham, MD: Rowman & Littlefield.

———, 2001. *Fissures in the Mediascape: An International Study of Citizens' Media,* Cresskill, NJ: Hampton Press.

Vidal, Gore. 1992. (The Great Unmentionable) Monotheism and its Discontents. *The Lowell Lecture,* Harvard University, Cambridge, MA. April 20. http://www.gorevidalpages.com/1992/04/gore-vidal-monotheism-and -its-discontents.html [accessed September 26, 2012].

Warhaft, Sally, 2006. *Personal interview with the author,* recorded August 3.

Weaver, David, Randal A. Beam, Bonnie J. Brownlee, Paul S. Voakes and G. Cleveland Wilhoit. 2003. *The American Journalist in the 21st Century: Key Findings,* Miami, FL: John S. and James L. Knight Foundation.

Weaver, David and G. Cleveland Wilhoit. 1996. *The American Journalist in the 1990s: US Newspeople at the End of an Era,* Mahwah, NJ: Routledge.

Weaver, David and G. Cleveland Wilhoit. 1994. The U.S. journalist in the 1990s and the question of quality in journalism, International Communication Association Annual Convention, Sydney, Australia, July.

Weaver, David H. and G. Cleveland Wilhoit. 1994. Daily Newspaper Journalists in the 1990s. *Newspaper Research Journal* 15, no. 3: 2–21.

Weaver, David H. and G. Cleveland Wilhoit. 1991. *The American Journalist: A Portrait of US News People and Their Work.* 2nd ed. Bloomington, IN: Bloomington University Press.

Weaver, David H. and G. Cleveland Wilhoit. 1986. *The American Journalist: A Portrait of US News People and their Work,* Bloomington, IN: Bloomington University Press.

Zelizer, Barbie. 2005. Definitions of journalism. In *The Press*, eds. Georgina Overholser and Kathleen Hall Jamieson, 66–80. Oxford: Oxford University Press.

Zhong, Bu and John E. Newhagen. 2009. How journalists think while they write: A Transcultural model of news decision making. *Journal of Communication* 59: 587–608.

Intellectual Property and Intellectual Freedom

Robert Tiessen

A s copyright activist, Robert Levine, frequently states, a fundamental right of authors is stated in the Universal Declaration of Human Rights from 1948: "Everyone has the right to the protection of the moral and material interests resulting from any scientific, literary or artistic production of which he is the author" (United Nations 1948). And of course the Universal Declaration of Human Rights also has the right of freedom of expression in article 19. "The freedom of expression includes the right to impart information and ideas through any media and regardless of frontiers" (United Nations 1948).

Intellectual Property and Intellectual Freedom should compliment each other. Intellectual Property is the concept that intangible items—ideas—can be owned and that one can profit from those ideas. There are three kinds of intellectual property: copyright, the fixed expression of an idea; patents, a method for accomplishing a process; and trademarks, marks or logos that identify a brand for commerce. This chapter will focus on copyright and its relationship with intellectual freedom. While patents and trademarks can also affect intellectual freedom, copyright has a long history of both complementing and conflicting with intellectual freedom. This chapter will explore how documentary filmmakers, users of social media, the blind, and librarians have wrestled with the competing demands of intellectual property.

Copyright is supposed to balance the rights of the creator, the owner (frequently not the creator), and the user. Among the most important rights for users in US and Canadian Copyright are the rights of fair use and fair dealing. Within the proper circumstances, these rights legally allow a user to copy copyrighted material without requiring permission. Do user rights within copyright law such as fair use or fair dealing provide sufficient protection to those who use someone else's intellectual property? The concept of fair use is found in Section 107 of the US Copyright Act: ". . . the fair use of a copyrighted work, including such use by reproduction in copies or phonorecords or by any other means specified by that section, for purposes such as criticism, comment, news reporting, teaching (including multiple copies for classroom use), scholarship, or research, is not an infringement of copyright" (US Copyright Office 2011, 19).

Fair dealing is a concept similar to fair use and is found in the copyright law of British Commonwealth countries. In Canada for example, the recently amended fair dealing provisions in the Canadian Copyright Act include research, private study, education, parody, satire, review, criticism and news reporting. In this chapter, the author will be referring to both fair use and to fair dealing. Within the limits of fair use or fair dealing, someone should be able to use a portion of copyrighted material while exercising their right to the freedom of expression. Yet in recent years, the right to use fair use while exercising freedom of speech has been increasingly challenged in court. Copyright creators and copyright owners (for example the publishing industry, the music industry and the movie industry) have frequently challenged the limits of fair use, seeking to make them as narrow as possible.

This chapter will explore several recent (since 2000) conflicts between intellectual property and intellectual freedom in the United States and Canada. Most of them involve fair use.

Documentary Films

Documentary filmmakers have long struggled with the issue of when to license material versus using fair use. These problems became much more widely known when the problems with Eyes on the Prize came to light (Dean 2004). In 2004, the popular documentary on the civil rights movement in the United States was no longer available for purchase in any format. It was no longer available for broadcast on television. Eyes on the Prize was released in 1987 to much acclaim. The producers of Eyes on the Prize licensed archival film footage to make their documentary. Unfortunately they could not afford to pay for perpetual rights to the footage they had licensed. Many of the rights they had licensed started to expire in the mid 1990's. After the rights expired, the only available copies were aging VHS tapes in libraries and private copies. No broadcaster would risk showing the film. In 2005, two philanthropists came to the rescue donating a combined $850,000.00 to relicense all the footage in Eyes on the Prize (Dean 2005).

Eyes on the Prize illustrates the copyright clearance culture that the documentary film industry lives under. Certainly some of the footage would have qualified as a fair use under copyright law, but licencing was chosen as the route for the footage that was used.

The Center for the Public Domain at Duke Law School created a comic book that illustrates some of the struggles that documentary filmmakers face

(Aoki, Boyle, and Jenkins 2006). Does one have to pay for rights to a television show or music that is playing in the background in footage of a documentary? What line does one have to cross to make a payment? Many filmmakers pay copyright clearance fees even when they feel that their use is fair in order to avoid drawn out lawsuits that they believe that they could win. Errors and omissions insurance which has to be paid if a documentary is shown as part of a television broadcast can often require payment where a filmmaker believes that something is a fair use. When a licence or copyright clearance expires, a documentary can no longer be shown or sold. Definitions of what is fair use have narrowed significantly in the US from the 1960's until now.

Two reports were created in 2004 and 2006 that further document the problems that documentary filmmakers face in both Canada and the US. *Untold Stories* is the result of interviews with 46 American documentary filmmakers and documents their issues with fair use and copyright clearance. While *Wired* magazine publicized the issues with *Eyes on the Prize*, *Untold Stories* was probably the report that started to get those problems noticed.

One of the biggest issues that filmmakers face is that broadcasters won't show films without errors and omissions insurance. Insurance companies won't provide the insurance unless all rights are paid for. Filmmaker Jon Else describes why he replaced a background shot that showed four seconds of *The Simpsons* playing on TV in the background rather than using fair use:

> *I've been in this business long enough, I've had enough depositions taken to know that it's not worth it. I'm willing to sacrifice a wonderful droll cultural moment—the stagehands watching* The Simpsons*—to avoid being taken to court. We did the same with this as the World Series. Literally at the 11ᵗʰ hour, a day before the online, I cut and pasted into the TV set a shot that I own to make the problem go away. Who loses is the audience in the end.* (Aufderheide and Jaszi 2004, 17)

His company couldn't afford to pay Fox the rights for *The Simpsons*, so he altered his documentary to put in footage that he owned the rights to. Fair use was not an option for John Else because of the need for insurance and Fox would not offer the rights for a price that John Else' company could afford.

> *"I haven't used fair use in the last ten years, because from the point of view of any broadcast or cable network, there is no such thing as fair use," said Jeffrey Tuchman. "I'm not speaking here of news networks. Every headline I use, even historical headline, even without news photographs, even without the masthead, every magazine cover, I have to get the rights to.* (Aufderheide and Jaszi 2004, 25)

While *Untold Stories* recommends that filmmakers make stronger use of fair use; and wants to work to persuade gatekeepers to take fair use more seriously, they also note that in the current environment that filmmakers feel that they cannot take that chance.

Working filmmakers by and large "know" that fair use is not a tool they can use. Those who are most familiar with the law are also aware that it is ultimately broadcasters and insurers who will decide whether they can use fair use, and that those entities, being risk-averse, regularly reject the claim. Broadcasters usually can achieve their main goal (e.g. a broadcast that engages an audience) without taking higher risks of legal liability. In sharp contrast, filmmakers talk about the loss to a society's memory, to the historical record, and to creative quality (Aufderheide and Jaszi 2004, 24). The substitutions that filmmakers are forced to make diminish the product and its historical accuracy. Showing theatre workers talking with the Simpsons in the background is different than showing background that they were not watching.

Copyright Clearance Culture and Canadian Documentaries, written by Howard Knopf for the Documentary Organisation of Canada, documents similar problems that Canadian documentary filmmakers face. Knopf points out that many of the problems of documentarians are similar: "While Canadian and American copyright laws are different in many material respects, both systems result in a similar "clearance culture" mentality and the consequential chill and censorship that follow" (Knopf 2006, 6).

But Canadian filmmakers who want distribution in both countries need to comply with both sets of laws. The clearance culture results in films not being made; scenes, cut, altered and censored; and quality suffers because of lack of money for clearance that may be unnecessary (Knopf 2006, 7). For an obituary broadcast on television of a famous actor, the clip will show show famous film clips of the actor as fair dealing. No permission is asked. But in contrast documentary films that are not quite as current are required to have copyright clearance rather than fair dealing. Why the difference? Finally Knopf points out two sections of the Canadian Copyright Act (CCA) that are useful to filmmakers, but that both filmmakers and errors & omissions lawyers ignore. Section 30.7 allows incidental inclusion of copyrighted material. Showing four seconds of the Simpsons playing on TV in the background while filming people talking does not infringe copyright in Canada. Filming buildings and sculptures permanently situated in a public place also does not infringe Section 32.2 of the CCA.

There are ongoing efforts on both sides of the border to deal with these concerns. In the US there is now a Documentary Filmmakers' Statement of Best Practice. (Association of Independent Video and Filmmakers 2005). In 2011, the Documentary Organisation of Canada went on a road show to promote stronger use of fair dealing in Canada. The struggle for clearer rules around the fair use/fair dealing of copyrighted works by documentary film-makers goes on.

Social Media

Social media also struggles with the limits around fair use and fair dealing. Similar to documentary filmmakers, does using a clip of a copyrighted work infringe copyright in social media? Does music playing in the background infringe copyright?

One of the most publicized incidents in the conflict between social media and IP is recounted by Lawrence Lessig in the introduction to his book *Remix* (Lessig 2008, 1–5). In 2007, Stephanie Lenz posted a video to YouTube showing her 13 month old son Holden dancing to the Prince song "Let's Go Crazy". She posted the 30 second video so that members of her family living far away could see her son learning to walk. Even though "Let's Go Crazy" is barely audible in the video, Universal Music Group did not find the video cute and filed a takedown notice with YouTube for copyright infringement. Lenz went to the Electronic Frontier Foundation and with their assistance filed a countersuit.

In 2008, a court ruled that the Universal Music Group (UMG) had acted in bad faith in filing the take down notice. UMG had acted in bad faith because they had failed to take into account the fact that Lenz' use of "Let's Go Crazy" was fair use. The main issue revolved around Section 512 of the Digital Millennium Copyright Act. In exchange for giving Internet service providers (ISPs) a safe harbour against copyright infringement, a notice and take-down system was established. Whenever a copyright owner sends a notice of copyright infringement, the ISP needs to respond by taking down infringing material. The DMCA didn't anticipate the massive growth in user generated content (UGC) with sites such as YouTube and Flickr. Corporate copyright owners responded to the massive growth in UGC by automating the notice and takedown system. In the automated system, there was no opportunity for creators of the videos to claim fair use. The Lenz decision should require a change in this process (Seidenberg 2006, 46–51).

Another aspect of the notice and take down system has been the ability of organizations to use notice and take down as a form of censorship. In the same year that Stephanie Lenz was dealing with the Universal Music Group, American environmentalist Liz Moore had to deal with a notice and takedown request from Syncrude Canada. Liz Moore had taken a company-organized tour of the oil sands and included some of her photos from the tour on her website. According to the company, all photos taken during the tour belong to Syncrude. Liz Moore did take the photos down, but ironically the publicity over the company's complaints significantly drove more traffic to her website (Mittelstaedt 2007). The mere threat of a lawsuit will typically make individuals fall into compliance with whatever a more powerful organization wants. Surely her use of the photos would have been considered a fair use, even if the rights to the photos were signed over to Syncrude.

Numerous groups have been accused of using notice and takedown as a form of censorship. In the United States one of the most mentioned groups is the Church of Scientology (Anderson 2008). In 2008, a mysterious group known as the American Rights Counsel issued 4,000 takedown notices for YouTube videos that were critical of Scientology. This led to criticism that the take down process was to open to abuse. Similar to Syncrude, an Australian mining group has been accused of using their country's notice and takedown laws to go after an Australian environmental group (Frew 2007). Rising Tide mocked the "Life brought to you by mining" website and ad campaign of the New South Wales Mineral Council, by creating their own website. The first take down notice was over using the Mineral Council's own photos and layout in Rising Tide's website. A second take down notice was issue after Rising Tide had removed all the photos and made considerable changes to the layout so that their website would not emulate the industry website.

While many countries have adopted some version of the notice and takedown system, Canada has a different system. Canada has a notice and notice system. An ISP is supposed to pass on a notice of copyright infringement to the ISP user being accused of copyright infringement. The copyright owner can then pursue the issue in court. There are a number of advantages to a notice and notice system. Notice and takedown forces an ISP to respond without being aware of the full situation. Notice and notice allows the person accused of copyright infringement to either take down the material or webpages on their own or communicate with the person issuing the notice to try to find out what the concerns are or to consider the option of going to court.

In 2012, the Canadian Parliament passed the Copyright Modernization Act which included a major effort to ensure that user generated content on the Internet was legal. The act added a new section, 29.21, to the Canadian Copyright Act entitled Non-commercial User-generated Content. This new section allows users to take pre-existing works and combine them to create new content for posting to YouTube and similar social media. If a provision like this had existed in US law in 2007, Stephanie Lenz almost certainly would not have needed to go to court when the Universal Music Group tried to takedown the video of her son. Section 29.21 requires content users to name the source of their material, use legal, not pirated, sources, and make only non-commercial use of the user-generated content (An Act to Amend the Copyright Act 2012).

It remains to be seen how useful these changes will be. Canadians tend to use American social media and servers located in the US, where American law applies. Like Syncrude, other Canadian organizations have been quite willing to use notice and takedown rules in the US. So it remains to be seen how much of an impact this new provision will have on Canadians or more globally.

Intellectual Property and the Blind

The blind struggle with intellectual property issues in ways that most of us cannot understand. Books and many more cultural products are not automatically available in a format that they can use. The ability to migrate formats to Braille or to an audio file that can be listened to is not an easy process even without considering intellectual property issues. According to the World Blind Union in 2012 only some 7% of published books are ever made accessible (in formats such as Braille, audio and large print) in the richest countries, and less than 1% in poorer ones (World Blind Union 2012).

This has created a book or information famine for the blind and the perceptually disabled. Copyright laws limit the ability of the blind to access the information that they need. Getting a hold of information in alternate formats is difficult. In 2006, the World Intellectual Property Organization studied the issue and discovered that fewer than 60 countries make provisions for the visually impaired in their copyright laws (Sullivan 2006, 9).

The US Copyright Act, Section 121, also known as the Chafee Amendment, makes special provisions for the blind and other people with disabilities. Authorized entities, which are non-profit organizations or government agencies with a primary mission of assisting the blind, may provide alternate format copies in formats which are exclusively for the use of the blind or for other people with disabilities. Neither payment of copyright royalties nor permission is required from the copyright owner to make a copy in a specialized format that is available exclusively for the blind or for other persons with disabilities.

In the Canadian Copyright Act, Section 32 provides similar provisions. One of the major differences between the Canadian and US copyright acts concerns authorized entities. Even though the Canadian National Institute for the Blind (CNIB) makes most of the alternate format copies in Canada, any non-profit organization including public libraries and school boards have the right to make alternate format copies for use by the perceptually disabled. A public library could act on its own to create an alternative format copy for a blind patron, if, for example, the required book that isn't available in an alternate format from the CNIB. This creates flexibility for the blind that is not available under US law.

The lack of flexibility in only allowing authorized entities to make copies has led to a back log of requests. The number of alternate format copies is limited to what authorized entities have the resources to produce. The authorized entities are not able to keep up with the demand. In the October 10, 2012 judgment in *Hathitrust vs. the Author's Guild*, the following expansion was made to authorized entities: "The ADA requires that libraries of educational institutions have a primary mission to reproduce and distribute their collections to print-disabled individuals, making each library a potential "authorized entity" under the Chafee Amendment (*HathiTrust vs. Author's Guild* 2012, 23). By interpreting authorized entities through the filter of the Americans with Disabilities Act (ADA), all American libraries that are part of educational institutions have now become authorized entities. This not only brings needed flexibility to educational institutions, this judgment may open the door to using the ADA to further open up the interpretation of authorized entities in the Copyright Act to include non-profit groups that do not have a narrow focus of just assisting the blind.

But there are other copyright issues that blind advocacy groups need to focus on globally. To that end after years of discussion and lobbying by blind advocacy groups, the World Intellectual Property Organization announced that there would be a diplomatic conference in July 2013 to negotiate an international treaty regarding the rights of the visually impaired to access copyrighted works (World Intellectual Property Organization 2012).

There appear to be two main reasons for the treaty; first, to make sure that all or at least most countries have exceptions in their copyright legislation to accommodate the blind. According to the WIPO survey fewer than 60 countries currently do. And second, to ensure that alternate format copies produced in one country can be shared across borders with the visually impaired in another country.

The main reason for wanting to share alternate format copies across international borders is that it limits duplication of effort. If the US National Library Service for the Blind and Physically Handicapped (NLS) has created an alternate format version of Arthur Miller's the Crucible, why should libraries in Canada, Australia, and the United Kingdom among others create their own alternate format copies? Given the limited resources that libraries for the blind have across the world, would not working together make more sense?

The Chafee Amendment, added in 1996, also allows the creation of alternate format copies without permission from the copyright owner. This raises the question of whether these copies are legal outside of the United States. Before 1996, alternate format copies required permission from the copyright owner. Under the old rules, the NLS would then share alternate format copies with other equivalent organizations around the world, because it had already received copyright permission from the owner.

With the Chafee Amendment this was all called into question. The NLS and other authorized entities no longer require copyright permission to make alternate format copies in the US, but how would that affect sharing and use with other countries? The National Library Service for the Blind and Physically Handicapped issued the following advice in 1997 and this continues to remain the standard advice:

> *If the braille or recorded versions of the books were distributed outside the United States, however, such act of distribution would not be covered by the exemption since U.S. copyright law has no extraterritorial effect. Since NLS loans material to eligible foreign agencies, NLS will continue to request permission for all books and periodicals published outside the U.S.* (US Library of Congress 1997)

And further down from the same document:

> *NLS will continue to lend to eligible foreign agencies through interlibrary loan. Such distribution is permissible under U.S. law and is unlikely to infringe the laws of other countries. However, foreign agencies must look to the law of the country where the use takes place to determine whether they might be liable for acts of unauthorized importation or distribution* of lawfully *made copies without permission of the copyright owner.* (US Library of Congress 1997)

The NLS will continue to loan physical copies via interlibrary loan if a foreign agency represents that the copies are legal in their country, but will only distribute alternate format versions (for reproduction to qualified individuals) outside the US if it has obtained copyright permission. Unfortunately the NLS rarely obtains copyright permission anymore since US law no longer requires it. Since 1997, other countries which had exceptions for the blind in their copyright law, have come to similar conclusions, especially regarding the export of alternate format copies. The Chafee Amendment which admirably sped up access to alternate format copies in the US by eliminating the need to request copyright permission or payment, simultaneously has had the effect of limiting international cooperation to make sure that blind people globally had access to alternate format copies. The 2013 WIPO negotiations led to a successful treaty that will hopefully soon be adopted by a sufficient number of nations to reduce or eliminate the information famine from which the blind are suffering.

Interlibrary Loan Across National Borders

Interlibrary loan allows libraries to share resources with other libraries. If an item is out of print or if in a library's judgment an item will receive little or no use, interlibrary loan can bring in that resource from another library. Libraries rely on fair use and fair dealing to make copies for interlibrary loan. As with making alternate format copies for the blind, fair use and fair dealing are based on national copyright laws. This has recently lead publishers to question whether interlibrary loan across national borders is legal. But, if intellectual freedom is an international right as stated in the UN Declaration on Human Rights, how can sharing information necessary for intellectual freedom stop at national borders?

In 1954, the International Federation of Library Associations came out with the first version of its guidelines for international interlibrary loan (International Federation of Library Associations 2009). The guidelines, which have been revised a number of times since, exist because libraries have been providing interlibrary loans across national borders for many decades. Interlibrary loan consists of both returnables (original books, microfilm, etc) and non-returnables (copies both digital and hard copy). International interlibrary loan has never been a secret. Governments and publishers have long been aware of this activity. National libraries like the Library of Congress and Libraries and Archives Canada have long been involved in the interlibrary loan system. The international standard practice for interlibrary loan has been to look in the home country first and then if necessary to look for items in other countries (Neal et al. 2011, 8).

The legal basis for making loans rests upon two points. The first is fair use or fair dealing. The second is that many countries in addition to fair use or fair dealing, have a legal provision for libraries to provide interlibrary loan. In the United States, that is Section 108 of the Copyright Act. In Canada's Copyright Act that is Section 30.2. With interlibrary loan the library is acting on behalf of the user to support their research and private study needs via fair use or fair dealing. But like provisions for the blind, the question as to whether or not these provisions extend internationally has been called into question. At least for libraries in the US, the conclusion of the Association for Research Libraries has been that international interlibrary loan is legal: "US copyright law supports the ability of domestic libraries to participate in ILL arrangements and to send copies of some copyrighted works to foreign libraries provided the libraries meet the requirements of the law" (Neal et al 2011, 3).

This has not stopped publishers' associations from challenging in recent years the rights of libraries to conduct interlibrary loan across international borders. The most prominent recent statement has come from the International Association of Scientific, Technical and Medical Publishers. This statement has five main principles, summarized below:

1.   The Berne Convention 3-step test should apply to all copyright exceptions including library supply.

2. Cross border interlibrary loan should be governed by licences with publishers. There is too much potential for conflicts between governing laws of different countries.

3. Digital document delivery directly to end users is best handled by the publishers. In other words libraries no longer need to provide this type of service.

4. There is a risk that interlibrary loan to individuals may end up being used for a commercial purpose. Therefore random sampling needs to take place to ensure that interlibrary loan is only for private, non-commercial use.

5. Interlibrary loan of copies should be restricted to print single copies for walk in library patrons. In other words, libraries should stop providing digital delivery of interlibrary loan (International Association of Scientific, Technical and Medical Publishers 2011).

Furthermore, the statement includes the following passage: "Journal publishers have been offering digital and online access to published content since the mid-1990's, and for most of that time have also been offering access to individual articles on a transactional basis for users who do not already have journal subscriptions" (International Association of Scientific, Technical and Medical Publishers 2011).

The publishers put forward the view that the transition to digital access has really eliminated the need for interlibrary loan of at least copies. Users can purchase any journal article that they need directly from the publisher. Interlibrary loan such as it does need to exist, should not cross international boundaries and it should only provide print copies for walk-in users of the library.

The STM Statement and similar other statements fail to recognize a number of things. First of all interlibrary loan is not really a separate copyright exception. Libraries make copies of journal articles and book chapters on the basis of fair use. In many respects the provisions regarding fair use/fair dealing are far more important than any additional legal provisions that allow libraries to act on behalf of the user.

Cross border interlibrary loan has existed legally for decades. Surely if interlibrary loan were illegal, publishers would have challenged the process in the 1960s or the 1970s. If cross border interlibrary loan has existed legally for decades, why should it now be challenged?

The STM Statement also ignores the fact that fair use and fair dealing are format neutral. There is no requirement that a fair use copy be in a specific format. Digital copies are as acceptable as print copies. Section 108 of the US Copyright Act which allows libraries to provide interlibrary loan is also format neutral. So it is clear that US libraries can provide digital copies for interlibrary loan. The recently revised Section 30.2 of Canada's Copyright Act again allows libraries to provide interlibrary loan, but requires digital copies to be controlled. ". . . (T)he providing library, archive or museum or person takes measures to prevent the person who has requested it from: a) making any reproduction of the digital copy, including any paper copies, other than printing one copy of it; b) communicating the digital copy to any other person; and, c) using the digital copy for more than five business days from the day on which the person first uses it" (An Act to Amend the Copyright Act 2012, 31–32).

However, many Canadian libraries no longer operate under section 30.2 of the Copyright Act. In 2004, when section 30.2 was even more restrictive than it is now, Canada's Supreme Court ruled that libraries could act directly under fair dealing rather than using 30.2:

> As an integral part of the scheme of copyright law, the s. 29 fair dealing exception is always available. Simply put, a library can always attempt to prove that its dealings with a copyrighted work are fair under s. 29 of the Copyright Act. It is only if a library were unable to make out the fair dealing exception under s. 29 that it would need to turn to s. 30.2 of the Copyright Act to prove that it qualified for the library exemption. (CCH Canadian Ltd. v. Law Society of Upper Canada, 2004, par. 49)

Since the CCH Supreme Court Judgment, a significant number of Canadian libraries provide interlibrary loan directly under the fair dealing provisions of the Copyright Act, rather than using section 30.2.

Given that fair use is format neutral, the idea that a move to the digital world eliminates the need for libraries to provide interlibrary loan is disingenuous. The primary argument seems to be that interlibrary loan now deprives publishers of a new market opportunity that they did not have in the pre-digital world for profit. One of the four factors for determining whether a use is fair is economic: ". . . the effect of the use upon the potential market for or value of the copyrighted work" (US Copyright Office 2011, 19).

So far there has been no relevant court case in US courts that interlibrary loan is having that kind of market effect on journal publishers. In the CCH Supreme Court judgment, the Canadian Supreme Court had a stronger ruling in the one case that involved libraries and fair dealing.

> If a copyright owner were allowed to license people to use its work and then point to a person's decision not to obtain a licence as proof that his or her dealings were not fair, this would extend the scope of the owner's monopoly over the use of his or her work in a manner that would not be consistent with the Copyright Act's balance between owner's rights and user's interests. (CCH Canadian Ltd. v. Law Society of Upper Canada, 2004, par. 70)

In other words, the simple refusal to purchase a product does not mean that the option to make a copy of an article would not be a fair dealing.

Libraries Licencing Digital Content

Since the 1990s, libraries have been purchasing increasing amounts of digital material (e-books, e-journals, etc.). For the 2010–2011 academic year, the median percentage of the budget spent on digital collections was 65% for libraries that were members of the Association of Research Libraries (Kyrillidou, et al 2012, 56). This compares with a median of 37% for ARL Libraries in 2004–2005. While statistics are not readily available for other groups and types of libraries, anecdotally all types of libraries are experiencing a significant increase in expenditures for digital material as opposed to print material.

Most digital materials are licenced rather than purchased. Licencing creates the possibility that uses might be forbidden under contract that would be allowed under a country's copyright laws. When a print book is purchased by a library, the use of it is governed by the copyright law of the country that it is in. Likewise if an e-journal is licenced by a library and the licence doesn't specifically mention copyright issues like fair use, then the use of it is governed by the copyright law of the country that it is in. What makes things different is when the licence has sections devoted to issues that used to rely on copyright law.

If the agreement does not mention fair use/fair dealing, then fair use/fair dealing is still applicable. However the licence may limit the scope of fair use/fair dealing. This is something that you may wish to discuss with the content owner (Harris 2009, 112).

The normal understanding of contract law is that when a licensee (library) waives a right in a contract (like fair dealing or interlibrary loan), the right is then lost to the user. In other words a library might waive the right to provide the resource as an interlibrary loan in exchange for a lower price. Or the content might be so valuable to the library's users that the library is willing to waive a right such as fair use copies for course reserves.

In 2008, the Canadian Association of Research Libraries studied issues relating to the licencing of e-books (Owen, et al 2008). It was felt at the time that e-books had new licencing issues compared to e-journals. On page 9 of the document, there is a table comparing the licencing provisions of nine different e-book contracts. One licence out of nine forbids interlibrary loan. Another forbid digital transmission of interlibrary loans and only allowed interlibrary loans to be sent via mail or fax. Another issue was that three of the licences required Canadian libraries to follow interlibrary loan provisions in the US Copyright Act, even though legally Canadian libraries have to follow the Canadian Copyright Act. One licence did not allow its resources to be used for ereserves.

Recall that the STM Statement on Document Delivery questioned the right of libraries to provide interlibrary loan requests across international borders. Given that publishers question that right, some publishers have started to put restrictions in their licences limiting interlibrary loan to the country of the licensee. Here is an example from one publisher: ". . . to an authorised user of another academic library in the same country . . ." (Hart Publishing n.d.)

Various guides have been written to help librarians through contract negotiations and to make sure that they do not sign overly restrictive agreements. Probably the most well known resource is LibLicense which is organized by Ann Okerson. LibLicence is an online discussion forum, and a website and also has a very prominent model licence that many libraries use to evaluate licences from a vendor. According to the LibLicense Model License these are common areas to watch for in licences:

- Electronic Reserves
- Education and Teaching
- Electronic Links or Hyperlinks
- Caching
- Scholar Sharing—Authorized users may transmit to a third party colleague insubstantial amounts of licenced material for personal or scholarly uses.
- Interlibrary Loan (LibLicense 2011)

While the LibLicense list is biased towards the needs of libraries that support educational institutions, these are all areas where a licence can unduly restrict or forbid library users from making use of material licenced by a library. Can teachers or faculty put a copy of licenced material on reserve or use licenced material in their teaching? Can a library user share a link of the licenced material with other library users? Could a library provide links to licenced material that discuss current topics or can they only provide a link to the licenced materials search interface? Could a friend or a family member who is a library user share licenced information about cancer treatments with someone who is not a library user? While some publishers insist that these kinds of uses are the thin edge of the wedge, this kind of use has always occurred with material that libraries have purchased rather than licenced. Historically, libraries have not been known for destroying the markets of publishers.

Currently the most common response to bad licences has been to educate librarians (especially the ones negotiating licences) about what poor provisions are and to encourage libraries not to accept bad licences, and to renegotiate the terms when necessary. But what happens when a library either mistakenly signs a bad licence or when it chooses to sign a bad licence because it cannot negotiate better terms for what it considers must have content?

On a practical level, libraries have chosen to assume that contract terms trump copyright law. At the same time there are other issues which libraries do not always explore. As Lesley Ellen Harris points out:

> Note that your patrons are not a party to the license agreement. As a result, they are not bound by the license agreement that you make with the content owner. Thus, even if you and the content owner agree to limit the fair use or fair dealing portions of the applicable copyright act in your license agreement, fair use and fair dealing are still available to the library's patrons. (Harris 2009, 34)

So a library user is not bound by the licence agreement. On the one hand, that means that if a library user breaks a licence but stays within the provisions of copyright law they are not liable to the content provider, but of course the library may very well be liable under contract law. Depending upon the breach of contract, the library and all of its users may find themselves cut off from access to a resource even if what the user has done does not violate copyright law.

Another issue is whether licences with provisions that go beyond copyright law are legal? For example in the Canadian Copyright Act, there is section 89: "No person is entitled to copyright otherwise than under and in accordance with this Act or any other Act of Parliament."

This has never been tested in court in terms of whether provisions in a contract that for example restrict the rights of consumers of content beyond the Copyright Act are legal. While the US Copyright Act does not have a section like section 89, similar arguments could be made that provisions that go beyond what is in the law might not be legal.

No doubt intellectual property and intellectual freedom will continue to have conflicts regarding which human right comes first. While conflicts between these two rights have gone on for centuries, the move to digital resources, and the recent pace of technological change has meant that conflicts are happening much more rapidly than in the past. From a library point of view, the biggest recent shift has to come from the fact that libraries no longer own their own content. Rather than purchasing books and journals, we are licencing content from vendors and our users are accessing that content over the Internet. This makes the licencing process far more critical than it was in the past.

A bigger issue is how law and societies define user rights such as fair use and fair dealing. Will they be defined broadly or narrowly? Will individuals and institutions feel capable of taking advantage of fair use? Or will the law be interpreted in a constrained way so that users do not feel that they can use fair use?

References

An Act to Amend the Copyright Act. 2012. Statutes of Canada. Chapter 20. http://www.parl.gc.ca/content/hoc/Bills/411/Government/C-11/ C-11_4/C-11_4.PDF (accessed December 18, 2012).

Anderson, Nate. 2008. Scientology fights critics with 4,000 DMCA takedown notices. *Ars Technica*. September 8. http://arstechnica.com/ uncategorized/2008/09/scientology-fights-critics-with-4000-dmca -takedown-notices/ (accessed December 14, 2012).

Aoki, Keith, James Boyle, and Jennifer Jenkins. 2006. Bound by the law? http://web.law.duke.edu/cspd/comics/pdf/cspdcomichigh.pdf (accessed November 23, 2012).

Association of Independent Video and Filmmakers, et al. 2005. Documentary Filmmakers' Statement on Fair Use. Washington, DC. http://www.centerforsocialmedia.org/sites/default/files/fair_use_ final.pdf (accessed December 7, 2012).

Aufderheide, Patricia, and Peter Jaszi. 2004. Untold stories: Creative consequences of the rights clearance culture for documentary filmmakers. Washington, DC. http://www.centerforsocialmedia.org/sites/default/ files/UNTOLDSTORIES_Report.pdf (accessed November 27, 2012).

CCH Canadian Ltd. v. Law Society of Upper Canada. 2004 SCC 13 (CanLII), [2004] 1 SCR 339. http://canlii.ca/t/1glp0 (accessed on November 30, 2012).

Dean, Katie. 2004. Bleary days for *Eyes on the Prize*. *Wired*. http://www.wired.com/culture/lifestyle/news/2004/12/66106 (accessed November 21, 2012).

Dean, Katie. 2005. "Cash rescues *Eyes on the Prize*." *Wired*. http://www.wired.com/entertainment/music/news/2005/08/68664 (accessed November 21, 2012).

Frew, Wendy. 2007. Industry closes anti-coal website. *Sydney Morning Herald*, March 5. http://www.smh.com.au/news/national/industry-closes -anticoal-website/2007/03/04/1172943275688.html (accessed December 14, 2012).

Harris, Lesley Ellen. 2009. *Licensing digital content: A practical guide for librarians*. 2nd Ed. Chicago: American Library Association.

Hart Publishing. n.d. Hart Publishing limited online journals institutional online agreement. http://www.hartjournals.co.uk/terms.pdf (accessed February 22, 2013).

HathiTrust Vs. Author's Guild. 2012. 11 CV 6351 (SDNY 2012). http://www.nysd.uscourts.gov/cases/show.php?db=special&id=232 (accessed December 20, 2012).

International Association of Scientific, Technical, and Medical Publishers. 2011. STM Statement on Document Delivery. http://www.stm-assoc.org/2011_06_08_STM_Statement_Document_Delivery.pdf (accessed June13, 2013).

International Federation of Library Associations. 2009. International resource sharing and document delivery: Principles and guidelines for procedure. http://www.ifla.org/files/assets/docdel/documents/international-lending-en.pdf (accessed January 3, 2013).

Knopf, Howard. 2006. The Copyright Clearance Culture and Canadian documentaries. Ottawa, Canada. http://www.macerajarzyna.ca/pages/publications/HPK_white_paper.pdf (accessed November 27, 2012).

Kyrillidou, Martha, Shaneka Morris, and Gary Roebuck. 2012. ARL Statistics 2010-2011. Association of Research Libraries: Washington. http://publications.arl.org/ARL-Statistics-2010-2011/56 (accessed February 22, 2013).

Lessig, Lawrence. 2008. *Remix*. New York: Penguin.

LibLicense. 2011. Liblicense model license agreement & commentary. http://liblicense.crl.edu/wp-content/uploads/2011/09/licenseagreements/standlicagree.pdf (accessed February 22, 2013).

Mittelstaedt, Martin. 2007. U.S. activist takes on syncrude; Colorado woman 'appalled' by the energy used at the alberta tar sands operation. *Globe and Mail*, May 3.

Neal, James G, Larry Alford, Mark Haslett, Catherine Murray-Rust, Winston Tabb, Lizabeth Wilson, and Prudence S Adler. Report of the Task Force on International Interlibrary Loan and Document Delivery Practices. 2011. *Research Library Issues* 275 (June):1–6. http://publications.arl.org/rli275/2 (accessed January 4, 2013).

Owen, Victoria, Robert Tiessen, Leslie Weir, Davina DesRoches, and Wanda Noel. 2008. E-Books in research libraries: Issues of access and use. Canadian Association of Research Libraries: Ottawa. http://carl-abrc.ca/uploads/pdfs/copyright/carl_e-book_report-e.pdf (accessed February 7, 2013).

Seidenberg, Steve. 2006. Copyright in the age of YouTube. *ABA Journal* 95: 46–51.

Sullivan, Judith. 2006. Study on copyright limitations and exceptions for the visually impaired. World Intellectual Property Organization: Geneva. http://www.wipo.int/edocs/mdocs/copyright/en/sccr_15/sccr_15_7.pdf (accessed December 20, 2012).

United Nations. 1948. Universal Declaration of Human Rights. http://www.un.org/en/documents/udhr/ (accessed July 19, 2013).

US Copyright Office. 2011. Circular 92: Copyright law of the United States and related laws contained in Title 17 of the United States Code. US Copyright Office: Washington. http://www.copyright.gov/title17/circ92.pdf (accessed February 28, 2013).

US Library of Congress. 1997. National Library Service for the blind and physically handicapped. Copyright law amendment—questions and answers. Update. July–September. http://www.loc.gov/nls/newsletters/update/1997/jul_sep.txt (accessed December 21, 2012).

World Blind Union. 2012. Press Release—WIPO negotiations treaty for blind people. http://www.worldblindunion.org/English/Documents/WBU Press Release RE- R2R 18 Dec 2012.doc (accessed February 28, 2013).

World Intellectual Property Organization. 2012. WIPO advances toward treaty to facilitate access to published works by persons with print disabilities, Morocco Offers to Host Diplomatic Conference. http://www.wipo.int/pressroom/en/articles/2012/article_0026.html (accessed December 20, 2012).

The Internet and Intellectual Freedom

Elizabeth A. Buchanan

Introduction: In My Own Backyard

In Fall, 2012, I sat in my office in the University of Wisconsin—Stout, oblivious to the ensuing social media frenzy surrounding a professor from our Theatre department, the television show "Firefly," and intellectual freedom. In fact, I would venture to say that the majority of our small 10,000 person campus was unaware that thousands of Firefly supporters, among others, were tweeting, posting, commenting, and conversing in every possible way via social media on the violation of Professor James Miller's intellectual freedom rights.

Here's the short version of the story, which is fully documented in a number of online newspapers and organizational web sites, for example in *The FIRE* (2012a). Professor Miller posted a flyer on his office door with one of Firefly's characters stating, "You don't know me, son, so let me explain this to you once. If I ever kill you, you'll be awake. You'll be facing me. And you'll be armed," a direct quote from the program which was cancelled in 2002. The poster was removed by a campus official, under the guise that it was threatening speech: Stout, like many other institutions of higher education, has a "threat assessment team." More will be said about this team later.

After its removal, a new poster was hung in its stead (fig. 1), which showed a cartoon beating another stick figure lying on the ground with the caption: "Warning Fascism: Fascism can cause blunt trauma and/or violent death. Keep fascism away from children and pets" (Kain 2011).

This poster, too, was removed, again under the guise that it was promoting violence and constituted threatening speech. Precedent exists in case law surrounding true threats, and neither poster constituted a true threat; but, in an attempt to balance safety and security, and to promote the standards of inclusive excellence to which Stout ascribes, there was some support for

Figure 1: Warning, Fascism can cause . . .

the removal of the posters. Achieving a balance between these standards of inclusive excellence, which includes:

> [a commitment] to this process to cultivate an environment that fosters and promotes diversity, equity, inclusion, and accountability at every level of university life. We value the presence and participation of diverse individuals and groups. We are engaged in creating learning environments in which students, faculty, and staff of all backgrounds can thrive and fulfill their academic, personal, and professional potential in a diverse nation and world. (University of Wisconsin—Stout 2012)

. . . while upholding legal rights to expression became a lightening rod. In response to the then millions (1.3 million, at last report) of tweets surrounding the controversy, the university responded, noting "This was not an act of censorship. This was an act of sensitivity to and care for our shared community and was intended to maintain a campus climate in which everyone can feel welcome, safe and secure." Tweets, including some from the writer of Firefly itself, circulated for weeks during the tumultuous time. It was not long before *The FIRE*, the Foundation for Individual Rights in Education, learned of the incident and began correspondence with the University's administration. After much discussion, Chancellor Charles Sorensen issued a statement that the professor could return the posters:

> *In retrospect, however, it is clear that the removal of the posters—although done with the best intent—did have the effect of casting doubt on UW—Stout's dedication to the principles embodied in the First Amendment, especially the ability to express oneself freely, . . . As many people have pointed out in the days since this issue surfaced, a public university must take the utmost care to protect this right.* (University of Wisconsin—Stout 2012)

Many, especially Professor Miller, took issue with the administration's statement, noting that rights to free expression were not his to give or take away.

To aid the campus in resolving its unrest, and moreover, understanding the deeper complexities of the law surrounding first amendment rights and system policy, Stout held three campus and community sessions to engage in a free and open discourse about speech and expression, legal rights, and the appropriate role of policies in an institution of higher education. The university experienced a collective learning moment, and used the controversy to work towards compatible policies for expression and rights with safety and inclusion. The university's final session included a lecture and discussion with Adam Kissel, of *The FIRE*, who described in detail the many violations ongoing across the country and world in the face of intellectual and academic freedoms (Kissel 2012). Many of us in education, ranging from primary through post-secondary, are unfamiliar with the case law surrounding free expression within the context of our institutions and more broadly. Students, in particular, are often unaware of their own rights, and to this end, *The FIRE* has issued educational materials on speech codes, institutional policies, and legal precedent (The Fire 2012b).

Stout, like many educational institutions today, is walking a fine line between support for academic and intellectual freedoms and concern for personal and communal safety. We balance the public trust and good with constitutional affordances, and this is not always a neat and clean relationship.

Readers shall see the struggle around this balance throughout this chapter, which will look at the impact and influence of the Internet on intellectual freedom. Since the inception of the World Wide Web, and in particular, social media, the many-to-many communicative mode and ease with which information or data are shared has been acknowledged, manipulated, and violated, simultaneously. Without Twitter, without social media, would 1.3 million Firefly viewers have known what was occurring in the small northwoods town of Menomonie, Wisconsin and its office doors? This is but one small example, of which there are many others: Think of the Jyllands-Posten Mohammed cartoons controversy of 2005, which certainly trumped, by social media standards, the Firefly controversy at Stout. Ess contends "Had these cartoons been restricted to print media, they would have had likely little impact outside of Denmark. But as made immediately available online, they sparked world-wide diplomatic furor and violent protest. . . . This example makes very clear how a globally distributed digital media thus amplifies the consequences for our communicative acts far beyond the boundaries familiar to us with traditional media" (Ess 2009, 16). The Danish courts upheld the publication of the cartoons, noting "the right to freedom of speech must be exercised with the necessary respect for other human rights, including the right to protection against discrimination, insult and degradation, but no apparent violation of the law had occurred" (2009, 16).

Across locales and jurisdiction, the right to speech and expression takes precedence over individual or collect outrage over offensive, violent, or "uncivil" expression. According to the advocacy group Reporters Without Borders, this year's index on expression is resuming some "normalcy:" "After the 'Arab springs' and other protest movements that prompted many rises and falls in last year's index, the 2013 Reporters Without Borders World Press Freedom Index marks a return to a more usual configuration" (Reporters Without Borders 2013). The European Commission has also acknowledged the specificity of technologies in relation to intellectual freedoms in the last few years: "The use of electronic communications technologies—on top of satellite broadcasting—greatly facilitated the wave of upheavals in the Mediterranean countries. The widespread use of mobile phones combined with social networking via internet—showed the importance of information society tools and technologies to the circulation of information. In countries where the circulation of information is partially restricted such tools can greatly contribute to the democratization of societies and the creation of public opinion through the promotion of freedom of expression" (2011).

While Ess, among others, acknowledges the power and influence of digital media, he also exercises caution: ". . . phrases such as a 'Facebook Revolution' or 'Twitter Revolution' indicate that we risk focusing more on the technologies involved than on the persons who are making use of them. (This

Figure 2: Freedom of the Press Worldwide in 2013, Reporters Without Borders

is, among other things, a form of technological determinism that should be carefully avoided)" (Ess 2013).

While fundamental principles of intellectual freedom remain, novel forms of expression, forms of protest, technological mediation are continually arising. New forms of protest and new forms of constraint fight for the lead in the ongoing battle over the rights of intellectual freedom. More broadly, Alfino rightfully recognizes the ongoing realities around intellectual freedom, technology-mediated or not: "Culturally and historically specific concepts such as 'intellectual freedom' will probably need to be rethought for a global environment that does not uniformly share the concerns of Western European culture. . . ." (2012, 15).

Fundamental Principles of Intellectual Freedoms

The Internet is not governed in the same ways as jurisdictional locales, though it has technological architectures, standards, protocols, and the like (Lessig 2006). But, when it comes to norms or rights, the Internet is schizophrenic and ambiguous. Fleeting causes or advocacy groups appear and disappear;

web pages go dark. Take-downs—sometimes government "coordinated" or "sponsored" and sometimes "industry-sponsored"—are frequent occurrences. Meanwhile, organized community protest in the forms of direct denial of service attacks, online petitions, and the like (recall the Grey Tuesday event chronicled by the Electronic Frontier Foundation or the mass Wikileaks protests (Electronic Frontier Foundation; Leiderman 2013) are not unfamiliar occurrences. So, how do we apply long-standing and fundamental principles from the "physical" world to the virtual? How do we find common ground, if indeed that is our goal, in the face of the diverse global environment Alfino acknowledges above?

The Universal Declaration of Human Rights, Article 19, acknowledges our freedoms *regardless of media and regardless of frontiers*: "Everyone has the right to freedom of opinion and expression; this right includes freedom to hold opinions without interference and to seek, receive and impart information and ideas through any media, regardless of frontiers" (United Nations 1948). Similarly, the European Convention for the Protection of Human Rights and Fundamental Freedoms, Article 10, asserts, "Everyone has the right to freedom of expression. This right shall include freedom to hold opinions and to receive and impart information and ideas without interference by public authority and regardless of borders" (European Council 1950). In the United States, there is a constitutional right to free exercise of thought and belief, as articulated in the Bill of Rights, the First Amendment to the Constitution, "Congress shall make no law respecting an establishment of religion, or prohibiting the free exercise thereof; or abridging the freedom of speech, or of the press; or the right of the people peaceably to assemble, and to petition the government for a redress of grievances." And in addition to the US Constitutional right, the right to intellectual freedom has been a cause for such professional associations as the American Library Association (ALA), which asserts ". . . the right of every individual to both seek and receive information from all points of view without restriction. It provides for free access to all expressions of ideas through which any and all sides of a question, cause or movement may be explored. Intellectual freedom encompasses the freedom to hold, receive and disseminate ideas" (ALA 2010, 466).

The ALA takes an absolute position that intellectual freedom is a pre-requisite to effective and responsible citizenship in a democracy: "Intellectual freedom can exist only where two essential conditions are met: first, that all individuals have the right to hold any belief on any subject and to convey their ideas in any form they deem appropriate; and second, that society makes an equal commitment to the right of unrestricted access to information and ideas regardless of the communication medium used, the content of the work/and the viewpoints of both the author and receiver of information." (ALA 2010)

However, we now engage and interact via social media and the Internet in non-democracies. In response, the ALA has issued the following supplement:

> *Intellectual freedom is not only the bulwark of our constitutional republic but also the rallying cry of those who struggle for democracy worldwide. The metaphorical circle of intellectual freedom has expanded to global proportions over the past two decades with the advent of potent new communications technologies and the growing international recognition of the Universal Declaration of Human Rights, Article 19, of which declares the right of all people to freedom of expression. As the free flow of information transcends national boundaries, it becomes increasingly clear that prohibitions on freedom of expression in one country will inhibit the freedom of those in many other countries around the world. In an age of multinational media corporations, international computer links, global telecommunications, and the World Wide Web, we can no longer think simply in local terms. Promoting and defending intellectual freedom requires thinking globally and acting locally.* (ALA 2010)

It is not only the ALA who is concerned about the dramatic changes, opportunities, and challenges brought on by informational and data flow. Since the 1980s in the early writings in computer ethics, digital data have been considered "greased" and "malleable," meaning they move and flow freely and take on different meanings in different contexts. This nature of digital data contributes now to the vehicle for global intellectual freedoms. But, as Mackinnon (2012a) has rightfully identified, our "Internet" is now a conglomeration of private forces, companies, and intermediaries who act as censors, who go above and beyond what extant speech and expression laws across the world may permit; these private intermediaries (e.g., Internet Service Providers (ISPs) or Internet Corporation for Names and Numbers (ICANN) have been found responding to requests from governments to censor, shut down, limit, or otherwise "interfere" on their behalves. Morozov (2011) identified the same reality in regards to the Iranian protests in 2009, where reports of US government influence over Twitter was exerted. The US government worked with Twitter to postpone a planned maintenance outage, so that protest tweets would not be interrupted (Buchanan 2011). What we are seeing in relation to intellectual freedom is a shift from control over individuals and human rights by nation states to an oddly unnatural control over our digital lives by private sovereignties (MacKinnon 2012a).

In response to this growing phenomenon of mediation and control over our digital lives, the Global Network Initiative (GNI) was founded. "All over the world—from the Americas to Europe to the Middle East to Africa and Asia—companies in the Information & Communications Technology (ICT) sector face increasing government pressure to comply with domestic laws and policies in ways that may conflict with the internationally recognized human rights of freedom of expression and privacy. In response, a multi-stakeholder group of companies, civil society organizations (including human rights and press freedom groups), investors and academics spent two years negotiating and creating a collaborative approach to protect and advance freedom of expression and privacy in the ICT sector, and have formed an Initiative to take this work forward. . . . The GNI is founded upon Principles on Freedom of Expression and Privacy that all its participants commit to uphold. These Principles are based on internationally recognized laws and standards for human rights, including the Universal Declaration of Human Rights (UDHR), the International Covenant on Civil and Political Rights (ICCPR), and the International Covenant on Economic, Social and Cultural Rights (ICESCR) (GNI 2011, 4). Interestingly, at last check, Twitter and Facebook, two of the major players in the so-called social media democracy movement, have not signed on to the GNI.

Determined entities, such as Reporters Without Borders, The International Freedom of eXchange, *The FIRE*, among others, are on constant vigil, as are dispersed collectives such as Anonymous to watch and protect against infringements to intellectual freedom in the globally-dispersed and interconnected world in which we share.

Let them Tweet?

Not everyone is in agreement about the role of social media and the Internet as the savior of and for intellectual freedoms world-wide. Morozov has asserted,

> *After all, Internet users can discover the truth about the horrors of their regimes, about the secret charms of democracy, and about the irresistible appeal of universal human rights on their own, by turning to search engines like Google and by following their more politically savvy friends on social networking sites like Facebook. In other words, let them tweet, and they will tweet themselves to freedom. By this logic, authoritarianism becomes unsustainable once the barriers to the free flow of information are removed.* (2011, xii)

Gladwell squarely questions the role of social media in the face of political activism: "It makes it easier for activists to express themselves, and harder for that expression to have any impact. The instruments of social media are well suited to making the existing social order more efficient" (Gladwell 2010).

The social order and protest are intimately connected with human rights and particularly, expression. Social media and Internet data are continually subjected to third party interference, and MacKinnon has found "Adding to the threat to free speech, recent academic research on global Internet censorship has found that in countries where heavy legal liability is imposed on companies, employees tasked with day-to-day censorship jobs have a strong incentive to play it safe and over-censor—even in the case of content whose legality might stand a good chance of holding up in a court of law. Why invite legal hassle when you can just hit 'delete'?" (2011).

Many institutions, businesses, and universities are doing just that, in a manner of speaking. That often untenable and uncomfortable line between ethics and law surfaces once again in the area of intellectual freedom and rights to expression. The rise of codes of conduct for social media usage for private, public, academic and business has been well documented, and Boudreaux (2012) has accumulated a sizeable collection of such policies. These policies reveal some commonalities around approaches to and restrictions on intellectual and particularly academic freedoms. For example, as an employee of a particular institution, one's participation in social media may be limited. Where universities are concerned, *The FIRE* has been examining such policies and calling attention where the constitutional right to speech and expression via social media have been infringed. But much future research on these specific questions and concerns surrounding the health of intellectual freedom, in light of social media policy, is critical.

Coming Full Circle

"Intellectual freedom implies a circle, and that circle is broken if *either freedom of expression or access to ideas is stifled*" (ALA 2010, emphasis added).

We are left with dissent and debate, not surprisingly, around intellectual freedoms, technologies, cultures, and securities. MacKinnon, who advocates strongly for a "citizen-centric" Internet that is governed by "consent of the networked," still admits, "We do not have good answers on how to balance the need for security and law enforcement on the one hand and protection of civil liberties and free speech on the other in our digital networks" (MacKinnon 2012a). The "consent of the networked" includes negotiation and balance, and awareness of the "otherness" in our world.

We began this chapter by reviewing one hot-button intellectual freedom case. The communities, both local and global, were torn on issues at the core of the case: Individual, intellectual freedom rights versus community and individual safeties. In response to the Firefly incident at UW Stout, a working group was formed to ensure consistency and adherence to extant first amendment rights with the assurance of personal and campus-wide security: Shiell and the Working Group (2012) produced a university-wide endorsed report and action protocol clearly grounded in first amendment rights, legal definitions and precedent around true threats, and university and system policy. It begins:

> The University of Wisconsin—Stout values freedom of speech and believes strongly in the right of all students, faculty and staff to express themselves freely about issues on and off campus. This freedom is fundamental on a public university campus. At the same time, it also is obligated to provide reasonable time, place, and manner regulations and to respond to unprotected harmful expression. Since expression can involve controversy and complaints, the university needs a process for dealing appropriately with complaints about expression, whether verbal or nonverbal. (2012)

Other institutions dealing with these tensions between rights and safety, and there are many, as documented on *The FIRE's* web page (2012a), or written about frequently in the Chronicle of Higher Education (for example, Fischman, 2011) who are encouraged to review the Stout policy. We at UW Stout learned a valuable lesson from this experience, one at the heart of intellectual freedom: Listen to your stakeholders, constituents, and opponents. It is in those places of passionate dissent and disagreement that meaningful engagement truly occurs.

Conclusion

The technologies we are surrounded by will continue to push our norms, our laws, our principles, and our dedication to basic human rights through new and novel tests and trials. The terrain is indeed different and novel, and we are seeing and experiencing a brave new world of expression: "Our best and brightest should be encouraged to find new methods of expression; direct action in protest must not stifle. The dawning of the digital age should be seen as an opportunity to expand our knowledge, and to collectively enhance our communication" (Leiderman 2013).

Epilogue

At the time of this writing, Aaron Swartz, founder of Demand Progress, who called attention to Facebook's censoring of political dissidents and bloggers, passed away, January 13, 2013. I want to thank Aaron for, among many other things, his contributions to intellectual freedom.

References

Alfino. Mark. 2012. Twenty years of information ethics. The *Journal of Information Ethics. Journal of Information Ethics* 21, no. 2: 13–16.

Buchanan, Elizabeth. 2011. E-research ethics and e-planning: emerging considerations for transformative research. *International Journal of E-Planning Research* 1, no. 1: 5–15.

American Library Association (ALA). 2010. *Intellectual Freedom Handbook*. Chicago: ALA.

Boudreaux, Chris. 2012. Social Media Governance Policy Database. http://socialmediagovernance.com/policies.php (accessed August 27, 2013).

Electronic Frontier Foundation. n.d. Grey Tuesday: A Quick Overview of the Legal Terrain. http://w2.eff.org/IP/grey_tuesday.php (accessed August 27, 2013).

Ess, Charles. 2009. *Digital Media Ethics*. Cambridge, UK: Polity.

European Commission. 2011. A Partnership for Democracy and Shared Prosperity with the Southern Mediterranean. *Joint communication to the European Council, the European Parliament, the Council, the European Economic and Social Committee and the Committee of the Regions*, Brussels (8.3.2011), COM. 200 final. http://eeas.europa.eu/euromed/docs/com2011_200_en.pdf (accessed August 27, 2013).

European Council. 1950. European convention for the protection of human rights and fundamental freedoms. http://conventions.coe.int/Treaty/en/Treaties/Html/005.htm (accessed August 27, 2013).

The Fire. 2012a. Schools. http://thefire.org/spotlight/schools/1844 (accessed August 27, 2013).

———. 2012b. About speech codes. Available: http://thefire.org/spotlight/about/ (accessed August 27, 2013).

Fischman, Josh. 2011. Will the internet destroy academic freedom? *The Chronicle of Higher Education*. http://chronicle.com/blogs/wiredcampus/will-the-internet-destroy-academic-freedom/31302. (accessed August 27, 2013).

Gladwell, Malcolm. 2010. Small change: Why the revolution will not be tweeted." *The New Yorker*. October 4. http://www.newyorker.com/reporting/2010/10/04/101004fa_fact_gladwell?currentPage=all. (accessed August 27, 2013).

Global Network Initiative (GNI). 2011. Protecting and advancing freedom of expression and privacy in information and communication technologies. Annual Report. http://www.globalnetworkinitiative.org/files/GNI_2011_Annual_Report.pdf. (accessed August 27, 2013).

Kain, Erik. 2011. How Firefly fans and Neil Gaiman used social media to save free speech. *Forbes Online*. December 11. http://www.forbes.com/sites/erikkain/2011/12/27/how-firefly-fans-and-neil-gaiman-used-social-media-to-save-free-speech/. (accessed August 27, 2013).

Kissel, Adam. 2012. "Speech police, campus speech codes, free speech and academic freedom." Stout Social Science Society. You Tube. http://www.youtube.com/watch?v=Qyw_L3VHdKA. (accessed June 20, 2013).

Leiderman, Jay. 2013. Justice for the PayPal WikiLeaks protesters: Why DDoS is free speech. *The Guardian.* 22 January. http://www.guardian.co.uk/commentisfree/2013/jan/22/paypal -wikileaks-protesters-ddos-free-speech. (accessed August 27, 2013).

Lessig, Lawrence. 2006. *Code: And Other Laws of Cyberspace, Version 2.0.* New York: Basic Books.

MacKinnon, Rebecca. 2011. Stop the great firewall of America. *The New York Times.* http://msl1.mit.edu/furdlog/docs/nytimes/2011-11-16_nytimes_ mackinnon_protect_IP_act.pdf (accessed August 27, 2013).

———. 2012a. *Consent of the networked world: The worldwide struggle for internet freedom.* New York: Basic Books.

———. 2012b. Consent of the Networked World. Ted Talk: http://consentofthenetworked.com/tedtalk/.

Morozov, Evgeny. 2011. *The net delusion: The dark side of internet freedom.* New York: Perseus Group.

Reporters without Borders. 2013. Press Freedom Index. http://en.rsf.org/ press-freedom-index-2013,1054.html (accessed August 27, 2013).

Shiell, T. and Working Group. 2012. First Amendment Protocol. http://www.uwstout.edu/ethicscenter/upload/protocol-narrative.pdf (accessed August 27, 2013).

University of Wisconsin—Stout. 2012. Inclusive excellence. http://www.uwstout.edu/about/diversity/index.cfm. (accessed August 27, 2013).

United Nations. 1948. The Universal Declaration of Human Rights. http://www.un.org/en/documents/udhr/ (accessed August 27, 2013).

The Open Access Movement

Olivier Charbonneau

Setting the Stage for Open Access

For many of us, the Internet now seems intertwined with our daily lives. Despite this, the emergence of a global interconnected digital network still rumbles the bedrock of many communities. It impacts how we interact with each other, as well as how we access and use documents and information (Ryan 2010). It also opens the door for new ways of thinking about these interactions, which, in many cases, imply paradigm shifts (Kuhn 1972). One such paradigm shift is open access.

According to Suber, open access involves documents or information that are "digital, online, free of charge, and free of most copyright and licensing restrictions" (2012, 4). As we will see in a moment, open access is often associated with the scholarly communication processes but, as Elkin-Koren and Salzberger judiciously point out:

> There is no strict definition of open access, or open content, and the term is often used to describe a wide range of activities with different strategies, goals and ideological commitments. Some initiatives focus on availability, promoting free and unrestricted access to all kinds of content, such as open access journals (e.g. BioMed, Public Library of Science (PLoS)) and courseware (e.g. MIT Open Courseware project). Other initiatives emphasize freedom to use copyrighted materials, and especially to modify, remix and tinker with pre-existing materials. The conviction shared by many open content initiatives is that the online environment facilitates new ways of sharing and collaborating in the production of creative works, and that copyright law in its current form creates an obstacle to exercise these new opportunities. (2012, 154)

It is important to understand that open access is a way to make materials available in digital environments, which was not afforded to us in such a direct manner before the advent of a global interconnected network. It involves a particular approach, that of openness, which also has ramifications in many domains.

In that sense, our goal with this paper is to provide sufficient insight into open access so that our readers may engage on the topic from an intellectual freedom perspective. That is why we will begin by exploring the relationship between these two topics. Then, we will succinctly present the theoretical issues related to open access, following Lessig's regulatory Framework (1999, 81). This framework provides for a structured analytical approach, dividing a complex digital issue in four themes: law, markets (or economics), norms and technology.

Afterwards, we will delve into more practical cases. The first one involves scholarly communication or, broadly speaking, publication of peer-reviewed scientific literature that originate from academic research projects. This first case is given more weight in this paper as it has generated much discussion. In fact, many confound this topic and open access, although it is applied to a myriad of other issues. Then, we will succinctly present a range of other cases where open access is seen as a viable solution or where advocates are pushing for it: free/libre open source software; open content and the public domain; open government; and free access to law. For each of these cases, we will highlight distinguishing features in order to orient the reader to more detailed information.

On the subject of terminology, we use the term "information" in a generic manner, which includes data, knowledge, information, culture or wisdom and the myriad products and documents that contain them, in digital (e.g.: electronic files) or physical (i.e.: books, CDs, vinyl records, etc.) form. Please excuse this shorthand.

One last point about epistemology, we borrow broadly from social systems theory as posited by Luhmann (1993; 1995; 2000; 2004), whereby agents in a social system interact through formal or informal communications, the sum of which form distinct sub-systems within their environments. Complexity arises when parameters or new factors influence impact how communications occurred—leading to systemic change.

Intellectual Freedom and Open Access

There is a clear consensus in the literature that intellectual freedom is directly linked with freedom of expression, the press and to access and use information and that it is a core value of librarianship. Michael Gorman famously stated that

> In the United States, [intellectual freedom] is constitutionally protected by the First Amendment to the Constitution, which states, in part,

"Congress shall make no law respecting an establishment of religion or prohibiting the free exercise thereof; or abridging freedom of speech, or of the press." There is, of course, no such thing as an absolute freedom outside the pages of fiction and utopian writings, and, for that reason, intellectual freedom is constrained by law in every jurisdiction. (2000, 88)

Gorman continues to state that rarely are proponents "for" or "against" intellectual freedom, but they articulate their views in absolute or relative terms. On these issues, Hauptman (2002, 16–29) as well as McMenemy, Poulter and Burton (2007) offer additional evidence and insight. The link between intellectual freedom and censorship is obvious.

Intellectual freedom is also linked with Article 19 of the United Nation's Universal Declaration of Human Rights, which states:

Everyone has the right to freedom of opinion and expression; this right includes freedom to hold opinions without interference and to seek, receive and impart information and ideas through any media and regardless of frontiers. (1948)

Samek (2007, 9–11) provides an account of how various groups, such as United Nations Educational, Scientific and Cultural Organization (UNESCO) and the International Federation of Library Associations and Institutions (IFLA) have further articulated the concept of intellectual freedom in various initiatives and declarations.

Barendt offers an interesting distinction between academic freedom, a well-known right professors enjoy in universities, and intellectual freedom:[a] cademic freedom is not identical to intellectual freedom or to freedom of the mind. Intellectual freedom is a right to which we are all entitled, wherever we work. Like freedom of speech or expression, it is a general right belonging to all citizens. (2010, 38) In discussing how intellectual freedom and freedom of expression are intertwined, Krug further articulates, in light of librarianship, that:

all people have the right to hold any belief or idea on any subject and to express those beliefs or ideas in whatever form they consider appropriate. The ability to express an idea or a belief is meaningless, however, unless there is an equal commitment to the right of unrestricted access to information and ideas regardless of the communication medium. Intellectual freedom, then, is the right to express one's ideas and the right of others to be able to read, hear or view them. (2006, 394–5)

From these points, we can draw a common thread for intellectual freedom, namely that it is universal in enshrining our right to access and use information. In light of this, intellectual freedom intersects or overlaps with open access in that the former is promoted as a way to maximize or optimize access and use of digital documents and information while the latter expresses a fundamental right of the same vein.

If open access and intellectual freedom are linked through their desired outcomes, that of increased access and use, they truly overlap when there is a clear case where an agent or an institution has a clear role in making the information they produce available under open access. That is to say, the imperative to make information available under open access. This linkage is implied in the literature, but more analysis of the relationship between these two concepts would undoubtedly be welcome.

Theoretical Insights Around OA

In order to dissect open access in more manageable bites, we will apply Lessig's regulatory Framework (1999, 81). This framework provides for a structured analytical approach, dividing a complex digital issue in four themes: law, markets (or economics), norm, and technology.

For law, we must first consider how public law and private ordering interact, namely through copyright and its interaction with freedom of expression. As for markets or economics, we will explore the rather revolutionary issue of "free" or "zero price" afforded to us by digital technologies. Then, gift giving and prestige provide insight to the norms of open access systems. And, we will explore how technology has shifted to open access in the past decades.

Private Relationships within Public Law

An important distinction must be made between the regimes established by public laws and the private relationships that are derived from them. Too often are these two confounded when analyzing how social systems interact with legal issues. In fact, agents in a social system interact according to rules established by law, but how they interact is rather a function of power asymmetries, such as access to capital. This is essential to understanding how open access is being brought forward in line with copyright.

Copyright establishes a general legal regime empowering a right-holder to forbid specific uses of qualifying information goods—generally referred to as "protected works" by jurists. In turn, one has two options if you wish to use a protected work in a way that constitutes a reserved right: (1) seek permission from a right-holder (which may not necessarily be the original creator); or (2) qualify for a limitation (such as through a collective licensing agency) or exception (such as fair use/dealings or other specific exceptions) to copyright, which depends directly on your jurisdiction (i.e. which country in the world you are in and that national Copyright Act). If you cannot, you must refrain from using the work or face reprimand. This general canvas explains how radio stations can play music; movie theatres show films; and how schools and universities can make copies of published works for students.

Now, the original goal of providing a "right to forbid" using protected works was to establish artificial scarcity around a work to allow markets to flourish. Many have raised significant issues with how this may limit the right to freedom of expression internationally (Griffiths and Suthersanen 2005; Strowel and Tulkens 2006) and within the United States (Nimmer 1969; Goldstein 1970; Litman 1986, 2006; Netanel 2001, 2008). Much can be said about how overzealous large corporations with a treasure trove filled with protected works muscle others to silence but this is not where our story is going.

Rather, open access focuses on cases where agents have an incentive (or should have an incentive) to allow others to use protected works. This is mainly achieved through contractual means, which fit completely within the logic of copyright (Lessig 1999, 2001, 2005, 2006, 2008). Contracts, also called licenses (Ellen 2009) when they cover non-exclusive rights, are a mechanism whereby a right-holder may authorize the use of a protected work in a way reserved by copyright.

In that sense, licensing schemes associated with open access, such as Creative Commons or the General Public licenses, are a twist of classic copyright because they constitute *pre-authorizations* for using a work (as opposed to asking for permission, you are allowed in advance) in specific cases. These licenses reflect the power of copyright permissions granted by contractual means, channeled to empower a community of creators to share, remix and use protected works.

Copyright establishes the general rules around using protected works. In it of itself, it is a means to an end, and can be wielded both to allow and forbid uses. The open access movement is using this tool to foster a system of pre-authorized uses, illustrating a fascinating case of judicious application of its principles to the digital environment.

The Economics of "Zero"

The economics of information goods are a fascinating and emerging field, particularly since the emergence digital technology (Varian, Farrell and Shapiro 2004). Not only do information goods expose a strange sequence of characteristics, they also test our assumptions of market dynamics (McKenzie 2003; Brousseau and Curien 2007).

Economic literature distinguishes between two types of goods: private goods and public goods. Economists use two concepts to distinguish them: rivalrousness and excludability. The case of private goods is easy to understand, as they are classic consumable goods. They generally respond to market dynamics of supply and demand, such as: an apple; a single copy of a paper book; a meal in a restaurant; etc. Private goods are rival in the same way that eating an apple means there is one less apple in the market and excludable because if the apple I own is in my lunch bag, I can exclude you from it (and society will back me up on my ownership claim if it is legitimate). Public goods are rather of a different breed, as they tend to have completely different consumption patterns. Take air, for example. It is difficult to say who owns it, if you consume air by breathing, it is hard to exclude others from doing so at the same time and your breathing of air does not deplete the total supply or air (on a global scale at least). As such, economists say that public goods are nonrival and nonexcludable.

More and more, digital information goods (without encryption) are seen as public goods in the economic sense (actually, so did the ideas behind physical information goods). For example, each copy of a non-encrypted PDF document on a government website is identical to the previous (nonrival) and can be copied at will (nonexcludable). Barring network congestion, it is easy to understand how digital documents on the Internet behave, in the economic sense, in the same manner as air (of course, you may say that accessing the Internet is not free and there may be network congestion in some cases—but this simplified example illustrates my point).

In that sense, open access can be construed as a way to maximize the aggregate social value of information goods. The more people share or participate in an information good, the more valuable it becomes for society. Shapiro and Varian present these issues from the perspective of network effects:

> There is a central difference between the old and the new economies: the old industrial economy is driven by economies of scale; the new information economy is driven by the economics of networks. [. . .] Whether real or virtual, networks have a fundamental economic characteristic: the value of connecting to a network depends on the number of other people already connected to it. (1999, 173–4)

In fact, digital technologies have decreased the costs of participating in digital environments. Anderson summarizes how the digital environment changes the economics of information goods:

> The democratized tools of production are leading to a huge increase in the number of producers. Hyperefficient digital economics are leading to new markets and marketplaces. And finally, the ability to tap the distributed intelligence of millions of consumers to match people with the stuff that suits them best is leading to the rise of all sorts of new recommendation and marketing methods, essentially serving as the new tastemakers. (2006, 57)

This has lead to a new category of information good: those produced socially. Benkler introduces an important point about the collaborative endeavor inherent to digital environments:

> Because social sharing requires less precise specification of the transactional details with each transaction, it has a distinct advantage over market-based mechanisms for reallocating the excess capacity of shareable goods, particularly when they have small quanta of excess capacity relative to the amount necessary to achieve the desired outcome. [. . .] If excess capacity in a society is very widely distributed in small dollops, and for any given use of the excess capacity it is necessary to pool the excess capacity of thousands or even millions of individual users, the transaction-cost advantages of the sharing system become significant. (2006, 114–5)

The reader will now understand the importance of copyright laws in economics of information goods. Because copyright forbids what technology allows, the economic nature of information goods changes from a public good to a private good. Said differently, the "right to forbid" granted to the rightholder by copyright creates artificial scarcity and a quasi-monopoly around the protected work. In that sense, the field of the economic analysis of law as applied to copyright and digital environments is rich (Frischmann 2012; Elkin-Koren and Salzberger 2012, 2004; Elkin-Koren, Netanel and Baker 2002).

Of Gifts, Prestige and Commons Management

Now that we have examined the legal and economic ramifications of open access, the question of "why?" begs itself. Why would creators elect to "give away" their content mostly for free on the Internet? What norms would dictate such a behavior in their communities?

Benkler (2005, 183) provides a partial answer in his discussion about perceived rewards of contributors of open access content, which he links to gift giving and alternative resource sharing networks. He posits that there are three main motivators for individuals to participate: monetary rewards; intrinsic hedonic rewards; and social-psychological rewards. Firstly, one may give away their intellectual property because doing so will allow them to profit down the line. This is the case for contributing to open source software projects, as one may obtain consulting contracts down the line, which may be much more lucrative than the small contribution of code to the overall software project. Secondly, some people derive intrinsic motivation from doing good deeds, hence the hedonistic rewards. Finally, social-psychological rewards stem from the prestige one can obtain from the community that produces the social good, for example by being recognized as an expert on a subject by your peers. Understanding how these three factors interact to motivate individuals in participating in peer-production systems will yield a better understanding of the norms that motivate a group.

Ostrom devised another approach through her analysis of how commons are managed outside of market mechanisms (Olstom 1990, 90–120). This framework highlights that the "tragedy of the commons" (Hardin 1968) can be averted if communities can manage to adhere to certain principles to guide their action. This model was recently applied to "knowledge commons" through the Institutional Analysis and Development framework or IAD (Ostrom and Hess 2007, 41–81), which aims to analyze commonly managed resources. First, the parameters of a case are described based on the biophysical characteristics of the resources used in common; the attributes of the community; and the rules in use. Then, action situations identify the salient processes as applied by the relevant actors—this constitutes the "Action Area" of the model, which yields patterns of interaction. Finally, evaluation criteria and outcomes provide feedback to all parts of the model. The IAD provides for another model to understand norms and parameters within a community that guide their collective actions.

Making it all Work

Digital technologies are at the forefront of open access. A loosely managed network of networks, where nodes can be added easily and at low cost as per the Open Systems Interconnection (OSI) Model (ISO/IEC 7498-1), provides for a flexible topography. Combined with inexpensive tools to create, edit and manage digital content, this topography provides for a fertile ground to sow the seeds of information.

The OSI Model is an important building block to understand: it is through open standards that a silent horde has coordinated the immense effort of cooperating to create the Internet. Each individual agent could interface with the broader network if they respected the basic rules with each application they added to the system. It also allowed small, simple projects to mushroom up to a global scale. When open standards are designed into a system, other agents can piggy-back on the value generated by each new user or information added to the system. Someone's free-riding becomes a vector for increased value for every member of the community. A great example of this process is the free/libre open source software (FLOSS) movement, which will be covered in a separate section below.

Tim O'Reilly (2005) famously proposed the phrase "Web 2.0" to describe this phenomenon, also known now as social media. To describe the potential of these new technologies, Coombs (2007, 16) has identified six pillars that underpin them:

1. Radical decentralization
2. Small pieces loosely joined
3. Perpetual beta
4. Remixable content
5. User as contributor
6. Rich user experience

These pillars—or philosophies—illustrates why social media have become so popular so quickly, namely through the network effect described above. Not all open access initiatives exhibit all of these factors, but the technological potential is there to innovate and shake the foundations of existing social processes. The next few sections present cases where communities have undertaken open access movements.

Scholarly communication

As famously posited by Harold J. Coolidge, a researcher's imperative is to publish or perish. This has given rise to the scholarly communication process, whereby submitted papers are peer-reviewed for quality and published in academic journals. Before digital technologies, this process was achieved through print dissemination. Researchers would give away the copyright to their papers to commercial publishers, who would organize the peer-review and printing processes, so that, in turn, university libraries would subscribe to them to provide access to scientific knowledge.

The problem arose when publishers saw an opportunity to deploy their business online, namely to leverage the intellectual assets given to them by researchers on the backs of university libraries, who are locked-in to subscribing to their journals. As Willinsky put it:

> Bodies of knowledge that would advance human understanding and benefit humankind seem so clearly a public good that it might well be hard for someone who is not part of the current system of scholarly publishing to understand why the research and scholarship literature is not being made as open as possible. One might argue that the print economy of journal publishing was once as open and far-reaching as is economically possible. Had journal prices not skyrocketed over the last few decades, it is possible that the idea of creating open access would not have taken the form that it has, or at least the idea would not have the force and urgency that it has now assumed. (2006, 36–7)

Studies abound of the skyrocketing cost of journal subscriptions in academic library (Association for Research Libraries 2004; Jacobs 2006; Suber

2012, 181) and are mostly cited as the main imperative of open access to scholarly communications.

In understanding the scope of open access to scholarly communications, some focus on the academic article submitted for peer-review, the workhorse of the research process, while others also include raw data generated by experiments as items to be made available in open access. In any case, open access is generally seen as both an alternative and a complement to the classic publication process.

Authors have the option of either choosing a fully open-access peer-reviewed journal (see the Directory of Open Access Journals at doaj.org), which is considered "gold" open access; publishing in classic journals (also called toll-access or subscription journals), as well as self-archiving their papers in open archives or institutional repositories, which is considered the "green" option. Most toll-access journals allow for the latter option and a summary of their self-archiving policies can be found on the SHERPA/RoMEO project page (http://www.sherpa.ac.uk/romeo/).

The open access journal "gold" option and the self-archiving "green" option were laid out in the Budapest Open Access Initiative statement (Open Society Foundation 2002) and the Berlin Declaration (Max Planck Society 2003). The latter is presented as something to foster while the latter as more of an imperative. Then, the Bethesda Statement (Suber 2003) provides guidance for institutions (universities) and grant-giving organizations on how to incorporate open access principles in their policies. It introduces a further distinction between "gratis" and "libre" open access. The former provides to access at no cost to the reader but still imposes copyright restrictions. The latter provides access that is free of charge and under a permissive license such as Creative Commons.

An important advocate for open access is the Scholarly Publishing and Academic Resources Coalition of the Association for Research Libraries (SPARC). It provides for many publications and guides to open access, such as alternate business models or model policies for universities (SPARC 2012). Another advocate for open access is the United Nations Educational, Scientific and Cultural Organization (UNESCO), which recently published a guide on developing open access policies for government and institutions (Swan 2012).

A final comment should be made on how institutions are implementing open access to scholarly communications. Some have voiced concerns that open access mandated from universities or grant-giving organizations are an impediment to academic freedom as they constrain the author of a scholarly communication to disseminate their creations in a particular way. Although these issues are very important, Suber points out that:

Academic authors remain free to submit their work to the journals or publishers of their choice. Policies requiring [open access] do so conditionally, for example, for researchers who choose to apply for a certain kind of grant. In addition, these policies generally build in exceptions, waver options, or both. Since 2008 most university policies have been adopted by faculty deeply concerned to preserve and enhance their prerogatives. (2012, 23)

The faculty autonomy argument is an important one to preserve academic (and, by extension, intellectual) freedom in scholarly communication. That is why so much attention is given to how institutions deploy their open access policies.

Other cases of OA

In this section, we briefly explore a few more cases where communities have been actively seeking open access to various types of resources. These are presented in no particular order.

Free/Libre and Open Source Software

Open source software is the original open access case. Software is created from code—computer code written by humans to operate computers. This code is then compiled or transformed into binary instructions that a computer's processor can implement in a program. When one installs a program on a personal computer, they copy the program's binary files to their computer. To modify a program, one needs to tinker with the source code, not the binary files.

That is why most commercial software is proprietary—we obtain a license to use the binary file and its corresponding program as is, not the right to tinker with the source code. As Stallman (2002) or Raymond (2001) have famously pointed out, in the early days of computers, one would receive the source code and were allowed to make local adjustments to ensure that the software would work properly. Proprietary software hinders our capacity to adapt the programs we use to our local needs.

The Free versus libre distinction is in line with the gratis or libre issue in scholarly communication. Giving software away for free is one thing, liberating it from copyright restrictions is quite another. The autonomy argument is foundational for the open source software movement.

Open Content and the public domain

The issues and philosophies of the open source software movement have repercussions in other areas, such as cultural production, social media and open educational resources. For example, Boyle (1996, 2008) explores how corporations attempt to enclose the public domain within their licensing businesses. Lessig (2006, 2005, 2001) proposes a structure by which we can share our cultural productions freely on the Internet. And Butcher, Kanwar and Uvalic-Trumbic (2011) envision a world where teachers and professors work together to create a global network of free online curricular documents for open education. All these are further examples of communities employing the open access principles

Open government

The term "open government" refers to a series of initiatives to increase access and use of public sector information, data and documents. It has gained broad acceptance within official governmental circles following a White House memorandum mandating United States agencies to follow its precepts (Orszag 2009) as well as an international declaration of principles aimed at governments (Open Government Partnership 2011).

Open government has drawn insight from many laws, policy instruments and institutions. For example, the right to access government records and documents is guaranteed in many jurisdictions around the world by freedom of information (FOI) laws (Mendel 2008). Similarly, many countries have launched e-government policies to modernize government processes (United Nations 2012). As well, many institutions support open access of public sector information, such as UNESCO (Uhlir 2004) and the OECD (2007, 2009). In a sense, open government builds momentum from these initiatives while introducing new concepts and processes.

A dynamic understanding of open government may be required to fully apprehend all ramifications (Gavelin, Burall and Wilson 2009). In fact, Lathrop and Ruma link open government with the philosophy of open source software:

> The concept of open government has been influenced—for the better—by the open source movement, and taken on a greater focus for allowing participation in the procedures of government. Just as open source software allows users to change and contribute to the source code of their software, open government now means government where citizens not only have access to information, documents and proceedings, but can also become participants in a meaningful way. Open governments also means improved communication and operations within various branches and levels of government. More sharing internally can lead to greater efficiency and accountability. (2010, xix)

These measures serve as a means of increasing accountability of government actions through transparency while involving citizens in the governance of the state through participation and collaboration. Similarly, open government implies a subtle argument about how the rhetoric of ownership inherent to copyright's logic of permission seeking hinders the broad use and sharing of government information.

Free Access to Law

"The Law" or legal information or primary legal materials generally refers to documents produced by competent legislatures and judiciary bodies within a jurisdiction, most notably court rulings as well as statutes and related documents. One would simply assume that these documents would constitute public record and therefore be freely available in digital format. Actually, securing open access to legal information is a much more complex endeavor primarily because of tradition (Martin 2006).

In the United States, private publishers traditionally provided for the dissemination of primary legal documents (Berring 2000). With the emergence of digital technologies, the industry consolidated around a few major players (Danner 2006). One of these publishers, West Publishing, sued Mead Data Center for copyright infringement of its pagination methodology, widely used by courts and lawyers at the time to write about the law. In 1986, the 8th Circuit Federal Appellate Court ruled in favor of West, effectively halting initiatives to provide open access to court cases (Berring 1997). This initiated the Neutral Citation movement (Martin 2006).

In many other English-speaking countries around the globe (notably former British colonies), primary legal documents are covered by "crown copyright" or a copyright claim by the government, as is the case in Canada (Foote 1997). This direct claim of ownership, and subsequent licensing agreements with private publishers, has posed unique challenges to making these materials available on the Internet (Tjaden 2005).

In order to counter private or public claims of ownership, the Free Access to Law movement aims to foster the open access publishing of primary legal documents through Legal Information Institutes, which, according to the Montreal Declaration on Free Access to Law:

- Publish via the internet public legal information originating from more than one public body;

- Provide free and anonymous public access to that information;

- Do not impede others from obtaining public legal information from its sources and publishing it; and

- Support the objectives set out in this Declaration. (WorldLII 2007)

These various Legal Information Institutes are aggregated within WorldLII (Greenleaf, Chung and Mowbray 2005). In fact, open access to law is seen as a way to foster the rule of law, particularly for developing countries (Poulin 2004) where as many as 4 billion people do not have access to the rule of law (Commission on Legal Empowerment of the Poor 2008, 1).

Conclusion

Our goal was to present the many dimensions of open access, as it represents a paradigm shift for many communities and it warrants study from multiple angles. More importantly, open access fosters intellectual freedom as it facilitates access to information and, if the appropriate factors are present, fosters a sense of engagement and stewardship in different contexts. This does not happen in a vacuum, individuals and institutions must operate a conscious choice to adhere to its principles in order to realize its potential for their communities.

We have explored cases where communities or agents have a direct interest in considering open access as their preferred method for interacting between themselves as well as documentation and information. Hopefully, this increased access does not simply lead to more complexity, but is met with new institutions and ways of doing so that society can recoup the benefits of open access to more information.

Acknowledgement

The author would like to thank his employer, Concordia University Libraries (http://library.concordia.ca/) for the time granted to work on this paper.

References

American Library Association. 2006. *Intellectual freedom manual*. 7th ed. Chicago: American Library Association.

Anderson, Chris. 2006. *The long tail: Why the future of business is selling less of more*. New York: Hyperion.

Aoki, Keith, James Boyle, and Jennifer Jenkins, eds. 2008. *Bound by law?: Tales from the public domain*. New expand ed. Durham, NC: Duke University Press.

Association for Research Libraries. Monograph and serial expenditures in ARL libraries, 1986–2004. http://www.arl.org/bm~doc/monser04.pdf.

Barendt, E. M. 2010. *Academic freedom and the law: A comparative study*. Oxford, UK: Hart Pub.

Benkler, Yochai. 2005. Coase's penguin, or, linux and the nature of the firm. In *CODE : Collaborative ownership and the digital economy*, ed. Rishab Aiyer Ghosh. Cambridge, MA: MIT Press.

Benkler, Yochai. 2006. *The wealth of networks: How social production transforms markets and freedom*. New Haven, CT: Yale University Press.

———. 2004. Sharing nicely: On shareable goods and the emergence of sharing as a modality of economic production, *The Yale Law Journal* 114, no. 2: 273–358.

———. 2002. Intellectual property and the organization of information production, *International Review of Law and Economics* 22, no. 1: 81.

———. 2001. The battle over the institutional ecosystem in the digital environment, *Association for Computing Machinery. Communications of the ACM* 44, no. 2: 84.

———. 2000. From consumers to users: Shifting the deeper structures of regulation toward sustainable commons and user access, *Federal Communications Law Journal* 52, no. 3: 561.

Berring, Robert C. 2000. Legal information and the search for cognitive authority, *California Law Review* 88, no. 6: 1673–1676.

———. 1997. Chaos, cyberspace and tradition: Legal information transmogrified, *Berkeley Technology Law Journal* 12, no. 1: 189–212.

Bloemsaat, B. and P. Kleve. 2009. Creative commons: A business model for products nobody wants to buy, *International Review of Law, Computers & Technology* 23, no. 3: 237.

Bobinski, George S. 2007. *Libraries and librarianship: Sixty years of challenge and change, 1945–2005*. Lanham, MD: Scarecrow Press.

Bollier, David. 2008. *Viral spiral: How the commoners built a digital republic of their own*. New York: New Press: Distributed by W.W. Norton & Co.

Boyle, James. 2008. *The public domain: Enclosing the commons of the mind*. New Haven, CT: Yale University Press.

Boyle, James. *Shamans, software, and spleens : Law and the construction of the information society*. Cambridge, MA: Harvard University Press, 1996.

Brousseau, Eric and Nicolas Curien, eds. *Internet and digital economics*. Cambridge, UK: Cambridge University Press, 2007.

Buchanan, Elizabeth A., and Katherine Henderson, eds. 2009. *Case studies in library and information science ethics*. Jefferson, NC: McFarland & Co.

Butcher, Neil, Kanwar, Ash and Uvalic-Trumbic, S. 2011. A basic guide to open educational resources (OER). Commonwealth of Learning ; UNESCO.

Commission on Legal Empowerment of the Poor. 2008. *Making the law work for everyone*. Vol. 1 ed. United Nations Development Programme.

Coombs, Karen A. 2007. "Building a library web site on the pillars of web 2.0," *Computers in Libraries* 27, no. 1: 16. http://www.infotoday.com/cilmag/jan07/Coombs.shtml.

Crawford, Brian D. 2003. "Open-access publishing: Where is the value?" *Lancet* 362, no. 9395: 1578–1580.

Creative Commons International. Creative commons publishes study of "noncommercial use". http://creativecommons.org/press-releases/entry/17721.

———. *Defining "noncommercial": A study of how the online population understands "noncommercial use"*. http://wiki.creativecommons.org/Defining_Noncommercial.

Custer, Joseph A. Information policy and intellectual freedom in american libraries before and after september 11, 2001: A global perspective. *International Association of School Librarianship. Selected Papers from the Annual Conference 2005*: 1–20.

Danner, R. A. 2007. "Legal information and the development of american law: Writings on the form and structure of the published law," *Law Library Journal* 99, no. 2: 193–228.

Dole, Wanda V., Jitka M. Hurych, and Wallace C. Koehler. 2000. Values for librarians in the information age: An expanded examination,. *Library Management* 21, no. 6: 285–297.

Dutton, William H. 2011. *Freedom of connection, freedom of expression : The changing legal and regulatory ecology shaping the internet*. Paris: UNESCO.

eIFL-IP. Handbook on copyright and related issues for libraries, advocacy for access to knowledge: Copyright and libraries http://plip.eifl.net/eifl-ip/issues/handbook/handbook-e.

Elkin-Koren, Niva and Eli M. Salzberger. 2013. *The law and economics of intellectual property in the digital age: The limits of analysis*. Abingdon, UK: Routledge.

Fitzgerald, Brian F., Jessica Coates, and Suzanne Lewis, eds. 2007. *Open content licensing: Cultivating the creative commons*. Sydney, N.S.W.: Sydney University Press.

Foote, Martha L. 1997. *Law reporting and legal publishing in canada: A history*. Kingston, ON: Canadian Association of Law Libraries.

Frischmann, Brett M. 2012. *Infrastructure: The social value of shared resources*. New York: Oxford University Press.

Gavelin, Karin, Simon Burall, and Richard Wilson. 2009. *Open government: Beyond static measures* OECD.

Ghosh, Rishab Aiyer, ed. 2005. *CODE : Collaborative ownership and the digital economy*. Cambridge, Mass.: MIT Press.

Giles, Jim. 2004. Societies take united stand on journal access, *Nature* 428, no. 6981: 356.

Goldstein, Paul. 1970. Copyright and the first amendment, *Columbia Law Review* 70: 983–1057.

Gorman, Michael. 2000. *Our enduring values: Librarianship in the 21st century.* Chicago: American Library Association.

Greenleaf, G., P. Chung, and A. Mowbray. 2005. Responding to the fragmentation of international law—WorldLII's international courts and tribunals project, *Canadian Law Library Review* 30, no. 1: 13-22.

Hamilton, Stuart and Niels Ole Pors. 2003. Freedom of access to information and freedom of expression: The internet as a tool for global social inclusion, *Library Management* 24, no. 8/9: 407-416.

Hardin, Garrett. 1968. The tragedy of the commons. *Science* 162: 1243-1248.

Harris, Lesley Ellen. 2009. *Licensing digital content : A practical guide for librarians.* 2nd ed. Chicago: American Library Association.

Jacobs, Neil. 2006. *Open access: Key strategic, technical and economic aspects.* Oxford: Chandos.

Jones, Barbara M. 2009. *Protecting intellectual freedom in your academic library : Scenarios from the front lines.* Chicago, IL: American Library Association.

Krug, Judith F. 2006. Libraries and the internet. Chap. 7.3, In *Intellectual freedom manual*, ed. Office for Intellectual Freedom. 7th ed., 394. Chicago, IL: American Library Association.

Kuhn, Thomas S. 1972. *La structure des révolutions scientifiques.* Paris: Flammario.

LaRue, James. 2007. *The new inquisition : Understanding and managing intellectual freedom challenges.* Westport, CT: Libraries Unlimited.

Lathrop, Daniel and Laurel Ruma, eds. 2010. *Open government: Collaboration, transparency, and participation in practice.* Sebastopol, CA: O'Reilly Media.

Lessig, Lawrence. 2006. *Code version 2.0.* New York: Basic Books.

Lessig, Lawrence. 2008. *Remix: Making art and commerce thrive in the hybrid economy.* New York: Penguin Press.

———. 2005. *Free culture: The nature and future of creativity.* New York: Penguin Books.

———. 2001. *The future of ideas: The fate of the commons in a connected world.* New York: Random House.

———. 1999. *Code and other laws of cyberspace.* New York: Basic Books.

Litman, Jessica D. 1986-1987. Copyright compromise and legislative history, *Cornell Law Review* 72 no. 5: 857-904.

Luhmann, Niklas. 2000. *The reality of the mass media.* Stanford, CA: Stanford University Press.

— — —. 1995. *Social systems*. Stanford, CA: Stanford University Press.

— — —. 1993. *Risk: A sociological theory*. New York: A. de Gruyter.

Luhmann, Niklas, Klaus A. Ziegert, and Fatima Kastner. 2004. *Law as a social system*. Oxford, UK: Oxford University Press.

Mahnke, Christel. 2006. WSIS, IFLA, UNESCO and GATS: Networking for libraries on an international level, *Library Hi Tech* 24, no. 4: 540.

Martin, Peter W. 2006. Neutral citation, court web sites, and access to authoritative case law, *Law Library Journal*. 99, no. 2: 329-364.

Max Planck Society. 2003. Berlin Declaration. http://oa.mpg.de/lang/en-uk/berlin-prozess/berliner-erklarung/. (accessed March 30, 2012).

McKenzie, Richard B. 2003. *Digital economics: How information technology has transformed business thinking*. Westport, CT: Praeger.

McLeod, Kembrew, and Peter DiCola. 2011. *Creative license: The law and culture of digital sampling*. Durham, NC: Duke University Press.

Mendel, Toby. 2008. *Freedom of information: A comparative legal survey*. Ed. UNESCO. 2nd ed. Paris : France: UNESCO.

Nelson, Cary. 2010. *No university is an island: Saving academic freedom*. New York: New York University Press.

Netanel, Neil. 2008. *Copyright's paradox*. Oxford, UK: Oxford University Press.

Netanel, Neil Weinstock. 2001-2002. Locating copyright within the first amendment skein, *Stanford Law Review* 54: 1-86.

Nimmer, Melville B. 1969-1970. Does copyright abridge the first amendment guarantees of free speech and press, *UCLA Law Review* 17: 1180-1204.

OECD Working Party on the Information Economy, Committee for Information, Computer and Communication Policy. Recommendation of the council for enhanced access and more effective use of public sector information http://www.oecd.org/sti/44384673.pdf.

— — —. Digital broadband content : Public sector information and content, [s.l.]. OECD Publishing. http://www.oecd.org/dataoecd/10/22/36481524.pdf.

Open Government Partnership. Open government declaration. http://www.opengovpartnership.org/open-government-declaration.

O'Reilly, Tim. 2005. What is web 2.0: Design patterns and business models for the next generation of software. http://oreilly.com/web2/archive/what-is-web-20.html

Orszag, Peter R. 2009. *Open government directive* The White House. http://www.whitehouse.gov/open/documents/open-government-directive

Ostrom, Elinor. 1990. *Governing the commons: The evolution of institutions for collective action.* Cambridge, UK: Cambridge University Press.

Owen, Tim Buckley. 2010. Crown copyright switches to creative commons, *Information World Review* 263: 1.

Poulin, D. 2004. Open access to law in developing countries, *First Monday* 9, no. 12: http://firstmonday.org/.

Raymond, E. S. 2011. *The cathedral and the bazaar: Musings on linux and open source by an accidental revolutionary.* Sebastopol, CA: O'Reilly.

Rezmierski, Virginia and Aline Soules. 2000. Security vs anonymity. *EDUCAUSE Review* 35, no. 2: 22-30.

Robinson, Lyn and David Bawden. 2001. Libraries and open society; popper, soros and digital information, *Aslib Proceedings* 53, no. 5: 167-178.

Roesch, Hermann. "IFLA code of ethics for librarians (draft)." International Federation of Library Associations and Institutions. Accessed March 30, 2012. http://www.ifla.org/files/faife/news/ICoE-Draft-111208.pdf

Ryan, Johnny. 2010. *A history of the internet and the digital future.* London, UK: Reaktion Books.

Samek, Toni. 2007. *Librarianship and human rights: A twenty-first century guide.* Oxford, UK: Chandos.

Schrader, Alvin. 1999. Internet censorship: Issues for teacher-librarians, *Teacher Librarian* 26, no. 5: 8-12.

Schrader, Alvin M. 2011. Intellectual freedom: Issues and information, *Feliciter* 57, no. 1: 10.

– – –. 1998. Internet censorship: Access issues for school librarians in a cyberspace world. *International Association of School Librarianship. Selected Papers from the Annual Conference*: 189-210.

Shapiro, Carl and Hal R. Varian, eds. 1999. *Information rules: A strategic guide to the network economy.* Boston, MA: Harvard Business Review Press.

Shearer, Kathleen and Andrew Waller. 2011. Open access, *Feliciter* 57, no. 3: 88-90.

SPARC. "Papers and guides." Scholarly Publishing and Academic Resources Coalition. http://sparc.arl.org/resources/resource-type/papers-guides

St. Laurent, Andrew M. 2004. *Understanding open source & free software licensing.* Sebastopol, CA: O'Reilly Media Inc.

Stallman, Richard and Software Foundation Free. 2002. *Free software, free society: Selected essays of richard M. stallman.* Boston, MA: Free Software Foundation.

Suber, Peter. 2003. Bethesda statement on open access publishing. http://www.earlham.edu/~peters/fos/bethesda.htm.

— — —. Open access overview. http://www.earlham.edu/~peters/fos/overview.htm.

Suber, Peter. 2012. *Open access*. Cambridge, MA: MIT Press.

Sundara Rajan, Mira T. 2006. *Copyright and creative freedom a study of post-socialist law reform*, New York, NY: Routledge.

Swan, Alma and UNESCO. 2012. *Policy guidelines for the development and promotion of open access*. Paris: United Nations Educational, Scientific, and Cultural Organization.

Takenouchi, Tadashi. 2006. Information ethics as information ecology: Connecting frankl's thought and fundamental informatics, *Ethics and Information Technology* 8, no. 4: 187-193.

Tjaden, Theodore John. 2005. Access to law-related information in canada in the digital age. Faculty of Law /z-wcorg/; http://worldcat.org

Uhlir, Paul F. 2004. *Policy guidelines for the development and promotion of governmental public domain information* UNESCO.

UNESCO Institute for Information Technologies in Education. Cost-benefit modelling for open learning. http://iite.unesco.org/pics/publications/en/files/3214686.pdf.

United Nations. Universal declaration of human rights. http://www.un.org/en/documents/udhr/index.shtml.

United Nations Economic and Social Affairs. 2012. *E-government for the people*.

Upshall, Michael. 2009. *Content licensing: Buying and selling digital resources*. Oxford, UK: Chandos.

Varian, Hal R., Joseph Farrell, and Carl Shapiro, eds. 2004. *The economics of information technology: An introduction*. Cambridge, UK: Cambridge University Press.

Winston, Mark D. and Susan Quinn. 2005, Library leadership in times of crisis and change, *New Library World* 106, no. 9/10: 395-415.

WorldLII. Montreal declaration on free access to law. http://www.worldlii.org/worldlii/declaration/montreal_fr.html

Part Three

Laws, Rights, and International Intellectual Freedom

Intellectual Freedom from within the International Human Right to Freedom of Thought, Conscience, and Religion

Leonard Hammer

The international human rights system begins to protect intellectual free-dom[1] through different avenues such as freedom of expression, intellectual property rights, the right to education, and protection against invasions of privacy. In each of these instances, the base protection for intellectual freedom is the capacity for an unencumbered thought process. Whether to allow thought to foster into expressed ideas and applications, or to prevent undue interference with an individual's private domain, the central notion is to preserve the capacity for thought. Ensuring protection of the internal recesses of the mind is a key factor that preserves intellectual freedom.

One particular international human right that can serve as an important source for intellectual freedom derives, perhaps surprisingly, from the human right to freedom of religion and belief. While the right to free thought in the framework of freedom of religion or belief is inherently linked to some form of belief system, the right provides an avenue for intellectual freedom by upholding the individual's internal capacities for engagement and analysis of ideas and notions. Referred to as the *forum internum*,[2] the elaboration of this normative form of protection goes quite far towards upholding intellectual freedom as it develops and emerges in other protected spheres.

---

1   Understood in this chapter as allowing for unfettered free thought(s).
2   While the international human rights system deems the *forum internum* as inviolable, manifesting the thought externally could result in curtailment if, for example, social convention deems such views as immoral or contrary to public policy.

Understanding the *Forum Internum*

The International Covenant on Civil and Political Rights (hereafter, "ICCPR") provides at Article 18(1) that:

> *Everyone shall have the right to freedom of thought, conscience and re-ligion. This right shall include freedom to have or to adopt a religion or belief of his choice, and freedom, either individually or in community with others and in public or private, to manifest his religion or belief in worship, observance, practice and teaching.* (United Nations 1976, 172)

The first line of this paragraph describes the *forum internum*, protecting 'religion conscience and thought'. The rest of the paragraph uses the terms 'religion or belief' to codify the manifestation of the right in the *forum exter-num*. The implication then is that the *forum internum* relates to wider aspects that includes all forms of thought.

'Thought' implies an infinite realm of ideas that a person might internally harbour. These can include a "personal" opinion, such as the merits of the colour blue in a bedroom, to a more developed form of constructed knowl-edge, such as understanding nuclear physics. The *forum internum* beliefs un-der Article 18 refer to an internal unit of knowledge deriving from specific mental processes. The unit of knowledge acquires its importance because individuals attribute to such knowledge some level of truth, which in turn leads to some form of compelling external action. The *forum internum* then en-compasses a broad swath of thought capacities, is subject to constant change as one considers new inputs into the thought processes, and is unique to each individual's social experiences and particular environment.

Furthermore, *forum internum* thoughts need not manifest themselves as *forum externum* beliefs since more general forms of expression could suffice.[3] For example, one's thought as to the merits of painting a prison wall bright red as opposed to brown based on the psychological benefits to the inmates can manifest itself through a number of general avenues. The typical mode might be by expressing one's opinion in governmental reports or profession-al journals relating to prisons. While the underlying 'belief' originates from an internal thought developed in the *forum internum*, the manifested action does not derive from a mandate to 'adhere' to the belief but results from a decision to express an opinion stemming from a thought. The thought itself does not demand any particular action from the person, even if it influences a person towards taking some form of external action, such as testifying to the benefits of the colour red before a governmental prison committee.

---

3   The typical example is freedom of thought manifesting via the freedom of ex-pression (vanDijk and vanHoof 1990, 398). See also discussion *infra*.

Of course, the individual is free to engage in particular actions that might be equivalent to the manifestation of a belief. Adhering to the belief that all prison walls are to be red might mandate a psychologist or prison worker to personally paint all such walls red or demand that it be carried out according to a belief.[4] The treaty terms 'to manifest his religion or belief in worship, observance, practice, and teaching' (ICCPR Article 18, *supra*) indicates that the treaty drafters were referring to cognitive beliefs that the individual relates to an underlying truth through one's existence (Partsch 1981; McDougal, Laswell, and Chen 1980; Benito 1989). Unlike a general thought, the manifestation of a 'belief' mandates specific modes of action pursuant to particular principles from which it is difficult to deviate. The narrower *forum externum* sphere of beliefs then derives from structured internal obligations that differ from the general units of knowledge protected in the *forum internum*.

ICCPR Article 18 further requires in subsection (2) that:

> *No one shall be subject to coercion which would impair his freedom to have or to adopt a religion or belief of his choice.* (ICCPR Article 18(2) *supra*)

The *travaux preparatoires* to the ICCPR note that the intention of the phrase 'to have or adopt' is to sanction the ability of the individual to change a religion or belief, a freedom to which various states severely objected. The drafters linked the ability to change a belief with the *forum internum* because such a change focuses on the internal, cognitive, abilities of the individual. The *travaux preparatoires* also refer to the issue of proselytising and the protection against missionaries from coercing individuals into changing their belief, as this interferes with one's internal free thought process (Tahzib 1996; Shaw 1992).

Of course, one can change a religion or belief and the change will be apparent through one's external actions. The change itself however occurred within the internal sphere of the *forum internum* due to a conscious decision to adopt a new form of belief.

Referring to the treaty language that prohibits coercion, the latter principally focuses on preventing a hindrance to the internal development of ideas and beliefs. The ICCPR Human Rights Committee's (hereafter "HRC") General Comment (hereafter "General Comment") to Article 18 defines coercion as incorporating:

> *the use of threat or physical force or penal sanctions to compel believers or non-believers . . . to recant their religion or belief or to convert. Policies*

---

4   Whether such demands are an accepted form of protected manifestation of a belief under the right is another determination.

or practices having the same intention or effect . . . are similarly inconsistent with Article 18(2). (United Nations 1993)

The HRC's General Comment to Article 18 refers not only to preventing the external practice of a belief (referred to as operating within the *forum externum*), but also to coercing one to recant a belief, the domain of the *forum internum*. Coercive actions of the state can violate the *forum internum* where the state is coercing an individual to alter an internal belief. Thus, in *Yong Joo-Kang v. Republic of Korea*, the Human Rights Committee found a violation of Article 18[5] by virtue of the attempt by the Korean authorities to discriminatorily engage in a coercive ideological conversion system to alter political opinions of inmates.

Commentators also have interpreted Article 18(2) as involving the *forum internum*. Coercion appertains to the individual's private, spiritual, or moral existence that cannot be subject to undue persuasion (Martinez-Torron 2005). The prohibited form of coercion differs from influences found in external forces, such as daily exposure to the media and advertising (Nowak 1993, 314; Sullivan 1988, 494). While 'appeals' to change a belief can include material inducements, the key factor is to avoid coercing the individual's freewill (Cumper 1995, 370; Sullivan 1988, 494).[6]

Krishnaswami's approach to the *forum internum* also focused on upholding the freedom of one's internal beliefs to prevent compulsion or coercion to belong or not to belong to a certain group (Krishnaswami 1960, 24–27). As described by Krishnaswami when studying the right to freedom of religion, a method for violating the *forum internum* is:

> *any instance of compelling an individual to join or of preventing him from leaving the organization of a religion or a belief in which he has no faith must be considered to be an infringement of the right to freedom of thought, conscience, and religion.* (Krishnaswami 1960, 16)

Pursuant to these comments, the protection accorded to the right to conscience in the *forum internum* is to prevent outside forces from violating an individual's internal thought or belief system, with the purpose of altering such a view. For example, brainwashing an individual is not so much concerned with a particular external practice or activity of the individual, but

---

5   Along with article 19, freedom of expression, see para. 7.2

6   Of course, advertising can be coercive as well. See *Church of Scientology v. Sweden* 1979. Restrictions on wording of advert for an 'E-meter', arguably a religious item, were upheld by the ECHR as not violating freedom of religion or free expression due to the commercial nature of transaction and perception that individuals joining the sect would feel compelled to purchase the item.

with a desire to change a belief or unit of knowledge harboured internally. The act of brainwashing, which also can entail a physical action that invokes other human rights violations (such as, for example, torture or inhumane treatment), consists of a desire to impose one's own beliefs or thoughts on the internal structure of the individual.[7]

The European Convention on Human Rights and Fundamental Freedoms (hereafter "ECHR") Court also distinguished between propagating a religion through missionary work, such as engaging a person in a general discussion, versus forcibly converting a person to another religion (*Kokkinakis v. Greece* 1993). Although not explicitly stated by the ECHR Commission in *Larissis v. Greece*, the prevention of coercion can be a reason for upholding an Air Force member's proselytising to civilians while prohibiting proselytising to fellow Air Force officers (*Larissis v. Greece* 1997). The Commission recognised the concern of the state that the inherent trust between Air Force personnel could be compromised to appease the desires of a superior officer,[8] thereby avoiding the potential for coercion.

The same can be said for a line of ECHR cases involving education and the minds of students. The *Folger* (*Folger v. Norway* 2007) and *Grzelak* (*Grzelak v. Poland* 2010) cases involved religious instruction in schools as being overly influential of a student's belief system; similar reasoning was used regarding sex education classes in schools (*Kjeldsen, Busk Madsen and Pedersen v. Denmark* 1976). These active forms of education can be compared to more passive attempts by educational institutions to, for example, have a student participate in a commemorative parade contrary to her beliefs (*Valsamis v. Greece* 1996) or have crucifixes hanging on the walls of Italian classrooms (*Lautsi v. Italy* 2011).[9]

Commentators further have noted the illegality of state brainwashing or other inhumane inquisitorial methods that rob the intellectual facilities and conscience of a person (Vermeulen 1993, 82). Coercion in this sense is comparable to losing one's autonomous ability to be a person (Shapiro 1983, 1289).

---

7   Note as well the contention concerning asylum law and individuals being persecuted for concealing a belief or (possibly) a political opinion (Smith 2012).

8   Note as well that limiting the beliefs of a particular group also affects the *forum internum* of other individuals who might have developed their beliefs by being exposed to the suppressed group. This broader aspect of the right shall be considered *infra* regarding the *forum internum* of groups.

9   For the active versus passive distinction (Witte and Arold 2011). Note as well that the *Lautsi* case was decided by the Grand Chamber of the ECHR court in holding that hanging a cross in public school classrooms is not considered indoctrination, especially upon accounting for the margin of appreciation. In the first *Latusi* case, decided in 2009, the Court held that hanging a cross in public school classrooms violated the objective notion of public education. See Lamb 2011.

Additional examples centre on denying the existence of personal moral or religious norms, such as coercing one to follow a particular religious belief system (Mcdougal, Laswell and Chen 1980, 655–660).

To further understand the *forum internum* and the protection accorded to an individual's *forum internum* in international human rights law, the prohibition against mental or psychological torture merits scrutiny. Article I of the *Convention Against Torture and other Cruel Inhuman or Degrading Treatment or Punishment* defines torture as including physical *and* mental torture with an intention to coerce or intimidate an individual.[10] The intention of adding the term 'mental' to the Torture Convention was to incorporate actions that force an internal change in the tortured individual's psyche (Macdonald 1989). Instances of such torture include implied threats or creating fear in the victim, thereby altering the victim's perception and forcing a change in one's will or conscience.[11]

Although the ICCPR Article 7 regarding the prohibition of torture does not specifically prohibit mental torture, the drafters discussed incorporation of the terms 'moral and mental' torture and indicated the prohibition against methods that paralyse the individual's will through non-physical, psychological, methods (See ECOSOC (1950) for a broad reading of Article 7). While the HRC has not always seized the opportunity to incorporate a prohibition against psychological torture when defining the term (McGoldrick 1991, 368), it has acknowledged that psychological torture is an important consideration.[12]

Mental torture focuses on instances where authorities desire to alter or change the internal belief of a person to extract information or convince the person of their guilt (Burgers and Danelius 1988). This understanding of

---

10 Article I of the 1984 Convention against Torture and Other Cruel, Inhuman or Degrading Treatment or Punishment provides in full: "For the purposes of this Convention, the term 'torture' means any act by which severe pain or suffering, *whether physical or mental*, is intentionally inflicted on a person for such purposes as obtaining from him or a third person information or a confession, punishing him for an act he or a third person has committed or is suspected of having committed, or *intimidating or coercing him or a third person*, or for any reason based on discrimination of any kind, when such pain or suffering is inflicted by or at the instigation of or with the consent or acquiescence of a public official or other person acting in an official capacity. It does not include pain or suffering arising only from, inherent in or incidental to lawful sanctions." [emphasis added]

11 See also European Commission (1969) which defined torture as driving an individual to act against his will or conscience.

12 McGoldrick (1991, 376) refers to *Quinteros v. Uruguay* (1990). Quinteros suffered psychological torture following the disappearance of her daughter.

mental torture is similar to the HRC's General Comment to Article 18 regarding the definition of coercion. Both torture and coercion centre on altering the internal mental framework of the individual to either extract information or force a change to a person's belief.

Analogous to the prohibition of brainwashing and the prohibition of mental torture may be a host of measures that oppress internal thoughts. Upholding the *forum internum* includes protection from dubious state practices against particular beliefs, especially a belief that need not be asserted in the *forum externum*. Because a person might internally adhere to a particular belief or ideology, as exemplified by external action such as associating with a group or engaging in various protests, the state authority might not only oppose the belief, but also desire to alter the belief. Thus, state harassment, such as constantly being followed by a state security agent due to one's association with a contrary belief or religion, is an example of a violation. The African Commission on Human Rights held that Zaire violated the African Convention on Human Rights and People's Rights (hereafter "AfrCHR") Article 8 right to freedom of conscience when the Zaire Government continually harassed Jehovah's Witnesses (*Les Temoins de Jehovah v. Zaire* 1997).[13] The African Commission found that the State targeted the Jehovah's Witnesses for harassment because they were associated with a different form of belief.

Further, many instances of a *forum internum* violation will spill over into the domain of the *forum externum* or other rights, especially where external state action might mask the underlying intentions of a state. As noted in the HRC's General Comment to Article 18, ICCPR Article 17 (right to privacy) and Article 19(1) (right to hold opinions without interference) serve to buttress the unlimited protection accorded to the *forum internum* (HRC General Comment to Article 18, paragraph 3.).[14]

Some ECHR cases link Article 8 (right to privacy) with instances of assertions centering on altering a belief. For example, the case of *Kjeldsen, Buck, & Pederson v. Denmark* (1980) entailed a challenge before the ECHR Court regarding the teaching of sex education in public schools. The applicants contended that such education violated a belief in privately educating one's children on the matter of sex. The ECHR distinguished between religious education, as involving private matters, and a sex education course, as relating to social public morals. The ECHR Court considered the right to privacy issue that the case raised in tandem with the asserted challenge to the applicant's belief regarding sexual education. Although the outcome of the case hinged on privacy grounds, the Court noted the inherent relationship between these

---

13 The Commission also accounted for the State's denial of access to education.
14 See also Nowak (1993, 294–295, 314–315) making a similar point regarding privacy and concluding that the private sphere is not subject to any limitations.

rights.[15] From a standpoint that accounts for the *forum internum* however the case is more of a contingent decision based on the subjective understanding of the ECHR Court of sexual mores because one may treat sex and religion as a public or private matter. Indeed one's attitudes towards sex and religion are generally linked, such that internally developing a belief on the matter, even if not entitled to manifestation, still demands some form of entitlement.

Freedom of expression in particular is intertwined with the individual's *forum internum* since it is internal free thought that serves as the venue for creating one's opinion (prior to actual expression). In the international sphere for example, thought relates to an individual's internal conscious process (United Nations 1960) (a rather broad range of "thoughts"), with manifestation of thought being placed within the confines of free expression.[16] The American Convention on Human Rights ("AmCHR") indicates such an approach by separating thought from conscience and religion and upholding its protection, along with opinion, in the right to free expression (American Convention on Human Rights, Inter-American Specialized Conference on Human Rights, November 22, 1969, at Articles 12 and 13).

Placing free thought within a free expression context[17] protects a broader range of thoughts than those reflecting an asserted conviction. Indeed, some commentators rely upon the right to free expression as an alternative method for manifesting a conscientious belief since it allows for a more direct application of a belief in a manner that avoids any reference or assessment of the asserted belief itself.[18]

---

15   See also *X Y & Z v. Sweden* 1984, holding that the right to privacy was not violated after state imposed restrictions on religious sect that believed in beating their children. Cf. *Hoffman v. Austria* 1994. The commission held that a state court decision to withdraw custody from a converted Jehovah Witness violated Articles 8 (right to family life) and 14 (right against discrimination).

16   See United Nations Secretary-General (1955) where the ICCPR drafters note the similarities between thought, as protected in Article 18, and opinion, as protected in Article 19 (freedom of expression) when referring to UDHR Article 4(2) (which prohibits any derogation to Article 18).

17   See Van Dijk and Van Hoof (1990, 413) (analysis of the European Convention on Human Rights and Fundamental Freedoms, where the authors equate the freedom to hold opinions under the right of free expression (Article 10 of the ECHR) with the freedom of thought under the right to freedom of religion (Article 9 of the ECHR)).

18   See Nickel (2005) (protecting the freedom of religion or belief can be accomplished through other rights, like freedom of expression) . . . US Courts also are inclined towards the right to free expression when dealing with the manifestation of more radical beliefs, such as burning the flag. See *Street v. New York* (1969). Note that linking free expression with the right to conscience is particularly

While the inclination of a court might be towards free expression when considering intellectual freedom as a human right, there are fundamental distinctions between free expression and the freedom of belief,[19] suggesting the need for also upholding the human right to free thought in the *forum internum* as a key starting point for protecting intellectual freedom.

Particularly, the identified grounds for free speech are the search for, and development of, truth in society,[20] the right to democratic participation,[21] and the need to allow for self-fulfilment and communicative integrity.[22] These cardinal grounds for free expression however overlook the underlying assertions and personal ideals involved in a thought process, especially when

---

suitable for the US where speech is a mechanism for refining and developing the communicative integrity of the individual. Free communication upholds the democratic ideal of evaluating ideas. Hence the broad grant of free speech in the US, since the right incorporates forms of action that relate to the 'communicative integrity' for the critical conscience. This basis justifies 'hate speech' because individuals, and not the state, are to use their inherent conscientious powers of rational conduct and reasonableness to assess the credibility of various expressions, even if the expression tends to offend the audience (Richards 1986, 180). Additionally, courts uphold acts such as burning the US flag or wearing black armbands to protest the Vietnam War because they relate to a symbolic communication that affects the conscientious perceptions of the greater community (Richards 1986, 194).

19 Concerning the manifestation of a religion or belief in the *forum externum*, see Dimitrijevic 1991, 64, noting how this fundamentally differs from merely harboring an opinion.

20 This basis can be viewed either as an argument that all assertions are fallible and therefore require a free speech challenge or that free expression ensures for the development of truth in the free marketplace of ideas, whereby all beliefs are ensured of vitality and guarded against undue suppression. See Cohen-Almogovar (1994) and Barendt (1992), 8–13, referring to Mill. Barendt notes however that the free marketplace of ideas will not incorporate all aspects of free speech, such as emotive speech or pornography, and the marketplace of ideas does not remove restraints on free speech for example due to public policy. See also Richards (1994, 35)

21 The notion is that a rational public should decide which ideas to accept or identify with and that free expression is a necessary component of democracy.

22 Cohen-Almogovar (1994) understand this basis as a means of preserving autonomy, whereby one can advocate ideas and beliefs, protect one's moral sovereignty and general spirit, and challenge accepted social standards. See also Barendt (1992, 8–23). Cf. Witte and Green (2009) noting not only the importance of freedom of religion or belief as providing a unique form of communal context, but also the identity-based dimension that the freedom entails.

involving a conscientious decision; nor do these free expression grounds retain the capacity to incorporate all forms of conscientious manifestation. Encouraging free expression assists society in achieving a broader understanding of what individuals view as the truth, thereby allowing for a more reasoned and measured approach to the truth. The link between this justification and the assertion of a belief derives from the focus on preserving the vitality of an individual's belief by tolerating its outward expression.[23] The problem is that the search for truth basis of free speech does not recognise the importance of a conscientious assertion nor that such an assertion derives from a need to adhere to personal belief as derived from within. Rather the basis involves a social oriented goal of allowing for an open society that encourages expression of a broad range of ideas, to enable individuals in a society to make their own reasoned determination of the truth. Adherence to a conscientious belief invariably derives from internal directives formed in the *forum internum*. Communicating a thought can entail an attempt to convince others of the merits of a belief, but it need not raise an action that manifests the belief.[24]

Another rationale is the importance of free speech as providing for full participation by all individuals in the democratic process (Barendt 1992, 20). This does not necessarily relate to free thought in the *forum internum*, although it assists with the *forum externum* manifestation of a belief by familiarizing the greater society with one's individual moral conceptions.[25] One must consider the individual internally engaging the grounds and reasons for making the assertion and not solely the desired effect that the communication is to have on other individuals within society,[26] otherwise the belief itself would

23 Cohen-Almogovar (1994) understands the truth basis as central to free expression. He relies on Mill to form a balancing of striving for the truth versus allowing for respect for others, thereby imposing limitations on free expression where its sole purpose is to incite and cause harm, rather than communicate an idea.

24 Additionally, this distinction highlights the problem surrounding proselytising. While a proselytiser certainly is attempting to express a belief, the additional key factor is that a proselytiser also is acting pursuant to the belief's directives to convince others of the religion's merits. See *Kokkinakis v. Greece* (1993).

25 Preserving a "democratic society" on utilitarian grounds of full social participation could diminish the individual values that the society is attempting to support since utilitarian grounds ignore the individual's conscientious calculation and basis for making an assertion (Barendt 1992, 16; Machan 1989).

26 The notion of engaging a thought without necessarily considering its social effect is recognized even by an 'absolutist' such as Richards (1986, 184) who notes the difference for example between upholding the right to maintain and express subversive ideas (which is subject to First Amendment free speech protection) versus actually conducting subversive action (which is not protected).

be quashed. A military conscientious objector, for instance, should not be denied the basis for creating and manifesting a belief due to the potential effect the objector's actions can have on other individuals within the military unit.

The Broad Scope of the *Forum Internum*

Noting the link between the *forum internum* and external actions such as torture demonstrates that the protection accorded to the *forum internum* is not exclusively limited to prohibitions of intrusive action by an outside party against one's internal thought processes, such as psychological (as opposed to physical) torture *contra* Dickson (1995, 328). The protection also can extend to prohibiting external actions that *lead* to a violation of the *forum internum*, since that is the forum where one forms a thought or belief and from which emanates an individual's direction for external action. Alternatively, just as the external actions of an individual need not be an actual manifestation of a belief, a *forum internum* violation can result from merely targeting an individual for identifying with a particular thought process or belief as a result of an internal thought process. The violation of the *forum internum* develops as the authority or external source acts to alter the internal thought. The key factor is the focus on altering the individual's adherence to a particular thought or belief.

A typical example would be discrimination against an individual for identifying with a group that professes a particular belief. While the state might be interfering with the individual's *forum internum* if the state desires that an individual alter a belief, the violating state action generally entails a claim of discrimination (See ICCPR Article 26). Thus even if initially a state might focus on an individual in a manner that seems to violate the *forum internum*, i.e. with a specific intention to alter the internal thought system of the individual, the eventual violation will centre on more explicit human rights breaches, such as torture or the right to security (e.g. *Delgado v. Columbia* 1990, discussed *infra*).

The odd result seems to be that while the protection accorded to the individual's *forum internum* is quite broad, the actual illegitimate activity is limited. This narrow application of the right derives from the difficulty in identifying violations of an internal belief when dealing with more extreme state action such as discrimination or the right to security, the general conflict between social interests and individual interests, and the ease in focusing on identifiable actions of the *forum externum*.

The lack of any practical application of the *forum internum* indicates the impossible situation that an unfettered right can create. For example, a state maintaining a religious belief (or secular ideal) inherently excludes other beliefs that might conflict with the state's belief system (Fish 1997). While the state may defer to the limitations provided for in the human rights treaties (like public policy), the limitations do not apply to the *forum internum*. Additionally, it is difficult to define the scope of the *forum internum* because it relates to all forms of thought and mental processes. This is especially the case when considering the broad manner in which external authorities can influence or violate an individual's thoughts. An authority might cause an alteration of the *forum internum* by forcing an individual to divulge certain information. Alternatively, an authoritative influence can result unintentionally by limiting an individual's education, which will hinder one's mental processes or by encouraging an excessively competitive society that can create frustrated individuals who cannot cope with social demands (Scharr 1967). One's internal thoughts also will be a reflection of one's own intellectual limitations that can hinder a person's overall mental perceptions. Such a drawback can result exclusive of any external authority. For example, it can derive as a result of one's upbringing or unduly traumatic childhood.

Obviously it was not the intention that an international human right would hold the state accountable for all forms of *forum internum* alterations regarding thought, even if they might be due to state oversight or error, such as not adopting a structured education policy (See also ICCPR Article 18(4) *infra*). The examples of brainwashing and coercion however suggest an authority with a specific end-goal (such as to punish or extract information). An example could be recently proposed legislation in Tajikistan to prevent anyone under the age of 18 from visiting a place of worship or attending religious ceremonies, except funerals. The proposed law includes a recommendation to parents to "give the child a worthy name consistent with national values" (i.e., no use of Islamic sounding names) (Parshin 2011).

The indication is that while the international human rights system accords the *forum internum* an unlimited scope of protection, the actual violation of the right by state activity is subject to a rather specific set of circumstances. While such an approach is practically sound, it does raise questions regarding the requirement on the state to protect all forms of thought and beliefs, including beliefs that are inherently contradictory to the state's basic tenets.

Analogy to *Forum Externum*

What if the mere existence of a particular thought or belief harms another, for example believing that homosexuality is morally and socially legitimate or that abortion is permissible might create feelings of disgust in another person? The question is especially relevant if the disgusted person is of a particular religious persuasion. Further, how is one to then achieve a balance between the individual's capacity for intellectual freedom as opposed to broader social interests? Can one limit pornography merely because one believes that it is indecent? Could a person's internal beliefs then be 'harmed' upon observing a pornographic book for sale in a local shop? What if the internal belief centred on a religious principle, such as the one cited by Mill regarding a Muslim not eating pork? Could the local butcher sell pork even if the sale might infringe the Muslim's internal belief system?

While the *forum internum* differs from the *forum externum* principally as a result of the physical realm of the right, one can make an analogy between the two to clarify the *forum internum's* scope. The *forum externum* has been grouped into two fundamental sections. The right applies to freedom *to* a belief, meaning to practise according to the beliefs' directives, as well as freedom *from* a belief, meaning to prevent applications of a belief's requirements on a non-believer. While this division does not alter the practical application of the right, international commentators use the approach to clarify the dimensions of the right (Krishnaswami 1960).

One also may divide the *forum internum* along similar lines, despite operating within a different context than the *forum externum*. Indications for this approach to the *forum internum* are found in ICCPR Article 18(2), where the terms 'have or adopt' have been interpreted as protecting the individual's right to change a religion, freedom *to*, as well as limiting the actions of excessively zealous missionaries, freedom *from* (Scheinen 1992, 267). The HRC also has noted that 'coercion' applies to not only impairing one's right to attain a thought or belief (freedom *to*) but also to protecting non-believers from compulsion to believe (freedom *from*) (HRC General Comment to Article 18, par. 5).

Freedom To

The principal considerations of the freedom *to* for the *forum internum* relate to situations where it is not necessarily the physical practice of the belief that merits protection but the ability to mentally adhere to a belief or thought. In such a case, the state might be imposing its will through various avenues that need not necessarily entail a physical violation but affect the person's psyche or mental process. The key factor here is the consequential desire of the state to alter the internal beliefs or thoughts of a person, even when associating the state violation with another form of human rights violation.

For example, a state's suppression of a person's freedom of expression also can violate one's *forum internum* if the state desires that the person alter the expressed belief rather than solely suppress the expression. It is one thing for a state to close the offices of a particular journal or limit the political abilities of a group that the state deems a public danger. It is quite a graver violation however for a state also to attempt to alter the internal beliefs of the journalists or the dissident group making the expression by way of mental or physical coercion.[27]

Because the *forum internum* right is quite broad, a potential violation focuses on more explicit actions, like a state altering an internal belief. This distinction in degree of state action reflects instances in which states can suppress other human rights, such as during national emergencies. Nonetheless, while there might exist grounds for suppressing the *forum internum* (along with other rights) during instances of say internal strife (where state stability might be paramount) (Fox and Nolte 1995), the suppression need not be to the extent that the state is altering the views and beliefs of the an opposition movement's members.

A 1990 case before the HRC demonstrates the manner in which to apply the freedom *to* right. In *Delgado v. Columbia* (1990), the state demoted the plaintiff, a teacher, from his position in a state school as a result of his insistence on teaching liberation theology along with the required curriculum mandated by the State's Church authorities. The school system forced the plaintiff to teach in areas not relating to his expertise, threatened him with criminal prosecution on false charges, and he was subjected to harassment and duress, for example, receiving threatening, anonymous, telephone calls.[28]

The HRC held that ICCPR Article 9 (right to security) was the applicable provision as it is a state's duty to safeguard individuals who are subject to such threats. The HRC limited its examination of ICCPR Article 18 to the manifestation of the belief, the *forum externum*, and held that there was no violation since the government can control state education of religion.

Considering the case from the *forum internum* standpoint however the state exerted pressure on the individual as a result of his identification with a set of beliefs. Granted that manifestation of the beliefs might have been properly curtailed by not allowing the plaintiff to preach his minority beliefs in

---

27	Coercive state tactics to alter a belief sometimes serve to strengthen the belief rather than diminish it. This result does not change the fact that the state is committing a *forum internum* violation.

28	See also *Bwala v. Zambia* (1993) where the HRC found a violation of the right to security for a political party member who was prevented from campaigning, was continually harassed, and was denied employment. A similar case was also raised before the American Convention on Human Rights ("AmCHR") Commission after the Nicaraguan Government published false information regarding the leader of an opposition political party. The applicant claimed that the Government violated AmCHR Article 12 because the government's actions effectively stifled his beliefs (Organization of American States 1986). The AmCHR Commission however decided the case on defamation grounds, AmCHR Article 5, rather than delve into the issue of freedom of belief.

a state school classroom.[29] However the subsequent treatment of the plaintiff as a result of his beliefs, including the alteration of his position from religious educator to teaching shop mechanics and on-going harassment through bogus telephone calls, created a different violation than a breach of the right to security.[30] The violations of the plaintiff's rights resulted in the State oppressing the plaintiff due to his internal beliefs that conflicted with the authorities. This is especially the case for the state church that had withdrawn initial support for the plaintiff as a religious teacher despite being aware of his liberation-theology beliefs. The State's actions indicated a desire to alter the plaintiff's belief before allowing him to continue teaching the religious course.

Freedom From

Freedom *from* in the *forum internum* involves protection from the imposition of an outside thought or belief with the purpose of impelling the individual to adopt a particular belief. The underlying objective of the imposing force is to replace one thought for another; however a person need not identify with a particular ideology to have this aspect of the *forum internum* violated. Freedom *from* primarily relates to developing a proper and fair system that protects one's beliefs while preventing imposition of such beliefs on another. Individual thoughts and beliefs should be able to develop independently of undue influences from ancillary sources, such as an authority's ideologically derived desire to entrench a particular thought in the psyche of its populace.[31]

The freedom *from* aspect of the *forum internum* is generally easier to identify than freedom *to* because in these cases a state is targeting a specific belief or mode of thought with a view towards changing it. Since the state is acting as an overseer of thought, the compulsion on the individual's *forum internum* and violation of one's intellectual freedom is more recognisable. The state is acting in a pro-active manner by creating a policy of desired change and forcing modification of one's internal thoughts and beliefs. Even if the targeted individual does not adhere to a belief, a violation occurs when a state acts to alter or instil a particular belief. For example, a state violates the right

---

29   Cf. *Ergul v. Turkey* 1996 in which the Commission upheld denial of judicial service due to claimant's membership in a political party. State policy was deemed a necessary condition established by law.

30   Some commentators limit the right to security to circumstances surrounding detention, such as an individual facing an unfounded threat of detention (Dinstein 1981, 128; Niemi-Kiesilainen 1992, 150). The HRC decisions seem to refute their conclusions.

31   A similar problem is raised when internal groups within the state impose their views with the goal of altering the individual's *forum internum*.

to free expression by requiring its teachers to accede to a 'duty of loyalty' oath to the state, especially if a teacher is a member of a dissident political faction (*Vogt v. Germany* 1996). In such a case, a violation to the *forum internum* also occurs. The state desires to alter the views of political dissent groups by imposing state ideology at the expense of an internal belief.

Significance for the *Forum Internum*

In forming a belief in the *forum internum*, the individual is subject to a host of internal and external influences that derive from constant interaction with society. While the thoughts or beliefs of an individual serve to structure the overall social and cultural construct, such thoughts and beliefs originated from objectively accepted knowledge that the individual had acquired from external sources. A person objectifies one's inner thoughts into an external reality and the thoughts are subsequently internalised back into the subjective consciousness.[32] Thus, external influences on a person (freedom *from*) also shape and form a person's beliefs (freedom *to*),[33] particularly when considering a person's development in a closely-knit social, religious, or group context.

The blurring of the freedom *from* and freedom *to* divide further enlightens our understanding of the *forum internum*. The relationship between the individual and society, and acknowledgment of both internal and external influences, highlights the importance of *how* we go about acquiring knowledge, engaging our thought processes, or shaping a belief. What is important for the conscientious process is not an understanding of the relationship between conscience and morals (or some other 'universal' form of ethical standard), but an analysis of the dynamic of the relation between conscience and the external world.

In discussing the epistemology of a person, Foucault indicated similar considerations even in more "objective" fields such as the natural sciences. For Foucault, discoveries do not soley occur because of scientific, empirical, experiments, but as a result of changes in the political and social arena that alter our perception and understanding of certain processes; discoveries happen as different discourses become acceptable and society removes previous social or language barriers (Foucault 1980, 115). Hence one may interpret a

---

32 As noted by Geertz, culture shapes the individual because the individual is dependent on culture to adequately define his or her behaviour (Geertz 1973, 43–44).

33 Hence the right to educate ones child pursuant to one's beliefs. See ICCPR *supra* Article 18(4) providing that: "The States Parties to the present Covenant undertake to have respect for the liberty of parents and, when applicable, legal guardians to ensure the religious and moral education of their children in conformity with their own convictions."

belief or ideology not as an objective truth, but as a result of the 'effects of truth [that] are produced within a discourse which in themselves are neither true nor false' (Foucault 1980, 118). The knowledge at one's disposal produces what the individual or society understands to be the truth.[34] The significance of such an approach is that the internal development of a belief is the result of a host of influences based on our particular regime of understanding; a belief need not relate to the truth of one's existence nor to some lofty ethical standard.

While the difference between *forum internum* and *forum externum* is that the exteriority is limited for the *forum internum* since it emanates from the individual's subjective understanding of the changes and discourses surrounding him, social factors, or transgressive considerations, will also influence and shape one's internal belief structure. Relying on a conscientious belief need not entail an individual's striving for a universal truth, but rather can be understood as an on-going search for a new understanding of one's position in the world and a sharper focus on the freedom that defines an individual's distinguished role in life (Bernauer and Mahon 1995, 153). The key factor is to acknowledge our derivation of knowledge, and understand our social interactions, with a view towards shaping a new understanding of ourselves (Rouse 1990, 216–220). As the external world shifts and different alternatives become available, one's approach to the truth of a particular thought or belief also will be subject to change. Beliefs then become contingent ideas, given different levels of knowledge and understanding in societies.

Notion of *Forum Internum* and Beliefs

One of the problems in making reference to the *forum externum* to elucidate protection for the *forum internum* is that it relies on the *ex post* manifestation to define the contours of a thought or belief. Not all thoughts or beliefs manifest or need to be manifested. Especially when considering the freedom *from* notion, where a belief is maintaining a passive role, there is no clarification regarding the scope of positive protection; rather the state's actions are to be limited to protect or preserve a particular belief. Discerning the belief might be difficult if it has not manifested, yet state action might require curtailment if a state's edicts or policies infringe the individual's *forum internum*. Alternatively, the *forum internum* might be so broad as to prove unworkable. Mill's example of pork being sold in a local shop as infringing the sensibilities of local Muslims clearly relates to the *forum internum*. No particular external action or manifestation of the belief is being infringed, yet one can conceive an infringement of an internal belief by the public sale of pork.

---

34   For Foucault, this was a rather important point given the inherent relation between one's acquisition of knowledge and one's use of power.

An additional problem with relying on the manifestation of a belief to discern the *forum internum* is that state imposed limitations on the *forum externum* affect the *forum internum*. Preventing the practice of a belief, even when justified, has an impact, as well, on the *forum internum*. Hence in instances where a state imposes limitations on the freedom of religion in accordance with public policy, such as to justify sex education or a 'neutral' religious education, an infringement on the *forum internum* of individuals who maintain contrary beliefs can occur.[35] The infringement is not only in a personal sense, such as Muslims who might not want pork sold in their neighbourhood,[36] but also one finds an infringement upon the foundational principles of a belief.[37] Preventing manifestation cannot but avoid some form of internal harm to the belief itself.

Conclusion

While the *forum internum* is entitled to absolute protection to preserve thought and intellectual freedom, analysis of the meaning of the *forum internum* as an international human right has been largely overlooked. As a result, this chapter focused on understanding how thought and intellectual freedom might be protected in the *forum internum*, given the importance of maintaining the internal, cognitive abilities of the individual to provide for the development of a thought. This includes protection against coercive action to not only suppress a belief, but also to alter it.

The *forum internum* differs from other conscious thought because it evaluates and develops particular conscientious beliefs, with a view towards upholding such beliefs in particular situations. Unlike a general thought, one can comprehend the *forum internum* by examining the manner in which an individual manifests a conscientious belief in the *forum externum*. Taking advantage of this two-way process provides the framework for elaborating upon the *forum internum*. The *forum internum* merits protection given its seminal

---

35 This contention regarding the violation of a person's belief seems to be the point raised by the dissent in *Valsamis v. Greece* 1996.

36 The disdain towards pork deriving from a religious edict.

37 Public policy for example might not only halt a religious practice, but also restructure a religious belief system. The US ban on polygamous Mormon marriages resulted in structural changes to the Mormon belief system (Harmer-Dionne 1998). Similarly, a doctor who subscribes to the right to life might be required to perform an abortion or lose her employment. While a state possibly may impose such a limitation on the manifestation of the belief pursuant to the treaties, an infringement on the internal belief system of the doctor also is occurring. The doctor has created a specific internal framework of belief that in turn has significance for her external actions.

epistemological role in shaping and creating an individual's thoughts or beliefs.

References

American Convention on Human Rights. 1969. Inter-American Specialized Conference on Human Rights, November 22, 1969

Barendt, Eric. 1992. *Freedom of speech*. Oxford: Clarendon Press.

Benito, Odio. 1989. *Elimination of all forms of racial discrimination*. New York: United Nations Press.

Bernauer, James, and Mahon, Michael. 1995 The ethics of Michel Foucault. In *The Cambridge Companion to Foucault*, ed. Gary Gutting. Cambridge, Mass: Cambridge.

Burgers, J. Hermann and Danelius, Hans. 1988. *The UN Convention against Torture: a Handbook on the Convention against Torture and Other Cruel Inhuman or Degrading Treatment or Punishment*. London: M. Nijhoff.

Bwala v. Zambia. 1993. HRC No. 314/1988

Church of Scientology v. Sweden. 1979. 16 D&R 68. ECHR No. 7805/77

Cohen-Almogovar, Rafael. 1994. *The boundaries of liberty and tolerance: The struggle against Kahanism in Israel*. Gainesville, Florida: University of Florida Press.

Cumper, Peter. 1995. Freedom of thought conscience and religion. In *The ICCPR and UK Law*, eds. David. Harris and Sara. Joseph. Oxford: Clarendon Press.

Delgado v. Columbia. 1990. HRC No. 195/1985 .

Dickson, Bruce. 1995. The United Nations and freedom of religion. *International and Comparative Law Quarterly* 44: 327.

Dimitrijevic, Vojin. 1991. Freedom of expression in the framework of the CSCE. In *The human dimension of the Helsinki Process: The Vienna follow-up meeting and its aftermath*, eds. Arie. Bloed and Pieter. van Dijk. The Netherlands: M. Nijhoff.

Dinstein, Yoram. 1981. The right to life, physical integrity and liberty. In *The International Bill of Rights*, ed. L. Henkin. New York: Columbia University Press.

ECOSOC , Commission on Human Rights, E/CN.4/SR. 1950

Ergul v. Turkey. 1996. 84 D&R 69. ECHR No. 23991/94.

European Commission. 1969. Report in the Greek case 1969, 12 Ybk of the ECHR 501 ECHR No. 00003321-3/67

Fish, Stanley. 1997. Mission impossible: Settling the just bounds between church and state, *Columbia University Law Review* 97: 2255.

Folgero v. Norway. 2007. Eur. Ct. H.R. 15472/02.

Foucault, Michel. 1980. *Power/Knowledge: Selected interviews and other writings 1972–1977.* Sussex: Harvester Press.

Fox, Gregory. & Nolte, Georg. 1995. Intolerant democracies, *Harvard International Law Journal* 36: 1.

General Assembly. 1960. 15th Session, Third Committee (Social Humanitarian and Cultural) mtg. 1021.

Geertz, Charles. 1973. *Interpretation of culture,* London: Hutchinson & Co.

Grzelak v. Poland. 2010. Eur. Ct. H.R. 7710/02.

Harmer-Dionne, Elizabeth. 1998. Once a peculiar people: Cognitive dissonance and the suppression of mormon polygamy as a case study negating the belief action distinction. *Stanford Law Review* 50: 1295.

Hoffman v. Austria. 1994. 17 EHRR 293. ECHR No. 12875/87.

Kjeldsen, Buck & Pederson v. Denmark. 1980. 1 EHRR 711. ECHR No. 5095/71.

Kokkinakis v. Greece. 1993. 17 EHRR 397. ECHR No. 14307/88.

Krishnaswami, Arcot. 1960. *Study of discrimination in the matter of religious rights and practices.* New York: United Nations.

Lamb, Rob. 2011. When human rights have gone too far: Religious tradition and equality in *Lautsi v. Italy. N.C.J. Intl L. & Com. Reg.* 36, 751.

Larissis v. Greece. 1997. VII(1) H.R. Case Digest 60. ECHR No. 23372/94.

Lautsi v. Italy. 2011. Eur. Ct. H.R. ECHR No. 30814/06.

Les Temoins de Jehovah v. Zaire. 1997. 4(1) IHRR 89. African Commission on Human and Peoples Rights No. 56/91.

Macdonald, Ronald. 1989. International prohibitions against torture and other forms of similar treatment or punishment. In *International Law at a Time of Perplexity: Essays in Honour of Shabtai Rosenne,* eds. Yoram. Dinstein and Mala. Tabory. The Netherlands: M. Nijhoff.

Machan, Tibor. 1989. *Individuals and their rights.* Illinois: Open Court.

Martinez-Torron, Javier. 2005. Limitations on religious freedom in the case law of the European Court of Human Rights. *Emory Intl L. Rev.* 19, 587.

McDougal, Myres., Lasswell, Harold. and Chen, Lung-chu. 1980. *Human rights and world public order.* New Haven, CT: Yale University Press.

McGoldrick, Dominick. 1991. *The human rights committee: Its role in the development of the International Covenant on Civil and Political Rights.* Oxford: Clarendon Press.

Nickel, James. 2005. Who needs freedom of religion? *U. Colo. L. Rev.* 76, 941.

Niemi-Kiesilainen, Johanna. 1992. Article 9. In *The Universal Declaration of Human Rights: A commentary,* eds. Asbjorn Eide, Gudmundur. Alfredsson, Goran. Melander, Lars. Rehof, and Allan. Rosas. Oxford: Oxford University Press.

Nowak, Martin. 1993. *UN Covenant on Civil and Political Rights: Commentary.* Germany: NP Engel.

Organization of American States. 1986. Res. No. 29/86, OAS Doc OEA/ Ser.L/V/II.68, Doc. 8 Rev. 1 (1986).

Parshin, Konstantin. 2011. Tajikistan: Dushanbe officials seek to assume some parenting responsibilities. Euraisanet.org. http://www.eurasianet.org/node/63052, March 11, 2011 (accessed September 1, 2011).

Partsch, Karl. 1981. Freedom of conscience and expression and political freedoms. In *The International Bill of Rights*, ed. Louis. Henkin. New York: Columbia University Press.

Quinteros v. Uruguay 1983, HRC No. 107/1981

Report of the SecretaryGeneral to the Tenth Session of the General Assembly. 1955. "Draft International Covenants on Human Rights: Annotation" A/2929, July.

Richards, David. 1986. *Toleration and the Constitution.* Oxford: Oxford University Press.

Rouse, Joseph. 1990, *Knowledge and power: Toward a political philosophy of science*, Ithaca and London: Cornell UP.

Scharr, John. 1967. Equality of opportunity and beyond. In *IX Nomos: Equality.* New York: Atherton Press.

Scheinen, Martin. 1992. Article 18. In *The Universal Declaration of Human Rights: A commentary*, eds Asbjorn Eide, Gudmundur. Alfredsson, Goran. Melander, Lars. Rehof, and Allan. Rosas. Oxford: Oxford University Press.

Shapiro, Robert. 1983. Of robots and persons and the protection of religious beliefs. *Southern California Law Review* 56: 1277.

Shaw, Malcolm. 1992. The definition of minorities in international law. In *The Protection of Minorities and Human Rights*, eds. Yoram. Dinstein and Mala. Tabory. The Netherlands: M. Nijhoff.

Smith, Peter. 2012. Suffering in silence: Asylum law and the concealment of political opinion as a form of persecution. Conn. L. Rev. 44, 1021.

Street v. New York. 1969. 394 US 576.

Sullivan, Donna. 1988. Advancing the freedom of religion or belief through the UN Declaration on the Elimination of Religious Intolerance and Discrimination. *American Journal International Law* 82: 487.

Tahzib, Bahiyyih. 1996. *Freedom of Religion or Belief: Ensuring Effective International Legal Protection.* The Netherlands: M. Nijhoff.

United Nations. 1950. Economic and Social Council. Commission on Human Rights, E/CN.4/SR., 141.

United Nations Secretary-General. 1955. Draft international covenants on human rights: Annotation. Report of the SecretaryGeneral to the Tenth Session of the General Assembly, A/2929, July 1.

United Nations. 1960. UN General Assembly, 15th Session, Third Committee (Social Humanitarian and Cultural) 1960, mtg. 1021.

United Nations. 1976. International Covenant on Civil and Political Rights, UNTS (United Nations Treaty System), 172.

United Nations. 1993. Human Rights Committee, General Comment No. 22, CCPR/C/21/Rev.1/Add.4, 7/30/1993.

Valsamis v. Greece. 1996. VI Rep. Judg. & Dec. 2312. ECHR No. 21787/93.

Van Dijk, Pieter. & Van Hoof, Fried 1990. *Theory and practice of the European Convention of Human Rights.* The Netherlands: Kluwer.

Vermeulen, Ben. 1993. Scope and limits of conscientious objection. In *Freedom of Conscience*, Council of Europe. Strasbourg: Council of Europe Press.

Vogt v. Germany 21 EHRR 205. ECHR No. 17851/91.

Witte, Jr., John. and Green, M. Christian 2009. Religious freedom, democracy, and international human rights. *Emory Intl L. Rev.* 23, 583.

Witte, Jr., John. and Arold, Nina-Louise. 2011. Lift high the cross?: Contrasting the new European and American cases on religious symbols on government property. *Emory Int'l L. Rev.* 25, 5.

X Y & Z v. Sweden 1984, 5 EHRR 147. ECHR No. 8811/79.

Yong-Joo Kang v. Republic of Korea, 1999. HRC No. 878/1999.

Hate Speech
Legal and Philosophical Aspects

Tomas A. Lipinski and Kathrine Henderson

This chapter analyzes hate speech in comparison and contrast to "hate crime" which is not speech at all but an act or course of conduct. The authors examine definitional issues raised by these concepts and review the protection for hate speech expressed in numerous judicial contexts. Courts, when confronted by hate speech, have deferred restrictions and embraced tolerance, placing faith in the "marketplace of ideas"—a concept often used to justify protection of hate speech. The authors offer that hate speech—to further exploit the marketplace analogy—is a form of market failure. Whether the failure is due to imperfect information (an opinion based on prejudice for example) or negative externalities (from a broader harm to society from such speech), there is justification for government intervention. In addition to harm, hate speech subverts the opportunity for true discourse. Whatever difficulties there are in defining hate speech, decades of United States jurisprudence illustrate that hate speech will be tolerated to ensure that freedom of speech is not chilled; however, free speech at all costs is difficult to justify.

The Difficulty in Defining Hate Speech

It is useful to define several terms that relate to speech and conduct that is colored by negative perspective or stained with prejudice or bigotry. A Westlaw search revealed that although the phrase "hate speech" appears in over 100 judicial opinions not a single court has clearly defined it. While the legal system accepts that hate crimes are subject to proscription, hate speech remains protected. Hate crime and hate speech often appear together in judicial discussions and it is from these discussions that we define the difference.

Courts make distinctions between hate speech and a hate crime. One court indicated that "racial slurs, profanities, and obscene gestures, while reprehensible" are not hate crimes (*State v. Sulick* 2012, n.p. and comparing W. Va. Code § 61-6-21(b)). The use of a racial slur itself is not a hate crime unless the use of force or threat of force is also present, but it is "hate speech" given the context. Sometimes it is a litigant rather than the court that characterizes certain words or actions as hate speech. In these instances courts do not correct such comments, implying at least a tacit endorsement of the concept where circumstances warrant. In *Stone v. Paddock Publications, Inc.*, the court referred to several anti-Semitic comments as hate speech (2011, 385). A similar recognition is found in *DiCarlo v. Potter*, where comments "negatively and derogatorily referenced DiCarlo's Italian-American heritage" (2004, 417). Courts also refer to hate speech in the context of criminal prosecutions or lawsuits based on claims of discrimination, defamation, or other harms or where one of the litigants has worked to combat hate speech. In other circumstances the court perceives neither a hate crime nor hate speech. For example in *Hafez v. Madison* (2009, 468), a reference made by a police detective calling Hafez an "Egyptian Muslim" when in fact he was both "Egyptian and Muslim" did not violate the due process rights of Hafez. As a result, a definition of hate speech remains, at least in the decisions of the courts, elusive, somewhat akin to Justice Potter Stewart's famous statement that he would not attempt to define obscenity: "perhaps I could never succeed in intelligibly [defining obscenity, but] ... I know it when I see it" (*Jacobellis v. State of Ohio* 1964, 197, Stewart, J., concurring). Obscenity was indeed later defined with a three-pronged standard in *Miller v. California* (1973). To date, however, hate speech has escaped similar judicial articulation.

Commentators have fared somewhat better in defining "hate speech," but not much. "Disagreement looms over the definition of hate speech" (Ryan 2012, 319, note 11). According to one commentator: "Hate speech may be defined as bigoted speech attacking or disparaging a social or ethnic group or a member of such a group" (Kohm 2010, 595). Black's Law Dictionary offers the following definition of hate speech: "Speech that carries no meaning other than the expression of hatred for some group, such as a particular race, especially in circumstances in which the communication is likely to provoke violence" (2009, n.p. in Westlaw).

As an alternative to providing a precise definition, other commentators focus on the destructive effects of the speech. Harmful or violent conduct are the easy cases. Some argue that we ought to incorporate a broader view. "Hate speech ... includes speech that is abusive, offensive, or insulting that targets an individual's race, religion, ethnicity, or national origin. ... Nations regulating hate speech as well as regulation advocates realize that hate speech is devoid of any value and therefore should be criminalized despite free speech ideals" (Webb 2011, 447–448). Whether such definitions would satisfy all stakeholders or prove useful to the courts is unclear. "Complicating things even further are cultural differences in how hurtful messages are typically interpreted, which means the impact of hate speech, as well as its definition, can vary from place to place. The importance of words varies by culture" (Shaw 2011, 288), and arguably within cultures or countries.

A third approach is reflected in foreign jurisdictions where a recognition of historical, systemic, or institutional political, social or economic disadvantage is admitted and addressed in law and based on constitutional guarantee. According to the Committee of Ministers of the Council of Europe, hate speech encompasses "all forms of expression which spread, incite, promote or justify racial hatred, xenophobia, anti-Semitism or other forms of hatred based on intolerance, including: intolerance expressed by aggressive nationalism and ethnocentrism, discrimination, and hostility against minorities, migrants, and people of immigrant origin" (1997, 107). Still others have observed the futility of arriving at a simple, one-size fits all definition, "We do not pretend that we can make hard choices easy, nor do we advocate for a particular definition of hate speech . . . efforts to define and proscribe hate speech should expressly turn on the harms to be targeted and prevented . . . outlining a menu of possible harm-based definitions" (Citron and Norton 2011, 1459). Citron and Norton identify the following harms: speech that threatens and incites violence; speech that intentionally inflicts severe emotional distress; speech that harasses; speech that silences counter-speech; and speech that exacerbates hatred or prejudice by defaming an entire group (2011, 1460–1468). However, as Waldron suggests, attempts to define hate speech miss the broader point of "tangible communications. . . . The word 'hate' suggests—we think misleadingly—that the task of legislation that restricts hate speech is to try to change people's attitudes or control their thoughts. . . . The issue is publication and the harm done to individuals and groups through the disfiguring of our social environment by visible, public, and semi-permanent announcements to the effect that in the opinion of one group in the community, members of another group are not worthy of equal citizenship" (Waldron 2010, 1601). In this context, hate speech is a negative externality in the marketplace of ideas. One person's actions, in this case their hate speech, negatively affects another person or even a whole group without cost to the speaker or benefit to society. The analogy of a negative externality provides an instructive frame of reference from which we can examine the unfairness that exists because, as discussed elsewhere in this chapter, the Court leans heavily toward free speech.

Hate Crimes

Numerous definitions of hate crimes are found in the various laws that attempt to punish crimes linked to some prejudicial characteristic of the victim and where the victim is targeted because of that characteristic. Black's Law Dictionary defines a hate crime as one that is "motivated by the victim's race, color, ethnicity, religion, or national origin. Certain groups have lobbied to expand the definition by statute to include a crime motivated by the victim's disability, gender, or sexual orientation" (Westlaw 2009). While a hate crime may include hate speech to prove an element of the offense, the two terms are not synonymous.

The concept of hate crime fares better in both the primary and secondary legal literature. For example, there is a treatise dedicated to the topic of hate crimes, collating the various state and federal approaches to legislating against crimes either motivated by such speech or with some hate speech connection to a crime (Wang 2012). While a federal statute proscribes certain conduct as a hate crime (28 U.S.C. § 249), most reported cases involve application of state law. Wang (2012) provides an overview of various codified iterations on a 50-state tabular form.

Politically Incorrect Speech

A final concept to distinguish is politically incorrect speech. While Black's Law Dictionary does not define politically incorrect speech, it does define its opposite: political correctness. "The inclination to avoid language and practices that might offend anyone's political sensibilities, especially in racial or sexual matters. An instance in which a person conforms to this inclination" (Westlaw 2009). Even within the same court, judges disagree on the use and meaning of this phrase. In one example a concurring judge criticized the use of the phrase, hinting at the difficulty of defining such phrases: "The majority, without any indication of having given any thought to the substance behind the use of the phrase, 'politically correct' . . . the amorphousness of 'political correctness' causes its meaning to shift depending upon who is using it and the context within which it is used. In any event, it is merely a way of denominating what its user thinks is acceptable in a particular political climate. In other words, it is a phrase of opinion, not definition" (*Seibert Security Services, Inc. v. Superior Court* 1993, 526, Timlin, J., concurring). Courts, cautious by nature to recognize new legal remedy to new harms appear to view political correctness as more driven by politics and other pressures than by the dictates of law. "Policy preferences of judges must not be advanced through the guise of newly created rights grounded in fads of political correctness" (*Andersen v. King County* 2006, 999). Fearful of legislating from the bench, as the expression goes, courts are reluctant to read such proscriptions into existing laws: "We are not inclined to reconcile the language of the statute with politically correct standards, in effect, defining public policy. This court is duty-bound to apply the law. Public policy is the prerogative of the legislature" (*State v. Logsdon* 2006). Some judges detest incorporating such standards or societal pressures into decision-making. As Justice Blackmun admonished: "I fear that the Court has been distracted from its proper mission by the temptation to decide the issue over "politically correct speech" and "cultural diversity," neither of which is presented here. If this is the meaning of today's opinion, it is perhaps even more regrettable" (*R.A.V. v. City of St. Paul, Minnesota* 1992, Blackmun, J., concurring). In general, courts appear suspicious of political correctness as a concept and even less capable in offering a standard by which to apply existing legal principles.

Commentators have been more forthcoming. Loury defines "political correctness" as "an implicit social convention of restraint on public expression, operating within a given community" (Loury 1994, 430). Raksin posits that political correctness combines elements of "official compulsion and censorship" with "progressive ideas about race, gender and power" and responds to those critical of political correctness: "By merging these meanings, the anti-PC party identifies progressive ideas with censorship and dresses up its own political agenda in the noble rhetoric of the First Amendment" (Raskin 1994, 70). A person who tells a politically incorrect joke is not engaging in a hate crime nor is he or she necessarily engaging in hate speech unless relayed specifically with that intent or at least with gross negligence (in a legal sense). One might proffer the politically incorrect comment by accident, by slip of the tongue or without meaning to breach a standard of comportment, i.e., negligence. However, it appears less believable to claim that one engaged in hate speech by the same (negligent) standard. Politically incorrect speech may not be targeted at a particular individual or group of individuals but can nonetheless offend both the target(s) as well as others not associated with the target or target group, whomever the disseminated speech reaches. A third broader social harm is also possible. Such speech may be offensive but not necessarily hateful.

Hate speech is offensive to many: target(s), non-target(s), and society on the whole. Intended to inflict specific harm, such speech precipitates a general harm, a societal malaise. While the politically incorrect speech offends it may not necessarily harm, that may not be its intent nor at times its effect. In other words not all politically incorrect speech is hate speech. So too, not all hate speech *occurs* in the context of criminal activity, a hate crime. Hate speech occurs with some measure of animus, politically incorrect speech need not. Though some readers may disagree with these observations, such disagreements underscore the difficulty of defining such concepts.

Hate Speech and the First Amendment in the Courts

In contrast to a weighing of factors or stakeholder interests, where, for example, the right of the speaker might be weighed against the harm to the subject, other listeners, or society at large and the magnitude of imposition assessed for each stakeholder, U.S. courts uphold the right of the speaker to speak. While courts recognize that speech is a tool that can be used for good or ill, courts remain constitutionally bound to protect the good or desirable speech along with the bad or undesirable speech. In a recent case involving protest by members of the Westboro Baptist Church at the funeral of an American soldier killed in Iraq the Chief Justice Roberts writing for a near unanimous Court (Justice Alito dissented) observed: "Speech is powerful. It can stir people to action, move them to tears of both joy and sorrow, and—as it did here—inflict great pain. On the facts before us, we cannot react to that pain by punishing the speaker. As a nation we have chosen a different course—to protect even hurtful speech on public issues to ensure that we do not stifle public debate. That choice requires that we shield Westboro from tort liability for its picketing in this case" (*Snyder v. Phelps* 2011, 1220). Such judicial coldness is rooted in decades of jurisprudence traced to the nation's founding: "If there is a bedrock principle underlying the First Amendment, it is that the government may not prohibit the expression of an idea simply because society finds the idea itself offensive or disagreeable" (*Texas v. Johnson* 1989, 414). While it can be argued that hate speech forecloses meaningful dialog or discussion, the Court values all speech, especially "in public debate our own citizens must tolerate insulting, and even outrageous, speech in order to provide adequate breathing space to the freedoms protected by the First Amendment" (*Boos v. Barry* 1988, 322).

Lower courts reiterate that the impact of the speech on listeners is not a factor to be considered in judging its merits. In *Monteiro v. Tempe Union High School District,* the Ninth Circuit Court of Appeals considered whether the required reading of *Huckleberry Finn* could form the basis of a discrimination claim. The court offered an "awareness that words can hurt, particularly in the case of children, and that words of a racist nature can hurt especially severely . . ." (*Monteiro v. Tempe Union High School District* 1998, 1026-1027). In spite of this acknowledgement the court feared the practical result if listeners (or in this instance the students and their parents) could object to offensive works in a process whereby works so classified could be removed from the curriculum and replaced by more palatable, blander substitutes. The court explained its refusal to side with the plaintiff:

> *the fact that a student is required to read a book does not mean that he is being asked to agree with what is in it . . . regardless of the fact that the*

work may be deemed to contain racist ideas or language. (Monteiro v. Tempe Union High School District 1998, 1031–1032)

Context is critical. In *Monteiro* above, the circumstances reflected no ill will, even though the plaintiff argued ill impact. "The hallmark of the protection of free speech is to allow 'free trade in ideas—even ideas that the overwhelming majority of people might find distasteful or discomforting" (*Virginia v. Black* 2003, 358). Courts are careful to protect even distasteful and offensive speech in hopes that the marketplace of ideas will sort out the truthful "sheep" from the offending "goats" (*Brown v. Entertainment Merchants Association* 2011, 2764).

To this point, the Supreme Court frequently considers expressions of quintessential hate; cross burning, for example, is a symbolic act to be sure, but no less speech as it does communicate a specific contextual message. In *R.A.V. v. City of St. Paul, Minnesota*, the Court struck down a city ordinance prohibiting bias-motivated disorderly conduct that prohibits the display of a symbol which one knows or has reason to know "arouses anger, alarm or resentment in others on the basis of race, color, creed, religion or gender" (Minn. Stat. § 609.2231(4)). By reaching "fighting words" with the stated bias or animus the city "proscribed fighting words of whatever manner that communicate messages of racial, gender, or religious intolerance. Selectivity like this creates the possibility that the city is seeking to handicap the expression of particular ideas. That possibility would alone be enough to render the ordinance presumptively invalid" (*R.A.V. v. City of St. Paul, Minnesota* 1992, p. 393–394). Such "selectivity" belies the position that the conduct alone is the target of regulation but also the underlying thought as well. This rendered the ordinance unconstitutional on the basis of viewpoint discrimination. The problem for Justice Scalia was not that cross-burning is not a bad thing, but that it cannot be treated differently than other forms of disorderly conduct.

Twenty years later the Court reviewed and upheld a Virginia statute making it a felony "for any person . . . with the intent of intimidating any person or group . . . to burn . . . a cross on the property of another, a highway or other public place" (Va.Code Ann. § 18.2-423). States had learned their lesson from *R.A.V.* and created statutes that penalized expressions of hate speech but added an extra element, in Virginia's instance an intent to intimidate, linking speech-thought to its impact; but the statute also provided that "[a]ny such burning . . . shall be prima facie evidence of an intent to intimidate a person or group" (Va.Code Ann. § 18.2-423). Like the fallacy of trying to define a word by using that word in its definition, the Court found flaw with the intent element as articulated in the statute. The state of Virginia, in basing the concept of intimidation on the act so proscribed engaged in a bit of circular logic. "We conclude that while a State, consistent with the

First Amendment, may ban cross burning carried out with the intent to intimidate, the provision in the Virginia statute treating any cross burning as prima facie evidence of intent to intimidate renders the statute unconstitutional in its current form" (*Virginia v. Black* 2003, 347–348). Intimidation as the thought behind the conduct and as an element of the crime must be determined apart from proscribed conduct; it must be a separate element, proved by evidence extrinsic to the circumstances of the act, i.e., the cross burning. The Supreme Court concluded that "Virginia's statute does not run afoul of the First Amendment insofar as it bans cross burning with intent to intimidate" (*Virginia v. Black* 2003, 362). As a result, states are free to proscribe such conduct. Cross burning (conduct) can be regulated when it ties such speech (speech can be non-verbal) to specific ill-intent (unlike campus speech codes discussed below that focus on the ill-intent without requiring ill-conduct). Cases that have one and not both or where the bias, animus or thought behind an act is targeted while other biases are left untouched are problematic. However, such distinctions may be lost on the subject-listener or upon those who are nonetheless offended or outraged because cross burning and other expressions of hate conflict with the dictates of a fair and just society.

Lessons from the Campus and School Speech Code Litigation

While many, many institutions of higher education have some form of campus speech code, those codes that have been challenged as unconstitutional have all met a similar demise. Such regulation is repeatedly struck down. While the courts appear to speak with one voice in these matters, the commentators are split. Some authors favor speech codes (Sunstein 1993; Hartman 1993; Byrne 1991; Lawrence 1990; Matsuda 1989; and Delgado and Yun 1994) while others oppose them (Rabe 2003; Calleros 1995; Sherry 1991; Smolla 1990; Siegel 1990; McGee 1990). The code detractors charge that speech codes cast a "pall of orthodoxy over the classroom" and suggest that education and dialogue is the better, constitutional approach to achieve the goals underlying the regulation, but without punishment or coercion: "The classroom is peculiarly the 'marketplace of ideas.' The nation's future depends upon leaders trained through wide exposure to that robust exchange of ideas which discovers truth out of a multitude of tongues" (*Keyishian v. Board of Regents* 1967, 603). Commentators supporting speech codes observe the Supreme Court's concern that educational environments should not impose conformity or "a pall of orthodoxy."

Courts distinguish between hate speech—protected by the First Amendment—and speech that causes cognizable legal harm. An example of the latter is speech that rises to a level of actionable harassment in the classroom or speech that harms a person's reputation, i.e., defamation (see Dale Herbeck's article on "Defamation and Intellectual Freedom" in this volume). In the educational setting courts are careful to distinguish between the two. "Harassment has never been a protected activity under the First Amendment" (*Saxe v. State College Area School District* 1999, 626–627). On appeal, the circuit court identified speech that while offensive, remains protected within the boundaries of the First Amendment: "But there is also no question that the free speech clause protects a wide variety of speech that listeners may consider deeply offensive, including statements that impugn another's race or national origin or that denigrate religious beliefs" (*Saxe v. State College Area School District,* 2001, 206). In the *Saxe* case the policy as written was overbroad, capturing far more speech than either federal or state anti-harassment statutes. The court concluded: "the Policy's 'Definitions' section lists as examples of covered harassment 'negative' or 'derogatory' speech about such contentious issues as 'racial customs,' 'religious tradition,' 'language,' 'sexual orientation,' and 'values.' Such speech, when it does not pose a realistic threat of substantial disruption, is within a student's First Amendment rights" (*Saxe v. State College Area School District* 2001, 217, footnote omitted).

As in *Monteiro,* courts are cautious to endow new rights that would allow a person or group to object to offensive speech. Courts are afraid that if adopted, and then applied equally to all, the results of such policy may do more harm than good, as each faction, empowered with a sort of preemptive strike or "heckler's veto" would exercise that right at every occasion. In this environment public discourse would be relegated to speech that is unpalatable to no one. As one court hypothesized:

> *All manner of other speech, from the innocuous to the laudable, could also be banned or punished under the school's hate speech policy. May a student wear a Black Pride t-shirt, or does this denigrate white and Asian students? May a student wear a t-shirt saying 'I love Jesus,' or will this make Jews, Muslims and Druids feel it's an attack on their religions? May a student wear a t-shirt saying 'Proud to be a Turk,' or will this cause bad vibrations for the Greeks and Armenians in the school? . . . The types of speech that could be banned by the school authorities under the Poway High School hate policy are practically without limit. (Harper v. Poway Unified School Dist. 2006, 1206–1207)*

In the K–12 school setting it is possible to regulate symbols or images that some argue are historically linked to representation of hate and oppression if the regulation complies with First Amendment sensitivities. The leading case is *Tinker v. Des Moines Independent Community School District.* "[T]he "*Tinker* standard" applies to all other student speech and allows regulation only when the school reasonably believes that the speech will substantially and materially interfere with schoolwork or discipline" (*Defoe ex rel. Defoe v. Spiva* 2010, 332). The circuit upheld the ban of the wearing or other display of the Confederate flag given the existing climate of racial tensions and open animus because of demonstrable substantial disruption or material interference with school processes such clothing displays would cause (*Defoe ex rel. Defoe v. Spiva* 2010, 335).

Other courts have upheld similar bans by school districts. In *A.M. ex rel. McAllum v. Cash* the court concluded that the "racially inflammatory meaning associated with the Confederate flag and the evidence of racial tension at [the high school] establish[ed] that [school officials] reasonably forecast that [displays of the Confederate flag] might cause substantial disruption of school activities" (2009, 233). In *B.W.A. v. Farmington R-7 School District* the court upheld a school district's ban on clothing depicting the Confederate flag based on evidence of "likely racially-motivated violence, racial tension, and other altercations directly related to adverse race relations in the community and the school" (2009, 741). Likewise, in *West v. Derby Unified School District No. 260* the court upheld a school district's clothing ban based on past racial incidents and a history of racial tension in the school district (2000, 1366–1367). Finally, in *Melton v. Young* the court concluded that the "continuing controversy over the use of the Confederate flag and the song "Dixie" at various school functions" caused the requisite disruption and interference to justify a ban on the use of both flag and song (1972, 1334).

Campus speech codes often proscribe protected speech. When this occurs and the code is challenged, courts conclude such codes are unconstitutional because the proscription reaches protected as well as unprotected speech. In addition, Courts conclude that such codes are over broad. Another problematic aspect of campus speech codes is definitional. Such codes are simply too vague to be constitutionally enforceable. College or university speech codes do not fare better than codes promulgated in the K–12 environment. Challenges in the early 1990s included *UWM Post, Inc. v. Board of Regents of University of Wisconsin System* (1991, 1165), *IOTA XI Chapter of Sigma Chi Fraternity v. George Mason University* (1991, 793) and, in more recent years, *McCauley v. University of the Virgin Islands* (2010); *DeJohn v. Temple University* (2008) to campus codes or policies using vague or imprecise language defining the targeted speech were also struck down as unconstitutional.

Legislative Approaches

Legislatures are often more aggressive in attempts to combat and proscribe hate speech. There are two main approaches. One is to proscribe a specifically defined act as a hate crime (Blum, 1994). This is the predominant legislative preference. While it is beyond the scope of this chapter to review the various state approaches, an excellent source for state-by-state review is found in Wang (2012). Variations include prohibitions on cross-burning or intimidating exhibit, anti-mask provisions (which would prohibit wearing a white conical hood), institutional vandalism such as the desecration of memorial or venerated monument or objects, obstructing free exercise of religion by disrupting a religious meeting. Some statutes contain an option for civil action and remedy in addition to a public collecting and reporting feature.

A second legislative approach is to enact penalty enhancement provisions. The two approaches are not mutually exclusive and are often found working in tandem in a particular instance. The Supreme Court offered a reason for treating crimes motivated by such bias as particularly pernicious and worthy of additional penalty: "The Wisconsin statute singles out for enhancement bias-inspired conduct because this conduct is thought to inflict greater individual and societal harm. . . . The State's desire to redress these perceived harms provides an adequate explanation for its penalty-enhancement provision over and above mere disagreement with offenders' beliefs or biases" (*Wisconsin v. Mitchell* 1993, 487–488). The attraction of penalty enhancement approaches is that it avoids the necessity of having to prove elements specific to the crime. Rather such provisions work in conjunction with a conviction under some other criminal statute such as assault, to add additional years to the sentence when there is evidence that the choice of victim was motivated by racial or other articulated animus. The Supreme Court has reiterated that this additional assessment must conform to Constitutional requirements of the Sixth Amendment (right to trial by jury), i.e., it must constitute a separate and provable element.

In *Apprendi v. New Jersey* (2000), the plaintiff was convicted of possession of a firearm for an unlawful purpose, a separate penalty "hate crime" enhancement statute authorized that an "extended term" of ten to twenty years imprisonment could be imposed if by a preponderance of the evidence the judge found that perpetrator "acted with a purpose to intimidate an individual or group of individuals because of race, color, gender, handicap, religion, sexual orientation or ethnicity" (N.J. stat. Ann 2C:44-3(e)). Under this standard Apprendi was sentenced to 12 years' imprisonment. The Supreme Court held that the Sixth Amendment prohibited the application of the New Jersey statute. A jury must prove any element-triggering enhancement beyond a reasonable doubt, i.e., requiring the same standards as the criminal prosecution itself. A preponderance of evidence standard often used in civil trials is a less exacting standard, requiring only that the greater weight of the evidence demonstrate the fact to be proved. It is the typical standard of civil trials.

Federal Statute Proscribing Hate Crimes

The leading federal statute is 18 U.S.C.A. § 249(a)(1), which punishes one who "willfully causes bodily injury to any person or, through the use of fire, a firearm, a dangerous weapon, or an explosive or incendiary device, attempts to cause bodily injury to any person, because of the actual or perceived race, color, religion, or national origin of any person." A second provision makes it a crime to "willfully cause [] bodily injury to any person or, through the use of fire, a firearm, a dangerous weapon, or an explosive or incendiary device, attempts to cause bodily injury to any person, because of the actual or perceived religion, national origin, gender, sexual orientation, gender identity, or disability of any person" (18 U.S.C.A. § 249(a)(2)(A)). There is scant case law regarding the federal statute, and no appellate decision though several lower courts have conclude that such statutes are constitutional under the Thirteenth, Tenth, and Fifth Amendments (*U.S. v. Beebe*, 2011).

Civil Remedies and the Tort of Outrage

In contrast to institutional regulatory models (codes or policies) or legislative prohibitions (crimes or penalty statutes), civil remedy may be an effective social option as it offers monetary compensation for inflicted harms. The tort of outrage falls within what is more commonly known as the tort of "intentional infliction of emotional distress" (IIED) and derives from a comment in the Restatement 2d of Torts discussing IIED inflicted by outrageous conduct: "The cases thus far decided have found liability only where the defendant's conduct has been extreme and outrageous. . . . Liability has been found only where the conduct has been so outrageous in character, and so extreme in degree, as to go beyond all possible bounds of decency, and to be regarded as atrocious, and utterly intolerable in a civilized community" (Restatements of Torts 2d § 46, Comment d.). The Restatement comment continues and delineates further what speech is not actionable: "The liability clearly does not extend to mere insults, indignities, threats, annoyances, petty oppressions, or other trivialities. The rough edges of our society are still in need of a good deal of filing down, and in the meantime plaintiffs must necessarily be expected and required to be hardened to a certain amount of rough language, and to occasional acts that are definitely inconsiderate and unkind. There is no occasion for the law to intervene in every case where some one's feelings are hurt" (Restatements of Torts 2d, § 46, Comment d.). Not all courts have embraced the concept. Commentators have proposed that the tort of outrage be adopted to include hate speech targeting "traditionally victimized minorities." The elements of the tort or harm as articulated by Delgado are as follows:

the plaintiff should be required to prove that language was addressed to him or her by the defendant that was intended to demean through reference to race; that the plaintiff understood as intended to demean through reference to race; and that a reasonable person would recognize as a racial insult. Thus, it would be expected that an epithet such as "You damn nigger" would almost always be found actionable, as it is highly insulting and highly racial. However, an insult such as "You incompetent fool," directed at a black person by a white, even in a context which made it highly insulting, would not be actionable because it lacks a racial component. . . . (1982, 179–180)

What would constitute outrage is often contextual as time, manner and audience. Evaluation of context should be made in the original context in which the speech occurred and not by more recent, exacting standards of comportment. As one court commented: "Although generations of high school and college football players can probably recall coaches who employed insensitive, insulting and what would now be politically incorrect language in an effort to motivate and inspire players, that approach is now as obsolete as the single wing offense. . . . Norman Lear's award-winning situation comedies *All in the Family* and *The Jeffersons* . . . might today produce gasps, and cries of 'outrageous' from the enforcers of political correctness, who are quick to label offensive utterances as 'hate speech'" *Civitella v. Pop Warner Football Team of Shelton, Inc.* 2010, *3).

Unfortunately, proponents of the civil remedy approach were dealt a blow by a recent Supreme Court decision. In *Snyder v. Phelps*, the Court held that the First Amendment prohibits the application of the tort of outrage to the nearby, peaceful picketing of military funerals. The Court observed that the picketing "addressed matters of public import on public property, in a peaceful manner, in full compliance with the guidance of local officials" (2011, 1220). The funeral protesters carried sign with a variety of messages including, "God Hates the USA/Thank God for 9/11," "America is Doomed," "Don't Pray for the USA," "Thank God for IEDs," "Fag Troops," "Semper Fi Fags," "God Hates Fags," "Maryland Taliban," "Fags Doom Nations," "Not Blessed Just Cursed," "Thank God for Dead Soldiers," "Pope in Hell," "Priests Rape Boys," "You're Going to Hell," and "God Hates You" (*Snyder v. Phelps* 2011, 1216–1217). The Court posited that even if the messages "were viewed as containing messages related to Matthew Snyder [the deceased soldier at whose funeral the protest was made] or the Snyders specifically, that would not change the fact that the overall thrust and dominant theme of Westboro's demonstration spoke to broader public issues" (*Snyder v. Phelps* 2011, 1217). Justice Roberts admitted that the juxtaposition of the speech at issue and funeral "made the expression of those views particularly hurtful to many, especially to Matthew's father" (*Snyder v. Phelps*, 2011, 1217). As the demonstrations were otherwise lawful Chief Justice Roberts concluded that "[s]imply put, the church members had the right to be where they were. . . . The picketing was conducted under police supervision . . . out of the sight of those at the church. The protest was not unruly; there was no shouting, profanity, or violence" (*Snyder v. Phelps* 2011, 1218–1219).

Maryland (where the *Snyder* case arose) and almost all of the other states now have laws imposing restrictions on funeral picketing. Although picketing is not prohibited in Maryland it is regulated; it cannot be "within 500 feet of a funeral, burial, memorial service, or funeral procession that is targeted at one or more persons attending the funeral, burial, memorial service, or funeral procession" (Maryland Code Ann., Crim. Law § 10-205(c)). A limitation on spatial (from 200 to 1,000 feet) and temporal (from 30–120 minutes before and/or after) proximity is common in these statutes.

Even if the tort would be established, in the online context federal tort immunity exists for intermediaries or operators of the online forum in which such speech would occur making such suits less attractive if not impossible (47 U.S.C. § 230). In *Noah v. America Online, Inc.* (2003) a subscriber made a "claim[] that the ISP wrongfully refused to prevent participants in an online chat room from posting or submitting harassing comments that blasphemed and defamed plaintiff's Islamic religion and his co-religionists" (*Noah v. America Online, Inc.* 2003, 534). The court concluded that the claim was barred by section 230 immunity. The only recourse would be to pursue action against the poster of the comment. A far less efficient remedy as the forum host has no legal responsibility in light of section 230 to edit or remove the offending speech.

Global Issues

While regulating expressions and displays of hate speech is restricted in the United States other approaches exist in many European countries such as France and Germany (Nrugger 2002). See for example *Yahoo! Inc. v. La Ligue Contre Le Racisme Et L'Antisemitisme* (2006), discussing a French law prohibiting the display for sale of Nazi memorabilia. A recent decision arising in a country that in the past had institutionalized and codified discrimination, the South Africa Equality Court observed: "Public speech involves a participation in political discourse with other citizens, in a manner that respects their own correlative rights. Hate speech has no respect for those rights. It lacks full value as political speech. Hate speech does not address the community in general but merely a portion of it; those who are the target group. Hate speech should not be protected merely because it contributes to the pursuit of the truth. If it denies recognition of the free and reasonable rights of others it makes no direct contribution to the process" (*Afri-Forum and Another v Malema and Others* 2011, 19). The South African court, in an opinion that cited a U.S. Supreme Court on free speech, concluded that singing the song "shoot the Boer" by ANC activist Julius Malema was hate speech prohibited under the South African constitution and legislation. The court's order prohibited the further singing of the song viewing alignment between the interpreted law protecting human dignity and the appropriate societal moral response as well: "The respondents are interdicted and restrained from singing the song known as Dubula Ibhunu at any public or private meeting held by or conducted by them. . . . The words and the song constitute hate speech. The morality of society dictates that persons should refrain from: using the words, singing the song" (*Afri-Forum and Another v Malema and Others* 2011, 63). The South African decision expresses a view that any positive effects of hate speech do not outweigh its negative effects. In the marketplace articulation, the social costs outweigh the social benefits producing a negative externality which causes, without out intervention through prohibition, the marketplace of ideas to fail.

Previous commentators have advanced this position (MacKinnon 1993; Waldron 2010). These commentators argued for a view of hate speech that constitutes a form of group defamation: "group defamation laws . . . look instead to the basics of social standing and to the association that is made—in the hate speech, in the libel, in the defamatory pamphlet or poster—between the denigration of that basic standing and some characteristic associated more or less ascriptively with the group or class . . . group defamation sets out to make it a liability by denigrating group-defining characteristics or associating them with bigoted factual claims that are fundamentally defamatory" (Waldron 2010, 1609). The point of this chapter is not to suggest that the law should move in one particular direction or another but rather to indicate and discuss the contrast between the moral and the legal result; in this contrast there is potential for discussion and hopefully understanding. The law in the United States protects the speech rights of the speaker as opposed to approaches that balance listener rights (not to be offended) or deleterious potential impact that such speech can have on the listener, bystanders or on society as a whole. In such a climate any concept of a marketplace of ideas cannot operate, any marketplace discourse is eliminated outright.

Philosophical Perspectives

Hate speech is not simply a matter of balancing the speaker's right of expression and the listener's right to not be offended—there is also the matter of a shared cultural history of oppression. This undercurrent of subordination, of continued racism, further complicates the ethical dilemma hate speech presents.

> *In the view of two commentators: The word "honky" is more a badge of respect than a put down. "Cracker," although disrespectful, still implies power, as does "redneck." The fact is that terms like "nigger," "spick," "faggot," and "kike" evoke and reinforce entire cultural histories of oppression and subordination. They remind the target that his or her group has always been and remains unequal in status to the majority group. . . . But not only is there no correlate, no hate speech aimed at whites, there is no means by which persons of color and others can respond effectively to this form of speech within the current paradigm. Our culture has developed a host of narratives . . . that render it difficult for the minority victim to talk back in individual cases, and to mobilize effectively against hate speech in general. (Richardson v. Sugg, 325 F.Supp.2d 919, 929–930 [E.D. Ark., 2004, citing Turner 1995])*

Hate speech and the Marketplace of Ideas

One critical concern of this chapter is that one of the most fundamental opportunities to contribute to the betterment of society is effectively denied for individuals and groups targeted for hate speech. Through its intentional suppression, hate speech erects barriers to entry for minorities, certain religious adherents, ethnic groups or others such as those identified as GLBT, into the marketplace of ideas.

From the previous discussion on hate speech policy and litigation, one can appreciate how difficult it is to disentangle hate speech from protected speech especially with the specter of chilled speech looming large. While it may be exceedingly difficult to legislate and adjudicate hate speech, fairness tells us we should not perpetuate injustice, which is what we are doing, albeit reluctantly, when we allow hate speech to continue unabated. Using the framework of justice as fairness, hate speech should be assessed on the basis of the harm it creates. Hate speech creates harm. It intimidates. It stirs up contempt, hatred, distrust, fear and more. It robs individuals of the opportunity to fully and outwardly express themselves by stating their opinions, hopes, beliefs and values. Hate speech burdens people who simply want to pursue their everyday lives—taking their children to school, shopping at K-mart, or having a meal at a neighborhood restaurant. Even those who argue that hate speech should not be legally restricted acknowledge the injustice that arises from hate speech. Hate speech stands in stark contrast to a society that strives to be egalitarian and democratic in its actions and within its social institutions and constructions.

John Rawls can be particularly instructive here. Rawls' first principle of justice in *A Theory of Justice* states that everyone "has an equal right to the most extensive liberties compatible with similar liberties for all" (Rawls 2001). Upholding hate speech is incongruous with Rawls' first principle and other ethical frameworks. Even John Stuart Mill in his essay, *On Liberty*, which eloquently and persuasively argues on behalf of the individual, recognizes that civilized communities should act to prevent harm to others, "the only purpose for which power can be rightfully exercised over any member of a civilized community, against his will, is to prevent harm to others" (Mill 1869, 8).

Rawls clearly promulgates the democratic ideal that everyone has an equal right to a basic set of rights. He also points out that the circumstances into which individuals are born or find themselves are quite different—some are born wealthy or poor, some are in the majority, some in the minority and so forth. Rawls' second principle—the difference principle—argues that these inequalities should be resolved in ways that provide the greatest benefit to those who are the least well off and further that society's institutions, which he calls "offices," must be open to all. That is, each person has an equal opportunity to participate.

If Rawls is correct, that everyone is entitled to a certain set of rights and that society should be arranged in ways that are fair and supported by reason, then what case could be made to support hate speech? Would racial slurs and other taunts be permitted? Would we permit "group libel" in which entire groups are negatively construed through statements that are unreasonable because they are not based on objective or scientific evidence? Hispanics are lazy, blacks are intellectually inferior, women are not rational enough to vote, or gay men are morally bankrupt. In this case, it seems reasonable that hate speech would not enjoy a protected position any more than shouting "fire" in a theater or 'fighting words' do under current United States jurisprudence, if citizens are truly regarded as "free and equal persons" (Rawls 2001, 7). Free and equal persons have the moral capacity for a sense of justice and they act *from* rather than merely *in* accordance with the principles of [political] justice that specify fair terms of social cooperation (Rawls 2001, 19). In this regard, hate speech itself cannot be justified. Actions, including speaking and publishing, which interfere with another person's opportunity to contribute their ideas are socially and ethically unacceptable in the justice as fairness framework.

Individual Rights, or, The Argument Against Hate Speech Legislation

But consider John Stuart Mill's defense of individual liberty again. Mill recognizes that the individual must be allowed to express his or her thoughts and values in ways that he or she sees fit in order to be happy. It is just this sort of case that lays the groundwork for two major arguments against hate speech legislation.

An exhaustive analysis of the morality of hate speech, which is beyond the scope of this chapter, is not needed to establish that injustice arises when an individual's chosen method of self-expression is protected, yet when such expression suppresses the rights of others. According to Waldron in, *The Harm of Hate Speech*, arguments against hate speech legislation include Baker's Autonomy Argument and Dworkin's Legitimacy argument. Hate speech, so the arguments go, is essential to freedom of speech. The speaker's right to say what he thinks about others, about the law, politics, or business or to express his belief in the superiority of Christians or fair-skinned people is protected because everyone has the "right" to express his or her ideas and beliefs. If expressing one's views with vehement hatred is inextricably linked to one's sense of autonomy—freedom of thought and will—then the hate speech must be allowed. In an over simplification of the individual rights arguments, it is possible that there would be a negative effect on the marketplace of ideas in that debates would be skewed, the playing field uneven, and individual expression foreclosed upon and so forth. Moreover, the Dworkin Legitimacy argument claims that enforcing hate speech laws would, "spoil the only democratic justification we have for insisting that everyone obey [the downstream] laws" (Dworkin in Waldron 2012). Waldron, in a moderate take on Dworkin's case, says, "I think what he wants to say is that there is something morally to regret when we enforce nondiscrimination laws against racists who were not allowed to influence the formal and informal political culture as they wished. But the *something to regret* might be more or less considerable" (Waldron 2009, 188). There is something too to regret if hate speech suppresses the opportunity of some individuals to influence the culture as they wish.

What ought to be done about the problem of hate speech?

"Our hope for the future of our society rests on the belief that the social world allows at least a decent political order, so that a reasonably just, though not perfect, democratic regime is possible" (Rawls 2001, 4).

As discussed in previous sections, advocates for hate speech legislation and countries that regulate hate speech "realize that hate speech is devoid of any value" and that it should not be permitted "despite free speech ideals" (Webb 2011). "Hate speech has no respect for those rights. It lacks full value as political speech. Hate speech does not address the community in general but merely a portion of it; those who are in the target group. Hate speech should not be protected merely because it contributes to the pursuit of the truth. If it denies recognition of the free and reasonable rights of others it makes no direct contribution to the process." (*Afri-Forum and Another v Male-ma and Others* 2011, 19). Protection of hate speech flies in the face of any notion of justice as fairness.

Charlotte H. Taylor aptly describes the chasm, "The two sides in the debate over hate speech might be called the anti-subordination camp and the free speech camp. Those in the anti-subordination camp understand hate speech to be a means of perpetuating systematic discrimination and oppression of minority groups. They are skeptical of the First Amendment and its emphasis on unfettered debate and protection of unpopular speech; they see 'freedom of speech' as a screen that protects racism, homophobia, misogyny, and other forms of discrimination. They urge that the equality values of the Fourteenth Amendment must not be sacrificed in the name of the First Amendment. Those in the free speech camp are, for their part, skeptical of the proposition that it is possible or advisable to regulate only that speech which contributes to subordination . . . debate between the two camps has ended at an impasse" (2010, 1117–1118).

This conflict is deeply rooted in competing philosophies, a quintessential ethical dilemma identified by Rawls "Here we focus on another root of the conflict: the different philosophical and moral doctrines that deal with how competing claims of liberty and equality are to be understood, how they are to be ordered and weighed against each other, and how any particular way of ordering them is justified" (Rawls 2001, 2). In the case of hate speech the conflict can be viewed as a competition between assuring equality under the law for all citizens, which is a democratic ideal and freedom of speech which is also a democratic ideal. Rulings that protect hate speech clearly indicate that more weight is given to the individual liberties found in free speech even in cases where individuals stir up hatred on the basis of skin color or belief or gender or sexual preference.

The Westboro case (see above) gives us a glimpse at one possibility—peripheral proscription. During its protests, Westboro positioned itself away from funeral procession and did not engage individual mourners. Ultimately, this has led to the enactment of funeral picketing laws across nearly every state where none existed before. Time and place restrictions if they are based on protecting dignity—that is upholding the 14th amendment—and not content-based—could be a step toward the social assurance that is rightfully expected by each member of society.

Forward

Bridging the gap between what is legal and what is fair regarding hate speech is an elusive task. In whatever ways we might work and rework our legal and philosophical considerations of hate speech in the future, as it stands now, there is no course of action that both ensures free speech, that allows the speaker to say what hateful thing he will, and also protects the targeted individual and greater society from the harm this hate speech produces. The reader might expect the authors to propose education, but as Waldron comments, we should not concern ourselves with changing the racist's view—he or she is entitled to those views.

Instead perhaps we should focus on the harm that is done and aspects of compensatory justice. Future legal strategies can take a variety of options. The first is to use allowable legal constructions to restrict hate related speech such as penalty enhancement statutes. A second and related approach attempts to minimize the impact of the speech at its outset but is unsatisfactory. Legal solutions such as the anti-picketing statutes, which afford some respect for the listener's rights, may be less satisfactory than other constructions because they provide an aura of social acceptance of hate speech. It seems implausible that a certain amount of distance between the speaker (500 feet for example) and the target could miraculously sanitize what is otherwise harmful, make hate speech less humiliating, less degrading, and less painful to those it targets. Third, proponents could still advocate for the creation of *sui generis* remedies such as group libel, although such restrictions could still face constitutional challenge. Fourth, advocates could continue attempts at proscription through the courts. The Supreme Court has excluded other sorts of speech such as defamation or child pornography from First Amendment protection, so too the courts could exclude hate speech because of the harm such speech wreaks upon the target or the subject. A similar argument might at some point similarly result in the exclusion of hate speech from constitutional protection.

References

A.M. ex rel. McAllum v. Cash. 565 F.3d 214 (5th Cir. 2009).

Abrams v. United States. 250 U.S. 616 (1919).

Abrams, Floyd. 1996. Hate Speech: The present implications of a historical dilemma, in Jane Duncan, Between Speech and Silence: Hate Speech, Pornography and the New South Africa. Quoted in Kohm, Lynne Marie. The First Amendment, homosexual unions, and "newspeak": Has the language surrounding the marriage debate altered the nature of marriage itself, or affected the truth of the issues Inherent in alternative marriage demands? *Liberty University Law Review* 4 (2010): 593–616.

Afri-Forum and Another v Malema and Others. CASE NO: 20968/2010 (South Africa Equality Court, September 12, 2011). http://www.saflii.org/za/cases/ZAEQC/2011/2.html (accessed October 22, 2013).

Andersen v. King County. 138 P.3d 963 (Wash. 2006).

Apprendi v. New Jersey. 530 U.S. 466 (2000).

B.W.A. v. Farmington R-7 School District. 554 F.3d 734 (8th Cir. 2009).

Bair v. Shippensburg University. 280 F.Supp.2d 357 (M.D. Pa. 2003)

Black's Law Dictionary. 2009. Ed. Bryan A. Garner. 9th ed. St. Paul, Minn: Thompson Reuters (Westlaw).

Blum, George L. n.d. Validity, construction, and effect of "Hate Crimes" statutes, "Ethnic Intimidation" statutes, or the like. 22 ALR 5th 261 (19194).

Boos v. Barry. 485 U.S. 312 (1988).

Brief for The American Legion as Amicus Curiae in Support of Petitioner, *Snyder v. Phelps.* 2010. WL 2224730, *18–*19. n. 2 (Dkt. No. 09-751, June 1, 2010).

Brown v. Entertainment Merchants Association. 131 S.Ct. 2729 (2011).

Brugger, Winfried. 2002. Ban on or protection of hate speech? Some observations based on German and American law. *Tulane European and Civil Law Forum* 17: 1.

Byrne, J. Peter. 1991. Racial insults and free Speech within the university. *Georgetown Law Journal* 79: 399–444.

Calleros, Charles R. 1995. Paternalism, counterspeech, and campus hate-speech codes: A reply to Delgado and Yun. *Arizona State Law Journal* 27: 1249–1280.

Christian Legal Society Chapter of the University of California, College of the Law. 130 S.Ct. 2971(2010).

Citron, Danielle Keats, and Northon, Helen. 2011. Intermediaries and hate speech: Fostering digital citizenship for our information age (note). *Boston University Law Review* 91: 1435–1484.

Civitella v. Pop Warner Football Team of Shelton, Inc. 2010 WL 5188760 (Conn. Super., 2010).

Commission of Ministers, Council of Europe. Recommendation No. R (1997) 20 of the Committee of Ministers to Member States on "Hate Speech" (1997). http://www.coe.az/pfddoc/committee_of_ministers/ Rec No.%CC20R% 20(97) 20 (e).pdf (accessed October 22, 2013).

Dambrot v. Central Michigan University. 55 F.3d 1177 (6th Cir. 1995)

Defoe ex rel. Defoe v. Spiva, 625 F.3d 324 (6th Cir., 2010).

DeJohn v. Temple University 537 F.3d 301 (3d Cir. 2008).

Delgado, Richard, and David Yun. 1994. The neoconservative case against hate speech regulation—Lively, D'Souza, Gates, Carter, and the tough love crowd. *Vanderbilt Law Review* 47: 1807–1826.

DiCarlo v. Potter. 358 F.3d 408 (6th Cir. 2004).

Doe v. University of Michigan. 721 F. Supp. 852 (E.D. Mich. 1989).

Hafez v. Madison. 348 Fed.Appx. 465 (11th Cir. 2009).

Hardy v. Jefferson Community College. 260 F.3d 671 (6th Cir. 2001)

Harper v. Poway Unified School Dist. 445 F.3d 1166 (9th Cir. 2006).

Hartman, Rhonda G. 1993. Hateful expression and First Amendment values: Toward a theory of constitutional constraint on hate speech at colleges and universities after *R.A.V. v. St. Paul. Journal of College and University Law* 19: 343–371.

In re Ohio Domestic-Violence Statute Cases, 872 N.E.2d 1212 (Ohio, 2007).

Iota XI Chapter of Sigma Chi Fraternity v. George Mason University. 773 F. Supp. 792 (E.D. Va. 1991), aff'd 993 F.2d 386 (4th Cir. 1993).

Jacobellis v. State of Ohio. 378 U.S. 184(1964)

Keyishian v. Board of Regents. 385 U.S. 589 (1967).

Lawrence, III, Charles R. 1990. If he hollers let him go: Regulating racist speech on campus. *Duke Law Journal* 431–483.

Lee v. K Mart Corp. 2011 WL 6740355 (D. Minn, 2011).

Little v. Robinson. 72 So.3d 1168 (Ala., 2011).

MacKinnon, Catharine A. 1993. *Only words.* Cambridge, MA: Harvard University Press.

Matsuda, Mari J. 1989. Public response to racist speech: Considering the victim's story. *Michigan Law Review* 87: 2320–2381.

McCauley v. University of the Virgin Islands. 618 F.3d 232 (3d Cir. 2010).

McGee, Robert W. 1990. Hate speech, free speech, and the university. *Akron Law Review* 24: 363–392.

Melton v. Young. 465 F.3d 1332 (6th Cir. 1972) *cert. denied,* 411 U.S. 951 (1973).

Mill, John S. 1869. On liberty. Raleigh, NC: Alex Catalogue.

Miller v. California. 413 U.S. 15 (1973).

Monteiro v. Tempe Union High School District. 158 F. 3d 1022 (9th Cir. 1998).

Noah v. America Online, Inc. 2003 U.S. Dist. LEXIS 8242 (E.D. Va. 2003), affirmed *Noah v. AOL-Time Warner, Inc.,* 2004 WL 602711 (4th Cir., 2004) (unpublished).

R.A.V. v. City of St. Paul, Minnesota. 505 U.S. 377 (1992).

Rabe, Lee Ann. 2003. Sticks and stones: The First Amendment and campus speech codes. *John Marshall Law Review* 37: 205–228.

Rawls, John. 2001. *Justice as fairness: A restatement.* Cambridge, MA: Harvard University Press.

Richardson v. Sugg. 325 F.Supp.2d 919 (E.D. Ark., 2004).

Roberts v. Haragan. 346 F.Supp.2d 853 (N.D. Tex., 2004).

Ryan, Sarah E. 2012. Fulfilling the U.S. obligation to prevent extermination-ism: A comprehensive approach to regulating hate speech and dis-mantling systems of genocide. *Loyola University Chicago Law Journal* 43: 317–356.

*Saxe v. State College Area School Dist.*77 F.Supp.2d 621 (M.D. Pa. 1999), re-versed, 240 F.3d 200 (3d Cir. 2001).

Seibert Security Services, Inc. v. Superior Court. 22 Cal.Rptr.2d 514 (Cal. App. 4 Dist. 1993).

Shaw, LaShel. 2011. Hate speech in cyberspace: Bitterness without boundar-ies. *Notre Dame Journal of Law, Ethics & Public Policy* 25: 279–304.

Sherry, Suzanna. 1991. Speaking of virtue: A republican approach to univer-sity regulation of hate speech. *Minnesota Law Review* 75: 933–944.

Siegel, Evan G. S. 1990. Closing the campus gates to free expression: The regulation of offensive speech at colleges and universities. *Emory Law Journal* 39: 1351–1400.

Smolla, Rodney A. Smolla & Nimmer on freedom of speech. Vol. 2 § 17:29 (Database updated March 2012).

Snyder v. Phelps. 131 S.Ct 1207 (2011).

State v. Logsdon. 2006 WL 1585447 (Ohio App. 3 Dist., 2006)

State v. Sulick. 2012 WL 602889.

Stone v. Paddock Publications, Inc. 961 N.E.2d 380 (Ill. App. Dist., 2 2011).

Strossen, Nadine. 1990. Regulating racist speech on campus: A modest pro-posal?. *Duke Law Journal* 1990: 483–573. Quoted in Calvert, Clay. Justice Samuel A. Alito's lonely war against abhorrent, low-value expression: A malleable First Amendment philosophy privileging subjective notions of morality and merit. *Hofstra Law Review* 4: 115–176.

Sunstein, Cass R. 1993. Liberalism, speech codes, and related problems, *Academe* 79: 14–25.

Taylor, Charlotte H. 2010. Hate speech and government speech. *University of Pennsylvania Journal of Constitutional Law* 12: 1115.

Texas v. Johnson. 491 U.S. 397 (1989).

Tinker v. Des Moines Independent Community School District. 393 U.S. 503 (1969).

Turner, Ronald. 1995. Regulating hate speech and the First Amendment: The attractions of and objections to, an explicit harms-based analysis. *Indiana Law Review* 29: 257–338.

U.S. v. Beebe. 2011 WL 3416734 (D. N.M.).

U.S. v. White. 670 F.3d 498 (4th Cir. 2012).

UWM Post, Inc. v. Board of Regents of University of Wisconsin System, 774 F.Supp. 1163 (E.D. Wis.1991).

Virginia v. Black. 538 U.S. 343 (2003).

Waldron, J. 2009. Dignity and defamation: The visibility of hate. *Harvard Law Review* 123: 1596–1657.

Waldron, Jeremy. 2012. *The harm in hate speech.* Cambridge, MA: Harvard University Press.

Webb, Thomas J. 2011. Verbal poison—criminalizing hate speech: A comparative analysis and a proposal for the American system (note). *Washburn Law Journal* 50: 445–482.

West v. Derby Unified School District No. 260, 206 F.3d 1358 (10th Cir.), *cert. denied,* 531 U.S. 825 (2000).

Wisconsin v. Mitchell. 508 U.S. 476 (1993).

Yahoo! Inc. v. La Ligue Contre Le Racisme Et L'Antisemitisme. 433 F.3d 1199 (9th Cir. 2006).

Intellectual Freedom and U.S. Government Secrecy[1]

Susan Maret

> *The idea of intellectual liberty is under attack from two directions. On the one side are its theoretical enemies, the apologists of totalitarianism and on the other its immediate, practical enemies, monopoly and bureaucracy.*
>
> ~George Orwell (1946)

Intellectual freedom assumes a free press, access to libraries, transparency of laws and regulations, open records and archives, and a social world that provides a foundation for exploration, expression, discussion of diverse perspectives, and the protection of rights. This rich climate potentially molds individual thought and action, but also civic participation, as "people do need novels and dramas and paintings and poems, 'because they will be called upon to vote'" (Meiklejohn 1961, 263). Intellectual freedom implies potential empowerment through information and communication regarding common life, for without knowledge there is no chance to exercise power (Bok 1989b). Through intellectual freedom, individuals are better able to come to terms with the times in which they live and the history they inherit. Essential for the creation of trust and confidence so critical in addressing issues of mutual concern, intellectual freedom is also related to a reduction of uncertainty, for in accessing certain kinds of information,[2] individuals as well as governments are able to assess risk and security (Daase and Kessler 2007; Edelstein 2004).

In this chapter, I investigate intellectual freedom in the United States within the confines of government secrecy. First, I discuss intellectual freedom through a lens of law and human rights, and in the following sections,

---

1   The author thanks Mark Alfino, Ivan Greenberg, and Mickey Huff for their feedback on this chapter.

2   Information as intended here means "knowledge communicated" (Capurro 2003),

I utilize political scientist Carl J. Friedrich's models of functional and disfunctional secrecy and tampering with communications in assessing "what
is and is not discreditable by examining particular practices of secrecy" (Bok
1989b, 9). Friedrich's modes of secrecy not only illustrate the demands secrecy places on intellectual freedom, but allow for the discussion of secrecy's
close cousins, propaganda, censorship, and surveillance.

Intellectual Freedom—A Global Right

The cornerstones of intellectual freedom, the ability to access and communicate information, including the "right to speak anonymously, the right to use
encryption tools and the right to be free from unwarranted monitoring and
surveillance" (Article 19 2003; United Nations General Assembly 1966) establish the power to research, write, publish, affiliate, protest, and assemble.
Furthermore, intellectual freedom is the right to hold beliefs, express opinions, and share information "regardless of frontiers" (United Nations General Assembly, 1948). Simply, intellectual freedom is defined as the "freedom
of the mind and as such it is both a personal liberty and a prerequisite for all
freedoms leading to action" (American Library Association 2010, xvii).

The Bill of Rights of the U.S. Constitution (1789) and laws such as the Ad-
ministrative Procedure Act P.L. 79-404 (1946), Freedom of Information Act
P.L. 89-487 (1966),[3] Federal Advisory Committee Act P.L. 92-463 (1972), the
Government in Sunshine Act P.L. 94-409 (1976), Paperwork Reduction Act
Amendments of 1996 P.L. 104-13, Electronic Freedom of Information Act
Amendments of 1996 (P.L. 104-231), and Open Government Act of 2007 (P.L.
110-175) extend political rights and civil liberties associated with intellectu-
al freedom.[4] In addition, rights associated with intellectual freedom in the
United States are affirmed through a variety of international declarations
and conventions.[5]

---

3   The Act was perceived by many in Congress and in federal agencies that admin-
     istered FOIA as a way to allow the release of legitimate secrets (Mackenzie 1997,
     12) and also began a longstanding "collision course" with the National Security
     Act and its provisions for secrecy (MacKenzie 1997, 12–13). FOIA was substan-
     tially amended in 1974, and de facto modified in 1984 by the CIA Information
     Act, which exempts operational files of the Agency from release.

4   A case can be made that intellectual freedom is furthered by environmental laws
     such as the Emergency Planning and Community Right-To-Know Act (P.L. 99-
     499), the National Environmental Protection Act of 1969 (P.L. 91-190), called the
     ecological *Magna Carta* (Auerbach 1972), and the Occupational Safety and Health
     Act of 1970 (P.L.91-596), which mandates a worker's right to know of chemical and
     radiation hazards in the workplace.

5   Such as the Universal Declaration of Human Rights (1948), particularly Articles
     18, 19, 26, and 27, the International Convention on the Elimination of All Forms

Intellectual freedom is also tied to the right to know (RTK) by way of an open media, of which Kent Cooper of the Associated Press observed that "a citizen is entitled to have access to news, fully and accurately presented. There cannot be political freedom in one country or the world, without respect for 'the right to know'" (*The New York Times* 1945, 18). It is with Cooper we witness the birth of the contemporary RTK movement in the United States during the 1940s, in part based on the ideal of an informed citizenship made possible through access to information. The RTK movement gained further ground with the work of Harold L. Cross, counsel to the *New York Herald Tribune*, who was enlisted by the American Society of Newspaper Editors (ASNE) to compile "a comprehensive report on customs, laws and court decisions affecting our free access to public information whether it is recorded on police blotters or the files of national government" (Cross 1953, xv). Among the rights identified by Cross is the "right of inspection," traced to English Common Law, where

> *Every person is entitled to the inspection, either personally or by his agent, of public records, including legislative, executive, and judicial records, provided he has an interest therein which is such as would enable him to maintain or defend an action in which the document or record sought can furnish evidence or necessary information.* (Cross 1953, 26)

In *The People's Right to Know: Legal Access to Public Records and Proceedings*, Cross reviewed statutes on the definition of a public record, privacy laws, and identified five "non-inspection doctrines" that outline instances where records can be withheld (1953, 203–213). In this work, Cross also argues for the addition of a constitutional amendment to clarify the First Amendment on access to information. Cross' book remains a groundbreaking early inventory of freedom of information laws and a measure of U.S. government secrecy and was an inspiration for the creation of the Freedom of Information Act of 1966, or FOIA (Lemov 2011). Both Cooper and Cross suggest that the RTK is best realized by an investigative press and media, coupled with publicity and transparency of government policies and actions.[6]

---

of Racial Discrimination (1969), the International Covenant on Civil and Political Rights (1976), the International Covenant on Economic, Social and Cultural Rights (1976), and the Convention against Torture and Other Cruel, Inhuman or Degrading Treatment or Punishment (1987). The Rio Declaration on Environment and Development, especially Principle 10, also reinforces the need for information in decisionmaking (United Nations Conference on Environment and Development 1992).

6   Note the distinctions between publicity and transparency as Daniel Naurin (2006) observes: "accountability is primarily a function of publicity rather than transparency. Publicity, one can say, is a causal mechanism linking transparency and accountability." (91).

Secrecy: Functional or Disfunctional?

Limits on intellectual freedom are associated with shades of government se-crecy, as the secret is "the ultimate sociological form for the regulation of the flow and distribution of information" (Hazelrigg 1969, 324). Secrecy may include the use of codes, disguises, markings, costumes, and specific colors (Bok 1989a; Simmel 1906) and is connected to the clandestine, or "any activ-ity or operation sponsored or conducted by governmental departments or agencies with the intent to assure secrecy and concealment" (Department of Defense 2012). But it is secrecy as the *consciously willed concealment of informa-tion* (Simmel 1906, 449) with sanctions for disclosure (Shils 1956) employed from the establishment of the United States across branches of government as a weapon, technique,[7] strategy, and policy that involves "conflicts of power that come through controlling the flow of information" (Bok 1989b, 18–19).

As Cass Sunstein observes, our current understanding of the Jeffersonian model of freedom of information, with its emphasis on the ability of citizens to make informed decisions by way of access to a wide variety of informa-tion, "oversimplifies the constitutional system, which delegates authority to representatives as well as to citizens" (1986, 891). Sunstein notes that political decisions are not always made by individuals but their elected representa-tives, who themselves are under legal and administrative constraints (1986, 894). What the Jeffersonian philosophy does accomplish, according to Sun-stein, is something interdependent, for if information "is kept secret, public deliberation cannot occur; the risks of self-interested representation and fac-tional tyranny increase dramatically. The Jeffersonian model thus calls for substantial limitations on governmental secrecy" (1986, 894). While this may be so in a general philosophical sense, as this chapter indicates, throughout U.S. history, government secrecy is often at odds with the rights associated with access to information.

Given this résumé, Friedrich's model of functional and disfunctional se-crecy is of value in examining government secrecy (Friedrich 1972, 175–176; Merton 1940, 561). First, Friedrich observes that in specific circumstances, secrecy can be system-developing, "system-maintaining and like conflict, may even be needed for the functioning of the system" (1972, 5). Friedrich associates official secrets, especially concerning foreign or military matters that are "subject to the strictest secrecy" with some functional secrecy, even though such secrecy "conflicts with the principle of popular control and re-lated freedom of the press and generally of expression" (1972, 177). In this way, specific conditions are reported in the research literature where secrecy

7   Technique as employed here reflects Merton's description of Ellul as "any complex of standardized means for attaining a predetermined result" (1964). Technique as used in this chapter may perhaps be extended to Foucault's (1972) "discursive practices."

is deemed protective and necessary, which fall into Friedrich's typology of the functional use of secrecy (Aftergood 1999; Blanton 2003; Commission on Protecting and Reducing Government Secrecy 1997; Hoffman 1981; McDermott 2011; Powers 1998; Schoenfeld 2011; Sunstein 1986; and Thompson 1999). To further support this view, historically, secrecy was frequently employed by the Framers during the establishment of the United States government to protect policies against foreign influence (Hoffman 1981; Halstuk 2002). Moreover:

> *Publicity was never opposed in principle; rather it was seen as unworkable in certain contexts or spheres of activity. As a result, the values of effective government and accountable government had to be balanced and reconciled. The favored device for accomplishing this was institutional pluralism.* (Hoffman 1981, 19)

The Framers' functional use of secrecy is perhaps an early form of deliberative privilege, which protects internal discussions as they are shaped by legislators and policymakers before opened for public discussion (Department of Justice 2009). For example, *The Resolution of Secrecy* adopted by the Continental Congress called for members

> *Not to divulge, directly or indirectly, any matter or thing agitated or debated in Congress, before the same shall have been determined, without leave of the Congress; nor any matter or thing determined in Congress, which a majority of the Congress shall order to be kept secret.* (Continental Congress 1775)

Historian Daniel N. Hoffman believes the Framers "made it clear that the Constitution had a place for secrecy, specifically with respect to the national security functions of the executive branch. No suggestion was made that secrecy would or should be practiced in other spheres, or that it would be absolute even as to these" (1981, 34). In this vein, Article I, Sec. 5, Cl. 3, of the U.S. Constitution offers Congress guidance for secret keeping (Amer 2008, 1) [8] and Article II Sec. 2 suggests a basis for executive secrecy, or "the right of the president and high-level executive branch officers to withhold information from those who have compulsory power" (Rozell 2002, 403). This right is not viewed as "absolute, as executive privilege is often subject to the compulsory powers of the other branches" (Rozell 2002, 403).[9] However, as Friedrich

---

8   "Injunction by secrecy," Standing Rule 36 (paragraph 3) of the U.S. Senate, authorizes publication of treaties after completion of secret negotiations. See Amer (2008) and Manley O. Hudson (1929) for a fascinating historical look at Rule 36.

9   *United States v. Nixon* (1974) recognized executive privilege, but declined to apply it to protect the Watergate tapes. The concept of the "unitary executive theory," held by the second Bush administration, holds that the president has authority over the Executive branch. For an extended discussion see Rosenberg (2008).

points out, the "functionality of secrecy is often too readily assumed with adequate proof." In his discussion of official secrecy, Friedrich observes that "many of the matters secreted by such agencies as the CIA and the FBI could just as well be a matter of public record, and other such matters subject to scrutiny by Congress and other administrative agencies" (1972, 190).

Conversely, secrecy is identified as "dysfunctional" by Friedrich when functionality "declines to a point where the particular part hurts and destroys the system" (1972, 7). In this way, disfunctional secrecy no longer includes and sustains an "adequately informed public opinion" (Friedrich 1972, 177). Historical and contemporary examples of disfunctional secrecy are plentiful in the scholarly and popular literature, ranging from subjects such as the overclassification of information, leaks and national security, intelligence budgets, trade policies, to confidential business information, covert actions, surveillance of U.S. citizens, dual-use technology, the environment, international relations, and military matters (Aftergood 2000; 2009; *American Civil Liberties Union and the American Civil Liberties Union Foundation v U.S. Department of Justice* 2013; Bok 1989b; Colby 1976; Cole 1987; Felbinger and Reppy 2011; Fisher 2006; Foerstel 1991; 1992; Gibbs 1995; 2011; Gravel 1972; Hinson 2010; Hook 1988; House Special Investigations Division 2004; House Subcommittee on National Security, Emerging Threats, and International Relations 2006; Johnson 2000; Lutter 2013; Mendelsohn 1996; *New York Times Co. v Department of Justice* 2013; Piltz 2011; Reporters Committee for Freedom of the Press 2005; Roberts 2006; Rourke 1957; 1960; Rozell 2002; Senate Select Committee to Study Governmental Operations with Respect to Intelligence Activities 1976; Senate Subcommittee on Constitutional Rights 1972; Shane 2006; Shils 1956; Thompson 1999; Turner 1994; Welsome 2000; Wise and Ross 1964).

The abundant literature on disfunctional secrecy also includes analysis of the state secrets privilege, a creature of judge-made law under the *Federal Rules of Evidence*, which lacks grounding in federal statutes and, many have argued, any grounding in the Constitution. Its use has frustrated judicial redress for constitutional wrongdoing, including "government assassination, torture, kidnapping, illegal surveillance" (Open the Government 2012, 17).

Disfunctional secrecy is associated with what might be considered "secret laws" such as classified National Decision Directives, which "do not appear to be issued under statutory authority conferred by Congress and thus do not have the force and effect of law" (General Accounting Office 1992, 1) and Presidential Study Directives (Federation of American Scientists 2011). In this way, disfunctional secrecy can exemplify sociologist Georg Simmel's "sociological expression of moral badness" (1906, 463) when it is utilized to restrict and rearrange information of a potentially embarrassing nature and to cloak corruption, abuse, and misconduct (Adams and Balfour 2011; Aftergood

1999; Bok 1989b; Blanton 2003; Cook 1996; Friedrich 1972; Gibbs 2011; Gup 2000; Halperin, et al 1976; Halperin and Woods 1990-1991; Kerry 1997; Leonard 2011, Olmsted 1996; Wise and Ross 1964).

The Moynihan Commission and Government Secrecy

Referred to as the Moynihan Commission for its chairman, Senator Daniel P. Moynihan, the Commission on Protecting and Reducing Government Secrecy applied sociologist Max Weber's analysis to dissect the "onion structure" of the bureaucracy, a system that is "organizationally shock-proof against the factuality of the real world" (Arendt 1968, 100). What Weber offers to the study of U.S. government secrecy is a description of a specialized, disciplined "power instrument of the first order" (1978, 987) highly dependent on control of information. The bureaucracy, according to Weber, is naturally secretive regarding knowledge and intentions whether out of functional or pure power motives (1978, 992-93). But there is more—a bureaucracy

> that uses its knowledge and capacity for concealment to escape inspection and control jeopardizes legal domination by usurping the rule-making or decision-making powers that should ideally result from the political and legislative process. (Bendix 1962, 452)

In his historical-sociological analysis, Weber identified rationality, technical superiority, reliance on "calculable rules" (1958, 215), and the "quantitative extension of administrative tasks" at the foundation of bureaucracy's inner workings (1968, 969). Bureaucracy, although "among those social structures which are the hardest to destroy" is also an "instrument for 'societalizing' relations of power" (Weber 1958, 228). Of deep relevance to the discussion of intellectual freedom and government secrecy, the bureaucracy's

> secretive tendency exists even in the absence of plausible justifications. Every bureaucracy will conceal its knowledge and operation unless forced to disclose them, and it will, if need be, simulate the existence of hostile interests to justify such concealment. (Bendix 1962, 452)

Although the finer aspects of Weber's work were not expressly discussed by the Moynihan Commission in its study, they nevertheless are essential to analyzing information practices and policies of U.S. federal agencies, for it is the files—the records of the bureaucracy, archives, all of it, print and digital, past and present—that are subject to secrecy, power, authority, rules, privilege, territory, and compartmentalization. Weber writes:

> Management of the modern organization is based upon written documents ("the files"), which are preserved in their original or draft form, and upon a staff of subaltern officials and scribes of all sorts. (1978, 957)

Increasingly all order in public and private organizations is dependent on the system of files and the disciplines of officialdom, that means, its habit of painstaking obedience within its wonted sphere of action. (1978, 988)

Utilizing Weber's sociological investigation into the nature of bureaucracy, the Commission describes secrecy in government in the following way:

A form of government regulation. There are many such forms, but a general division can be made between regulations dealing with domestic affairs, and those dealing with foreign affairs. In the first category, it is generally the case that government prescribes what the citizen may do; in the second category, it is generally the case that government prescribes what the citizen may know. (1997)

These distinctions led Senator Moynihan to remark that two regulatory "regimes" exist in the United States: the first regime allows for freedom of information through public disclosure, discovery, and due process, and is under public scrutiny. The second regime is "concealed within a vast bureaucratic complex," wherein "some congressional oversight may take place and some presidential control" (1997). In this latter regime, the public is not excluded altogether, but the system is fraught with "misadventure." Misadventure, where limited oversight and public review takes place, also suggests possibilities for betrayal and corruption (Friedrich 1972, 175), ethical failures (Bean 2011; Colby 1976; Farrall 2011; Leonard 2011; and Piltz 2011) and administrative evil (Adams and Balfour 2009; 2011).

By far the most noteworthy of the Commission's contributions to advancing theory, secrecy by regulation acts as a barometer of sorts for gauging secret keeping in government. While Weber never expounded on the uses of secrecy and its forms in relation to the files, he brought together the essential ingredients for the Moynihan Commission's model of secrecy by regulation, or "'government secrecy,' which more properly could be termed 'administrative secrecy.'"[10] That is, secrecy by regulation provides a means to study those techniques that establish norms for secrecy through custom, law, regulation, politics, and specific techniques, and/or administrative tools such as nondisclosure agreements, compartmentalization, over-classification and reclassification.[11] In characterizing government secrecy as a form of regulation,

---

10   Political scientist Frances E. Rourke (1957; 1960), the Moynihan Commission, and Friedrich all refer to government secrecy as "administrative secrecy" following Max Weber (1968, 993).

11   Reclassification is also termed "retroactive secrecy." See *United States of America, Plaintiff v. The Progressive Inc., Erwin Knoll, Samuel Day, Jr., and Howard Morland, Defendants,* where the plaintiff "advanced the concept of retroactive secrecy,

the Commission's historical review reports an almost cyclical use of secrecy that includes the use of propaganda, censorship, and surveillance by the U.S. government in response to concerns over national security, conspiracy, and domestic subversion.[12]

For example, the Commission drew parallels between the Alien Sedition Act of 1798, where "John Adams could say that 'a free press maintains the majesty of the people' and champion the Sedition Act that threatened five years in prison to anyone whose opinions besmirched the good name of a government official or sowed confusion among the people" and the Espionage Act of 1917 that quelled political speech and public protest over the World War I (WW1) draft as the "United States Government grew reckless in its infringement of liberty" (Schultz 2003, 39). The conviction of Charles Schenk under the Espionage Act for distributing anti-draft pamphlets during WWI—the "peoples' war" as Woodrow Wilson termed it—led the Supreme Court to deny Schenk's argument that his activities were protected by the First Amendment. Writing the opinion for the Court, Justice Oliver Wendell Holmes proposed distinctions for speech rights in the concept of "clear and present danger":

> *Words which, ordinarily and in many places, would be within the freedom of speech protected by the First Amendment may become subject to prohibition when of such a nature and used in such circumstances a to create a clear and present danger that they will bring about the substantive evils which Congress has a right to prevent. (Schenck v. United States 1919)*

Moreover, the Committee on Public Information (CPI), or Creel Committee, played a significant role in shaping public opinion shortly after America's entry into World War I. In 1917, eighteen categories of information were published in *The New York Times* and proposed for restriction via "voluntary censorship" by the Committee on grounds of providing information to the enemy. The list of categories, from boat schedules, battle plans, and "technical inventions," were disclosed by the Committee after Washington correspondents "declined to consider them" (*The New York Times* 1917, 4). One reason offered for rejection of the regulations by the press is that they "would

---

declaring that previously published articles contained secrets" (*The Progressive* 1979).

12   For example, see the Central Intelligence Agency's *Dispatch: Countering criticism of the Warren Report*, which sought to "provide material for countering and discrediting the claims of the conspiracy theorists, so as to inhibit the circulation of such claims in other countries (1967, 1). The *Dispatch* contains a lengthy analysis of books written on the assassination of President Kennedy. Also see Chang (2002) and Greenberg (2012).

bar speculation about possible peace or differences of opinion with allies or neutrals" (*The New York Times* 1917, 1). Through its domestic and foreign divisions, the CPI placed the press and movie industry "upon their honor, and made them partners of Government in guarding military information of tangible benefit to the enemy" (Committee on Public Information 1920, 10). These features of the National Security State (NSS) suggest great opportunities for "misadventures" as observed by Senator Moynihan. They also imply opportunities for disfunctional secrecy, which endanger the very enjoyment of rights that sustain intellectual freedom, including the ability of elected representatives to provide oversight and individuals to exercise the responsibilities of citizenship and assume a right to privacy. As a side note, these voluntary press restrictions are similar to those proposed by President John F. Kennedy in 1961 to the Association of Newspaper Editors during the Cold War, and in more recent times, information was voluntarily withheld by *The New York Times* regarding an American drone base located in Saudi Arabia (Fresh Air 2013). Cases of dual-use research where "journal editors screen, review, and potentially reject manuscripts on the basis of their weapons potential" such as H5N1 influenza research (Gottron and Shea 2012, 8; Felbinger and Reppy 2011) have also been proposed for informal press restrictions on the basis of harm to national security.

Secrecy by Regulation and the National Security State

A combination of Executive Orders (EOs) and legislation further institutionalizes the use of secrecy by the U.S. government. The Roosevelt administration's 1940 EO 8381 built on an 1869 Army order concerning forts to allow the "Secretary of War or the Secretary of the Navy as 'secret,' 'confidential,' or 'restricted' and all such articles or equipment which may hereafter be so marked with the approval or at the direction of the President (Quist 2002, 46; Committee on Government Reform, 2004). Issued in 1942, EO 9182, "Consolidating Certain War Information Functions into an Office of War Information" outlined the security categories of SECRET, CONFIDENTIAL, and RESTRICTED (Executive Order 1942). Truman Executive Order 10290 further formalized the security classification system with the creating of TOP SECRET, SECRET and CONFIDENTIAL classifications (Executive Order 10290 1951). The EO also defined classified security information as "official information the safeguarding of which is necessary in the interest of national security." This same Order moved philosophy into policy by defining information as "knowledge which can be communicated, either orally or by means of material" (Part III. Definitions). Legislation such as the Atomic Energy Act of 1946 (P.L. 79-585) and1954 (P.L. 83-703) especially placed protections on "atomic" information and created security categories such as Restricted Data (RD), Formerly Restricted Data (FRD), and "born classified" (Commission on

Protecting and Reducing Government Secrecy 1997, Appendix A).[13] The National Security Act of 1947 (P.L. 80-253) advanced intelligence collection and analysis in creating the Central Intelligence Agency,[14] the Department of the Army, Navy, and Air Force in the "coordination of the activities of the National Military Establishment."[15]

With this history in mind, Weber's "permanent character of the bureaucratic machine" (1958, 228) is melded to secrecy by regulation, and finds a home in the contemporary model of the national security state (NSS). The NSS model advances Weber's observations on the technical superiority of the bureaucracy in its ability to capture, analyze, manipulate, quantify, share, categorize,[16] and preserve a variety of personal and public information. It also provides support for the Moynihan Commission's secrecy by regulation and post 9/11, the bureaucratic reorganization of U.S. government,[17] and policies such as the Global War on Terror (GWOT)[18] and secret cyber-warfare

---

13   "Born classified" or classified at birth protects "sensitive information which would not be divulged before the United States had an opportunity to assess its importance and take appropriate classification action" (DeVolpi et al. 1981, 59).

14   The National Security Act created the National Security Council, which provided for the supervision of the Central Intelligence Agency as an independent agency (Central Intelligence Agency 2008). The Act further mandated that the Director of Central Intelligence "shall be responsible for protecting intelligence sources and methods from unauthorized disclosure" (National Security Act 1947, Section 102 2 d (3)).

15   The National Security Act, Sec. 101 outlines "national security" and refers to all intelligence, regardless of the source from which derived and including information gathered within or outside the United States, that: A) pertains, as determined consistent with any guidance issued by the President, to more than one United States Government agency; and, B) that involves: 1) threats to the United States, its people, property, or interests; 2) the development, proliferation, or use of weapons of mass destruction; or 3) any other matter bearing on United States national or homeland security.

16   Such as CUI, or Controlled Unclassified Information that requires safeguarding or dissemination controls pursuant to and consistent with law, regulations, and government-wide policies. CUI excludes classified information (Executive Order 13556, 2009).

17   The creation of the Department of Homeland Security through the Homeland Security Act of 2002 (P.L.107-296) for example, was the largest reorganization of U.S. government since the Truman administration with its enactment of the National Security Act.

18   The GWOT is described as the "elements of war and non-war . . . an orchestrated mélange of combat operations, military operations other than war, and operations conducted by various nonmilitary departments of government (Record 2003, 6). O'Connell argues the GWOT does not meet formal definitions of war under international law (2005, 1).

(Sangar and Shanker 2013). The NSS is described as having the following elements:

- Control of the public sphere (Raskin and LeVan 2005)

- Covert actions and the rise of secrecy regarding state actions (Raskin and LeVan 2005)

- Federal (and local) law enforcement metamorphosing into security enforcement and surveillance (Raven-Hansen 2005)

- Limiting or undermining individual rights (Raskin and LeVan 2005)

- Nuclear weapons are a key component of the NSS (Dwyer and Dwyer 2005)

- Organizing for war, cold war, and limited war (Raskin and Le-Van 2005)

These features of the NSS suggest great opportunities for "misadventures" as observed by Senator Moynihan. They also imply opportunities for disfunctional secrecy, which endanger the very enjoyment of rights that sustain intellectual freedom, including the ability of elected representatives to provide oversight and individuals to exercise the responsibilities of citizenship and assume a right to privacy.

Friedrich's "Tampering with Communications"

Friedrich, in addition to theorizing that secrecy has a functional use but may also be a disfunctional state, ties secrecy to the "tampering with communications" especially when it is coupled to propaganda. That is, as Friedrich observes, while secrecy withholds information, propaganda "distorts information or even adds misinformation" (1972,176). For Friedrich, propaganda, like secrecy,, seems to conflict with the norm of candor and sincerity, which are considered ethically good" (1972, 176). Friedrich also theorized the "crucial function of both political propaganda and secrecy is to manipulate men in relation to the political order" (Friedrich 1972, 176). As with secrecy, Friedrich is clear that propaganda can play a functional (1972, 230) or disfunctional (pathological) role in politics and political systems (1972, 192).

As one scholar writes of propaganda, there is a "lingering uncertainty" as to the concept's "definability and indeed, its very utility" (Cunningham 2002, 37).[19] Categories range from agitation propaganda, black propaganda,

---

19 See Cull, Culbert, and Welch (2003) for multiple definitions of propaganda; while there is no set definition, propaganda generally, is a technique to influence public opinions.

disinformation (from the Russian, "dezinformatsia") to counterpropaganda (Cunningham 2002, 66–71) and been classed as a type of communication (Cunningham 2002, 77). While Friedrich never defines propaganda in his *The Pathology of Politics*, which makes it difficult to fully carve out its territory with secrecy, he does associate propaganda with manipulation of information and communication. The American Library Association's (2005) "Resolution on Disinformation, Media Manipulation, and Destruction of Public Information" comes close to suggesting Friedrich's intent in that propaganda is "Inaccurate information, distortions of truth, excessive limitations on access to information." Nevertheless, in connecting secrecy and propaganda, Friedrich opens the theoretical door to expand on additional, significant relationships secrecy has with censorship and surveillance. These specific conditions of information are discussed below as they relate to government secrecy and the tampering with communications.

Censorship

According to Cull, Culbert, and Welch (2003), censorship takes two forms: the selection of information to support a particular viewpoint, or the deliberate manipulation or doctoring of information to create an impression different from the original one intended. The latter issue of "doctoring" not only suggests Carl Friedrich's tampering but also a dynamic where secrecy, propaganda, and censorship work in tandem:

> In order to conduct propaganda, there must be some barrier between the public and the event. Access to the real environment must be limited, before anyone can create a pseudo-environment that he thinks is wise or desirable. (Lippmann 1922)

Censorship is characterized as "not only a story that was never published, it is any story that does not get widespread distribution regardless of its factual nature and significance to the society at large and its systems of democratic government" (Phillips and Huff 2011, 156). Much like secrecy, censorship is intentional in prohibiting access to controversial works and/or materials characterized as "any expression or its author as subversive or dangerous" (American Library Association 2002).

Though "many forms of censorship are invisible and difficult to trace, since censorship normally takes place in an atmosphere of secrecy" (De Baets 2011, 54), we can identify the paths censorship may take. Recalling Weber's bureaucracy and the Moynihan Commission, censorship can be promoted through administrative-regulatory controls and techniques such as security classification and markings, historical engineering (Chomsky 1989; Patterson 1988), thought control (Patterson, 1988), redaction, or the blacking out or exclusion of information,[20] and prepublication review. If we follow Friedrich, these activities can be functional or disfunctional in nature; if we recall the Moynihan Commission and its nod to Weber, secrecy by regulation allows for the very bureaucratic techniques and institutionalized controls that enable secrecy tied to censorship.

One particular institutionalized technique, prepublication review, regulates the communication and transmission of federal agency information. An example from the National Security Agency/Central Security Service describes the types of the materials that federal employees and contractors must submit for review:

> *Any Agency-related material that is intended for publication or dissemination must undergo pre-publication review. This includes, but is not limited to: books, biographies, articles, book reviews, videos, co-op reports, speeches, press releases, conference briefings, research papers and internet postings.* (National Security Agency 2009)

Although Hedley describes prepublication review as a functional means to "assist authors in avoiding inadvertent disclosure of classified information which, if disclosed, would be damaging to national security—just that and nothing more" (2007), there are cases of former federal employees who followed agency prepublication review policies only to have it censored through redaction and in some cases, contested for public release. The first book published in the United States that contained 168 blank pages marked "deleted" by the CIA "to indicate portions censored by the government" was Victor Marchetti and John D. Marks' (1974) *The CIA and the Cult of Intelligence* (Mackenzie 1997, 51). Works by Phillip Agee (1975), Frank Snepp (1977), James Bamford (1982), Ralph McGehee (1983), T.J Waters (2006), Ishmael Jones (2008), and Anthony Shaffer (2010)[21] were contested in varying ways by U.S. intelligence agencies. These titles remain valuable documentary works in that they reveal the inner dynamics of the intelligence community, its successes and failings, and post 9/11, enhanced interrogation and extraordinary renditions.[22] For example, Ali H. Soufan, a former FBI interrogator and counterterrorism specialist who authored *The Black Banners: The Inside Story of 9/11 and the War*

---

20 A simple perusal of the Declassified Documents Reference System will indicate the majority of declassified documents are redacted, some in sections of released records and others, entire documents. Public documents are also redacted, as in the case of the 9/11 Commission report with 28 missing pages (Elliott 2011).

21 On January 18, 2013, the Department of Defense declassified 198 redactions in the 2010 edition of Shaffer's book *Operation Dark Heart* (Department of Defense 2013).

22 See AccessInfo Europe and Reprieve (2011), Singh (2013) and the Rendition Project (n.d.).

Against Al Qaeda, revealed details about the USS Cole and 9/11 investigations in the book. Deletions

> *seem hard to explain on security grounds. Among them, according to the people who have seen the correspondence, is a phrase from Mr. Soufan's 2009 testimony at a Senate hearing, freely available both as video and transcript on the Web.* (Shane 2011)

In another challenge, former FBI translator Sibel Edmonds submitted her book *Classified Woman: The Sibel Edmonds Story* twice to the FBI, which prolonged the review. In 2012, the National Whistleblowers Center (NWC) issued a statement documenting Edmonds' illegal termination from the FBI, continuing harassment, and censorship of her book (Boiling Frogs 2012). Although prepublication review implies a comprehensive review in terms of identification and removal of classified information before it is disclosed (e.g., published), Lt. Colonel Daniel Davis came under questioning for distributing an unclassified paper he wrote titled *Dereliction of Duty II: Senior Military Leader's Loss of Integrity Wounds Afghan War Effort.* Davis voluntarily submitted his report to an internal Army review for approval, but the Pentagon refused permission for Davis to publish the report (Hastings 2012). *Rolling Stone* eventually published *Dereliction* in February 2012, but without approval from the Army. Davis' disclosure offers insight into Friedrich's disfunctional secrecy and tampering of communications:

> *What I witnessed in my most recently concluded 12 month deployment to Afghanistan has seen that deception reach an intolerable high. I will provide a very brief summary of the open source information that would allow any American citizen to verify these claims. But if the public had access to these classified reports they would see the dramatic gulf between what is often said in public by our senior leaders and what is actually true behind the scenes.* (Davis 2012, 2)

Another example of prepublication review is reminiscent of the Creel Committee's attempt to restrict specific categories of information during combat, the Office of the Army Surgeon General's (2005) *Release of Actionable Medical Information Policy Memorandum,* which

> *sets forth procedures to review abstracts, manuscripts, journal articles, speeches, and other open source venue where professional medical activities, analyses, and/or research are reported using medical information derived from a combat Theater. This includes medical information on service members, civilians, and enemy combatants (in any status: enemy prisoner of war, retained personnel, etc.) injured in combat Theater but treated outside of the Theater.* (Office of the Army Surgeon General 2010, 2)

This policy was issued during a period of increasing concerns that medical information "provided in a variety of forums (professional journals, national meetings, discussed in the media) was "aiding the enemy" (Cordts, Brosch, and Holcomb 2008, S16). However, the use of prepublication review in this case raises concerns related to censorship as a tampering: first, the restriction of "actionable medical information" has not been subject to open debate in Congress, the press, or in public venues. Secondly, if freely reported and discussed in the peer reviewed medical literature and at medical conferences, emergency medicine/trauma techniques devised in the field and in DOD facilities have the potential ability to benefit society at large.[23] Lastly, as actionable medical information is restricted, there remain questions as to the veracity of existing public information, including government generated statistics, on "service members, civilians, and enemy combatants (in any status: enemy prisoner of war, retained personnel, etc.)"[24]

Censorship as a tampering of communications also extends to regulation of speech by federal agency employees. In one example, a NOAA climate research scientist "whose published modeling research suggested the likelihood of increased hurricane intensity under projected future global warming was kept away from the [Katrina] briefing" (Piltz 2011, 228). In addition, James Hansen, Director of NASA's Goddard Institute for Space Studies, reported that NASA officials at headquarters ordered the public affairs staff "to review his coming lectures, papers, postings on the Goddard Web site and requests for interviews from journalists" (Piltz 2011, 229). The suspension and reinstatement of wildlife biologist Dr. Charles Monnett by the Bureau of Ocean Energy Management, Regulation & Enforcement (BOEMRE, formerly the Minerals Management Service) raises continuing concerns as to the ability of scientists in federal employ to freely conduct scholarly research, as well as interpret and communicate their results to the large scientific community (Barringer 2011; PEER 2010; 2012; and Union of Concerned Scientists 2009).

Censorship also can be thought of as regulative, where information "can be amended or revolutionized in ways that raise or lower body counts, number of books banned or citizens ghettoized or 'gulaged'" (Jansen 1991, 8). Regulative censorship is illustrated by techniques used by the U.S. government to "limit and shape news coverage" during the Vietnam, Grenada, Panama, and the Gulf Wars (Sharkey 1991, 1). Images of war were "sanitized,"

---

23   For additional cases of military secrecy, see Maret (2011c) on the manipulation of Sarin research at Rocky Mountain Arsenal, Coser on the Cold War (1963), and photos of U.S. military casualties obtained through FOIA by The Memory Hole (Carter 2004).

24   For example, the Congressional Research Service report on military causalities (Fischer 2013).

and "control is exercised over journalists, restricting their access to theaters of operation, misinforming about specific military operations, concealing information, and minimizing discussion of causalities" (Sharkey 1991, 23–26). During the invasion of Grenada in 1983, the Pentagon applied the British media model utilized during the 1982 Falklands War with Argentina (Sharkey 1991, 4). During Operation Desert Storm, or the First Gulf War (1990–91), the Pentagon "was unwilling to disclose what it knew about the likelihood of civilian casualties caused by the U.S. and allied bombing" (Sharkey 1991, 3). Discrepancies in reported numbers of Iraqi civilian deaths beginning with the 2003 invasion and into the Iraqi occupation by coalition forces continue. In 2010, Wikileaks released the Iraqi war logs, which document approximately 109,000 deaths in the Iraq war; the Opinion Research Business study reported at least one million Iraqi deaths (Phillips and Huff 2011). A recent investigation approximates "half million deaths in Iraq could be attributable to the war" between 2003–2011 (Hagopian et al. 2013).

Two additional cases illustrate the link between secrecy and censorship as a tampering with communications. First, the President John F. Kennedy Assassination Records Collection Act of 1992 (P.L. 102-526), or the JFK Act, legislated the "opening of the files [that] would quash unmerited speculation and paranoia that was having a corrosive effect on faith in our government's institutions" (Horne 2009, 18). However, per the JFK Act, release of assassination records can be postponed beyond the year 2017 if "the President certifies" that: 1) "continued postponement is made necessary by an identifiable harm to the military, defense, intelligence operations, law enforcement, or conduct of foreign relations;" and, 2) "the identifiable harm is of such gravity that it outweighs the public interest in disclosure" (Assassination Records Review Board 1998, 8).

The second case concerns release of records from the National Commission on Terrorist Attacks Upon the United States (P.L. 107-30) hearings, hereafter referred to as the 9/11 Commission. The Intelligence Authorization Act for Fiscal Year 2003 (P.L. 107-36) Sec. 602 (3) (4) directed the Commission to "make a make a full and complete accounting of the circumstances surrounding the attacks" (2003). The 9/11 Commission encouraged the release of records after its investigation for those records "not already publicly available should be made available to the public, to the greatest extent possible consistent with the terms of this letter, beginning on January 2, 2009 (National Commission on Terrorist Attacks upon the United States 2004). However, only 35% of the Commission's archived textual records are presently declassified (National Archives and Records Administration n.d.) and many are redacted. As legislative branch records are exempt from FOIA, the Act cannot be utilized by researchers to obtain the remaining 526 cubic ft. of 9/11 Commission records, which include a thirty page summary of an April 29,

2004 interview by the Commission with former President George W. Bush and Vice President Dick Cheney (Paltrow 2011). As in the case of the JFK records, there are stipulations placed on the release of records:

> Records should not be disclosed if they (a) contain information that continues to be classified; (b) disclose private information that the Commission agreed to protect from public disclosure; or (c) are otherwise barred from public disclosure by law, as determined by the Archivist. (National Commission on Terrorist Attacks upon the United States 2004)

Surveillance

Secrecy and censorship take on new ground through watching and spying, especially when the latter is considered as a form of surveillance (Jansen 1991, 14). Censorship then becomes a "bad police measure, for it does not achieve what it intends, and it does not intend what it achieves" (Marx 1842). In recent times, revelations by former NSA contractor Edward Snowden of the National Security Agency (NSA) secret global surveillance exemplifies Friedrich's disfunctional secrecy and tampering with communications. The Snowden leak of NSA documents present a case where secrecy, censorship, and surveillance intersect not only in terms of the range and depth of spy programs by federal agencies, but public understanding of government surveillance of personal communications. As shocking as the Snowden disclosures are, they also call into question the integrity of government information used by the public, the media, and researchers as critical oversight tools. For example, the nonprofit "Open the Government" reported its disillusionment with government generated information, which the organization analyzes in its annual Secrecy Report. Open the Government's concern with the veracity of data from federal agencies is worth reporting in full below as it exposes how government generated information may not be an accurate portrayal of federal policies and programs (emphasis added):

> For the last few years we have been reporting on the use of National Security Letters (NSLs) and on the government's applications to the Foreign Intelligence Surveillance Court (FISC). Now, however, we have to question the accuracy and meaningfulness of such numbers and are not including them in this year's Report. Our distrust of the government's reported numbers is focused in four areas: demands for records under Section 215 of the USA PATRIOT Act; the applications made to the FISC under Section 702 of the FISA Amendments Act of 2012; the failure of congressional oversight; and our new understandings of the interactions between the FISC and the intelligence community, and the expanded role of the Court. (2013, iii)

> Previous to the Snowden leaks of NSA records, Senators Ron Wyden and Mark Udall questioned Agency officials on the widespread surveillance of

U.S. citizens, whose communications were collected or reviewed under Section 702 of the Foreign Intelligence Surveillance Act of 1978 (P.L. 95-511) or the FISA Amendment. The Senators were informed by the NSA Inspector General that "he and NSA leadership agreed that an IG review of the sort suggested would itself violate the privacy of U.S. persons" (Ackerman 2012; Webster 2012). This is not only a significant finding in terms of the reaches of government secrecy; it is also a serious affront to intellectual freedom and privacy, particularly in terms of past reports by the press and whistleblowers of domestic warrantless wiretapping and global surveillance of communications by the NSA and the FBI, with the assistance of telecommunications carriers and contractors (Bamford 2012; Cohn 2010; Cole 2011; Gorman 2008; Government Accountability Project n.d.; Markey 2012; Greenwald 2013; Risen 2006).

NSA surveillance, coupled with compilation of secret watchlists (e.g., the Terrorist Identities Datamart Environment, Investigative Data Warehouse, Secure Flight, No Fly List and Selectee List), Suspicious Activity Reporting (Farrall 2011), the InfraGard program[25], and the RIOT or Rapid Information Overlay Technology program (Gallagher 2013), often implemented with assistance from contractors in the "privatization of national security" (Monahan and Palmer 2009; Bean 2011) indicate the reach of the national security state bureaucracy where information is mined, classified, shared, and restricted by federal agencies, national and regional Joint Terrorism Task Forces (JTTF), fusion centers[26], the private sector[27], and international law enforcement and intelligence agencies. While the public is left to speculate as to the criteria for such secrecy, censorship, and spying, Friedrich reminds us that if "secrets

---

25   Infragard is a "partnership" between FBI Field offices and "businesses, academic institutions, state and local law enforcement agencies, and other participants dedicated to sharing information and intelligence to prevent hostile acts in the United States." See https://www.infragard.net.

26   According to *Washington Post* reporters Dana Priest and William M. Arkin (2010) there are 1,271 government organizations and 1,931 private companies working on programs related to counterterrorism, homeland security and intelligence, and an estimated 854,000 people hold top-secret security clearances. The exact number of individuals who hold clearances is "murky" (Open the Government 2013, 21).

27   See *Summary and Recommendations*, Secretary's Advisory Committee on Automated Personal Data Systems *Code of Fair Information Practice* or FIPS, especially: 1) There must be no personal data record keeping systems whose very existence is secret; and, 2) There must be a way for an individual to find out what information about him is in a record and how it is used (U.S. Department of Health and Human Welfare, 1973).

are suspected on all sides, confidence vanishes and political life becomes a nightmare of terrorized suspicions" (1972, 233).

The Tragedy of Democracy

The tampering with communications through secrecy, propaganda, censorship, surveillance, or all techniques working as a complex of information control, influences historical understanding, social memory, and the fulfillment of human rights that support intellectual freedom. Leaving researchers with an incomplete understanding of events and actors, and individuals with a less than ideal toolbox to form judgments regarding policies, tampering has the potential to erode trust in government. In his observations on the influence of bureaucracy in society—perhaps anticipating secrecy by regulation by several decades—Max Weber made a remarkable statement: democracy, he wrote, is "defeated not so much by conditions external to itself but by its own inner tendencies. The tragedy of democracy occurs when it cannot defeat the organizational forces that evolve, quietly, and almost invisibly to take possession of it" (quoted in Diggins 1996, 85).

Through Thomas Emerson's First Amendment "possibilities," perhaps we can judge the weight of secrecy on intellectual freedom. Emerson's four possibilities, which mirror the outcomes of the numerous civil and human rights declarations and laws mentioned earlier in this chapter, consist of "individual self-fulfillment, advancement of knowledge and discovery of truth, and participation in decision making by all members of the society." Emerson suggests that a "more adaptable and hence stable community" is attainable through these values (quoted in Baker 1989, 47). As guiding principles, Emerson's utopian principles are a means to evaluate the avenues to which both functional and disfunctional secrecy may curb intellectual freedom in the lives of individuals and broadly in the social world. Whether functional or disfunctional secrecy or the tampering with communication utilized in the drive to protect national security, all of these conditions of information may carry the seeds of disfunction within.

References

AccessInfo Europe and Reprieve. 2011. Rendition on record. http://www.accessinfo.org/en/civil-liberties/212-rendition-on-record (accessed June 14, 2012).

Ackerman, Spencer. 2012. NSA: It would violate your privacy to say if we spied on you. *Wired* June 18. http://www.wired.com/dangerroom/2012/06/nsa-spied/ (accessed January 6, 2013).

Adams, Guy and Danny L. Balfour, 2011. "Open secrets": The masked dynamics of ethical failures and administrative evil. In *Government Secrecy, Research in Social Problems and Public Policy*, 19, Ed. Susan Maret, 403–419. Bingley, UK: Emerald Group Publishing Limited.

Adams, Guy B. and Danny L. Balfour. 2009. *Unmasking administrative evil.* 3rd ed. Armonk, NY: M.E. Sharpe.

Aftergood, Steven. 2009. Reducing government secrecy: Finding what works. *Yale Law and Policy Review* 27:399–416. http://www.fas.org/sgp/eprint/aftergood.pdf (accessed March 12, 2012).

Aftergood, Steven. 2000. Secrecy is back in fashion. *Bulletin of the Atomic Scientists* 56, no. 6: 24–30.

Aftergood, Steven. 1999. Government secrecy and knowledge production: A survey of some general issues. In *Secrecy and Knowledge Production*, Ed. Judith Reppy, 17–29. Occasional Paper #23, Cornell University. http://www.einaudi.cornell.edu/peaceprogram/publications/occasionapapers/occasional-paper23.pdf (accessed March 12, 2012).

Agee, Philip. 1975. *Inside the company: CIA diary.* New York: Stonehill.

Amer, Mildred. 2008. Secret sessions of Congress. CRS reports to Congress RS20145, March 27. http://www.fas.org/sgp/crs/secrecy/RS20145.pdf (accessed April 7, 2012).

American Civil Liberties Union and the American Civil Liberties Union Foundation v .U.S. Department of Justice. 2013. January 3. 12 Civ. 794 (CM). http://www.aclu.org/national-security/anwar-alawlaki-foiarequest-district-court-opinion (accessed January 7, 2013).

American Library Association. 2010. *Intellectual freedom manual.* 8th ed. Chicago, IL: American Library Association.

American Library Association. 2005. Resolution on disinformation, media manipulation, and destruction of public information. http://www.ala.org/aboutala/governance/policymanual/updatedpolicmanual/section2/52libsvcsandrespon - 52.8 (accessed March 12, 2012).

American Library Association Council. 2002. Resolution reaffirming the principles of intellectual freedom in the aftermath of terrorist attacks. http://www.ala.org/offices/oif/statementspols/ifresolutions/resolutionreaffirming (accessed April 7, 2012).

Arendt, Hannah.1968. *Between past and future: Eight exercises in political thought.* New York: Viking Press.

Article19.org. 2003. Statement on the right to communicate. http://www.article19.org/pdfs/publications/right-to-communicate.pdf (accessed April 17, 2012).

Assassination Records Review Board. 1998. Final report. September. http://www.archives.gov/research/jfk/review-board/report (accessed June 5, 2012).

Atomic Energy Act of 1954. P.L. 83-703. https://forms.nrc.gov/aboutnrc/governing-laws.html (accessed January 17, 2013).

Atomic Energy Act of 1946, P.L. 79-585. http://www.osti.gov/atomicenergyact.pdf (accessed January 17, 2013).

Auerbach, S. I. 1972. Ecology, ecologists and the E.S.A. *Ecology* 53, no. 2:206–207.

Baker, C. Edwin. 1989. *Human liberty and freedom of speech.* New York: Oxford University Press.

Bamford, James. 2012. The NSA is building the country's biggest spy center (Watch what you say). March 10. http://www.wired.com/threatlevel/2012/03/ff_nsadatacenter/all (accessed April 17, 2012).

Bamford, James. 1982. *The puzzle palace: A report on America's most secret agency.* Boston: Houghton Mifflin.

Barringer, Felicity. 2011. Report on dead polar bears gets a biologist suspended. *The New York Times* July 28, https://www.nytimes.com/2011/07/29/science/earth/29polar.html?_=1 (accessed June 1, 2012).

Bean, Hamilton. 2011. Is open source intelligence an ethical issue? In *Government Secrecy, Research in Social Problems and Public Policy,* 19, Ed. Susan Maret. 385–402. Bingley, UK: Emerald Group Publishing Limited.

Bendix, Reinhard. 1962. *Max Weber: An intellectual portrait.* New York: Anchor Books.

Blanton, Thomas. 2003. National security and open government in the United States: Beyond the balancing test. In *National Security and Open Government: Striking the Right Balance.* Campbell Public Affairs Institute and the Open Society Justice Initiative, 33–73. http://www.maxwell.syr.edu/campbell/events/past/papers/NSOG.pdf. (accessed March 12, 2012).

Boiling Frogs. 2012. Press release: FBI attempts to hold Sibel Edmonds' book hostage: Investigation shows agency used contract to censor whistleblowers. April 10. http://www.boilingfrogspost.com/2012/04/10/press-release-fbiattempts-to-hold-sibel-edmonds-book-hostage-illegallyunconstitutionally (accessed May 1, 2012).

Bok, Sissela. 1989a. *Lying: Moral choice in public and private life.* New York: Vintage Books.

Bok, Sissela. 1989b. *Secrets: On the ethics of concealment and revelation.* New York: Vintage Books.

Capurro, Rafael and Birger Hjørland. 2003. The concept of information. http://www.capurro.de/infoconcept.html (accessed May 1, 2012).

Carter, Bill. 2004. Pentagon ban on pictures of dead troops is broken. *The New York Times.* April 23. http://www.nytimes.com/2004/04/23/national/23PHOT.html (accessed May 1, 2012).

Central Intelligence Agency. 2008. A look back. https://www.cia.gov/newsinformation/featured-story-archive/2008-featured-storyarchive/national-security-act-of-1947.html (accessed May 1, 2012).

Chang, Nancy. 2002. *Silencing political dissent.* New York: Seven Stories Press.

Chomsky, Noam. 1989. *Necessary illusion: Thought control in democratic societies.* Cambridge: South End Press.

Cohn, Cindy. 2010. Lawless surveillance, warrantless rationales. *Journal on Telecommunications & High Technology Law* 8: 351–357.

Colby, William E. 1976. Intelligence secrecy and security in a free society. *International Security* 1, no. 2: 3–14.

Cole, David. 2011. After September 11: What we still don't know. *The New York Review of Books.* September 29. http://www.nybooks.com/articles/archives/2011/sep/29/afterseptember-11-what-we-still-dont-know (accessed January 12, 2012).

Cole, David and James X. Dempsey. 2006. *Terrorism and the constitution: sacrificing civil liberties in the name of national security.* New York: New Press.

Cole, Leonard. 1987. *Clouds of secrecy: The Army's germ warfare tests over populated areas.* New York: Rowman and Littlefield.

Commission on Protecting and Reducing Government Secrecy. 1997. Report of the Commission on Protecting and Reducing Government Secrecy: Hearing before the Committee on Governmental Affairs. United States Senate, 105th Congress, first session, May 7. Washington, Government Printing Office. http://www.gpo.gov/fdsys/pkg/GPOCDOC105sdoc2/contentdetail.html (accessed May 1, 2012).

Committee on Government Reform. 2004. Secrecy in the Bush administration. September 14. U.S. House of Representatives. https://www.fas.org/sgp/library/waxman.pdf (accessed May 13, 2013).

Committee on Public Information. 1920. Complete report of the chairman. Washington: Government Printing Office. http://archive.org/details/completereportof00unit (accessed May 1, 2012).

Continental Congress. 1775. Resolution of secrecy adopted by the Continental Congress. November 9. http://avalon.law.yale.edu/18th_century/const01.asp (accessed April 19, 2012).

Cook, Blanche Wiesen. 1996. Presidential papers in crisis: Some thoughts on lies, secrets, and silence. *Presidential Studies Quarterly* 26:285–92.

Cordts, Paul R., Laura A. Brosch, and John B. Holcomb. 2008. Now and then: Combat casualty care policies for Operation Iraqi Freedom and Operation Enduring Freedom compared with those of Vietnam. *The journal of trauma injury, infection, and critical care*. February supplement: S14–S20.

Coser, Lewis. 1963. The dysfunctions of military secrecy. *Social Problems* 11, no.1: 13–22.

Cross, Harold L. 1953. The people's right to know: Legal access to public records and proceedings. Morningside Heights, NY: AMS Press.

Daase, Christopher and Oliver Kessler. 2007. Construction of danger: Knowns and unknowns in the `war on terror': uncertainty and the political construction of danger. *Security Dialogue* 38: 411–434.

Davis, Daniel. 2012. Dereliction of duty II: Senior military leader's loss of integrity wounds Afghan war effort. January 27. http://www1.rollingstone.com/extras/RS_REPORT.pdf (accessed January17, 2013).

Davis, David Brion. 1971. *The fear of conspiracy: Images of un-American subversion from the revolution to the present.* Ithaca: Cornell University Press.

De Baets, Antoon. 2011. Taxonomy of concepts related to censorship of history. In *Government Secrecy, Research in Social Problems and Public Policy,* 19, Ed. Susan Maret, 53–65. Bingley, UK: Emerald Group Publishing Limited.

Department of Defense. 2013. Request for prepublication review of Operation Dark Heart manuscript. Ref: I 0-S-271 011. http://www.fas.org/sgp/jud/shaffer/012413-review.pdf (accessed January 25, 2013).

Department of Defense. 2012. *Dictionary of military and associated terms.* JP 1-02. March 12. http://www.dtic.mil/doctrine/dod_dictionary/ (accessed April 19, 2012).

Department of Justice. 2009. Guide to the Freedom of Information Act, Exemption 5. http://www.justice.gov/oip/foia_guide09/exemption5.pdf (accessed June 10, 2013).

DeVolpi, Alexander, Gerald E. Marsh, Ted A. Postol, and George Stanford. 1981. *Born secret: The H-bomb, the Progressive case and national security.* New York: Pergamon Press.

Diggens, John Patrick. 1996. *Max Weber and the spirit of tragedy.* New York: Basic Books.

Dodd, Christopher J. 1997. Human rights information act. *Congressional Record* September 25. https://www.fas.org/sgp/congress/s1220.html (accessed January 16, 2013).

Donner, Frank. 1990. *Protectors of privilege: Red squads and police repression in urban America.* Berkeley: University of California Press.

Dwyer, Anabel L. and David J. Dwyer. 2005. Courts and universities as institutions in the national security state. In *Democracy's shadow: The secret world of national security*, Ed. Marcus G. Raskin and A. Carl LeVan, 165–204. New York: Nation Books.

Earl, Jennifer. 2009. Information access and protest policing post-9/11: Studying the policing of the 2004 Republican National Convention. *American Behavioral Scientist* 53:44–60.

Edelstein, Michael R. 2004. *Contaminated communities: Coping with residential toxic exposure.* Boulder, CO: Westview Press.

Edmonds, Sibel. 2012. *Classified woman: The Sibel Edmonds story: A memoir.* Alexandria, VA: Sibel Edmonds.

Elliott, Justin. 2011. The enduring mysteries of 9/11. *Salon*, September 7. http://www.salon.com/2011/09/07/sept_11_unanswered_questions (accessed January 19, 2013).

Ellul, Jacques. 1964. *The technological society.* Trans. John Wilkinson. New York: Alfred Knopf.

Executive Order 13556. 2009. Controlled unclassified information. http://www.archives.gov/cui (access January 16, 2013).

Executive Order 10290. 1951. Prescribing regulations establishing minimum standards for the classification, transmission, and handling by departments and agencies of the executive branch of official information which requires safeguarding in the interest of the security of the United States. http://www.trumanlibrary.org/executiveorders/index.php?pid=262 (accessed April 19, 2012).

Executive Order. 1942. Consolidating certain war information functions into an Office Of War Information. June 13. http://www.presidency.ucsb.edu/ws/index.php?pid=16273&st=Executve+Order+9182&st1= (accessed June 14, 2013).

Farrall, Kenneth. 2011. Suspicious activity reporting: U.S. domestic intelligence in a postprivacy age? In *Government Secrecy, Research in Social Problems and Public Policy*, 19, Ed. Susan Maret, 247–276. Bingley, UK: Emerald Group Publishing Limited.

Federation of American Scientists. 2011. Presidential Study Directives [PSD] Barack Obama administration. https://www.fas.org/irp/offdocs/psd/index.html (accessed January 11, 2013).

Felbinger, Jonathan and Judith Reppy. 2011. Classifying knowledge, creating secrets: Government policy for dual-use technology. In *Government Secrecy, Research in Social Problems and Public Policy*, 19, Ed. Susan Maret, 277–299. Bingley, UK: Emerald Group Publishing Limited.

Finan, Christopher M. 2007. *From the Palmer raids to the Patriot Act: A history of the fight for free speech in America.* Boston: Beacon Press.

Fischer, Hannah. 2013. U.S. military casualty statistics: Operation new dawn, operation Iraqi freedom, and operation enduring freedom. February 5. RS22452.http://www.fas.org/sgp/crs/natsec/RS22452.pdf (accessed February 8, 2013).

Fisher, Louis. 2006. *In the name of national security: Unchecked presidential power and the Reynolds case.* Lawrence: University Press of Kansas.

Foerstel, Herbert. N. 1992. *Secret science: Federal control of American science and technology.* Westport, CT: Praeger.

Foerstel, Herbert. N. 1991. *Surveillance in the stacks: The FBI's library awareness program.* New York: Greenwood Press.

Foucault Michel. 1972. *The archaeology of knowledge and the discourse on language.* Pantheon Books, New York.

Fresh Air. 2013. The sticky questions surrounding drones and kill lists. Interview with Scott Shane. NPR. February 11. http://www.npr.org/2013/02/12/171719082/the-sticky -questionssurrounding-drones-and-kill-lists (accessed February 12, 2013).

Friedrich, Carl J. 1972. *The pathology of politics.* New York: Harper Row.

Gallagher, Ryan. 2013. Software that tracks people on social media created by defence firm. *The Guardian* February 10. http://www.guardian.co.uk/ world/2013/feb/10/software-tracks-socialmedia-defence (accessed February 10, 2013).

General Accounting Office. 1992. The use of presidential directives to make and implement U.S. policy. January 14. NSIAD-92-72. http://www.gao.gov/products/NSIAD-92-72 (accessed January 11, 2013).

Gibbs, David N. 2011. Sigmund Freud as a theorist of government secrecy. In *Government Secrecy, Research in Social Problems and Public Policy,* 19, Ed. Susan Maret, 5–22. Bingley, UK: Emerald Group Publishing Limited.

Gibbs, David N. 1995. Secrecy and international relations. *Journal of Peace Research* 32, no.2: 213–228.

Gorman, Siobhan. 2008. NSA's domestic spying grows as agency sweeps up data. *Wall Street Journal,* March 10. http://online.wsj.com/article/ SB120511973377523845.html (accessed April 26, 2012).

Gottron, Frank and Dana A. Shea. 2012. Publishing scientific papers with potential security risks: Issues for Congress. July 12. R42606. http://www.fas.org/sgp/crs/secrecy/R42606.pdf (accessed July 19, 2012).

Government Accountability Project. n.d. NSA whistleblower Tom Drake. http://whistleblower.org/action-center/save-tom-drake (accessed April 17, 2012).

Gravel, Mike. 1972. The secrecy system. *Social action* 38, no. 5: 13–20.

Greenberg, Ivan. 2010. *The dangers of dissent: The FBI and civil liberties since 1965*. Lanham, MD: Lexington Books.

Greenwald, G. 2013. NSA whistleblower Edward Snowden: 'I don't want to live in a society that does these sort of things.' *The Guardian*, June 9. http://www.guardian.co.uk/world/2013/jun/09/edward-snowden -nsawhistleblower-surveillance (accessed June 10, 2013).

Gup, Ted. 2000. *The book of honor: Covert lives and classified deaths at the CIA*. New York: Doubleday.

Halperin, Morton H., Jerry J. Berman, Robert L. Borosage, and Christine Marwick. 1976. *The lawless state: The crimes of the U.S. intelligence agencies*. New York: Penguin Books.

Halperin, Morton and Jeanne M. Woods. 1990–1991. Ending the Cold War at home. *Foreign Policy*, no. 81: 128–143.

Halstuk, Martin E. 2002. Policy of secrecy-pattern of deception: What federalist leaders thought about a public right to know, 1794–98. *Communication Law and Policy* 7: 51–76.

Hamilton, Alexander. 1788. Certain general and miscellaneous objections to the Constitution considered and answered. *The Federalist* No. 84. http://avalon.law.yale.edu/18th_century/fed84.asp (accessed June 14, 2013)

Hastings, Michael. 2012. The Afghanistan report the Pentagon doesn't want you to read. *Rolling Stone*, February 10. http://www.rollingstone.com/ politics/blogs/national-affairs/theafghanistan-report-the-pentagon -doesnt-want-you-to-read-20120210 (accessed November 4, 2013).

Hazelrigg, Lawrence. 1969. A reexamination of Simmel's 'The secret and the secret society': Nine propositions. *Social forces* 47, no. 3:323–330.

Hedley, John Hollister. 2007. Reviewing the work of CIA authors: Secrets, free speech, and fig leaves. https://www.cia.gov/library/center-forthe -study-of-intelligence/kentcsi/docs/v41i3a01p.htm (accessed May 1, 2012).

Hinson, Christopher L. 2010. Negative information action: Danger for democracy. *American Behavioral Scientist*, 53:826–847.

Hoffman, Daniel N. 1981. *Governmental secrecy and the founding fathers: A study in constitutional controls*. Westport, CT: Greenwood Press.

Hook, Glenn. 1988. Roots of nuclearism: Censorship and reportage of atomic damage in Hiroshima and Nagasaki. *Multilinga* 7, no.1–2: 133–156.

Horne, Douglas P. 2009. *Inside the Assassination Records Review Board: The U.S. government's final attempt to reconcile the conflicting medical evidence in the assassination of JFK*. Falls Church, VA: D.P. Horne.

House Special Investigations Division. 2004. *Secrecy in the Bush administration.* U.S. House of Representatives, Committee on Government Reform, Minority Staff. Washington: Government Printing Office.

House Subcommittee on National Security, Emerging Threats, and International Relations. 2006. *Drowning in a sea of faux secrets: Policies on handling of classified and sensitive information:* Hearing before the Subcommittee on National Security, Emerging Threats, and International Relations of the Committee on Government Reform, House of Representatives, 109 2nd session, March 14. Washington: Government Printing Office.

Hudson, Manley O. 1929.The 'injunction of secrecy' with respect to American treaties. *The American Journal of International Law* 23 no. 2: 329 335.

Intelligence Authorization Act for Fiscal Year 2003. P.L. 107-36. 116 Stat. 2383. http://govinfo.library.unt.edu/911/about/107-306.htm (accessed January 15, 2013).

Jansen, Sue Curry. 1991. *Censorship: The knot that binds power and knowledge.* Oxford: Oxford University Press. http://avalon.law.yale.edu/18th_century/fed64.asp (accessed April 25, 2012).

Jay, John. 1788. The powers of the Senate from the New York packet. *The Federalist* No. 64. March 7. http://avalon.law.yale.edu/18th_century/fed64.asp (accessed May 11, 2013).

Johnson, Chalmers. 2000. *Blowback: The costs and consequences of American empire.* New York: Metropolitan Books.

Jones, Ishmael. 2008. *Human factor: Inside the CIA's dysfunctional intelligence culture.* New York: Encounter Books.

Kennedy, John F. 1961. *The president and the press: Address before the American Newspaper Publishers Association.* April 27. http://www.jfklibrary.org/Research/Research-Aids/ReadyReference/JFK-Speeches/The-President-and-the-Press-Address-beforethe-American-Newspaper-Publishers-Association.aspx (accessed January 11, 2013).

Kerry, John. 1997. Growing intelligence budgets. *Congressional Record,* May 1. http://www.fas.org/sgp/congress/kerry.html (accessed May 1, 2012).

Kunstler, William M. 2004. *The emerging police state: resisting illegitimate authority.* Ed. Michael Steven Smith, Goldman, Karin Kunstler, and Kunstler, Sarah. New York: Ocean Press.

Lemov, Michael R. 2011. *People's warrior: John Moss and the fight for freedom of information and consumer rights.* Lanham, MD: Rowman & Littlefield.

Leonard, J. William. 2011. The corrupting influence of secrecy on national policy decisions. In *Government Secrecy, Research in Social Problems and Public Policy,* 19, Ed. Susan Maret, 421–434. Bingley, UK: Emerald Group Publishing Limited.

Lutter, Randall, Craig Barrow, Christopher J. Borgert, James W Conrad Jr., Debra Edwards, and Allan Felsot. 2013. Data disclosure for chemical evaluations. *Environmental Health Perspectives* 121, no.2: 145–148.

McDermott, Patrice. 2011. Secrecy reform or secrecy redux? Access to information in the Obama administration. In *Government Secrecy, Research in Social Problems and Public Policy,* 19, Ed. Susan Maret, 189–217. Bingley, UK: Emerald Group Publishing Limited.

McGehee, Ralph W. 1983. *Deadly deceits: My 25 years in the CIA.* New York: Sheridan Square Publications.

Mackenzie, Angus. 1997. *Secrets: The CIA's war at home.* Berkeley: University of California Press.

MacKenzie, Debra. 2002. U.S. Non-lethal weapons report suppressed. *New Scientist,* May 2. http://www.newscientist.com/article/dn2254 -usnonlethal-weapon-reports-suppressed.html (accessed May 1, 2012).

Marchetti, Victor and John D. Marks. 1974. *The CIA and the cult of intelligence.* New York, Knopf.

Markey, Edward. 2012. Letters to mobile carriers regarding use of cell phone tracking by law enforcement. http://markey.house.gov/content/ letters-mobile-carriers-reagrdinguse-cell-phone-tracking-law -enforcement (accessed July 1, 2012).

Meiklejohn, Alexander. 1961. The First Amendment is an absolute. *The Supreme Court Review* 1961: 245–266.

Mendelsohn, William R. 1996. In camera review of classified environmental impact statements: A threatened opportunity? *Boston college environmental affairs law review* 23, no.3: 679–698.

Merton, Robert K. 1940. Bureaucratic structure and personality. *Social forces* 18, no. 4: 560–568.

Monahan, Torin and Neal A. Palmer. 2009. The emerging politics of DHS fusion centers. *Security Dialogue,* 40:617–636.

Monnett, Charles and Jeffrey S. Gleason. 2006. Observations of mortality associated with extended open-water swimming by polar bears in the Alaskan Beaufort Sea. *Polar biology* 29 no. 8: 681–687. doi:10.1007/s0030000501052 (accessed May 1, 2012).

Moynihan, Daniel P. 1997. Secrecy as government regulation. *Congressional record* May 1. http://www.fas.org/sgp/congress/kerry.html (accessed May 1, 2012).

National Archives and Records Administration. n.d. *9/11 Commission records.* http://www.archives.gov/research/9-11 (accessed June 2, 2012).

National Commission on Terrorist Attacks Upon the United States. 2004. *Letter to Honorable John W. Carlin.* August 20, http://www.archives.gov/foia/9-11-commission-letter.pdf (accessed June 2, 2012).

National Security Act. 1947. Pub.L. 80-253, 61 Stat. 495. http://intelligence.senate.gov/nsaact1947.pdf (accessed January 2, 2013).

National Security Agency/Central Security Service. 2009. Pre-publication review. http://www.nsa.gov/public_info/prepub/index.shtml (accessed March 1, 2012).

The New York Times. 1945. The right to know. January 23.

The New York Times. 1917. Censor Creel gives out rules for newspapers. May 28.

The New York Times v. United States Department of Justice. 2013. 11 Civ. 9336 (CM). January 3. http://www.aclu.org/nationalsecurity/anwar-al-awlaki-foia-request-district-court-opinion (accessed January 7, 2013).

The New York Times Co. v. United States. 1971. 403 US 713. Retrieved from https://supreme.justia.com/cases/federal/us/403/713/case.html

O'Connell, Mary Ellen. 2005. When is a war not a war? The myth of the global war on terror. *ILSA Journal of International & Comparative Law* 12, no.2: 1–5.

Office of the Army Surgeon General. 2010. *Release of actionable medical information.* http://www.ddeamc.amedd.army.mil/clinical/investigation/documents/10032_Release_of_Actionable_Medical_Information%5B1%5D.pdf (accessed May 1, 2012).

Office of the Army Surgeon General. 2005. Release of actionable medical information policy memorandum. http://www.epinews.com/files/TAB_B_AMI_Policy_Letter_and_PolicyMemo.pdf (accessed May 1, 2012).

Olmsted, Kathryn S. 2011. Government secrecy and conspiracy theories. In *Government Secrecy, Research in Social Problems and Public Policy*, 19, Ed. Susan Maret, 91–100. Bingley, UK: Emerald Group Publishing Limited.

Olmsted, Kathryn S. 1996. *Challenging the secret government: The post Watergate investigations of the CIA and FBI.* Chapel Hill: University of North Carolina Press.

Openthegovernment.org. 2012. Secrecy report. http://www.openthegovernment.org/node/3578 (accessed October 10, 2012).

Orwell, George. 1946. *The prevention of literature.* http://gutenberg.net.au/ebooks03/0300011h.html - part46 (accessed May 1, 2012).

Paltrow, Scot J. 2011. National Archives sits on 9/11 Commission records. *Reuters*, September 8. http://www.reuters.com/article/2011/09/08/us-sept11-archiveidUSTRE7872QI20110908 (accessed June 2, 2012).

Patterson, Thomas G. 1988. Thought control and the writing of history. In *Freedom at risk: Secrecy, censorship and repression in the 1980s*, Ed. Richard O. Curry, 60–68. Philadelphia: Temple University Press.

PEER. 2012. Polar bear probe lumbers into its third year. April 5. http://www.peer.org/news/news_id.php?row_id=1570&title=POLAR20BEAR PROBE LUMBERS INTO ITS THIRD YER (accessed June 2, 2012).

PEER. 2010. Ocean scientists' work screened by public relations staff. November 10. http://www.peer.org/news/news_id.php?row_id=1423 (accessed June 2, 2012).

Phillips, Peter and Mickey Huff. 2011. Project Censored international: Colleges and universities validate independent news and challenge global media censorship. *Research in Social Problems and Public Policy* 19:153–169.

Piltz, Rick. 2011. Secrecy, complicity, and resistance: Political control of climate science communication under the Bush-Cheney administration. In *Government Secrecy, Research in Social Problems and Public Policy*, 19, Ed. Susan Maret, 219–246. Bingley, UK: Emerald Group Publishing Limited.

Powers, Robert Gid. 1998. Introduction. In *Secrecy*. Ed. Daniel Patrick Moynihan, 1–58. New Haven: Yale University Press.

Priest, Dana and William M. Arkin, 2010. A hidden world, growing beyond control: Top secret America. The Washington Post, July 19. http://projects.washingtonpost.com/top-secret-america/articles/ahidden-world-growing-beyond-control (accessed May 28, 2012).

The Progressive. 1979. The H-bomb secret: How we got it, why we're telling it. http://www.progressive.org/images/pdf/1179.pdf (accessed March 1, 2012).

Quist, Arvin S. 2002. Security classification of information. Oak Ridge, TN: Oak Ridge Classification Associates, LLC. https://www.fas.org/sgp/library/quist/index.html (accessed May 28, 2013).

Raskin, Marcus G. and Carl A. LeVan. 2005. The national security state and the tragedy of empire. In *Democracy's shadow: The secret world of national security*, Ed. Marcus G. Raskin and A. Carl LeVan, 3–42. New York: Nation Books.

Raven-Hansen, Peter. 2005. Security's conquest of federal law enforcement. In *Democracy's shadow: The secret world of national security*, Ed. Marcus G. Raskin and A. Carl LeVan, 217–236. New York: Nation Books.

Record, Jeffrey. 2003. Bounding the global war on terrorism. Strategic Studies Institute, U.S. Army War College, December. http://www.strategicstudiesinstitute.army.mil/pdffiles/pub207.pdf (accessed January 11, 2013).

Rendition Project. n.d. Timelines. http://www.therenditionproject.org.uk/timeline/index.html (accessed June 10, 2013).

Reporters Committee for Freedom of the Press. 2005. Homefront confidential: How the war on terrorism affects access to information and the public's right to know. 6th ed. September. http://www.rcfp.org/homefrontconfidential (accessed February 25, 2012).

Risen, James. 2006. *State of war: The secret history of the CIA and the Bush administration.* New York: Free Press.

Roberts, Alasdair. 2006. *Blacked out: Government secrecy in the information age.* New York: Cambridge University Press.

Rosenberg, Morton. 2008. Presidential claims of executive privilege: History, law, practice and recent developments. August 21. *CRS report to Congress* RL30319. http://www.fas.org/sgp/crs/secrecy/RL30319.pdf (accessed April 27, 2012).

Rourke, Francis E. 1960. Administrative secrecy: A congressional dilemma. *American political science review* 54, no. 3: 684–694.

Rourke, Francis E. 1957. Secrecy in American bureaucracy. *Political Science Quarterly,* 72 no. 4: 540–564.

Rozell, Mark J. 2002. Executive privilege revived? Secrecy and conflict during the Bush administration. *Duke Law Journal* 52, no.2: 403–421. http://scholarship.law.duke.edu/dlj/vol52/iss2 (accessed April 28, 2012).

Sangar, David E. and Thom Shanker, 2013. Broad powers seen for Obama in cyberstrikes. *The New York Times,* February 3. https://www.nytimes.com/2013/02/04/us/broad-powers-seen-forobama-in-cyberstrikes.html?pagewanted=1&_r=1&ref=global-home& (accessed February 3, 2013).

Schenck v. United States. 1919. 249 U.S. 47. http://www.oyez.org/cases/19011939/1918/1918_437 (accessed April 28, 2012).

Schoenfeld Gabriel. 2011. *Necessary secrets: National security, the media, and the rule of law.* New York: W. W. Norton & Co.

Schultz, William F. 2003. *Tainted legacy: 9/11 and the ruin of human rights.* Thunder's Mouth Press/Nation Books.

Senate Select Committee to Study Governmental Operations with Respect to Intelligence Activities. 1976. *Intelligence activities—Senate Resolution 21: Hearings before the Select Committee to Study Governmental Operations with Respect to Intelligence Activities of the United States Senate*, 94-1. 7 vols. http://www.aarclibrary.org/publib/contents/church/contents_church_eports.htm (accessed May 1, 2012).

Senate Subcommittee on Constitutional Rights. 1972. *U.S. army surveillance of civilians: A documentary analysis*, 92d Congress, 2d session. Washington, DC: Government Printing Office. https://bkofsecrets.wordpress.com/2009/06/17/army-surveillancedoc/ (accessed May 1, 2012).

Shaffer, Anthony. 2010. *Operation dark heart: Spycraft and special ops on the frontlines of Afghanistan and the path to victory*. New York: Thomas Dunne Books.

Shane, Peter, M. 2006. Social theory meets social policy: Culture, identity and public information policy after September 11. *I/S: A Journal of Law and Policy* 2, no.1: i–xxi.

Shane, Scott. 2011. CIA demands cuts in book about 9/11 and terror fight. *The New York Times*. August 25. https://www.nytimes.com/2011/08/26/us/26agent.html (accessed May 1, 2012).

Sharkey Jacqueline. 1991. *Under fire: U.S. military restrictions on the media from Grenada to the Persian Gulf War*. Center for Public Integrity. http://www.publicintegrity.org/assets/pdf/UNDERFIRE.pdf (accessed May 1, 2012).

Shils, Edward. 1956. *The torment of secrecy: The background and consequences of American security policies*. Glencoe, IL: The Free Press, 1956.

Simmel, Georg. 1906. The sociology of secrecy and secret societies. *The American Journal of Sociology* 11, no.4: 441–498.

Singh, Amrit. 2013. Globalizing torture: CIA secret detention and extraordinary rendition. Open Society Foundations. http://www.opensocietyfoundations.org/reports/globalizing-torturecia-secret-detention-and-extraordinary-rendition (accessed February 5, 2013).

Snepp, Frank. 1999. *Irreparable harm: A firsthand account of how one agent took on the CIA in an epic battle over secrecy and free speech*. New York: Random House.

Snepp, Frank. 1977. *Decent interval: An insider's account of Saigon's indecent end*. New York: Random House.

Soufan, Ali. 2011. *The black banners: The inside story of 9/11 and the war against Al-Qaeda*. New York : W.W. Norton & Co.

Sunstein, Cass R. 1986. Government control of information. *California Law Review* 74, no. 3: 889–921.

Theoharis, Athan G. 2011. *Abuse of power: How Cold War surveillance and secrecy policy shaped the response to 9/11.* Philadelphia: Temple University Press.

Theoharis, Athan G. 2004. *The FBI & American democracy: A brief critical history.* Lawrence: University Press of Kansas.

Theoharis, Athan G. 1978. *Spying on Americans: Political surveillance from Hoover to the Huston plan.* Philadelphia: Temple University Press.

Thompson, Dennis F. 1999. Democratic secrecy. *Political Science Quarterly* 114, no.2: 81–193.

Turner, Robert F. 1994. Testimony, secret funding and the `statement and account' clause: Constitutional and policy implications of public disclosure of an aggregate budget for intelligence and intelligence related activities https://www.fas.org/irp/congress/1994_hr/turner.htm (access January 11, 2013).

Union of Concerned Scientists. 2009. Freedom to speak: A report card on federal agency media policies. http://www.ucsusa.org/scientific_integrity/abuses_of_science/freedomtospeak.html (accessed May 1, 2012).

United Nations Conference on Environment and Development. 1992. Rio declaration on environment and development. http://www.unep.org/Documents.Multilingual/Default.asp?documenti=78&articleid=1163 (accessed January 18, 2013).

United Nations General Assembly. 1948. Declaration of human rights. http://www.un.org/en/documents/udhr/ (accessed March 12, 2012).

United Nations General Assembly. 1966. International covenant on civil and political rights. http://www2.ohchr.org/english/law/ccpr.htm (accessed March 12, 2012).

U.S. Department of Health, Education & Welfare, Secretary's Advisory Committee on Automated Personal Data Systems. 1973. *Records, computers and the rights of citizens: Report of the Secretary's advisory committee on automated personal data systems.* Washington DC: Government Printing Office. https://epic.org/privacy/hew1973report/Summary.htm (accessed January 18, 2013).

Washburn, Patrick S. 1986. J. Edgar Hoover and the Black press in World War II. ED271749. Paper presented at the *Annual Meeting of the Association for Education in Journalism and Mass Communication* 69th, Norman, OK, August 3–6.

Waters, T.J. 2006. *Class 11: Inside the CIA's first post-9/11 spy class.* New York: Dutton.

Weber, Max. 1978. *Economy and society: An outline of interpretive sociology.* Trans. Ephraim Fischoff. Ed. Guenther Roth and Wittich, Claus. Berkeley: University of California Press.

Weber, Max. 1968. *Economy and society: An outline of interpretive sociology.* Trans. Ephraim Fischoff. Ed. Guenther Roth and Wittich, Claus. Berkeley: University of California Press.

Weber, Max. 1958. *From Max Weber: Essays in sociology.* Ed. and Trans. H.H. Gerth and Mills, C. Wright. New York: Oxford University Press.

Webster, Stephen C. 2012. NSA: Revealing how many Americans we've spied on would violate their privacy. *The Raw Story,* June 19. http://www.rawstory.com/rs/2012/06/19/nsa-revealing-how-manyamericans-were-spied-on-would-violate-their-privacy (accessed June 19, 2012).

Welsome, Eileen. 2000. *The plutonium files: America's secret medical experiments in the Cold War.* New York: Dell.

Wise, David and Thomas B. Ross. 1964. *The invisible government.* New York: Random House.

Intellectual Freedom and Privacy

Neil M. Richards and Joanna F. Cornwell

Intellectual freedom and privacy are distinct concepts, but they are related and mutually reinforcing. Certain kinds of privacy protections can be essential to the meaningful exercise of intellectual freedoms. Particularly when individuals are engaged in intellectual activities (broadly defined), privacy protections can operate to provide a shield from the scrutiny and interference of others so that intellectual inquiry—thinking, reading, and private conversations—can occur. The absence of such protections for "intellectual privacy" (whether physical, social, or legal) can shine the light of surveillance onto intellectual activities, driving them to the conventional, the mainstream, and the uncontroversial. (Richards 2013a; 2013b; 2008).

Americans have long understood the links between a well-educated citizenry and the preservation of democratic self-government (ALA 2012c). For example, Benjamin Franklin started the first public subscription library in 1731 in Philadelphia, Pennsylvania (Morse 1989). Nine signers of the Declaration of Independence were members of Benjamin Franklin's Library Company (Library Company 2012). Modern librarians continue this commitment. The American Library Association asserts that intellectual freedom has two main dimensions: 1) "the right of every individual to hold any belief of any subject and to convey their ideas in any form they deem appropriate," and 2) "that society make an equal commitment to unrestricted access to information and ideas" (ALA, 2012c). Legally, the concept of intellectual freedom in the United States is associated with the First and Fourth Amendments of the U.S. Constitution. The First Amendment protects the right of freedom of speech and press, and their associated freedoms of thought, belief, and inquiry. The Fourth Amendment protects an individual's "persons, houses, papers, and effects" from unreasonable government searches and seizures, and had its genesis in the need to protect private correspondence from government surveillance. As William Stuntz has explained, the origins of the

Fourth Amendment have much in common with the origins of the First. Stuntz has shown how the eighteenth century British Crown frequently used criminal prosecutions for seditious libel to suppress dissidents and other government critics, and used searches of private property for diaries and other incriminating texts in order to advance such prosecutions. Such prosecutions were also common in the colonies, and formed the context out of which the Fourth Amendment was drafted and ratified (Stuntz 1995). From this perspective, the First Amendment protects the right to speak, while the Fourth protects the ability to develop ideas away from the interference of the state. Both protections thus work together to guarantee intellectual freedom as a constitutional matter.

Modern understandings of intellectual freedom reflect these constitutional origins. The First Amendment's protections extend beyond those of speakers to those of listeners as well, and include the right to know or receive information (Emerson 1976; Solove & Richards 2009). The right to know is an important liberty because it provides individuals with the ability to seek the truth, to aid collective decision-making for political processes, and to obtain personal fulfillment (Emerson 1976). Moreover, the right of free speech also includes the right to speak anonymously or under a pseudonym, a well-established practice in American public debate since James Madison, John Jay, and Alexander Hamilton penned *The Federalist* under the pseudonym Publius. Readers and listeners of public speech may similarly want to remain anonymous and to consume this information in a quiet space (such as a library) without observation (Blitz 2006). It is in such contexts that privacy has the most meaningful role to play in providing protection for intellectual pursuits.

Privacy is a wide-ranging, complex concept and it continues to change as information technology and social norms evolve (Nissenbaum 2004; Solove 2010). The first well-known legal definition of privacy came from the 1890 Warren and Brandeis article "The Right to Privacy," which famously defined privacy as the "right to be let alone" (Warren & Brandeis 1890). In response to this article, state legislatures and courts created or recognized privacy rights as a matter of state tort law. These decisions were ultimately categorized into four distinct torts by William Prosser during the middle decades of the twentieth century, and through Prosser's influence over the course of tort law most jurisdictions today recognize four separate causes of action under the right to privacy: intrusion into seclusion, disclosure of private facts, appropriation of likeness, and false light (Richards & Solove 2010).

While the tort law of privacy has remained relatively stable, scholarly understandings of privacy have continued to evolve as legal scholars have subsequently developed new analytic frameworks to better understand what privacy can mean. Moreover, the emerging world of information and electronic communications technologies has placed increased importance on the idea of privacy. Scholarly understandings of "information privacy" have struggled with the definition of privacy and the values it protects. Responding to the first "data bank" technologies in the 1960s, Alan Westin argued that privacy is not an absolute right, but rather a claim for individuals and institutions "to determine for themselves when, how, and to what extent information about them is communicated to others" (Westin 1967). Westin's intuitive understanding of privacy as having something to do with control over one's personal information remains influential in today's scholarly and policy understandings of privacy. However, definitions of privacy have remained elusive.

Two recent conceptual advances are also worthy of mention. First, Daniel Solove has offered a four part "taxonomy" of information privacy (Solove 2010). Solove divides harmful activities in information privacy into the four principal categories of: 1) information collection, 2) information processing, 3) information dissemination, and 4) invasion (Solove 2010). Solove proceeds to break down these four parts into more specific harmful sub-activities. Information collection involves surveillance and interrogation or probing for information (Solove 2010). Information processing describes how outside entities such as the government and businesses process and manipulate an individual's data by engaging in activities such as aggregation, identification, insecurity, exclusion, and secondary use (Solove 2010, 104). Information dissemination describes what happens to an individual's data when it is shared with third parties, including potentially: breach of confidentiality, disclosure, exposure, increased accessibility, blackmail, appropriation, and distortion (Solove 2010). Finally, invasion details the specific harm to an individual's privacy, namely intrusion into their tranquility and decisional interference (Solove 2010). While Solove admits these categories are artificial, he advocates for a bottom-up approach to examining privacy problems (Solove 2010). By using this approach, privacy problems will not be overlooked and privacy principles will be better informed to understand such privacy problems in the first place (Solove 2010).

Also recognizing the difficulty in defining privacy, Helen Nissenbaum provides three principles for guiding contemporary privacy policy: "1) limiting surveillance of citizens and use of information about them by agents of government; 2) restricting access to sensitive, personal, or private information; and 3) curtailing intrusions into places deemed private or personal" (Nissenbaum 2004). In subsequent work Nissenbaum notes that few people actually want their information to be kept confidential under all circumstances, but rather that most people want their information to flow, but to flow within appropriate norms. These norms, she asserts, vary from context to context, such that the key to sensible privacy policy is to maintain what she calls "contextual integrity"—the appropriate balance between privacy and flow depending on social norms (Nissenbaum 2010). In this essay, we provide an account of the ways in which intellectual freedom and privacy are interrelated. We pay particular attention to both the constitutional dimensions of these important values, as well as the important roles that social and professional norms play in their protection in practice. Our examination of these issues is divided into three parts. Part I lays out the law and legal theory governing privacy as it relates to intellectual freedom. Part II examines a special context in which law and professional norms operate together to protect intellectual freedom through privacy—the library. Finally, Part III discusses how government actions and other threats can infringe individuals' privacy, potentially threatening intellectual freedom.

Privacy Law and Intellectual Freedom

First Amendment Theory and Intellectual Freedom

The First Amendment's guarantees of free speech and press protect many things, but at their core is a commitment to intellectual freedom. We can see this commitment in the seminal free speech texts from the early twentieth century, texts which have become the core of First Amendment theory today (Richards 2008). For example, Justice Oliver Wendell Holmes' famous dissent in *Abrams v. United States* quite clearly linked the purposes of constitutional protection free speech with the search for truth, a statement of intellectual freedom in its most stark and philosophical form. The underpinnings of intellectual freedom in First Amendment theory can be seen even more clearly in Justice Brandeis' opinions in *Whitney v. California* and *Olmstead v. United States*. In *Whitney*, the Court was examining the constitutionality of California's criminal syndicalism statute under the First Amendment. In Justice Brandeis' concurrence, he noted that:

> *Those who won our independence believed that the final end of the state was to make men free to develop their faculties. . . . They believed that freedom to think as you will and to speak as you think are means indispensable to the discovery and spread of political truth.* (Whitney 1927)

Although Brandeis' opinion did not have the effect of law when it was published, over time it has been recognized by courts and legal scholars as one of the most important statements regarding how the First Amendment should be protected, and why it should be protected broadly to promote intellectual freedom. In *Whitney*, Brandeis was not merely making a historical comment on our nation's founders, but rather was describing how essential freedom of speech is to self-government (Richards 2010). In order to have an effective self-government resulting in more democratic decisions, there must be an educated and democratic citizenry (Richards 2010). The recognition of how critical free speech is to producing an informed, educated and democratic citizenry is one of Brandeis' most innovative and novel contributions to First Amendment jurisprudence (Richards 2010). A democratic citizenry must have robust free speech protections and access to new opinions, as what lawyers call "counter-speech" is the best remedy to dangerous and harmful ideas (Richards 2010). Brandeis describes this concept:

> If there be time to expose through discussion the falsehood and fallacies, to avert the evil by the process of education, the remedy to be applied is more speech, not enforced silence. (Whitney 1927)

Brandeis' connections between free speech, self-government, a democratic citizenry, and intellectual freedom have since become a cornerstone of modern First Amendment speech theory (Richards 2010). Brandeis further explained the linkages between privacy and intellectual freedom in his well-known dissent in *Olmstead v. United States* (1928) (Richards 2008; Richards 2010). *Olmstead* was a Fourth Amendment case in which the majority of the Supreme Court held that federal wiretapping did not require a warrant under the Fourth Amendment. Brandeis argued that:

> The makers of our Constitution undertook to secure conditions favorable to the pursuit of happiness. They recognized the significance of man's spiritual nature, of his feelings and of his intellect. They knew that only a part of the pain, pleasure and satisfactions of life are to be found in material things. They sought to protect Americans in their beliefs, their thoughts, their emotions and their sensations. They conferred, as against the government, the right to be let alone—the most comprehensive of rights and the right most valued by civilized man. (Olmstead 1928)

Brandeis' dissenting arguments in *Olmstead* eventually carried the day, and his arguments were accepted by the Supreme Court in *Katz v. United States* (1967), which ruled that the Fourth Amendment protects a person's "reasonable expectation of privacy." *Olmstead* was, of course, a Fourth Amendment case, but in his opinion, Brandeis revealed some of the ancient connections between the First and Fourth Amendments in the context of intellectual freedom. Brandeis thus illustrated how privacy could provide a shelter for free thought and intellectual freedom (Richards 2008). He went on to warn prophetically that in the future it might be possible for "the government, without removing papers from secret drawers, [to] reproduce them in court, and by which it will be enabled to expose to a jury the most intimate occurrences of the home. Advances in the psychic and related sciences may bring means of exploring unexpressed beliefs, thoughts and emotions" (Olmstead 1928).

In order to prevent this, Brandeis argued, novel and unjustifiable intrusions into domestic and intellectual privacy must be considered a violation of the Fourth Amendment.

Brandeis's connections between privacy and freedom of speech nevertheless run somewhat against the grain of the traditional ways that courts have approached the relationship between these two values. Traditionally, the Supreme Court and First Amendment scholars have considered privacy as a hostile or competing value to free speech. This typically occurs when a privacy cause of action is brought against the press for disclosing true but newsworthy facts about the subject of a news story (Richards 2008). In such cases, the Supreme Court usually holds that the constitutional right of free speech under the First Amendment value prevails against the tort right in protecting one's emotions from distress (Richards 2008). Most recently for example, in *Snyder v. Phelps*, the Court examined an invasion of privacy claim by a deceased military veteran's father subjected to horrific anti-gay protesting by the Westboro Baptist Church at his son's funeral (Snyder 2011). The Court held that the veteran's father did not prove the elements for an invasion into privacy tort and that the First Amendment "protect[s] even hurtful speech on public issues to ensure that we do not stifle public debate" (Snyder 2011). A long line of earlier cases have held that the First Amendment protects the ability of the press to publish emotionally damaging but true statements, such as the names of rape victims notwithstanding civil and criminal laws to the contrary (Richards 2011).

Notwithstanding these precedents, privacy is able to survive challenges from the First Amendment when it protects spaces or relationships from intrusion (Richards 2011). This is especially the case when government actors are the ones seeking to intrude, as the robust body of Fourth Amendment law protecting the privacy of the home can attest to. Thus, in *Kyllo v. United States*, the Court held it to be a violation of the Fourth Amendment when the government had used an infrared thermometer to measure the temperature of the exterior of a house they suspected was harboring an indoor marijuana farm. And in *Wilson v. Layne*, the Court also found a violation where police brought a reporter along with them to observe the execution of an arrest warrant in a private home. The Court has also on limited occasions recognized that the First Amendment protects intellectual freedom in the privacy of one's home directly. In *Stanley v. Georgia*, the Court famously recognized the right of an individual to read books and watch films, even pornographic films that were otherwise illegal to possess, in the privacy of one's home, against government intrusion. The Court held that:

> *If the First Amendment means anything, it means that a State has no business telling a man, sitting alone in his own house, what books he*

may read or what films he may watch. Our whole constitutional heritage rebels at the thought of giving government the power to control men's minds. (Stanley 1969)

Intellectual Privacy

Within First Amendment law and theory, Neil Richards has located and illustrated "intellectual privacy," the "ability, whether protected by law or social circumstances, to develop ideas and beliefs away from the unwanted gaze or interference of others" (Richards 2008). Although intellectual privacy as an identified term is relatively new, its roots in First Amendment theory are much older, and can be traced back to Brandeis and *Stanley*. Intellectual privacy strengthens the right to speech as it provides a theory of protection for the freedom of thought; it protects the way in which our minds develop to say something before the speech actually occurs (Richards 2008). Richards argues the "First Amendment should protect cognitive activities even if they are wholly private and unshared because of the importance of individual conscience and autonomy" (Richards 2008). A theory of intellectual privacy also "creates a screen against such surveillance" as surveillance can chill First Amendment activities when readers in fear of being watched do not access certain articles on the Internet or do not check out certain books (Richards 2008; Richards 2013a; 2013b).

Legal Scholar Julie Cohen has also recognized the value of intellectual privacy in a number of contexts (Cohen 1996). She notes that "reading is so intimately connected with speech, and so expressive in its own right, that the freedom to read anonymously must be considered a right that the First Amendment protects" (Cohen 1996). Under the current copyright law, there is no obligation for companies to maintain a reader's anonymity when using their product (Cohen 1996). Therefore, she stresses that the law be amended to ensure autonomy-based rights are recognized and provide "breathing space for thought, exploration, and personal growth" (Cohen 2003). In her recent book *Configuring the Networked Self*, Cohen expands this theory, arguing that informal opportunities and spaces for private experimentation allow for the development of the self, whether alone or in the company of others. Cohen notes that intellectual privacy is important not just for high-minded "intellectual" ideas, but also for whatever we wish to experiment with as part of our engagement in the formation of culture—a phenomenon she calls "the play of everyday practice" (Cohen 2012).

Daniel Solove argues that government actions and subpoenas that request reading lists, diaries, internet search histories, computer hard drives, and emails implicate an individual's First Amendment liberties (Solove 2007). Solove proposes that the First Amendment can be used alongside the Fourth and Fifth Amendments as a source of criminal procedure to prevent invasive government intrusion when the intrusion implicates the First Amendment (Solove 2007). He recommends that courts should determine whether or not the First Amendment applies when the government seeks a subpoena for information gathering purposes and then determine if the request would have a sufficient chilling effect on the First Amendment activity (Solove 2007). In the event the First Amendment applies, the court must then determine whether or not the government had "a significant interest in gathering the information, and, if so, whether the process was narrowly tailored to the government interest" (Solove 2007).

State Laws on Protecting Reader Privacy

There is no federal statute protecting reader privacy, but 48 states and the District of Columbia have passed library reader confidentiality laws (Klinefelter 2010). The remaining states, Kentucky and Hawaii, have no express legislative protection of librarian privacy, though their state Attorneys General have each issued opinions declaring that the state protects the privacy of library users (Klinefelter 2010). State library privacy laws vary widely in scope, as some states only protect public libraries, rather than (for example) private university libraries. Operating on top of the state laws are library privacy policies, which can provide higher levels of privacy protection to their patrons. Klinefelter notes that the state may offer more reader privacy protection, a library's own policy may offer the reader more protection, or a reader may be protected by both a state law and library policy (Klinefelter 2010).

Beyond libraries, several states offer protections for reader records generally, such as those created by bookstores and websites, though the type of protections and type of mediums protected also varies widely from state to state (Richards 2013b). In Michigan's Preservation of Personal Privacy Act of 1988, all records of selling, renting or lending books and other written materials shall not be disclosed to any third party unless provided by law, broadly defined (MICH. § 445.1712). In California, the Reader Privacy Act of 2012 protects all reading records, including e-books, from disclosure to third parties unless the government has a proper court order or a private entity has a user's informed and affirmative consent for a specific use of this record (CAL. CIV. CODE § 1799.3). In contrast to other states statutes' providing for reader protection, Colorado protects the right to purchase books anonymously through Article II, Section 10 of its state Constitution (Richards 2013). The Colorado Supreme Court upholds the importance of reader privacy and sets forth a balancing test that requires law enforcement officials seeking specific book records from a bookstore to first demonstrate a compelling government need for these records and the court can consider whether there are reasonable alternative methods of meeting this need, whether the warrant is too broad, and whether the reason for seeking these records are valid (Tattered Cover 2002, 1047). As evidenced by this sample of state protections, the type of reading materials protected and the regulation of disclosure to third parties provides an uneven treatment of reader records under our law (Richards 2013).

Social Norms

Librarians' History in Advocating for Privacy to Secure Intellectual Freedom

As the previous discussion of library policies suggests, libraries and librarian ethics play a central role in any discussions of intellectual freedom and privacy. Indeed, the professional work of librarians is perhaps the context in which the linkages between privacy and intellectual freedom have been recognized the most. This is true both as a matter of the theory of librarianship as well as a series of practices and norms that embody these theories into everyday institutions and interactions. As a center for "uninhibited intellectual inquiry," libraries are places where individuals can self-direct their learning towards a collection of books, periodicals, digital information, and other media without bias or scrutiny (ALA 2012c). Courts have also noted that libraries play an important role in providing a citizen with access to the printed word, and more broadly to all ideas (US vs. ALA 2003).

As such, librarians have a long history in advocating for privacy as an instrumental goal in furtherance of their broader commitment to the intellectual freedom of their patrons. The American Library Association (ALA) first affirmed a right to privacy in 1939 (ALA 2002). The ALA Library Bill of Rights outlines the duties and the principles for how librarians should protect and defend intellectual freedom (ALA 2012c). Today, the ALA Code of Ethics states: "[w]e protect each library user's right to privacy and confidentiality with respect to information sought or received and resources consulted, borrowed, acquired or transmitted" (ALA 2012b). The ALA believes that the right of privacy ensures an individual may openly learn, read, and research without intrusion (ALA 2002). When individuals fear surveillance or that their privacy is threatened, the ALA's position is unequivocal that true intellectual freedom no longer exists (ALA 2002).

Librarians' Advocacy for Protecting Users' Confidentiality and Privacy

While library records have been recently targeted for national security reasons under the USA Patriot Act of 2001, government agencies have been seeking library records in criminal investigations for decades. In response to these government actions, in 1970 the ALA adopted a policy that library records are to be deemed confidential and not considered public records, even for public libraries (ALA 2012c). The ALA's Office of Intellectual Freedom publishes an Intellectual Freedom Manual, which sets forth a policy on confidentiality of library records (ALA 2012c). The Manual states that not only does the Librarian Code of Ethics include a duty to protect the privacy and confidentiality of library patrons, but also that librarians should not release an individual's records to a government agency without an authorized process, order, or subpoena (ALA 2012c). Upon receiving the subpoena, the librarian should consult with legal counsel to determine if the subpoena is proper and if there is a showing of good cause for its issuance (ALA 2012c). The ALA also recommends that libraries create and publish a privacy policy, so that users are aware of and consent to how their personal information is being collected, used, and stored (ALA 2012c).

Library Privacy Policies as a Model for the Digital World

By thus making duties of confidentiality and respect for patron reading privacy an important part of the professional ethics of librarianship, the ALA shows how social and ethical norms can place an additional level of privacy protection on top of whatever legal rules might be in place. With the advent of new digital technologies, librarian and legal scholar Ann Klinefelter argues that libraries are confronted with new opportunities for reader records to be shared instead of discarded (Klinefelter 2010). With respect to these online sharing systems, libraries have proceeded cautiously "with a policy of opt-in, rather than opt-out for those services that have the potential to compromise reader privacy" (Klinefelter 2010). Although some librarians might question a need for privacy in a "culture fueled by Facebook, blogs, Twitter and celebrity" or would like to study readers' data for social sciences purposes, Klinefelter notes that most librarians are "committed advocates for the privacy of thought through reading" (Klinefelter 2010). Moreover, the set of professional rules and practices that librarians have developed to protect free reading and intellectual inquiry could be extended to other areas. Klinefelter suggests that the rules librarians have developed could serve as a model for other digital environments such as Google Books, e-readers, and other digital mediums (Klinefelter 2010, 561). Other legal scholars have made similar arguments (Richards 2013; Blitz 2006; Cohen 1996; 2003).

The Advent of Social Reading Applications Have Impacted Reader Privacy

A new phenomenon on the Internet in recent years has been the rise of "social reading." This is the idea that automatic disclosure of one's friends' reading habits gives Internet users suggestions of new and interesting things to read. Accordingly, companies like Facebook and Twitter, in collaboration with many newspapers, have created "social reading" opportunities for online users. Once a reader provides a one-time consent to a website newspaper application, then "the application can be used to allow the automatic disclosure of their reader records to their friends on social networks" (Richards 2013b). This automatic disclosure is known as "frictionless sharing." Richards argues that while some sharing may appear to be "cool," there are inherent dangers in frictionless sharing that threaten a reader's intellectual freedom and privacy (Richards 2013b). First, frictionless reading is not frictionless as the application can inadvertently invade a reader's privacy when they do not intend to share an embarrassing article that they read by posting the article automatically on their social network page. Second, frictionless sharing eliminates conscious or meaningful sharing. Third, frictionless sharing does not guarantee our intellectual freedom will advance, but rather it hinders our ability to freely engage with any ideas "on our own terms with meaningful guarantees that we will not be watched or interfered with" (Richards 2013b). If readers are worried that our reading habits might be disclosed automatically or accidentally, then readers would become less likely to engage or experiment with unpopular or deviant ideas (Richards 2013b).

Richards suggests that social reading applications should build applications based on an opt-in and conscious choice, so that reading is confidential and that sharing an article can be conscious and valuable (Richards 2013b). Although social reading creates significant threats to reader privacy, millions of readers have signed up for reading applications on Facebook in 2012, indicating that some readers enjoy the frictionless sharing application (Purewal 2012). By May 2012, millions of users had stopped using such applications, suggesting that some readers were turned off by frictionless sharing; nonetheless, some readers suggest that the drop-off is merely because Facebook altered how shared articles were displayed on a reader's Facebook page (Purewal 2012). The threat of social reading to intellectual privacy is thus likely to persist in the future.

Threats and Public Policy Considerations

Government Threats and Impacts on Intellectual Freedom and Privacy

National Security

Throughout history, governments have interfered with an individual's intellectual freedom and privacy in the name of national security. As noted earlier, such efforts by the British Crown during the colonial period resulted in the protections of persons, houses, and papers in the text of the Fourth Amendment. More recently, during the McCarthy era in the 1950s, the United

States government used library records to uncover suspected communists and other political dissidents (Martin 2003). In the 1970s, government officials sought reader records on political radicals and anti-Vietnam activists; and in the 1980s the Federal Bureau of Investigation (FBI) sought circulation records for "suspicious looking foreigners" through a Library Awareness Program (ALA 2012c). A Freedom of Information Act (FOIA) Request in 1989 revealed that 266 critics of the Library Awareness Program were subjected to FBI index checks (ALA 2012c). Local law enforcement has also attempted, albeit unsuccessfully, to use library records for fishing expeditions to build evidence for a criminal prosecution (ALA 2012c).

USA PATRIOT Act Section 215

The most recent government action in this sphere is Section 215 of the USA PATRIOT Act of 2001, which authorized the government to obtain "any tangible thing," including confidential library reader records, book sale records, and book customer lists for a national security investigation (USA PATRIOT Act of 2001, § 215). Proponents of the act argued that opening up library and book records was critical to national security, so that law enforcement agents could have access to more information, enhancing their ability to uncover terrorist plots (Martin 2003). Section 212 of the Act also authorized librarians to pass over any information to a government entity if the librarian, "in good faith, believes that an emergency involving danger or death or serious physical injury to any person requires disclosure" (USA PATRIOT Act of 2001, § 212).

Pursuant to Section 215, a federal agent can apply to a federal District Court or magistrate judge to obtain library records providing "a statement of facts showing that there are reasonable grounds to believe that tangible things sought are relevant to an authorized investigation . . . to obtain foreign intelligence information not concerning a United States person or to protect against international terrorism or clandestine intelligence activities" (PATRIOT Act of 2001, codified at 50 U.S.C.A. § 1861(a)(1); 2012). This standard is lower than a probable cause standard and does not require the government to provide specific, articulable facts that there is a reasonable belief that these records will assist with an authorized investigation (Martin 2003; Woods 2005). These orders are also subject to a gag order, mandating that the recipient of an order cannot reveal the order, so that the content of the FBI application remains secret. The Act also specifically states that the FBI is not authorized to obtain records on US citizens who are carrying out "activities protected by the First Amendment of the Constitution" (PATRIOT Act of 2001, codified at 50 U.S.C.A. § 1861(a)(1).

The ALA and other privacy and intellectual freedom advocates severely criticized Section 215 for having a chilling effect on First Amendment liberties and violating Fourth Amendment rights by lowering the standard required to obtain the records (Martin 2003; ALA 2009). In response to some of this criticism, Section 215 was amended to allow for enhanced oversight in 2006 (USA PATRIOT Act 2006). This amendment provides a librarian with the right to consult with an attorney about a PATRIOT Act order and requires the Attorney General to inform and submit reports about all of the requests under Section 215 to the U.S. House of Representatives' Permanent Select Committee of Intelligence of the House and the U.S. Senate's Select Committee on Intelligence and Committee on the Judiciary in April of every year (50 U.S.C.A. § 1862).

Nonetheless, the ALA and privacy and intellectual freedom advocates argue that the enhanced oversight amendment does not go far enough. The ALA recently launched a campaign to address the USA PATRIOT Act's intrusions into reader privacy (ALA 2012a). This campaign advocates for restoring reader privacy prior to the PATRIOT Act by allowing the Act to sunset (ALA 2012a).

In 2007, the Office of Inspector General (OIG) in the Department of Justice (DOJ) conducted an assessment of Section 215 and discovered the following:

- The first Section 215 request was not made until May 2004

- From May 2004–2005, 21 solely Section 215 orders were obtained and 141 Section 215 orders were obtained in combination with a pen register or wiretap order

- All 162 of these requests were approved by the Foreign Intelligence Surveillance Act Court and only four were slightly modified from the original request by the Court

- Two of these Section 215 orders were improperly requested

- There was no evidence that information obtained from these orders helped uncover a terrorist plot

- None of these orders were used to obtain library records (US Department of Justice 2007)

The USA PATRIOT Act has been reauthorized several times, the last in May 26, 2011 when President Obama signed S. 990 the "PATRIOT Sunsets Extension Act of 2011," extending certain surveillance provisions, including Section 215, for four years (White House 2011). While the latest DOJ Office of the Inspector General (OIG) report from 2012 mentions that the Office is reviewing Section 215 applications filed between 2007 to 2009, there is no information provided on whether there has been any improper or illegal uses of this Section (US Department of Justice 2012, 16–17).

Cybersecurity Programs

In addition to Section 215, the National Security Agency (NSA) and the Department of Homeland Security (DHS) have invested billions of dollars in cybersecurity and have discussed launching such cybersecurity programs as "Perfect Citizen" and "EINSTEIN," some of which may include electronic surveillance of users on the Internet (Adhikari 2010). As recently as February 2012, DHS was under congressional scrutiny when news media reported that the government monitors social networking activity and the postings of comments on online newspapers sites (Stone 2012). DHS maintained that these actions are not intended to curb online speech, but rather capture "situational awareness" during breaking news events and natural disasters (Stone 2012).

Gregory Nojeim suggests that there should be more transparency in how cybersecurity programs protect civil liberties and that the National Security Agency, the lead agency in this area, may not be the most appropriate agency to safeguard civil liberties (Nojeim 2010).

Government Action in the Private Sector

Government action has also affected the private sector's privacy and confidentiality policies. In 2006 in an action concerning COPA, the Child Online Protection Act, the U.S. Department of Justice filed a court order seeking a random sample of 50,000 URLs and 5,000 user search queries from Google's online search engine database over a one-week period without seeking any personally identifiable information to the user's identity[1] (Gonzales 2006). Many leading search engines apparently handed the information over without protest, but Google challenged the subpoena, stating that their user policy assured users of their privacy and anonymity (Gonzales 2006). Google won a partial victory. The Court held that Google had to produce a random selection of 50,000 URLs from Google's database as long as proprietary information was not compromised, but that it did not need to disclose user search terms as the DOJ did not meet its burden under discovery standards (Gonzales 2006). While the Court did not make an express ruling on privacy, it did recognize that considerable privacy issues are raised when discussing a user's search data (Gonzales 2006).

Some private online companies like Facebook, Twitter, and Google play a unique role in society as networking tools that connect millions of users to each other. On these networking sites or search engines, users may consider that their activity is limited or private, but in reality this information may be shared with third parties and used to provide targeted advertisements (Ghitis 2012). To what extent actions on Facebook or Google are private or can

1   The Child Online Protection Act (COPA) was struck down in 2007.

be shared with the government is still an open issue and is hotly debated. As these companies have access to millions of users' information, habits, and opinions, it should be no surprise that the government is keenly interested in this data. At the time of writing, the government is interested in obtaining cyber threat information from online web companies. The Cyber Intelligence Sharing Protection Act (CISPA) was passed by the House in April 2012 and authorizes companies to share vital information on cyber threats with the government (Tsukayama 2012). President Obama states that he would veto the bill in its current form, citing privacy concerns (Tsukayama 2012). Privacy advocates are concerned that this cybersecurity mission will be a mechanism for the government to obtain all kinds of personally identifiable information and private user data and that the government will use this data for national security, outside of cyber threats (Tsukayama 2012).

Emerging Technologies and the Free Flow of Information

Emerging technologies can have a dual effect on intellectual access and privacy. Instead of inhibiting the right to know, such technologies can also enhance individuals' access to information. New technologies, including web-based applications that share articles and books within a person's network, promote an open and collaborative learning environment (Zu 2009). Therefore, patrons may prefer relaxed privacy policies (Zu 2009).

The free flow of information can be valuable to both businesses and consumers. Fred H. Cate emphasizes the importance of a balanced approach to privacy on the Internet and that too much regulation in the private sector can interfere with information flows (Cate 2000). Protecting an individual's privacy can create high transaction costs, resulting in inaccurate and incomplete information (Cate 2000). Technology companies such as Facebook and academics like Journalism Professor Jeff Jarvis have also advocated for the values of sharing (Jarvis 2011).

Julie Cohen notes, however, that copyright management technologies are used to monitor readers' habits once they access reading materials, so that owners of this information can prevent widespread infringement; however, she stresses that these technologies can "entail total loss of reader anonymity in cyberspace" (Cohen 1996). Therefore, she urges for Congress to adopt copyright laws that protect readers against anonymity-destroying practices (Cohen 1996).

While technologies continue to advance and develop, breaking down more barriers to reader data, Richards recommends that policymakers keep in mind four principles: 1) reader data is sensitive and may cause harm if wrongly disclosed; 2) readers require real notice on data collecting practices so they can behave accordingly; 3) readers must be provided with a real conscious choice to share information instead of frictionless sharing; and 4) confidentiality rules can be a best practice for ensuring information is properly shared without invading intellectual privacy. Adherence to these principles, he argues, could allow us to obtain some of the benefits of new digital technologies without sacrificing our intellectual privacy (Richards 2013).

References

Adhikari, Richard. 2010. "Report: NSA heads up 'Perfect' plan to hunt down cyberthreats. *TechNewsWorld*, July 18. http://www.technewsworld.com/rsstory/70374.html (accessed October 18, 2013).

American Library Association (ALA). 2002. Privacy: An interpretation of the Library Bill of Rights, June 19. http://www.ala.org/advocacy/sites/ala.org.advocacy/files/content/intfreedom/librarybill/interpretations/privacyinterpretation.pdf (accessed October 18, 2013).

American Library Association (ALA). 2009. Resolution on the reauthorization of Section 215 of the USA PATRIOT Act, 2009. http://www.ala.org/offices/oif/ifissues/2009usapatriotactreauthorize (accessed June 13, 2012).

American Library Association (ALA). 2012a. Campaign for reader privacy. http://www.readerprivacy.org (accessed June 13, 2012).

American Library Association (ALA). 2012b. Code of ethics of American Library Association. http://www.ala.org/advocacy/proethics/codeofethics/codeethics (accessed June 13, 2012).

American Library Association (ALA). 2012c. Intellectual freedom manual. 8th ed. American Library Association Office for Intellectual Freedom.

Blitz, Marc Jonathan. 2006. Constitutional safeguards for silent experiments in living: Libraries, the right to read, and a First Amendment theory for an unaccompanied right to receive information, 74 UMKC L. Rev. 799, 805.

CAL. CIV. CODE § 1799.3 (2012).

Cate, Fred H. 2000. Principles of Internet Privacy, 32 Conn. L. Rev. 877.

Cohen, Julie E. 2012. *Configuring the networked self: Law, code, and the play of everyday practice.* New Haven: Yale University Press.

Cohen, Julie E. 2003. Drm and privacy, 18 Berkeley Tech. L.J. 575.

Cohen, Julie E. 1996. A right to read anonymously: A closer look at "copyright management" in cyberspace, 28 Conn. L. Rev. 981.

Emerson, Thomas. 1976. Legal foundations for the right to know, Wash. Univ. L.Q. 1.

Ghitis, Frida. 2012. Google knows too much about you, CNN, February 9. http://www.cnn.com/2012/02/09/opinion/ghitis-google-privacy/index.html (accessed October 18, 2013).

Gonzales v. Google, Inc. 2006. 234 F.R.D. 674 (N.D. Cal. 2006).

Jarvis, Jeff. 2011. *Public parts: How sharing in the digital age improves the way we work and live. place?* New York: Simon & Schuster.

Katz v. United States, 389 U.S. 347 (1967).

Klinefelter, Ann. 2010. Library standards for data privacy: A model for the digital world? 11 N.C. J. L. & Tech.

The Library Company. 2012. At the instance of Benjamin Franklin: A brief history of The Library Company of Philadelphia. The Library Company. http://www.librarycompany.org/about/Instance.pdf (accessed July 16, 2012).

Martin, Kathryn. 2003. The USA PATRIOT Act's application to library patron records, 29 J. Legis. 283.

MICH. COMP. LAWS § 445.1712 (1988).

Morse, John T. 1989. Benjamin Franklin (1st ed. 1898).

Nissenbaum, Helen. 2010. Privacy in context: technology, policy and the integrity of social life.

Nissenbaum, Helen. 2004. Privacy as contextual integrity. 79 Wash. L. Rev. 119.

Nojeim, Gregory T. 2010. Cybersecurity and freedom on the internet. 4 J. Nat'l Security L. & Pol'y 119.

Olmstead v. United States, 277 U.S. 438 (1928).

Purewal, Sarah Jacobsson. 2012. Facebook social reader users are fleeing in droves, *PCWorld*, May 8. http://www.pcworld.com/article/255210/facebooks_social_reader_users_are_fleeing_in_droves.html (accessed October 18, 2013).

Richards, Neil M. 2013a, The dangers of surveillance. 126 Harv. L. Rev. 1934.

Richards, Neil M. 2013b. The perils of social reading, 101 Geo. L. J. 689.

Richards, Neil M. 2011. Limits of tort privacy, 9 J. Telecom. & High Tech. L. 357.

Richards, Neil M. 2010. The puzzle of Brandeis, privacy and speech, 63 Vand. L. Rev. 1295.

Richards, Neil M. 2008. Intellectual privacy, 87 Tex. L. Rev. 387.

Richards, Neil M., and Daniel J. Solove. 2010. Prosser's privacy law: A mixed legacy, 98 Calif. L. Rev. 1887.

Snyder v. Phelps, 131 S. Ct. 1207 (2011).

Solove, Daniel J. 2010. Understanding privacy.

Solove, Daniel J. 2007. The First Amendment as criminal procedure, 82 N.Y.U. L. Rev. 112.

Solove, Daniel J. and Neil M. Richards. 2009. Rethinking free speech and civil liability. 109 Colum. L. Rev. 1650.

Stanley v. Georgia, 394 U.S. 557 (1969).

Stone, Andrea. 2012. DHS monitoring of social media under scrutiny by lawmakers. Huffingtonpost.com, February 16. http://www.huffingtonpost.com/2012/02/16/dhs-monitoring-of-social -media_n_1282494.html (accessed October 18, 2013).

Stuntz, William J. 1995. The substantive origins of criminal procedure. 105 Yale L.J. 393, 395.

Tattered Cover, Inc. v. City of Thornton. 44 P.3d 1044 (Colo. 2002).

Tsukayama, Hayley. 2012. CISPA: Who's for it, who's against it and how it could affect you, *Washington Post*, April 27. http://www.washingtonpost.com/business/technology/cispa-whos -for-it-whos-against-it-and-how-it-could-affect-you/2012/04/27/ gIQA5ur0lT_story.html (accessed October 18, 2013).

United States v. Am. Library Ass'n, Inc. 539 U.S. 194 (2003).

Uniting and strengthening America by providing appropriate tools required to intercept and obstruct terrorism (USA PATRIOT Act). USA Patriot Act of 2001 § 215, 50 U.S.C.A. §§ 1861–1862 (West Supp. 2002).

USA PATRIOT and Improvement Act of 2005, PL 109–177, March 9, 2006, 120 Stat 192.

U.S. Department of Justice. 2007. A review of the Federal Bureau of Investigation's use of Section 215 orders for business records office of inspector general. Office of the Inspector General, March. http://www.justice.gov/oig/special/s0703a/final.pdf (accessed October 18, 2013).

U.S. Department of Justice. 2012. Report to Congress on implementation of Section 1001 of the USA PATRIOT Act. Office of Inspector General, February. http://www.justice.gov/oig/special/2012/s1202.pdf (accessed October 18, 2013).

Warren, Samuel D., and Louis D. Brandeis. 1890. The right to privacy, 4 Harv. L. Rev. 193.

Westin, Alan. 1967. *Privacy and freedom.* New York: Atheneum.

White House. 2011. Statement by the press secretary on S. 990. Press Release. May 26. http://www.whitehouse.gov/the-press-office/2011/05/26/ statement-press-secretary-s-990.

Whitney v. California. 1927 274 U.S. 357.

Woods, Michael J. 2005. Counterintelligence and access to transactional records: A practical history of USA PATRIOT Act Section 215. 1 *J. Nat'l Security L. & Policy* 37.

Zu, Chen, et. al. 2009. The academic library meets web 2.0—applications and implications, 35 *J. Acad. Librarianship* 324. http://eprints.rclis.org/bit-stream/10760/10750/1/The_Academic_Library_Meets_Web_2.0_-_Applications_%26_Implications.pdf (accessed October 18, 2013).

Defamation Law and Intellectual Freedom

Dale A. Herbeck

Karin N. Calvo-Goller is a senior lecturer at the Academic Center of Law and Business in Israel. In 2006, she wrote *The Trial Proceedings of the International Criminal Court*, a book published by Martinus Nijhoff, a prominent Dutch publishing house. The following year, Thomas Weigand, a law professor at the University of Cologne, reviewed the work for *Global Law Books*, a web site associated with the *European Journal of International Law*. The review, a scant four paragraphs in length, praised the book as "timely and welcome." While acknowledging that the book "meticulously covers all relevant topics," Weigand went on the fault Calvo-Goller for "rehashing the existing legal set-up," an unproductive exercise because "a large part of the volume consists of a reprint of the ICC Statute and its Rules of Procedure and Evidence" (Weigand 2007).

What happened next was unexpected. An outraged Calvo-Goller contacted the site's editor, Joseph H. H. Weiler, a law professor at New York University, and demanded that the critical review be withdrawn on the grounds that the review "goes beyond the expression of an opinion, fair comment and criticism" (quoted in Weiler 2009, 968). The editor refused, arguing that granting such a request would "have dealt a very serious blow to notions of freedom of speech, free academic exchange and the very important institution of Book Reviewing" (Wiler 2009, 974). Weiler did, however, invite Calvo-Goller the opportunity to write a "comment" that would appear alongside Weigand's review. This offer did not satisfy Calvo-Goller, who promptly filed a criminal libel complaint against the editor in a court in Paris, France. While Calvo-Goller was a French citizen, this seemed an odd place to initiate legal proceedings. After all, the lawsuit involved a review by a German professor about a book published in the Netherlands that had been written by an author residing in Israel. Further confounding matters, the review was published in a forum devoted to European law that was edited by an American.

While the web site was available in France, the review was written in English (Liptak 2011).

The French court ultimately ruled in favor of Weiler. The much anticipated decision, issued in early 2011, held that the review expressed a legitimate scholarly opinion and fell within the range of commentary that an author might reasonably expect when publishing scholarly work. The larger significance of the lawsuit, however, is not so easy to dismiss as the case has "disturbing implications for all those who write, edit, and publish critical scholarly work" (Sutherland 2010, 657). In an editorial, the *American Journal of International Law* detailed some of the "implications of the pending action for academic freedom and scholarly debate" (Damrosch 2010, 227). If reviewers feared that a harsh assessment might trigger legal action, they might be tempted to soften criticism. For their part, editors and publishers might be reluctant to feature work that could trigger costly court proceedings. "Disagreements of the sort involved in this matter," the editorial concluded, "should be addressed through normal scholarly channels, free from apprehension that critical comments about scholarship could subject a reviewer or an editor to legal liability" (Damrosch 2010, 227).

This case is not, moreover, an aberration. In a growing number of instances, aggrieved parties have attempted, with varying degrees of success, to use defamation law as a way to attack or even silence their critics. The threat of such litigation poses a serous threat to intellectual freedom. To appreciate the full magnitude of this danger, it is necessary to briefly review the fundamentals of defamation law, to consider how defamation suits might impinge on intellectual freedom, and to understand how the strategic use of litigation might be used to silence speakers and limit speech.

Defamation Law

A defamation suit offers a legal remedy for any person or corporation whose reputation has been damaged by a false statement of fact. Under the common law, the medium by which the defamatory statement was communicated is an important factor in determining the seriousness of the offense. Before the advent of broadcasting, print was the major means for permanently recording and widely distributing information. With the advent of the printing press, a defamatory statement that took a written form was a serious offense called libel. In contrast, a defamatory statement that was spoken was a less serious matter known as slander. This distinction recognized the fact that the audience for spoken words was smaller and that slanderous statements were transitory in nature.

New communication technology—radio, television, film, and tape recording—blurred the simple distinction between libel and slander. A defamatory

remark, broadcast over the public airwaves, might reach an audience of millions. Because the statement was spoken, the common law suggested it constituted slander. In contrast, a defamatory email, circulated among a handful
of employees of a company might be considered libelous, even though its
audience was much smaller.

The old common law distinction quickly gave way to the new communication technology. In 1977, the American Law Institute took the position that
defamatory remarks that are broadcast should be treated as libel rather than
as slander. According to the influential legal treatise, *The Restatement of Torts*,
"defamation by any form of communication that has the potentially harmful
qualities characteristic of written or printed words is to be treated as libel"
(Restatement 1977, 182).

To prove defamation, an aggrieved party traditionally had to satisfy three
distinct elements: publication, identification, and defamation. In 1964, the
United States Supreme Court added a fourth element, that being fault.

Publication is generally the easiest element to prove. When used in this
way, the term "publication" means the message must be communicated to
a third party. The question of whether a work was published is easily answered when the defendant is a newspaper or a television station. Publication is not, however, always as simple as it appears. There are a number of
cases, for example, in which the defendant claims they were simply "repub-
lishing" statements made by someone else. *Vanity Fair* correspondent and
courtroom observer Dominick Dunne offered this defense against a defamation suit filed by Congressman Cary Condit. When Dunne reported that the
Congressman might be involved in the disappearance of Chandra Levy, one
of his legislative interns, Condit sued the journalist for defamation. In his
defense, Dunne argued he was simply repeating statements made by others.
A federal court rejected Dunne's defense and the case was settled out of court
for an undisclosed sum.

In addition to publication, the aggrieved party must prove identification.
In many cases, the plaintiff is identified by name. It is possible, however, for
a party to be identified without using his or her name. It would be possible,
for example, to identify someone by referring to them as the star of a popular
television show or as the chief of the local police department. It is even possible to identify someone by offering enough descriptive characteristics. This
has become more of a consideration in recent years with the blurring of the
line between news and entertainment. Consider, for example, the novel *Primary Colors*, which was subtitled "A Novel of Politics." The book is ostensibly
about Governor Jack Stanton, a politician from a southern state who was running for president of the United States. Many readers, however, undoubtedly
thought the book was likely based on the presidential primary campaign of
Arkansas Governor Bill Clinton. A library site adviser sued the publisher for

defamation on the grounds that a character in the book, who loosely resembled her, was portrayed as a promiscuous woman. The court dismissed her lawsuit, concluding that "superficial similarities are insufficient" to prove identification (*Carter-Clark* 2003, 293). In other cases, however, aggrieved parties have demonstrated enough similarity to demonstrate identification.

There is also series of cases in which individuals claimed that they were identified by defamatory statements made about a group of people. In general, courts have held that the larger the group, the less likely it is that any one individual has been identified. So, for example, the claim that "all politicians are crooks" refers to a class so large that it would be unreasonable to conclude that the speaker was referring to any specific politician. The issue becomes more complicated, however, as the group shrinks in size. One of the most influential group libel cases is *Neiman-Marcus v. Lait*. In an expose about the Neiman Marcus store in Dallas titled *U.S.A. Confidential*, the author alleged that the saleswomen and models who worked in the store were "call girls" and that the "most of the sales staff" in the men's section were "fairies." Some of the saleswomen, most of the salesmen, and all of the models sued the publisher for defamation. In resolving the suit, the court held that the 382 saleswomen were not individually identified because their group was too large. At the same time, the court held that the twenty-five salesmen and nine models were small enough groups that a specific could claim they were identified. "It is not possible to set definite limits as to the size of the group or class," the *Restatement of Torts* concludes, "but the cases in which recovery has been allowed usually have involved numbers of 25 or fewer" (1977, 4564a).

The third element is defamation. Speech is defamatory, under the common law, if it tends to lower a person's or an entity's reputation before others, cause that person to be shunned, or exposes that person to hatred, contempt, or ridicule. If a statement is defamatory at face value, and without further proof, it is said to constitute libel per se. A classic example of libel per se is an assertion of criminal activity, as when Dominick Dunne accused Congressman Condit of being implicated in the disappearance of Chandra Levy. In contrast with libel per se, libel *per quod* occurs when a statement is not defamatory at face value, but is defamatory with additional information. A good example often used to illustrate the distinction is *Morrison v. Ritchie*. In this case, which occurred in Scotland in 1902, a local newspaper announced that a woman had given birth to twins. The statement was not defamatory at face value, but it damaged the woman's reputation because members of the local community knew that she had only been married for a single month. This added bit of information, not contained in the newspaper's story, made the innocuous reporting of the twin's births defamatory.

There are, however, some limitations on defamation. A statement cannot be defamatory if it is true. According to the *Restatement of Torts*, "there can be no recovery in defamation for a statement of fact that is true, although the statement is made for no good purpose and is inspired by ill will toward the person about whom it is published and is made solely for the purpose of harming him" (1977, 325). This means, Michael Traynor concludes, "researchers who study objectively, verifying their work through careful peer review and editing, as well as the institutions that publish such work, have little to fear from defamation claims" (1990, 381).

Under the common law, the burden of proving the truth of an allegedly defamatory statement was placed on the defendant. This is important because it meant that the burden of proving falsity was not on the party alleging the defamation, but rather on the speaker or publisher. Fearing this arrangement might burden free speech, the United States Supreme Court assigned the burden of proof to the party alleging defamation. In *Philadelphia Newspaper v. Hepps*, the Supreme Court acknowledged that placing "the burden of proving truth upon media defendants who publish speech of public concern deters such speech because of the fear that liability will unjustifiably result" (1986, 777). Recognizing that such a "'chilling' effect would be antithetical to the First Amendment's protection of true speech on matters of public concern," the Court held the "plaintiff must bear the burden of showing that the speech at issue is false before recovering damages for defamation from a media defendant" (1986, 777). "To do otherwise," the Court concluded, could 'only result in a deterrence of speech which the Constitution makes free'" (1986, 777).

To prove defamation, not only must the statement be false, it must also damage reputation. Traynor observes that, "Given the focus of defamational law in reputational harm to individual persons or entities, much research, even if false, will be immune by definition from the threat of a defamation lawsuit" (Traynor 1990, 381–382). This is significant because it means the abstract discussion of ideas cannot be defamatory because they do not harm the reputation of a specific person or entity. As the discussion becomes less abstract, however, it might become defamatory. So, by way of example, it would not be defamatory to claim that chemical runoff causes cancer. This assertion might become defamatory, however, if it was falsely charged that a particular company is killing children in the neighborhood adjacent to one of its manufacturing plants.

Finally, with respect to defamation, it is important to distinguish between a false statement of opinion and a false statement of fact. This distinction was recognized by the United States Supreme Court in *Gertz v. Welch*, a case involving a defamation suit brought by an attorney who alleged he was defamed in a story published in *American Opinion*. In sorting out the issues raised by the case, the Court distinguished between an opinion and a fact. "Under the First Amendment," the Court continued, "there is no such thing as a false idea" (1974, 339). This protection did not extend, the Court continued, to "the intentional lie nor the careless error" (1974, 340). To many observers, this suggested that an opinion was protected by the First Amendment and could never be defamatory.

The Supreme Court has not, however, fully embraced this position. In *Milkovich v. Lorain Journal,* the Court recognized the possibility of a defamatory opinion. To illustrate this point, Chief Justice William Rehnquist offered a hypothetical:

> *If a speaker says, "In my opinion John Jones is a liar," he implies a knowledge of facts which lead to the conclusion that Jones told an untruth. Even if the speaker states the facts upon which he bases his opinion, if those facts are either incorrect or incomplete, or if his assessment of them is erroneous, the statement may still imply a false assertion of fact. Simply couching such statements in terms of opinion does not dispel these implications; and the statement, "In my opinion Jones is a liar," can cause as much damage to reputation as the statement, "Jones is a liar." (19–20)*

While Rehnquist was willing to extend a measure of protections to some opinions, the Chief Justice was not willing to embrace the idea that all opinions are entitled to a full measure of First Amendment protection. To aid in distinguishing between protected and unprotected opinions, Rehnquist offered a single criterion: whether the statement can be proved true or false.

Prior to 1964 and the landmark case of *New York Times v. Sullivan,* if these three conditions were met, libel was presumed to have occurred (and no fault on the part of the defendant had to be proved) and damages followed automatically. In *Sullivan,* however, the Court added a fourth requirement: fault.

To appreciate the significance of this landmark decision, it is necessary to briefly recount the facts of the case. On March 26, 1960, the *New York Times* published a full-page advertisement under the headline "Heed Their Rising Voices" that was placed by the Committee to Defend Martin Luther King and the Struggle for Freedom in the South. The text of the ad—ten brief paragraphs—offered a brief account of events in Southern cities to document the widespread prevalence of racism. The only person specifically named in the ad is Martin Luther King Jr., and he is only singled out because of the intimidation and violence that was directed against him and his family. In the final paragraphs, the ad calls on "men and women of good will" to make a financial contribution to the campaign.

Lester Bruce Sullivan, who went by the initials L.B., sent a letter to the New York Times demanding a "full and fair" retraction because, as an "official of the City of Montgomery," the ad had accused him of grave misconduct" (Lewis 1992, 11). When the paper declined to issue a formal retraction, Sullivan filed a defamation action in Alabama Courts. Under Alabama law at the time, Sullivan need only prove that the ad referred to him by name and that he was defamed to recover damages. Testifying in his own behalf, Sullivan claimed he was libeled by the ads reference to the "truckloads of police armed with shotguns and tear-gas ringed the Alabama State Campus" in Montgomery. He also objected to the reference to "Southern violators" who have answered Dr. King's peaceful protests with intimidation and violence." Although his name never appeared in the ad, Sullivan claimed he was identified by these demeaning references to the police. An all-white, all-male jury agreed, awarding Sullivan a total of $500,000 in damages.

The New York Times appealed to the Alabama Supreme Court, but that Court denied relief holding that defamation is not "within the area of constitutionally protected speech" (*New York Times v. Sullivan* 1962, 266). Although the United States Supreme Court had shown little interest in defamatory speech, attorneys for the newspaper appealed and the Justices agreed to hear the case. The decision that resulted, authored by Justice William Brennan, set aside the judgment against the *New York Times* and set out a new standard for assessing defamatory speech.

To lay the foundation for his decision, Justice Brennan traced the role of free speech in the United States from James Madison and the Sedition Act of 1798 to more contemporary times. Along the way, the opinion referred to political philosophers such as John Stuart Mill, and distinguished jurists such as Judge Learned Hand and Justice Louis Brandeis, and landmark decisions. From these fragments, Justice Brennan created a First Amendment that embraced "a profound national commitment to the principle that debate on public issues should be uninhibited, robust, and wide-open, and that it may well include vehement, caustic, and sometimes unpleasantly sharp attacks on government and public officials" (*New York Times v. Sullivan 1964*, 271).

Having come this far, it might seem that Justice Brennan would conclude that the First Amendment should protect any and all criticism of public officials. Justice Brennan was not, however, willing to go that far. Rather, he recognized the possibility that some criticism might be so outrageous as to be unworthy of constitutional protection. To distinguish between protected and unprotected speech, Justice Brennan crafted an "actual malice" rule. Under this formulation, public officials would need to demonstrate that a defamatory statement was made "with knowledge that it was false or with reckless disregard of whether it was false or not" (1964, 280).

In the years since *Sullivan*, the Supreme Court has expanded the actual malice rule to include both public figures as well as public officials, it has broadened the definition of public officials to include those who have substantial responsibility for the conduct of government affairs, and it has defined official conduct to include private matters that touch on a person's fitness for public office. These protections have created "breathing space" for speech on matters of public concern, even speech that includes false statements. Defamatory statements regarding matters of public concern are only subject to liability if it can be shown that they are made with actual malice. It should be noted, however, that false statements of facts about either private matters or private persons receive limited First Amendment protection.

While the "actual malice" test has received most of the scholarly attention, Justice Brennan's opinion had a practical dimension too. In his concurring opinion, Justice Hugo Black warned that "malice" is "an elusive, abstract concept, hard to prove and hard to disprove. The requirement that malice be proved provides at best an evanescent protection for the right to critically discuss public affairs and certainly does not measure up to the sturdy safeguard embodied in the First Amendment" (1964, 294). In this instance, Justice Black's concern was more than theoretical. If *New York Times v. Sullivan* was remanded to the lower courts, a sympathetic Alabama jury might simply conclude that the newspaper had acted with malice. The paper had, after all, failed to validate the truth of the various assertions contained in the advertisement.

To make sure that lower courts applied the actual malice test with rigor, Justice Brennan set out a series of "procedural safeguards" to protect defendants in defamation cases (Herbeck 2013, 2). He assigned the burden of proof to the plaintiff, he required that "judges conduct an independent examination of the whole record" to determine whether the heightened burden had been satisfied (*New York Times v. Sullivan* 1964, 285), and he demanded that actual malice be proven with "convincing clarity" (1964, 285–286). These standards, combined with the "actual malice test," created the space for the discussion and debate that Justice Brennan thought was demanded by the First Amendment.

Defamation Law and Intellectual Freedom

The attempt to apply defamation law to academic scholarship is, according to Amy Gadja, a "relatively recent phenomenon. In the century or so following the first reported U.S. case involving alleged defamation by a professor only about a dozen reported cases involved an academic suing for defamation and not a single one was directed against a fellow academic or an academic journal" (Gadja 2009, 161–162). Two of the early cases, for example, involved suits brought by academics against newspapers for publishing falsehoods (*Edwards v. National Audubon Society*) or allegations of sexual misconduct (*McClean v. Scripps*).

This pattern abruptly changed in *Neary v. Regents of the University of California*, a 1988 case brought by a rancher who sued the university and three of its professors for defamation. The suit involved a herd of pregnant heifers purchased by George Neary. Fearing that the herd was infested with scabies mites, state and federal authorities sprayed the herd with the chemical toxaphene. The following spring, when the heifers began calving, roughly one-quarter of the 400 newborn calves died. In an effort to understand why this happened, officials arranged for an investigation by veterinarians from the University of California at Davis. After reviewing the facts, the veterinarians concluded that the death of the calves were not caused by the spraying of toxaphene, but rather due to inadequate care and feeding. At outraged Neary sued, alleging among other things, that the report was defamatory because it contained false statement of facts.

Since he was a public figure, Neary was required to prove actual malice. After hearing the evidence, the jury found that twelve statements in the report were defamatory and awarded Neary a total of $7 million in general damages. University officials were stunned by the outcome and warned of dire consequences. An attorney for the school, John F. Lundberg, claimed the decision "will have a chilling effect on the research and expert opinion we expect of university professors, even in areas of controversy" (Hager 1988). "A preoccupation with avoiding litigation, and its risk of exorbitant damages," Michael Traynor warned, "could discourage not only forthright factual reporting, but also the publication of innovative ideas" (Traynor 1990, 376). To determine whether there is any merit to these warnings, it is important to delineate some of the ways in which defamation law has been used to limit expression.

Defamation Law as Censorship

As traditionally conceived, defamation law offers aggrieved parties a means to restore their damaged reputation. In recent years, however, some individuals and corporations have attempted to use defamation law as a weapon to suppress speech. While there may be limited chance of actually prevailing in court or collecting damages, defamation suits are sometimes filed in an effort to intimidate or even silence speakers who might lack the financial or legal resources to defend them. Even those with resources sometimes decide that it is cheaper to capitulate than to risk losing a defamation case.

The Chilling Effect

The threat of litigation is often sufficient to deter speech. "If punishment is the motive," Rodney Smolla speculates, "plaintiffs do not have to win to win, and whatever the parties' motives, plaintiffs do not have to lose to lose" (Smolla 1986, 794). In a very real sense, the cost of defending a defamation suit constitutes a "private fine" levied by the plaintiff on the defendant. If the plaintiff is blessed with sufficiently deep pockets, it is possible to impose financial hardship on anyone who makes disparaging remarks. Such expenses do not restore the plaintiff's reputation, Lee Levine notes, yet they have "a very real inhibiting effect on the press" (Levine 1985, 90). The only way to prevent such suits, unfortunately, is to avoid any publication that might be remotely actionable. This could be accomplished by ignoring controversial topics or individuals, diluting critical commentary, or by adding restrictive language to qualify harsh judgments. "The very essence of a chilling effect," Frederick Schauer has suggested, "is an act of deterrence" (Schauer 1978, 689).

An excellent example of this effect involved a critical review by Frederic Townsend of *Born to Rebel*, a significant book by Frank Sulloway dealing with birth order and political drive. When the review was accepted for publication, the referees suggested it might form the basis for a productive roundtable discussion. Since Sulloway's work was being featured, Gary Johnson, the editor of *Politics and the Life Sciences* invited Sulloway to participate. According to Johnson's account, Sulloway initially agreed to participate, but later had a change of heart and alleged that the review was defamatory. Sulloway threatened to defend his reputation in court and the controversy spilled over into the popular press. Johnson stood his ground and, after a five-year delay, the roundtable was finally published in September 2000. In an editorial response to the essay, Johnson lamented that "Scholars, scientists, and publishers cannot focus properly on what should be their principal concerns if the threats of catastrophic legal costs hangs over them and their organizations and journals" (2000, 241). To solve this problem, Johnson proposed a "multidisciplinary legal defense fund" that could be invoked to "reduce the likelihood that important research, analysis, or criticism will not be carried out or will remain unpublished because of potential legal complications" (Johnson 2000, 241).

"In a series of recent cases," Gajda notes, "small, poorly funded academic journals have simply withdrawn published articles when faced with threats of a defamation lawsuit" (Gadja 2009, 176). In 2005, for example, both the author and the *University of San Francisco Law Review* were threatened with legal action for an article about how child custody cases involving allegations of domestic violence were treated under international law. In the article, Professor Merle Weiner made two passing references to one such case and one of the parties threatened to sue. Simply defending against such a suit would be expensive and, when Weiner's home institution, the University of Oregon, renounced any legal obligation to defend the professor, Weiner reluctantly decided not to contest the case and agreed to withdraw the offending paragraph. The law review subsequently concluded that it would cost less to expunge the objectionable paragraph than to defend against a defamation action. The content at issue was promptly removed from the journal's electronic archives.

In both of these cases, the mere threat of a defamation action had consequences. The risk of legal action alone was enough for Professor Weiner to modify her article. The roundtable on *Born to Rebel* was eventually published, but only after the editor carefully considered whether it was worth the financial risk. In other cases, the threat of legal action likely might mean a work will never be published. Malicious speech does not deserve to be published, but the threat of a defamation action likely deters some legitimate criticism.

Strategic Lawsuits Against Public Participation (SLAPPs)

In the 1960s and early 1970s a special and disturbing use of defamation law emerged: some real estate oil, and mining interests began to file defamation suits against individuals and groups who had publicly criticized their activities or testified against their plan for development. Initially the suits were directed at environmental organizations, such as the Sierra Club. Soon, however, the companies discovered that suits against individual critics, such as those who circulated petitions or spoke at public hearings, were more effective in silencing critics than were suits against organizations. These suits raise important free speech concerns because the primary purpose is not to protect reputation (as in a standard defamation suit) but to use legal procedures to silence critics by forcing them to spend time and money defending themselves in court.

The growing number of such cases caught the attention of Professors George W. Pring and Penelope Canan of the Political Litigation Project at the University of Denver. In 1984 Pring and Canan began an in-depth investigation of civil suites intended to punish citizens for speaking out, characterizing such actions as Strategic Lawsuits Against Public Participation, or SLAPPs. After more than a decade of work, including studies of more than 200 cases, Pring and Canan published the results of their research in a book called *SLAPPs: Getting Sued for Speaking Out.*

The authors set out a four-part definition to distinguish these cases from more traditional defamation suits. In order to be classified as a SLAPP, a case had to involve speech that: (1) was intended to influence a governmental action, (2) resulted in a civil complaint (usually filed for monetary damages), 3) was filed against nongovernment groups or persons, and (4) concerned a significant public issue. Pring and Canan documented that such cases occurred in all 50 states and that it took defendants an average of four years to win a dismissal.

The study reported that, in many cases, a SLAPP is made possible by a speaker's use of hyperbole, exaggeration, or incorrect information in the course of petitioning a governmental body. Because no "actual malice" is involved, the person filing the suit—usually a party with a vested interest—is unlikely to win the case if it goes to trial. Nevertheless, the extreme language, inaccurate statements, or strong charges do provide the opening for a lawsuit.

Sometimes the suit will threaten the author, but it can also target the publisher. In Missouri, a high school English teacher wrote a letter to the editor opposing a company's request for a permit to operate a medical waste incinerator, claiming such incinerators cause headaches, nosebleeds, and "other health problems" and accusing the company of having "little regard for the public health, safety or the environment." In response, the incinerator company sued the teacher for $1,000,000 in damages. Along the same lines, Boise Cascade, a wood and paper products maker, threatened to sue the *Denver Journal of International Law and Policy* after the journal published an article criticizing the company for "greed and arrogance." The most inflammatory of the accusations focused on the company's dealings in Mexico. Rather than contest the case, the University of Denver had the article withdrawn from several legal data bases and issued an "errata" notice stating "this article has been withdrawn for its lack of scholarship and false content."

The growth of the Internet has created a new variation on the traditional SLAPP. Many Internet forums allow for anonymous speech and there are web sites for complaining about defective goods and poor services, rotten neighbors or promiscuous classmates, and even mediocre professors. In an effort to hold anonymous speakers accountable for allegedly defamatory statements made on these forums, some aggrieved parties have tried to learn the identity of their critics. Since the web site and the ISP promises to protect a speaker's privacy, these parties have asked judges to issue subpoenas ordering the web site or ISP involved to divulge the name of the anonymous critic. If the speaker were identified, it would be possible to file a traditional defamation suit. The fear of being unmasked, or of having to go to court to prevent being identified, functions much like a traditional SLAPP. Recognizing this possibility, the phrase "cyber-SLAPP" has been coined to refer to these actions (Spencer 2001, 493).

Finally, it should be noted that SLAPPs are not always defamation actions. Plaintiffs have also claimed business torts, civil rights violations, conspiracy to commit tortuous acts, or misuse of the judicial process. While the basis for the lawsuit varies, the effect is the same. According to Rodney Smolla, "plaintiffs do not have to win to win, and whatever the parties' motives, defendants do not have to lose to lose" (Smolla 1986, 803). The cost of defending such a lawsuit is a kind of "private fine" that the plaintiff levies on the defendant.

A plaintiff blessed with sufficiently deep pockets can impose significant financial hardship even in a case with no real merit. Such costs do not restore the plaintiff's reputation, but they do have an inhibiting effect on individual citizens, organized groups, and the press.

In an effort to level the playing field, more than half of the states have enacted statutory protections against SLAPPs. Under California law, for example, a defendant can ask a court to dismiss a lawsuit that violates the freedom of speech. Since this determination is made before the case goes to trial, the statute seeks to reduce the financial burden that chills speech. Not all of the states, however, have adopted anti-SLAPP statutes and there is no currently federal anti-SLAPP law. This leaves open the potential for "forum shopping," a practice where plaintiffs search for the state that offers the most favorable treatment. In some cases, aggrieved parties have even gone to foreign countries in the hope of obtaining redress.

Libel Tourism

Most of the aforementioned cases were brought in the United States. Under *New York Times v. Sullivan*, it is difficult for plaintiffs to prove defamation and recover damages. In an effort to obtain more favorable treatment, some plaintiffs have sought relief in foreign countries such as England, Brazil, Australia, Indonesia, and Singapore, which have lower standards for proving defamation. This extreme forum shopping has been characterized as "libel tourism" because it involves lawsuits that are brought in foreign countries against United States citizens. In extreme cases, neither party to the lawsuit is a citizen or a resident of the country in which the defamation action is filed.

An early example of libel tourism involves the 2003 book *Funding Evil: How Terrorism is Financed – and How to Stop It*, in which Dr. Rachel Ehrenfeld, an Israeli-born writer and United States citizen, alleged that billionaire Saudi businessman Sheikh Khalid bin Mahfouz (residing in Ireland) and his sons, Abdulrahman bin Mahfouz and Sultan bin Mahfouz, were fundraisers for Islamic terrorist groups. Although *Funding Evil* was published and distributed in the United States, 23 copies were purchased from online bookstores in Great Britain. Those sales allowed the Mahfouzes to sue Ehrenfeld in England, which places more emphasis on whether speech is fair and accurate and does not have the equivalent of the "actual malice" rule set out in *Sullivan* at the time. (A recent British decision, *Reynolds v. Times Newspapers*, provides qualified protection for the publication of defamatory statements that serve the public interest.) Although she was aware of the lawsuit, Ehrenfeld chose not to travel to Great Britain to defend herself, and the court issued a default judgment in favor of the Mahfouzes. The High Court of Justice found Ehrenfeld's accusations were false, ordered her to apologize and pay $250,000 in damages and costs, and prohibited her from selling additional copies of *Funding Evil* in Great Britain. Ehrenfeld attempted to have the judgment declared unenforceable by a United States court, but her lawsuit was dismissed. The court determined it had no jurisdiction over the Mahfouzes unless and until they came to the United States to enforce their claim.

This was not, however, the only lawsuit brought by Sheikh Khalid bin Mahfouz. Over the past decade, he has either threatened or successfully sued more than 40 authors and publishers (including several Americans) in Great Britain for reports on terrorism that mentioned him by name. Since few of these parties were willing to face these allegations in court, Mahfouz was able to obtain apologies, force retractions, and extract financial concessions. In other cases, he obtained default judgments because the defendant did not appear in court and the judge ruled in favor of Mahfouz without hearing arguments.

The impact of such defamation cases is significant. In July 2008, the United Nations Human Rights Committee issued a damning critique of British libel law, warning the "practical application of the law of libel has served to discourage critical media reporting on matters of serious public interest, adversely affecting the ability of scholars and journalists to publish their work." This was a serious problem, the U.N. report concluded, because in the age of the Internet, it "creates the danger that a State party's unduly restrictive libel law will affect freedom of expression worldwide on matters of valid public interest."

Even though the defamation judgments of foreign courts are generally not enforceable in the United States, these lawsuits still have a "chilling effect" on the freedom of expression. Random House and Cambridge University Press, for example, refused to publish controversial books about Middle East politics for fear of running afoul of English libel law and being sued in Great Britain. The impact of libel tourism will be even greater if foreign courts manage to create a fear of liability among authors and publishers for works published and marketed in the United States. While the Mahfouz suit involved terrorism, cases have already been brought in foreign jurisdictions involving a broad range of plaintiffs with diverse issues. The possibility of such lawsuits is the reason why libel tourism poses such a significant threat to academic freedom.

In an effort to protect U.S. citizens like Ehrenfeld and publishers like Random House, several states adopted libel tourism laws. The New York legislature was the first state to act when it adopted a "Libel Terrorism Protection Act" (also known as "Rachel's Law") in January 2008. California, Florida, Illinois, Maryland, Tennessee, and Utah quickly followed suit. The laws differ, but they all prevent the enforcement of defamation judgments unless it can be proved that the judgment is valid under United States law. Under the

California Libel Tourism Act, for example, California courts will not recognize a foreign court decision "unless the court determines that the defamation law applied by the foreign court provided at least as much protection for freedom of speech and the press as provided by both the United States and California Constitutions" (*California Code of Civil Procedure* Sec. 1716(c)(9)). Assuming the Mahfouzes were public figures, they would have to demonstrate that Ehrenfeld acted with "actual malice" before a California court would enforce the judgment rendered by the British court.

Because state laws provide only a patchwork of protection, a federal libel tourism bill was introduced in Congress, which unanimously passed the Securing the Protection of our Enduring and Established Constitutional Heritage (SPEECH Act). President Obama signed the measure into law on August 13, 2010. From a First Amendment perspective, the SPEECH Act is notable on three counts. First, the law would bar enforcement of a foreign defamation judgment if the speech at issue was not defamatory under U.S. law. Second, the law specifically protects internet service providers (ISPs) from foreign defamation judgments unless an American court determines that the foreign judgment would be consistent with Section 230 of the Communications Decency Act. This section limits the liability of ISPs for defamatory content created by a third party. Finally, the law creates a cause of action that allows an author or publisher to go to court and seek a declaratory judgment holding a foreign judgment unenforceable under American law, even if the foreign party has not attempted to enforce the judgment in the United States.

The SPEECH Act is not the end of the story. First Amendment law was born in a world with national boundaries firmly grounded in physical geography. In such a world, it was possible for each country to make and enforce its own notion of free speech. With the advent of global media, a system of law grounded in a physical world with firm national boundaries will necessarily come under attack. The SPEECH Act attempts to respond to this challenge by refusing to recognize foreign defamation judgments that do not adhere to the tenets of U.S. defamation law. This law addresses the immediate issues raised by libel tourism, but it avoids the larger problem. At some point, Congress and the court will be forced to reconcile the American commitment to freedom of expression with communication technology that transcends the boundaries of traditional nation states.

Legendary media critic and columnist A. J. Liebling famously asserted that "freedom of the press is guaranteed only to those who own one." While Liebling was complaining about the corrosive effect of media monopolies of his era, his remarks take on a different meaning today. With the threat of libel actions, strategic lawsuits against public participation, and the prospect for libel tourism, a new set of threats to the freedom of thought has emerged. The threat of media ownership remains, but it might now be said that the freedom to exercise academic and intellectual freedom is only guaranteed to those with both deep pockets and the fortitude to stand strong when threatened with a defamation lawsuit.

References

Carter-Clark v. Random House. 768 N.Y.S.2d 290 (N.Y. Sup. Ct. 2003).

Condit v. Dunne. 317 F. Supp. 2d 344 (S.D. N.Y. 2004).

Damrosch, Lori Fisler, Bernard H. Oxman, Richard B. Bilder, and David D. Caron. 2010. Editorial comment: Book reviews and libel proceedings. *American Journal of International Law* 104: 226–227.

Edwards v. National Audubon Society, 556 F.2d 113 (2d. Cir. 1977).

Gadja, Amy. 2009. *The trials of academe: The new era of campus litigation.* Cambridge, MA: Harvard University Press.

Gertz v. Welch. 418 U.S. 323 (1974).

Hager, Philip. 1988. Rancher wins $7 million in UC libel suit. *Los Angeles Times.* September 10, 1988. http://articles.latimes.com/1988-09-10/news/mn-1494_1_libel-suit (accessed July 1, 2013).

Herbeck, Dale A. 2013. Rereading *New York Times v. Sullivan*: The importance of procedure in libel cases. *First Amendment Studies* 47: 1–19.

Johnson, Gary R. 2000. Editorial. Science, Sulloway, and birth order: An ordeal and an assessment. *Politics and the Life Sciences* 29: 211–245.

Levine, Lee. 1985. Judge and jury in the law of defamation: Putting the horse behind the cart. *American University Law Review* 35: 3–92.

Lewis, Anthony. 1992. *Make no law: The Sullivan case and the First Amendment.* New York, NY: Vintage Books.

Liptak, A. 2011. From a book review to a criminal trial in France. *New York Times*, February 21. http://www.nytimes.com/2011/02/22/us/22bar.html (accessed July 1, 2013).

McClean v. Scripps. 17 N.W. 815 (Mich. 1883).

Milkovich v. Lorain Journal. 497 U.S. 1 (1990).

Morrison v. Ritchie & Co. 39 Scot. L. Rep. 432 (Scot. 1902).

Neary v. Regents of the University of California. 230 Cal. Rptr. 281 (Ct. App. 1986).

Neiman Marcus v. Lait. 13 F.R.D. 311 (S.D. N.Y. 1952).

New York Times v. Sullivan. 273 Ala. 656 (Ala. 1962).

New York Times v. Sullivan. 376 U.S. 254 (1964).

Philadelphia Newspaper v. Hepps. 475 U.S. 767 (1986).

Pring, George W., and Penelope Canan. 1996. *SLAPPs: Getting sued for speaking out.* Philadelphia, PA: Temple University Press.

Restatement (Second) of Torts. 1977. Section 581A.

Reynolds v. Times Newspapers Ltd. All ER 609 (1999).

Schauer, Frederick. 1978. Fear, risk and the First Amendment: Unraveling the chilling effect. *Boston University Law Review* 58: 685–732.

Segal, Jonathan. 2009. Anti-SLAPP make benefit for glorious entertainment industry of america: *Borat, Reality Bites*, and the construction of an anti-SLAPP fence around the First Amendment. *Cardozo Arts & Entertainment Law Journal* 26: 639–665.

Smolla, Rodney A. 1986. Symposium, Taking Libel Reform Seriously. *Mercer Law Review* 38: 793–808.

Spencer, Shaun B. 2001. CyberSLAPP suits and John Doe subpoenas: Balancing anonymity and accountability in cyberspace. *John Marshall Journal of Computer and Information Law* 19: 493–521.

Sutherland, Kate. 2010. Book reviews, the common law tort of defamation, and the suppression of scholarly debate. *German Law Journal* 11: 656–670.

Traynor, Michael. 1990. Defamation law: Shock absorbers for its ride into the groves of academe. *Journal of College and University Law* 16: 373–398.

Weigand, Thomas. 2007. Review of *The trial proceedings of the International Criminal Court*, by K. N. Calvo-Goller. Global Law Books, April 3. http://www.globallawbooks.org/reviews/detail.asp?id=298 (accessed July 1, 2013).

Weiler, Joseph H. H. 2009. Editorial: Book reviewing and academic freedom. *European Journal of International Law* 20: 967–976.

Part Four

The Arts, Social, Cultural, and Professional Life

Religion and Intellectual Freedom

Emily J. M. Knox

Every year the American Library Association's Office for Intellectual Freedom (OIF) collects statistics for books that have been challenged in libraries across the United States. The reasons for the challenges run the gamut from sexuality to political content. One reason that has been cited many times over the years by librarians that report the challenges is "religion." In some respects, it is difficult to know how this reason for challenging books is defined. For example, at the height of its popularity, the *Harry Potter* series was challenged for including witchcraft. There are several verses in the Bible that condemn witchcraft (Deuteronomy 18:10; Galatians 5:20) and these challenges could be interpreted as "religious" challenges. In another example, *The Da Vinci Code* was challenged by Catholic sources for its "blasphemous nature" (Karolides, Bald, and Sova 2011, 221). In her reference book, *Banned Books: Literature Suppressed on Religious Grounds*, Margaret Bald discusses the suppression histories of books as varied as *Oliver Twist* and the *Bible* (Bald 2006). Although the books that Bald catalogs are challenged for different reasons that range from promotion of evolution to blasphemy, they can all be classified as "religious." However, it should be noted that these varied explanations make it problematic to discuss religion as it relates to intellectual freedom.

If religion is defined narrowly, the United States is becoming a much less religious nation in the 21st century. According to the most recent Pew Forum on Religion & Public Life survey, 16.1% of Americans state that they have no religious affiliation (Pew Research n.d.). Although the survey accounts for many different types of religious beliefs (Christian, Agnostic, Hindu), this chapter will argue that this is a narrow construction of religion based on a conceptualization of the term that associates religiosity with organized religious practices. In order to have a less antagonistic relationship—as exemplified by the challenges given above—between religion and intellectual freedom, it is necessary to have more expansive definitions of both concepts. This chapter argues that the relationship between religion and intellectual freedom centers on how one understands the practice of reading and its effects on the reader. It begins with a review of previous literature and discussion on religion and intellectual freedom. It then offers a brief history of reading in a religious context and an overview of the connection between religious reading and positive or negative reading effects. The chapter then shifts to the modern era to discuss the development of an agnostic view toward reading effects which informs practices in contemporary librarianship. Finally, the chapter presents a conceptualization of religion based on a concept of "process of valuation" and a definition of intellectual freedom rooted in social justice. Overall, the chapter argues that because librarians can afford to be agnostic on the issue of the effects of reading, they are empowered to take a broader view of both religion and intellectual freedom. With these less limiting definitions in mind, it is easier for librarians and other information professionals to fulfill their professional duty to provide the best information on religion for the least cost to the people who use their institutions.

Previous Literature

Although there are many reference works concerning the censorship of individual works for religious reasons, there is little scholarly literature on intellectual freedom and religion. This might be true for several reasons but one of the primary ones seems to be related to the difficulty of defining "religion." Religion is a broad term and, as noted above, it can mean different things to different people. As Ann Taves noted in her 2010 presidential address to the American Academy of Religion, it is both difficult to specify as an object of study and a difficult area in which to formulate means to study (Taves 2011). The category covers theistic and non-theistic religions, animistic and organized religions, as well as broader social movements (e.g., Marxism as religion). It is also possible that the so-called secularization thesis, which holds that the modern world is continually becoming less religious, is also related to the lack of literature on the topic of intellectual freedom and religion. That is, it might be that as religion is perceived to be a less potent social force in our society, there is less interest in studying its influence within the academy. Although the rise of evangelical and fundamentalist movements in the later 20th century reduced general acceptance of this theory (Riesebrodt 1998), it is possible that its influence reduced the amount of research on intellectual freedom and religion. Finally, there also seems to be a stronger association between religion and *censorship* but not between religion and *intellectual freedom*. As demonstrated in the examples above, there seems to be an overall view that religions are focused on abridging intellectual freedom through the censorship of materials.

One article that exemplifies this viewpoint discusses the relationship between Catholicism and censorship. Ted G. Jelen argues that the Roman Catholic Church's position on intellectual freedom has remained unchanged over time and is linked to the Church's overall view of itself as a teacher to its members (Jelen 1996). This is in direct contrast with what Jelen calls the classical liberal viewpoint of John Stuart Mill on which much of modern society bases its view of intellectual freedom. This viewpoint stresses liberty without constraint as long as it does not harm other people. The Catholic Church, on the other hand, rests its views of intellectual liberty on three pillars: first, that objective truth exists; second, that scripture is vital but is not the final source of authority for correct living; and, finally, on the long tradition of natural law. In light of this, the Catholic tradition is very suspicious of individual reason. If one follows one's own reason one is, for all intents and purposes, obeying the demands of the flesh rather than the spirit. The Church does not want to remove all books but provide guidance on what books and media are best for the soul. Jelen bluntly states the "Roman Catholic Church is not committed to intellectual freedom as that term is conventionally understood" (Jelen 1996, 48). The church is instead focused on teaching people to live responsibly within the strictures of natural law.

Note that this is the conceptualization that many bring with them to the topic of religion and intellectual freedom. That is, since religion is focused on living a correct life, it cannot—by definition—be committed to the possibility of intellectual liberty. This conceptualization, however, is based in a very narrow understanding of religion. Although the Roman Catholic Church as an institution may not be dedicated to intellectual freedom, this has little bearing on individual Catholics, the wider Western world, or other religious traditions. The conflation of the idea of "religion" with the "Church" or "fundamentalist Christians" or "Muslims" is one of the issues that increases the difficulty in reconciling religion and intellectual freedom.

In 2000, *Indiana Libraries* wrestled with the question of religion and intellectual freedom. Doug Archer's article on the topic is one of the few works to look at the topic from a positive point of view about religion (Archer 2000). Archer begins by noting that religion and intellectual freedom come from common philosophical and theological starting points and need not be in conflict with one another. Archer offers three possible reasons for this. First, religion is not a monolithic category. There are, to paraphrase William James, varieties of religious experience and diverse viewpoints mean that there is a multiplicity of standpoints regarding questions of intellectual freedom. Second, Archer notes that the freedoms given in the First Amendment to the Constitution are rooted in the Reformation. Through a fairly detailed exploration of the history of Baptists and Anabaptists, Archer makes a case for the foundations of intellectual freedom as having roots in established religions. Clashes between various Reformist sects led, somewhat paradoxically, to the disestablishment of religion. "People argued for the right to hold a variety of beliefs and to print and circulate those beliefs. Diversity had become the rule rather than the exception" (Archer 2000, para. 10). This crucial point leads to the third reason for harmony between religion and intellectual freedom—both are rooted in the "soil of personal liberty." Although many Reformers wished for "religious freedom for me and not for thee," this attitude gradually shifted to one in which religious belief became part of an overall free market of ideas. "By the insight that religious wars had not, could not and should not settle the truth, and by the practical act of constitutionally removing the right of any one viewpoint, be it religious or political to official status, freedom for all was guaranteed" (Archer 2000, para. 13). Since there was no established religion, the marketplace of ideas—including religious ideas—became the law of the land.

Archer continues with a discussion of differing definitions of religion and ends by stating that librarians should view religion as "an inextricable element in human society" (Archer 2000, para. 18) noting that information professionals must be sure to remember that people, including religious people, have the right to advocate for any views they wish even if others disagree. Most importantly Archer states that librarians should see the religious community as an "opportunity for service" and not a professional roadblock.

There are two responses to Archer's article in the *Indiana Libraries* issue. The first is from Christian Pupont who argues that part of the issue with religious freedom centers on the semantics of the term "freedom." Religious ideas concerning freedom indicate that "believers do not simply claim that they have certain freedoms, but rather that they are free" (Pupont 2000, para. 2). He advocates instead for using the term "liberty" instead of "freedom." Liberty "better denotes the passive state of being able to act without fear of repression" (Pupont 2000, para. 3). This is discussed in more detail below.

The second response is from Barbara Luebke who describes some of the problems concerning intellectual freedom and religion in her small town in Indiana. She views religious censorship, particularly in the form of challenges to what is perceived to be unsuitable material and the use of internet filters in the library, as essentially a community issue. Those who move to her community because of its conservative character are surprised to find that the community is more heterogeneous than they expected. Most complaints come from this group, who are "very vocal about what they believe should be acceptable for everyone" (Luebke 2000, para. 2). Luebke ends by emphasizing policy and its importance for making all people feel that they have a chance to explain their own viewpoints.

In 2005 the Office for Intellectual Freedom Round Table of the American Librarian Association addressed the issue of religion and intellectual freedom in a sponsored program on the subject at the ALA Annual Conference. The speakers addressed two questions. First, "how can libraries serve both the religious and secular demands made by members of their communities? Second: Does demonstrating respect for religious life conflict with the separation of church and state. There were four respondents to the question. Each of their arguments is briefly described below.

Martin Marty began by addressing the growing controversial nature of religion in the U.S. He offers four seminal quotations on this topic. The first is from George Santayna who, in the early part of the 20th century, addressed the question of intellectual freedom (though not by using that term) through the lens of religious liberty. Santayana noted that religious liberty for all comes with a lack of certainty that is the basis for intellectual freedom. An agreement among those who were religious skeptics and those who were fervent believers laid the foundations for the first amendment freedoms found in the U.S. Constitution. In particular, Marty points to religious fervor of Anne Hutchinson on the one hand followed by Thomas Jefferson's skepticism on the other. This argument is similar to the one given by Archer described above.

Marty then focuses on Hannah Arendt and the importance of religious diversity to civil society. He states Arendt's thesis as follows: "if a society [has] one religion, they'll kill everybody else; if it has two they'll kill each other. Look at the map today, anywhere you'd like, if you have more [than two religions], they have to find a way and freedoms come with that" (Office for Intellectual Freedom 2005, 271). Marty is concerned that the polarization of the U.S. population is leading to a lessening of freedoms. He describes these poles as the "aggressively religious and the aggressively nonreligious" (Office for Intellectual Freedom 2005, 272). Marty offers four possible explanations for these changes: First, the end of Communism, millennialism and other movements led to a certain kind of unrootedness for many individuals. Second, he notes that the marketplace of ideas is working hard to fill this vacuum. Third, we have become a more individualist and less communitarian society. Finally, technology allows those who have previously not had a seat at the table to gain a voice.

Similarly to Luebke above, Marty argues that many religious controversies are nativist expressions. The campaign to put the 10 Commandments in courthouse is "not about religion at all, it's about who belongs here and who doesn't" (Office for Intellectual Freedom 2005, 308). Finally, Marty argues that librarians must work to make others aware that all arguments, both religious and nonreligious, have ideological underpinnings.

The second speaker at the forum was Susan Jacoby, an independent scholar whose remarks will be discussed in more detail below. The third speaker was a Pentecostal pastor and librarian, Mike Wessells, who argued that libraries should collect a wide array of opinions in their collections. He stated that "in order to affirm everyone, we have to be able to be offensive to everyone in some fashion, and it's important to remember that we also have to be offensive to ourselves" (Office for Intellectual Freedom 2005, 312). The final speaker was Doug Archer whose argument is given above. At the presentation he also offered a few practical tips for librarians trying to be inclusive in their collection development policies.

To return to Jacoby, she noted that "libraries are in no way responsible for what any reader takes away from a book" and librarians should focus on providing good reading material and not on "meeting religious demands of their community" (Office for Intellectual Freedom 2005, 309). She is particularly concerned with the issue of "demonstrating respect" to religious voices. Jacoby describes some religions as insular and notes that these will inevitably be "undermined" by the mission of the library. Since the library attempts to make all information accessible, it cannot help but make information available that is at odds with these religions.

Jacoby argues that the act of reading has consequences and it is because of these consequences that people attempt to censor books. She looks back at the Roman censor and then discusses her own brushes with religious censors. Her own magazine, *Free Inquiry*, which has a distinctly new atheist bent, was censored by a local library in New Jersey which refused to accept a gift subscription to the magazine because it did not fit with the "values of the community." She ends by noting that libraries should collect books that will not be easy to read. It is not the library's place to make sure that all reading materials contained within it are simple and easy to digest. This means that, inevitably, that they will be offensive to religious readers. These two combined issues—that libraries are not responsible for how readers interpret a book and that reading has consequences—are discussed in more detail in the next section.

Religious Reading and Reading Effects

The concept of reading effects can be traced directly to particular ideas of religious reading that can be found in the history of reading practices. For example according to common sources, in the Middle Ages, although many people could not read, those who could often did so for religious purposes (Lyons 2010). Religious reading was seen as a path to redemption. During the early modern era, the doctrine of *sola scriptura* (by scripture alone) led followers of Reformation leaders to read the Bible for themselves in search of salvation. Scholars note that among Reformers, although they argued that the Bible was a simple text to understand, there was pervasive fear that certain interpretations of scripture might lead to heresy (Gilmont 2003). What is most important here is that reading was understood to be a practice with consequences for individuals. Although the formulations of this fear changed over time, few argue that reading has no effects on the character or behavior of the reader.

The idea that reading can have effects is one of the reasons why one might choose not to support intellectual freedom. A traditional view of reading holds that reading "good" books is best because it will lead to good outcomes in the individual. For example, during debates in the late 18th and early 19th centuries over the so-called "fiction question" and throughout the public library movements dogma of "social improvement," librarians held the view that the general public should be indoctrinated to read "quality" books (Garrison 2003). Reading "bad" books would have a detrimental effect on both individual moral character and the democratic nature of society.

A few examples of this viewpoint come from articles from the *Library Quarterly*, published by the Graduate Library School of the University of Chicago in the 1930s and '40s. One example is Douglas Waples's article "On Developing Taste in Reading," which argues that there are both "meritorious" and "meretricious" types of reading and taste has little to do with what people like to read (Waples 1942). Another is William Stanley Hoole's 1938 article, a course in recreational reading, which was intended to provide "close contacts with books which lead to broader cultural improvement" (Hoole 1938, 2). Even earlier, in 1931, A.H. Starke explicitly stated that there is a marked "influence of reading on character" (Starke 1931, 180).

Although there was quite a bit of research in the area of reading effects early in the first half of the 20th century, such research fell out of favor later in the century probably due to shifting attitudes towards paternalism in the public sphere as well as the adoption of the Library Bill of Rights. This latter document states that "materials should not be excluded because of the origin, background, or views of those contributing to their creation" and "should not be proscribed or removed because of partisan or doctrinal disapproval" (American Library Association 1996). Wayne Wiegand argues that librarianship found support for intellectual freedom a more fruitful area of research than studying reading habits and outcomes (Wiegand 1999).

Another influence upon reading research can be found in what might be called a modernist view of reading effects which developed in the 1970s. This viewpoint was most clearly articulated by Jesse Shera in his monograph *Introduction to Library Science* in which he writes that "because we do not know, with any precision, 'what reading does to people,' or how it affects social behavior the profession can be magnanimous in admitting to library shelves books that present all sides of a subject" (Shera 1976, 56). Modern librarianship does not argue that there are no effects when one reads a particular text but that there is no way of knowing what those effects might be. Agnosticism toward the effects of reading and knowledge might be understood as one of the primary epistemological positions of modern librarianship. This conceptualization of reading also allows modern librarians and information professionals to provide a variety of viewpoints regarding a particular subject, including religion, on their shelves.

Religion and Religiosity: An Expanded Definition

When one thinks of "religion," what comes to mind? One might think of a figure like Pat Robertson of the 700 Club or James Dobson of Focus on the Family who embody a particular type of Evangelical Christianity. Others might think of the Tenzing Gyatso considered by Tibetan Buddhists to be the 14th incarnation of the Dalai Lama. For many in the United States, "religion" might have a political dimension associated with the Christian Right and their many social campaigns. Other images that might come to mind include churches, shrines, crosses, headscarves and other material of religious observance.

There is often a "public" aspect to these conceptualizations of religion. Religious people display their religion by discussing what they believe. In many cases, being religious also has a theistic cast involving a belief in an omniscient, omnipotent, and omnipresent higher being or at the very least in a transcendent "higher power." Religious people "do things" and/or "believe things." Religion is also strongly associated with values and practices that may be in conflict with modern secular society.

These formulations all have several things in common. First, they are images of organized religion often associated with the five major religions. Second, these ideas of religion do not include people who are agnostic or atheist. Third, they incorporate a narrow definition of religion that focuses on public actions. They are all somewhat limited conceptualizations of religion that would, in turn, have strong implications for whether or not religious people support intellectual freedom. That is, if one thinks of being religious in these ways, then how could a religious person be open to other ideas? How can one respect the free speech of others?

As discussed above, although one might have a general idea of what religion is in a decidedly "I know it when I see it" kind of way, religion is, in fact, notoriously difficult to define. In the most recent *Encyclopedia of Religion*, Gregory D. Alles states that it is difficult to "denote religious experience in a way that is not obscure . . . or circular" (Alles 2005, 7701). Since its establishment as an area of academic study in the late 19th century, there have been many efforts to define just what "religion" is. This section of the article does not attempt to discuss all of the many definitions given over time or even give its own definition of religion; instead, this section will provide the reader with some sense as to why religion is contested in the hopes of broadening the conceptualizations of religion given above.

Alles' article provides a good starting point for understanding why the concept of "religion" is not stable. He begins with an overview of Ernst Feil's three meanings of the term starting with religion as a collection of moral behaviors that are directed to spiritual beings, then religion as "an intuition of the universe as a whole and of oneself as a part of it" and, finally, religion as faith (Alles 2005, 7702). Alles then discusses strategies that scholars have used to define religion. For example, there are scholars of religion who focus on how religion functions; that is, they "describe what religions do." Other scholars employ Wittgenstein's idea of "family resemblances" among religions while others focus on religion as prototype. This final category is probably most familiar to many non-scholars in that religions are often classified based on how much they resemble one's own understanding of religion. As Alles states, "for North American and European scholars, religion is a category whose prototypes are Judaism, Christianity, and Islam, perhaps not in that order. Other religions are religions to the extent that they are more or less analogous to these prototypes" (Alles 2005, 7704). One could argue that the definitions of religion given above fall into this category of using a prototype for classification.

In her presidential address to the American Academy of Religion, Ann Taves also focused on the definition of religion as an object of study within the academy. She argues that rather than thinking of a religion as a "thing" one should consider religion to be a process, specifically a *process of valuation*. The term "valuation" refers to "things that matter":

> What we as scholars think of as religions, philosophies, paths . . . etc., could be construed as more or less formalized, more or less coherent systems of valuation that people call upon consciously and unconsciously when making claims regarding what happened, what caused it, and whether or why it matters. They are not, however, the only systems of valuation and may be drawn upon by some but not all participants in an action or event. Nor are highly elaborated, formalized, and coherent systems required for people to make such judgments. Indeed, I would suggest that the more formalized and coherent systems stand in explicit tension with less coherent, but more pragmatic, more automatic, seemingly intuitive processes of valuation. (Taves 2011, 292)

Here religion is a process of making judgments regarding life events. This definition pulls religion out of the realm of the how humans relate to the mystical, spiritual, occult, and supernatural and into the domain of focusing on how individuals understand particular happenings in their lives.

For the purposes of conceptualizing the relationship between religion and intellectual freedom, this definition is helpful because it moves religion from simply a domain of "doing things" and/or "believing things" into something more dynamic. If religion is a "process of valuation" rather than a series of proscriptions and demands, one can more clearly see why it is important to provide access to information that will aid this process.

Although the conceptualization of religion as a "process of valuation" provides a broader starting point for understanding religion, it is still somewhat abstract. In light of this, it is helpful to consider the varied ways in which people actually live out this process. Here we turn to social science and the measurements that are used to identify the religiosity and spirituality of a particular individual or population.

One of the most popular of these models is the Fetzer multidimensional measure which is used by many scholars and practitioners (Neff 2006). Developed by a group of scholars to study various dimensions of religion and spirituality, the Fetzer measure is composed of 12 dimensions of spirituality and religion (Fetzer Institute and National Institute on Aging 1999). These 12 domains are as follows: Daily Spiritual Experiences, Meaning, Values, Beliefs, Forgiveness, Private Religious Practices, Religious/Spiritual Coping, Religious Support, Religious/Spiritual History, Commitment, Organizational Religiousness, and Religious Preferences. These dimensions cover a wide-range of concepts that might be included in the "process of valuation."

Items in the measurement run the gamut from "I ask for God's help in the midst of daily activities" to "I think about how my life is part of a larger spiritual force." Note that almost all of the questions are answered using a Likert scale. That is, it is possible to state that "'I feel God's presence' 1—Many times a day; 2—Every day; 3—Most days; 4—Some days; 5—Once in a while; 6—Never or almost never" (Fetzer Institute and National Institute on Aging 1999, 15). It is the dimensionality of this measure that is of particular interest here. One might think of religion as an all or nothing proposition—one either believes or one does not. However, the array of questions and answers in the Fetzer Measure demonstrate that lived religion and spirituality is rarely static. When thinking of religion in relation to intellectual freedom it is important to consider both the process of valuation and all of the dimensions that encompass religious and spiritual life.

Intellectual Freedom and Social Justice

In the United States, intellectual freedom is strongly associated with first amendment of the Constitution. The amendment which states "Congress shall make no law respecting an establishment of religion, or prohibiting the free exercise thereof; or abridging the freedom of speech, or of the press; or the right of the people peaceably to assemble, and to petition the Government for a redress of grievances" provides the legal basis for freedom of both speech and religion in the United States. Although there are categories of speech that are not protected, American citizens are generally allowed to engage in a speech that is not incitement, libel, or slander. The concept of intellect freedom flows from this right but is somewhat broader.

The term conveys the idea that individuals are free to believe in, share, and have access to any intellectual materials. The *Intellectual Freedom Manual*, for example, defines the term as follows: "intellectual freedom accords to all library users the right to seek and receive information on all subjects from all points of view without restriction and without having the subject of one's interest examined or scrutinized by others" (American Library Association 2010, 3). Supporting intellectual freedom means that one is against censorship. This means that someone who supports intellectual freedom is, by definition, against religious challenges against material described above.

It is more helpful to define intellectual freedom as a right to access the whole of the information universe without fear of reprisal from social, institutional, or governmental powers. This definition is rooted in ideas of "liberty" rather than "freedom." As noted above, liberty denotes a state of independence from oppression—one has the agency to seek whatever information one wishes. This definition approaches intellectual freedom as a social justice issue and is based on the work of Peter Lor and Johannes Britz, who use philosopher John Rawls' theory of justice to support their view that knowledge societies must have freedom of access to information (Lor & Britz, 2007). Their thesis states that knowledge societies cannot exist without freedom of access to information. The authors use their own country, South Africa, as an example in order to demonstrate how lack of access to information can have deleterious effects on a society. "Our experience in South Africa during the apartheid years," the authors write, "taught us that restrictions on access can cause a regime to lose touch with reality. Curtailment of freedom of information is invariably associated with the dissemination of disinformation" (Lor & Britz, 2007, 394). Lor and Britz describe four pillars of information societies (information and communication technology infrastructure, usable content, human intellectual capacity, and physical delivery infrastructure) which cannot be brought to fruition without access to information. It is the third pillar—human intellectual capacity—that relates directly to religion and intellectual freedom.

Conclusion

The relationship between religion and intellectual freedom is difficult to articulate. At first glance, they seem to be opposing domains. If the original conceptualizations of religion and intellectual freedom given above are used, adhering to a particular religion means, by definition, that one does not support access to any and all information. This article argued for a broad understanding of religion to mitigate the oppositional stance between religion and intellectual freedom.

In library and information science it is imperative that, instead of focusing on religion as a negative domain when it comes to intellectual freedom, we focus on the human intellectual capacity for the process of valuation and the multiple dimensions of religiosity and spirituality. Although librarians' interactions with "religious" people who challenge materials in collections might be of the negative variety, librarians and other information professionals must recall that we are there to serve all members of our communities including both those who are certain of their religious beliefs and those who are not.

References

Alles, Gregory D. 2005. Religion [further considerations]. In *Encyclopedia of religion*, Ed. Lindsay Jones, 11:7701–7706. Detroit: Macmillan Reference USA.

American Library Association. 1996. Library Bill of Rights. American Library Association. http://www.ala.org/ala/issuesadvocacy/ intfreedom/librarybill/index.cfm (accessed November 24, 2012).

– – –. 2010. *Intellectual freedom manual*. Eighth Edition. Chicago, IL: American Library Association.

Archer, J. D. 2000. Religion and intellectual freedom. Indiana Libraries 19, no.2.

Bald, Margaret. 2006. *Banned books: Literature suppressed on religious grounds*. 2nd Edition Revised. New York, NY: Facts On File.

Fetzer Institute, and National Institute on Aging. 1999. Multidimensional measurement of religiousness/spirituality for use in health research : a report of the Fetzer Institute/National Institute on Aging Working Group. Kalamazoo, MI: Fetzer Institute.

Garrison, Lora Dee. 2003. Apostles of culture: Public libraries and American society, 1876–1920. Madison, WI: University of Wisconsin Press.

Gilmont, Lydia G. 2003. Reading and the Counter-Reformation. In *A history of reading in the West*, Ed. Guglielmo Cavallo and Roger Chartier, 238–268. Amherst, MA: University of Massachusetts Press.

Hoole, William Stanley. 1938. The course in recreational reading in Birmingham-Southern College. *The library quarterly* 8, no. 1 (January 1): 1–12.

Jelen, T. G. 1996. Catholicism, conscience, and censorship. In *Religion and mass media: Audiences and adaptations*, Eds. D. A. Stout and J. Buddenbaum, 39–50. Thousand Oaks, CA: Sage.

Karolides, Nicholas J, Margaret Bald, and Dawn B Sova. 2011. *120 banned books: Censorship histories of world literature*. New York, NY: Facts on File, Inc.

Lor, Peter Johan, and Johannes Jacobus Britz. 2007. Is a knowledge society possible without freedom of access to information? *Journal of information science* 33, no. 4 (August 1): 387–397.

Luebke, Barbara. 2000. Religion and intellectual freedom: a response. *Indiana Libraries* 19, no. 2 (January 3): 11–12.

Lyons, Martyn. 2010. *A history of reading and writing in the Western world*. New York, NY: Palgrave Macmillan.

Neff, James Alan. 2006. Exploring the dimensionality of 'Religiosity' and 'Spirituality' in the Fetzer Multidimensional Measure. *Journal for the Scientific Study of Religion* 45, no. 3: 449–459.

Office for Intellectual Freedom. 2005. Religion and intellectual freedom: Divine revelation in the marketplace of ideas. *Newsletter on Intellectual Freedom* 54, no. 6 (November): 270–314.

Pew Research. Religion and Public Life Project. n.d. Religious Landscape Survey. http://religions.pewforum.org/affiliations (accessed November 11, 2013).

Pupont, Christian. 2000. Religion and intellectual freedom: a response. *Indiana libraries* 19, no. 2 (January 3): 13–14.

Riesebrodt, Martin. 1998. *Pious passion : the emergence of modern fundamentalism in the United States and Iran*. Berkeley, CA: University of California Press.

Shera, Jesse. 1976. *Introduction to library science: Basic elements of library service*. Littleton, CO: Libraries Unlimited.

Starke, A. H. 1931. Children's reading. *The library quarterly* 1, no. 2 (April 1): 175–188.

Taves, Ann. 2011. 2010 Presidential address: 'Religion' in the humanities and the humanities in the University. *Journal of the American Academy of Religion* 79, no. 2 (June 1): 287–314.

Waples, Douglas. 1942. On developing taste in reading. *The library quarterly* 12, no. 3 (July 1): 740–747.

Wiegand, W. A. 1999. Tunnel vision and blind spots: What the past tells us about the present; reflections on the Twentieth-century history of American librarianship. *The library quarterly* 69, no. 1: 1–32.

Art Censorship Today

Svetlana Mintcheva

The Impulse to Censor

On an otherwise peaceful October afternoon in 2010, a woman armed with a crowbar entered the Loveland Museum/Gallery in Colorado and smashed the plexiglass case holding a multi-panel lithograph that collaged various images from popular culture and religion. As she reached in and ripped out the work, the woman was screaming: "How can you desecrate my Lord?" The lithograph, by Mexico-born artist Enrique Chagoya had become the subject of controversy because, among multiple other images, it collaged a pop image of Jesus Christ with a drawing of the body of a woman engaged in a sexual act. However, as it was displayed in a city owned gallery, the First Amendment had so far protected it from the censorious zeal of a city councilman and local church groups (Frosch 2010).

A few months later, in April 2011, two unidentified men entered the Yvon Lambert Collection in Avignon, France, and attacked American photographer Andres Serrano's 24-year old photograph, *Piss Christ*, with screwdrivers and a ice pick. The vandalism followed a protest against the exhibition led by the Civitas Institute and other organizations dedicated to "defend[ing] the honor of the Son of God" (Chrisafis 2011).

Such acts of violence against inanimate objects tell us something about the power of images to arouse strong emotions, which include the desire to suppress, or even destroy them. Periods of iconoclasm, when images are destroyed on a massive scale in an effort to eradicate the dangerous symbolism they contain, recur through history and invariably accompany shifts in political and religious power. Long before the Taliban blew up the images of the Buddha in Bamiyan Valley in 2001, King Hezekiah purged the Temple of Jerusalem of idols and destroyed Moses' bronze serpent; early Christians destroyed sculptures of the Roman gods; Protestant reformers attacked

Catholic statues; Pueblo Indians burned and destroyed crucifixes in their war against Spanish colonizers; and the Soviet revolution destroyed churches. Less than a century later images of Soviet leaders were themselves destroyed, proving that secular political idols can be just as hated—and potentially dangerous—as religious ones. Political power battles find both expression and additional fuel in attacks on symbolic objects.

The classic image of censorship is, indeed, that of officials in power physically destroying books and art in public rituals: It could be Savonarola's so-called "Bonfires of the Vanities" in 15th century Florence, where "immoral" books, paintings and art

Figure 1: Seal of The New York Society for the Suppression of Vice

were cast into the bonfire along with other "sin-producing" objects like mirrors, cosmetics, fine dresses, playing cards, and musical instruments; the actions of Anthony Comstock's New York Society for the Suppression of Vice in late 19th century U.S.A., eloquently represented in the Society's seal, whose surface is split between an image of a man being thrust into a jail cell and another of a man in a top hat casting a book into a bonfire (fig.1); or the ritualistic Nazi book burnings of the 1930s.

This kind of dramatic grand scale censorship accounts for a very small fraction of the work suppressed today. Regimes of wholesale overt censorship do exist but not as part of developed democracies, which all hold freedom in general and freedom of speech in particular, as core principles. And nowhere is freedom of speech as cherished a principle as it is in the United States. The First Amendment of the United States Constitution prohibits government officials from suppressing speech based on the viewpoint it expresses. While initially interpreted to protect mainly political speech (hence Comstock could attack "obscenity" undisturbed), the interpretation gradually broadened to the point where today the First Amendment protects entertainment as well as the press, images as well as words. Artistic expression, whether in film, painting, or even video games, conveys views and opinions and thus participates in the democratic marketplace of ideas.

As a result of broad constitutional protections the heavy hand of government rarely falls directly on artistic expression, yet subtler forms of censorship are ubiquitous. New incarnations of censorship resist being identified as such and may, indeed, fall outside the legal definition of censorship, which is limited to public officials discriminating against viewpoints. If a private entity—be it an Internet intermediary like Google or a private museum—removes a work of art from its virtual or real walls, this is not censorship in the eyes of the law. Neither is the removal of public funding from an arts institution censorship under the law unless there is a direct and proven link between the funding decision and the suppression of a particular viewpoint. Nevertheless, both private acts of suppression and the political manipulations of the public purse strings have constraining effects on artistic freedom. As discussed later in this chapter, they can be even more efficient than direct government censorship in forcing both artists and art institutions to censor themselves.

This is not to say that government has entirely surrendered its role as censor. As we shall see, government officials are not always aware of their responsibilities under the law and often misidentify their actions as being sensitive to community values or protecting children rather than recognizing them as the suppression of objectionable ideas, i.e. censorship. Moreover, the First Amendment does not protect all speech. There is, indeed, no country today where free speech is an absolute. Obscenity, child pornography, defamation and libel, incitement to violence, and threats are all refused the mantle of constitutional protection in the U.S. Unfortunately, it is sometimes hard to draw a clear line between protected and unprotected material, which tends to lead down the slippery slope of self-censorship.

Multifaceted as the censorship of art is in its methods, its targets are stunningly consistent: sex (including nudity), commentary on religion, and political content. I will focus on each of these in turn, tracing the various manifestations of censorship in each category. I will then cast a critical eye on a compromise solution art institutions tend to use so as to deflect calls for the removal of artwork because it offends someone: the warning label. No essay on art censorship today would be complete without mentioning money, the market and copyright law and their joint effect on artistic freedom. Alongside these relatively new neo-liberal modes of constraining artistic freedom, I will briefly note some current-day incarnations of that oldest of censorship techniques: vandalism. Throughout I use the word censorship not in its narrow legal sense, but according to its common dictionary definition as suppression of speech considered objectionable by anyone with the power to do so.

1. Sex: Art is Never Obscene (But What is Art?)

The 1989 retrospective of the work of photographer Robert Mapplethorpe, *The Perfect Moment*, had traveled—among heated controversy, but free of legal problems—to several venues before coming to the Cincinnati Contemporary Arts Center (CAC). In Cincinnati, Citizens for Community Values, a conservative group, convinced the District Attorney to press obscenity charges against CAC and its then-director, Dennis Barrie. At issue were several photographs representing sexually explicit scenes from the black leather s & m gay subculture, as well as two images of young children with visible genitals. CAC and Barrie fought back and the case went to trial. After hearing testimony from art experts, the jury had to decide whether the work was obscene based on the three-prong test, which has been used to define obscenity since the 1973 case of *Miller v. California*. The answer to the first two prongs of the test, which ask whether the material appeals to the prurient interest in sex and whether it is patently offensive by local community standards, was clearly yes. The decision of the jury thus hinged on the third prong of the test: whether the material lacked serious literary, artistic, political, or scientific value.

Contrary to the work's "patent offensiveness", however, its artistic value, according to *Miller*, must be judged not by local community, but by national standards. The defense summoned prominent national art experts who spoke highly of the artistic significance of Mapplethorpe's photographs. Deferring to their opinion, the jury found that the work had serious artistic value and was, therefore, not obscene. The high profile failure of the prosecution in securing a guilty verdict in the Mapplethorpe case has pretty much inoculated art, at least art recognized as such by the experts, from obscenity charges (*City of Cincinnati v Contemporary Arts Center* 1990).

This is good news for artists with recognition, but not so good news for those without an established place in the art world, like the young underground comic book artist Mike Diana, whose drawings earned him an obscenity conviction in 1994 in Pinellas County, Florida (Comic Book Legal Defense Fund n.d.).

Aside from obscenity the First Amendment protects representations of adult sexuality. This is not the case when images of minors are involved, even when the sexual content of those images is entirely in the eye of the beholder.

So called "child pornography" or images featuring sex acts involving children is the most recent category of expression that has been refused constitutional protection (*New York v Ferber* 1982). The rationale is that the production of such images is inherently related to the abuse of actual children. Indeed, the exploitation and abuse of children in the production of pornography is a despicable crime that merits strict penalties.

However, the legal definition of child pornography has been expanded to include not only the representation of actual sex acts involving minors, but also any representation of minors, nude or clothed, in which there is a "lascivious" focus on the genitals. But who is to decide if a photograph of a child "lasciviously" focuses on the genitals? What if a straightforward image of a child playing on the beach arouses the "lascivious" interest of a pedophile? Should it be the potential reaction of a pedophile that becomes the standard by which we judge images of children? Vague as it is, the law leaves it up to the beholder to judge whether an image of a child or teen is pornographic or not. Worse, it loads the dice by often compelling prosecutors who look at the image of a child to think of how that image could be seen by a pedophile (Adler 2006).

In 1990, FBI officers raided the studio of photographer Jock Sturges and seized his equipment. The reason: his images of adolescents shot at a naturist resort in France were suspected of constituting child pornography. Charges were never filed, but uneasiness over images of naked minors has been growing ever since. In 2012, the Kohler Art Center in Sheboygan, Wisconsin removed photographer Betsy Schneider's work documenting the growth of her daughter from birth to age eleven, because of complaints regarding the nudity present in some of the images. The group exhibition, on the topic of family and children, contained images of full frontal adult nudity, yet the only work removed was Schneider's, one that represented a baby and a four-year old naked.

Vague child pornography laws have claimed victims among innocent mothers or grandmothers who had taken pictures of their children or grandchildren. In 2000, for instance, amateur photographer Marian Rubin was charged with child endangerment for taking pictures of her granddaughters, ages three and eight, frolicking naked before taking a bath. Police seized the photos from a commercial processing lab in New Jersey. Rubin was suspended from her job as a social worker, and put on probation. A year later the case was dismissed but not before taking a heavy emotional and financial toll on Rubin (Rubin 2002).

Established art is not exempt: In 2009, the Tate Modern in London removed a 1983 work by Richard Prince from a retrospective of the artist's work because of concerns that the image of a naked 10-year old actress, Brooke Shields, within it could be found to be sexually suggestive and thus to violate the law (Searle 2009). The same image was featured in a Guggenheim Museum show in New York in 2007 without controversy. But, given the growing panic around images of children and their possible use by pedophiles, a future exhibition of the image may well cause problems even on this side of the Atlantic.

There is no clear artistic value defense in alleged child pornography cases. Yet, few prosecutors are likely to try to test child pornography laws against an old and established work by an artist of Richard Prince's stature. If a young and less recognized artist produced a similar image today he or she would be taking a serious risk. Moreover, the institution exhibiting the work can also be charged under child pornography laws, which carry a sentence of a minimum of five years. All this makes artists who explore the liminal moment of adolescence extremely vulnerable. At the same time, art spaces willing to exhibit the work are becoming scarcer.

For a few years at the end of the last century it looked like child pornography law might expand to include even simulated images of children, so-called "virtual child porn." In 2002, however, in the case of *Ashcroft v The Free Speech Coalition*, the US Supreme Court found unconstitutional a provision in the 1996 Child Pornography Prevention Act, which prohibited "any visual depiction, including any photograph, film, video, picture, or computer or computer-generated image or picture" that "is, or appears to be, of a minor engaging in sexually explicit conduct" (18 U. S. C. §2256(8)(B), cited in *Ashcroft* 2002). Such an expanded law could have had disastrous consequences on art, whether a theatrical production of *Romeo and Juliet*, which, indeed, may feature actors appearing to be minors having sex or a film based on *Lolita* where a filmmaker may use body doubles to shoot sexually explicit scenes involving an adult male and pubescent girl. The actors in both cases would be adult, but would appear to be minors.

Still, representations of entirely fictional children in sexual situations pose a risk for their creator and distributor, as well as to the consumer. While such images cannot be classified as child pornography as they do not involve the participation of real children, they can be and are prosecuted under obscenity law, but carry penalties equivalent to those related to the child pornography. The severe penalties are a disincentive to those who would want to challenge an obscenity charge in courts. Thus, in 2010, a man pled guilty to obscenity charges for receiving, through the mail, Japanese manga featuring sexually explicit images of (cartoon) children. The case never went to trial, so it is unclear whether experts could have convinced the jury of the artistic value of manga (Kravets 2009). Essentially, the expression of pure fantasy is penalized as if it were a deed connected to the abuse of actual children.

The problems created by child pornography laws are a result of their vague and expansive formulation (i.e. the extremely subjective character of determining the presence of a "lascivious" focus on the genitals) and not of their original intent, which is to protect children from exploitation and abuse. On the contrary, the refusal of constitutional protection for forms of sexual expression under the label of obscenity remains singular in that no proof of harm to an individual has been required.

The definition of obscenity merely refers to an offense caused to "local community standards" by sexually explicit material that "lacks serious literary, artistic, political or scientific value" (*Miller v. California* 1973). However, the category of "community standards" applied to today's diverse society raises the question of who has the power to decide on where the line of offense is to be drawn. Many members of a community may find representations of homosexual acts offensive, but should government help impose their views on the whole community? The question of who decides becomes even more acute when it comes to determining the value of a work: few agree on the value of contemporary art, and this makes for exciting academic debate, but in a court of law such a determination may lead to a jail sentence.

Obscenity, by definition, does not affect work with recognized artistic value. Still, the very existence of an obscenity exception to the First Amendment perpetuates a cultural atmosphere where sexual expression, even non-sexual nudity, automatically raises a red flag. In fact, some of the most frequently targeted artwork today contains nudity or sexual content.

Simple nudity is fully protected by the Constitution, as the Supreme Court has repeatedly affirmed. Nevertheless, nudes are perhaps the most frequently suppressed category of art in the United States. This may be one feature that makes this country's censorship mores unique (religious and political controversies abound elsewhere). Controversy regularly accompanies the display of nudes in a public space that is not solely dedicated to art, be it a library, town hall, or county center. Often, in response, the work is removed.

On the rare occasions when the removal of nudes is challenged in court, the results are generally in favor of the artists. In *Hopper v City of Pasco* (2001), for instance, the 9th Circuit Court of Appeals held that city officials' removal of works by artists Janette Hopper and Sharon Rupp from City Hall Gallery violated their First Amendment rights. The two artists' work had been rejected with the justification that it could be misconstrued as "sexual" or "prurient." However, because the City Hall Gallery was a designated public forum, i.e. a space open to all kinds of expressive activity, the City had to show that any restriction was necessary to serve a compelling state interest and that it was narrowly drawn to achieve that end. The court found that the restriction on potentially controversial work did not serve any compelling state interest, and, since the City never claimed the works were obscene or offered evidence that children would even see let alone be harmed by them, the removal had violated the artists' First Amendment rights.

But the story does not have the happiest of endings for artistic freedom: In the wake of their loss in court the City of Pasco terminated the City Hall exhibition program in its entirety. Similarly, in 2003, Nevada County (California) officials ordered the cancellation of the entire Annual Open Studios Art Show at the County's Administrative Center because they realized the First Amendment barred them from censoring the exhibition by removing five individual works containing nudity (Fineman 2003). In both cases, unable to impose their views on what art should be exhibited in a public space, public officials opted to cancel valuable showcases for local artists. The organizations behind such programs are thus placed in the unenviable position

Figure 2: Janette Hopper, Comedy and Tragedy—1995 (9.5
X 7.25) Linoleum Print, permission courtesy of the artist.

of having to choose between accepting censorship or losing an exhibition space. No wonder they often choose to self-censor.

But there is also another reason why public officials get away with removing nudes: To pursue a legal challenge is a costly and labor-intensive process. Hence, for every legal challenge to the removal of a nude from a show, there are many removals that go unquestioned. A legal challenge is, however, not the only recourse in confronting censorship: public pressure by local individuals, civil society networks, and media exposure often succeed in preventing the removal of artwork. The National Coalition Against Censorship launched, in 2000, an Arts Advocacy Project, whose goal is to confront censorship through advocacy and education, without recourse to legal action.

Figure 3: Caption: Betsy Schneider Januarys 1998–2008, part of her series, Quotidian, removed from an exhibition at Wisconsin's Kohler, Art Center in response to complaints, permission courtesy of the artist.

A letter from the Project, coupled with media exposure and grassroots involvement, has often been enough to convince a public official to reconsider a decision to censor.

But why are nudes so controversial? To the casual observer of US culture—the observer who is aware of the nation's hypersexualized advertising techniques, avid consumption of porn, as well as of the proliferation of all kinds of sexual subcultures—the claim that nudes are so frequently censored in this country may appear to be an exaggeration. After all, audiences of all ages attended the 2010 Museum of Modern Art Marina Abramovic retrospective and not only witnessed plenty of nudity, but had to squeeze between live nude performers. The acceptability of nudes is to a high degree a question of location or, one may say, a form of keeping up appearances. The "sex sells" philosophy of advertising is pervasive but never explicit (sexual innuendo can be easily denied), porn and sexual subcultures are relegated to the private sphere and, in the context of specialized art institutions, the risqué character of the body has long become a rather tired cliché. Yet, in spaces that do double duty as exhibition venues and educational art centers or other public purpose buildings, even the most abstract or stylized suggestion of a nude body can be considered off limits.

Whatever the deep reasons for the exacerbated sensitivity to nudes in public spaces may be—whether it be the country's religious past, the obsessive discomfort with the body characterizing its dominant religious traditions, the guilt associated with the nation's insatiable consumption of porn, or the combination of these factors—the most frequent overt justification for the removal of nudes is the claim that children may happen to see them.

It seems that this fear is strongest in cases where children—and their parents—may encounter nudes inadvertently, for instance in the hallway of an arts center offering drawing classes. Yet, no harm has befallen children visiting large museums, where nudes are ubiquitous, nor has anyone even made an argument that children may be subjected to any specific harm by seeing a nude. In spite of that, time and again, the potential presence of children is used as a justification for the removal of nudes and few challenge the reasoning behind such an argument. Perhaps it is not any actual harm to the children that makes adults try to shield them from representations of the human body, perhaps adults are protecting *themselves* from the embarrassment they feel when seeing a nude in the company of children. The strong reaction to representations of nudes is much more understandable as a result of adults' unease at the erotic interest that a nude may arouse in themselves, than as a result of the effect of nudes on children.

Occasionally, another rationalization for removing nudes emerges: that nudes in a work place create a hostile work environment for women (in the case of female nudes; male nudes are rarely exhibited in the first place, which is a whole different story of power, patriarchy and tradition— when they are exhibited, they are not spared controversy). The courts have agreed, however, that a single painting of a nude is far from the type of repeated and systematic behavior that defines sexual harassment. In one case, for instance, where the City of Murfreesboro, Tennessee removed a painting of a nude from City Hall after receiving a complaint that the display of the painting constituted sexual harassment, the court held that the removal of the painting violated the artist's First Amendment rights as it was an "arbitrary decision . . . guided by nothing other than the subjective perceptions of municipal officials" (*Henderson v. City of Murfreesboro* 1997).

To this day, however, public officials are frequently in a hurry to remove a work in response to a complaint, rather than stand by free speech principles. As late as 2011, when an employee of the Marin County Civic Centre in California claimed the image of a nude in the annual Arts Council member show created a "hostile work environment," the work was immediately removed. After national free speech organizations NCAC and the First Amendment Project intervened the work was put back on display.

The censorship of sex and nudity has been practiced for such a long time that potential controversy over this type of content is taken for granted. Few stop to consider the cultural roots of the distaste for sexual representation. Many of these roots lead, of course, to religion. Yet, the religious grounds for censoring sex are rarely explicit because it is much more efficient to censor sex on the more seemingly "universal" grounds of "decency" (few question the universality of the concept) and the protection of the vulnerable. When art is censored on overtly religious grounds, it is, most often, because of the use of religious symbols.

2. Religion (or Should Taxpayer Money be Spent on Art that Offends Religious Sensitivities?)

Organized religion has a very long and well-documented history of censorship. Just think of the Index of Prohibited Books, the burning of heretics or the punishment of blasphemy. But the First Amendment not only guarantees freedom of speech, it establishes the separation of church and state which dictates that government cannot promote one religion over others.

Notwithstanding almost two and a half centuries of separation of church and state religious groups in the US have never given up the desire to impose their values and beliefs on society at large. In the late 20th century, such groups, in spite of their insistence on being the "moral majority," were finding themselves increasingly weaker. The values they espoused were no longer unquestioningly accepted as universal. Perceiving the loss of cultural and political hegemony in an increasingly diverse and secular society, religious groups needed to mobilize their constituencies and increase their influence. In the late 1980s a solution was found: target the arts!

The ensuing fight over what art public money should fund and what art public museums should exhibit became both a common ground and an organizing principle for a coalition between the religious right and fiscal conservatives. The religious right wanted to prevent any challenge to their beliefs from entering the public sphere blessed by federal funds (and that included discussions of homosexuality, AIDS, sex, feminism, as well as criticism of the

Church). Fiscal conservatives just didn't want federal funds to go to the arts: Of all social programs they would consider "inessential" the arts were, perhaps, the most vulnerable. In a brilliant move, religious activists took hold of the rhetoric of victimhood from feminism and identity politics and turned it to their own ends: this was not about blasphemy, they claimed, but about offended sensibilities and the taxpayer supported promotion of "hate speech" against religion. Fiscal conservatives gladly supported a movement that attacked public funding for the arts.

The work that was used to trigger right-wing activism was an image of a crucifix: Andres Serrano's photograph *Piss Christ*, a provocatively titled photograph of a plastic crucifix in a golden fluid. The photograph had been part of an exhibition that had travelled to ten cities without incident, and by the end of January of 1989, had finished its tour. Three months later the Rev. Donald E. Wildmon, a minister from Tupelo, Miss. and founder of the American Family Association, a conservative fundamentalist Christian advocacy organization, sent a letter to members of Congress and others claiming *Piss Christ* represented "demeaning disrespect and desecration of Christ." A month after Wildmon raised the alert, United States Senator Alfonse D'Amato dramatically ripped apart a copy of the exhibition catalogue containing the work and denounced it on the Senate floor as an "outrage," an "indignity," and a "deplorable, despicable display of vulgarity." (Comments 1989) This marked the launch of a decade long attack on the National Endowment for the Arts (NEA), the federal arts funding agency that had provided support for the exhibition.

Nobody is obliged to like an artwork, and Wildmon was free to rally his constituency against art that he perceived as offensive. But government officials do not have the same freedom: while they may dislike an artwork, they cannot use the power of their office to impose their personal likes and dislikes on the whole nation. Faced with this conundrum, Congressional opponents of art that was homoerotic, too stridently feminist or critical of religion found the formula "sponsorship not censorship": they claimed artists could make any art they wanted, but that they were not entitled to have this art supported by public funds. The very real threat was that, if the NEA did not clean up its act, the agency could be entirely abolished.

The ensuing decade-long war on the NEA enacted publicly in Congress and the media led, in 1995, to the termination of the NEA individual grants to artists program. The agency survived, but in 1998 the United States Supreme Court upheld a clause requiring the NEA to take into consideration "general standards of decency and respect for the diverse beliefs and values of the American public" when awarding grants (*National Endowment for the Arts v Finley* 1998) But what do those standards of decency require? Judging by the work that was targeted for Congressional attack, decency meant pulling public funding away from art about sexuality, and more specifically homosexuality or AIDS, as well as from art representing religious symbols in ways unsanctioned by the religious right. The reason the Supreme Court upheld the "decency clause" was that it was advisory and not imperative: the NEA was only required to "take into consideration" decency and respect as one factor among many.

However, this was not the way some public officials interpreted it. It was in the name of respect for the beliefs of Catholics that New York Mayor Rudy Giuliani decided in 1997 to take public offense at a mixed media work by British-Nigerian artist Chris Ofili to be displayed at the city-funded Brooklyn Museum of Art blockbuster visiting exhibition, *Sensation*. Among the list of materials used in the piece, called *The Holy Virgin Mary*, was "elephant dung." A federal district ruled that Giuliani's attempt to cut funding for the Museum and evict it from its city-owned space in retaliation for *Sensation* was a violation of its First Amendment rights.

Giuliani had to resort to more subtle methods. A few years after *Sensation*, another Brooklyn Museum exhibition included Renee Cox's staged photograph *Yo Mama's Last Supper*, with the artist, nude, in the position of Christ in the center of her re-creation of the last supper. In response, and aware this time that he could not force the Museum to remove the piece, Giuliani announced the formation of a "decency commission" to supervise art at city funded museums. The initiative was forgotten when the World Trade Center was destroyed by terrorists on September 11, 2001, and the Mayor faced more urgent issues.

Controversies around art with religious content persist with some regularity, generally spurred by private religious groups, conservatives, or just sensation seeking media. The groups protesting an artwork are invariably small, but their strident voice is amplified by media coverage and often appears representative. This rhetoric focuses on offended feelings and the misuse of tax dollars, but controversies always stem from underlying cultural conflicts about the acceptability of homosexuality, about the role of women, or about social power. It is these long-standing conflicts that account for the intensity of passion, which would seem excessive if it were no more than a reaction to a piece of artwork safely ensconced in a museum gallery.

The 2010 controversy over *Hide/Seek: Difference and Desire in American Portraiture* provides a useful example. A month after the exhibition opened at the Smithsonian's National Portrait Gallery, a right wing media group, Cybercast News Service (CNS), published an inflammatory article attacking some of the works in the show for their homoerotic content. The Catholic League, an advocacy organization, claimed offense and, soon after, two leading Republicans in Congress, Reps. John Bohner and Eric Cantor, threatened the Secretary of the Smithsonian with funding cuts if a 1987 video included in the show, *Fire in My Belly* by David Wojnarowicz, was not removed. Smithsonian Secretary G. Wayne Clough, in what many considered an overly hasty move, had the piece taken down within hours. The stated reason for requesting the removal of the work was that the representation in the video of a crucifix with ants crawling on it was a deliberate insult to Catholics. Leaving aside the fact that Wojnarowicz, raised a Catholic himself, identified with the suffering Christ, whose image he used repeatedly in his work (Cotter 2010). The disproportionate focus on a few seconds of highly ambiguous video footage was somewhat strange. Indeed, this was only one of several works that the original CNS article singled out—all the other works referred to homosexuality (and so did Wojnarowicz' video, with the difference that it also featured religious imagery). It seems much more likely, given heated political debates about gay marriage, that the true offense offered by the show was the very fact that the venerable institution like the Smithsonian had dared to devote an exhibition to art by and about homosexuals.

The exclusive focus on the crucifix is indicative of a cultural shift since the early 1990's culture wars, when federal arts funding was challenged by right-wing republicans in Congress specifically objecting to representations of homosexuality. In 1989, while discussing an amendment to the 1990 appropriations bill, which would limit National Endowment for the Arts funding for "depictions of homoeroticism" among others, Senator Jesse Helms stated "The American people . . . are disgusted with the idea of giving the taxpayers' money to artists who promote homosexuality insidiously and deliberately. . . ." (Quigley n.d.). After years of gay activism around AIDS and civil rights, attacks on homosexuality are, in general, more careful and less acceptable. Yet the discourse of believers taking vocal offense at the abuse of sacred symbols continues unabated.

Globally, constraints on art for religious reasons are on the rise. In traditionally repressive Islamic regimes, the glimmer of hope offered by the blossoming of somewhat open international art events like the Sharjah Bienial were soon darkened by overt censorship. Even in a nominally democratic country, like Russia, the "incitement to religious hatred" law has repeatedly been used against curators, museum directors, and artists (Human Rights Watch 2005).

But who owns religious symbols? For secular artists religious symbols are part of a shared cultural heritage and thus a language, a tool of communication. Yet, in the context of religious dogma, these same symbols have a fixed and vigilantly guarded meaning. Depending on how much political power religion wields in a specific place, clashes between artists and organized religion can result in the suppression of art and punishment of curators, in physical attacks and threats or in the subtler pulling of the purse strings.

3. Political Art (or Best Tolerated Behind a Velvet Rope)

When it comes to political art in the US, its suppression is generally left to private entities or becomes a matter of self-censorship. The First Amendment bars public officials from censoring art because of the political point of view it expresses, even when it irreverently uses a revered national symbol like the flag (*US v Eichman* 1990). Nevertheless, I will argue, decisions on funding or allocating exhibition space have censorious effects, especially when there are hidden political motivations behind them, and so do disingenuous calls for "balance". The bulk of opposition to political art, however, is encountered when the work occupies open public space—political art, just like the nude, is well tolerated in a museum and often controversial outside.

a. The War on Terror

A major test to the nation's tradition of tolerance towards political art presented itself in the brief period after September 11, 2001, a time when sensitivity to the victims and heroes of 9/11 was threatening to stifle any politically critical discourse. As plans for the reconstruction of Ground Zero were developing, New York Governor George Pataki pressed The Drawing Center Museum and the International Freedom Center (IFC), cultural organizations invited to occupy space at Ground Zero, to guarantee that their programming would never denigrate America or offend the families of 9/11 victims. The reason for this somewhat unusual request was that the Drawing Center had exhibited, in the past, such political work as drawings by Amy Wilson, which incorporated text bubbles featuring political opinion on both on the left and right, as well as a tiny stylized figure referring to the Abu Ghraib abuses; or Mark Lombardi's understated but revealing graph visualizing President Bush's personal and financial connections. Apparently, in his request for a kind of loyalty oath on part of the two institutions, the Governor equated political critique with denigration of America and offending the families of 9/11 victims (Dunlap 2005).

The Lower Manhattan Development Corporation, responsible for development at Ground Zero, went even further and asked to review the "detailed plans, program and governance structure" of the IFC—presumably to ensure that no content would be featured that could potentially be deemed unpatriotic and offend some groups.

The climate of fear which spread in the wake of 9/11 and was perpetuated by the War on Terror directly impacted artists working with unconventional materials. In May 2004, the Joint Terrorism Task Force detained artist and SUNY Buffalo professor Steve Kurtz of the Critical Art Ensemble (CAE) on suspicions of bioterrorism and seized documents, computers, and equipment used in CAE's projects, including scientific equipment used to test food for the presence of genetically modified organisms. It was the scientific equipment, which was to be used in a forthcoming art installation and performance at Massachusetts Museum of Contemporary Art (Mass MOCA) that drew the attention of law enforcement. Even after the New York State Commissioner of Public Health determined that the materials posed no public safety risk, the District Attorney continued to press mail and wire fraud charges against Kurtz. A judge dismissed the case four years later, declaring that even if the actions alleged in the indictment were true, they would not constitute a crime (CAE Defense Fund 2008).

Targeting artists like Steve Kurtz, even after the initial suspicion has been proven wrong, does not counter terrorism so much as inhibit intellectual and creative activities. The District Attorney's actions raise the suspicion that government officials perceive an interest in using the pretext of a ubiquitous threat of terror to pursue frivolous prosecutions and thus to intimidate artists whose work is critical of corporate actions and government policies.

b. The demand for "balance"

Having become a buzzword when politically controversial topics are broached, the search for balance often functions as a subtle disguise for censorship. In 2004, for instance, the Arizona State University (ASU) Museum was hosting a show, *Democracy in America*, featuring historical and contemporary examples of political caricature. The show was to run parallel to the pre-election debate between John Kerry and George W. Bush, which led to intense scrutiny on the part of local legislators. Conscious of the scrutiny, the ASU president forcefully insisted on the show being "balanced."

Balance is, of course, a responsible ambition. But the political pressure to introduce balance in practice often requires the silencing of critical voices. In the ASU case, it meant a mechanical counter-balancing of any criticism of the policies of the Bush administration with criticism of Democratic presidential candidate John Kerry. As a result, the curators were confronted with a thorny problem: Kerry had not been in the position to make as momentous decisions as the President, so there was not much artwork criticizing him; on the other hand there was not much cutting edge work celebrating George W. Bush. So what were the museum director and curators to do to achieve "balance"? They eliminated from the show the work of several artists who had been invited to participate, not only work that was explicitly critical of the president, but work that could potentially be interpreted as expressing anger at the status quo. Because the decision was made as part of the curatorial process—even though under administrative pressure—it was hard to allege outright censorship. Yet some voices were excluded from the show, casting a dark shadow over what should have been a celebration of the clamor of political voices in American democracy (Watson 2004).

Demands for balance have also featured prominently in attacks on programming relating to the Israeli–Palestinian conflict. In 2011, for instance, the Museum of Children's Art in Oakland, CA, cancelled a show of drawings by Palestinian children partly because the images depicted realities that bothered some groups concerned about a possible one-sided representation of the Israeli–Palestinian conflict (Tucker 2011).

c. Political Art Inside and Outside the Museum

As with the nude, political art's acceptability appears to wane when it leaves the museum. This is likely due to the fact that, while remaining within the confines of contemporary art institutions, most political art tends to preach to the converted, since the majority of art audiences today share similar political beliefs. Its political message thus tends to provoke much less response than its aesthetic stature.

Yet there is another reason why museum-ensconced political art rarely bothers even the not-fully-converted: the inoculating effect of the museum. Visitors enter a museum with the expectation that this is a space apart, where you just look on quietly, where you do not touch and do not take action. This, of course, goes against the very nature of political art, which invites more than mere contemplation.

As a result political art has the potential for stronger impact when it stages its interventions in spaces where it is not sequestered as "art." It is when it appears in those spaces—public streets and squares, multi-use buildings, airports or subway stations—that political art becomes subject to the most virulent censorship.

In 2011, African-American artist Fred Wilson's proposed monument to slavery, *E Pluribus Unum*, was cancelled due to pressure from parts of the community in Indianapolis, Indiana. The proposed work featured a replica of the figure of a liberated slave from the city's iconic Soldiers and Sailors Monument. The figure, which is a small part of the original ensemble, was to be displayed on its own at a different location. By thus highlighting a rarely noticed part of a familiar monument, Wilson's work would make visible attitudes and assumptions that informed the city's past, but were rarely brought out in the open. The complexity of connotations inflamed controversy in some small but vocal sections of the local African-American community. After much discussion, the whole project was cancelled (The Fred Wilson Public Art Project n.d.).

In the course of the debate the artist was, tellingly, invited to take his art to a museum rather than to a public space. Viewed as a museum piece the work would apparently be acceptable, its complexity of connotations less inflammatory. Unlike a museum piece, a disruptive intervention in the city fabric affects our perceptions before we can take the distancing attitude of aesthetic appreciation. Taken-for-granted expectations about public space, property rights, and corporate discourse can be jolted out of their routine complacency.

Public art, which has the capacity of transforming a lived environment, is increasingly restricted by various committees and permission processes and often just simply removed upon receiving a complaint. Sometimes not even a complaint is needed: a 2010 mural by graffiti artist Blu, commissioned by LA MOCA for the museum's show on street art, proved too uncomfortably political for museum director Jeffrey Deitch, who had it painted over less than 24 hours after it was created. Deitch was concerned about the proximity of the mural, which depicted rows of coffins covered with dollar bills, to the LA Veteran's Affairs Hospital and a Japanese war memorial (Finkel 2010).

Given the restrictions put on public space, which appears as hostile to art as it is friendly to advertising, and the often-quarantined space of the museum, artists are most successful in creating meaningful artistic interventions by doing it with no permit—often transgressing laws and regulations. Their work counters what I would call a "structural pre-censorship." Contrary to censorship, which happens after a work has been produced and put on display, structural pre-censorship regulates what can be said before it is said. Structural pre-censorship thus constrains the very possibility of production.

Structural pre-censorship is a result not so much of specific regulations on speech, but of laws and other economic and cultural practices that determine what constitutes "legitimate" artistic expression and where it can be displayed. Though by definition outside the law and thus beyond any free speech protection, guerilla cultural tactics are worth mentioning as a suggestion of how some of the most effective political art today entirely bypasses the free speech debate: its very creation breaks regulations and hence cannot hope to be protected as free speech.

Such cultural tactics comprise illegal street art or graffiti, altering the messages of corporate advertising billboards, and, today, with the extension of public space into virtual space, creating Internet hoaxes to expose the perceived rapacity and social irresponsibility of corporate culture. In one such intervention, for instance, artist collective the Yes Men, created a complex hoax, impersonating Dow Chemical spokesmen and creating fake websites for the company, with the goal of drawing attention to Dow's refusal to ever provide sufficient compensation for the disastrous effects of the 1984 Bhopal chemical leak. Running afoul of various laws, such tactics cannot claim First Amendment protection, yet they account for some of the most effective political art today.

4. Handling Controversial Content: Warning Labels

Wary of controversy but determined to show cutting-edge work, some exhibition spaces opt for the compromise of a warning label. It is much harder for a parent to complain if they have led their child through an entrance graced by a sign warning them of "adult" or "mature" content. If they then encounter risqué material with their child, presumably to mutual embarrassment, well, they have been forewarned.

Warning labels are used increasingly to protect the sensibilities of adult eyes as well (or, rather, leave it to the viewer to make a conscious decision to risk offense). The New York Jewish Museum's 2002 exhibition, *Mirroring Evil*, for instance, prominently featured a warning that explained that the works to follow had hurt and offended Holocaust survivors who had seen them. Patrons were offered the option of leaving through a door immediately to the left. Such warnings labels are by now standard practice; you can see them everywhere (and this particular viewer confesses to a tinge of excitement when she spots one). But how purely informative are they?

Preparing us to see something disturbing or prurient, such warnings may be seen as performative prophecies, which ask us to look at the work as disturbing or prurient and thus skew our perception of it.

One of the more creative—and self-reflective—uses of a warning sign was the advertising for the Brooklyn Museum's notorious 1999 *Sensation* show. Capitalizing on controversy, the ad featured a tongue-in-cheek warning that the show: "may cause shock, vomiting, confusion, panic, euphoria and anxiety." The ad was true to the show's title, but it also smartly criticized other such, more matter of fact, museum warnings. What the *Sensation* ad was saying, through hyperbole, was that art can have many strong effects. But that is obvious: images are powerful, otherwise why would we even care to spend time with them? It also, however, pointed at the absurdity of flagging a specific image as potentially dangerous, unless all we want from art is to reconfirm our pre-conceptions and inoculate ourselves against an unprotected encounter with the image.

Almost universally accepted as a political expedient way of protecting institutions against complaints, warning signs are not just an easy solution: they change the way we look at art and affect the expectations we bring to it.

5. The Role of Money and Markets in Censorship

In neo-liberal democracies the subtle regulation accomplished by means of pulling the strings of the public or private purse or by the mechanisms of the seemingly neutral market is sometimes far more successful than any attempt at overt suppression. It is telling that many of the controversies mentioned in this article are framed as debates around the use of money: one of the most successful slogans of those seeking to censor an artwork has become "taxpayer money should not be used to support art that is offensive." In spite of the legal protections of the First Amendment, government officials can continue to censor art by punishing—or threatening to punish—those who dare exhibit challenging work.

A publicly funded art institution can choose to be daring, but that means it will risk alienating legislators and then having its funds slashed the following year for the ostensible reason that there are other fiscal priorities. Indeed, as mentioned earlier, the mere suggestion of a threat to the Smithsonian's future budget made its Secretary, G. Wayne Clough, order—within hours— the removal of a controversial video from a curated exhibition at one of the institution's member museums.

If public money is always potentially accompanied by pressures to censor or self-censor, wouldn't art be better off if left to the free market? Not necessarily. What happens when public financial support for the arts shrinks, as it has been doing, is that foundations and private donors, corporate or individual, take its place. Private patronage, from Gaius Maecenas in Ancient Rome to David Koch and the Bank of America today, has many advantages, but unconditional support for artistic freedom is not one of them. And why should it be? For a corporation, supporting the arts is a way to advertise their brand, a goal better accomplished through backing popular blockbuster shows than socially critical and possibly disturbing programs. Individuals, on the other hand, can exercise subtle political pressure on institutions that have become dependent on their support.

Donors at a private museum don't have to try to avoid First Amendment imperatives by finding neutral reasons to cut funds to an offending institution: being private, they are free to use their financial clout in any way they like. For instance, big institutional donors may insist that a show that dares pose questions they do not like is inappropriate for a particular art institution.

This was the case in 2008, when the Spertus Museum in Chicago, a Jewish institution, was pressured to close down *Imaginary Coordinates*, a show combining historical Holy Land maps and contemporary artwork. Officers of the Jewish United Fund/Jewish Federation of Metropolitan Chicago, which contributes 11 percent of the Museum's operating budget, were extremely critical of the exhibition. They interpreted its questioning of boundaries as anti-Israel and insisted it was not appropriate for a Jewish institution. While the Museum denied that the cancellation had anything to do with funding, it was hard for anyone to ignore the connection between the Museum's sudden decision that the exhibition was, indeed, inappropriate and the pressure exercised by one of its largest donors. So much for the "new civic agenda"

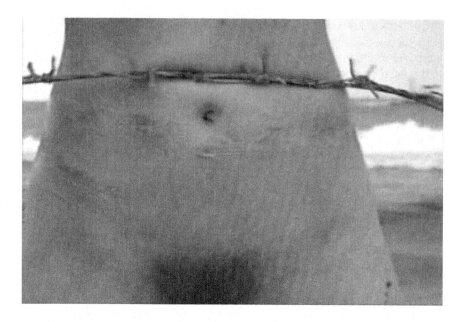

Figure 4: Sigalit Landau, Barbed Hula, 2000. Still from a single-channel video, 2 minutes, permission courtesy of the artist.

declared by the museum in the preface to the exhibition's catalogue, which promised not to be sectarian and to examine and question "broadly accepted Jewish assumptions" (Brachear, Snodgrass, and Rosen 2008).

It is hard to document the extent of widespread donor pressure on art institutions: the majority of decisions are made behind closed doors and before an exhibition opens. However, the large role private donors, corporate or individual, play in supporting high-profile expensive exhibitions is public information. Three and a half decades ago, Philippe de Montebello, the venerable former director of the Metropolitan Museum of Art, famously characterized corporate sponsorship of exhibitions as "an inherent, insidious, hidden form of censorship" (McGuigan 1985). Today, however, the Metropolitan, like other large art institutions, is deeply beholden to corporations. The Museum's 2005 marquee-name summer show, *Chanel*, for instance, was sponsored by no other than the House of Chanel. The exhibition, rather curiously, omitted any mention of the fashion icon's use of Nazi-era laws to consolidate her business interests in Vichy France. Was that blind spot related to the interests of the exhibition's sponsor? There is no evidence, but the abandonment of a critical perspective in favor of a simply celebratory one does provide grounds for suspicion.

The increasing dependence on private donors (Lerner 2006) has the potential to compromise art institutions' independence in many ways, rarely identifiable as censorship but with similar constraining effects. Donors rarely give money for general support, instead they give works, sponsor specific shows, or endow a wing. Their support is thus not neutral, but aims at leaving the mark of their vision or personality. What a museum visitor may see would then be determined by the arbitrary desires of patrons rather than by any consideration of the educational or aesthetic significance of the work (Thompson 2008, 219).

A hot commercial art market coupled with underfunded art institutions gives rise to further entanglements between aesthetic choice and money-oriented decisions. It is well established that museum purchases give legitimacy to an artist and a retrospective significantly increases the value of an artist's work (Thompson 2008, 221). A show sponsored by a specific artist's dealer then raises questions: Has the dealer's contribution influenced the programming decision? Such processes are, like the effects of private money donated to art institutions in general, quite opaque. The multiple entanglements between money, programming and art institutions, however, suggest that the mechanisms of government suppression are increasingly replaced, in neoliberal democracies, by the subtle pressures exercised by those who control financial resources.

6. Censorship as Collateral Damage of Copyright Law Enforcement

Though not intended to suppress viewpoint, but, on the contrary, to "promote the Progress of Science and useful Arts," copyright law has begun to function as one of the most active contemporary censors. Sometimes suppressing an artwork is "collateral damage" in the process of asserting intellectual property rights, at other times such rights are used as a straightforward means of controlling the terms of the conversation around a particular subject.

Digital reproduction technologies coupled with a postmodern backlash towards the cult of originality persisting from Romanticism into Modernism, have generated many forms that can be all grouped under "appropriation art." Such art takes images from popular culture or from other artists with the various goals of paying homage to the original, parodying or deconstructing it, or offering a social and cultural critique. Fair use, a U.S. specific exception to copyright protections, allows the use of copyrighted work for purposes of parody or commentary or if the derivative work is sufficiently transformative of the original (Stanford University Libraries 2010). But judgments of what is fair use can be subjective: The parties in a fair use dispute may disagree in their interpretation as to whether an artwork is sufficiently transformative in comparison with the original or as to whether it is indeed a parody of the source.

Copyright, originally extending for 14 years and renewable for another 14, to a total of 28, has now been stretched to life plus 70 years for individuals and 95 years for corporations. This means that pop-culture icons like Mickey Mouse or Barbie, which have long become part of the vernacular, still cannot be freely used. If an artist does use them and claims fair use, he or she may be forced to defend this claim in court. For an individual artist, however, to challenge a corporation in court is extraordinarily expensive, while enforcing trademark and copyright is often a well-funded job for members of a corporation's legal staff.

It took five years of litigation and over 2 million dollars in legal costs before photographic artist Tom Forsythe's right to use Barbie in his parodic series *Food Chain Barbie* was vindicated (*Mattel, Inc. v. Walking* 2003). While Forsythe was eventually awarded legal costs, few artists can afford the risk of having to carry the burden of hefty costs if a copyright case is not resolved favorably. In 2012, for instance, the law firm representing DLT Entertainment, the owners of the 1970s sitcom *Three's Company*, sent playwright David Adjmi a letter claiming copyright infringement. The offending material was Adjmi's play, *3C*, a parody of the sitcom. DLT demanded that Adjmi cease further performances of the play anywhere. Yes, the playwright probably has a fair use right to use elements of *Three's Company* so as to parody the show, but could he afford to assert that right in a court of law when faced by a corporation with much deeper pockets? Fearful of the costs of litigation and reluctant to engage in a long legal battle Adjmi decided not to fight DLT (Healy 2012).

Most cases regarding fair use and appropriation art hinge on the question of whether the new work sufficiently "transforms" the original. Other factors taken into account are whether there is substantial similarity between the two works, whether the new work is a parody referring to the original (parody is always fair use), whether the new work usurps the market for the original, and whether the use is commercial or not. The details of a 2013 case involving the work of Richard Prince, an artist whose work builds on the appropriation of images from popular culture, make clear the rather complex and rarely predictable workings of copyright law.

In a long anticipated decision and apparent win for appropriation art, the Second Circuit reversed a lower court's ruling and held that Richard Prince's use of images by photographer Patrick Cariou in his "Canal Zone" series was, indeed, fair use. The appeals court disagreed with the lower court that to be fair use a work must directly comment on or critique the original. On the contrary, it was sufficient that Prince's work transformed the original by employing it in a different manner in order to produce a new message. Based on its own aesthetic analysis the court held that the majority of the works in

"Canal Zone" constituted a transformative fair use of Cariou's photographs, even though the series did not comment on or critique Cariou's "Yes Rasta." In a passage resembling testimony from an art expert, the majority opinion stated, "Where Cariou's serene and deliberately composed portraits and landscape photographs depict the natural beauty of Rastafarians and their surrounding environs, Prince's crude and jarring works, on the other hand, are hectic and provocative. . . . Prince's composition, presentation, scale, color palette, and media are fundamentally different and new compared to the photographs, as is the expressive nature of Prince's work" (*Cariou v Prince* 2013).

But who is to decide what use is transformative—and how sure can an appropriation artist be of the consistency of future decisions? The appeals court in *Cariou v Prince* found Prince's works transformative simply by looking at them side by side with Cariou's. Yet, the judges hesitated as to five of the works: "Certainly, there are key differences in those artworks compared to the photographs they incorporate. *Graduation*, for instance, is tinted blue, and the jungle background is in softer focus than in Cariou's original. Lozenges painted over the subject's eyes and mouth—an alteration that appears frequently throughout the Canal Zone artworks—make the subject appear anonymous, rather than as the strong individual who appears in the original. Along with the enlarged hands and electric guitar that Prince pasted onto his canvas, those alterations create the impression that the subject is not quite human. Cariou's photograph, on the other hand, presents a human being in his natural habitat, looking intently ahead. Where the photograph presents someone comfortably at home in nature, *Graduation* combines divergent elements to create a sense of discomfort. However, we cannot say for sure whether *Graduation* constitutes fair use or whether Prince has transformed Cariou's work enough to render it transformative" (*Cariou v Prince*). The judges eventually abandoned the struggle to decide whether *Graduation* and the other four pieces were sufficiently transformative and left it to the lower court.

Cariou v Prince emphasizes the difficulty in predicting whether a court's aesthetic analysis would result in support or rejection of a fair use claim. Indeed, one of the judges, in a partial dissent, argued the court was in no position to make its own aesthetic judgments and should have remanded all the works to the lower court. Presumably that court would then hear expert witnesses on whether the use of Cariou's photographs in each of Prince's works is transformative or not. But would even the experts agree?

Since this is all about money, it should be noted here that, contrary to the situation where a big corporation like Mattel goes after an artist with limited resources, the Prince case—as a number of other cases where artists confront other artists—pitted a previously unknown photographer against a famous artist whose work sells for millions of dollars and his dealer Larry Gagosian (also a defendant in the case), one of the most powerful dealers in the art world. While a corporation may be motivated by the desire to retain control over its trademark products and maximize its profits, a photographer like Cariou may simply want a degree of compensation for being used as "raw material" in Prince's enormously lucrative paintings. The system of copyright law is blind to this important distinction.

Copyright can also work as a much more straightforward means of censorship in cases where the copyright holder refuses reproduction rights to those who want to use a work in a context of which he or she disapproves. Thus those who may be critical of an artist's *oeuvre* or whose approach simply does not suit the tastes of the artist or her estate can be prevented from illustrating or documenting their analysis. For years photographer Diane Arbus' estate would refuse the reproduction rights for her work unless it was to appear in the context of an article approved by the estate. Thus many writings on Arbus were published without reproductions of some of her most famous work.

In another representative instance, the Gagosian Gallery rejected a request to reproduce an image by one of the gallery's artists after asking "which other artists would be discussed in the same chapter, the size and prominence of the picture, the publisher, the size of the press run" (Thompson 2008, 222). The rejection appeared to have been based solely upon the desire to maintain the artist's exclusive brand.

In an economy that is increasingly reliant on intellectual product rather than manufactured goods, the protection of intellectual property is a top priority. Artists themselves have an interest in making a living from their work by licensing its reproduction; otherwise being an artist would be even less viable a career choice than it already is. Yet, as copyright laws tighten and the fair use exception to these laws shrinks, and as the limited term of copyright is extended to exceed the human lifespan, the regulation of intellectual property appears to be less and less about promoting the "Progress of Science and useful Arts" and more and more about extracting maximum profit with no consideration for the arts or science at large.

7. Vandalism and Threats of Violence as Censorship

Censorship, by definition, can only be perpetuated by those who have the power to suppress: public officials or, in cases of private censorship, heads of institutions, as well as owners of media and communication platforms. What recourse does that leave for those who don't have that power but are unable to tolerate an artwork? They can protest, but their protests may not get the desired results. So, occasionally, frustrated by the inability to impose their views on others, aspiring censors decide to act outside the law and destroy the work that offends them.

Destruction of offensive images has a long tradition from early Christians destroying pagan "idols" to the Taliban destroying historic Buddha statues in Afghanistan—but it has generally been deployed by those newly in power so as to establish a new symbolic regime. On the contrary, vandalism today is making its presence felt increasingly in multicultural liberal democracies as a tactic of those who perceive a loss of cultural hegemony as the two examples in the beginning of this text testify: the destruction of Enrique Chagoya's lithograph at a gallery in Colorado and of Andres Serrano's *Piss Christ* in Avignon, France. These are not isolated incidents; recent instances of vandalism of art spread from the Australia and South Africa to Sweden.

Another tactic of suppression exercised by those deprived of the power to censor directly is the issuing of threats of violence. One goal of such threats is to provoke enough fear in an institution that it decides to cancel a show thus avoiding vandalism or violence against those involved. In 2001, the Los Angeles City Cultural Affairs Department cancelled *WAR*, an exhibition by L.A. artist Alex Donis, before its opening at the Watts Towers Arts Center (Reich 2001). A Watts community group had warned that the show, a series of fictionalized pairings of LAPD officers and gang members in same-sex dancing poses, might have provoked gang violence.

More recently, in 2008, concerned about numerous death threats by animal rights activists, San Francisco Art Institute (SFAI) decided to close French Algerian artist Adel Abdessemed's installation *Don't Trust Me*, which featured video footage of animals being slaughtered by the blow of a sledgehammer (Baker 2008).

While both institutions' responses are understandable, closing a show for fear that some groups may respond violently leads down a dangerous path: it empowers violent hecklers to suppress ideas they do not like. In a society where privacy has been surrendered to safety, will free speech be the next sacrifice?

Conclusion: The Future of Art Censorship

Overt government censorship is only the tip of the iceberg of repression today, at least insofar as a neo-liberal state like the U.S. is concerned. The suppression of art and ideas is accomplished far more successfully by market mechanisms, self-censorship, and the very structures of art-exhibiting practices and institutions, which allow only a limited range of work to be shown in environments that often inoculate the work. Concerned about offending donors, jeopardizing corporate funds, or unwilling to engage in the possibility of months of media controversy, art institutions frequently prefer to self-censor, tone down political shows, turn off video installations at prime visiting hours, or even reconsider their programming.

This trend is likely to continue in the future: public space is increasingly the province of advertising companies and our fastest growing commons—the Internet—consists of private platforms (Google, Facebook, YouTube) with more or less restrictive terms of service. Public funds for the arts have consistently shrunk and are likely to go on shrinking thus leaving art to the whims of large private and corporate patrons; and just as the technology to create new works from existing material has expanded, the use of our shared storehouse of images and sounds has been restricted by more and more rigid legal chains.

Censorship is in effect being privatized and this is bad news. The First Amendment may protect artists from direct government suppression, but it does not protect against private censorship or from more insidious methods of state censorship like funding cuts. Whether it is public or private, overt or masquerading as something else, censorship has the same classic effects: it deprives a particular audience of the opportunity to see an artwork, it perpetuates the views and tastes of those with political, economic or cultural power, and it encourages artists to self-censor if they want their art to be shown.

References

Adler, Amy. 2006. Knowing it when you (don't) see it: Mapping the pornographic child in order to diffuse the paedophilic gaze. In *Censoring culture: Contemporary threats to free expression*. eds. Robert Akins and Svetlana Mintcheva. New York: The New Press.

Ashcroft v. The Free Speech Coalition. 535 U.S. 234; 122 S. Ct. 1389; 152 L. Ed. 2d 403; 2002 U.S.

Baker, Kenneth. 2008. Show's cancellation a rare case of artists advocating censorship. *San Francisco Chronicle*, April 1.

Brachear, Manya A. and Charles Storch. 2008. Controversy closes show at museum. *Chicago Tribune*, June 21.

CAE Defense Fund Press Release. 2008. Artist cleared of all charges in precedent-setting case. June 11. http://www.caedefensefund.org/releases/cleared_6_11_08.html (accessed September 30, 2013).

Cariou v Prince. 714 F.3d 694 (2d Cir. 2013), 2013.

City of Cincinnati v. Contemporary Arts Center. City of Cincinnati v. Barrie. 57 Ohio Misc. 2d 15; 566 N.E.2d 214; 1990 Ohio.

Chrisafis, Angelique. 2011. Hit with a Hammer and Slashed with an Ice Pick. *The Guardian*, April 19.

Comic Book Legal Defense Fund. n.d. BLDF Case Files, *Florida v. Mike Diana.* http://cbldf.org/about-us/case-files/cbldf-case-files-mike-diana/ (accessed June 14, 2013).

Comments on Andres Serrano by Members of the United States Senate. 1989. *Congressional Record* http://www.csulb.edu/~jvancamp/ 361_r7.html (accessed September 30, 2013).

Cotter, Holland. 2010. As ants crawl over crucifix, dead artist is assailed again. *New York Times,* December 10.

Dunlap, David W. 2005. Freedom museum is headed for showdown at ground zero. *New York Times,* September 22.

Fineman, Carol. 2003. It's nude. Is it lewd? *The Union,* September 28.

Finkel, Jori. 2010. Museum of Contemporary Art commissions, then paints over, artwork. *Los Angeles Times,* December 14.

The Fred Wilson Public Art Project. n.d. http://www.fredwilsonindy.org (accessed June 15, 2013).

Frosch, Dan. 2010. Provocative image of Christ sets off a debate punctuated with a crowbar. *New York Times,* October 11.

Healy, Patrick. 2012. If three constitutes company, add lawyers to make it a crowd. *New York Times,* July 17.

Henderson v. City of Murfreesboro. 960 F. Supp. 1292; 1997 U.S. Dist. LEXIS 4078.

Hopper v. City of Pasco. 241 F.3d 1067; 2001 U.S.

Human Rights Watch. 2005. Russia: Art conviction undermines free expression, March 28 http://www.hrw.org/en/news/2005/03/27/ russia-art-conviction-undermines-free-expression (accessed April 11, 2013).

Kravets, David. 2009. U.S. Manga obscenity conviction roils comics world. *Wired,* May 28.

Lerner, Ruby. 2006. Private philanthropy and the arts: Does anybody want an artist in the house? In *Censoring culture: Contemporary threats to free expression.* Eds. Robert Atkins and Svetlana Mintcheva. New York: The New Press.

Mattel, Inc., v. Walking Mountain Productions. Mi353 F.3d 792; 2003 U.S.

McGuigan, Cathleen, et al. 1985. A word from our sponsor: Increasing ties between big business and the art world raise some delicate questions. *Newsweek,* November 25.

Miller v. California. 413 U.S. 15; 93 S. Ct. 2607; 37 L. Ed. 2d 419; 1973 U.S.

National Endowment for the *Arts v. Finley* (97–371) 524 U.S. 569 (1998)

New York v. Ferber, 458 U.S. 747 (1982).

Quigley, Margaret. n.d. The Mapplethorpe Censorship Controversy: Chronology Of Events. Political Research Associates. http://www.publiceye.org/theocrat/Mapplethorpe_Chrono.html (accessed April 11, 3013).

Reich, Kenneth. 2001. Yanking of Art Spurs Protests. *Los Angeles Times*, October 13.

Rosen, Rhoda. 2008. Imaginary Coordinates (exhibition catalogue). Chicago: Spertus Press.

Rubin, Marian. 2002. Naked Truths. Lincoln, Nebraska: Writer's Showcase.

Searle, Adrian. 2009. Tate Modern removes naked Brooke Shields picture after police visit. *The Guardian*, September 30.

Stanford University Libraries. 2010. Stanford Copyright & Fair Use Overview, Chapter 9. http://fairuse.stanford.edu/Copyright_and_Fair_Use_Overview/chapter9/index.html (accessed January 16, 2013).

Thompson, Donald N. 2008. *The $12 million stuffed shark: The curious economics of contemporary art and auction houses.* London: Aurum.

Tucker, Jill. 2011. Oakland museum cancels Palestinian kids' war art. *San Francisco Chronicle*, Friday, September 9.

U.S. v Eichman. 496 U.S. 310; 110 S. Ct. 2404; 110 L. Ed. 2d 287; 1990 U.S.

Watson, Joe. 2004. Bush League: ASU's museum cut anti-Bush art from its upcoming political exhibition—for purely political reasons. *Phoenix New Times*, Thursday, Aug 19.

Sex and Intellectual Freedom

Robert P. Holley

Intellectual freedom is an abstract concept. As applied to libraries, it is a much broader principle than judging whether a book about male penguins raising a chick is suitable for a school library collection. The American Library Association gives the following definition of intellectual freedom: "Intellectual freedom is the right of every individual to both seek and receive information from all points of view without restriction. It provides for free access to all expressions of ideas through which any and all sides of a question, cause or movement may be explored." (American Library Association) Within a literal reading of this definition, intellectual freedom on sexual topics is sorely lacking in American culture and its libraries.

This entry will focus on the United States since a cross cultural understanding of intellectual freedom is a topic too large to deal with in any detail. Intellectual freedom in public and school libraries is emphasized with broader cultural trends added as needed. The American ideal of intellectual freedom developed within the context of First Amendment rights. "Congress shall make no law respecting an establishment of religion, or prohibiting the free exercise thereof; or abridging the freedom of speech, or of the press; or the right of the people peaceably to assemble, and to petition the Government for a redress of grievances" (Bill of Rights 1789). The corollary of freedom of speech is the freedom to access what others have said. Legislation and court decisions have established certain exceptions to freedom of speech such as libel, child pornography, and obscenity; but the United States is more liberal, at least legally, in regard to political speech than many Western democracies (Cohen Henry 2003). Canada, France, and Austria, among others, prohibit, for example, hate speech or advocating Nazi doctrines (Rosenberg 2000). On the other hand, many Western democracies are much more liberal, at least in practice, about matters of sexual expression (Herzog 2011).

Legalities are much less important in the area of sex and intellectual freedom than are cultural values. Viewing adult pornography on the Internet is legal. Estimates vary on the number of adults who visit porn sites but are in the range of 25–34 million weekly (Covenant Eyes). The number of users who would admit doing so is decidedly less. In many parts of the United States, working in the sex industry may offer the best economic prospects for both women and men. "Sex workers receive $25–30 per hour, roughly four times what they could expect outside prostitution" ("Finance And Economics: Selling sex; Economics focus" 2008). In addition, more women entered the sex industry during the economic downturn because traditional jobs were less available or paid too little (Sotelo 23). Providing career counseling for these jobs could be viewed as a useful and legitimate public library function and meet a legitimate information need. One book on this topic, *Turning Pro* by Magdalene Meretrix, includes such practical topics as "Continuing Education Within the Field" and "Planning for the Future" but, according to WorldCat, only one public library holds this item (Full text of "Loompanics 2003 Catalog"). American public libraries generally do not provide materials on alternate heterosexual lifestyles such as cross dressing, swinging with multiple partners on a permanent or temporary basis, and "deviant" behaviors such as sadomasochism though these activities are legal in most jurisdictions. Lesbian, gay, bisexual, and transgender (LGBT) individuals may receive even less support for and representation of their lifestyle.

Many jurisdictions use various strategies to regulate the sex industry rather than directly prosecuting the sexual activities that might well be found to be legal. There are "four main tools available to regulate adult businesses: obscenity, zoning, licensing, and nuisance control. It is not surprising to learn that it's easier to regulate activities with no speech content than it is to regulate adult bookstores or movie houses" (Henderson 2004) Another effective tactic is to focus on concerns about children up to the age of eighteen because they have fewer legal rights than adults. Fortunately for intellectual freedom in the United States, the Supreme Court most often decides that legislation cannot be written in a way that reduces adult access to materials to the level that would be suitable for children. In the filtering cases like CIPA, "the Supreme Court ruled emphatically that any such restriction of adult access must be removed at the request of an adult. The filter must be disabled immediately in order to ensure that the rights of adult patrons are not being trampled" (Mauger 2012). Finally, libraries, especially public libraries, most often follow community cultural standards and are more subject to pressure from individuals and organized groups because public libraries depend upon the community for their funding. In the same way, school libraries find it hard to argue against concerned parents who ask why their innocent children should be exposed to "smut."

Difficulties in Assessing Intellectual Freedom

Assessing the state of intellectual freedom in American society at large and in public libraries is a formidable task for many reasons.

The Diversity of American Culture

The diversity of American culture complicates any generalization about sex and intellectual freedom in libraries. Different areas and cultures in America are more conservative or liberal in sexual matters overall; but the public library, at least in principle, is supposed to meet the needs of all its users and represent multiple viewpoints. Some communities may not have a clear majority for any viewpoint. These viewpoints may even differ from one library branch to another within a large public library system.

Differences in the Attitudes of Librarians toward Intellectual Freedom

Intellectual freedom is given as a core value of librarianship and accepted as such by most librarians, at least in theory. It is doubtful, however, that many librarians follow a hard line in support of intellectual freedom especially in the hot button area of sex. In addition, librarians possess varying degrees of courage in their willingness to take on conflicts arising from defending intellectual freedom. These librarians may also make different judgments on the possibilities of intellectual freedom conflicts arising in their communities. The simplest path to avoid purchasing some sexual materials is to discover some superficially valid reason for not adding them to the library's collection. One such case is Madonna's *Sex*, a *New York Times* best seller. "An often-stated reason for not buying *Sex* was the likelihood of its being stolen. Other reasons were the probability of its falling apart (though DeCandido indicated it can be rebound), the multimedia design, and the high cost ($49.95 retail) even after a library distributor's discount" (Fialkoff 1992). Another example is the 2013 bestseller *50 Shades of Grey* where some librarians avoided purchasing this tremendously popular novel because "the reviews weren't good. They said the book was very poorly written . . ." (ALA Intellectual Freedom Committee 2012, 147). In both cases, for such high demand items, the libraries most likely would have purchased similar non-controversial books with the same "flaws."

Publication Availability

Librarians cannot buy sexual materials if they are not available. Most public libraries, especially smaller ones, depend upon traditional library vendors who stock most of their wares from traditional trade publishers. Traditional publishers are not adverse to publishing edgy works, mostly fiction, if the sales potential is high. For example, they publish urban fiction with its profanity, sex, and violence since it sells well within the African-American community and is most often bought by urban public libraries with few attempts at censorship. Trade publishers have become, however, risk adverse on more controversial sexual topics.

Traditional publishers, however, are not the only source for publications on sexual topics. The Internet has opened up publishing sexual materials by non-traditional sources. Smaller "niche" publishers compete successfully with the traditional publishers by understanding their narrower markets and the authors who write for them. According to blogger Scarlett Stevens, examples of specialized publishers of erotica include Elora's Cave, Carnal Desires Publishing, Phaze Books, Liquid Silver Books and Excessiva. (Stevens). In addition, digital publishing and print-on-demand has reduced the need for large print runs and reduced overhead costs.

The two factors above have led to another important development for the availability of erotica to libraries—the growth of self-publishing. Authors can make their books available at a relatively small cost and market them online. Amazon aggressively courts authors and provides support for self-publishing with its service CreateSpace (CreateSpace). Amazon, in fact, has a relatively good record for avoiding censorship as can be seen by its initial defense of publishing *The Pedophile's Guide to Love and Pleasure* though the company later caved to public pressure (Shepherd). Statistically, the growth in self-publishing has been enormous. "A staggering 764,448 titles were produced in 2009 by self-publishers and micro-niche publishers, according to statistics released this morning by R.R. Bowker. The number of "nontraditional" titles dwarfed that of traditional books whose output slipped to 288,355 last year from 289,729 in 2008" (Milliot 2010). Libraries, however, are less likely to purchase materials from smaller presses and self-published materials because these items seldom are reviewed except in specialized sources, are often difficult to identify, and may require inefficient separate purchases from the publisher or author (Grobelny 2013). Some libraries even have difficulty in getting authorization to purchase from Amazon even though Amazon has "launched a new Corporate Accounts program (http://www.amazon.com/corporate), accepting online purchase orders from qualified businesses, libraries, schools, government institutions and other organizations that want to purchase items from across the Amazon.com Web site without using a credit card" (Amazon.com).

Focus on Challenges

Much of the current publicity for intellectual freedom focuses on challenges in public and school libraries. The American Library Association (ALA)

Office of Intellectual Freedom (OIF) sponsors a highly effective Banned Books Week each year. This emphasis on challenges inhibits a more serious discussion of intellectual freedom for several reasons. To be challenged, the book must have been purchased for the library. Furthermore, the list of most challenged books most often includes a high percentage of children's materials or adult books assigned to be read by teenagers. Thus, it can be argued that this emphasis upon challenges may trivialize the concept of intellectual freedom. By focusing on objections that are often ludicrous, librarians can easily say that they have no problems with these materials while overlooking the seriousness of providing information on controversial but important sexual matters (Holley 2012).

Children and Young Adults

Court decisions have affirmed that children and young adults have intellectual freedom rights though to a more limited extent than adults. They also have more rights as they get older until the day they have full adult rights at the age of eighteen. (Kelsey, 2007) (Chmara & Mach, 2004) A complicating issue is that parents have some but not total control over their children's access to information. While many parents give their children relatively broad freedom in their reading and viewing, some wish to restrict access to only materials of which they approve. Public libraries have taken the stance that parents should accompany their children to the library if they wish strictly to restrict their access. Some libraries do, however, have policies in place partially to block access. Some examples include requiring parents to approve checking out certain types of materials such as videos, restricting access to the adult collection, and the legal requirement as stated above to filter Internet access to be eligible for E-rate discounts. Many consider that exceptions exist to the rights of parents to control access to information where children or, more frequently, young adults need parentally prohibited information to deal with urgent information needs such as sexual orientation or sexual abuse. (Kniffel 1999)

School media centers have a more difficult task in defending their libraries from intellectual freedom challenges because school librarians do not have the public library defense that parents have the duty to supervise their children's library use by coming with them to the library (Aftab, Herb and Klipsch . The school acts *in loco parentis* and thus shoulders a greater responsibility. The problem of age appropriate materials becomes more pronounced when the same media center serves a broad age range such as early middle school through advanced placement high school seniors. (Chelton 2011) No simple solutions exist for the media center though some have collections restricted to advanced classes or requiring parental approval. Some strategies to minimize the possible confrontation with parents include not book talking or displaying potentially objectionable materials and avoiding making controversial reading recommendations unless the media specialist knows the student well. Some media specialists sacrifice intellectual freedom by not purchasing items with the slightest hint of controversy including a broad range of sexual materials. As for Internet filtering, many school librarians have no choice but to accept filtering since the E-rate discount applies to the entire school district; and school administrators impose filtering to gain the cost savings.

Print Materials

Sex instruction should be considered a health or human development issue that would not engender much controversy, but this is seldom the case within schools. The initial question is the age at which to start "sex ed." While the experts recommend starting early, some parents believe that they should be able to preserve the "innocence" of their children as long as possible, perhaps in extreme cases for women until they get married as was the case in prior generations. In 1999, Landry, Singh, and Darroch investigated sexuality education including the attitudes of teachers and parents as well as the importance of abstinence only education (Landry, Singh and Darroch 2000). They concluded that "a large proportion of schools are doing little to prepare students in grades five and six for puberty, much less for dealing with pressures and decisions regarding sexual activity." State laws present another complicating factor. Teachers may be forbidden from discussing anything but traditional morality and gender orientation. Any discussion of birth control, masturbation, LGBT issues, and any option except abstinence and heterosexual sex within marriage can be illegal. In Michigan, for example, one of the summary headings states the following: "Required Content Including Emphasis on Abstinence" The section goes on to require teaching the benefits of abstaining from sex until marriage and the negative consequences of having sex before then. The possibility of gay or lesbian sex is not mentioned in this summary document that also omits, of course, any mention of the human value of sexual pleasure (Michigan Department of Education 2007).

For librarians, an essential book that crosses the boundaries by age and type of library is *For SEX EDUCATION, See Librarian: A Guide to Issues and Resources* by Cornog and Perper. The authors have written a comprehensive resource on sexual matters (Perper and Cornog 1996). To quote the description on Amazon.com:

> At long last, here is the definitive practical guide to sexuality materials in libraries and an annotated bibliography of nearly 600 recommended books for school and public libraries. Cornog and Perper, the preeminent

experts on sexuality materials for libraries, provide guidelines for materials selection, reference, processing, access, programming, and dealing with problems of vandalism and censorship. The bibliography, organized into 5 topics and 48 subtopics, annotates a collection of recommended books and nonprint materials on sexuality information for children and adults, most published since 1985. Recommended works represent a wide variety of views, including Christian and conservative. (Amazon.com)

This book is the best place to start for a general overview of this topic for public and school libraries.

These strictures may extend to the school media center. These laws contradict in some sense parental control because some parents hold values that go against these limited choices in sexual education. While strict neutrality in these areas is impossible because accepting multiple viewpoints is in itself a value, accepting multiple values in this area would appear to be a logical extension of the multiplicity and non-exclusivity of viewpoints extended to differing religious and moral viewpoints by the first amendment. Surprisingly, beyond the discussion of individual titles, no general research article on this topic appears to exist.

The public library has much greater flexibility in matters of sexual education and other sexual topics. Since the public library is not subject to the same legal standards as public schools, any constraints will be self-imposed. Cohen concluded, however, in her research study that "it is clear that many librarians view the role of the public library as a peripheral source for sexual-health information for young adults. They do not believe that it is within the purview of the public library to advocate sexual-health education, develop or promote programs, or highlight relevant sections within their collections" (Cohen, R. 2008).

Adults also need factual information about sex and sexual health. Sexual health is less controversial for adults because our society assumes that adults are sexually active and accepts the reality, if not the philosophy, of sexual activity outside of marriage. Society has an interest in preventing the spread of sexually transmitted diseases so that public libraries encounter less opposition to providing this type of information. AIDS prevention has been a particularly strong collection area though other diseases such as syphilis, herpes, gonorrhea, etc. also receive attention. While somewhat overlapping the issue of sexual technique, adults of both sexes seek out information on erectile dysfunction, how to achieve orgasm, and the effects of aging upon sexual activity and performance. Adults may also seek out materials on the norms of sex within American culture to learn where they fit in. *The Joy of Sex* by Alex Comfort remains one of the most recognizable titles (Comfort 2009) along with *The Joy of Gay Sex* by Silverstein and Picano (Silverstein and Picano 2004).

Lifestyle choices and other sexual information make up a second category with high sexual content. This category includes both fiction and non-fiction, but this article will stress non-fiction except for younger children. For them, the main reasons for challenges are sex, violence, and homosexuality. One common theme found objectionable is having the child live in a non-traditional family that does not include a man and a woman who are married to each other. Examples include *Heather Has Two Mommies* by Leslea Newman and *Daddy's Roommate* by Michael Willhoite. This category is related more to the sexual activity of the parents than that of the child. Other common themes that lead to banning include sexual content in general, violence, disrespect, and just plain scariness (University of Illinois at Urbana-Champaign Social Sciences 2013).

Post-puberty children in middle or high school usually have great interest in learning about courtship and mating rituals. Most non-fiction materials focus on heterosexual relations with broad discussion of the role of dating in teenage life. Many of these materials could be seen as etiquette with a sexual component. Topics can include how to attract the opposite sex, rules for dating, and sometimes discussions of sexual options. Such materials also exist for LGBT students but are less common and less likely to be purchased by public libraries and school library media centers. One example is *Friendship, dating, and relationships* by Simone Payment, which is held by 159 libraries in WorldCat (Payment 2010). One interesting area for graduating high school students is career guidance for working in the legal sex industry, where resources are almost totally lacking. Working in the legal sex industry can be one of the more lucrative career choices for both men and women and has the same legal status as working in a minister's office. Cultural prohibitions exist, however, about talking about such options. Providing some sort of career guidance would help reduce the potential risks of such careers. The same comments would apply for adults. Beyond the example already mentioned above, one such book is *1, 2, 3, be a porn star: a step-by-step guide to the adult sex industry for men and women* by Ana Loria (Loria 2000). While working as a porn star is legal, only five libraries in WorldCat hold this title of which only one is a public library. On Amazon.com, the book is, however, surprisingly popular with 35 customer reviews and a respectable sales rank of #3,248,734 (Amazon.com).

The range of materials for adults is theoretically much larger because adults have much more freedom in sexual matters. The public library can provide access to much non-controversial materials on heterosexual lifestyles including dating, courtship, marriage, and sexual issues within the traditional married couple. This literature can be on the advice columnist level or include serious research studies. This advice often is in keeping with cultural norms so that literature on how to snag a husband is acceptable, while a text on how to seduce a woman is not as can be seen by the multiple titles from mainstream publishers with significant library holdings on the first topic compared with mostly self-published titles without library holdings on the second. Some topics may deal with controversial topics such as affairs and visits to prostitutes but within the context of an exclusive heterosexual relationship as the desired norm with advice on how to "correct" the problem. The sexual literature may even include religious perspectives on maintaining a "moral" and "traditional" lifestyle.

The public library is less likely to collect materials on non-traditional heterosexual and gay/lesbian lifestyles. The research that follows identifies practical non-scholarly materials in Amazon.com and then checks their availability in libraries by checking WorldCat holdings. An exception is cohabitation, which is well represented in public library collections. The results are as follows: *Shacking Up: The Smart Girl's Guide to Living in Sin without Getting Burned* by Stacy Whitman, 373 holding libraries;. *Unmarried to Each Other: The Essential Guide to Living Together as an Unmarried Couple* by Dorian Solot and Marshall Miller, 613 holding libraries; and *How to Move in with Your Boyfriend (and Not Break up with Him)* by Tiffany Curent, 215 holding libraries. Bondage is another subject with some holdings in public libraries. Amazon includes a long list of practical titles including the following two recent publications. *The Ultimate Guide to Kink: BDSM, Role Play and the Erotic Edge* by Tristan Taormino is held by 31 libraries, including many public libraries. It is also available as an Ebrary title as an ebook. The second title, *Fifty Shades of Bondage & Submission: A Beginner's Guide to BDSM* by Renee Dubois, has 15 library holdings, almost all public libraries.

A very popular area, at least as seen in Amazon sales rankings, is swinging. This topic, however, appears to be completely off limits since no American public library claims ownership in WorldCat to the following three books: *Swinging for Beginners: An Introduction to the Lifestyle* by Kaye Bellemeade; *The Swinger Manual* by JustAsk Julie with a high Amazon best seller ranking of #123,524; and *Recreational Sex : An Insider's Guide to the Swinging Lifestyle* by Patti Thomas. It appears that materials on this legal activity are more objectionable to libraries than discussions of how to engage in sexual activities such as prostitution that remain illegal in most jurisdictions.

On the other hand, finding publications on how to navigate the legal and quasi-legal sex scene of bars, night clubs, sex shows, and prostitution is difficult. Books on these topics are often available only as self-published ebooks. Furthermore, trying to find additional items by using the *Library of Congress Subject Headings* in relevant books discovered from Amazon is next to impossible. One item, held by 32 libraries, is *Veronica Monet's sex secrets of escorts: tips from a pro*, but it would be difficult to find it in the library catalog from its three subject headings, "Sex instruction." "Man-woman relationships," and "Tantrism." Amazon lists two gay items with a focus on hustling. The first by Joseph Itel, *A Consumer's Guide to Male Hustlers*, is surprisingly from a mainstream publisher, Routledge, and has 35 holdings though many are academic institutions. The second, *Hustling: a gentleman's guide to the fine art of homosexual prostitution* by John Preston, on the other hand, is held by only eight libraries. I was not able to find commercially published materials on sex in public places and cross dressing.

For polygamy or plural marriage publications, it is impossible to distinguish among personal narratives, scholarly resources, and practical advice. Furthermore, the prominence of this topic in the history of the LDS Church and its offshoots and its acceptance in Islam results in 12,818 entries in WorldCat from a search on the keyword "polygamy." Second, the acceptance of pornography as a means of enhancing sexual relationships of all types has enough mainstream support to be eliminated as a serious intellectual freedom issue. Evidence for this view includes *Defending Pornography: Free Speech, Sex, and the Fight for Women's Rights* by Nadine Strossen and the many sexual education titles by Dr. Ruth K. Westheimer.

Media

Music

Music shares many traits with publishing. Sexual content is harder to overlook in music than in the printed word though mumbling sometimes makes the words harder to discern. Music depends upon public airplay, mostly on the radio, for publicity. The major record labels are willing to include a high level of sexual content; but to get airplay they often make available a censored version of the recording, especially for radio play in conservative parts of the country. To give an example, "wishing you could get inside her pants" becomes "wishing she would give you a chance" in *Good Girls Don't* by The Knack. (http://www.youtube.com/watch?v=QaELi92uwwc original http://www.youtube.com/watch?v=Sc4l5EpCMEc censored)

A bibliography on music censorship in general is available in a LibGuide produced by the University Libraries at Bowling Green University (Bowling Green State University 2012). Libraries do not appear to have faced many intellectual freedom challenges in this area. The only censorship example found in *Library Literature Online* describes a case where Kansas Attorney General Phill (sic) Kline defended "his decision this spring to refuse some 1,600 music CDs officials believed to contain inappropriate content." (Goldberg 2004) Overall, libraries may have avoided complaints in this area by purchasing the edited versions of controversial music.

Film

Film poses increased intellectual freedom concerns since visual materials make sexual material more difficult to overlook. As stated above, print materials depend upon the imagination of the reader and thus are sometimes excluded from attempts to craft censorship legislation at national and state levels. Within the American context, film has a long history of censorship from the Production Code (1930), which was challenged and then abandoned in the late 1960s, led to the current voluntary MPAA system that replaced it in 1968 (Pollard 2009). While the American Library Association *Library Bill of Rights* does not support the use of these ratings, the same document also disapproves of their removal when present. Many libraries clearly label films with these ratings. Since these ratings are created by a private body, they have no legal standing and cannot be incorporated into the law (Caldwell-Stone 2004). The mainstream movie studios depend upon widespread distribution of their films and normally modify any film with a proposed NC rating (the former X) not because of legal concerns but because most leases prohibit movie theaters from showing NC films (Eberts 2000). From another perspective, removing "objectionable" parts of commercial films to make them more acceptable for conservative audiences was judged to be a violation of copyright (Gustafson 2006). Libraries sometimes have a separate process for circulating films to minors to enable parents to determine the rules for their children. As stated above, the MPAA ratings have no legal standing so that having minors check out R rated films is a library policy decision and not a legal requirement. This policy is contentious and has been challenged in many jurisdictions (Annoyed Librarian 2008).

The Internet

The Internet poses the greatest challenge for libraries and intellectual freedom. Unlike all the other categories above, the individual library does not control the content that is made available. The Internet has become the favored way to distribute legal pornography. Legal pornography accounted for $13 billion in revenue in 2006 (Covenant Eyes). Pornography Web sites have historically been early adopters of the technology that provides new distribution channels. The major search engines provide settings that allow any user to find easily large quantities of legal pornography. The following discussion does not include child pornography, which is illegal for its violation of the rights of those under eighteen who are not able to give their legal consent. This issue is complicated, however, by the fact that the Internet provides access to international Web sites in countries where the age of consent may be lower than in the United States. The international aspect of the Internet also makes it difficult to attempt any Internet regulation since the United States cannot control content outside its borders except through filtering and blocking payment.

While Congress has attempted to regulate sexual content on the Internet, the courts have overturned these efforts on the principle that any legislation must allow adults access to legal content and not impose unreasonable restraints such as requiring the adult to have a credit card. Efforts at the state level have also failed for the same reason. To overcome this setback, Congress has tied Internet filtering to receiving subsidies under the Children's Internet Protection Act. To receive these funds, libraries must filter access for those under eighteen while at least in theory allowing adults to have access to the full Internet upon request (Caldwell-Stone 2013). Many libraries do not follow these guidelines and filter all computers, often with success because adult library users are afraid of the negative consequences of challenging this policy. Other libraries have decided not to filter because of the costs of doing so and the negative effects upon computer speed. The intellectual freedom community has great concern about filters. While libraries can sometimes choose which categories to filter, the filter vendor can choose the specific sites to block through the construction of the filtering algorithms (Kolderup 2013). Of particular concerns has been the blocking of LGBT sites without explicit sexual content while allowing sites hostile to gays (Chmara 2012).

The second risk for libraries is the issue of creating a hostile work environment in which employees are forced to see images that they find offensive. Library employees at the Minneapolis Public Library sued and won a preliminary judgment in such a complaint (Oder 2001). The general advice to libraries is to have at least some computers with privacy screens so that a passersby cannot easily see what users are viewing. Doing so also increases user privacy for all types of materials (Holt 2001). A final issue is whether to filter the Internet for those who use the library's wireless access on their own computers (Landry et al. 2000).

Conclusion

Sex remains a contentious issue in American culture. On the one hand, political rhetoric and popular opinion still often support adherence to Judeo-Christian sexual morality. Many outwardly voice support for the traditional view of sex only within a heterosexual marriage. Counter evidence is the increasing acceptance of cohabitation, children outside marriage, and equal sexual rights including marriage for the LGBT community. Much evidence further suggests, however, that American behavior does not conform to these stated principles. Reliable research studies show that around 50% of

U.S. teenagers are sexually active (Youth Risk Behavior Survey 2012) and that between 30–60% of spouses have had sex outside marriage (Facts and Statistics About Infidelity). Sex sells in the media. Pornography is a $13 billion industry. Finally, the difference in sexual values may vary more in the United States than is true for most other Western democracies. This variance puts self-censorship pressures on the national media.

School librarians are often constrained to avoid sexual materials since a curricular focus mainly determines what they add to their collections. As seen above, state legislation often determines what schools can teach with the result than an abstinence only policy often prevails. Some school librarians, perhaps a near majority according to a recent research study, face resistance from their principals over including sexual education materials (Richey 2012). In a similar fashion, school librarians are "under-collecting LGBTQ-themed titles. Although LGBTQ teens are estimated to make up 5.9 percent of the students in American high schools, the average number of LGBTQ-themed titles held by these school libraries was 0.4 percent" (Hughes-Hassell, Overberg, and Harris 2013). These statistics make it even more important for school librarians to be aware of the intellectual freedom issues surrounding sexual content and the need to have the courage to provide information on sexual health and sexual choices for students.

The typical public library reflects the ambiguity over sexual content. On average, the library follows the decisions of the American public over what is acceptable or not although exceptions can occur such as was the case for Madonna's *Sex* whose erotic visual content caused many libraries to avoid its purchase because of its visual elements even though the book was a best seller. The public library is often sensitive to challenges from the conservative elements of the community where a few concerned patrons can create strong negative publicity. The media contributes to this paranoia by occasionally running segments about unfiltered Internet access to legal pornography (Libraries walk a tightrope on porn 2012). In general, most intellectual freedom challenges deal with access by children and young adults to material that does not reflect the challenger's view of their innocence and appropriate behavior.

From the point of view of the public library as an information resource, a more important issue is the lack of factual information on sex health issues including support for alternative life styles, exploration of LGBT issues, and guidance on legal alternative careers such as working in the sex industry. The public library that represents America as a culture of married, traditional, heterosexual couples does not reflect the realities of American society today.

References

Aftab, Parry, Steve L. Herb and Pamela R. Klipsch. 2000. Kids have rights/ parents have responsibilities/librarians have ulcers! *Newsletter on Intellectual Freedom*, 49 no. 1: 5–37.

Amazon.com. 1-2-3 Be a porn star! A step-by-step guide to the adult sex industry. http://www.amazon.com/1-2-3-Step---Step-Guide-Industry/ dp/0965119025/ref=sr_1_1?s=books&ie=UTF8&qid=1381447758&sr=1 -1&keywords=0965119025 (accessed October 10, 2013).

Amazon.com. Amazon.com introduces corporate accounts program; Libraries, small businesses and other organizations can now purchase from Amazon.com without using credit cards. *News release.* http://phx.corporate-ir.net/phoenix.zhtml?c=176060&p=irol -newsArticle_Print&ID=502802&highlight= (accessed October 10, 2013).

Amazon.com. For SEX EDUCATION, see librarian: A guide to issues and resources: Book description http://www.amazon.com/For-SEX -EDUCATION-See-librarian/dp/0313290229/ref=sr_1_2?ie=UTF8&qid =1381435383&sr=8-2&keywords=cornog+martha (accessed October 10, 2013).

ALA Intellectual Freedom Committee. 2012. fifty shades of censorship?. *Newsletter on Intellectual Freedom*, 61, no.4: 145–148.

American Library Association. "Intellectual freedom and censorship Q & A." http://www.ala.org/Template.cfm?Section=basics&Template=/ ContentManagement/ContentDisplay.cfm&ContentID=164089 (accessed October 10, 2013).

Annoyed Librarian. 2008. Libraries and parental control. *Library Journal Blog.* http://lj.libraryjournal.com/blogs/annoyedlibrarian/2008/12/15/ libraries-and-parental-control/ (accessed October 11, 2013).

Bill of Rights. 1789. http://www.archives.gov/exhibits/charters/bill_of_ rights_transcript.html (accessed October 8, 2013).

Caldwell-Stone, Deborah. 2004. Movie ratings are private, not public policy. *ILA Reporter* 2, no. 22: 10–13.

_____. 2013. Filtering and the First Amendment. *American Libraries* 45, no. 3/4: 58–61.

Chelton, Mary. K. 2011. Musings on intellectual freedom and YA services. *Voice of Youth Advocates* 34, no.2: 121.

Chmara, Theresa. 2012. Why recent court rulings don't change the rules on filtering. *American Libraries* 43, no. 7/8: 17.

Chmara, Theresa, and Mach, Daniel. 2004. Minors' rights to receive information under the First Amendment. http://www.ala.org/offices/oif/ ifissues/issuesrelatedlinks/minorsrights (accessed October 10, 2013)

Cohen, Henry. 2003. *Freedom of speech and press : exceptions to the First Amendment*. New York: Novinka Books.

Cohen, Rebecca J. 2008. Sex education and the American public library: A study of collection development, reference services, and programming for young adults. *Young Adult Library Services* 6, no.3: 40–45.

Comfort, Alex. Q. S. 2009. *The joy of sex* (Rev. ed.). New York: Three Rivers Press.

Covenant Eyes. http://www.discernement.com/fichs/10141.pdf (accessed October 8, 2013).

CreateSpace. https://www.createspace.com/ (accessed October 9, 2013).

Eberts, Roger. 2000. Ugly reality in movie ratings. *Roger Ebert's Journal.* http://www.rogerebert.com/rogers-journal/ugly-reality-in-movie-ratings (accessed October 9, 2013)

Facts and statistics about infidelity. *Truths about deception: Advice about lying, infidelity, love and romance.* http://www.truthaboutdeception.com/cheating-and-infidelity/stats-about-infidelity.html (accessed October 11, 2013).

Fialkoff, Francine. 1992. Sex in the library; Madonna's book raises acquisition, censorship, and practical issues. *Library Journal, 117*, 63.

Finance and Economics: Selling sex; economics focus. 2008. *The Economist* January 19: 86.

Full text of "Loompanics 2003 catalog". http://archive.org/stream/Loompanics_Catalog_2003/Loompanics-Catalog-2003_djvu.txt (accessed October 9, 2013.

Goldberg, Beverly. 2004. Kansas librarians embroiled in CD flap. *American Libraries* 35, no. 8: 15–16.

Grobelny, Joseph D. 2013. Self-Publishing: A bibliographic essay. *Against the Grain* 25, no. 3: 35–36.

Gustafson, Rod. 2006. Why the end of "Sanitized" movies is a good thing. *Parenting and the media.* http://parentstv.org/PTC/publications/rgcolumns/2006/0713.asp (accessed October 11, 2013).

Henderson, Harold. 2004. Review of *You can't do that here!* by Jules B. Gerard *Planning* 70, no. 7: 50.

Herzog, Dagmar. 2011. *Sexuality in Europe: a twentieth-century history.* New approaches to European history Cambridge, UK: Cambridge University Press.

Holley, Bob. 2012. Random ramblings—Does the focus on banned books subtly undermine intellectual freedom. *Against the Grain* 24, no. 6: 82–85.

Holt, Eric A. 2001. Patron privacy and the computer screen. *Louisiana Libraries* 64, no.2: 37–38.

Hughes-Hassell, Sandra, Elizabeth Overberg and Shannon Harris. 2013. Lesbian, gay, bisexual, transgender, and questioning (LGBTQ)-themed literature for teens: Are school libraries providing adequate collections? *School Library Research*, 16: 1–18.

Kelsey, Marie. 2007. Are we lucky for the First Amendent? A brief history of students' right to read. *Knowledge Quest* 36, no. 2: 26–29.

Kniffel, Leonard. 1999. Children's access: protection or preparation? *Library Journal*, 30 no. 10: 59–62).

Kolderup, Gretchen. 2013. The First Amendment and internet filtering in public libraries. *Indiana Libraries*, 32 no.1: 26–29.

Landry, David J., Susheela Singh and Jaqueline E. Darroch. 2000. Sexuality education in fifth and sixth grades in U.S. public schools, 1999. *Family Planning Perspectives*, 32 no. 5: 212–219.

Libraries walk a tightrope on porn. 2012. *Los Angeles Times*. January 3. http://articles.latimes.com/2012/jan/03/opinion/la-ed-library-20120103 (accessed October 9, 2013).

Loria, Ana. 2000. *1, 2, 3, be a porn star: a step-by-step guide to the adult sex industry for men and women*. Malibu,CA: InfoNet Publications.

Mauger, Jeremy. 2012. COLLECTION MANAGEMENT, CONCEPTUAL ANACHRONISMS, AND CIPA. *Progressive Librarian*, (Spring):25–33.

Michigan Department of Education. 2007. HIV/STD and sex education in Michigan public schools. A summary of legal obligations and best practices. http://www.michigan.gov/documents/mde/3_Four_Page_Summary_of_Legal_Obligations_249414_7.pdf (accessed October 10, 2013).

Milliot, Jim. 2010. Self-Published titles topped 764,000 in 2009 as traditional output dipped. *Publishers Weekly* April 14. http://www.publishersweekly.com (accessed October 20, 2013).

Oder, Norman and Michael Rogers. 2001. Feds back Minnesota staffers' complaint. *Library Journal*, 126 no. 12: 20–22.

Payment, Simone. 2010. *Friendship, dating, and relationships* 1st ed. New York, NY: Rosen Pub.

Perper, Timothy and Martha Cornog. 1996. *For sex education, see librarian: a guide to issues and resources*. : Greenwood Press.

Pollard, Tom. 2009. *Sex and violence: the Hollywood censorship wars*. Boulder: Paradigm Publishers.

Richey, Jennifer. 2012. Motivators and Barriers to Sexual-Health Information Provision in High School Libraries: Perspectives from District-Level Library Coordinators and High School Principals. *School Library Research*, 15, 1–17.

Rosenberg, Richard S. 2000. Who Will Censor? BC Tel and the Oliver "Hate" Web-Site. *The International Information & Library Review*, 32 no. 3–4: 359–377. doi: http://dx.doi.org/10.1006/iilr.2000.0142

Shepherd, Jack. The Pedophile's Guide To Love And Pleasure. *BuzzFeed*. from http://www.buzzfeed.com/expresident/the-pedophiles-guide-to -love-and-pleasure

Silverstein, Charles and Felice Picano. 2004. *The joy of gay sex* 1st ed. New York: HarperResource.

Sotelo, Nicole. 2009. Women hit hardest in bad economy. *National Catholic Reporter*, 45 no.13: 23.

Stevens, Scarlett. Top Five Erotica Publishers. http://scarlettstevens.word-press.com/2011/08/25/top-five-erotica-publishers/ (accessed October 9, 2013).

University Libaries. Bowling Green State University. 2012. Music Censorship. http://libguides.bgsu.edu/content.php?pid=9333&sid=61254 (accessed October 11, 2013).

University of Illinois at Urbana-Champaign Social Sciences, Health and Education Library. 2013. Challenged children's books. *The school collection: Children's literature at the Social Sciences, Health, and Education Library*. http://www.library.illinois.edu/sshel/s-coll/findbks/addlbibs/ challengedbooks/index.htm (accessed October 10, 2013).

Youth Risk Behavior Survey. 2012. Trends in the prevalence of sexual behaviors and HIV testing national YRBS: 1991–2011 http://www.cdc.gov/ HealthyYouth/yrbs/pdf/us_sexual_trend_yrbs.pdf (accessed October 11, 2013).

Sexual Orientation and Gender Expression

James V. Carmichael

> *Coming from the insularity and prejudices of England
> . . . she [Madge Garland] also found something as elusive
> and enduring as this aesthetic awakening: an instinct for
> the possibilities of friendship and an understanding of the
> world as her home. She called it "freedom of thought."*
>
> ~Lisa Cohen, *For All We Know* (2012)

Our ability to use words as we see fit is perhaps the primary measure of our intellectual freedom. Otherwise, we would live in a dream world, largely unexpressed. We form hierarchical classifications of value, create laws by which we function as societies, interpret law and custom, and make decisions that in turn are justified by ethical and moral understandings through words. This essay discusses words and their changing meanings over time as they have referred to sexual orientation and gender expression, and how language generally engages intellectual freedom. How humans have designated meaning by symbols and signs is one of the enduring objects of study. Words conceal as well as reveal meaning too. Minority members invent local *patois* understood only by initiates so that they may communicate with one another without being understood by members of the usually oppressive majority. Sometimes members of minorities also reclaim pejorative terms of oppression by which they own their own socially-constructed identities (Grahn 1984; Smitherman 2000). Such words and phrases become objects of study in the university where the power relations unleashed by words are deconstructed and refashioned into theory. Most importantly, words and their expressive power mutate with poetic license in verse, history, and legend, whether in print or in performance. As Virginia Woolf declared, words ". . . hate being useful; they hate making money; they hate being lectured about in public. In short, they hate anything that stamps them with one meaning or confines them to one attitude, for it is their nature to change" (Woolf 2011, 627). The words associated with sex, sensuality, and gender are among the most mutable, socially charged, and misunderstood of any subset in English. This entry therefore employs many historical examples to illustrate change.

Consider camp usages. While a portion of the educated general public may recognize camp's origins in the gay community, most of the public probably doesn't. In addition to Sontag's seemingly exhaustive notes on sophisticated uses of camp (Sontag 1964), one may add the much more basic function of discretion, since in addition to its humorous elements, camp provides safety for homosexuals and comfort for oblivious heterosexuals nearby. The use of verbal innuendo or intonation (indirect) or by using "another mother tongue," for example, by referring to other gay or lesbian people in the room as "family," or using "festive," as we did in the fifties and sixties, as a synonym for "gay," lesbian and gay people historically employed camp usages to avoid being "obvious" homosexuals in conversation. This codification has been habitually referred to in the LGBT community as "discretion" (Cohen 2012, 329–30). If it is true, as Halperin (2013) suggests, that the greater part of gay identity is in fact cultural association, sensitivities, and humor, then sex eventually assumes a secondary role in gay identity, whether the general public recognizes that fact or not. It is the confusion of sex with the rest of gay life that creates many of the misunderstandings about the import of LGBT issues and identity.

There are performative elements of gay identity that demand intellectual freedom. With greater social acceptance of homosexuality since the AIDS crisis, for example, public performance has provided a creative venue for individuals to negotiate and express their sexual identity. Bell describes the career arcs of fashion designers John Galliano (b. 1960) and Alexander McQueen (1969–2010), two innovators of the runway show as performance art who express not only sexual themes such as bondage, S&M, but political and autobiographical themes (cf. "The Widow of Culloden") in their work. One important aspect of their creations has been their own appearances and costumes at the end of the show, Galliano usually as outrageously theme-styled as his models, McQueen in work clothes, outwardly eschewing the queenly celebrity persona. Thus the artist as well as his message is subject to invention, masquerade, interpretation, and such extravaganzas may well be the last gasp of the playfulness of camp in a world of increasingly flat-lined and relentless entertainment (Bell n.d.). Such aspects of mass entertainment may in fact be less controversial than more private aspects of gay identity, such as displays of affection in public spaces that would not raise an eyebrow if the individuals were straight.

Throughout this essay, a distinction is made between sex, the reproductive physical attributes with which one is born, and gender, societal expectations of behavior or roles associated with sex. As much as sex and gender have been used interchangeably in recent years (Butler 1990), the polarities of masculinity and femininity remain entrenched in popular consciousness, and some distinction between the terms "sex" and "gender" is as necessary as ever. Intellectual freedom with respect to sexual orientation and gender expression can be usefully discussed in terms of self-determination of sexual identity and gender behavior, access to information, and censorship of information. Associated with these intellectual, spiritual, and expressive dimensions, political engagement and ethical considerations also have an impact on aspects of thought and expression.

Self-Determination: Nomenclature and Dimensions of Identity

Intellectual freedom forms the very core of self-imagining, but it also attends various forms of self-expression in the public sphere. Those whose behaviors and preferences conform to expectations of conventional behavior experience their own conflicts with authority in the course of the life cycle, but those who are "obviously" different in any significant respect—sexuality, race, sex, degree of masculinity/femininity in a given environment—usually feel initially compelled to adapt by either self-segregating with others who appear to be similar, or adjusting their behavior in such a way that they *seem* to exhibit majority characteristics, hence the "closet" (Sedgwick 1990). While it is true that racial identity is more immediately obvious than one's sexual orientation, gay and lesbian individuals are not invisible, and are frequently the target of bullying even before they reach puberty. Historically, the social penalties for sexual minorities have included death, criminal incarceration, banishment, and social exclusion. In some cultures, penalties are still severe (Crompton 2003; Fishman 1998; Cooper 1998; Eskridge 2008; Leavitt 2006; West 1972, esp. 37–39). As the collective experiences of all minorities attest, however, the moral or spiritual cost of "passing" in the majority culture can be high. Whatever forms of intimidation an individual faces—burning at the stake, murder, brutal beatings, bullying, verbal slurs, shunning, disowning by family, friends, and community, or discrimination in the law or at the workplace—to enjoy the full entitlement to life as defined by that nebulous phrase "the pursuit of happiness" in *The Declaration of Independence*, at a minimum, and the entitlement to love proffered to every human being by *The United Nations Declaration of Human Rights* at a maximum, those threats must be removed. In terms of the LGBT climate in the United States, the community is comprised of people who have experienced or continue to experience varying degrees of liberation and oppression, both from without and within (e.g., internalized homophobia), and thus, for all the media attention to *the* LGBT community, especially in television and films, there are in fact multiple LGBT realities based on demographics, experience, and individual responses to life factors.

A Historical Sketch of Politics Surrounding LGBT Nomenclature

In the political and social advancement of sexual dissidents over the past fifty years or so, one must ask whether freedom of expression and the growth of the LGBT community, represented by the exhaustive inclusiveness of its constantly expanding acronym, have in fact clarified the personhood of the individuals it represents beyond their sexual preferences or biological history. A "complete" typology of sexual variance, one greatly expanded since about 1970, has evolved (Greenblatt 2011, 5–6). For the purposes of this essay, the explicit terms *gay, lesbian, bisexual, transsexual, transgender, queer* and the collective term *LGBT* are used depending on context, although many writers prefer the acronym (e.g., LGBTTIQQA) which, while thorough and explicit, usually adds precision at the point where individual elements of sexual identity are being defined, defended, or claimed.

LGBT here refers collectively to those not exclusively committed to heteronormative modes of being, namely: gay men or homosexual males, lesbians or female homosexuals, bisexuals, those not attracted exclusively to the opposite sex, transgender people, those whose "gender behavior, expression, or identity does not conform to the sex they were assigned at birth" (Greenblatt 2011, 6), transsexuals, those who are transitioning or have transitioned from their birth sexual identity, and intersex individuals who are born with biological sexual anomalies. "Queer," a formerly pejorative broad term used to refer to any "non-heterosexual-identified person or act" is also used in several contexts (Greenblatt 2011, 6). "Questioning individuals" refers to those engaged in an exploration of their sexual identity, orientation, or form of gender expression, and the "allies" of all or some of the above people are included under the acronym "A" although none of these latter categories are the primary focus of this discussion. It should be noted also that "I" has been used to stand for "inquiring;" and that "A" is also used for "asexual," those individuals who claim antipathy or indifference to sex.

Given the desire for acceptance by at least a part of the LGBT community, does the perpetuation of an awkwardly elaborate form of labeling also limit how humans define their own expressive possibilities or simply make the assignment of gender roles less problematic? Or both? One of the informal tenets of LGBT etiquette is not to assume that anyone has a particular identity until that person willingly discloses it. A male who has undergone hormone therapy and wears cosmetics, for example, but has not fully transitioned may prefer to be referred to by masculine pronouns until his transformation is complete, but that is not a given. Perhaps labels do serve an educational purpose for the uninitiated, but the education may come at the point where a label is misapplied. While this opportunity to explain his identity may broaden his social freedom, it may in fact limit his own conception of his own or other gendered possibilities. At the very least, we have categorical preferences not accounted for by the oppressive binary implicit in heterosexuality. A typology of sexual difference certainly allows for less ambiguity in purely sexual terms, but fails to address the question of why choosing any sexual category, publicly or not, should be a desirable end of the search for not only sexual, but human, identity, especially given the findings of the various Kinsey reports on the ubiquity of same-sex experience. Where is the person behind the label, and do the labels offer more than a means of meeting the exigencies of political correctness or of fending off unwanted sexual attentions? The question in all minority struggles may ultimately be at what price social equality is forged and what limits a lack of social equality places on how individuals imagine themselves. Hence, the ever-expanding acronym reduces the identity of the person to a sexual function or gender identification, as if personhood consisted of little else (Ghaziani 2011, 117–120). To be fair, however, in many historical contexts that is exactly how the law and society treated people whose sexual identity was unmasked.

What people are called, as Michel Foucault's brilliant historical analysis demonstrates, and how they refer to themselves, are both demonstrations of power (1990). Far from being "the love that dare not speak its name," homosexuality and its variants at times seem like "the love that won't shut up" (Willis 2012). Foucault remarks that a prominent characteristic of modern societies is not so much that they "consigned sex to a shadow existence, but that they dedicated themselves to speaking of it ad infinitum, while exploiting it as the 'secret'" (1990, 35). Foucault views sexuality as a locus of power exploited by the state, the professions, and society. According to him, the eighteenth and nineteenth centuries, far from repressing sexuality, denatured it through excessive discourses on sex:

> First, there was medicine, via the "nervous disorders;" next, psychiatry, when it set out to discover the etiology of mental illnesses, focusing its gaze first on "excess," then onanism, then frustration, then "frauds against procreation," but especially when it annexed the whole of sexual perversions as its own province; criminal justice, too which had long been concerned with sexuality, particularly in the form of "heinous crimes and crimes against nature". . . and lastly all those social controls, which screened the sexuality of couples, parents and children, dangerous and endangered adolescents . . . intensifying people's awareness of it as a constant danger, and this in turn created a further incentive to talk about it. (1990, 30–31)

Foucault demonstrates how, by appropriating the naming and discussion of sexual variants, medical practitioners specializing in sexual disorders stigmatized homosexuality as sexual "deviance." Marcel Proust's father, for example, was a doctor specializing in routine sexual maladies, and that fact may explain why so much attention was paid to young Marcel's "chronic" masturbation, a trait which would be considered normal today (White 1999, 20). The medical authority by which sexual behaviors were named and classified, whether they were sanctioned or condemned by the state, was eventually assumed by psychiatric practitioners who, ironically, were wedded to the idea of homosexuality as a disease until the late twentieth century. This is where the "scientific" paradigm had led them (Dreischer and Merlino 2007).

The principle of intellectual freedom ultimately suggests that individuals be allowed to describe themselves by whatever terms they choose. Such labeling practices as those outlined above do not serve the purposes of government bureaucracy and, in particular, the antiquated classification schemes of the U. S. Census. Recognition of the inadequacy of the categories of race and sex has long been acknowledged by the scholarly community, and limited changes in the past two censuses have not helped. (See also Gates and Ost (2004), who devised a method for estimating the gay and lesbian population in spite of the government's failure to collect such information). Frank Kameny (1925–2011), the United States astronomer fired for his sexual orientation during the 1949–1953 McCarthy "lavender scare" purge of the federal government (Johnson 2004), frequently reminded his audiences that government consists of *we the people* rather than just the office-holders the people elect. Categories must accommodate people, not people, categories.

The "contested terrain" of LGBT identity since the 1990s has made frictionless discussion of non-heterosexual sex, sexual identity, and expression difficult and some would say, undesirable in the LGBT community, at least within the academy (Lovaas, Elia, and Yep 2006; Berlant and Warner 1995; Morland and Willox 2005; Warner 2012). Gore Vidal, for example, became somewhat of a pariah in the gay community for rejecting the label "gay," since he did not believe in gay identity, only homosexual acts. His refusal to embrace the stereotyped gay identities such as the "Castro Street clone" of the 1970s—mustachioed, muscular macho-acting men in regulation tight faded jeans, T shirt or flannel plaid, and Ray Ban aviator glasses—as anything but sexual play-acting, spoke to a more *intellectual* approach to freedom than could be afforded by the sexual abandon of the bath houses and raunchy bars of the pre-AIDS sexual revolution, his own fictional contribution to which, *Myra Breckinridge* (1970), anticipated the trans movement *avant la lettre*. His rejection of the gay party line stung all the more since he was a pioneer of the modern homosexual novel, and had sacrificed critical acceptance of his work by publishing just as the McCarthy era began (Vidal 1948; 1995; and 1999).

Other reasons for the mercurial nature of the LGBT intellectual terrain are complex, but can be explained at the most basic level by individual differences and by the fact that many pioneer gay organizations such as the Gay Task Force of the American Library Association (ALA)[1] had an 'open-door policy' for anyone who wanted to attend its meetings, including "hundreds of gay men and lesbians across the United States who [otherwise] wouldn't dream, of being involved with professional meetings . . . except perhaps to demonstrate against them" (Gittings 1998, 87). Barbara Gittings (1932–2007), longtime leader of the ALA Gay Task Force during its formative years, used the term *gay* to refer to anyone who wanted to join the Task Force, including lesbians (Gittings, quoted in Carmichael 1998, n4). The term also included those, such as bisexuals and transsexuals, whose sexual identities were less comfortably accommodated, if at all, by other existing organizations at the time they became allied with gay/lesbian groups. While there have been complaints of racial and ethnic discrimination by the greater LGBT movement, it is fair to say that individuals of many sorts gradually gained a voice in the relatively non-threatening environment of groups such as the ALA Gay Task Force in the early days of sexual liberation. The common ground of all groups within the gay community lay in the articulation of non-normative sexual identity and expression.

The national gay movement of the 1960s and 1970s followed in the wake of the civil rights and second wave feminist movements. Its renegade status made its precise nature more open and fluid within the (heterosexual) sexual revolution already in progress (see, for example, Chesser (1940), which over its successive editions dropped "for Every Married Adult" in its subtitle; Friedan (1963) and *The Sexual Revolution* (1972) that gave some idea of the wider dimensions of sexual concerns of gay and straight people at that time). Separatist groups provided asylum and guarantees of exclusivity, anonymity, and safety, especially for lesbians and other women whose experience with men had been physically or emotionally violent (Thistelethwaite 1998). Many aspects of formal sociological analysis of countercultural social movements have not been fully developed, but it is generally understood that the early gay movement and its academic correlate, Lesbian and Gay Studies[2], gradually expanded to include other aspects of sexuality. The AIDS crisis of the 1980s and 1990s, however, and particularly the militant protests of the

---

1   Recognized as the first gay professional group in the world, the ALA LGBT Round Table was originally formed under the Social Responsibilities Round Table of the American Library Association in 1970 as the Gay Task Force, and has changed its name periodically as its membership has expanded and the LGBT community has evolved.

2   The movement achieved academic respectability as an independent entity with the publication of *The Journal of Homosexuality* in 1976, but had existed until that time on the periphery of criminological, psychological, sexological, and medical practice (Dynes 1987).

ACT UP and Queer Nation movements in response to government indifference to the disease at the federal, state, and local level led to a more aggressive critique of sexual convention and incorporated various elements of postmodern theory into a critique of heteronormativity under the academic rubric of "Queer Studies."

The theoretical concerns of Queer Studies were those of the postmodern era: post-colonialism, interdisciplinarity, deconstruction, and globalism, what Lyotard calls "incredulity towards metanarratives"—grand historical accounts that treated the rulers, military leaders, and policies of the white western world to the exclusion of women, people of color, lower classes, and of course, sexual minorities (1984, xxiv). While as an academic project, queer theory, like postmodernism generally, has provided insight and—why not?—playfulness into humanist analysis (Eagleton 2003), at its extreme end (as, for example, in interpreting Caravaggio's "The Sacrifice of Isaac" as a symbolic representation of father/son rape (Hammill, cited in Warnke 2007, 101) its value has been questioned. According to such satirical depictions as *The Lecturer's Tale* (2001) by James Hynes, extremes of queer theory and political correctness have run their course, and the excesses of the modern academy, particularly the threat to academic freedom, make it deservedly ripe for a *Götterdämmerung*, one that seems to have already begun in the gutting of the humanities and the growing proportion of non-tenured faculty and administrative positions (Ginsberg 2011). Without gay and lesbian studies or queer theory, however, the LGBT community might never have been gained respectable academic footholds in the university, and thus, the opportunity to educate upcoming generations about LGBT issues as human issues.

Queer Theory set itself up in generational opposition to Lesbian and Gay Studies, which came to be associated negatively with the post-Victorian modernist project of the first half of the twentieth century and with quantitative research dominated by gay white males, with insufficient attention to qualitative aspects of research and feminist, racial, and class concerns generally. But Queer Studies has also been accused of lack of diversity (Lovaas, Elia, and Yep, 2006; Warner, 2012). It is not the purpose of the present essay to judge the fairness of that appraisal or to dwell on divisions within the LGBT community except insofar as they illuminate the basic concerns of intellectual freedom *vis-à-vis* the greater society, but it is perhaps worth noting that the promise of LGBT novels, as exemplified by the early twentieth century canon, e.g. "the modernist canon well stocked with homosexuals . . . Proust, Mann, Gide, Genet, Forster, Woolf, Stein, Langston Hughes, Djuna Barnes, and Henry James . . . Vidal, Isherwood, Baldwin, and Capote" (Glazek, 2013, 25) has not been fulfilled by the return to literary realism in the novels of Michael Cunningham, Alan Hollinghurst, and Cólm Tóibín. The creative experimentation of Edmund White's ambitious but commercially unsuccessful

Nocturnes for the King of Naples (1978), according to Glazek, has been short-circuited by the author's shift from experimental fiction to the lightly fictionalized memoir and popular literary criticism; he has "graduated from the desperation of the closet to the glamour of life as a gay high society tag-along" (Glazek 2012, 25). Thus, as with other groups, the avant-garde of the gay world is pressured to mainstream for the popular market. Success, then, in terms of societal acceptance, can itself be an impediment to intellectual freedom.

LGBT issues can't be easily extricated from issues of race and sex without considerable loss of intellectual integrity. Since at least the eighteenth century due to the slave trade and its after effects, race has led all other minority concerns, from which sex and sexual orientation have gained both momentum and moral force. Sex and gender, however, are more universal concerns: Pharr was the first observer to explicitly tie homophobia to sexism (1988), and one only has to consider the relative invisibility of lesbians in comparison to gay men to perceive how sexism has worked its way through the LGBT community, from McCarthyite purges to the AIDS crisis, and not always to male advantage. Punishments, for example, are not always dealt out equally for gay men and lesbians. Robbins' (1994) study of the purge of gay Library of Congress employees in 1950 found that only men were fired for homosexuality; although statistically it is almost certain that there were more lesbians than gays in the profession. No female employees were fired. Just as female experience was at that time discounted relative to that of men, so lesbians were considered less of a security risk—less susceptible to blackmail and exposure—than gay men. Moreover, due to the prevalence of the widely accepted phenomenon of women living together in "Boston marriages" to save living expenses, female companionate relationships were less suspect than male ones (The History Project 1998). Thus, the gender binary is active especially in the LGBT community, and women are subject the same disadvantages that they experience elsewhere. Lesbian caretakers of men with AIDS emerged early in the 1980s, and the experience for women led in some cases to burn out and desertion of the ALA's Gay Task Force for the Feminist Task Force.

The question of what kinds of identities the LGBT community includes is thus a very complex question because of the differences between the individuals, and the perceptions about those individuals that constitute it. Whether one believes that there is a quality of being that characterizes all gay and (or) lesbian people—the so-called *essentialist* position—or, like Gore Vidal, one views one's same-sex sexual activity as merely one feature of one's identity, depends on all of the factors that have contributed to that individual's life: socio-economic, cultural, generational, educational, and the accidents of individual fortune. The kinds of pressures these identities exert in turn on society will vary according to time, place, and circumstance, and determine their reception. Hyne's mysterious Trans (transsexual or transgender) English instructor at the center of *The Lecturer's Tale* may be the very intellectual force who drives the curriculum of the modern university, or the intellectual weight of postmodern identity politics may drive the university to collapse and revert to vocational schools where tenure is only a distant memory. Scenarios of intellectual freedom for LGBT people have been and will be as kaleidoscopic as their individual names, and we may therefore expect that the vocabulary used to identify them within and without that community will coalesce and expand with time.

Bending Gender Nomenclature

As discussed in the previous section, homosexuality needs "a more generous vocabulary . . . than is provided by the dichotomy of 'freely chosen' on the one hand and 'fated' or 'determined' on the other" (Card, quoted in Wilkerson 2009, 97). In a sense, gay and lesbian experience reflects the tension found in heterosexual culture between the duality of "rigid aspects of the self like sexuality that seem determined and aspects of the self that seem freely chosen" (Wilkerson 2009, 97). Historically, these tensions have been addressed, or ignored, by religion and the law. The gay and lesbian communities have evolved in spite of the dogged opposition of some churches, synagogues, mosques and councils of government, and its success speaks to its ability— some might even say, genius—for communications, especially through film and television as well as in traditional print media formats (Streitmatter 1995; Meeker 2006). Expressions of identity and sexuality in the public forums of the parade, the concert, the news, and the stage, and the ubiquitous camp aside in television and film, have ensured progress since the 1960s because of, as well as in spite of, adversity. Much the same may be said to apply of the Trans community.

   It seems difficult to remember a time when sexual orientation was not a central political issue, and it may be even harder to remember a time when the physical possibility of sex reassignment surgery was as rare as a successful heart transplant—perhaps more rare. The exemplar for decades was Christine Jorgensen, (1926-1989), although Wikipedia's article on Jorgensen reminds readers that German doctors had performed successful sex reassignment surgery by 1930, and two of the residents of the Magnus Hirschfeld Institute in Berlin were transsexuals. The relationship of sex reassignment surgery to sexual orientation is complex and likewise the issues faced by transsexuals can be analogized with those of homosexuals only with difficulty. Their commonality lies in their position as objects of persecution due to their sexual difference. Bisexuality is also a much more complex phenomenon than is commonly depicted as it encompasses not only those who are genuinely attracted to both sexes, but those who have had sexual experiences with both sexes and, while preferring one sex over another, do not exclude the possibility of being attracted to their secondary preference later (Bogle 2012). For some individuals, such attractions may be seamless or fluid.

As Talbot notes "transgenderism has replaced homosexuality as the new civil rights frontier, and Trans activists have become vocal and organized" (2013, 59). The term transgender, however, is an umbrella category that includes the full range of individuals who resist gender categories, e.g., those who only cross dress or wear makeup or take hormones or by "styling their appearance in gender-confounding ways but abstaining from medical procedures" (2013, 62). Yet gender dysphoria, the sense of being in the wrong biological body, is experienced by only one out of every 10,000 for males and females, and "long term studies of children with gender dysphoria have found that only fifteen per cent continue to have this feeling as adolescents and adults" (65), so parents and counselors are waiting longer to resort to radical surgery, and this is true for intersex individuals as well. The progressive idea is to allow individuals the maximum amount of autonomy in determining their sexual identity, and to resist rushing into irremediable surgical procedures. For a complementary perspective, see Ruth Padawer's recent article, "boygirl" (2012).

Yet while a degree of permissiveness with gender bending is generally acceptable to the general public—it has certainly not hurt the popularity of a rock star like David Bowie—Americans seen hard-wired to masculinity and femininity, whether they are gay or straight. "Metrosexualism," urban sexual sophistication (straight-but-not-narrow), and a loosening of certain symbolic gender rigidities such as the use of cosmetics for males, body building for women, or indifference towards sexual orientation in the heterosexual population, has received a certain amount of attention in the press. There remains resistance to the idea of a sexual continuum among males, however, and this may be the personal limit of intellectual freedom for some individuals. Although research has shown that both straight and gay males are aroused by gay and straight pornography, attachment to the gender binary so far as identity is concerned is adamant. Tye posits that ". . . the myth of the straight male is integral to our culture's conceptualization of masculinity. Acknowledging the truth is too threatening—both for men and women. Furthermore, keeping the myth alive is essential to social conservatives' goal of keeping gender and sexuality in check. This is nothing if not a power issue" (2008, 83).

Gender fluidity receives lip service from the educated public, yet men who play female roles in a dramatic production, for example, may resist the idea that it is part of their identity or something more indicative than role play. In the creative realm, it is all very well to insist as Virginia Woolf did, that, "It is fatal to be a man or woman pure and simple; one must be woman-manly or man-womanly" (Woolf 1991, 108), but workaday androgyny plays knowingly with the appearances of masculinity and femininity, so that even as we defy the shallowness of gender roles, we are held captive by them, and nowhere more so than on the surfaces of sexual attraction. Medical and psychological publications of the 1930s, especially the two-volume *Sex Variants*, linked homosexuality with cross-gender identification and were responsible for "perpetuating a clear distinction between masculine and feminine roles" (Minton 1986, 1). These studies succeeded all too well in their aims, for as Ross noted in his recent review of gay culture, "A Web site devoted to culling obnoxious messages from gay hookup sites included the following: 'Don't be gay,' 'No fats or fems,' 'If you have a broken wrist, keep movin.' Fleeing stereotypes, gay men too often fall into a deeper conformity—the rigid choreography of the average male" (2012, 52). Such notices don't speak well for the gender tolerance of these individuals. Much as the gay community may deplore the stereotypes of butch and nelly, Academy Awards go to high camp Trans *Kinky Boots* and hunky queer cowboys in brokeback marriages (Handley 2011; Butler 2006). The reality is usually more ambiguous, however.

The importance of the Trans movement is that it has expanded the ways that we think about gender and the words we use to describe gendered experience, although it may also be presumed to have posed a challenge to some aspects of traditional gay, lesbian, and bisexual identities. It is the assumption of this essay that lesbian, gay and bisexual identities are may be spoken of separately, i.e., that many if not most gays, lesbians, and bisexuals do not experience gender dysphoria or the sense of being in the wrong body. Nevertheless, the Trans movement has made room for people within the LGBT community who have only partially transitioned, and mandated a customary respect for individual's choices with regard to choice of pronoun, appearance, and behavior.

Nomenclature and Censorship

Homosexuality and its attendant list of sexual crimes was reduced to an act rather than a feeling (e.g., *love*) well into the twentieth century, and the various acts were euphemized into Latin (*fellatio*) lest the epidemic be spread by use of the vernacular. Over time, it became less and less mentionable in polite society. The last European public burning for a homosexual, a sodomy case concerning a priest who had also stabbed his victim, occurred in France in 1784. By 1791, France had become the first western country to decriminalize homosexuality under the *Code Pénal de la Révolution*, and became the twentieth century publishing capital for erotic books of all stripes, whatever their literary value (Crompton 2003, 450, 524–528; Kearney 2007). But, in America, literary depictions of homosexuals in mainstream literature were rare in the nineteenth century. They were usually secondary characters, as was the hustler Harry Bolton in Herman Melville's *Redburn* (1849). The Comstock Act of 1873 made the distribution of pornography through the mails illegal and expanded the powers of the Postmaster General. At various times throughout the twentieth century, the subject of homosexuality in a non-medical context was enough to bring a book to court, as was the case with *The Well of Loneliness* by Radclyffe Hall in 1929. In *People vs. Friede* (1955), the American publishers of Hall's novel were found guilty under the New York obscenity statute as it extolled a "female invert" and "unnatural and depraved relationships" in an idealized fashion (Green 1990, 355). During the McCarthy era, affinities with either homosexuals or interracial activities were often conflated with Communism (Johnson 2004). Thus over the course of the nineteenth century, much as Foucault has noted, literary discussion of homosexuality was pushed to the background and the law appropriated proper determination of the terms of discussion through censorship. This in turn affected the ways in which gay and lesbian people thought about the acceptability of their behavior, and molded the codes of etiquette by which homoexuality could (not) be discussed.

The most basic form of suppression after bodily harm and death is censorship. If information about identity and the words that describe and explore it are sequestered or destroyed, the individual can receive no affirmation. If untruths become orthodoxy, lies are codified. When Barbara Gittings, as a library aide, searched for information on same-sex attraction in her college library, she encountered the full panoply of psychiatric studies that viewed homosexuality as a disease. As an early lesbian activist and editor of the East Coast edition of the Daughters of Bilitis journal, *The Ladder*, she made both psychiatry and librarianship the focus for her activist energies. She promoted positive gay and lesbian literature, developed a gay bibliography that became the first of its kind for library users, joined a group of founding members of the National Gay Task Force, stormed the 1972 annual meeting of the American Psychiatric Association in order to protest the disease classification of homosexuality in the American Psychological Association's *Diagnostic and Statistical Manual*, and "combatted the lies in libraries" (Gittings 1979; 1998; Drescher and Merlino 2007). Thus, library history provides one of the earliest and richest examples of how misinformation and mislabeling work to the disadvantage of sexual minorities, and how intellectual freedom changes the climate in which oppression operates. LGBT Round Table history is a refreshing founding counter-narrative in a profession in which prudery was often mistaken for literary taste and conflated with censorship (Markun, 621).

The liberality of the Supreme Court of the 1950s and 1960s under the leadership of Justice Earl G. Warren had a positive effect on all erotic literature, whatever its orientation. D. H. Lawrence's *Lady Chatterley's Lover* (1926) was banned in the United States until 1959; and Jean Gênet's *Our Lady of the Flowers* had to wait until 1964 for American publication. Meanwhile the illicit pornographic subculture flourished hand-in-hand with the more respectable gay publications, which skirted various prohibitions with regards to male frontal nudity until 1967, when advocates of sexual freedom gained a victory in *United States of America vs. Lloyd Spinar and Conrad Germain* (Sears 2006, 517–535). Since that time, the courts have tended to employ the vague standard of community values as a general guide. Community values are, of course, highly determined by the words used to describe them.

The internet and multiplicity of media have stymied the effectiveness of conventional monitoring of content and access to controversial materials, through filtering, for example (Schrader and Wells 2009). However fine the distinctions between erotica and pornography, artistic expression and obscenity (Lawrence 1953), the best censorship is probably no censorship; let readers outgrow their prurient tastes if they can, for no legislation can curb curiosity (Deacon 1926). While LGBT books have consistently been near the top on the ALA Banned Books lists, particularly those written for youth, no one argues unopposed any more that writings by or about LGBT concerns, or expressions of such sensibilities, are by their very nature obscene. The fact that the British Museum Press offers among its 2013 summer books R. B. Parkinson's *A Little Gay History: Desire and Diversity across the World* suggests that the climate for LGBT publications has undergone a profound ontological change in the western world.

Nomenclature, Conformity, and Normalization

Conformity to social norms is one of the ways individuals acquiesce their need for attention. It indicates maturity to a certain degree, although conformity acquired negative connotations in periods such as the 1920s and 1960s when upheaval and revolt against social structures and conventions prevailed. Although the LGBT movement was born during a socially conservative era (D'Emilio 1983), it did not flourish until a revolutionary one (Hirschman 2012) when it acquired its reputation for flamboyant color and outrageousness (dykes on bikes, males dressed as nuns on roller skates, drag generally, hyper-masculine musculature and nudity). The choice of gay marriage as a unifying focus for the LGBT movement may therefore seem regressive in that it conforms to a conservative social norm, but queering marriage may also be a revolutionary act in the same sense that "living in sin" with a lover was once considered a radical flouting of convention.

Same-sex attachments have been recorded throughout human history in all advanced cultures (Crompton 2003; Malcolm 2007; Muhlstein 1999;

Rowbotham 2008; and White 1999) and there is a long tradition of same-sex attachments among aboriginals, repressed by Christian colonization as part of the imperial project (Parkinson 2013). Modern western cultures including American settler culture have no valid ontological basis for appraising or interpreting native same-sex relationships, since as settlers they are also occupiers and invaders; there can't be rapprochement with the new-age "two spirit" culture (Rifkin 2011, 275).

Marriage as a legally binding act among same-sex couples was rare before the twenty-first century, and even heterosexual marriage was limited to the upper classes in England before the eighteenth century and particularly the Marriage Act of 1752 (Boswell 1994; Callón 2011; Stone 1992). Although it is common today to hear marriage bruited about as a 'God-given" institution without any attempt to distinguish among its customary, legalistic and religious elements, Lawrence Stone (1992, 3) draws attention to the fact that many eighteenth century married couples in England could not be sure if they were married or not due to the prevalence of common-law marriage and defects in the marriage laws.

Since the "decriminalization' of homosexual acts in *Lawrence v. Texas* in 2003, the political energies of the LGBT community have been refocused on normalization (Lithwick 2012), although the Supreme Court ruling does not ensure immunity from entrapment on the local level (Huffman 2011). The current political emphasis on marriage is a product of generational change within the LGBT community, one which the conservative Right has predictably exploited as an example of LGBT exceptionalism to divert media attention from more substantive issues such as economic inequality and its corrosive social effects (Judt 2010).

There are LGBT individuals who believe the push for gay marriage is misdirected (Warner 1999, 81–14) and historian John D'Emilio, in a presentation before the ALA LGBT Round Table (2009). Particularly among members of the generation coming to maturity in the sixties there is no consensus about the role gay marriage will play in social acceptance for the LGBT community as "just like us," if only because nonconformity was the byword of the sixties. As one Minnesota commentator remarked, to some observers, it seems at times as if the gay marriage movement may be "leading down the aisle to nowhere" (Burns 2012, 8).

Naming, Labeling and Ethical Considerations

Intellectual freedom is literally, free. Freedom of the Press extends only to those who own one; if you have the money to buy the press, the freedom to print what you please extends to you. Where intellectual freedom becomes sticky is in an unequal power relation (e.g., teacher/student, political advertiser/television consumer) in which a person or organization vested with authority uses that authority to intimidate a vulnerable party. The moral or ethical concerns of those who understand non-binary sexual orientation and gender expression as a direct threat to their intellectual freedom and lifestyle, and those whose very identity is inextricably bound to that expression, test the limits of the possibilities of civil discourse in a democratic society. The fact that polarization has characterized that discourse since about 1980 (cf. Anita Bryant's, "Family Values," Reagan and the emergence of the Christian Right in politics; the AIDS crisis) does not so much reflect the breakdown of society as it does the deafening volume of a partisan debate that is occurring à haute *voix*. For the first time, thanks to the internet and the popular media there are virtually no limits on expression. Mrs. Grundy is not dead, but even she knows that in a world where pornography is available in multiple formats to every person of whatever age with the ability to plug into the internet and pay, the argument is no longer about sex or even national security. The argument is about power, money, diminishing resources, and establishing conventions of engagement. The question then becomes, how does another's *freedom of expression* (verbal or actual) limit one's own *intellectual freedom*?

Outside of a small section of the LGBT community and perhaps philosophy and English departments in universities, most people do not understand or care about the torturous distinctions made by the intelligentsia of the queer community among shades of meaning between labels, inclusivity *et al*. To such people, whom we may refer to as the general public, individualism may have more to do with conformity and how one votes, while sexual orientation and gender expression may be fancy ways of referring to little more than the sexual activities of those people who frequent same-sex bars. Articulation and elaboration of our identities does not necessarily convert people in the non-LGBT community to a more respectful attitude. The historical problems of queer individualism, stereotyping, and problematical categorization and nomenclature may be as remote to the general public as the intricacies of mathematical reasoning in nuclear science, though they may function in a world that benefits from aspects of both worlds. You don't have to understand how a combustion engine works to operate an automobile, as the saying goes.

Especially within the context of the publicly-funded university, however, practical aspects of functioning in an era of identity politics and taste-group marketing become obvious. As with problems of public expression regarding race and sex (e.g., female clergy, a mixed-race President), equitable expression for *all* citizens of the United States is threatened by the current judicial iteration of free speech (*Citizens United vs. Federal Election Committee* 2010) since the First Amendment of the U. S. Constitution forbids the government from limiting political contributions made by corporations, associations, or labor unions. The ruling means that ordinary interest groups with limited funds will have very little defense against more wealthy groups. More money means more speech. While the case may evoke the Gilded Age with its atmosphere of capitalism run amok, it has direct implications for current day citizens given that many voting Americans are influenced by news media and political advertising on television. This is significant in that money not only works against LGBT interests, but for them as well. For example, the most recent study of funders for LGBT issues found that of $123 million spent for LGBT work across the United States, only $3.8 went to the South. In North Carolina, where the Amendment One anti-gay marriage measure passed into the Constitution by 61 percent in 2011, follow up interviews with pro-amendment voters found confusion among them about what the amendment actually was about. Funders tend to believe the stereotypes about the region and consider change in the region hopeless. Media-made Dixie extends to negative stereotypes.

There is not always adequate traditional redress available to the citizen who protests. While rallies in Minnesota in 2011 reversed the governor's attempt to outlaw collective bargaining, repeated weekly "Moral Mondays" in North Carolina seem to have little effect. North Carolinians have demonstrated against cuts in public education and healthcare that target the most vulnerable citizens and have been arrested for their trouble. Governor Pat McCrory and other lawmakers have spoken respectfully to the press about the demonstrators, but are not making any adjustments to the budget (Berman 2013). World opinion does not count for much in Washington at present, either, so the United Nations' LGBT-rights declaration in 2011 can not necessarily be relied on to have much effect in Mayberry, let alone the rest of the world, where homosexuality is still illegal in approximately seventy-eight countries, and, at least theoretically, punishable by death in five of them (Parkinson 2013, 23).

There are clearly ethical issues related to LGBT intellectual freedom that call for more individual responsibility than they do government action. Moshman presents three case studies that illustrate practical ways to protect the academic freedom of all parties to a discussion of sexual orientation in the classroom environment (2002, 147–161). Universities are supposed to be relatively safe environments for intellectual freedom, at least according to the charter documents of the American Association of University Professors. There are clearly limits to how far thought may be translated into action, as the notorious case of Pennsylvania State University's assistant coach Jerry Sandusky illustrates.

More troubling for the LGBT community and western culture generally is the ancient Greek legacy conjoining pederasty and pedagogy, by which associations such as the North American Man/Boy Love Association (NAM-BLA), which advocates for this ancient inheritance and combats legal age limitations on non-coercive sex, exist on the edge of culturally acceptable practice (Percy 2005). Many people in the LGBT community will not even discuss the issue because it raises the specter that has haunted their efforts to achieve mainstream status within the larger culture, namely the conflation of pedophilia with same-sex desire.

Jordan's (2011) content analysis of the treatment of homosexual themes in Christian literature—gay and straight—sheds light on the question of youth and sexuality in a refreshing way and deserves to be widely read. He begins his exegesis with a discussion of G. Stanley Hall's 1904 *Adolescence: Its Psychology and Its Relations to Physiology, Anthropology, Sociology, Sex, Crime, Religion, and Education*, whose "scientific" study of youth is nevertheless tinted by Hall's own religious convictions, unveiling an "ephebic decade" from the onset of puberty to "conversion" "rebirth" in the firmly heterosexual institution of marriage. It is a delicate and disordered period of life, subject to the dangers, temptations, and trials which religious teaching will cure. As Rifkin reads Hall,

> This "best decade of life" merits "reverence" perhaps more than "anything else in the world." In adolescence, the divine energies for change are the most active. They align the individual with divine purposes through sex. The "rich and varied orchestration" of sexual life "brings the individual into closest rapport with the larger life of the great Biologos [God]." (Jordan 2011, 4)

Adolescent desire can alight almost anywhere and then become fixed through habit.

It is not difficult to understand from this beginning point where Jordan is leading the reader in twentieth century discussions of homosexuality and religion. He provides a context through close reading of diocesan literature, texts from the homophile era of the 1950s as well as the Christian Right backlash of the 1970s and the homosexual recovery movement, for the spiritual alienation of gay youth. Christian thinking about youth and homosexuality led to the establishment by Troy Perry of the Metropolitan Community [LGBT] Church in 1968, now numbering 222 congregations in 37 countries. Perhaps Jordan's most poignant reading concerns John Rechy's controversial gay novel about a Los Angeles teen-aged hustler, *City of Night* (1963), which he brilliantly interprets as a gay *Divine Comedy* "except that in this undivine comedy *Purgatario* is undistinguishable from *Inferno* because there is no further paradise." He describes the novel as "one of the great works of gay religion—precisely because it is a prolonged meditation on adolescence" (2011, 79). For Rechy, a Catholic author, absolution resides in "recognizing the form of another's telling," although the novel itself is far more than autobiography: "self-narration becomes theodicy" (Jordan 2011, 80). In his concluding chapter, aptly titled "How Not to Talk about Sex in Church," he reminds readers of the important role church rhetoric plays not only in enforcing laws and customs, but also, in spite of explicit teachings to the contrary, in providing a place and inspiration for inventing an "alternate self." Thus, the institution of the church may ignite musical or artistic aspirations while it restrains expression of queer or non-reproductive sexuality. It comes to symbolize the investiture of meaning in life even while its self-seriousness inspires mockery. "They offer material for that curious queer mimicry known as camp, but they also and inevitably trouble tidy schemes for regulating loves" (2011, 213). Thus, spiritual ownership of sexual identity, orientation, and gender expression may provide the most durable foundation of intellectual freedom for those we now refer to as *LGBT*, whatever they are called—whether it comes in the twenty-first century church, an alternate form of enlightenment or a program of recovery, or both, or all three (Borden 2007). Of course, spiritual freedom may also come through agnosticism.

A second very important ethical area relates back to the indispensable value of self-knowledge regarding one's sexual orientation and sex identity. As Battaly notes, given the constraints of our categorically-inclined culture, and the assumption that sex identity is "exhausted by the concepts of male and female" (2007, 151), many people may not discover their true identity until later in life. The news archives are stuffed with examples of politicians, actors, and other public figures who claim self-ignorance rather than hypocrisy when their sexual apostasy is revealed. The emphasis in the past thirty years on exposing children to information about LGBT issues long before adolescence represents in part an attempt to encourage self-knowledge and ownership of identity before others can exploit the LGBT individual. More importantly, self-knowledge and openness may prevent the LGBT individual from persecuting other like individuals in an attempt to conceal or distance herself from a "hidden" identity, (Battaly 2007; Padawer 2012).

Hidden identities raise still a third very controversial ethical dilemma that concerns the "outing" of public figures, and especially those who are assuming anti-LGBT stances or pursuing anti-LGBT policies, or have done so in the past (Mohr 1992; Stramel 2008). This strategy is not unique to the queer community: throughout human history, various groups have exacted justice for past persecutions. To the LGBT community, defamation or exposure can in some ways be likened to death-in-life, but in the case of particularly vulnerable individuals it can also lead to death. For example, Tyler Clementi committed suicide in 2010 after his college roommate streamed video of him having sex with a man on the internet. Outing of public figures by LGBT activists first occurred during the AIDS crisis to engage public discussion about the disease. It has become customary in modern biographical practice both for prurient and explanatory reasons. In the case of Roger Casement, the Irish hero who had exposed the inhumanity of Leopold III's imperial regime in the Congo, the neutrality of the Irish in World War I, the Irish uprising against Britain in 1916, and Casement's attempt to recruit Germans to the "Irish Brigade" to fight against the British in Ireland led to his conviction for treason. After the conviction, photographs of his diaries for 1903, 1910, and 1911 including evidence of his homosexuality were circulated by the government to his mainly Irish Catholic supporters. Needless to say, the evidence undermined the case for commutation, and he was executed (Ó Síocháin 2008).

How words and labels may be used to endanger or harm an individual have in recent years received considerable attention from advocates of the anti-bullying movement, and the LGBT community has benefitted perhaps more than other groups from the focus on the unacceptability of bullying, although it is worth reiterating that silence about the subject characterized previous generations because individual adults were free to punish bullies with impunity, and children who suffered were expected to rise above their travails, which supposedly made them stronger. In the present era, emphasis on ethical behavior seems to focus on protecting those too young, weak, or incapacitated for self-defense, but no doubt in the future a different articulation of social ethics will emerge. It is always to question where any conventions of ethical behavior leave the interests of individual versus societal intellectual freedom, and how lines between ethical behavior and intellectual freedom are drawn.

References

Baker, Jack. 1972. Homosexual is an oppressive term. In *The sexual revolution: Traditional mores versus new values*, ed. Gary E, McCuen and David L. Bender, 61–64. Minneapolis, MN: Greenhaven Press.

Battaly, Heather D. 2007. Intellectual virtue and knowing one's own sexual orientation. In *Sex and ethics: Essays on sexuality, virtue, and the good life*, ed. Halwani, Raja, 149–161. New York: Palgrave Macmillan.

Bell, Deborah L. n.d. Masquerade motivations behind the fashion shows of Alexander McQueen and John Galliano. Unpublished manuscript.

Berlant, Lauren and Michael Warner. 1995. What does Queer Theory teach us about X? *PMLA* 110 (May): 343–349.

Berman, Ari. 2013. Carolina's moral mondays. *The Nation* 5 no. 12: 9–10.

Bogle, Donald. 2012. *Heat wave: The life and career of Ethel Waters*. New York: Harper Collins.

Borden, Audrey. 2007. *The history of gay people in Alcoholics Anonymous: from the beginning.* New York: Haworth Press.

Boswell, John. 1994. *Same-sex unions in pre-modern europe.* New York: Villard.

Burns, Rebecca. 2012. Beyond gay marriage. *In these times.* (August 2012): 8–9.

Butler, Judith. 1990. *Gender trouble: Feminism and the subversion of identity.* New York: Routledge, 1990.

Butler, Kathy. 2006. Many couples must negotiate terms of 'Brokeback Marriages.' *New York Times,* March 7. http://search.proquest.com/hnpnewyorktimes/docview/93217249/13F96A0E0B722F90E03/1?accountid=14604 (accessed July 30, 2013).

Callón, Carlos. 2011. Amigos e sodomitas. A configuración da homosexualidade na Idade Media, merecente do XVI Vicente Risco de Ciencias Sociais. http://www.galiciae.com/nova/78210.com (accessed August 6, 2013).

Carmichael, James V. Jr. ed. 1998. *Daring to find our names: The search for lesbigay library history.* Westport, CT: Greenwood Press.

Chesser, Eustace. 1940. *Love without fear: A plain guide to sex technique for every married adult.* London: Cowan.

Clarke, Eric O. 2000. *Virtuous vice: Homoeroticism and the public sphere.* Durham, NC: Duke University Press.

Cohen, Lisa. 2012. *All we know: Three lives.* New York: Farrar, Straus & Giroux.

Cooper, Janet. 1998. Librarians as cultural enforcers. In *Daring to find our names: The search for lesbigay library history.* ed. James V. Carmichael Jr., 113–120. Westport, CT: Greenwood Press.

Crompton, Louis. 2003. *Homosexuality and civilization.* Cambridge, MA: Belknap Press of Harvard University Press.

Dalzell, Tom. 2010. *Flappers 2 rappers: American youth slang.* Minneola, NY: Dover.

Deacon, William A. 1926. A note on the censorship. In *Poteen: a pot-pourri of Canadian essays,* 29–50. Ottawa: The Graphic Publishers, Ltd.

D'Emilio, John. 1983. *Sexual politics, sexual communities: The making of a homosexual minority in the United States, 1940–1970.* Chicago: University of Chicago Press.

Drescher, Jack and Joseph P. Merlino. 2007. *American psychiatry and homosexuality: An oral history.* New York: Harrington Park Press.

Dynes, Wayne R. 1987. *Homosexuality: A research guide.* New York: Garland.

Eagleton, Terry. 2003. *After theory.* New York: Basic Books.

Eskridge, William N., Jr. 2008. *Dishonorable passions: Sodomy laws in America. 1861–2003*. New York: Viking.

Fishman, Israel. 1998. Reclaiming a founding. In *Daring to find our names: The search for lesbigay library history*. Ed. James V. Carmichael Jr., 107–112. Westport, CT: Greenwood Press, 1998.

Foucault, Michel. 1990. *The history of sexuality, volume I: An introduction*. New York: Vintage Books.

Friedan, Betty. 1963. *The feminine mystique*. New York: Norton.

Gates, Gary J. and Jason Ost. 2004. *The gay and lesbian atlas*. Washington, DC: Urban Institute Press.

Ghaziani, Amin. 2011. Post-gay collective identity construction. *Social Problems* 58 (February): 99–125.

Ginsberg, Benjamin. 2011. *The fall of the faculty: The rise of the all-administrative university and why it matters*. New York: Oxford University Press.

Gittings, Barbara. 1978. Combatting the lies in libraries. In *The gay academic*, ed. Louie Crews, 107–118. Palm Springs, CA: ETC Publications.

– – –. 1998. Gays in library land: The gay and lesbian task force of the American Library Association: The first sixteen years. In *Daring to find our names: The search for lesbigay library history*. Ed. James V. Carmichael Jr., 81–93. Westport, CT: Greenwood Press, 1998.

Glazek, Christopher. 2012. mid-century male. *London Review of Books* 34 (July 19): 25–26.

Grahn, Judy. 1984. *Another mother tongue: Gay words, gay worlds*. Boston: Beacon Press.

Green, Jonathan. 1990. *Encyclopedia of censorship*. New York: Facts on File.

Greenblatt, Ellen. 2011. *Serving LGBTIQ Library and Archives Users: Essays on Outreach, Service, Collections and Access*. Jefferson, NC: McFarland.

Handley, William R., ed. 2011. *The brokeback book: From story to cultural phenomenon*. Lincoln: University of Nebraska Press.

Hirschman, Linda. 2012. *Victory: The triumphant gay revolution*. New York: Harper.

Huffman, M. Blake. 2011. North carolina courts: Legislating compulsory heterosexuality by creating new crimes under the crimes against nature statute post-*Lawrence v. Texas*. *Law & Sexuality* 20: 1–30.

The History Project. 1998. *Improper Bostonians: Lesbian and gay history from the Puritans to playland*. Boston: Beacon Press, 1998.

Johnson, David K. 2004. *The lavender scare: The cold war persecution of gays and lesbians in the federal government*. Chicago: University of Chicago Press.

Jordan, Mark D. 2011. *Recruiting young love: How Christians talk about homosexuality*. Chicago: University of Chicago Press, 2011.

Judt, Tony. 2010. *Ill fares the land.* New York: Penguin Press.

Kearney, Patrick J. 2007. *The Paris Olympia press.* 2nd ed. Liverpool: Liverpool University Press.

Lawrence, D. H. 1953. Pornography and obscenity. In *Sex, literature, and censorship: Essays,* ed. Harry T. Moore, 69–88. New York: Twayne Publishers.

Leavitt, David. 2006. *The man who knew too much: Alan Turing and the invention of the computer.* New York: W. W. Norton.

Lithwick, Dahlia. 2012. Extreme makeover: The story behind the story of *Lawrence v. Texas. The New Yorker* (March 12): 76–79.

Lovaas, Karen E, John P. Elia, and Gust A. Yep. 2006. Shifting ground(s): Surveying the contested terrain of LGBT Studies and Queer Theory. *The Journal of Homosexuality* no. 52 (1–2): 1–18.

Lyotard, Jean-Francois. 1984. *The postmodern condition: A report on knowledge.* Minneapolis, MN: University of Minnesota Press, 1984.

Malcolm, Janet. 2007. *Two Lives: Gertrude and Alice.* New York: Yale University Press.

Markun, Leo. 1930. *Mrs. Grundy: A history of four centuries of morals intended to illuminate present problems in Great Britain and the United States.* New York: Appleton.

Meeker, Martin. 2006. *Contacts desired: Gay and lesbian communications and community, 1940s–1970s.* Chicago: The University of Chicago Press.

Melville, Herman. 1948. *Redburn: His first voyage.* London: Jonathan Cape.

Minton, Henry L. 1986. Femininity in men and masculinity in women: American Psychiatry and Psychology portray homosexuality in the 1930's. *Journal of Homosexuality* 13 (Fall): 1–21.

Mohr, Richard D. 1992. *Gay ideas: Outing and other controversies.* Boston: Beacon Press.

Morland, Iain and Annabelle Willox, eds. 2005. *Queer theory.* New York: Palgrave Macmillan.

Moshman, David. 2002. Homophobia and academic freedom. *Journal of Lesbian Studies* 6 nos. 3/4: 147–161.

Muhlstein, Anka. 1999. *A taste for freedom: The life of Astolphe de Custine.* New York: Helen Marx Books.

Ó Síocháin, Séamus. 2008. *Roger Casement: Imperialist, rebel, revolutionary.* Dublin: Lilliput Press.

Padawer, Ruth. 2012. boygirl. *New York Times Magazine* (August 12): 19–23.

Parkinson, R. B. 2013. *A little gay history: Desire and diversity across the world.* London: The British Museum Press.

Percy, William A. III. 2005. Reconsiderations about Greek Homosexualities. *Journal of Homosexuality* 49, no. 3-4: 13-61.

Pharr, Suzanne. 1988. *Homophobia: A Weapon of Sexism.* Little Rock, Ark.: Chardon.

Rifkin, Mark. 2011. *When did Indians become straight? Kinship, the history of sexuality, and native sovereignty.* New York: Oxford University Press.

Robbins, Louise S. 1994. The library of congress and federal loyalty programs, 1947-1956: No 'communists or cocksuckers'. *The Library Quarterly* 64 (October): 365-385.

Ross, Alex. 2012. Love on the march. *The New Yorker* (November 12): 48-53.

Rowbotham, Sheila. 2008. *Edward Carpenter: A life of freedom and love.* New York: Verso.

Schrader, Alvin and Kristopher Wells. 2009. *Challenging Silence, Challenging Censorship.* Ottawa: Canadian Teachers Federation.

Sears, James T. 2006. *Behind the mask of the Mattachine: The Hal Call Chronicles and the early movement for homosexual emancipation.* New York: Harrington Park Press.

The Sexual Revolution: Traditional mores versus new values, ed. Gary E, McCuen and David L. Bender. Minneapolis, MN: Greenhaven Press.

Sedgwick, Eve K. 1990. *Epistemology of the closet.* Berkeley: University of California Press.

Sontag, Susan. 1964. Notes on camp. *Partisan Review* 31 (Fall): 515-530.

Smitherman, Geneva. 2000. *Black talk: Words and phrases from the hood to the amen corner.* Boston: Houghton Mifflin.

Stone, Lawrence. 1992. *Uncertain unions: Marriage in England, 1660-1753.* New York: Oxford University Press.

Stramel, James S. 2008. Coming out and outing. *Metaphilosophy* 39 (October): 438-442.

― ― ―. 2007. Coming out, outing, and virtue ethics. In *Sex and ethics: Essays on sexuality, virtue, and the good life,* ed. Raja Halwani, 162-176. London: Palgrave Macmillan.

Streitmatter, Roger. 1995. *Unspeakable: The rise of the gay and lesbian press.* Boston: Faber and Faber.

Talbot, Margaret. 2013. About a boy. *The New Yorker* (March 18): 56-65.

Thistlethwaite, Polly J. 1998. Building 'A home of our own:' The construction of the lesbian herstory archives. In *Daring to find our names: The search for lesbigay library history.* Ed. James V. Carmichael Jr., 153-174. Westport, CT: Greenwood Press, 1998.

Tye, Marcus C. 2008. Bye-bye bi? Bailey, biphobia, and girlie-Men. In *Men speak out: Views on gender, sex, and power,* ed. Shira Tarrant, 80–85. New York: Routledge.

Vidal, Gore. 1948. *The city and the pillar.* New York: Dutton.

———. 1995. *Palimpsest: A memoir.* New York: Random House.

———. 1999. *Sexually speaking: Collected sex writings.* San Francisco: Cleis Press.

Warner, Michael. 1999. Queer and then? *The Chronicle Review* (January 6): B6–B9

———. *The trouble with normal: Sex, politics, and the ethics of queer life.* New York: The Free Press.

Warnke, Georgia. 2007. *After identity: Rethinking race, sex, and gender.* New York: Cambridge University Press.

West, Celeste and Elizabeth Katz, eds. 1972. *Revolting librarians.* San Francisco: Booklegger Books.

White, Edmund. 1999. *Marcel Proust.* New York: Viking.

Wilkerson, William. 2009. Is it a choice? Sexual orientation as interpretation. *Journal of Social Philosophy* 40 (Spring): 97–116.

Willis, Steve. 2012. *Oscar Wilde's christmas carol.* Unpublished manuscript.

Woolf, Virginia. 2011. Craftsmanship. British Broadcasting Corporation transcript, April 29. In *The essays of Virginia Woolf, Volume Six: 1933 to 1941,* ed. Stuart M. Clarke, 624–627 London: The Hogarth Press.

———. 1991. *A room of one's own.* New York: Harcourt, Inc.

Intellectual Freedom and Libraries

Loretta Gaffney

In 1999, the American Family Association (AFA) produced and promoted a videocassette entitled *Excess Access: Pornography, Children, and the American Library Association*. Part dramatization of a family's clash with their local public library, and part call to arms for conservative activists, the video marked a turning point in conservative media: while it fanned the flames of community fears over pornography on public library terminals, its main target was not the pornographers, but the American Library Association (ALA). Conservative groups like the AFA and Focus on the Family tended to target individual books for protest during the early- to mid-1990s, such as *Heather Has Two Mommies* and *Daddy's Roommate*, but by the turn of the millennium the so-called pro family movement had switched tactics, targeting intellectual freedom policies and documents such as the *Library Bill of Rights* directly. While their campaign for mandatory Internet filtering of sexually explicit imagery in schools and public libraries was ultimately successful, fueling the momentum necessary support the Supreme Court upholding the Children's Internet Protection Act (CIPA). In 2003, pro family activists had launched a much larger project with no end in sight: a critique of librarianship itself. *Excess Access* packed a skillful one-two punch: clearly intended to shock and outrage viewers about pornography in libraries, it also leveraged viewer outrage toward a challenge to the professional authority and judgment of librarians.

During the 1990s and 2000s, conservative activists not only appropriated libraries as battlegrounds for causes like antigay activism, but also incorporated libraries and librarianship into the issue base of the pro family movement. A collection of loosely linked, well-organized grassroots campaigns around issues like opposition to abortion and gay marriage, the pro family movement was a resurgence of conservative activism in the late 20th and early 21st centuries that brought libraries into the culture wars crossfire. Pro family library challenges went beyond objections to particular materials in order to target library policies of open access, collection diversity, and patron privacy. Pro family activists also mounted an explicit critique of the American Library Association (ALA), opposing the ALA's defenses of intellectual freedom for all ages and all types of media. These activists described their own struggle as a quest to wrest libraries away from the ALA and restore them to parental and taxpayer control.

Excess Access' dramatization opens with a mother dropping her young son off at the public library, where a shifty-eyed, nervous-looking middle-aged man is downloading pornography from the Internet. After printing the pornography out, the man follows the boy into the men's room. As the bathroom door swings shut and the scene fades to black, the man hisses in voice-over: "Hey kid! Look at this." Meanwhile, the librarian preoccupied with chiding children for chewing gum in the library, is apparently powerless to intervene when sexual predators threaten children's safety. When the outraged mother returns to the library, demanding to know how the predator got the pornography in the first place, the librarian immediately pulls out the *Library Bill of Rights*, explaining that there's nothing she can do to interfere with the man's intellectual freedom to view pornography in the library. The mother muses in a later scene that she's "known [the librarian] for years. Her hands must be tied, or something." That "something" turns out to be the American Library Association, and the ethics of a profession the video aims to expose as corrupt and illegitimate.

While conservative activists were certainly concerned about the cultural consequences of pornography generally, their concern about porn in libraries suggests a deeper critique of librarianship at the root of the movement. In the process of organizing opposition to libraries' anti-filtering policies, pro family activists advanced a competing vision of librarian professionalism, calling for evaluation, judgment and intervention during an era when library leaders were championing a neutral stance toward Internet content. At the same time, conservative activists clearly doubted the ability of librarians to make decisions, often characterizing them as either dupes of the American Library Association, or too cowed and intimidated to challenge the intellectual freedom party line. Though they believed librarians should be cultural "gatekeepers," activists ultimately put more faith in the values of some of the community and the anxieties of parents than they did in librarians' professional judgment.

This article explores how pro family activists portrayed librarians and critiqued librarianship during the height of the movement to pass and uphold the Children's Internet Protection Act (2000), legislation that compelled all public and school libraries accepting federal funds to use software to filter their Internet access. Examining key pro family movement media, I analyze the competing vision of librarianship advanced by pro family activists. As they argued that librarians needed to protect patrons by filtering their Internet access, pro family library activists ultimately advocated for a narrowly defined service role for librarianship. After exploring the history of the Children's Internet Protection Act and the ALA's positions on filtering, I analyze how the pro family movement attempted to discredit the American Library Association in order to promote its own vision of librarians as the servers of a homogenous community. Pro family activists urged librarians not simply to filter Internet access, but to passively reflect community standards and anticipate the wishes of conservative, protectionist parents.

"An Imperfect and Robotic Technology:" How (and Why) the ALA took on Filtering and CIPA

In 1998, a group of Loudoun County, VA citizens and library patrons, dubbing themselves Mainstream Loudoun, challenged their public library's decision to filter Internet access as a violation of their First Amendment rights. It was a case that many librarians watched with great interest; indeed, the ALA lent its extensive lobbying and legal resources ALA uses the Freedom to Read Foundation for legal cases (not sure if you need to distinguish) to the case, as it had done in two previous cases related to regulating Internet content. However, this previous legislation aimed at limiting access to Internet content (CDA 1996 and COPA 1998) had focused on limiting the expression of the originator of the speech, or the publisher. *Mainstream Loudoun v. Loudoun County Board of Trustees* was the first legal case directly involving the *receivers* of online information, and not coincidentally, the first to rule on the use of Internet filters in public libraries (Hein 2007, x).

A federal district court eventually struck down the Loudoun County Library filtering policy, ruling that, when the public library purchased internet access, they made an acquisitions decision that included everything available on the Internet. Any attempt to restrict Internet access would thus be tantamount to removing books from the library shelves. Citing *Pico v. Island Trees*, a 1982 case that sanctioned the removal of books from libraries for partisan or doctrinal reasons, the court concluded that content-based restrictions could only be justified by a compelling government interest. Though protecting children from harmful materials might be considered a compelling interest, the court ultimately decided that the filters in question were not narrowly tailored enough to protect that interest because they blocked constitutionally protected speech.

The issue of filtering in libraries seemed to be settled. However, pro-family activists continued to organize for some kind of filtering mandate for public libraries and schools. The result was the Children's Internet Protection

Act, passed by both houses and signed into law by President Clinton in 2000. It contradicted the Mainstream Loudoun ruling, but avoided some of the pitfalls that had doomed its predecessors, the Communications Decency Act (1996) and the Children's Online Protection Act (1998). While it mandated the use of filtering in libraries and schools that accepted the e-rate, it also included a provision for adults to request unfiltered access by request for "bona fide research and other lawful purposes" and for minors to request access to wrongfully blocked sites. Most significantly, it allowed some wiggle room for financially secure libraries to opt out if they were willing to forgo the e-rate. The ALA challenged CIPA in a federal district court, citing Mainstream Loudoun ruling that Internet filters were not sufficiently tailored enough to serve state interest, as well as charging that managing requests for unfiltered access would represent a serious professional burden for librarians (American Library Association CIPA 2010). However, the Supreme Court upheld CIPA in 2003 over the ALA's objections, ruling that all libraries using the e-rate must submit a statement of intention to comply with CIPA by July 2005.

The ALA's opposition to CIPA and to filters had its roots in more general intellectual freedom principles they believed to be applicable in both print and online environments. In general, librarians were urged to apply these principles regardless of the medium in question. The most recent editions of the *Intellectual Freedom Manual* (2002, 2006, and 2010) attempt to apply general intellectual freedom principles in an online context. While the authors of the *Intellectual Freedom Manual* acknowledged that "time, place and manner" restrictions can be levied on patrons' access to electronic information, they insist that such restrictions "should not be based on content"(American Library Association 2006, 93). In addition, the authors caution against denying access to information "perceived to lack value" and reiterate that as with print resources, "[t]he provision of access does not imply sponsorship or endorsement" (Ibid). Moreover, they defend minors' access with arguments identical to those submitted to defend their access to print materials, noting the need for youth to become "thinking adults" and participate in "an informed electorate," as well as noting their essential First Amendment right to all information (American Library Association 2002a, 85). ALA argues that libraries should make online content available under the same "constitutional protections that apply to the books on libraries' shelves" (American Library Association 2002b, 245).

However, the Internet offers some different challenges and opportunities for librarians. The first is in the need to educate patrons in how to navigate the vast and often confusing fields of information in an online format. The authors of the *Intellectual Freedom Manual* write that the way that libraries ". . . empower individuals to explore ideas, access and evaluate information, draw meaning from information presented in a variety of formats, develop valid conclusions, and express new ideas" may be even more crucial in navigating the online environment (American Library Association 2006, 147). Overall, the Internet is viewed quite optimistically as an opportunity for libraries to provide more diverse kinds of information to their patrons, information they might not be able to access otherwise. The authors cite the online environment as opportunity, rather than challenge, offering minors a chance "to participate responsibly in the electronic arena . . . nurturing the information literacy skills demanded by the Information Age." The Internet's ability to enable "individuals to receive speech from the entire world and speak to the entire world" is also cited by the authors, noting the provision of global information as not simply a right for patrons, but an opportunity for libraries to correct inequities of access to these resources.

Yet the Internet also proves to be a challenging venue for intellectual freedom when principles meet collection development practice. Despite the Loudoun ruling, any analogies between the Internet and the library's physical shelves ultimately broke down when it came to collection development and control over the content (and quality) of the library's resources. The Internet's sheer vastness and diversity of material meant that librarians' professional practices of selection and evaluation were no longer practical or even possible. The *Intellectual Freedom Manual* authors write that "[p]roviding connections to global information, services, and networks is not the same as selecting and purchasing materials for a library collection" (American Library Association 2002a, 75). In fact, some material online may not meet the library's collection development requirements at all. Still, this need not be the librarian's concern; rather, the role of active selection is delegated to the patron, with ". . . each user [left] to determine what is appropriate" (Ibid). This boundary between providing access and making selections puts the onus on the patron to decide what is suitable or unsuitable for her purposes. The librarians' responsibility in the online environment is only to provide access to information, without judgment, leaving it to the users to determine whether that information meets their needs and interests—unless of course the users are minors, in which case parents have the final say. Interestingly, librarians are explicitly cautioned to police the line between personal belief and professional practice when dealing with online materials; they "should not deny or limit access to electronic information because of its allegedly controversial content or because of the librarian's personal beliefs or fear of confrontation . . . [or] on the grounds that it is perceived to lack value" (Ibid, 83).

While the 5th edition of ALA's *Intellectual Freedom Manual* did acknowledge the Internet as a potential source for library challenges in 1996 (Hopkins 1996, 275–276), it was the 6th edition in 2002 that fully codified the library field's position on the use of filtering software. In an article on challenges and issues facing the field, Shaevel and Becker argue that filters compromise not simply patrons' First Amendment rights, but the "core values of librarianship," particularly the protection of access to all library materials for all categories of users (Ibid). They also critiqued the "imperfect and robotic technology" for imposing the biases of "corporate entities" on the community, limiting "the community's right to govern its own library and that library's selection policies" (Ibid). Given all these factors, the ALA Council affirms that filters "block access to Constitutionally protected speech violat[ing] the *Library Bill of Rights*" (Ibid, 246). The "Statement of Library Use of Filtering Software Policy Statement" enumerates other problems with filtering technology, including viewpoint or content discrimination, vague and subjective criteria for site blocking, the propriety nature of information about how sites are blocked, and the imperfections of the technology, leading to "over-blocking" legitimate sites. The policy statement characterizes filters as "designed for the home market . . . to respond to the preferences of parents making decisions for their children" and thus ultimately "dissonant" with the mission of libraries serving diverse communities and providing information access to all users (American Library Association 2002b, 249).

In general, librarians' professional judgment is constructed as a uniquely civic-minded and public one, in contrast to both the commercial interests of filtering software companies, and the religious and moral convictions of the pro-family activists. With no professional ethics or responsibilities to curb them, software companies were thought free to impose their viewpoints on a community, forcing it to ". . . conform its library's selection policies to the biases and beliefs of the corporate entities which design filtering software, while disregarding the community's right to operate its library according to its own norms and values" (Shaevel and Becker, 2002, 35). ALA believes that filtering software imposes commercial values and norms on communities, interfering with librarians' ability to interpret community needs and to connect community members with the necessary resource. Thus, the professional roles and responsibilities of librarians are explicitly linked to the empowerment of the public, and of citizens in a democracy. While filtering is definitely framed as a violation of citizens' rights, it is also deemed to interfere with the ability of librarians to make professional judgments in the service of those rights, disrupting the delicate balance between professionalism and civic responsibility that lies at the heart of the ethic of intellectual freedom.

ALA continues to oppose the use of filters in libraries on both ideological and professional bases, though it grants that some libraries may have to filter because of CIPA, or state, municipal, or board policies. In these cases, libraries are advised to use filters at the least restrictive level, and to educate patrons about their right to request unblocked access. Arguments about patron rights and librarians' obligation to uphold and advocate for them are common in the professional discourse, and find their most iconic and power-ful expression in the *Library Bill of Rights*. As in other areas of potential con-flict and challenges, the *Manual* advises librarians to adopt policies that "em-phasize the library's support for the principles of intellectual freedom and its respect for the diversity of the community." Shaevel and Becker also counsel librarians to make use of time limits, privacy screens, and Internet education rather than resorting to filtering their terminals' Internet access (Ibid, 36).

Difficulties with selecting and evaluating information on the Internet aside, it is notable that, while acknowledging wrinkles and complexities, ALA has maintained—and, in some cases, intensified—its case for libraries as institutions that are vital to citizen education and democracy. In fact, no-tions of citizenship and community are interwoven into not only defenses of patrons' rights of access, but also into the professional work of librarianship. Intriguingly though it is the patrons whose intellectual freedom rights are being asserted, without libraries it is suggested such a right would be mean-ingless. "In a democracy, libraries have a particular obligation to provide li-brary users with information necessary for participation in self-governance" (American Library Association 2002a, 92). In order to fulfill this obligation, librarians must be free to exercise professional judgments, judgments that are hampered by filtering, certainly, but also by any challenges to library collections and policies, as well as by librarians who fail to counter these challenges with the *Library Bill of Rights*.

Taking on the ALA: The Pro Family Filtering Campaign

The passage of the Children's Internet Protection Act (CIPA) in 2000, and ALA's subsequent challenge to CIPA's constitutionality were in many ways tailor-made catalysts for pro family activism. Pro family organizations such as the American Family Association had long made fighting pornography their primary political focus, while Family Friendly Libraries' explicit attacks on the ALA meant that many activists' consciousness were already attuned to the relationship between "offensive" library materials and library policy. The controversy over CIPA offered pro family library activists a boost from conservative and religious anti-porn organizations, while allowing those groups to give their faithful a more concrete blueprint for grassroots activ-ism. The American Family Association launched a campaign, along with the release of "Excess Access," to arm local activists with the tools they needed to challenge ALA policies in their public libraries. Even Dr. Laura Schless-inger got in on the action, using her popular radio program to goad listeners into becoming "Warriors" against the ALA (Schlessinger 1999b, 18). Thus, the perceived threat of pornography to young minds, coupled with a persistent idealized image of library space as "safe" space, brought anti-ALA activism into the conservative mainstream.

Pro family activists took on the filtering issue not simply because it was timely, but because for many, the combination of kids, pornography, and libraries was an unthinkable combination. Factor in the ease and accessibility of Internet access, and the alarm factor was raised significantly. Though Family Friendly Libraries founder Karen Jo Gounaud admitted that so-called "adult" materials in libraries were not a new concern, she thought the "introduction of unfiltered Internet" had hastened public libraries' decline into "library licentiousness and parental rights denial," drawing pornography and libraries into an un-acceptably close embrace as "shameful bedfellows" (Gounaud Online Summit). Metaphors abounded for libraries with unfiltered Internet. "Excess Access" deemed such a library "a playground for children and the adversaries of parents" (Excess Access 1999) while Dr. Laura referred to public libraries as "a peep show booths" (Schlessinger 1999a, 8). In a packet of information distributed by the American Family Association, a document entitled "Arguments Used by the ALA and Your Local Librarian," called the library "the equivalent of an adult book store. Pornography and children have no business with one another, especially not in a public library" (American Family Association 1999a).

Part of the genius of the pro family campaign to compel public libraries to filter was their skillful maneuvering between the very real problems of pornography in libraries and a socially conservative response framed as "common sense." While "Excess Access" offered glimmers of sexual conservatism, warning that children would learn about "the joys of gay sex" as a hand pulls the title *Gay American History* from the stacks, most of the campaign's rhetoric was studiously bipartisan (Excess Access 1999). David Burt, founder of Filtering Facts, a pro-filtering advocacy organization, was often quoted in the pro family press while explicitly being identified as a non-religious person. His profile made him the perfect one to argue that "[p]rotecting children is of interest to people of all beliefs. . . . Whether or not branches of government—libraries—should use taxpayer dollars to provide free hard-core pornography to children isn't about 'religion' or even politics. It's about common-sense" (Boyd 2000, 27). Further, having "decent" communities where parents feel that their children are safe was framed by anti-porn activist Phil Burress as an issue of values and standards, rather than politics: "Community standards are not left or right. They are high, low, or somewhere in between. . . . Liberals and conservatives alike, for the most part, want a wholesome, clean community in which to raise their families. They want a community free of sex shops on every corner" (Wildmon 1999, 16). After presenting the pro-filtering case as the overwhelmingly reasonable one, pro family critics generally go on to bemoan the current state of ALA-fueled library insanity. "I can't believe one trip to the library has turned our lives upside down," the mother in "Excess Access" remarks, in palpable disbelief (Excess Access, 1999). Dr. Laura is similarly aghast that enemy has become the once-beloved public library: "What is going on in the world? I never imagined I would one day be fighting to protect children from pedophiles *and* from their own public libraries! . . . Is this some Orwellian vision of the future, where the safest place in the world suddenly becomes the most dangerous?" (Schlessinger 1999a, 8). How did the "most dangerous" place in the world become that way? The pro family media cite three culprits, all of whom they claim molest children in some way: the pedophiles who use the library, the pornographic images themselves, and ALA. Because its policies are depicted as aiding and abetting the first two culprits, ALA emerges in the pro family media as the clear enemy.

The presence of pedophiles and child molesters in the library is highlighted in almost every pro-filtering argument in the pro family media. It is not simply that porn might be accessed, but what behaviors it could stimulate in unscrupulous patrons. Libraries without filters, argues Focus on the Family Citizen writer Karla Dial, are "magnets for molesters" (Dial 2004, 20). Pedophiles are drawn to the library by the promise of free porn and the carte blanche to look at it and even print it out in public. Once they have access, "their desires are fueled by what the library allows them to have" and the almost certain presence of children creates a temptation comparable to "giving an alcoholic access to alcohol. They are looking for this, and we shouldn't give them the opportunity" (Ibid, 23). Dick Black, a Loudoun county library board member and longtime conservative activist, concurs. "[T]he only purpose for viewing pornography is sexual gratification. . . . And the public library is not the kind of place where you want men coming in and becoming sexually aroused. This creates a dangerous situation for children, even if they're protected from seeing it" (Boyd 2000, 27). Even if the porn viewers don't act out as a direct result of what they see, they can use their viewing itself as a form of harassment of patrons and library staff. And "acceptable use" policies (enforced with the infamous "tap on the shoulder" by a supervising librarian) won't do the trick if the patron is consulting an innocuous-looking "training manual on kidnapping and rape for sexual pleasure, or for ways to lure children into seemingly harmless, but dangerous situations" (Sharp 1999). It is clear from the pro family media that the problem is not simply porn, but the behaviors and intent of those who view it at the library.

The theme of molestation continues in pro family pro-filtering discourse, where pornography is claimed to have the ability to attack kids even without the aid of a human intermediary. The accidental viewing of a pornographic image not only shocks the viewer, but burrows into his or her mind, never to be erased. According to the AFA's Randy Sharp, stumbling upon hardcore pornography "instantly penetrate[s] the computer user's mind, [and] the damage done to a child's innocence is permanent and cannot be reversed" (Ibid). Similarly, Dr. Laura asks readers to imagine a scenario wherein they are a parent accompanying their preschooler to the library, "anticipating a pleasant visit and the armful of new books you'll take home." But then, as they pass the library's new computers, they are ". . . assaulted by the site of hard-core pornography splashed across one of the screens. 'Mommy, what's that?' your preschoolers says, confusion in his voice. You hurriedly usher him away and out of the library—but how can you remove the image now planted in his brain?" (Schlessinger 1999a, 8) The greatest fear of conservative activists is that children will be exposed to pornography and be virtually "molested" and irrevocably damaged by the experience. Accordingly, in "Parent Alert: Beware the Public Libraries," Gounaud writes that "[t]hese electronic playgrounds can almost instantly molest young minds with free samples of topless Playboy Playmates, masturbating Hustler models, obscene ads for 'Cybersex Toys' and sites like 'Anybody want to molest me?' and 'It feels good to molest animals and children.'" (Gounaud Parent Alert). In their defense of filtering technology, Family Friendly Libraries contrasts the supposed malleability of filters with the irrevocable damage done to children by pornography: "Restoration of access to legitimate sites is easy. Restoring a child's molested mind is not" (Gounaud Realities of Library Porn).

Despite the sinister aims of pornography and its denizens, it quickly becomes clear that ALA is the real enemy of the piece in the pro family media. Intriguingly, many pro family critics promote their pro-filtering mission as a rescue mission to recover the quality of librarians' work lives. First, they make it clear that it is not the local librarian's fault for not defying ALA policy, because the organization is so powerful that it effectively intimidates its membership into toeing the party line. "Though the ALA strenuously denies it," Dr. Laura warns, "many librarians have written to tell me that crossing the ALA can also mean losing your job" (Schlessinger 1999a, 9). Donald Wildmon cites ALA's influence in the training and hiring of librarians as a way to keep them "hostages" to ALA policy. "Many decent hard-working, God-fearing librarians are fed up with the ALA. But they fear what the ALA will do to them if they speak out" (Wildon 1999). Wildmon exhorts readers to become activists in order "to rescue our libraries and librarians from the morally bankrupt American Library Association" (Ibid). In a sound bite for "Excess Access," Phil Burress calls ALA's influence "institutional inbreeding" and cites it as the reason that librarians are "told what to think and how to react by the American Library Association." David Burt concurs, arguing that librarians are taught to hold up the Library Bill of Rights "so that it sounds like it's a legal document, it sounds like it's the law," meanwhile giving "lip service" to the notion of patron input in collection development decisions. Reconsideration forms are offered, "as if they were actually going to consider the request, when in reality they're never going to reconsider their request" (Excess Access).

After intimidating librarians into following their dictates, according to the pro family activists, ALA then hangs them out to dry in the sordid, stressful workplace permeated by pornography and sexual harassment. The "Minneapolis 12," a group of female public librarians who sued the EEOC because their bosses would not protect them from a "hostile workplace" of patrons viewing pornography on library Internet terminals, are often featured in the pro-family media as evidence that the ALA does not care about—or take care of—its own. As York argues in an article for Concerned Women for America's *Family Voice*, "[t]hey—and their innocent patrons—were exposed to the vilest obscenity imaginable: child porn, bestiality, sodomy, torture" (York 2002, 9). Randy Sharp argues that acceptable use policies (as opposed to filters) put "employees in the potentially dangerous position of challenging a sexual predator, pedophile or addict, who historically, is prone to violence" (Sharp 1999). And yet the ALA filed a suit to block implementation of CIPA ". . . despite the sordid effect Internet porn has on its own librarians" (Morse 2001, 14). Libraries with unlimited access to the Internet are presumed to attract troublesome patrons, luring them into proximity with children and even female library workers. They might harass librarians or take pleasure from librarians and other patrons noticing what they are looking at online. As Gounaud puts it, "[f]ree pornography attracts a different breed of library patron than those who would use the net for legitimate educational and entertainment purposes. They are not ashamed of others seeing what they are pursuing. In fact, these porn pursuers, usually male, seem to enjoy watching the reaction of the librarians, usually female, and others who are within range of their sexually explicit surfing escapades" (Gounaud Loudoun County).

This discourse of librarians in distress is overlaid with a subtle dismissal of library work and librarian professionalism. Morse writes that the age of the Internet makes librarians "long for the days when their worst problems were collecting nickel fines for overdue books and shushing noisy children" (Morse 2001, 14). In the face of the problems presented by Internet porn access in libraries, librarians are portrayed as helpless to correct behavioral problems, their hands tied by ALA. Pro family activist Tallie Grubenhoff reported visiting her local library in Selah, WA, only to be shocked by a group of 11 and 12 year old boys and girls "whooping it up" while looking at porn. "The librarian explained that she couldn't do anything about it" so Grubenhoff was obliged to discipline them herself (Boyd 2000, 26). The librarian in "Excess Access" chides her young patron for chewing gum—"no gum in the library!"—yet she is helpless to prevent ill-intentioned patrons from downloading and printing out porn (Excess Access).

Tellingly, pro family activists argue that filters are in librarians' best interests too, freeing them from the "police work" of monitoring patrons' online behavior. They cannot imagine another role for librarians with regard to the Internet other than "policing," and argue that this job should be "automated and technical." Presumably, this will allow librarians to spend more time doing "the real work" of librarianship, and thus improve their relationships with community members. "Librarians," argues Gounaud, "should not have to police and confront patrons who choose to operate in prurient web sites outside of recommended library policy guidelines . . . it places librarians in the uncomfortable, even dangerous role of being confrontational cyber-activity cops instead of friendly information professionals" (Gounaud Realities of Library Porn).

The answer, then—even beyond installing filters in public libraries—is to take on ALA and its policies. Guidelines for library activists urge them to educate themselves on the ALA and their "political and cultural agenda" (Schlessinger 1999a, 11). Dan Kleinman of Safelibraries is also adamant that the battle begins with the ALA, warning activists to "beware that the ALA will attempt to mislead you every step of the way" and encouraging them to "speak up, speak out, and attend library board meetings. . . . Do not be afraid of the ALA" (Kleinman 2007, 49). The AFA sends its would-be activists on research missions to determine whether or not their local libraries are infiltrated by ALA policies. Detective work to figure out whether your library is "a community friend or foe" includes fishing for porn sites: "Search for "XXX, hardcore, nude [and] follow one of the search result links. If you successfully link to a porn site, your library has unrestricted Internet access" (American Family Association 1999b). Once educated about the ALA, activists are empowered to make their own decisions about which issue or issues on which to focus library campaigns. Acknowledging the power in multiple, diffuse grassroots movements, Donald Wildmon exclaims that "[t]his fight is a local fight. There is no way we can conduct it from our AFA headquarters. YOU must fight for your own libraries; you, and the members of your local community" (Wildmon 1999). Similar language of empowerment characterizes Gounaud's "Ten Ways to Create a Family Friendly Library." As she argues, "in the battle to restore decent limits and common sense to public libraries, remember that you are protecting *your* children, *your* tax money, and *your* community. Public libraries are supposed to answer to *you*—not to the American Library Association" (Gounaud 1999a). Meanwhile, Dr. Laura urges activists to "draw up your list of concerns and prioritize them, describing as clearly as possible what they desired solutions would be and practical ideas for their implementation . . . [and] "[d]on't forget that the ballot box is the ultimate opportunity for you to affect public policy—including public library policy—by selecting moral and ethical leaders and de-selecting those less honorable" (Schlessinger 1999a, 11). Though activists are allotted significant freedom in how they take on the ALA in local library theaters, one message is clear: "intellectual freedom" is merely a green light for pornography in libraries. Similarly, efforts to fight ALA policy are reasonable actions taken by concerned parents, and pro family activists are advised to propose them that way. "Take great care not to appeal like a book-burner," cautions Wildmon (Wildmon 1999). "Don't accept the censor label," agrees Burress. "The real censors are the librarians [and their directors] who choose every day what will and won't be in the library." The territory of the First Amendment and of free speech is not to be ceded to the ALA. As Dick Black argues, "[i]f you get into theoretical speak about the First Amendment and freedom of speech, you're on their turf. You need to talk about whether or not libraries should provide pornography to children or if libraries should be places for the sexual gratification of adults" (York 2002, 12). By staying "on message" and keeping pornography center stage, pro family critics believe that they will be better equipped to dodge the charge of "censorship", which Gounaud argues is "one of the most abused words in the American Library Association's campaign against parents" (Excess Access). Meanwhile, ALA itself is charged with hypocrisy, for upholding values like "intellectual freedom" and "diversity" while attempting to shut down parental and community dissent. "I hear and read the words 'inclusive' and 'diversity' in everything the ALA does," Burress declares, "but have quickly learned they are neither 'inclusive' nor 'diverse' when only ALA-approved persons can serve the community as a trustee or employee of the library" (American Family Association 1999a, 9). Perhaps the most memorable denunciation of the profession is from "Don," a disgruntled former librarian featured in a sidebar in *Dr. Laura's Perspective*. "The biggest censors I have ever met have been librarians," he claims. "They're the most discriminatory, most censorious, narrow-minded bunch I've ever been around. . . . They hide behind 'Intellectual Freedom' because it protects them; they can buy anything they want, and it makes a martyr of them. Then there's no more discussion: 'You are a bigot, we are open-minded, end of conversation'" (Schlessinger 1999a, 10).

Conclusion

In the wake of CIPA, ALA has been careful to make provisions for the law, remaining critical of filters but not opposing their use in libraries outright. In the 8th edition of the *Intellectual Freedom Manual*, the ALA *"does not recommend the use of filters to block access to constitutionally protected speech on* computers located in publicly funded libraries" (Morgan 2010, 39). However, the reasoning behind this position is still framed both in terms of patron rights and in terms of the core values of the profession. Patrons seeking digital resources ". . . enjoy the same rights to publish information and receive information as do those who use the print media" and filters violate not just these rights, but also ". . . the core values of librarianship" (Ibid). In addition, ALA continues to argue that filters don't work, even for their supposed purpose of protecting children. The answer to the need for safety is information literacy instruction furnished by the librarian. The characterization of filtering as "an imperfect and robotic technology" remains, and ALA insists ". . . education offers the best means of addressing the issue of Internet safety for both children and adults" (Ibid, 40). Nevertheless, ALA recognizes that libraries accepting the e-rate are legally bound to filter their Internet terminals. In this environment, it becomes even more crucial for librarians to alert adult patrons to their right to have filtering software disabled, and to be diligent about unblocking wrongly blocked sites for minors. The ALA also continues to recommend that filters be set "at the least restrictive level" and warns that ". . . public libraries must remain cautious about using filtering. Ultimately, the *CIPA scheme* was upheld because it was tied to funding and the government conceded that an adult's request for disabling of the filter could never be denied and did not have to be justified [emphasis added]" (Chmara 2010, 345).

Difficulties with selecting and evaluating information on the Internet aside, it is notable that, while acknowledging wrinkles and complexities, ALA has maintained—and, in some cases, intensified—its case for libraries as institutions that are vital to citizen education and democracy. In fact, notions of citizenship and community are interwoven into not only defenses of patrons' rights of access, but also into the professional work of librarianship through ALA's *Code of Ethics*. Intriguingly, though it is the patrons whose intellectual freedom rights are being asserted, without libraries, it is suggested, such a right would be meaningless. In order to fulfill this obligation, librarians must be free to exercise professional judgments, judgments that are hampered by filtering, certainly, but also by any challenges to library collections and policies, as well as by librarians who fail to counter these challenges with the *Library Bill of Rights*. In maintaining these responsibilities to citizens and communities, librarians will also have to consider online access in light of the ever-prevalent reliance on filtering technology.

While the ALA's views on filtering have remained the same since the passage of CIPA, their anti-filtering rhetoric has softened and become more understated. The 6th and 7th editions of the *Intellectual Freedom Manual* describe filtering as a violation of both patrons' freedoms and of ". . . the core values of librarianship, which esteem a person's right to read and hear ideas without limitation" (Shaevel and Becker 2002, 35). Filtering is decried as inconsistent with the library's purpose, imposing a pall of exclusion over what should, by democratic rights, be an arena of inclusion. By interfering with an atmosphere of unfettered access, filtering is deemed disruptive of the library's ability to provide access to a diverse range of points of view, corrupting what would otherwise (presumably) be a free marketplace of ideas. The very ideal of an informed citizenry is thought to rely upon libraries themselves, not only providing a range of choices, but providing the opportunity to exercise those choices. Thus, filtering and materials challenges are accused of threatening democracy itself, because a democracy ". . . operates best when information flows freely and is freely available" (Ibid, 33). Moreover, there is no other institution that can fulfill this responsibility to its citizens; it is "the library's unique responsibility" to make sure that citizens "have the tools necessary for self-improvement and participation in the political process" (Ibid).

In sum, through its opposition to the use of Internet filters in libraries, the ALA is able to articulate a professional role for librarians that includes creating and maintaining a community of citizens. This role can only be hampered by "the imperfect and robotic technology" of filters (American Library Association 2002a). In fact, ALA believes that education offers the best means of addressing issues of Internet safety, a task which obviously cannot be left in the hands of either filtering software companies, or censorious individuals who want to impose their morality on the community. Yet pro-family activists have also taken up the language of community and citizenship, casting the activities of ALA (and librarianship itself) as "private interference" with what should be the free exercise of democracy. Should the ALA fail to recognize this, they risk becoming "tone deaf" to how their own rhetoric can (and has) been used against them in the public debate. This could result in many missed opportunities, but especially the opportunity to organize the general public around intellectual freedom issues; a public for whom "community" and "values" may resonate more deeply than "information" and "access."

References

American Family Association. 1999a. A guide to what one person can do about pornography. Tupelo, MS: American Family Association.

— — —. 1999b. How safe is your public library? Tupelo, MS: American Family Association.

American Library Association. 2002. "Access to digital information, services, and networks." In *Intellectual Freedom Manual* 6th ed. Chicago: ALA.

— — —. CIPA. http://www.ala.org/advocacy/advleg/federallegislation/cipa (accessed April 1, 2012).

———. 2006. "The importance of education to intellectual freedom." In *Intellectual Freedom Manual* 7th ed. Chicago: ALA.

———. 2002a. "Questions and answers: Access to electronic information, services, and networks." In *Intellectual Freedom Manual* 6th ed. Chicago: ALA.

———. 2002b. "Statement on Library Use of Filtering Software." In *Intellectual Freedom Manual* 6th ed. Chicago: ALA.

———. 1997. Resolution on the Use of Filtering Software in Libraries. http://www.ala.org/advocacy/intfreedom/statementspols/ifresolutions/resolutionuse (accessed April 9, 2012).

Boyd, Clem. 2000. Libraries Feel the Pressure. *Focus on the Family Citizen* 14, no. 4 (April): 26-7.

Burt, David. 2000. *Dangerous access 2000: Uncovering porn in american public libraries*. Washington, D.C.: Family Research Council.

Chmara, Teresa. 2010. "Public Libraries and the Public Forum Doctrine." In *Intellectual Freedom Manual* 8th ed. Chicago: ALA.

Dial, Karla. In harm's Way. *Focus on the Family Citizen Magazine* 18, no. 8 (2004): 18-23.

"Excess Access": Pornography, Libraries, and the American Library Association.* Videocassette. AFA, 1999.

Gounaud, Karen Jo. 1999a. 10 Ways to Create a Family Friendly Library." *Dr. Laura Perspective* (July): 11.

———. 1999b. ALA is a big contributor to public library internet porn problem. Letter to the Editor, *Washington Times*, March 26.

———. Loudoun County, Virginia Support Document. http://web.archive.org/web/19981203071402/www.fflibraries.org/ALAMinefieldsInCyberspace.htm (accessed December 11, 2011.)

———. Online Summit: Focus on Children. http://web.archive.org/web/19981205141305/www.fflibraries.org/interrec.htm (accessed December 11, 2011).

———.Parent Alert: Beware the Public Libraries. http://web.archive.org/web/20010110183900/www.fflibraries.org/Speeches_Editorials_Papers/stlmetro.htm (accessed March 3, 2010).

———. Realities of Library Porn: Another Perspective on the Loudoun Decision. http://web.archive.org/web/20010117005900/www.fflibraries.org/Speeches_Editorials_Papers/FairfaxColumnThree12-98.htm (accessed April 9, 2012).

Heins, Marjorie. 2007. *Not in front of the children: "Indecency", censorship, and the innocence of youth*. 2nd ed. New Brunswick, NJ: Rutgers University Press.

Hopkins, Diane McAfee. 1996 "School library media centers and intellectual freedom," In *Intellectual Freedom Manual* 5th ed. Chicago: ALA, 275–276.

Kleinman, Dan. 2007. Libraries, children, and value voters. *New Jersey Family Magazine*: 47–51.

Morgan, Candace. 2010. Challenges and issues today. in *Intellectual Freedom Manual* 8th ed. Chicago: ALA.

Morse, Anne. 2001. Hitting the Escape Button. *Focus on the Family Citizen Magazine* 15, no. 12 (December): 14–15.

Schlessinger, Laura. 1999a. Is Your Library Friend or Foe? *Dr. Laura Perspective* (July): 8–10, 13.

– – –. 1999b. Dr. Lauraland: The warriors are on the march! *Dr. Laura Perspective* (July): 18.

Shaevel, Evelyn and Beverly Becker. 2002. "Challenges and Issues." In *Intellectual Freedom Manual* 6th ed. Chicago: ALA.

Sharp, Randy. 1999. Supplement to the Arguments Used by the ALA and Your Local Librarian. Tupelo, MS: American Family Association.

Wildmon, Don. 1999. How You Can Take Back Your Local Library. Tupelo, MS: American Family Association.

York, Frank. 2002. Porn-Free zone? *Family Voice* (July/August): 8–14.

Journalism and Intellectual Freedom

Joe Cutbirth

Chauncey Bailey was a free thinker who died for journalism. The *Oakland Post* editor was taking his regular morning walk to work in 2007 when a man in dark clothes and a ski mask stepped-up with a shotgun and fired two blasts: one into Bailey's back, another into his face execution style as he lay on the sidewalk (Heredia 2007). The man testified at trial that he had been ordered to find, track and kill Bailey before the seasoned journalist printed his latest in a series of articles that questioned the political relevance of Your Black Muslim Bakery, an iconic local establishment and former model of African-American pride (Lee 2011).

Bailey was working on a story about the moral direction of the bakery, including possible criminal activities by a number of people at various levels in the powerful organization (KTVU.COM 2007). He had stepped forward as a counterrevolutionary of sorts, asking questions that some people in the black community didn't want to answer. He was exposing corruption and showing an ugly side of a para-political movement some considered sacred. He was applying the principle of intellectual freedom in his profession. It's what journalists do in a free society.

Intellectual freedom guarantees individuals the right to think freely and to express their thoughts openly. It is a key distinction between free societies and authoritarian governments that routinely suppress the practice. Educators, librarians and more recently, the Free Software Movement, have taken the lead in promoting the practice, which developed historically from opposition to book censorship (American Library Association 2010).

Concern that censorship and print licenses would erode intellectual freedom has existed for centuries, but after World War II founders of the United Nations were so intent on keeping similar atrocities from reoccurring that they included a global commitment to free thought and expression in the UN Charter. Known as the Declaration of Human Rights, it reads: "Everyone has

the right to freedom of opinion and expression; this right includes freedom
to hold opinions without interference and to seek, receive and impart information and ideas through any media and regardless of frontiers" (United
Nations 1948).

Still, many journalists fight for that right and some pay the ultimate price
to practice it. So few journalists in the United States are killed—or even intimidated in ways that resemble trouble their colleagues in other countries
face—that it's easy to overlook what happened to Bailey and others.[1] The
Committee to Protect Journalists counts more than 900 journalists killed
(at least 580 of them murdered with impunity) since 1992 covering political upheaval and conducting dangerous investigations, virtually all of them
abroad (Committee to Protect Journalists 2013).

Scholars often scoff at the idea that journalism is an intellectual pursuit.
Many journalists do, too, despite the fact that journalism's ultimate award—
the Pulitzer Prizes—recognizes opinion and criticism, historical research and
writing, biographical works, drama, music and poetry. Walter Lippmann,
the iconic public intellectual known for his syndicated newspaper column,
"Today and Tomorrow," earned his first Pulitzer Prize in 1962 for a landmark
series of articles based on an extended interview with Nikita Khrushchev.
Lippmann's reports suggested that Russia and China's powers lay "not in
their clandestine activity but in the force of their example" on the developing states of Africa, Asia and Latin America and, more important, that free
nations in the West could counter that example by demonstrating that it was
possible to raise backward societies without sacrificing democracy (Steel
1980, 511).

Indeed, a review of Pulitzer citations shows an extraordinary pattern
of awards for intellectual work. Pulitzer winners have offered: an historic
examination of America as empire, sociologies of a jungle colony in South
America founded by Henry Ford, and biographies of historic figures as
diverse as George Kennan and Malcolm X. Recently, jurors gave the prize

---

1   The relatively few deaths that occurred inside the United States, include: William
     Biggart, a freelance news photographer, who rushed to the World Trade Center
     with his camera after hearing about the attacks and whose body was found in
     the four days later rubble; Robert Stevens, a photo editor at a Florida tabloid who
     died after inhaling the same strand of anthrax mailed to a number of journalists
     including NBC anchor Tom Brokaw in that spate of post-911 domestic terror-
     ism; Dona St. Plite, a Haitian-born reporter in Miami murdered at a benefit for
     the family of a colleague after his name was placed on a hit list of supporters of
     ousted Haitian president Jean-Gertrand Aristide; and Manuel de Dios Unanue, a
     Cuban-American magazine editor shot in the head in a New York City restaurant
     in retaliation for stories he had written about drug trafficking and money laun-
     dering operations.

to Stephen Greenblatt of Harvard for "recounting how an obscure work of philosophy discovered 600 years ago changed the course of history by anticipating the science and sensibilities of today" (The Pulitzer Prizes 2012a). Greenblatt's work recalls an epic by the Roman poet Lucretius that argued "the universe functions without the aid of gods, that religious fear was damaging to human life, and that matter was made up of very small particles in eternal motion, colliding and swerving in new directions" (The Pulitzer Prizes 2012b).

Sinclair Lewis, the first American writer to receive the Nobel Prize for literature, took a stand for intellectual freedom when he declined the 1926 Pulitzer Prize for his novel *Arrowsmith* because the award description noted that the winner should contribute to the "wholesomeness of American life." In a letter explaining his decision, Lewis told the Pulitzer board:

> *Seekers for prizes tend to labor not for inherent excellence but for alien rewards: they tend to write this, or timorously to avoid writing that, in order to tickle the prejudices of a haphazard committee. . . . This phrase (wholesomeness of American life), if it means anything whatever, would appear to mean that the appraisal of the novels shall be made not according to their actual literary merit but in obedience to whatever code of Good Form may chance to be popular at the moment.* (Sinclair Lewis Society 2012)

Still, journalism in the form most of us encounter it and think about it—the news report—isn't a scholarly endeavor, though it is a form of inquiry. Like social science, journalism has methods and ethics, and those practices and standards are designed to ensure the veracity of what journalists find. Like social scientists, journalists use observation, interviews and archival research (though usually in briefer forms) to examine occurrences, events, circumstances and people who shape events and policies, and who come into conflict with each other as those events play out.

Dick Blood, the great city editor at the *New York Daily News* who nurtured a generation of young journalists during two decades as a professor at Columbia and New York University, once told an incoming class at NYU that journalism is actually pretty simple. "You take a torch to the back of the cave and see if there is a monster. If there is one, you come out and tell the tribe. If there isn't, you don't make one up."

Blood's monsters, of course, translate metaphorically to all sorts of things. They can be thugs and bullies who take over noble institutions and turn them on the public they were formed to serve, such as the ones who murdered Chauncey Bailey, or they can be social conditions like unsafe neighborhoods, decaying schools and stagnant economies. The list is vast, and it changes constantly. That's what keeps news organizations in business. People have to think about these monsters in order to face them. They need facts, and they need to be free to share those facts with each other and to form opinions about them. Journalism helps shape public opinion, and in doing so helps us with that intellectual activity.

If anything in the realm of mass journalism seems likely to inhibit intellectual freedom, it would be the ethos of objectivity, which often is seen as the goal of mainstream news media during much of the twentieth century. Objectivity conjures images of detachment, fairness and an adherence to facts. Casual observers equate it with a perception of neutrality. Sociologist Michael Schudson defines it simply as the belief that one should separate facts from values (Schudson 1978, 3). Is that possible? And if so, is objectivity a goal that journalists always should strive for? Should a journalist writing about a hate crime or the Holocaust detach from the horror and inhumanity of utterly immoral violence and strive for neutrality? What is fair in terms of facts in a situation like that?

These are complicated notions with complicated and subtle relationships that demand highly nuanced thinking and writing. That is where intellectual freedom can serve journalism, not stifle it. At times intellectual freedom is part of the decision whether to pursue a story at all. At times it influences how journalists gather factual information, decide what to write and later how to edit. These notions and the decisions made around them often are tied to audience expectations. Journalism considered objective by a Fox News audience may look very different than journalism considered objective by a regular reader of the *Village Voice*. None of these decisions is made in an intellectual or commercial vacuum. As Schudson notes:

> *Objectivity is a peculiar demand to make of institutions which, as business corporations, are dedicated above all to economic survival. It is a peculiar demand to make of editors and reporters who have none of the professional apparatus which, for doctors or lawyers or scientists, is supposed to guarantee objectivity.* (Schudson 1978, 3)

James Carey cautions us to view journalism as a body of work, not a set of individual or isolated stories (Carey 1997, 148). He warns against a tendency to see journalism as even the multiple treatment of a single event in the newspaper and urges us also to consider forms that surround, correct and complete the daily newspaper, such as television, documentary, docudrama, news weeklies, journalism of opinion and even book-length journalism. He sees journalism as a particular form of social practice, "a form of inscribing the world, first in speech, then in print, then in the modern advanced arts of broadcasting and electronics" (Carey 1997, 239). What unifies the practice across time, media, and organization, is its democratic context. Carey takes the position that journalism as a practice is unthinkable except in the context of democracy; in fact, he sees the two as virtually indistinguishable.

Indeed, history bolsters that idea: the more democratic the society, the more news and information it tends to have (Kovach and Rosenstiel 2007, 16). Bill Kovach and Tom Rosenstiel note that as ancient democracies began to develop, they tended toward a kind of pre-journalism. The Greeks used the oral tradition in the Athenian marketplace and offered almost everything important to public life for public consumption (Hohenberg 1973, 2). The Romans developed a daily account of the Senate along with their political and social happenings known as *acta diurna*, which was transcribed onto papyrus and posted in public places (Stephens 1996, 27).

That type of communication declined in Europe and written news virtually vanished with the collapse of the Western Roman Empire. Additionally, plagues, poverty, and centuries of violent authoritarian rule kept common people illiterate and in a social regime where the idea of them constituting a "public"—much less having "public opinion"—was virtually nonexistent until the Renaissance economy gave rise to a new merchant class.

Journalism, Revolution and the Public Sphere

Commercial expansion, religious conflict and the rise of nation-states—not advances in technology—radically changed the economic and political context of communications in Europe and America during the seventeenth and eighteenth centuries (Starr 2004, 23). It is important not to overlook the contribution Johannes Gutenberg made to the publication and distribution of ideas in 1440 with moveable type, but as Paul Starr notes, a printer from the 1500s magically catapulted into a print shop of the late 1700s would have found hand-operated wooden presses barely altered from those in his own time (Moran 1973, 30–31).

Yet, during that period, the changes in what people knew about their world and how they got that information were enormous. Europe and the American colonies benefitted from the introduction of regularly available postal service; scientific journals and other periodicals appeared; and journalism began to emerge in its early modern form (Starr 2004, 23). The market for printed texts expanded, and the law of intellectual property began to take shape—but more important, these developments led to a new sphere of public information, public debate and public opinion (Starr 2004, 23).

Journalism historically does its intellectual work in the public sphere in the form of texts that move beyond daily dispatches. Jurgen Habermas argues that during the Enlightenment a bourgeois public sphere emerged and provided a social framework where citizens exchanged ideas and developed public opinion. Habermas sees this "public realm" as "a space where men could escape from their roles as subjects and gain autonomy in the exercise and exchange of their own opinions and ideas" (Outram 1995, 11). That relationship frequently is traced to late-seventeenth century British coffee houses and in a more complex and nuanced way to French salons, which Habermas claims emerged in cultural-political contrast to court society (Habermas 1968).[2]

The English Civil War, a series of armed conflicts between Parliamentarians and Royalists that led to the execution of Charles I, established the ideological precedent that a monarch could not govern without some popular consent. It engulfed England for most of the 1640s, and as often is the case, the national crisis sparked both legitimate and devious arguments for public safety that led to actions designed to quash free association and expression.

At the height of the turmoil, Parliament passed The Licensing Act of 1643, which required a government-approved license for authors to publish their works. The following year, John Milton, whose writings typically championed freedom and self-determination, wrote *Areopagitica* (Kendall 1960). The tract drew on historic facts from classical democracies (Greece and Rome had no such licensing for written ideas) and Biblical mores to offer a passionate defense of a free press and free speech. He argued: "Who kills a man kills a reasonable creature, God's image; but he who destroys a good book, kills reason itself, kills the image of God, as it were in the eye."

Milton failed to convince Parliament to repeal the act, but scholars credit *Areopagitica* for influencing intellectual freedom in ideas later espoused by John Locke and John Stuart Mill (Kendall 1960). It's key points also are visible in the United States Constitution, whose writers and contributors believed prior restraint would have a chilling effect on speech and on the type of publications citizens need to participate in a publicly driven society. In fact, the U.S. Supreme Court has referred to *Areopagitica* by name in four twentieth-century cases involving the First Amendment, such as *New York Times v. Sullivan, Times Film Corp v. City of Chicago et al, Eisenstadt Sheriff v. Baird,* and *Communist Party of the United States v. Subversive Activities Control Board.*

Copyright, another British custom with implications for journalism and intellectual freedom, initially helped governments restrict printing; however, these days it is used to encourage creative work by giving authors control over their product's use and profit. Copyright generally lasts for the creator's

---

2   Others have argued that salons were closer to an extension of court society. In *The History of Manners,* Norbert Elias contends the dominant concepts of the salons—politeese, civilite, and honnete were used almost as synonyms by which courtly people designated in a broad or narrow sense, the quality of their own behavior. Steven Kale and others compromise in a position that the public and private spheres overlapped in the salons.

life plus fifty to one hundred years after his or her death. Most jurisdictions give the public some leeway for limited and fair use of material that is widely recognized in the public domain.

In the wake of the British debate over censorship (beginning about 1650) English coffee houses sprung up around Oxford, where their clientele consisted largely of professors and others interested in experimental ideas (Cowan 2005, 91). Known as "penny universities," because a penny was the combined price of admission and a cup of coffee, they were a place for like-minded scholars to congregate, to read, to learn from and to debate with each other; however, they emphatically were not a university institution, and the discourse there was far different from what was offered by prevailing universities (Cowan 2005, 91).

Coffeehouses naturally became a focus of news culture as news became available in a variety of forms in many locations. That included: print, both licensed and unlicensed; manuscripts; aloud, as gossip, hearsay, and word of mouth (Cowan 2005, 87).

The Spectator and the *Tatler*, published by Richard Steele and Joseph Addison, were two widely distributed and influential publications found in English coffeehouses. They brought politeness to coffeehouse conversation with the explicit purpose of reforming English morals through a veiled critique of English society (Mackie n.d.). Addison and Steele relied on coffeehouse conversation as a source of news and gossip, and they relied on the houses themselves as a distribution network to spread that information back to their clientele (Bramah 1972, 48). Edward Bramah argues that the good standing of the press during the era of *The Tatler* and *The Spectator* can be directly attributed to the popularity of the coffeehouse, which was increasingly recognized as a locus for the public sphere (Bramah 1972, 48).

It is important to note, however, that large categories of people were excluded from the public life of the coffeehouses and from issues addressed in newspapers that constituted this early public sphere. Schudson reminds us that women were outside the magic circle, as were men without property. Those who were included, it can also be added, had a limited capacity to arrive at reasoned public choice not only because their circle was small but also because their information about public affairs was restricted. Government operated in much greater secrecy than would be true later. Even when information was available, a culture of deference left to only a few of those propertied white males in the coffee house the capacity to speak authoritatively (Schudson 2009).

Some of the key class and economic structures that offered access to and participation within coffeehouses can be found in nuanced forms in salons that are widely associated with pre-revolutionary France. An obvious difference between French salons and British coffee houses is the important and visible role that women played in salons. In general, *salonnieres* were more than social climbers; they were intelligent, self-educated women who lived by Enlightenment values and used them to shape the salon to meet their own social intellectual and educational needs (Goodman 1994, 14). Dena Goodman argues in *The Republic of Letters* that the relevance of the salons waned with the French Revolution as "the literary public sphere was transformed into the political public" (Goodman 1994, 280). Stephen Kale offers a subordinate analysis that extends their relevance to the Revolution of 1848. He notes:

> . . . *a whole world of social arrangements and attitudes supported the existence of French salons: an idle aristocracy, an ambitious middle class, an active intellectual life, the social density of a major urban center, sociable traditions and a certain aristocratic feminism. This world did not disappear in 1789.* (Kale 2006, 9)

Outside the salons, pamphlets and periodicals served as a standard source of ideas for the intense ideological awareness and commitment that defined the Revolution. Pamphlets predate periodicals as instruments for forging public opinion during times of great crisis in the seventeenth century (Chisick 1988, 625). In the eighteenth century, the periodical press emerged as more important in forming and directing opinion. Harvey Chisick offers a concise description of the evolution:

> *Under the Old Regime, most periodicals were concerned with literature and the arts and sciences or acted as channels for local news and advertising. The government exercised close censorship of periodicals and did not tolerate independent political reporting. Forced underground or across the frontiers, much political journalism of the Old Regime was irregular in appearance and harsh in tone. With the Revolution, true political periodicals began to appear.* (Chisick 1988, 626–627)

Chisick finds an interesting equilibrium between pamphlets and newspapers; some of the more successful dailies of the early Revolution also produced pamphlets on a massive scale. So much was happening in these years that reporting and commenting on events could not be contained within the framework of four crammed quarto pages of tiny print, and news and commentary naturally spilled over into supplements and pamphlets (Chisick 1988, 643).

But no face of the Revolution is as eerily prominent as that of Jean-Paul Marat, the radical journalist murdered in his bathtub by a Girondist sympathizer and immortalized that way in *The Death of Marat*, a painting by Jaques-Louis David, himself a member of one of the two "Great Committees" (the Committee of General Security). Marat's essays and newspaper journalism, known for absolute defense of the under class and opposition to enemies of the Revolution, made him a hero of the masses and their ersatz ambassador to the radical Jacobians who seized authority in 1793. His targets routinely were the powerful influential groups in Paris, including the Constituent Assembly, court ministers and the *Corps Municipal.*

Marat launched his own newspaper in September 1789. He first called it *Moniteur Patriote* (Patriotic Watch); four days later renamed it *Publiciste Parisien;* and he eventually settled on *L'Ami du Peuple* (Friend of the People.) Historian Jeremy Popkin dubbed it "the most celebrated radical paper of the Revolution" (Danton and Roche 1989). Marat's passionate writing challenged conservative revolutionaries and incited violence, and forced him more than once to flee Paris or go into hiding. In a pamphlet from July 26, 1790, titled *C'en est fait de nous* (We're done for) he wrote:

Five or six hundred heads would have guaranteed your freedom and happiness but a false humanity has restrained your arms and stopped your blows. If you don't strike now, millions of your brothers will die, your enemies will triumph and your blood will flood the streets. They'll slit your throats without mercy and desembowel your wives. And their bloody hands will rip out your children's entrails to erase your love of liberty forever (Marat 1790).

Any recap of journalism, intellectual freedom, and European revolution would be remiss without acknowledging the enormous role played by Karl Marx who, among many other things, spent more than a decade (1851–62) as London correspondent for Horace Greeley's *New-York Tribune (sic).* Greeley tried to steer the *Tribune* away from the sensationalism of the popular mass penny papers of that era. Robi Chakravorti describes Marx's work as "academic or conceptual journalism . . . philosophical-analytical insights based chiefly on research using as news pegs general issues affecting societies" (Chakravorti 1993, 1856–1859). Isaiah Berlin saw his work as ahead of its time and with a "highly twentieth century flavor" because it gave readers sketches of events or characters and emphasized hidden interests and the sinister activities likely to result from them rather than the explicit motives furnished by the actors themselves or the social value of public policy (Berlin 1963, 169–170). He gave his New York audience columns largely focused on international affairs such as "Elections in England" (1852), "The Greek Insurrection" (1854), and "The Right Divine Hohenzollerns" (1857). The arrangement with Greeley also allowed the *Tribune* to carry works by his colleague Friedrich Engels, whose columns included "the British Army in India" (1858), "Military Reform in Germany" (1860), and "Could the French Sack London?" (1860).

The work Marx did from London for Greely came during a stretch of relative stability that followed a decade of economic uncertainty, writing for a series of radical papers in Cologne and elsewhere in Western Europe. It was during that tenuous time immediately after Marx finished his studies that he developed his ideas concerning dialectical materialism and penned *The Communist Manifesto* (1848). His writing freely criticized national governments across the continent and challenged liberals and other members of the socialist movement whose ideas he thought were ineffective or outright anti-socialist (Wheen 2001, 42–44). Marx used an inheritance from his father to launch his own brief effort as a newspaper publisher, founding *Neue Rheinische Zeitung*, which he used to promote European news with his own socioeconomic interpretation. Police regularly harassed Marx and other socialists, and when Prussia's democratic government collapsed in 1848 King Frederick William IV's government passed counter-revolutionary measures designed to cleanse leftist elements from the country (Wheen 2001, 137–146). As a result, *Neue Rheinische Zeitung* was shut down. Marx fled the country that spring and was unable to move back to Germany or Belgium, so he found refuge in London in August 1849 (Watson 2010, 250; Wheen 2001, 147).

The First Amendment, News Magazines and the Public Intellectual

Nothing in American culture ensures the simultaneous viability of journalism and intellectual freedom more than the First Amendment to the United States Constitution. It is the founding principle for free expression in artistic and academic work as well as in the nation's news industry. Enlightenment ideas of democracy and individual liberty energized colonists during the American Revolution and guided the founding fathers afterward as they set about the business of starting a new country.

Thomas Paine, known as "a corset maker by trade, a journalist by profession and a propagandist by inclination," made a passionate case for independence in two highly successful pamphlet series, *Common Sense* (1776) and *The American Crisis* (1776–83) (Padover 1952, 32). *Common Sense* was a monograph published on January 10, 1776, and signed "Written by an Englishman." Paine abandoned lofty tones typical of the publications read by his highly educated peers and reduced political arguments to a level designed for an average citizen. His chief contribution was raising the public debate about independence to an overt public discussion, though he also believed in the peaceful nature of republics; his views were an early and strong conception of what scholars would come to call the "democratic peace" theory (Levy 2011). *Common Sense* quickly spread among the literate. An estimated 500,000 copies including pirated editions sold during the course of the revolution through the American British colonies, which had only two million free inhabitants; it was the best-selling American book of its day (Hitchens 2006, 37). The tract was so influential that John Adams said, "Without the pen of the author of *Common Sense,* the sword of Washington would have been raised in vain" (Lepore 2006).

After the revolution, leaders had to establish laws around the institutions that would have an impact on new American life. James Madison, considered the principle author of the Bill of Rights, considered the First Amendment as an action clause of sorts to the entire social contract, and he enshrined the philosophical and political principles set forth in these famous words:

> *A popular government without popular information or the means of acquiring it is but a prologue to a farce or a tragedy; or perhaps both.*
>
> *Knowledge will forever govern ignorance; and a people who mean to be their own governors must arm themselves with the power which knowledge gives.* (The First Amendment Center n.d.)

The amendment contains four clauses—religion, speech, press, and assembly—but contrary to some popular belief, it does not give citizens unfettered freedom in those areas. Congress, state legislatures, and the courts generally have been sympathetic to claims of free speech and freedom of the press—especially in the areas of politics and public life—but they also have upheld reasonable restrictions on those claims through laws that address libel, privacy, public safety, and copyright.

Carey cautions against the trap of viewing the First Amendment through the overly simplistic "rights tradition" and urges us to consider its clauses as a compact way of describing a political society (Carey 1997, 216-217). He interprets the amendment as "an attempt to find the nature of public life as it existed at the time or as the founders hoped it would be." To put it plainly, Carey reads it as a blueprint for a public sphere where people are free to gather without the intrusion of the state; once gathered, they are free to speak openly and freely; they are further free to write down what is said and distribute it to citizens who could not gather on that occasion (Carey 1997, 217). Viewed that way, the First Amendment links journalism directly to the public sphere and also provides guidance for how relevant statutes should or shouldn't be written as future needs arise.

As America grew, sensationalism came to be the chief characteristic of the penny papers that replaced the colonial press and dominated American journalism for much of the nineteenth century. Greeley tried to elevate intellectual discourse in his *New York Tribune* by creating a paper that would exclude the "immoral and degrading" police reports loved by readers of the *Herald* and appeal to an audience of the "virtuous and refined" (Tucher 2012). He was explicit about his goal not just to publish the first cheap paper with a Whig sensibility but also to improve the moral tone of the cheap press generally. Additionally, a literature of reform began to emerge in the late nineteenth century that would influence a movement known as "muckraking," which began to appear in journalistic publications around 1900. Magazines such as *Colliers Weekly* and *McClure's Magazine* were widely read by a growing middle class at the turn of the century. The January 1903 issue of *McClure's* is considered the official beginning of muckraking journalism for that single issue contained: "The History of Standard Oil" by Ida Tarbell, "The Shame of Minneapolis" by Lincoln Steffens, and "The Right to Work" by Ray Stannard Baker. Muckrakers were considered more investigative journalists than public intellectuals, but their work clearly set a moral agenda for intellectual discussion in the public sphere. Tarbell and Steffens' turned their magazine articles into books where they honed their intellectual arguments and further raised the level of public discourse about their ideas. Not long after the muckrakers, Lippmann and Herbert Croly founded *The New Republic* (1914), where Lippmann's essays on national affairs so impressed President Woodrow Wilson that he asked Lippmann to help formulate the Fourteen Points, develop the League of Nations, and travel to the postwar peace negotiations at Versailles.

This rise in social and economic criticism and the intellectual focus on international affairs did not go unfettered. As World War I raged in Europe, the old tension between free expression and public safety that marked the British, French and American revolutions emerged in the form of the Espionage Act of 1917 and its companion, the Sedition Act of 1918. These laws were used to prosecute socialist and pacifist Americans who distributed materials with antiwar ideas. In one case, the secretary of the Socialist Party of America printed and mailed about 15,000 leaflets to prospective military draftees urging them not to submit to intimidation and to assert their rights against involuntary servitude. In the other, two leaflets thrown from windows of a building in New York City (one written in Yiddish) and signed "revolutionists" denounced the decision to send troops to Russia and called on businesses to stop producing weapons that would be used against the Soviets.

The Supreme Court ruled unanimously in *Schenck v. United States* (1919) that the First Amendment did not give a citizen the right to express printed opposition to the draft. Justice Oliver Wendell Holmes wrote: "When a nation is at war, many things that might be said in time of peace are such a hindrance to its effort that their utterance will not be endured so long as men fight" (Holmes 1919). His opinion also established the "clear and present danger" test:

> *The most stringent protection of free speech would not protect a man in falsely shouting fire in a theatre and causing a panic. . . . The question in every case is whether the words used are used in such circumstance and are of such a nature as to create a clear and present danger that they will bring about the substantive evils that Congress has a right to prevent.*

Holmes support for the espionage and sedition acts softened a few months later. In the second case, *Abrams v. United States* (1919), he and Louis Brandeis dissented. They argued that the founding fathers protection of free expression was "as experiment as all life is an experiment" and that the First Amendment left no room for the government to suppress ideas, except where a threat was imminent (Holmes 1919).

> *Persecution for the expression of opinions seems to me perfectly logical. If you have no doubt of your premises or your power and want a certain result with all your heart you naturally express your wishes in law and sweep away all opposition. . . . But when men have realized that time has upset many fighting faiths, they may come to believe even more than they believe the very foundations of their own conduct that the ultimate good desired is better reached by free trade in ideas.* (Holmes 1919)

Nonetheless, the clear-and-present-danger test lasted until 1969, when the court moved the standard for criminal prosecution to expression that provoked "imminent lawless action," making it harder to prosecute expression of ideas that potentially conflicted with public safety. That case, *Brandenburg v. Ohio*, came during the height of the Vietnam War but had nothing to do with the conflict. It involved a speech given by a Ku Klux Klan leader who made statements law enforcement officials perceived as threats for future violence.

Unencumbered by notions of objectivity and neutrality that newspaper publishers adopted to reduce the influence of government and stem the practice of sensationalism, it was magazines—not newspapers—that became a launching ground in the twentieth century for the careers of public intellectuals and for journalism with intellectual ramifications. John Hersey's 31,000-word masterpiece, *Hiroshima*, captivated readers of *The New Yorker*, which made the unprecedented decision to displace virtually all other editorial content to run the account of six people who survived the bombing that launched the era of potential nuclear war. Fifteen years later, the magazine serialized *Silent Spring* by Rachel Carson, a well-known writer of natural history but relative newcomer to social criticism. Indeed, *The New Yorker* helped establish a modern tradition of a journalism of ideas by publishing compelling writers, such as Irwin Shaw, Alice Munro, Haruki Murakami, and J.D. Salinger.

The Nation, founded in 1865 and known as the oldest continuously published weekly magazine in the United States, was a consistent voice of liberalism during the twentieth century, supporting the New Deal and calling for nationalization of industry. It was consistently left of *The New Republic*, and the FBI had files on its editors as far back as 1915. In fact, virtually every editor of *The Nation* from the 1920s to 1970s was examined for subversive activities and ties (Kimball 1986, 399–426). Its notable contributors include: Albert Einstein, H.L Mencken, Edward Said, Christopher Hitchens, Leon Trotsky and Jean Paul-Sartre.

It's important to note that American magazine journalism, magazine writers and their ideas have not been exclusively progressive or liberal. A grand example is William F. Buckley, who used the magazine format to launch a revival of conservatism in America and arguably to change the course of world history by sewing the seeds for the Reagan presidency. He published *The National Review* in 1955 with the goal of mainstreaming the conservative movement through a blend of American political conservatism, laissez-faire economics and global anticommunism. Buckley used the magazine to create a new pedigree for modern conservatism and to exclude people, ideas or groups he thought were unfit to be associated with the cause (Chapman 2009). He denounced Ayn Rand, the John Birch Society, George Wallace and anti-Semites. Historian George Nash, a key interpreter of American conservatism, called Buckley "arguably the most important public intellectual in the United States in the past half century. . . . For an entire generation, he was the preeminent voice of American conservatism and its first great ecumenical figure" (Nash 2008).

Conclusions

In sum, journalism has a long, rich history as a vehicle for spreading ideas with intellectual implications, but that doesn't mean all journalism is an intellectual process. Many of us experience journalism as a consumer product with information simplified and condensed for mass markets and quick delivery. It comes to us in all sorts of forms, including *USA Today, Headline News*, half-hourly updates on commercial radio, and reactive conversation through social media. Breaking local news, personality features, urban crime stories (If it bleeds, it leads!), weather updates, and sports scores give corporate media plenty of information to market and sell with little if any intellectual context. Yet, even in those brief and basic forms, journalism is a type of inquiry, and inquiry is fundamental to intellectual freedom.

A broader look at journalistic practices and traditions shows the work of determining what information is important for widespread circulation, compiling it in ways that it is intellectually digestible, then distributing it to an intended audience has varied over centuries, across cultures and even within particular cultures at specific times. Journalism as we know it took shape about 150 years ago, though its role in the great European and American revolutions, grounded in Enlightenment ideology and political theory, is distinct and undeniable. This journalism of ideas comes to salience at times of great cultural questioning, and it does its social and intellectual work in what

Habermas has identified as the bourgeois public sphere. Its ability to bolster freedom, to reshape society, and even to help create a government is so great that constitutions, laws and court decisions in free societies recognize it as a bulwark against authoritarianism.

Still, licensing, copyright, issues of public safety, and the modern era ethos of neutrality and objectivity can shape, constrain and threaten the journalistic practice of intellectual freedom even in open societies. The United States balked at the European traditions of licensing publishers, which often led to official censorship. Our founding fathers wrote copyright protections into the Constitution not to inhibit publication but to give citizens the right to control their written ideas for reasonable times, and then to allow widespread public access so they can be modified, further developed, and add to our intellectual life. They crafted the First Amendment of the Bill of Rights, which American journalists like to brandish as a shield against government intimidation. However, courts have steadfastly ruled that in some cases—particularly matters of public safety—free expression and the publication of inflammatory ideas may be limited or curtailed. And ironically, the ethos of objectivity and neutrality that became the voluntary guiding principle of mainstream journalism in the twentieth century may have actually dampened critical reporting in newspapers and allowed magazines to emerge as the fundamental training ground for public intellectuals and a journalism of ideas.

As the Internet Age unfolds, access to journalism from all over the globe and the ideas that come with it are greater than ever. So are the tensions over the exercise of intellectual freedom both among sovereign nations and within nations themselves. Journalists at home and abroad are at the forefront of the legal and ethical practices of intellectual freedom, and their work is not without personal risk. Virtually every type of idea—routine to contentious— is at our disposal. And the lessons of history show that intellectual freedom has the power to cause revolution and ensure democracy and that journalism plays a key role in determining whether and how that happens.

References

American Library Association. 2010. *Intellectual Freedom Manual*. 8th ed. Chicago, IL: American Library Association.

Berlin, Isaiah. 1963. *Karl Marx: His Life and Environment* Berlin: Oxford University Press.

Bramah, Edward. 1972. Tea and Coffee. *A Modern View of Three Hundred Years of Tradition*. Tiptree, Essex: Hutchinson & Co, Ltd.

Carey, James. 1997. A republic if you can keep it. In *James Carey: A Critical Reader*. eds. Munson, Eve Stryker and Catherine A. Warren. Minneapolis: University of Minnesota Press.

Carey, James. 1997. The Dark Continent of American Journalism. In *James Carey: A Critical Reader*. Eds. Munson, Eve Stryker and Catherine A. Warren. Minneapolis: University of Minnesota Press.

Carey, James. 1997. The Press, Public Opinion and Public Discourse. In *James Carey: A Critical Reader*. Eds. Munson, Eve Stryker and Catherine A. Warren. Minneapolis: University of Minnesota Press.

Chakravorti, Robi. 1993. Marx the journalist. *Economic and Political Weekly* 28, no. 36 (Sept. 4).

Chapman, Roger. 2009. *Culture wars: an encyclopedia of issues, viewpoints, and voices*. Vol. 1. New York: M. E. Sharpe.

Chisick, Harvey. 1988. Pamphlets and journalism in the early French Revolution: The offices of the Ami du Roi of the Abbe Royou as a center of royalist propaganda. *French Historical Studies* 15, no. 4 (Autumn).

Committee to Protect Journalists. 2013. Journalists killed since 1992. http://cpj.org/killed (accessed August 24 2013).

Cowan, Brian William. 2005. *The Social Life of Coffee: The Emergence of the British Coffeehouse*. New Haven: Yale University Press.

Danton, Robert and Daniel Roche, eds. *Revolution in Print: the Press in France, 1775–1800* Berkeley: University of California Press.

The First Amendment Center. n.d. *James Madison*, Vanderbilt University and the Newseum. http://www.firstamendmentcenter.org/hall-of-fame/james-madison (accessed August 24, 2013).

Goodman, Dena. 1994. *The Republic of Letters: A Cultural History of the French Enlightenment*. Ithaca: Cornell University Press.

Habermas, Jurgen. 1989. *Structural Transformation of the Public Sphere*, Vol. 30. Cambridge, Mass: MIT Press.

Heredia, Christopher, Leslie Fulbright, and Marisa Lagos. 2007. Hit man kills newspaper editor on Oakland street. *San Francisco Chronicle*, Aug. 2.

Hitchens, Christopher. 2006. *Thomas Paine's Rights of Man*. New York: Grove Press.

Hohenberg, John. *Free Press, Free People: The Best Case*. New York: Free Press.

Holmes, Oliver Wendell. *Schenck v. United States* 249 U.S. 47 (1919). http://supreme.justia.com/cases/federal/us/249/47/case.html (accessed August 24, 2013).

Holmes, Oliver Wendell. 1919. *Abrams v. United States* 250 U.S. 616 (1919) http://supreme.justia.com/cases/federal/us/250/616/case.html (accessed August 24, 2013).

Kale, Steven. 2006. *French Salons: High Society and Political Sociability from the Old Regime to the Revolution of 1848.* Baltimore: Johns Hopkins University Press.

Kendall, Willmoore. 1960. How to Read Milton's Areopagicita. *The Journal of Politics* 23, no. 3: 439–473.

Kimball, Penn. 1986. The History of *The Nation* According to the FBI. *The Nation.* New York: The Nation Company.

Kovach, Bill and Tom Rosenstiel. 2007. *The Elements of Journalism.* New York: Three Rivers Press.

KTVU.COM. 2007. Handyman Charged in Newsman's Sidewalk Murder. Aug. 7, 2007.

Lee, Henry K. 2011. Chauncey Bailey shooter laughed at killings. *San Francisco Chronicle.* March 28.

Lepore, Jill. 2006. The sharpened quill. *The New Yorker,* October, 16.

Levy, Jack S. and William R. Thompson. 2011. *Causes of War* New York: Wiley and Sons.

Mackie, Erin. n.d. *The Commerce of Everyday Life: Selections from The Tatler and The Spectator.* Boston: Bedford Cultural Editions.

Marat, Jean-Paul. 1790. Jean C'en est Fait de Nous! Saricks, French revolutionary pamphlets, 3839 (Imp. de Marat 1790) http://www.worldcat.org/title/cen-est-fait-de-nous/oclc/607059886 (accessed August 24, 2013).

Milton, John. 2006. *Areopagitica,* Project Gutenberg EBook http://www.gutenberg.org/files/608/608-h/608-h.htm (accessed August 24, 2013)

Moran, James. 1973. *Printing Presses: History and Development from the Fifteenth Century to Modern Times.* Berkeley and Los Angeles: University of California Press.

Nash, George H. 2008. Simply Superlative: Words for Buckley. *National Review Online,* Feb 28.

Outram, Dorinda. 1995. *The Enlightenment.* Cambridge, Cambridge University Press.

Padover, Saul K. 1952. *Jefferson: A Great American's Life and Ideas.* The New American Library.

The Pulitzer Prizes. 2012a. The Pulitzer Prize Winners General Nonfiction, 2012. http://www.pulitzer.org/citation/2012-General-Nonfiction (accessed August 24, 2013).

The Pulitzer Prizes. 2012b. The Pulitzer Prize Winners General Nonfiction, 2012. http://www.pulitzer.org/works/2012 (accessed August 24, 2013).

Schudson, Michael. 1978. *Discovering the News: A Social History of American Newspapers.* New York: Basic Books.

Schudson, Michael. 2009. A Family of Public Spheres. *Transformations of the Public Sphere*. Social Science Research Council website. http://publicsphere.ssrc.org/schudson-a-family-of-public-spheres (accessed August 24, 2013).

The Sinclair Lewis Society. 2012. Why did Sinclair Lewis decline the Pulitzer Prize? Illinois State University. http://english.illinoisstate.edu/sinclairlewis/sinclair_lewis/faq/faq2.shtml (accessed August 24, 2013).

Starr, Paul. 2004. *Creation of the Media*. New York: Basic Books.

Steel, Ronald. 1980. *Walter Lippmann and the American Century*. Boston: Little Brown and Company.

Stephens, Mitchell. *History of News*. Fort Worth, Texas: Hardcourt Brace Publishers.

Tucher, Andie. 2012. professional correspondence Nov. 25.

United Nations. 1948. Article 19. Universal Declaration of Human Rights. http://www.un.org/en/documents/udhr/index.shtml#a19 (accessed August 24, 2013).

United Nations. 1948. Universal Declaration of Human Rights. http://www.un.org/en/documents/udhr/index.shtml (accessed August 24, 2013).

Watson, Peter. 2010. *The German Genius: Europe's Third Renaissance, the Second Scientific Revolution and the Twentieth Century*. New York: Harper Collins.

Wheen, Francis. 2001. *Karl Marx: A Life*. New York: Norton.

Academic and Intellectual Freedom

Mark Alfino

A cademic Freedom, in the modern form it takes at teaching and research universities, refers to the freedom to research and teach without fear of reprisal, including the loss of one's job, for one's viewpoint. It is a form of intellectual freedom that attaches to particular professional roles (the teacher, professor, researcher, student) and allows claims and privileges that can be recognized not only in a court, but in the intramural judgments of university grievance and contract compliance processes, and therefore, also in the distribution and balance of power and work relationships in a faculty.

This somewhat formal definition, which betrays the common preference for thinking of academic freedom as a faculty right—it is also an institutional right—still makes a good start. Many of the problems of academic freedom involve determining legitimate boundaries between the freedoms it protects in teaching, research and expression, and the prerogatives of the academic institution, as well as of other faculty. How does the institution's authority to restructure curriculum affect and intersect with the faculty's authority to create it, for example? Can one faculty's protected expression create a hostile environment for another? Can particular ways of teaching violate student academic freedom? When one looks closely at how boundary questions like these are settled, one comes to know that academic freedom is a particular cultural practice that will draw on local understandings of reasonableness, manifested through the particular history and institutions of its time and place. We shall see how the emergence of academic freedom in the United States in the nineteenth century, for example, was conditioned in some very historically specific ways.

By contrast, contemporary challenges to academic freedom come from large and recent changes in the academy and global economy. So it will have to remain an open question what lessons from the US experience of the emergence of academic freedom from the late 19th century to about 1980 apply to the new, post-1980 challenges to academic freedom. My hypothesis is that since both historic and contemporary problems of academic freedom have to be understood in reference to underlying social institutions, comparative study is likely to be valuable. Some of these underlying institutions, such as the percentage of tenure/tenure-track faculty, have suffered dramatic declines. As Hansmann reports, "From 1975 to 2009, the proportion of faculty on the tenure track in US colleges fell by nearly half, from 57 to 30 percent" (Hansmann 2012, 176). As we shall see, strong arguments link academic freedom to tenure and faculty governance. If tenure does not rebound as a social institution supporting academic freedom, then how can academic freedom be realized in the future academy? This is probably the most pressing problem for realizing academic freedom in the emerging global higher education environment.

In this chapter, we will come to know academic freedom both theoretically, as a manifestation of enlightenment thought first seen in Germany, and through its US manifestation in the 19th century. The US context, while particular, is important as site for the growth of a culture of academic freedom because it developed, through the American Association of University Professors (AAUP), an extensive case record on violations of academic freedom. The AAUP itself has developed reflection on the nature of academic freedom through a period of almost 100 years, starting with the 1915 Declaration of Principles on Academic Freedom and Academic Tenure (AAUP 1915).

Breaches of academic freedom still involve the classic stereotype of a faculty member lecturing or publishing something controversial. But it can also arise from a faculty member or student at a U.S. university's campus in Dubai or Singapore experiencing a limitation of academic freedom due to cultural differences. It can arise between two faculty members, or a faculty member and a student. It can arise along with research conflict of interest issues, in a faculty member over-defending or being unwilling to defend the research or activities of a funded institute or sponsor on his or her campus. It arises in distinctive ways for religious institutions, where questions of institutional identity are often understood as an institutional prerogative that ought to affect curriculum. Finally, since academic freedom disputes often involve claims of reprisal, they come with a whole set of facts that are often difficult to interpret. Some cases will be mentioned along the way, but many are still in process at the time of writing and I would not presume to judge them, especially by press reports. But the image of academic freedom cases as predominantly featuring pure benighted faculty members speaking truth to power (let's call it the Galilean ideal), while inviting, and one that we will shortly indulge, would, if over-generalized, conceal the diversity and structure of actual cases.

History of Academic Freedom

We start our inquiry in this chapter the well-established and recent record of thought on academic freedom and then we will try to use this common understanding to present and critically assess contemporary trends in the practice of academic freedom, including the internationalization of academic freedom, the increasingly complex relationship of corporate donors and academic freedom, and an uncertain legal environment for academic freedom in the US following the US Supreme Court decision in *Garcetti v. Ceballos*. By the end of this discussion, we will try to pose some critical questions about the best ways to think about the changes occurring in the area of academic freedom and its supporting institutions.

We can talk about a special or protected status for academics in the medieval period, but the best place to locate the modern understanding of academic freedom is in Enlightenment Germany, the 18th century culture of Christian Wolff, a professor of mathematics and physics at University of Halle. Wolff outraged the Pietists of Halle by claiming that theological claims can be based on mathematical reasoning, and, for example, by praising Confucianism as evidence of the use of reason to find moral precepts. Wolff, as good a post-Enlightenment candidate for the Galilean ideal as we will have to offer, was suppressed by the King Frederick William I in 1723 for his views, but reinstated, as an imperial baron, in 1745 by his successor, Frederick the Great. From the early nineteenth century, German academic culture adopted the language and thinking of "akademische Freiheit." "A half century later the philosopher Johann Gottlieb Fichte could proclaim that "free investigation of every possible object of thought is without doubt a human right" (Finkin and Post 2009, 19).

As 19th century American culture developed the wealth and motivation to create more colleges and universities, it found its own "Christian Wolfs" and its own equivalent of "pietist Generals," and the culture of academic freedom developed from these incidents as well. The one most often told, because it appears to have been the most consequential, is the case of the dismissal of Edward A. Ross, a European trained economist who took an academic position in 1896 at 5 year old Stanford University. Mrs. Stanford was already understood to be willing and able to dismiss faculty for their viewpoint. Ross held unpopular viewpoints in economics. For example, he favored "free silver," which was a radical view for an academic economist to hold at that time. But Ross also gave racially chauvinistic speeches, objecting to the arrival of Chinese guest workers and immigrants. As Haskell points out in his excellent account of the story, Ross' social views were not out of line with his contemporaries. But Mr. Stanford had banned political activity by the faculty and Ross' condemnation of immigrant labor was felt to be a rebuke to the

Stanford fortune. Ross was not reappointed in the 1900 academic year. While many Stanford faculty supported Ross by resigning their own positions, requiring extensive rebuilding of departments, the importance of the Ross case lay in the attention it received from Ross's professional society, the American Economic Association, which launched an investigation of the incident that many consider a model for the approach the AAUP would adopt after its formation fifteen years later.

The Christian Wolff and Ross cases define the classic stereotype of the academic freedom hero, even if our modern one is tarnished a bit by his apparent racism. As we have said, the Galilean ideal is a perfection of the genre. Galileo was even a pious hero of the truth. The nineteenth and twentieth century have offered plenty of occasions for testing academic freedom—state loyalty oaths, local conflicts between state university professors and state politicians or enterprises, war and anti-war speeches, reform movements—all of these have afforded opportunities for testing and deepening our understanding of academic freedom (Jones 1949). But we should be careful not to over-idealize the stereotype. Academic freedom also protects the faculty member with unpopular views or even widely repudiated views. When, for example, John C. Yoo, the author of many of the "torture memos" which came from the second Bush Administration's Justice Department, resumed his work at UC Berkeley, he was protected from significant protests calling for his removal by academic freedom (Glenn 2009).

Another lesson we get from cases and history is that social institutions play a big role in the defining academic freedom. Following the formation of the AAUP, a private and non-profit organization, cases came to be heard before "Committee A on Academic Freedom and Tenure" and institutions could be censured for violating academic freedom. Because academic freedom existed as a cultural value, at least since the Ross case, and could affect faculty recruitment and morale, universities have generally wanted to defend their reputations for protecting academic freedom. But as Thomas Haskell points out, along with the emergence of the AAUP we also find professional academic organizations that formed during the late 19th century, such as the Modern Language Association (1883), the American Historical Association (1884), the American Economic Association (1885) (Haskell 1996, 45). These gave authority to judgments about what counts as legitimate professional activity, something that is essential not only in adjudicating disputes, but in faculty governance and selection. So the social matrix of academic freedom in the US is defined by a voluntary common "horizontal" recognition of the AAUP's authority to investigation alleged breaches of academic freedom combined with participation in professional academic societies, which can authoritatively evaluate published work. These provide a kind of vertical integration with AAUP protection, which has the same need as all stakeholders for some source of authoritative judgment in cases alleging incompetence, for example. In fact, if we follow Thomas Haskell's argument in "Justifying the Rights of Academic Freedom" a bit more directly, we can see how central to academic freedom these supporting institutions were. Haskell pushes the connection between academic freedom and professionalization by suggesting that we can even define academic freedom in terms of the aims of these and related institutions. "This is how I, as a historian, would define academic freedom: as the capstone of the institutional edifice that Victorian reformers constructed in hopes of establishing authority and cultivating reliable knowledge" (Haskell 53). While we often see academic freedom as an end in itself, it also works in the service of the cultivation of knowledge. Professional associations and publication practices, such as peer and blind review, that produce authoritativeness can be seen both as protectors of academic freedom, and as a crucial institutional component in a knowledge-seeking or knowledge-oriented culture.

Haskell's essay occurs in a great collection of articles edited by Louis Menand for University of Chicago Press in 1996. The volume is sufficiently recent to include a retrospective look at the culture wars, but not recent enough to reflect the era of outcomes assessment. The reduction of tenure was well underway by the 1990s. In Haskell's case, the key question, reflecting the legacy of postmodernism and the culture wars, was this: If there is no special status to knowledge, if knowledge is simply a concealment of power, then how can we make the kinds of authoritative claims for different fields of knowledge that those Victorians wanted us to make? And if we can not identify standards of quality in academic work now, then on what basis could a claim of violating academic freedom rest? As Haskell and others argue, academic freedom gains its legitimacy by delivering authoritative judgments about eccentric and boundary cases. If positions like Stanley Fish's in "There's No Such Thing as Free Speech and It's a Good Thing Too" were sound, then academic life would just be another scene for political conflict. The possibility of academic freedom assumes that we can make some valid or sound judgments about both the quality of work in our fields and the effectiveness of our teaching. Some versions of postmodernism, such as Fish's, seemed to have threatened these assumptions.

Without generalizing too much from a small number of cases, we can now see *faculty* academic freedom (institutional academic freedom remains to be discussed) as a role-specific right to pursue the academic profession without external interference or fear of reprisal. It is sustained in the US context by a set of faculty-run institutions related to scholarship—field-specific associations and societies, but also journals and conferences and the faculty-run AAUP, whose investigations and judgments are perceived as consequential to most colleges and universities. We can also see how important the specific institutional history of higher education and academic societies was to the specific form that academic freedom took in the US. Academic freedom depends upon disciplines of knowledge that can make authoritative judgments about their work. Therefore, intellectual societies and systems of publication and recognition of new work play a significant role in sustaining academic freedom.

This arrangement among universities, academic societies, and the AAUP is not without its weaknesses. As Haskell argued, radical critiques of the basis of knowledge, such as we experienced in the post modern period, undermined academic freedom. As noted, tenure is a minority position in academia today and does not exist at many universities. Faculty governance is increasingly replaced by professional administration which directs the production of reports from faculty departments (related to specific, directed activity) and manages curriculum revision. Defenses of academic freedom, such as we will read about in the next section, have cogent arguments for connecting the freedom to research, teach, express oneself intra- and extramurally and share in governance. But the modern university is changing, and on a global scale, in ways that do not preserve this wholistic image of faculty vocation and university enterprise. After looking at some theoretical defenses of academic freedom and some of the lines of thought that emerged in AAUP casework, we will turn to recent trends and developments.

Theoretical Justifications for Academic Freedom and the Development of Committee A's work

One of the best recent theoretical defenses of academic freedom is given in the 2009 book, *For the Common Good*, co-authored by Matthew Finkin, a highly accomplished legal scholar, long serving professional staff member, and past legal counsel at the AAUP and Robert Post, current Dean of Yale Law School. Their short treatment works from the consensus view, among supporters of academic freedom, that it is "for the common good" of creating and disseminating knowledge. Each domain of activity protected by it: research, teaching, intra and extramural speech, and governance each has its own rationale, often one that developed as well from the logic of the case histories of the AAUP. Along with a general defense of academic freedom, Finkin and Post explain the evolution of the AAUP's 1915 Declaration of Principles on Academic Freedom and Academic Tenure in the 1940 Statement of Principles of Academic Freedom and Tenure, as well as the so-called "Wolf Trap" agreement of 1970.

Perhaps the most straightforward way to think about academic freedom as supporting the common good is to credit academics with the production of reliable knowledge, and to rest one's case then on the idea that knowledge is a good. The crucial link in this argument will be between academic freedom and knowledge production. This will puzzle many people who encounter universities primarily as places that teach and confer degrees. Even college students are sometimes puzzled about how faculty research works and how it fits into university employment. Many people looking at higher education from a business standpoint are puzzled by the idea that faculty have "divided loyalties" to the teaching work of the institution and to faculty research work, which need not be related to any teaching interest and often connects the faculty member more to extramural resources and experiences, such as conferences and partnerships, than to intramural ones.

Faculty do traditionally consider themselves as having a personal research agenda whose progress their university employer has agreed to support and reward (or not hinder), in exchange for contributing to the degree conferring activity of the university. Evidence of the development of this agenda is still traditional evidence for promotion to full professor. Devoting a portion of faculty time and compensation to research might be parallel to the way that many professional work groups spend money maintaining and developing the credentials of their professionals through continuing education or further degrees. However, in the social and institutional environment of the 1915 Declaration, one finds a different approach. The Declaration encourages us to think of faculty as "appointees" rather than "employees," ". . . the relationship of the professor to the trustees may be compared to that between judges of the federal courts and the executive who appoints them" (1915 Declaration, cited in Finkin 2009, 34). The judges' status emerges in part because her job requires not only continuing education and technical correctness, but also some particular protections to maintain independence of thought and judgment. The pressure to change the outcome of a judicial process is not so different from the pressure to change a grade or research result. Whether we are talking about justice or knowledge production, we cannot let the employer, whether the government or a private founder of a university, determine the outcome of the investigation.

Should we place this sort of status in academics? The goal of producing knowledge—and its admittedly expensive requirement, independence of thought—might require allowing academics to self-regulate many aspects of their professional life, such as employment, ranks, and compensation. When these goods are held at the discretion of non-faculty employers, so the argument goes, faculty can be pressured or penalized for non-compliance.

It is also true, and Finkin acknowledges the problem as a paradox, that in this self-regulatory model of academic freedom we rely on faculty to come up with the intellectual standards they will live by and judge each other by and yet faculty are often, in the humanities in any case, in open critical discussion of such standards (Finkin 2009, 39). Because academic freedom is based on a freedom to pursue knowledge, and not merely on the desirability of being free from constraint, the professorate must be able to show that its privileges and responsibilities are being exercised to that end, even though the standards for judging knowledge are often difficult to recognize in emerging research and ideas. In other words, standards are needed but contested. And the contest is taking place largely among the very same individuals who will be using the standard in making judgements.

This sort of justification might work for academic freedom in research, where the goal is to expand knowledge, but how does it apply to teaching, much less intra and extra-mural speeches and other activity? One general consideration is that the professing of new research is often closely connected with the criticism and development of it. As many teaching researchers will attest, often by teaching material we gain insights into theories and ideas, and this often leads to new writing and research. So the teaching and research domains do not always need to be thought of as completely separate.

However, Finkin adds another sort of argument which he also finds in the 1915 Declaration. Teaching is not just the conveyance of information but a matter of modeling inquiry. Students should be learning not just a particular subject matter, but how to evaluate new and contested results in a field. Teachers can only model this independence of judgment if they can practice it with students. "The essentially American premise of the *Declaration* is that students cannot learn how to exercise a mature independence of mind unless their instructors are themselves free to model independent thought in the classroom" (Finkin 2009, 81).

Again, we should note that this approach involves a substantive commitment about the nature and purpose of higher education (though one which might be challenged at an empirical level). Higher education is crucially about modeling critical inquiry skills from the elementary level that permits college level work to the level at which a graduate (or post graduate) could venture critical comments and hypotheses about work in the field. It is true that in many fields, especially in the humanities, faculty are among the primary producers of new work and comprise a primary audience for that work. Faculty therefore play a crucial role in the dissemination process of new knowledge. In addition, but perhaps more central to the 1915 Declaration, "modeling independence of thought" (which is after all the practice of academic freedom itself) is a central learning goal for students at the university level.

Because this approach involves a substantive commitment to knowledge and the circumstances of its study and production, it has a moral focus that positions it well (at least theoretically) to respond to recent challenges such as the integration of "hostile environment law" into university life. Because

the freedom to teach is directed to the goal of producing critical and independent learners, the creation of a hostile environment, which by definition com-
promises learning, should not pose an unwelcome or additional constraint
on the professional ethics of academic freedom (Finkin 105). That does not
mean that it might not be perceived that way, or in some cases may actually
function that way. But at least in theory, a hostile learning environment is
already inimical to the substantive goals of academic freedom.

Academic freedom also applies to intramural speech. Intramural speech
concerns the speech that faculty will engage in with an administration in
the course of their shared governance role. If a faculty member could face
reprisal for criticizing an administrator, it could inhibit their professional
judgment about how to govern their department. Academic freedom in intramural expression is protected by a grant of status in which an agent who
is otherwise an employee is given explicit authority to speak freely and critically. As we shall see, it is not necessarily well protected by the First Amendment.

When it comes to extramural speech, whether under one's faculty or civic
identity or within or outside one's subject area expertise, academic freedom
traditionally provides various degrees of protection, but carries with it correlative responsibilities. In particular, the 1940 Statement references the "special position" of a faculty member in a community as a ground for specific
responsibilities of care for an institution's reputation, for truth, etc. A 1970
joint statement (with the Association of American Colleges) and interpretation of the 1940 Statement rather streamlined this language to simply say that
extramural speech was only relevant to the assessment of competence of the
faculty member (Finkin 2009, 131).

Academic freedom is probably best justified by connecting it to the needs
of knowledge production and the need to model critical inquiry to advanced
students, especially those who have been brought far enough into their subject matter to need such skills. It does seem to follow from this justification
that participation of faculty in governance of the university and the weight
typically given to their judgments about curriculum, hiring, and promotion
are well justified traditions supporting this view of academic freedom. Also,
guarantees of tenure, now at historic lows, seem integral to this understanding of academic freedom.

One lesson we should recall from section one of this chapter is that our
understanding of academic freedom is not only defined theoretically, but in
the actual configuration of social institutions at work in a particular culture
of academic freedom. The traditional model of academic freedom presumes
a somewhat traditional and "nuclear" college or university in which faculty are in regular interaction over many years, producing curriculum and
degrees in a fairly stable educational environment. That still characterizes

many colleges and universities, but higher education is changing dramatically in some areas. Compared to the mid-20th century, in the US a greater percentage of university life is devoted to basic and mass instruction of a larger percentage of the population. In a purely instructional environment, and with increasingly technical material, the cultivation of independence of thought looks more like one value among many. In the last few decades universities have been under increasing pressure, from a society skeptical of the costs, to demonstrate specific outcomes for their graduates. Many programs are accumulating valid data on the effectiveness of their methods. At some point, a faculty might have to wonder if they harm their students more by not adopting better teaching methods rather than by preserving a high degree of "freedom to teach."

The more uncertain the higher education environment becomes, whether from pressures to demonstrate effectiveness or from global market changes in higher education as an industry, the more pressure traditional faculty governance models may experience. This in turn affects academic freedom.

Academic freedom for faculty is a kind of professional guarantee to protect independence of judgment. Other professions provide similar guarantees when they want to express the importance of an employee acting on their best professional judgment. For example, it would be a breach of ethics for an employer to pressure an engineer to sign a technical drawing or document affirming the integrity of a structure if he or she did not feel confident about it. But we do not feel that the engineer's independence of judgment requires giving her anything like the protections of academic freedom. A critic of traditional academic freedom could ask whether tenure and faculty governance are really needed to guarantee that a worker will not be penalized for independent thought. As a traditionalist about academic freedom, I have more confidence in a system in which faculty have a great prerogative in governance, but I must admit that the protections and status afforded by academic freedom is disproportionate to the engineer's case.

Arguably, however, the academic's research and teaching responsibilities need to be given wider protection because they can touch on a wider range of interests and conflicts. It is not just the case that new knowledge can upset powerful interests, it is also the case that in the practice of understanding new and old ideas (through study and teaching and writing) we may need more room to wander than the engineer building a bridge. Faculty fill a range of analogues from engineer to judge.

As we saw with the 19th century growth of academic freedom in the US, faculty cultivated their status and authority by showing, in part through their professional societies, that they do, in fact, play a critical role in the growth of knowledge and that this role cannot be effective without independence of thought and expression. That in turn requires faculty participate in governance and are able to earn tenure. This picture still describes faculty life, but now for a minority of faculty in higher education. Interestingly, the aspirations of higher education to produce independent and critical thinkers remain as high as ever, at least in rhetoric. What is very unclear today is how much of the traditional environment of research and teaching is needed to optimize the production of knowledge and the level of critical discussion in society at large, especially through its most educated members.

Topics, Developments, and Trends

There are some perennial topics in academic freedom, such as the role of religion, which bear mention in this context either because of particularly interesting writing on the topic or because there have been developments in the area. Also, there are relatively new topics, such as the internationalization of education (and of academic freedom) that raise new and difficult issues. Finally, we will provide a very brief summary, with reference to more detailed treatments, of legal trends in academic freedom in US constitutional and federal court decisions. The news there, since 2006, has been the *Garcetti* case, which we will consider from diverse expert perspectives.

Religious institutions face particular challenges in observing academic freedom depending upon the degree to which they wish to see their religious traditions and dogmas reflected in the curriculum or wish the curriculum to be restricted by religious belief. One long term strategy for facing these challenges is to screen faculty for "mission-fit," but in the end religious institutions also do generally want to commit themselves to academic freedom because they want competitive programs and degrees to offer. The flashpoints for academic freedom for faculty at religious institutions occur less at the hiring stage than in controversial events such as the staging of the Vagina Monologues and controversial faculty teaching or extramural expression.

Religious academic freedom is not only about faculty academic freedom. Some of the most challenging arguments advancing the right of religious institutions to mix religious mission with curriculum depend upon claims about the *institutional academic freedom* of the college or university. In important and lucid papers from 1990, Michael McConnell, professor of law at University of Chicago, exchanged views with philosopher Judith Jarvis Thompson and Matthew Finkin. In his paper, "Academic Freedom in Religious Colleges and Universities," McConnell argued for restoring the so-called "limitations clause" to official AAUP language on academic freedom at religious institutions. The 1940 Statement seemed to allow colleges and universities to disclose limitations to academic freedom to job candidates. The 1970 Statement deleted the limitations clause, consolidating the position that a religious university should be able to realize academic freedom completely, and when religion is added to the mission of the university it ought not to compromise academic freedom. Thus, there is no need to allow limitations. McConnell makes a good first glance case that people who want to promote diversity of thought should be open to more diversity in the meaning of a university education than the AAUP appears to be. It is an especially interesting case to make in a culture which certifies its colleges and universities by private accrediting associations which do introduce some variation into the definition of a university education. Less persuasive are McConnell's arguments that promoting academic freedom at religious universities will lead to their extinction or undermine religious freedom.

In their reply article, Thompson and Finkin accept the idea that religious colleges and universities make distinctive contributions to higher education, but deny that this requires limitation of academic freedom. Indeed, it is difficult, argumentatively, to accept the premise of academic freedom being about the production of truth and yet argue that if an exception is not made for religious ideas then their truths will not be heard. Thompson and Finkin suggest that in the end McConnell may be selling religious thought short by suggesting that it needs support from the limitations clause. Note that the reply to McConnell does not depend upon a claim about the intrinsic desirability of diversity of thought, but upon diversity of thought which promotes truth seeking.

An interesting recent case at University of Illinois Champaign involving religious academic freedom illustrates some of the modern complexity of the issue in ways that perhaps discussions of the limitations clause cannot. Kenneth Howell was teaching a Newman Center funded course on Catholicism for the University of Illinois at Champaign. Howell was allegedly non-reappointed after student complaints about his instruction on the Catholic Church's view of homosexuality (Gillen 2010). Without confirming details of the original problem, the University reversed itself and rehired Howell, this time paying his contract through the university rather than the Newman Center . While it is hard to tell from this distance, in this case what seemed to matter was making sure that a UI faculty member was really reporting to his university colleagues regarding standards of teaching and academic freedom.

We have been writing about academic freedom so far largely within the US cultural context, but two international trends have been creating a more global environment for thinking about academic freedom. Increasingly, international bodies, such as the United Nations Educational, Scientific and Cultural Organization UNESCO (UNESCO 1999) and the European Union (2013) have written or updated statements of academic freedom, including an important 2009 joint statement by the AAUP and the Canadian Association of University Teachers, "On the Conditions of Employment at Overseas

Campuses." (AAUP and CAUT 2009). Higher education is internationalizing fast and in new ways. There has been a sharp growth in global university partnerships for example. This brings about a predictable clash between US academic freedom culture and the cultures of the host partner's campus.

Amid reports that New York University's partnership with the National University of Singapore would not honor all facets of academic freedom, the AAUP wrote an open letter to the Yale community probing Yale's approach to managing academic freedom in their partnership (AAUP 2012). Judging from press reports, it is clearly Yale's intention to comply with American academic freedom standards (Davie 2012). While some imply that there is a fundamental incompatibility between the way the overseas programs work (largely with non-tenured faculty) and the way that host cultures operate (with different norms for dissent or public protest), other voices are more moderate. In an article written by Simon Chesterman, who worked on an earlier law school partnership between NYU and a Singaporean university, we are reminded that part of the point of an international collaboration such as NYU seeks is to experience and negotiate conflicting norms and values. Also, we should remember that in our own cultural contexts, political correctness operates to limit academic freedom. Partnerships always involve the possibility of compromising one's values for a common endeavor. But with the right of intercultural understanding, the exportation of US higher education could also serve the goal of exporting cultures of academic freedom. Because, as we have noted, academic freedom has an institutional embodiment that will be unique to the circumstances of its development, we should expect the meaning of "global academic freedom" to be only partially informed by the US cultural experience.

"Donor Effects" on academic freedom concern the way in which donors and founders of colleges, universities and institutes compromise academic freedom. Of course this is not itself a new topic. We started, for example, with one of the classic stories of founder influence in Mrs. Stanford and Professor Ross. But donor effects have become more complicated to untangle in recent years as corporate sponsorship of research has created a number of new ways that conflicts of interest and loyalty can affect academic freedom. For example, is it acceptable for a donor of an institute to have representation on a Board that may engage in recommendations for faculty hiring? Donors often have specific agendas, which may naturally lead them and the universities that accept their money to unduly influence either the hiring process or the academic freedom of hired faculty. In a recent controversy exemplifying this pattern, Eric Barron, President of Florida State University, taking issue with earlier reports, claimed that a sufficient separation had occurred between a Koch Foundation advisory board and the university's economic department, which hired a faculty member with Foundation donated funds (Barron 2011).

In other cases, such as the separate cases of two Brown university medical researchers David Kern and Martin Keller, the conflicts of interest and protections against fraud and abuse of academic freedom are particularly complex. Kern worked fifteen years as a Brown medical school faculty member and was also a clinician at Brown affiliated Memorial Hospital, where he directed an occupational health clinic. Kern noticed patients with a pattern of lung ailments who were also workers at Microfibres, a significant hospital donor, represented on the hospital's board. Kern visited a Microfibres factory to take air tests and eventually sought to present evidence about the causes of the workers illness at a professional conference. Because Kern signed a confidentiality agreement when he took the air samples, Microfibres and Brown objected to Kern presenting his paper. Kern sought legal advice and decided that his confidentiality agreement did not cover this circumstance, but Brown responded to the controversy by shutting down Kern's clinic immediately and letting his five year contract with the Brown Medical School expire.

In a contrasting case, however, we have the story of Martin Keller, another Brown university faculty member and past chair of the Psychiatry Department, who has brought over 8 million dollars of research money to Brown from major pharmaceutical companies such as GlaxoSmithKline (GSK). In 2001, Keller was the lead author of a major study supporting the safety and effectiveness of GSK's anti-depressant, Paxil. When irregularities in Keller's research emerged, including the use of a GSK ghost-writer, Brown defended Keller. These two cases were reported by Jennifer Washburn in *Academe* (Washburn 2011) and drawn from her book, *University Inc.*

Fortunately, our goal is not to make an armchair assessment of the merits of these or related cases discussed by Washburn and others. The modern university has benefited from significant research partnerships with other countries and cultures as well as with major donors, including corporations and foundations. But these stories also suggest that donor effects require universities to not only protect faculty from donor pressure, but also protect themselves against research fraud which may result if a researcher's interests are too closely aligned with a donor or the product they are studying.

International partnerships and "donor effects" are important topics today because of changes in a variety of institutions, especially the connection between research (government and private sector) and commercial institutions. As competitive institutions, universities have acquired increasingly sophisticated approaches to working with industry, governments, and other organizations, including other higher education organizations. International partnerships are driven by both traditional study abroad demand and a perception that the best national universities can only maintain their status in a global higher education environment by making partnerships that add "value" to their "brand," giving them access to global faculty resources and authoritative learning on a wide range of global topics. These topics also remind us that academic freedom issues do not just involve faculty and outspoken speech. The business of running a university can create situations in which academic freedom can be spread or put in jeopardy; an institutions' primary intent in a new or untraditional venture might be to maintain or increase its status and competitiveness.

Our last substantive task in this review of academic freedom is to look at developments and trends in a line of US Supreme Courts cases related to academic freedom for faculty. Does the US constitution protect academic freedom for faculty? Should a society look to its constitution (or similar expression of rights) to articulate the protections of academic freedom for faculty?

Before discussing those cases, we should acknowledge again, and in more detail this time, that academic freedom as a concept is not just a faculty right, but is extensively treated in the US as an institutional right of the university. That is why you will find courts deferring to universities on a wide range of questions, such as whom to admit, what may be taught, how it should be taught (especially cases involving off-topic speech in the classroom), and assigning grades (Tepper and White 2009, 136–145). Each of these questions has its case history, but the general temper of case law is to grant the university a significant deference of judgment in conducting its fundamental business. For example, even when courts have reigned in universities in areas of affirmative action admissions, they have deferred to the educational goals behind such policies.

That said, the spotlight remains on faculty speech cases. And there have been recent important developments in this case law that not only help us understand US judicial thought on academic freedom in relation to constitutionally protected speech, but also how any international system for protecting academic freedom might operate in relationship to similar rights.

Beginning with the more settled part of the legal story, there are a variety of classic cases in which Supreme Court justices have said supportive things about academic freedom and even decided cases in recognition of the concept. Early Supreme Court cases on academic freedom involved external threats to faculty, such as from laws regulating political viewpoint or membership (*Adler v. Board of Education* 1952) or loyalty oaths (*Wieman v. Updegraff*, cited in Areen 2009, 969). The 1957 *Sweezy v. New Hampshire* case was the first in which a majority decision of the court affirmed academic freedom. Sweezy, the editor of a progressive economics journal, refused to answer questions from the New Hampshire Attorney General about his classroom teaching and lectures. His contempt citation was overturned by a Supreme Court which explicitly acknowledged the importance of academic freedom.

The Sweezy case has its critics (White 2009), but subsequent cases have also afforded the courts a similar opportunity to extol the values of academic freedom. Part of the theoretical difficulty with protecting academic freedom as a First Amendment right is that it may not be well suited to acknowledge specific rights and privileges of specific professions or vocations. It is, after all, intended to articulate a right that applies uniformly to all citizens.

Experts acknowledge that direct jurisprudence on academic freedom is vague and inconclusive (White 2009, 814). So it might be more helpful to ask the question this way: To what extent does a right to free speech exist for anyone at the workplace? Does it matter if your employer is the state or federal government?

In an interesting line of cases involving speech protection for government employees, we see a continuation of the Supreme Court's thinking about whether specific speech protections apply to specific conditions of employment. The traditional default assumption about this is often identified with a quote from Oliver Wendell Holmes, who said in the famous 1892 case, *McAuliffe v. Mayor of New Bedford*, in which a police officer was fired for violating restrictions on political activity, "The petitioner may have a constitutional right to talk politics, but he has no constitutional right to be a policeman" (Areen 2009, 974). Constitutional rights are distinct from privileges such as employment.

But subsequent cases have developed this picture in complex ways. The so-called rights-privileges distinction was eroded in the case of *Pickering v. Board of Education*. Marvin Pickering was a school teacher who wrote an editorial to the local paper criticizing the school board for spending too much money on athletics and not enough on academics (Areen 2009, 974). His dismissal was upheld by Illinois courts but overturned by the State Supreme Court, which argued that "the proper inquiry when determining whether Pickering was afforded First Amendment protections was to look at the 'balance between the interests of the [employee], as a citizen, in commenting upon matters of public concern and the interest of the State, as an employer, in promoting the efficiency of the public services it performs through its employees'" (Houle 273). In a related case, *Connick v. Myers*, the court applied this test from Pickering and found against the claimant, Connick, who had been fired for pursuing a personal job matter in a way that did not raise a public concern and which arguable worked against the smooth functioning of the workplace.

The so-called Pickering/Connick test balancing employee speech rights and employer rights to control employee behavior in the workplace remained unchanged until the more recent case of *Garcetti v. Ceballos*, widely seen as the most consequential Supreme Court case on academic freedom in many years. This might be puzzling on a first reading of the case since neither party was an academic. Ceballos was a deputy district attorney on Los Angeles who claimed to have uncovered improprieties in an affidavit used to file for search warrant. Ceballos pursued his viewpoint with his employers in meetings and memoranda and eventually testified for the defense in the case. Ceballos claims that after these events he experienced retaliation in the form of adverse job assignment and denial of promotion (Houle 2012, 280). After an initial adverse judgment, the Ninth Circuit Court sided with Ceballos, arguing that his memorandum on the case raised a matter of public concern—potential misrepresentation of an affidavit. But the Supreme Court of the United States reversed the decision, saying that because Ceballos was acting "pursuant to his duties as a calendar deputy" his speech cannot be protected. The presumption behind the Pickering/Connick test was that if a matter raised a public concern, then the employee pursuing it might be protected if the facts showed an appropriate balance with the employer's right to control the workplace. Now, with Garcetti, the court seems to be saying that even if the issue does raise a matter of public concern, if the public employee was acting within their assigned duties, then their speech does not enjoy first amendment protection.

The Garcetti decision has been the subject of a considerable literature, which is only sampled here. The dissenting opinions from Justices Souter and Ginsberg warn that the case drew too bright a line for excluding first amendment protection. Souter favored a more flexible standard, that would ask whether the defendant "was speaking on a matter of 'unusual importance and satisfies high standards of responsibility in the way he does it'" (Rosborough 2009, 589). Breyer was specifically concerned that the court's approach could limit disclosure of misleading evidence, which officers of a court have a duty to disclose. After Garcetti, it seems quite plausible that a public university faculty member could be fired for criticizing his or her administration. In other words, Garcetti seems to threaten academic freedom by undermining faculty governance, which includes, at least by tradition, the ability to speak candidly to the administration. The Court was aware that its decision might be construed as destructive of academic freedom, so it included this language, which conspicuously omits reference to faculty governance, and which has come to be known as the "Garcetti reservation":

> *There is some argument that expression related to academic scholarship or classroom instruction implicates additional constitutional interests that are not fully accounted for by this Court's customary employee-speech jurisprudence. We need not, and for that reason do not, decide whether the analysis we conduct today would apply in the same manner to a case involving speech related to scholarship or teaching.* (Tepper and White 2009, 157)

While many commentators (including the AAUP) are critical of the Garcetti decision, there are a variety of ways to look at it. It is still possible that the Supreme Court will determine that not all forms of public employment work by the same rules. This is part of the argument that Judith Areen makes: "the best way to resolve the problems posed by Garcetti and other employee-speech cases to academic freedom is to focus on the role of government-as-educator and to develop a jurisprudence for the role that is tailored to the distinctive goals, needs, and characteristics of higher education" (Areen 2009, 989). Others argue that academic freedom has never been an appropriate topic for constitutional interpretation. This goes along with practical post-Garcetti advice, from the AAUP and others, to include appropriate protections for academic freedom into contracts and handbook language (AAUP 2011).

Conclusion

It is ironic that even as international organizations seek to affirm academic freedom for faculty as a global professional right, in the US context there may be more uncertainty about the protections of academic freedom for US faculty than at any time since the mid-20th century. Not only has constitutional protection become more ambiguous than ever, but also the institutions that support academic freedom—a largely tenured faculty with recognized and supported traditions of shared governance, an authoritative network of professional learned societies and journals, and public support for the unique project of higher education—are increasingly in decline or under pressure.

As we have seen, academic freedom is a traditional culture concept, most recently identifiable with the German Enlightenment of the 18th century and then with US university traditions of the 19th and 20th centuries. In the US context, the AAUP developed some of the most extensive thinking about the nature of academic freedom over a 100 year period starting with the formation of the organization and its famous "Committee A on Academic Freedom and Tenure." The AAUP adopted a strong and substantive vision of the university as a special kind of community that had to protect freedom of thought, teaching, and research with unique rules and governance institutions. When academic freedom is tied to the knowledge-producing functions of university life it can be effectively defended as the price of a vibrant knowledge community.

The deepest challenges to academic freedom are probably not from the US Supreme Court, but from changes in the actual institutions of higher education and their self-image. Also, as with the health care industry, society is asking for more accountability from universities to demonstrate the effectiveness of their services. Academic freedom, tenure, and traditional forms of faculty governance are very expensive and it will be hard for institutions under scrutiny to show that there might not be more effective methodologies for delivering some forms of instruction than traditional faculty governance allow for. Some new kinds of "universities" are not so much traditional communities of intellectuals trying to live an intellectual life of research and discovery and model that to students while doing some teaching, but rather, teaching institutions devoted to instruction in an increasingly technically defined post-secondary curriculum. As the shape and function of universities changes, the substantive vision of university life that gave so much support to academic freedom in 20th century United States will need revision. At a minimum, we will need to think harder about how to protect academic freedom without tenure, assuming that is possible.

Works Cited

Adler v. Board of Education of City of New York, 342 U.S. 485 1952.

American Association of University Professors. 2009. Protecting an independent faculty voice: Academic freedom after *Garcetti v. Ceballos*.

— — —. 2011. Defending academic freedom in the age of Garcetti. *Academe*. January–February.

— — —. 2012. An open letter from the AAUP to the Yale community. (accessed May 26, 2013).

— — —. 2013a. 1940 statement of principles on academic freedom and tenure.

— — —. 2013b. 1915 Statement on Academic Freedom and Tenure. AAUP 1915 http://www.aaup.org/AAUP/pubsres/policydocs/contents/1915.htm (accessed May 28, 2013).

American Association of University Professors and Canadian Assoication of University Teachers. 2009. On conditions of employment at overseas campuses. http://www.aaup.org/aaup/comm/rep/a/overseas.htm (accessed May 28, 2013).

Areen, Judith. 2009. Government as educator: A new understanding of first amendment protection of academic freedom and governance. *Georgetown Law Review* 97: 945–1000.

Barron, Eric J. 2011. FSU advisory board is not hurting academic freedom. *St. Petersburg Times* (Florida), May 13.

Chesterman, Simon. 2012. Academic freedom in New Haven and S'pore. *The Straits Times*, March 30.

Davie, Sandra. 2012. US dons: Freedom at Yale-NUS a concern. The *Straits Times* (Singapore), December 6.

European Union. 2013. Charter of Fundamental Rights of the EU 2013 Available from http://ec.europa.eu/justice/fundamental-rights/charter/ (accessed May 18, 2013).

Finkin, Matthew and Robert C. Post. 2009. For the Common Good: Principles of American academic freedom. New Haven, CT: Yale University Press.

Garcetti v. Ceballos, 547 US 410 –2006

Gillen, Patrick T. 2010. University faces a test of academic freedom *The Washington Times* 3, July 20.

Glenn, David. 2009. 'Torture memos' vs. Academic freedom *The Chronicle of Higher Education* 55, no. 28.

Hansmann, Henry. 2012. The evolving economic structure of higher education. *University of Chicago Law Review* 79: 159-83.

Haskell, Thomas L. 1996. Justifying the rights of academic freedom in an era of "power/knowledge". In *The future of academic freedom*. Chicago: University of Chicago Press.

Houle, Suzanne R. 2012. Is Academic Freedom in Modern America on Its Last Legs after *Garcetti v. Ceballos? Capital University Law Review* no. 40.

Jones, Howard M, ed. 1949. *Primer on intellectual freedom*. Cambridge, MA: Harvard University Press.

McConnell, Michael W. 1990. Academic freedom in religious colleges and universities. *Law and Contemporary Problems* 53, no. 3: 303-24.

Menand, Louis. 1996. *The future of academic freedom*. Chicago: University of Chicago Press.

Rosborough, Robert S. 2009. A "Great" Day for academic freedom: The threat posed to academic freedom by the Supreme Court decision in *Garcetti v. Ceballos. Albany Law Review* no. 72.

Sweezy v. New Hampshire, 354 U.S. 234 (1957)

Tepper, Robert J. and Craig G. White. 2009. Speak no evil: Academic freedom and the application of *Garcetti v. Ceballos* to public university faculty. *Catholic University Law Review* 59: 125.

Thompson, Judith Jarvis and Matthew Finkin. 1990. Academic freedom and church-related higher education: A reply to professor McConnell. *Law and Contemporary Problems* 53, no. 3: 419-29.

United Nations (UNESCO). 1999. Implementation of the international covenant on economic, social and cultural rights. http://www.unhchr.ch/tbs/doc.nsf/(Symbol)/ae1a0b126d068e868025683c003c8b3b?Opendocument.

Washburn, Jennifer. 2011. Academic freedom and the corporate university. *Academe* 97, no. 1 (January–February): 8-13.

White, Lawrence. 2009. Fifty years of academic freedom jurisprudence. *Journal of College and University Law* 36: 791-842.

Wieman v. Updegraff, 344 U.S. 183 (1952).

Index

CPSIA information can be obtained
at www.ICGtesting.com
Printed in the USA
LVOW13s0548040117

519661LV00011B/143/P

9 781936 117574